T0234567

Lecture Notes in Computer Science 10323

Commenced Publication in 1973
Founding and Former Series Editors:
Gerhard Goos, Juris Hartmanis, and Jan van Leeuwen

More information about this series at http://www.springer.com/series/7410

Michael Brenner · Kurt Rohloff
Joseph Bonneau · Andrew Miller
Peter Y.A. Ryan · Vanessa Teague
Andrea Bracciali · Massimiliano Sala
Federico Pintore · Markus Jakobsson (Eds.)

Financial Cryptography and Data Security

FC 2017 International Workshops
WAHC, BITCOIN, VOTING, WTSC, and TA
Sliema, Malta, April 7, 2017
Revised Selected Papers

 Springer

Editors

Michael Brenner 🆔
Leibniz Universität Hannover
Hannover
Germany

Vanessa Teague
University of Melbourne
Parkville, VIC
Australia

Kurt Rohloff 🆔
New Jersey Institute of Technology
Newark, NJ
USA

Andrea Bracciali 🆔
University of Stirling
Stirling
UK

Joseph Bonneau
New York University
New York, NY
USA

Massimiliano Sala 🆔
University of Trento
Trento
Italy

Andrew Miller
University of Illinois at Urbana-Champaign
Urbana, IL
USA

Federico Pintore 🆔
University of Trento
Trento
Italy

Peter Y.A. Ryan
University of Luxembourg
Luxembourg
Luxembourg

Markus Jakobsson
Agari Inc.
San Mateo, CA
USA

ISSN 0302-9743   ISSN 1611-3349   (electronic)
Lecture Notes in Computer Science
ISBN 978-3-319-70277-3   ISBN 978-3-319-70278-0   (eBook)
https://doi.org/10.1007/978-3-319-70278-0

Library of Congress Control Number: 2017959723

LNCS Sublibrary: SL4 – Security and Cryptology

Printed on acid-free paper

This Springer imprint is published by Springer Nature
The registered company is Springer International Publishing AG
The registered company address is: Gewerbestrasse 11, 6330 Cham, Switzerland

Preface

WAHC 2017: 5th Workshop on Encrypted Computing and Applied Homomorphic Cryptography

The hype over the cloud and recent disclosures show there is demand for secure and practical computing technologies. The WAHC workshop addresses the challenge in safely outsourcing data processing onto remote computing resources by protecting programs and data even during processing. This allows users to outsource computation over confidential information independently from the trustworthiness or the security level of the remote delegate. The workshop serviced these research needs by collecting and bringing together some of the top researchers and practitioners from academia, government, and industry to present, discuss, and share the latest progress in the field relevant to real-world problems with practical approaches and solutions. The workshop was uniformly attended by academia, government, and industry, with participants from previous years with experience in the domain and new attendees contributing and learning from the community for the first time. Specific encrypted computing technologies focused on homomorphic encryption and secure multiparty computation. The technologies and techniques discussed in this workshop are key to extending quality of implementation and the range of applications that can be securely and practically outsourced. Presentations and discussion at the workshop were of the high quality and deep insights we have come to expect from our community. Topics of conversation included insights and lessons learned from experience implementing encrypted computing schemes and experience reports on applying these technologies. Special thanks to the invited speakers: Kim Laine from Microsoft Research and Yuriy Polyakov from the New Jersey Institute of Technology, who shared their experiences implementing open-source homomorphic encryption libraries. The workshop received 19 submissions. All contained unique and interesting results. Each was reviewed by at least three Program Committee members. While all the papers were of high quality, only seven papers were accepted to the workshop. We thank the authors for all submissions, the members of the Program Committee for their effort, the workshop participants for attending, and the FC organizers for supporting us.

April 2017

Michael Brenner
Kurt Rohloff

WAHC 2017 Program Committee

Dan Bogdanov	Cybernetica, Estonia
Zvika Brakerski	Weizmann Institute, Israel
David Cash	Rutgers, USA
Hao Chen	Microsoft Research, USA
Rosario Gennaro	CUNY, USA
Seung Geol Choi	US Naval Academy, USA
David Cousins	BBN, USA
Marten van Dijk	UConn, USA
Dario Fiore	IMDEA, Spain
Sergey Gorbunov	University of Waterloo, USA
Debayan Gupta	MIT, USA
Vlad Kolesnikov	Bell Labs, USA
Kim Laine	Microsoft Research, USA
Tencrède Lepoint	SRI International, USA
Pascal Paillier	CryptoExperts, France
Benny Pinkas	Bar-Ilan University, Israel
Erkay Savas	Sabancı University, Turkey
Berk Sunar	WPI, USA
Mehdi Tibouchi	NTT, Japan
Fre Vercauteren	KU Leuven, Belgium
Adrian Waller	Thales, UK

BITCOIN 2017: 4th Workshop on Bitcoin and Blockchain Research

The past year leading up to the 4th Bitcoin and Blockchain Workshop in 2017 has seen a continued booming trend: increased adoption and development in cryptocurrencies like Bitcoin, Ethereum, Zcash, and many more, as well as investment in blockchain - related technologies from industry broadly. Cryptocurrency and blockchain technology are emerging as a significant and productive research topic in computer security.

Much like the price of Bitcoin and the market capitalization of the cryptocurrency ecosystem, our workshop has also grown year by year. This year we received a record number of submissions (38), and after our peer-review process we accepted a record number of papers (14), and yet increased in selectivity (37% acceptance rate). We were very happy to convene an outstanding Program Committee (listed here) comprising not just leading academics, but also top PhD students and prominent developers.

From our strong technical program emerged several themes of focus, including privacy analysis and privacy-preserving enhancements; smart contract scripting functionality and applications in both Bitcoin and Ethereum; game theoretic analysis of consensus protocols; and scalability improvements for cryptocurrency transactions. We note also that our host conference accepted five papers on blockchain technology to its main track, and also featured a keynote talk on a new cryptocurrency protocol from Turing Award winner Silvio Micali. A new workshop dedicated to smart contract security hosted in parallel also featured 11 talks and a keynote from Vitalik Buterin.

We would like to thank our Program Committee for the hard work they put into producing high-quality and useful reviews, and the authors and speakers for contributing to our program. We especially thank Nicolas Christin for once again hosting the conference management server, and the organizers and sponsors of Financial Cryptography for guiding us through a successful event.

April 2017

Andrew Miller
Joseph Bonneau

BITCOIN 2017 Program Committee

VOTING 2017: Second Workshop on Advances in Secure Electronic Voting Schemes

Voting 2017 was the second of what looks like turning into an ongoing series of workshops on verifiable voting systems associated with Financial Crypto.

Voting 2017 occurred at a time of hightened global interest in election security. Attacks, attributed to Russia, deliberately interfered with the politics of the US presidential election. Much remains murky about what exactly occurred, but it is clear that hackers breached the Democratic campaign system and selectively leaked material. It is also clear that various registration systems were hacked, although the resulting damage is unclear.

In the wake of this, many European countries discontinued Internet voting or electronic counting plans over fears that their elections would also be targeted.

In France we witnessed similar attempts to meddle with the democratic process, although in this case the Kremlin's favored candidate did not carry the day. Interestingly in this case it appears that the Macron team were forewarned and detected the attempted meddling, and indeed staged some counter-meddling of their own: injecting fake items for the hackers to uncover.

The most interesting statement about US election security came from Former CIA Acting Director Michael Morell, who said of Russian interference: "They tried, and they were not successful, but they still tried, to get access to voting machines and vote counting software, to play with the results."

This raises the obvious question, "How does he know they were not successful?"

This is what Voting 2017 was about: the quest to design election systems that produce evidence of an accurate election result, or a clear indication of a problem.

We began with an inspiring keynote by Prof. Philip Stark from The University of California at Berkeley, who explained that the absence of meaningful post-election audits implies that we will never know who truly deserved to be elected US president in 2016. Efforts to perform recounts in Pennsylvania, Michigan, and Wisconsin were thwarted by either technical obstacles, e.g., absence of a paper audit trail, or legal, e.g., judges using absurd "Catch 22" style arguments that to justify a recount required evidence of fraud. He explained how routine post-election risk-limiting audits would allow us to be confident, every election, that the result was correct.

In "BatchVote: Voting Rules Designed for Auditability," Perumal, Rivest, and Stark investigated voting schemes that were designed for efficient auditability. First-past-the-post elections (the most common style in the USA) are very easy to audit, but can suffer from the spoiler effect and other distortions. Other, more expressive, voting systems such as IRV and STV are very difficult to audit, or even to find the winning margin for. This paper considers both democratic qualities and ease of auditing to design voting systems that meet both criteria.

In "Existential Assertions for Voting Protocols," by Ramanujam, Sundararajan, and Suresh, a new type of formal verification of e-voting protocols is introduced. The term-based model of e-voting protocols is replaced with assertions, e.g., signatures or zero-knowledge proofs are replaced with assertions idealizing their desired behavior. This firstly makes the model quite intuitive to read, but more importantly allows us to model how the adversary can logically infer based on the assertions he has seen, and capture if this gives new attacks. The main novelty from the authors is an existential quantifier that allows the authors to give an equivalence-based notion of privacy in e-voting protocols and check privacy for FOO and Helios 2.0.

In "A Roadmap to Fully Homomorphic Elections," Gjøsteen and Strand describe how to use fully homomorphic encryption to provide universal verifiability while protecting privacy for Norway's complex ballots. Norway's current system requires the verification process to be restricted to a few auditors due to privacy concerns. The main challenge is that a Norwegian ballot has so many possible values that a voter may choose to identify herself by choosing a unique vote. If individual votes are exposed, this can result in bribery or coercion. Fully homomorphic encryption would allow for universal verification, although at present it is not fast enough to run on real elections.

The next paper considers the voter's end of verifiable Internet voting. In "Using Selene to Verify Your Vote in JCJ," Rial, Iovino, Roenne, and Ryan describe how the transparent voter verification techniques of the Selene scheme can be combined with the rather strong coercion resistance mechanisms of JCJ (Juels, Catalano, and Jakobsson).

In "Enabling Vote Delegation for Boardroom Voting," Kulyk, Neumann, Marky, and Volkamer consider the privacy and verifiability of vote delegation, in which a voter may choose to nominate someone else to determine his vote. In their setting there are a relatively small number of voters, who all participate actively in the protocol.

We had a valuable tutorial on complex proofs for mixnet verification. Haenni, Locher, Koenig, and Dubuis wrote "Pseudocode Algorithms for Verifiable Re-encryption Mixnets" to explain to a general audience how these sophisticated proofs work and facilitate implementations.

Finally, Yang and Clark described a new protocol for "Practical Governmental Voting with Unconditional Integrity and Privacy." This scheme (probably inevitably) has to sacrifice universal verifiability, but it represents an interesting part of the solution space that deserves exploration, and may be appropriate for some elections.

The threat of electoral fraud is not new, and is not going away. Introducing computers expands the opportunity, possibly allowing for very large scale fraud from all over the world. We hope this volume has contributed to a global effort to ensure that our voting systems are robust, privacy-preserving, and not trusted until they provide meaningful evidence of having produced an accurate election result.

We would like to thank the Program Committee for their hard work and careful reviews of the papers.

April 2017   Peter Y.A. Ryan
                                                                    Vanessa Teague

VOTING 2017 Program Committee

Roberto Araujo	Universidade Federal do Pará (UFPA), Brazil
Jeremy Clark	Concordia University, Canada
Chris Culnane	University of Melbourne, Australia
Jeremy Epstein	SRI International, USA
Aleksander Essex	Western University, Canada
David Galindo	University of Birmingham, UK
Kristian Gjøsteen	Norwegian University of Science and Technology, Norway
Rajeev Gore	The Australian National University, Australia
Jens Groth	University College London, UK
Rolf Haenni	Bern University of Applied Sciences, Switzerland
Reto Koenig	Berne University of Applied Sciences, Switzerland
Steve Kremer	Inria Nancy - Grand Est, France
Olivier Pereira	Universite catholique de Louvain, Belgium
Ron Rivest	MIT, USA
Peter Roenne	SnT, University of Luxembourg, Luxembourg
Alon Rosen	IDC Herzliya, Israel
Mark Ryan	University of Birmingham, UK
Steve Schneider	University of Surrey, UK
Berry Schoenmakers	Eindhoven University of Technology, The Netherlands
Carsten Schuermann	IT University of Copenhagen, Denmark
Philip Stark	University of California, Berkeley, USA
Melanie Volkamer	Karlstad University, Sweden
Poorvi Vora	The George Washington University, USA

WTSC 2017: First Workshop on Trusted Smart Contracts

These proceedings collect the papers and posters accepted at the First Workshop on Trusted Smart Contracts (WTSC 2017) associated to the Financial Cryptography and Data Security 2017 (FC 2017) conference held in Malta in April 2017.

WTSC 2017 focused on smart contracts, i.e., self-enforcing agreements in the form of executable programs and other decentralized applications that are deployed to and run on top of blockchains. These technologies introduce a novel programming framework and execution environment, which, together with the supporting blockchain technologies, carry unanswered and challenging research questions. Multidisciplinary and multifactorial aspects affect correctness, safety, privacy, authentication, efficiency, sustainability, resilience, and trust in smart contracts and decentralized applications.

WTSC 2017 aimed to address the scientific foundations of Trusted Smart Contract engineering, i.e., the development of contracts that enjoy some verifiable "correctness" properties, and to discuss open problems, proposed solutions, and the vision on future developments among a research community that is growing around these themes and brings together users, practitioners, industry, institutions, and academia. This was reflected in the Program Committee of this first edition of WTSC, comprising members from companies, universities, and research institutions from 11 countries worldwide, who kindly accepted to support the event. The association with FC 2017 provided an ideal context for our workshop to be run in. WTSC 2017 was partially supported by the University of Stirling, UK, the University of Trento, Italy, and FC 2017 IFCA-ICRA. This first edition of WTSC 2017 received 19 submissions by about 50 authors, of which nine were accepted after peer review as full papers and three as posters, and have been collected in the present volume. These analyzed the current state of the art, addressed aspects of privacy, models for contract composition and concurrency, incentives and penalties, taxonomies of smart contract applications, legal implications of smart contracts, theorem-proving-based verification for smart contracts, decentralized markets, and smart-contract-based consensus protocols.

WTSC 2017 also enjoyed Vitalik Buterin (Ethereum Foundation) as keynote speaker. Vitalik, a prominent contributor to the world of smart contracts, gave a talk on the challenging topic of the cryptoeconomics of smart contracts.

April 2017

Andrea Bracciali
Federico Pintore
Massimiliano Sala

WTSC 2017 Program Committee

Massimo Bartoletti	University of Cagliari, Italy
Andrea Bracciali	University of Stirling, UK (Chair)
Eimear Byrne	University College Dublin, Ireland
Martin Chapman	King's College London, UK
Tiziana Cimoli	University of Cagliari, Italy
Nicola Dimitri	University of Siena, Italy
Stuart Fraser	Wallet.Services, UK
Laetitia Gauvin	ISI Foundation, Italy
Davide Grossi	University of Liverpool, UK
Iain Henderson	Jlink Lab, UK
Yoichi Hirai	Ethereum DEV, Germany
Camilla Hollanti	Aalto University, Finland
Ioannis Kounelis	Joint Research Centre, European Commission
Loi Luu	National University of Singapore
Michele Marchesi	University of Cagliari, Italy
Peter McBurney	King's College London, UK
Neil Mclaren	Avaloq Innovation Ltd, UK
Philippe Meyer	Avaloq Innovation Ltd, UK
Mihail Mihaylov	Vrije Universiteit Brussel, Belgium
Sead Muftic	KTH Royal Institute of Technology, Sweden
Igor Nai Fovino	Joint Research Centre, European Commission
Daniela Paolotti	ISI Foundation, Italy
Federico Pintore	University of Trento, Italy
Massimiliano Sala	University of Trento, Italy (Chair)
Ilya Sergey	University College London, UK
Jason Teutsch	University of Chicago, USA
Roberto Tonelli	University of Cagliari, Italy
Yaron Velner	Hebrew University, Israel
Luca Vigano	King's College London, UK

TA 2017: First Workshop on Targeted Attacks

A targeted attack is one in which contextual information about the intended victim is used to configure the attack; for example, a spear phishing attack is targeted, while a typical spam blast is not. Targeting is performed in order to maximize yield and minimize detection. Being able to assess the yield of attacks enables efforts to predict the likely growth of these attacks, as soaring profits fuel more attacks. Similarly, it is important to understand how targeted attacks avoid detection in order to improve detection methods.

It is commonly believed that targeted attacks are enabled by data from account compromises, breaches, and public resources, but the risk associated with various types of data is poorly understood. It is also important to better understand new methods or communication media used for targeted attacks, and how attackers tailor targeted attacks to the media and to their goals whether this is to distribute malware, obtain data, or coerce a user to perform an action.

Targeted Attacks 2017 was the first workshop addressing this threat. Its success rested both on the insightful submissions we received and the excellent Program Committee that guided the selection.

April 2017   Markus Jakobsson

TA 2017 Program Committee

David Maimon	UMD
Damon McCoy	NYU
Angela Sasse	UCL
Hossein Siadati	NYU
Elaine Shi	Cornell
Gianluca Stringhini	UCL
Gary Warner	PhishMe
Moti Yung	Snap

Blockchain and Smart Contract Mechanism Design Challenges (WTSC17 Keynote Talk)

Vitalik Buterin

Ethereum Foundation

Abstract. Arguably, the true genius behind the success of Bitcoin, Ethereum and similar systems was not the specific design of their blockchain, or their use of algorithms that resemble forms of distributed consensus in order to maintain security; rather, it is the innovation of *cryptoeconomics* - the art of combining cryptographic techniques and economic incentives defined and administered inside a protocol in order to encourage users to (correctly) participate in certain roles in the protocol, and thereby preserve and maintain certain desired properties of the protocol. I describe the key ideas in the abstract, then apply them to Bitcoin proof of work, the Schellingcoin oracle, Casper, as well as describing several key open problems in blockchain-based system design.

Contents

Advances in Secure Electronic Voting Schemes

Poster Papers

Encrypted Computing and Applied
Homomorphic Cryptography

Simple Encrypted Arithmetic Library - SEAL v2.1

Hao Chen[1(✉)], Kim Laine[1], and Rachel Player[2]

[1] Microsoft Research, New York, USA
haoche@microsoft.com , kim.laine@microsoft.com
[2] Royal Holloway, University of London, London, UK
rachel.player.2013@live.rhul.ac.uk

Abstract. Achieving fully homomorphic encryption was a longstanding open problem in cryptography until it was resolved by Gentry in 2009. Soon after, several homomorphic encryption schemes were proposed. The early homomorphic encryption schemes were extremely impractical, but recently new implementations, new data encoding techniques, and a better understanding of the applications have started to change the situation. In this paper we introduce the most recent version (v2.1) of Simple Encrypted Arithmetic Library - SEAL, a homomorphic encryption library developed by Microsoft Research, and describe some of its core functionality.

1 Introduction

In many traditional encryption schemes (e.g. RSA, ElGamal, Paillier) the plaintext and ciphertext spaces have a tremendous amount of algebraic structure, but the encryption and decryption functions either do not respect the algebraic structure at all, or respect only a part of it. Many schemes, such as ElGamal (resp. e.g. Paillier), are multiplicatively homomorphic (resp. additively homomorphic), but this restriction to one single algebraic operation is a very strong one, and the most interesting applications would instead require a ring structure between the plaintext and ciphertext spaces to be preserved by encryption and decryption. The first such encryption scheme was presented by Craig Gentry in his famous work [21], and since then researchers have introduced a number of new and more efficient *fully* homomorphic encryption schemes.

The early homomorphic encryption schemes were extremely impractical, but recently new implementations, new data encoding techniques, and a better understanding of the applications have started to change the situation. In 2015 we released the *Simple Encrypted Arithmetic Library - SEAL* [19] with the goal of providing a well-engineered and documented homomorphic encryption library, with no external dependencies, that would be equally easy to use both by experts and by non-experts with little or no cryptographic background.

R. Player—Much of this work was done during an internship at Microsoft Research, Redmond.

M. Brenner et al. (Eds.): FC 2017 Workshops 2017, LNCS 10323, pp. 3–18, 2017.
https://doi.org/10.1007/978-3-319-70278-0_1

SEAL is written in C++11, and contains a .NET wrapper library for the public API. It comes with example projects demonstrating key features, written both in C++ and in C#. SEAL compiles and is tested on modern versions of Visual Studio and GCC. In this paper we introduce the most recent version, SEAL v2.1, and describe some of its core functionality. The library is publicly available at http://sealcrypto.codeplex.com and is licensed under the Microsoft Research License Agreement.

1.1   Related Work

A number of other libraries implementing homomorphic encryption exist, e.g. HElib [2] and $\Lambda \circ \lambda$ [18]. The FV scheme has been implemented in [1,9], both of which use the ideal lattice library NFLlib [30]. Perhaps the most comparable work to SEAL is the C++ library HElib [2] which implements the BGV homomorphic encryption scheme [12].

A comparison of popular homomorphic encryption schemes, including BGV and FV, was presented by Costache and Smart in [14]. An comparison of the implementations, respectively, of BGV as in HElib and of FV as in SEAL would be very interesting, but appears challenging. One reason for this is that the documentation available for HElib [23–25] does not in general make clear how to select optimal parameters for performance, and in [25, Appendix A] it is noted '[t]he BGV implementation in HElib relies on a myriad of parameters ... it takes some experimentation to set them all so as to get a working implementation with good performance'. On the other hand, we know better how to select good parameters for performance for SEAL (see Sect. 4 below). Such a comparison is therefore deferred to future work.

2   Notation

We use $\lfloor \cdot \rfloor$, $\lceil \cdot \rceil$, and $\lfloor \cdot \rceil$ to denote rounding down, up, and to the nearest integer, respectively. When these operations are applied to a polynomial, we mean performing the corresponding operation to each coefficient separately. The norm $\|\cdot\|$ always denotes the infinity norm. We denote the reduction of an integer modulo t by $[\cdot]_t$. This operation can also be applied to polynomials, in which case it is applied to every integer coefficient separately. The reductions are always done into the symmetric interval $[-t/2, t/2)$. $\log_a$ denotes the base-a logarithm, and log always denotes the base-2 logarithm. Table 1 below lists commonly used parameters, and in some cases their corresponding names in SEAL.

3   Implementing the Fan-Vercauteren Scheme

In this section we present our implementation of the Fan-Vercauteren (FV) scheme [20].

As described in [20], the FV scheme consists of the following algorithms: SecretKeyGen, PublicKeyGen, EvaluateKeyGen, Encrypt, Decrypt, Add, Mul, and Relin (version 1). In SEAL we generalize the scheme a little bit, as will be discussed below.

Table 1. Notation used throughout this document.

Parameter	Description	Name in SEAL
q	Modulus in the ciphertext space (coefficient modulus)	`coeff_modulus`
t	Modulus in the plaintext space (plaintext modulus)	`plain_modulus`
n	A power of 2	
$x^n + 1$	The polynomial modulus which specifies the ring R	`poly_modulus`
R	The ring $\mathbb{Z}[x]/(x^n + 1)$	
R_a	The ring $\mathbb{Z}_a[x]/(x^n + 1)$	
w	A base into which ciphertext elements are decomposed during relinearization	
$\log w$		`decomposition_bit_count`
ℓ	There are $\ell + 1 = \lfloor \log_w q \rfloor + 1$ elements in each component of each evaluation key	
δ	Expansion factor in the ring R ($\delta \leq n$)	
Δ	Quotient on division of q by t, or $\lfloor q/t \rfloor$	
$r_t(q)$	Remainder on division of q by t, i.e. $q = \Delta t + r_t(q)$, where $0 \leq r_t(q) < t$	
χ	Error distribution (a truncated discrete Gaussian distribution)	
σ	Standard deviation of χ	`noise_standard_deviation`
B	Bound on the distribution χ	`noise_max_deviation`

3.1   Plaintext Space and Encodings

In FV the plaintext space is the polynomial quotient ring $R_t = \mathbb{Z}_t[x]/(x^n + 1)$. The homomorphic addition and multiplication operations on ciphertexts (that will be described later) will carry through the encryption to addition and multiplications operations in R_t. Plaintext polynomials are represented by instances of the `BigPoly` class in SEAL. In order to encrypt integers or rational numbers, one needs to encode them into elements of R_t. SEAL provides a few different encoders for this purpose (see Sect. 5).

3.2   Ciphertext Space

Ciphertexts in FV are vectors of polynomials in R_q. These vectors contain at least two polynomials, but grow in size in homomorphic multiplication operations, unless relinearization is performed. Homomorphic additions are performed by computing a component-wise sum of these vectors; homomorphic multiplications are slightly more complicated and will be described below. Ciphertexts are represented by instances of the `BigPolyArray` class in SEAL.

Textbook-FV only allows ciphertexts of size 2, resulting in minor changes to the homomorphic operations compared to their original description in [20]. We will describe below the algorithms that are implemented in SEAL.

3.3   Encryption and Decryption

Ciphertexts in SEAL are encrypted exactly as described in [20]. A SEAL ciphertext $\mathtt{ct} = (c_0, \ldots, c_k)$ is decrypted by computing

$$\left[\left\lfloor \frac{t}{q}[\mathtt{ct}(s)]_q \right\rceil \right]_t = \left[\left\lfloor \frac{t}{q} \left[c_0 + \cdots + c_k s^k \right]_q \right\rceil \right]_t .$$

Encryption are decryption are implemented in SEAL by the `Encryptor` and `Decryptor` classes, respectively.

3.4   Addition

Suppose two SEAL ciphertexts $\mathtt{ct}_1 = (c_0, \ldots, c_j)$ and $\mathtt{ct}_2 = (d_0, \ldots d_k)$ encrypt plaintext polynomials m_1 and m_2, respectively. Suppose WLOG $j \leq k$. Then

$$\mathtt{ct}_{\mathrm{add}} = ([c_0 + d_0]_q, \ldots, [c_j + d_j]_q, d_{j+1}, \ldots, d_k)$$

encrypts $[m_1 + m_2]_t$.

In SEAL homomorphic addition is implemented as `Evaluator::add`. Similarly, homomorphic subtraction is implemented as `Evaluator::sub`.

3.5   Multiplication

Let $\mathtt{ct}_1 = (c_0, c_1, \ldots, c_j)$ and $\mathtt{ct}_2 = (d_0, d_1, \ldots, d_k)$ be two SEAL ciphertexts of sizes $j + 1$ and $k + 1$, respectively. The output of $\mathtt{Mul}(\mathtt{ct}_1, \mathtt{ct}_2)$ is a ciphertext $\mathtt{ct}_{\mathrm{mult}} = (C_0, C_1, \ldots, C_{j+k})$ of size $j + k + 1$. The polynomials $C_m \in R_q$ are computed as

$$C_m = \left[\left\lfloor \frac{t}{q} \left(\sum_{r+s=m} c_r d_s \right) \right\rceil \right]_q .$$

In SEAL we define the function `Mul` (or rather family of functions) to mean this generalization of the Textbook-FV multiplication operation (without relinearization). It is implemented as `Evaluator::multiply`.

Algorithms for Polynomial Multiplication. Multiplication of polynomials in $\mathbb{Z}[x]/(x^n + 1)$ is the most computationally expensive part of Mul, which in SEAL we implement using Nussbaumer convolution [16]. Note that here polynomial multiplication needs to be performed with integer coefficients, whereas in other homomorphic operations it is done modulo q, which is significantly easier, and can always be done more efficiently using the Number Theoretic Transform (NTT).

It is also possible to implement a Karatsuba-like trick to reduce the number of calls to Nussbaumer convolution, reducing the number of polynomial multiplications to multiply two ciphertexts of sizes k_1 and k_2 from $k_1 k_2$ to $c k_1 k_2$, where $c \in (0, 1)$ is some constant depending on k_1 and k_2. For example, if $k_1 = k_2 = 2$, then $c = 3/4$, which is currently the only case implemented in SEAL.

3.6 Relinearization

The goal of relinearization is to decrease the size of the ciphertext back to (at least) 2 after it has been increased by multiplications as was described in Sect. 3.5. In other words, given a size $k + 1$ ciphertext $(c_0, \ldots, c_k)$ that can be decrypted as was shown in Sect. 3.3, relinearization is supposed to produce a ciphertext $(c'_0, \ldots, c'_{k-1})$ of size k, or—when applied repeatedly—of any size at least 2, that can be decrypted using a smaller degree decryption function to yield the same result. This conversion will require a so-called *evaluation key* (or *keys*) to be given to the evaluator, as we will explain below.

Let w denote a power of 2, and let $\ell + 1 = \lfloor \log_w q \rfloor + 1$ denote the number of terms in the decomposition into base w of an integer in base q. We will also decompose polynomials in R_q into base-w components coefficient-wise, resulting in $\ell + 1$ polynomials. Now consider the EvaluateKeyGen (version 1) algorithm in [20], which for every $i \in \{0, \ldots, \ell\}$ samples $a_i \xleftarrow{\$} R_q$, $e_i \leftarrow \chi$, and outputs the vector

$$\mathsf{evk}_2 = \left[\left([-(a_0 s + e_0) + w^0 s^2]_q, a_0 \right), \ldots, \left([-(a_\ell s + e_\ell) + w^\ell s^2]_q, a_\ell \right) \right].$$

In SEAL we generalize this to j-power evaluation keys by sampling several a_i and e_i as above, and setting instead

$$\mathsf{evk}_j = \left[\left([-(a_0 s + e_0) + w^0 s^j]_q, a_0 \right), \ldots, \left([-(a_\ell s + e_\ell) + w^\ell s^j]_q, a_\ell \right) \right].$$

Suppose we have a set of evaluation keys $\mathsf{evk}_2, \ldots, \mathsf{evk}_k$. Then relinearization converts $(c_0, c_1, \ldots, c_k)$ into $(c'_0, c'_1, \ldots, c'_{k-1})$, where

$$c'_0 = c_0 + \sum_{i=0}^{\ell} \mathsf{evk}_k[i][0] c_k^{(i)}, \quad c'_1 = c_1 + \sum_{i=0}^{\ell} \mathsf{evk}_k[i][1] c_k^{(i)},$$

and $c'_j = c_j$ for $2 \le j \le k - 1$.

Note that in order to generate evaluation keys access to the secret key is needed. This means that the owner of the secret key must generate an appropriate number of evaluation keys and share them with the evaluating party in advance of the relinearization computation, which further means that the evaluating party needs to inform the owner of the secret key beforehand whether or not they intend to relinearize, and if so, by how many steps. Note that if they choose to relinearize after every multiplication, only evk_2 will be needed. SEAL implements the above operation as `Evaluator::relinearize`.

3.7   Other Homomorphic Operations

In addition to the operations described above, SEAL implements a few other useful operations, such as negation (`Evaluator::negate`), multiplication by a plaintext polynomial (`Evaluator::multiply_plain`), addition (`Evaluator::add_plain`) and subtraction (`Evaluator::sub_plain`) of a plaintext polynomial, noise-optimal product of several ciphertexts (`Evaluator::multiply_many`), exponentiation with relinearization at every step (`Evaluator:exponentiate`), and a sum of several ciphertexts (`Evaluator::add_many`).

SEAL has a fast algorithm for computing the product of a ciphertext with itself. The difference is only in computational complexity, and the noise growth behavior is the same as in calling `Evaluator::multiply` with a repeated input parameter. This is implemented as `Evaluator::square`.

3.8   Key Distribution

In Textbook-FV the secret key is a polynomial sampled uniformly from R_2, i.e. it is a polynomial with coefficients in $\{0, 1\}$. In SEAL we instead sample the key uniformly from R_3, i.e. we use coefficients $\{-1, 0, 1\}$.

4   Encryption Parameters

Everything in SEAL starts with the construction of an instance of a container that holds the encryption parameters (`EncryptionParameters`). These parameters are:

- `poly_modulus`: a polynomial $x^n + 1$;
- `coeff_modulus`: an integer modulus q;
- `plain_modulus`: an integer modulus t;
- `noise_standard_deviation`: a standard deviation σ;
- `noise_max_deviation`: a bound for the error distribution B;
- `decomposition_bit_count`: the logarithm $\log w$ of w (Sect. 3.6);
- `random_generator`: a source of randomness.

Some of these parameters are optional, e.g. if the user does not specify σ or B they will be set to default values. If the the decomposition bit count is not set (to a non-zero value), SEAL will assume that no relinearization is going to be performed, and prevents the creation of any evaluation keys. If no randomness source is given, SEAL will automatically use `std::random_device`.

In this section we will describe the encryption parameters and their impact on performance. We will discuss security in Sect. 7. In Sect. 4.4 we will discuss the automatic parameter selection tools in SEAL, which can assist the user in determining (close to) optimal encryption parameters for many types of computations.

4.1 Default Values

The constructor of `EncryptionParameters` sets the values for σ and B by default to the ones returned by the static functions

> `ChooserEvaluator::default_noise_standard_deviation()`, and
>
> `ChooserEvaluator::default_noise_max_deviation()`.

Currently these default values are set to 3.19 and 15.95, respectively. As we also mentioned above, unless they want to use relinearization, the user does not need to set `decomposition_bit_count`. By default the constructor will set its value to zero, which will prevent the construction of evaluation keys.

SEAL comes with a list of pairs (n, q) that are returned by the static function

> `ChooserEvaluator::default_parameter_options()`

as a keyed list (`std::map`). The default (n, q) pairs are presented in Table 2.

Table 2. Default pairs (n, q).

n	q
1024	$2^{35} - 2^{14} + 2^{11} + 1$
2048	$2^{60} - 2^{14} + 1$
4096	$2^{116} - 2^{18} + 1$
8192	$2^{226} - 2^{26} + 1$
16384	$2^{435} - 2^{33} + 1$

4.2 Polynomial Modulus

The polynomial modulus (`poly_modulus`) is required to be a polynomial of the form $x^n + 1$, where n is a power of 2. This is both for security and performance reasons (see Sect. 7).

Using a larger n decreases performance. On the other hand, it allows for a larger q to be used without decreasing the security level, which in turn increases the noise ceiling and thus allows for larger t to be used. A large value of t allows the scheme to support larger integer arithmetic. When CRT batching is used (Sect. 5.3), a larger n will allow for more elements of $\mathbb{Z}_t$ to be batched into one plaintext.

4.3   Coefficient Modulus and Plaintext Modulus

Suppose the polynomial modulus is held fixed. Then the choice of the coefficient modulus q affects two things: the upper bound on the inherent noise that a ciphertext can contain[1] (see Sect. 6), and the security level[2] (see Sect. 7.2 and references therein).

In principle we can take q to be any integer, but taking q to be of special form provides performance benefits. First, if q is of the form $2^A - B$, where B is an integer of small absolute value, then modular reduction modulo q can be sped up, yielding overall better performance.

Second, if q is a prime with $2n|(q-1)$, then SEAL can use the Number Theoretic Transform (NTT) for polynomial multiplications, resulting in huge performance benefits in encryption, relinearization and decryption. SEAL uses David Harvey's algorithm for NTT, as described in [26], which additionally requires that $4q \leq \beta$, where β denotes the *word size* of q:

$$\beta = 2^{64\lceil \log(q)/64 \rceil} .$$

Third, if $t|(q - 1)$ (i.e. $r_t(q) = 1$), then the noise growth properties are improved in certain homomorphic operations (recall Table 3).

The default parameters in Table 2 satisfy all of these guidelines. They are prime numbers of the form $2^A - B$ where B is much smaller than 2^A. They are congruent to 1 modulo $2n$, and not too close to the word size boundary. Finally, $r_t(q) = 1$ for t that are reasonably large powers of 2, for example the default parameters for $n = 4096$ provide good performance when t is a power of 2 up to 2^{18}.

We note that when using CRT batching (see Sect. 5.3) it will not be possible to have t be a power of 2, as t needs to instead be a prime of a particular form. In this case the user can try to choose the entire triple (n, q, t) simultaneously, so that $t = 1 \pmod{2n}$ and q satisfies as many of the good properties listed above as possible.

4.4   Automatic Parameter Selection

To assist the user in choosing parameters for a specific computation, SEAL provides an automatic parameter selection tool. It consists of two parts: a `Simulator` component that simulates noise growth in homomorphic operations using the estimates of Table 3, and a `Chooser` component, which estimates the growth of the coefficients in the underlying plaintext polynomials, and uses `Simulator` to simulate noise growth. `Chooser` also provides tools for computing an optimized parameter set once it knows what kind of computation the user wishes to perform.

---

[1] Bigger q means higher noise bound (good).
[2] Bigger q means lower security (bad).

5   Encoding

One of the most important aspects in making homomorphic encryption practical and useful is in using an appropriate *encoder* for the task at hand. Recall that plaintext elements in the FV scheme are polynomials in R_t. In typical applications of homomorphic encryption, the user would instead want to perform computations on integers or rational numbers. Encoders are responsible for converting the user's inputs to polynomials in R_t by applying an encoding map. In order for the operations on ciphertexts to reflect the operations on the inputs, the encoding and decoding maps need to respect addition and multiplication.

5.1   Integer Encoder

In SEAL the *integer encoder* is used to encode integers into plaintext polynomials. Despite its name, the integer encoder is really a *family* of encoders, one for each integer base $\beta \geq 2$.

When $\beta = 2$, the idea of the integer encoder is to encode an integer a in the range $[-(2^n - 1), 2^n - 1]$ as follows. It forms the (upto n-bit) binary expansion of $|a|$, say $a_{n-1} \ldots a_1 a_0$, and outputs the polynomial

$$\texttt{IntegerEncode}(a, \beta = 2) = \text{sign}(a) \cdot \left(a_{n-1}x^{n-1} + \ldots + a_1 x + a_0\right) .$$

Decoding (`IntegerDecode`) amounts to evaluating a plaintext polynomial at $x = 2$. It is clear that in good conditions (see below) the integer encoder respects addition and multiplication:

$$\texttt{IntegerDecode}\left[\texttt{IntegerEncode}(a) + \texttt{IntegerEncode}(b)\right] = a + b \,,$$

$$\texttt{IntegerDecode}\left[\texttt{IntegerEncode}(a) \cdot \texttt{IntegerEncode}(b)\right] = ab \,.$$

When β is set to some integer larger than 2, instead of a binary expansion (as was done in the example above) a base-β expansion is used. SEAL uses a *balanced* base-β representation to keep the absolute values of the coefficients as small as possible [19].

Note that the infinity norm of a freshly encoded plaintext polynomial is bounded by $\beta/2$, and the degree of the polynomial encoding a is bounded by $\lceil \log_\beta(|a|) \rceil$. However, as homomorphic operations are performed on the encryptions, the infinity norm and degree will both grow. When the degree becomes greater than or equal to n, or the infinity norm greater than $t/2$, the polynomial will "wrap around" in R_t, yielding an incorrect result. In order to get the correct result, one needs to choose n and t to accommodate the largest plaintext polynomial appearing during the computation. For a very nice estimate on how large n and t need to be, we refer the reader to [15].

The integer encoder is available in SEAL through the `IntegerEncoder` class. Its constructor will require both the `plain_modulus` and the base β as parameters. If no base is given, the default value $\beta = 2$ is used.

5.2 Fractional Encoder

There are several ways for encoding rational numbers in SEAL. One way is to simply scale all rational numbers to integers, encode them using the integer encoder described above, and record the scaling factor in the clear as a part of the ciphertext. We then need to keep track of the scaling during computations, which results in some inefficiency. Here we describe what we call the *fractional encoder*, which has the benefit of automatically keeping track of the scaling. Just like the integer encoder, the fractional encoder is really a family of encoders, parametrized by an integer base $\beta \geq 2$. The function of this base is exactly the same as in the integer encoder, and we will only explain how the fractional encoder works when $\beta = 2$.

Consider the rational number 5.8125, with the finite binary expansion

$$5.875 = 2^2 + 2^0 + 2^{-1} + 2^{-2} + 2^{-4}.$$

First we take the integer part and encode it as usual with the integer encoder, obtaining the polynomial $\texttt{IntegerEncode}(5, \beta = 2) = x^2 + 1$. Then we take the fractional part, add n (degree of the polynomial modulus) to each exponent, and convert it into a polynomial by changing the base 2 into the variable x. Finally we flip the signs of each of the terms, in this case obtaining $-x^{n-1} - x^{n-2} - x^{n-4}$. This defines $\texttt{FracEncode}(r, \beta = 2)$ for rational numbers $r \in [0, 1)$. For any rational number r with a finite binary expansion, we set

$$\texttt{FracEncode}(r, \beta = 2) = \text{sign}(r) \cdot [\texttt{IntegerEncode}(\lfloor |r| \rfloor, \beta = 2)$$
$$+ \texttt{FracEncode}(\{|r|\}, \beta = 2)],$$

where the fractional part is denoted by $\{\cdot\}$. Concluding our example, $\texttt{FracEncode}(5.8125, \beta = 2)$ yields the polynomial $-x^{n-1} - x^{n-2} - x^{n-4} + x^2 + 1$. Decoding works by reversing the steps described above. It is easy to see that $\texttt{FracEncode}$ respects both addition and multiplication [19].

The fractional encoder is implemented by the class $\texttt{FractionalEncoder}$. Its constructor will take as parameters the $\texttt{plain\_modulus}$, the base β, and positive integers n_f and n_i with $n_f + n_i \leq n$, which describe how many coefficients are reserved for the fractional and integer parts, respectively.[3] If no base is given, the default value $\beta = 2$ is used.

Comparing the Two Fractional Encoding Approaches. The *scale-to-integer* technique mentioned above, and our fractional encoder, have similar performance and limitations, but are not equivalent. In some cases the fractional encoder is strictly better.

For example, suppose the homomorphic operations result in some cancellations in the underlying plaintext. Since the level of a scaled encoder never

---

[3] More precisely, n_f describes how many coefficients are used when truncating possibly infinite base-β expansions of rational numbers.

drops, it does not recognize this cancellation, and once the level reaches its maximum (n coefficients), decoding will fail. For the fractional encoder, however, cancellations take care of themselves, permitting potentially more homomorphic operations. As a concrete example, consider $n = 8$, base $\beta = 2$, and the computation $(12 \cdot 0.25)^3$. With the scale-to-integer technique, a rational number $a/2^i$ is encoded as $(p(x), i)$, where $p(x)$ is an integer encoding of a. Hence, the inputs are encoded as $(x^3 + x^2, 0)$, and $(0, 2)$. The result of the computation is $(3x^7 + x^6 - x - 3, 6)$, which does not decode to the correct result since the first entry wrapped around $x^n + 1$. On the other hand, with the fractional encoder, the two inputs are encoded as $x^3 + x^2$ and $-x^6$, and the resulting plaintext polynomial is equal to $(x + 1)^3$, which decodes correctly.

Remark 1. In [15] the authors claimed that the two fractional encoding methods above are equivalent, by claiming the existence of an isomorphism between the underlying rings. We would like to point out that their object R_1 does not satisfy the distribution law, hence is not a ring. This was likely an innocent typo (indeed, with a sign mistake fixed R_1 does become a ring), but even then the map $\phi : R_1 \rightarrow R_2$ in their paper is only a surjective homomorphism, and not injective, due to the fact that encoding is not unique: e.g. (x^i, i) encodes the integer 1 for all i.

5.3   CRT Batching

The *CRT (Chinese Remainder Theorem) batching* technique allows upto n integers modulo t to be packed into one plaintext polynomial, and operating on those integers in a *SIMD (Single Instruction, Multiple Data)* manner. For more details and applications we refer the reader to [11, 19, 34].

Batching provides the maximal number of plaintext slots when the plaintext modulus t is chosen to be a prime number and congruent to 1 (mod $2n$), which we assume to be the case. Then there exists (see e.g. [19]) a ring isomorphism `Decompose` : $R_t \rightarrow \prod_{i=0}^{n-1} \mathbb{Z}_t$, whose inverse we denote by `Compose`. In SEAL, `Compose` and `Decompose` are computed using a negacyclic variant of the Number Theoretic Transform (NTT).

When used correctly, batching can provide an enormous performance improvement over the other encoders. Note, however, that for computations on encrypted integers rather than on integers modulo t one needs to ensure that the values in the individual *slots* never wrap around t during the computation.

SEAL provides all of the batching-related tools in the `PolyCRTBuilder` class.

6   Inherent Noise

Definition 1 (Inherent noise). *Let* $\mathtt{ct} = (c_0, c_1, \ldots, c_k)$ *be a ciphertext encrypting the message* $m \in R_t$. *Its inherent noise is the unique polynomial* $v \in R$ *with smallest infinity norm such that*

$$\mathtt{ct}(s) = c_0 + c_1 s + \cdots + c_k s^k = \Delta m + v + aq$$

for some polynomial a.

It is proved in [20], that the function (or family of functions) `Decrypt`, as presented in Sect. 3.3, correctly decrypts a ciphertext as long as the inherent noise satisfies $\|v\| < \Delta/2$.

6.1 Overview of Noise Growth

We present in Table 3 probabilistic estimates of noise growth in some of the most common homomorphic operations. Even though these are estimates, they are simple and work well in practice. For input ciphertexts $\texttt{ct}_i$ we denote their respective inherent noises by v_i. When there is a single encrypted input `ct` we denote its inherent noise by v.

Table 3. Noise estimates for homomorphic operations in SEAL.

Operation	Input description	Estimated output noise
`Encrypt`	Plaintext $m \in R_t$	$2B\sqrt{2n/3}$
`Negate`	Ciphertext ct	$\|v\|$
`Add/Sub`	Ciphertexts $\texttt{ct}_1$ and $\texttt{ct}_2$	$\|v_1\| + \|v_2\| + r_t(q)$
`AddPlain/` `SubPlain`	Ciphertext ct and plaintext m	$\|v\| + r_t(q)$
`MultiplyPlain`	Ciphertext ct and plaintext m with N non-zero coefficients	$N\|m\| \left(\|v\| + r_t(q)/2 \right)$
`Multiply` (with integer encoders)	Ciphertexts $\texttt{ct}_1$ and $\texttt{ct}_2$ of sizes $j_1 + 1$ and $j_2 + 1$	$t\left(\|v_1\| + \|v_2\| + r_t(q) \right)$ $\times \left\lceil \sqrt{2n/3} \right\rceil^{j_1+j_2-1} 2^{j_1+j_2}$
`Multiply` (with `PolyCRTBuilder`)	Ciphertexts $\texttt{ct}_1$ and $\texttt{ct}_2$ of sizes $j_1 + 1$ and $j_2 + 1$	$nt\left(\|v_1\| + \|v_2\| + r_t(q) \right)$ $\times \left\lceil \sqrt{2n/3} \right\rceil^{j_1+j_2-1} 2^{j_1+j_2}$
`Square`	Ciphertext ct of size j	Same as $\texttt{Multiply}(\texttt{ct}, \texttt{ct})$
`Relinearize`	Ciphertext ct of size K and target size $L < K$	$\|v\|$ $+(K - L)\sqrt{n}B(\ell + 1)w$

6.2 Maximal Levels for Default Parameters

In Table 4 we give the maximal supported levels for various power-of-2 plaintext moduli, only taking the noise growth into account. The coefficient moduli are chosen to be the defaults, given in Table 2. We chose to use a uniformly random polynomial in R_t as the plaintext.

Table 4. Maximal levels for different choices of polynomial modulus and plaintext modulus.

n	$\log_2 q$	$\log_2 t$	Max. level
2^{10}	35	6	1
2^{11}	60	7	2
		16	1
2^{12}	116	1	6
		8	4
		20	2
2^{13}	226	8	8
		20	5
		30	3
2^{14}	435	8	15
		32	7
		64	4

7   Security of FV

7.1   Ring-Learning with Errors

The security of the FV encryption scheme is based on the apparent hardness of the famous *Ring-Learning with Errors (RLWE)* problem [29]. Each RLWE sample can be used to extract n *Learning with Errors (LWE)* samples [27,32]. The concrete hardness depends on the parameters n, q, and the standard deviation of the error distribution σ.

7.2   Security of the Default Parameters in SEAL v2.1

We now give an estimate of the security of the default parameters in SEAL v2.1 based on the LWE estimator of [7].[4] The estimator takes as input an LWE instance given by a dimension n, a modulus q, and a *relative error* $\alpha = \sqrt{2\pi}\sigma/q$. For various attacks it returns estimates for the number of bit operations, memory, and number of samples required to break the LWE instance. In Table 5 we give the expected number of bit operations required to attack the LWE instances induced by the SEAL v2.1 default parameters, assuming that the attacker has as many samples, and as much memory, as they would require. Recall from Sect. 4.1 that in SEAL the default standard deviation is $\sigma = 3.19$, so we always have $\alpha q = \sigma\sqrt{2\pi} \approx 8$, and we use $\alpha = 8/q$. We use the default n and q as presented in Table 2.

Recently, Albrecht [3] described new attacks on LWE instances where the secret is very small, and presented estimates of the cost of these attacks on

---

[4] We used the version available on February 23rd, 2017 (commit `d70e1e9`).

Table 5. Estimates of log of the bit operations required to perform the above named attacks on the SEAL v2.1 default parameters. The symbol '—' denotes that the estimator did not return a result.

n	q	α	small sis	bkw	sis	dec	Kannan
1024	$2^{35} - 2^{14} + 2^{11} + 1$	$8/q$	97.6	237.4	126.5	116.1	116.6
2048	$2^{60} - 2^{14} + 1$	$8/q$	115.1	391.2	136.2	129.0	129.5
4096	$2^{116} - 2^{18} + 1$	$8/q$	119.1	615.3	132.7	128.2	129.2
8192	$2^{226} - 2^{26} + 1$	$8/q$	123.1	1168.6	132.2	—	131.1
16384	$2^{435} - 2^{33} + 1$	$8/q$	130.5	1783.5	134.4	—	135.9

the default parameters used in SEAL v2.0. Estimates for cost of the attacks described in [3] have been included into the LWE estimator of [7]. In Table 5 we have included the attack presented in [3, Sects. 3 and 4], labelled 'small sis', which performs best against the SEAL v2.1 parameters. To label the other attacks we follow the notation of [7]: 'bkw' denotes a variant [22] of the BKW attack [5,10], 'sis' denotes a distinguishing attack as described in [31]; 'dec' denotes a decoding attack as described in e.g. [28]; 'kannan' denotes the attack described in [6]. The estimator was not run for Arora-Ge type attacks [4,8] or for meet-in-the-middle type attacks, since these are both expected to be very costly.

Remark 2. At the time of writing this, determining the concrete hardness of parametrizations of (R)LWE is an active area of research (see e.g. [7,13,17]), and no standardized (R)LWE parameter sets exist. Therefore, when using SEAL or any other implementation of (R)LWE-based cryptography, we strongly recommend the user to consult experts in the security of (R)LWE when choosing which parameters to use.

References

1. FV-NFLlib. https://github.com/CryptoExperts/FV-NFLlib. Accessed 17 Feb 2017
2. HElib. https://github.com/shaih/HElib. Accessed 21 Nov 2016
3. Albrecht, M.R.: On dual lattice attacks against small-secret LWE and parameter choices in HElib and SEAL. Cryptology ePrint Archive, Report 2017/047 (2017). http://eprint.iacr.org/2017/047
4. Albrecht, M.R., Cid, C., Faugère, J.-C., Fitzpatrick, R., Perret, L.: Algebraic algorithms for LWE problems. IACR Cryptology ePrint Archive 2014:1018 (2014)
5. Albrecht, M.R., Cid, C., Faugère, J.-C., Fitzpatrick, R., Perret, L.: On the complexity of the BKW algorithm on LWE. Des. Codes Crypt. **74**(2), 325–354 (2015)
6. Albrecht, M.R., Fitzpatrick, R., Göpfert, F.: On the efficacy of solving LWE by reduction to unique-SVP. In: Lee, H.-S., Han, D.-G. (eds.) ICISC 2013. LNCS, vol. 8565, pp. 293–310. Springer, Cham (2014). https://doi.org/10.1007/978-3-319-12160-4_18
7. Albrecht, M.R., Player, R., Scott, S.: On the concrete hardness of learning with errors. J. Math. Cryptol. **9**(3), 169–203 (2015)

8. Arora, S., Ge, R.: New algorithms for learning in presence of errors. In: Aceto, L., Henzinger, M., Sgall, J. (eds.) ICALP 2011. LNCS, vol. 6755, pp. 403–415. Springer, Heidelberg (2011). https://doi.org/10.1007/978-3-642-22006-7_34
9. Bajard, J.C., Eynard, J., Hasan, A., Zucca, V.: A full RNS variant of FV like somewhat homomorphic encryption schemes. Cryptology ePrint Archive, Report 2016/510 (2016). http://eprint.iacr.org/2016/510
10. Blum, A., Kalai, A., Wasserman, H.: Noise-tolerant learning, the parity problem, and the statistical query model. J. ACM **50**(4), 506–519 (2003)
11. Brakerski, Z., Gentry, C., Halevi, S.: Packed ciphertexts in LWE-based homomorphic encryption. In: Kurosawa, K., Hanaoka, G. (eds.) PKC 2013. LNCS, vol. 7778, pp. 1–13. Springer, Heidelberg (2013). https://doi.org/10.1007/978-3-642-36362-7_1
12. Brakerski, Z., Gentry, C., Vaikuntanathan, V.: (Leveled) fully homomorphic encryption without bootstrapping. In: Proceedings of the 3rd Innovations in Theoretical Computer Science Conference, pp. 309–325. ACM (2012)
13. Buchmann, J.A., Büscher, N., Göpfert, F., Katzenbeisser, S., Krämer, J., Micciancio, D., Siim, S., van Vredendaal, C., Walter, M.: Creating cryptographic challenges using multi-party computation: the LWE challenge. In: Emura, K., Hanaoka, G., Zhang, R. (eds.) Proceedings of the 3rd ACM International Workshop on ASIA Public-Key Cryptography, AsiaPKC@AsiaCCS, Xi'an, China, May 30–June 03, 2016, pp. 11–20. ACM (2016)
14. Costache, A., Smart, N.P.: Which ring based somewhat homomorphic encryption scheme is best? In: Sako, K. [33], pp. 325–340
15. Costache, A., Smart, N.P., Vivek, S., Waller, A.: Fixed point arithmetic in SHE schemes. Technical report, Cryptology ePrint Archive, Report 2016/250 (2016). http://eprint.iacr.org/2016/250
16. Crandall, R., Pomerance, C.: Prime Numbers: A Computational Perspective, vol. 182. Springer Science and Business Media, Heidelberg (2006). https://doi.org/10.1007/0-387-28979-8
17. Crockett, E., Peikert, C.: Challenges for ring-LWE. Cryptology ePrint Archive, Report 2016/782 (2016). http://eprint.iacr.org/2016/782
18. Crockett, E., Peikert, C.: Λoλ: functional lattice cryptography. In: Weippl, E.R., Katzenbeisser, S., Kruegel, C., Myers, A.C., Halevi, S. (eds.) Proceedings of the 2016 ACM SIGSAC Conference on Computer and Communications Security, Vienna, Austria, 24–28 October 2016, pp. 993–1005. ACM (2016)
19. Dowlin, N., Gilad-Bachrach, R., Laine, K., Lauter, K., Naehrig, M., Wernsing, J.: Manual for using homomorphic encryption for bioinformatics. Technical report, Microsoft Research (2015). http://research.microsoft.com/apps/pubs/default.aspx?id=258435
20. Fan, J., Vercauteren, F.: Somewhat practical fully homomorphic encryption. Cryptology ePrint Archive, Report 2012/144 (2012). http://eprint.iacr.org/
21. Gentry, C.: Fully homomorphic encryption using ideal lattices. STOC **9**, 169–178 (2009)
22. Guo, Q., Johansson, T., Stankovski, P.: Coded-BKW: solving LWE using lattice codes. In: Gennaro, R., Robshaw, M. (eds.) CRYPTO 2015. LNCS, vol. 9215, pp. 23–42. Springer, Heidelberg (2015). https://doi.org/10.1007/978-3-662-47989-6_2
23. Halevi, S., Shoup, V.: Design and implementation of a homomorphic-encryption library (2013). http://people.csail.mit.edu/shaih/pubs/he-library.pdf
24. Halevi, S., Shoup, V.: Algorithms in HElib. In: Garay, J.A., Gennaro, R. (eds.) CRYPTO 2014. LNCS, vol. 8616, pp. 554–571. Springer, Heidelberg (2014). https://doi.org/10.1007/978-3-662-44371-2_31

25. Halevi, S., Shoup, V.: Bootstrapping for HElib. In: Oswald, E., Fischlin, M. (eds.) EUROCRYPT 2015. LNCS, vol. 9056, pp. 641–670. Springer, Heidelberg (2015). https://doi.org/10.1007/978-3-662-46800-5_25
26. Harvey, D.: Faster arithmetic for number-theoretic transforms. J. Symb. Comput. **60**, 113–119 (2014)
27. Lepoint, T., Naehrig, M.: A Comparison of the homomorphic encryption schemes FV and YASHE. In: Pointcheval, D., Vergnaud, D. (eds.) AFRICACRYPT 2014. LNCS, vol. 8469, pp. 318–335. Springer, Cham (2014). https://doi.org/10.1007/978-3-319-06734-6_20
28. Lindner, R., Peikert, C.: Better key sizes (and attacks) for LWE-based encryption. In: Kiayias, A. (ed.) CT-RSA 2011. LNCS, vol. 6558, pp. 319–339. Springer, Heidelberg (2011). https://doi.org/10.1007/978-3-642-19074-2_21
29. Lyubashevsky, V., Peikert, C., Regev, O.: On ideal lattices and learning with errors over rings. In: Gilbert, H. (ed.) EUROCRYPT 2010. LNCS, vol. 6110, pp. 1–23. Springer, Heidelberg (2010). https://doi.org/10.1007/978-3-642-13190-5_1
30. Aguilar-Melchor, C., Barrier, J., Guelton, S., Guinet, A., Killijian, M.-O., Lepoint, T.: NFLLIB: NTT-based fast lattice library. In: Sako [33], pp. 341–356
31. Micciancio, D., Regev, O.: Post-quantum cryptography. In: Bernstein, D.J., Buchmann, J., Dahmen, E. (eds.) Lattice-based Cryptography. Springer, Heidelberg (2009). https://doi.org/10.1007/978-3-540-88702-7_5
32. Regev, O.: On lattices, learning with errors, random linear codes, and cryptography. In: Gabow, H.N., Fagin, R. (eds.) Proceedings of the 37th Annual ACM Symposium on Theory of Computing, Baltimore, MD, USA, 22–24 May 2005, pp. 84–93. ACM (2005)
33. Sako, K. (ed.): CT-RSA 2016. LNCS, vol. 9610. Springer, Cham (2016). https://doi.org/10.1007/978-3-319-29485-8
34. Smart, N.P., Vercauteren, F.: Fully homomorphic SIMD operations. Des. Codes Crypt. **71**(1), 57–81 (2014)

Towards Privacy-Preserving Multi-party Bartering

Stefan Wüller[1]([⊠]), Ulrike Meyer[1], and Susanne Wetzel[2]

[1] RWTH Aachen University, Aachen, Germany
{wueller,meyer}@itsec.rwth-aachen.de
[2] Stevens Institute of Technology, Hoboken, NJ, USA
swetzel@stevens.edu

Abstract. Both B2B bartering as well as bartering between individuals is increasingly facilitated through online platforms. However, typically these platforms lack automation and tend to neglect the privacy of their users by leaking crucial information about trades. It is in this context that we devise the first privacy-preserving protocol for automatically determining an actual trade between multiple parties without involving a trusted third party.

1 Introduction

The Encyclopedia Britannica defines *bartering* as "the direct exchange of goods or services—without an intervening medium of exchange or money—either according to established rates of exchange or by bargaining". Bartering is considered to be the oldest form of trading and has been practiced since the early days of humanity. In this traditional form, bartering typically requires a party to find a single trade partner that offers what the party demands and at the same time demands what the party offers. Alternatively, it may try to find a larger trade cycle in which more than two parties will exchange their goods or services in a cyclic fashion. While the former may not even exist, the latter is difficult if not even impossible to find. In any case, the offer and demand of each party needs to be satisfied simultaneously.

The introduction of currencies resolved these issues to some extent. In particular, it allows to decouple the search for a trade partner that satisfies a partys demand from the search for a trade partner that demands what that party offers. In addition, traditional trading with (cash) currencies guarantees that each party only learns how much of what it is selling to whom and how much of what it is buying from whom but nothing about what their trade partners do in return. Also there is no bank or any other trusted third party directly involved in the trading, observing who buys what from whom. The importance of these privacy guarantees offered by cash currencies are widely recognized and have led to the introduction of many successful digital counterparts (e.g., Bitcoin [11]).

Despite the benefits of using money as a mediator in trading, bartering has become popular again in recent years. This is due, among other reasons, to the

© International Financial Cryptography Association 2017
M. Brenner et al. (Eds.): FC 2017 Workshops 2017, LNCS 10323, pp. 19–34, 2017.
https://doi.org/10.1007/978-3-319-70278-0_2

fact that online bartering platforms greatly facilitate the cumbersome search for trade partners (e.g., U-Exchange, BarterQuest, or TradeYa). However, these platforms typically disclose what (and how much) parties seek or offer at least to the operator of the platform and typically also to other parties even if a trade between these parties is not possible. Thus the privacy guarantees offered by traditional bartering (i.e., a party merely learns what it gets and what it gives away and there is no third party observing the transactions) are lost.

The goal of our work is to follow suit with digital cash and enable electronic bartering with privacy guarantees equivalent to the guarantees provided by traditional bartering or trading using (cash) currencies. In our bartering process, each party specifies a quote defining its offered and desired commodity and the corresponding quantity ranges. A party keeps its quote private at all times from all other parties. Upon completion of the privacy-preserving bartering process, each party learns nothing but its direct trade partners as well as the commodities and quantities to be sent and received. Thus, for a given set of parties and their quotes, our bartering process privately determines an actual trade which includes the actual trade constellation of the parties (i.e., which party trades with which other party) as well as the actual commodities and quantities to be traded. The actual trade can be selected based on different selection strategies including the maximization of the number of parties able to trade. At the core of our bartering process (designed as a secure multi-party protocol based on homomorphic threshold encryption) is a novel protocol that privately determines the actual trade constellation. This protocol makes use of a novel privacy-preserving mapping operation that is based on the uniqueness of prime factorization, which is of independent interest beyond the context of electronic bartering.

Obviously, given their local view of the actual trade constellation, the parties can negotiate the quantities at which the commodities are to be exchanged outside of the bartering process described above. Yet, it is important to recognize that in practice this requires one of the parties to first state its intentions. In order to compensate for such a disadvantage, a party may elect to lie about the range it is willing to accept. As a first step to mitigating this problem, we enable to negotiate the actual quantities in an automatic and unbiased fashion by randomly sampling out of a private interval (defined by the private limits of the parties). As such, this approach motivates the parties to privately specify their true negotiation ranges.

2   Related Work

For the two-party case, secure multi-party computation (SMPC) protocols for privacy-preserving bartering have been proposed, e.g., in [5,7]. While these two-party protocols can obviously be used to find pairwise trades in the multi-party setting with more than two parties as well, they cannot be used to determine trade cycles between more than two parties. The particular challenge of finding such cycles in a privacy-preserving way in the SMPC setting has already been recognized in [6] but has not been addressed so far.

To the best of our knowledge, there is only one approach to privacy-preserving multi-party bartering that has been proposed in the past [9]: Kannan et al. introduce a protocol where each party holds an indivisible commodity from a publicly known finite set of commodities as well as a totally ordered preference list over all commodities in the set. Their goal is then to determine an actual trade between multiple parties such that the computed commodity allocation is pareto optimal while the input of each party (commodity and preference list) is kept private. Specifically, the protocol protects the parties' input under the notion of *marginal differential privacy* [9] which is a relaxation of *differential privacy* [4]. In contrast to differential privacy, marginal differential privacy is restricted to an adversary that has access to the protocol output of only one single party which corresponds to the assumption that there are no colluding parties participating in the protocol which try to subvert the privacy of another party. The substantial difference between the approach from [9] and our approach is that the former one focalizes on the privacy of the parties' input after the functionality is computed while the major goal of our approach is to provide privacy during the computation of an actual trade. Further differences to our work are that the protocol from [9] requires a trusted third party in order to determine an actual trade and that they use a weaker privacy notion that assumes non-colluding parties. In our approach, an actual trade is computed without the help of a trusted third party and we allow that all but one colluding parties may be controlled by an adversary. In addition, our approach supports divisible commodities.

In contrast to e-commerce (and auctions), bartering transactions are not necessarily reduced to money which allows for a richer structure of exchanges [10]: A trade takes place if the involved parties are satisfied w.r.t. the specification of their offered and desired commodities and the corresponding quantities. If the commodities first have to be converted into money (as it is the case for e-commerce and auctions), the prices of the commodities have to be individually determined. Consequently, a party desiring a commodity which is more expensive than its offered commodity is not able to barter, although a trade could have taken place if the commodities were traded directly [10]. Thus, privacy-preserving protocols for e-commerce scenarios (e.g., [1]) or auctions (e.g., [12]) can not directly be applied to implement privacy-preserving bartering.

3 Preliminaries

By $a \leftarrow_\$ A$ we indicate that a is drawn uniformly at random from A. $\mathbb{N}_u :=$ $\{1, ..., u\}$ refers to the set of natural numbers less than or equal to $u \in \mathbb{N}$. The set of all prime numbers within an integer interval I is referred to as $\mathbf{P}_I$. We denote the index set of all parties P_i participating in a multi-party protocol as $\mathscr{P} := \{1, \ldots, \iota\}$ where $i \in \mathscr{P}$. Furthermore, λ denotes the empty string.

3.1 Threshold Paillier

Our design approach assumes an additively homomorphic cryptosystem which is semantically secure against chosen-plaintext attacks and provides a (τ, ι) threshold variant, i.e., the decryption key is distributed amongst ι parties such that at least $\tau \leq \iota$ parties have to collaborate in order to decrypt a ciphertext.

In the following, we summarize the (τ, ι) threshold variant of the Paillier cryptosystem [13] from [3] along with the Paillier-related notation used throughout the paper.

The public key corresponds to an RSA modulus $N = p \cdot q$ of bit length k, where p, q are safe primes (i.e., there are prime numbers p' and q' such that $p = 2p' + 1$ and $q = 2q' + 1$) and k refers to the security parameter. The private key $d \in \mathbb{Z}_{p'q'N^s}$ with $s > 0$, $s \in \mathbb{N}$ satisfying $d = 0 \bmod p'q'$ and $d = 1 \bmod N^s$ is polynomially shared between $P_1, \ldots, P_\iota$ such that at least τ parties have to cooperate for decryption. The encryption of a message m in the *plaintext space* $\mathbb{P} := \mathbb{Z}_{N^s}$ is computed as $c = E(m) := (N+1)^m r^{N^s} \bmod N^{s+1}$ where $r \leftarrow_{\$} \mathbb{Z}^*_{N^{s+1}}$ and c is an element in the *ciphertext space* $\mathbb{C} := \mathbb{Z}^*_{N^{s+1}}$. Throughout the paper we assume $s = 1$. We have that the plaintext space $\mathbb{P}$ forms the additive group $(\mathbb{Z}_N, +)$, and the ciphertext space $\mathbb{C}$ forms the multiplicative group $(\mathbb{Z}^*_{N^2}, \cdot)$. For further details we refer to [3].

Let $m, m_1, m_2 \in \mathbb{P}$ and $\kappa \in \mathbb{N} \setminus \{0\}$. The Paillier $((\tau, \iota)$ threshold) cryptosystem provides for *homomorphic addition*

$$E(m_1) +_h E(m_2) := E(m_1) \cdot E(m_2) = E(m_1 + m_2)$$

and *homomorphic scalar multiplication*

$$E(m) \times_h \kappa := \underbrace{E(m) \cdot E(m) \cdots E(m)}_{\kappa \text{ times}} = E(\kappa \cdot m).$$

A ciphertext $E(m)$ can be *randomized* (or *re-randomized*) by homomorphically adding a fresh encryption of zero. For the remaining sections $\mathbb{P}$, $\mathbb{C}$, $E(\cdot)$, and $D(\cdot)$ refer to the plaintext space, the ciphertext space, the encryption function, and the decryption function of (τ, ι) threshold Paillier, respectively. Note that for convenience, we omit the keys from the notation.

3.2   Secure Multi-party Computation

In order to define security comprising privacy and correctness, we have to specify the capabilities of an adversary under whose presence a protocol has to be secure. We prove our protocols to be secure in the semi-honest model. A semi-honest adversary controls a set of corrupted parties which correctly follow the protocol specification with the exception that each corrupted party keeps record of all data it generates itself and all messages it receives from other parties.

We assume that the parties communicate over authentic channels, i.e., the transferred data is resistant to tampering but can be wiretapped.

Let $\widehat{X} := (X_1, \ldots, X_\iota)$ and let $\mathcal{F} : (\{0,1\}^*)^\iota \to (\{0,1\}^*)^\iota, \widehat{X} \mapsto (\mathcal{F}_1(\widehat{X}), \ldots, \mathcal{F}_\iota(\widehat{X}))$ be a multi-party ($|\mathscr{P}| = \iota \geq 2$) functionality computable in polynomial time where P_i provides input X_i and obtains output $\mathcal{F}_i(\widehat{X})$ ($i \in \mathscr{P}$). Let π be an ι-party protocol for computing functionality $\mathcal{F}$. We write $I_C :=$

$\{i_1, ..., i_\kappa\} \subset \mathscr{P}$ for the index set of $1 \leq \kappa < \iota$ corrupted parties controlled by the adversary. The view of P_i during an execution of π on input $\widehat{X}$ and security parameter s is denoted as $\text{VIEW}_i^\pi(s, \widehat{X}) := (s, X_i, \mathring{r}_i, m_{i,1}, ..., m_{i,n})$, where $\mathring{r}_i$ represents P_i's internal random tape and $m_{i,j}$ represents the j-th message P_i received during a protocol execution of π. We write $\text{OUTPUT}^\pi(s, \widehat{X}) := (\text{OUTPUT}_1^\pi(s, \widehat{X}), ..., \text{OUTPUT}_\iota^\pi(s, \widehat{X}))$ in order to refer to the output of protocol π on input $\widehat{X}$ and security parameter s. Let $\widehat{X}_{I_C}, \mathcal{F}_{I_C}(\widehat{X})$, and $\text{VIEW}_{I_C}^\pi(\widehat{X})$ denote the κ-tuples $(X_{i_1}, ..., X_{i_\kappa})$, $(\mathcal{F}_{i_1}(\widehat{X}), ..., \mathcal{F}_{i_\kappa}(\widehat{X}))$, and $(I_C, \text{VIEW}_{i_1}^\pi(\widehat{X}), ..., \text{VIEW}_{i_\kappa}^\pi(\widehat{X}))$, respectively.

Definition 1 (Security: Semi-Honest Model, Multi-Party Setting [8]). *π securely computes $\mathcal{F}$ if there exists a probabilistic polynomial time algorithm $\mathcal{S}$ such that for every I_C it holds that $\{(\mathcal{S}(1^s, I_C, \widehat{X}_{I_C}, \mathcal{F}_{I_C}(\widehat{X})), \mathcal{F}(\widehat{X}))\}_{\widehat{X}, s}$ and $\{(\text{VIEW}_{I_C}^\pi(\widehat{X}, s), \text{OUTPUT}^\pi(s, \widehat{X}))\}_{\widehat{X}, s}$ are computational indistinguishable.*

For convenience, we omit s from the remaining considerations. We call $\mathcal{S}$ a *simulator* and enclose the values it *simulates* by square brackets $\langle \cdot \rangle$ in order to distinguish between simulated values and those occurring during a protocol run.

In order to facilitate the security proof of a protocol π implementing functionality $\mathcal{F}$ where π consists of a finite set of sub-protocols $\rho_1, ..., \rho_n$ securely computing functionalities $\mathcal{G}_1, ..., \mathcal{G}_n$ in the semi-honest model, we can apply the *Modular Composition Theorem* [2] which states that if π' securely computes $\mathcal{F}$ in the semi-honest model where the sub-protocol calls of π are replaced by calls to a trusted third party computing $\mathcal{G}_1, ..., \mathcal{G}_n$, then π securely computes $\mathcal{F}$ in the semi-honest model.

To prove our protocols to be secure in the semi-honest model, we first prove that $\{\mathcal{F}(\widehat{X})\}_{\widehat{X}} \stackrel{c}{\equiv} \{OUTPUT^\pi(\widehat{X})\}_{\widehat{X}}$. This step is referred to as *Correct Output Distribution* (COD). Second, we prove that $\text{VIEW}_{I_C}^\pi$ can be simulated under consideration of the given inputs and outputs of all corrupted parties such that $\text{VIEW}_{I_C}^\pi$ and the corresponding simulated view are computationally indistinguishable, referred to as *Correct View Distribution* (CVD).

To refer to a concrete functionality or protocol, we use the templates $\mathcal{F}_{name}^{[affix]}$ and $\pi_{name}^{[affix]}$ where protocol $\pi_{name}^{[affix]}$ is an implementation of functionality $\mathcal{F}_{name}^{[affix]}$ with *name* and *affix* describing the functionality to be computed where the use of *affix* is optional. For convenience, we omit *name* and *affix* for the case that the target functionality and protocol is clear from the context. Furthermore, we write $\mathcal{F}(X_1, ..., X_\iota, X)$ to denote that X is a public input that is known by all parties. $(o) \leftarrow \mathcal{F}(X)$ indicates that all parties have common input X and common output o.

4   Overview

4.1   Bartering Related Terminology

For a set of parties, a trade generically indicates which party receives (or sends) which quantity of which commodity from (or to) which other party. In this

Table 1. Bartering related acronyms used throughout the paper.

$TPT(S)$	Trade partner tuple (Set)	Definition 2 (below Definition 10)
$TPC(S)$	Trade partner constellation (Set)	Definition 3 (below Definition 4)
$PTPC(S)$	Potential trade partner constellation (Set)	Definition 4 (below Definition 4)
$ATPC$	Actual trade partner constellation	Definition 5
AT	Actual trade	Definition 6

paper, we focus on so-called (1:1) *trades* with one offered and one desired commodity for each party. In such a trade, each party receives some quantity of its desired commodity from at most one party and sends some quantity of its offered commodity to at most one other party.

More specifically, we consider a set of ι parties $\{P_i | i \in \mathscr{P}\}$ with $\mathscr{P} := \mathbb{N}_\iota$ and a publicly known finite set $\mathscr{C} := \{c_1, \ldots, c_n\}$ of divisible commodities. Each party P_i specifies exactly one *quote* $\mathbf{q}^{(i)} := (\mathbf{o}^{(i)}, \mathbf{d}^{(i)})$ where $\mathbf{o}^{(i)}$ and $\mathbf{d}^{(i)}$ is P_i's *offer* and *demand*, respectively. We model $\mathbf{o}^{(i)}$ as a 3-tuple $\mathbf{o}^{(i)} := (c_o^{(i)}, \underline{q}_o^{(i)}, \overline{q}_o^{(i)})$ where $c_o^{(i)} \in \mathscr{C}$ specifies the commodity offered by P_i and $\underline{q}_o^{(i)} \in \mathbb{N} \backslash \{0\}$ ($\overline{q}_o^{(i)} \in \mathbb{N} \backslash \{0\}$) denotes the minimum (maximum) quantity of $c_o^{(i)}$ offered. Similarly, we model $\mathbf{d}^{(i)} := (c_d^{(i)}, \underline{q}_d^{(i)}, \overline{q}_d^{(i)})$ with $c_d^{(i)} \in \mathscr{C}$ and $\underline{q}_d^{(i)}, \overline{q}_d^{(i)} \in \mathbb{N} \backslash \{0\}$. With $\mathbf{q}^{(i)}$ a party P_i indicates that it is *satisfied* with a trade if it receives at least $\underline{q}_d^{(i)}$ and at most $\overline{q}_d^{(i)}$ units of commodity $c_d^{(i)}$ and sends at least $\underline{q}_o^{(i)}$ and at most $\overline{q}_o^{(i)}$ units of $c_o^{(i)}$. For convenience, we assume that $\underline{q}_o^{(i)} = 1$ and $\overline{q}_d^{(i)} = \infty$. The *quantity ranges* of the offered and desired commodities of a party P_i ($i \in \mathscr{P}$) are thus defined as $Q_o^{(i)} := [1, \overline{q}_o^{(i)}]$ and $Q_d^{(i)} := [\underline{q}_d^{(i)}, \infty]$. We write $q_{c_o^{(i)}}^{(i,i')}$ in order to indicate at which quantity $P_{i'}$ will receive commodity $c_o^{(i)}$ from P_i ($i, i' \in \mathscr{P}$).

We introduce the following bartering related terms which are summarized in Table 1 and illustrated in Fig. 1:

Definition 2 (Trade Partner Tuple). *A trade partner tuple $TPT^{(i)} := (x^{(i)}, y^{(i)})$ for P_i ($i \in \mathscr{P}$) with $x^{(i)}, y^{(i)} \in \mathscr{P} \backslash \{i\}$ is a 2-tuple which specifies the indices of the trade partners $P_{x^{(i)}}$ and $P_{y^{(i)}}$ of P_i: $P_{x^{(i)}}$ is the offerer of party P_i, i.e., P_i receives some quantity of some commodity from $P_{x^{(i)}}$, while $P_{y^{(i)}}$ is the demander of P_i, i.e., P_i has to send some quantity of some commodity to $P_{y^{(i)}}$. If a party P_i neither sends nor receives any commodity in a trade, i.e., it does not participate, we write $TPT^{(i)} = (0, 0)$.*

Definition 3 (Trade Partner Constellation). *A trade partner constellation $TPC := (TPT^{(1)}, TPT^{(2)}, ..., TPT^{(\iota)})$ is an ι-tuple which specifies exactly one trade partner tuple for each P_i ($i \in \mathscr{P}$) and has the following property: for each trade partner tuple $TPT^{(i)} = (x^{(i)}, y^{(i)})$ it either holds that $x^{(i)} = y^{(i)}$ or it holds that there exist exactly two distinct entries $TPT^{(i')}$ and $TPT^{(i'')}$ with $i \neq i', i''$ such that $TPT^{(i')} = (y^{(i)}, y^{(i')})$ and $TPT^{(i'')} = (x^{(i'')}, x^{(i)})$.*

Definition 3 ensures that each party that participates as offerer (demander) in some TPT of a TPC also participates as demander (offerer) either in the same or in exactly one other TPT of the TPC.

For a fixed context of quotes $\mathbf{Q} := \{\mathbf{q}^{(1)}, ..., \mathbf{q}^{(\iota)}\}$ with $\mathbf{q}^{(i)} = ((c_o^{(i)}, \underline{q}_o^{(i)}, \overline{q}_o^{(i)}),$ $(c_d^{(i)}, \underline{q}_d^{(i)}, \overline{q}_d^{(i)}))$, a TPC is transformed into a *trade partner constellation formula*, written $\varphi \overset{\mathbf{Q}}{\sim} TPC$, such that:

$$\varphi := \bigwedge_{\substack{i=1 \\ (x^{(i)}, y^{(i)}) \neq (0,0)}}^{\iota} \mathcal{C}(\mathbf{q}^{(i)}, \mathbf{q}^{(x^{(i)})}) \wedge \mathcal{R}(\mathbf{q}^{(i)}, \mathbf{q}^{(x^{(i)})}) \tag{1}$$

with

$$\mathcal{C}(\mathbf{q}^{(a)}, \mathbf{q}^{(b)}) := \begin{cases} 1 & \text{if } (\mathbf{q}^{(a)}, \mathbf{q}^{(b)}) \in C \\ 0 & \text{otherwise} \end{cases}, \ \mathcal{R}(\mathbf{q}^{(a)}, \mathbf{q}^{(b)}) := \begin{cases} 1 & \text{if } (\mathbf{q}^{(a)}, \mathbf{q}^{(b)}) \in R \\ 0 & \text{otherwise} \end{cases}$$

where

$$C := \{(\mathbf{q}^{(a)}, \mathbf{q}^{(b)}) | c_d^{(a)} = c_o^{(b)}\}, \ R := \{(\mathbf{q}^{(a)}, \mathbf{q}^{(b)}) | \underline{q}_d^{(a)} \leq \overline{q}_o^{(b)}\}.$$

Evaluating φ (for a given context of quotes) denoted as $[\![\varphi]\!] \in \{0, 1\}$ allows one to check whether or not there is a trade which all parties P_i (with $TPT^{(i)} \neq (0,0)$) in the corresponding trade partner constellation are satisfied with. The trade partner constellations for which this holds for a given context of quotes $\mathbf{Q}$ are referred to as *potential trade partner constellations*:

Definition 4 (Potential Trade Partner Constellation). *For a context of quotes* $\mathbf{Q}$, *a trade partner constellation* TPC *is a potential trade partner constellation* $(PTPC)$, *iff* $\varphi \overset{\mathbf{Q}}{\sim} TPC$ *and* $[\![\varphi]\!] = 1$.

We write $TPCS := \{TPC_1, \ldots, TPC_t\}$ for a set of trade partner constellations. Given $TPCS$ and $\mathbf{Q}$, the set of potential trade partner constellations is denoted as $PTPCS$. Furthermore, given $TPCS$ and $\mathbf{Q}$, we define $\Phi := \{\varphi_j | \varphi_j \overset{\mathbf{Q}}{\sim} TPC_j, j \in \mathbb{N}_{|TPCS|}\}$ and $\Phi_{\text{sat}} := \{\varphi_j | \varphi_j \in \Phi, [\![\varphi_j]\!] = 1\} \subseteq \Phi$.

Definition 5 (Actual Trade Partner Constellation). *An actual trade partner constellation* $ATPC$ *is a specific* $PTPC$ *drawn from* $PTPCS$ *based on a specified selection strategy.*

For matters of convenience, we first assume that $ATPC$ is drawn uniformly at random from $PTPCS$. In Sect. 5.4, we sketch a modification of our protocol allowing to select an $ATPC$ maximizing the number of traded commodities (without reducing the level of privacy). Other optimization criteria can be integrated analogously.

Definition 6 (Actual Trade). *An actual trade* AT *for an* $ATPC$ *specifies the actual commodities and actual quantities for the commodities traded between the parties involved in* $ATPC$.

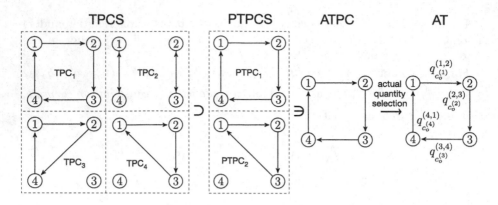

Fig. 1. Illustration of the bartering related terms and their relations.

Figure 1 illustrates the interdependency of the introduced terms. A trade partner constellation can be visualized as a directed graph, i.e., a node represents a party and a directed edge between two nodes represents the exchange direction of a commodity between two parties. For example, according to the node labels and the direction of the edges we have that TPC_4 in Fig. 1 is equal to $(TPT^{(1)}, TPT^{(2)}, TPT^{(3)}, TPT^{(4)}) = ((3,2),(1,3),(2,1),(0,0))$. A potential trade partner constellation set is a subset of a given trade partner constellation set containing those trade partner constellations which form the basis for a trade all involved parties are satisfied with when taking the given context of quotes into account. In Fig. 1, we assume a context of quotes such that $TPC_1 = PTPC_1$ and $TPC_4 = PTPC_2$ are potential trade partner constellations. An actual trade partner constellation is an element from the set of potential trade partner constellation selected w.r.t. a specific strategy. In Fig. 1, the actual trade partner constellation is chosen such that it maximizes the number of traded commodities. The determined actual trade partner constellation is transferred into an actual trade by selecting the actual quantities of the commodities to be traded. In Fig. 1, the actual trade indicates that P_1 has to send $q_{c_o^{(1)}}^{(1,2)}$ units of commodity $c_o^{(1)}$ to P_2, that P_2 has to send $q_{c_o^{(2)}}^{(2,3)}$ units of commodity $c_o^{(2)}$ to P_3, and so on.

4.2   Bartering Process and Intuition

The overall goal of a bartering process between parties $P_1, ..., P_\iota$ with a context of quotes $\mathbf{Q} = (\mathbf{q}^{(1)}, ..., \mathbf{q}^{(\iota)})$ is to determine an actual trade, i.e., one specific trade with which all parties are satisfied. Our bartering process introduced in this paper can determine such an actual trade from the set of all possible trade partner constellations. However, for matters of efficiency, it is also possible to use a smaller trade partner constellation set, e.g., one which may contain only trade partner constellations of 5-trade cycles or constellations in which specific parties get to trade (cf. $TPCS$ in Fig. 1). Upon input of the trade partner constellation

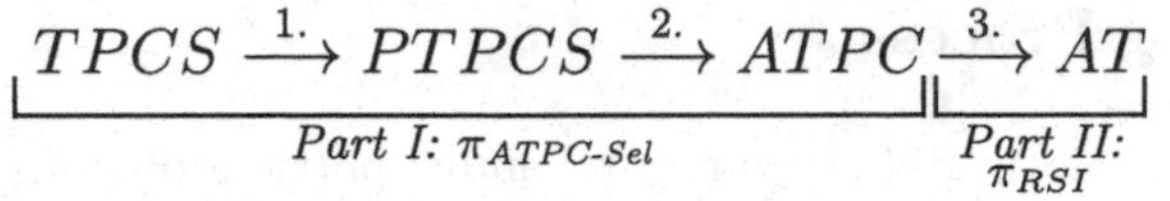

$$TPCS \xrightarrow{1.} PTPCS \xrightarrow{2.} ATPC \xrightarrow{3.} AT$$

$$\underbrace{\hspace{5cm}}_{\text{Part I: } \pi_{ATPC\text{-}Sel}} \quad \underbrace{\hspace{2cm}}_{\substack{\text{Part II:} \\ \pi_{RSI}}}$$

Fig. 2. Illustration of the overall bartering process.

set, the bartering process tries to find an actual trade consistent with the trade partner constellations in the given trade partner constellation set.

Finding an actual trade first requires the determining of the set of potential trade constellations, i.e., those trade constellations in the trade partner constellation set for which the commodities and quantities of the involved parties in their roles of offerer and demander match (Transition 1, Fig. 2). Subsequently, one of the potential trade constellations is selected as actual trade partner constellation (Transition 2, Fig. 2). This constellation then already indicates which parties will send (resp., receive) some commodity to (from) which other party in the (yet to be determined) actual trade. Finally, the parties have the option to individually engage in a two-party protocol with each one of their trade partners (determined by the actual trade partner constellation) in order to select the actual quantities for the commodities to be traded (Transition 3, Fig. 2).

In order to implement such a bartering process securely, the input of the parties, i.e., their quotes, have to be kept secret throughout the process. Moreover, at the end of the process the parties should learn no more than their local view of the selected actual trade, i.e., their own trade partners and the commodities and quantities to be traded with them. Our newly developed bartering process consists of two parts (cf. Fig. 2).

(Part I.) For the first part, we design a secure multi-party protocol $\pi_{\text{ATPC-Sel}}$ that takes a context of private quotes $\mathbf{Q}$ as well as a (publicly known) set of trade partner constellations as input and then performs the following steps: (1) securely determine the potential trade partner constellation set, (2) securely select an actual trade partner constellation, and (3) provide each party P_i with (nothing but) its actual trade partner tuple in the actual trade partner constellation as output (see Sect. 5.2).

(Part II.) In the second part, we propose the option that each party is involved in the two-party protocol π_{RSI} for the secure computation of a random sub-interval (see Sect. 5.3) with each of its trade partners to automatically and fairly determine the actual quantities traded.

For a more comprehensive intuition, we refer to the extended version of this paper [15]. Moreover, the extended version provides an intuition of the novel privacy-preserving mapping operation based on the uniqueness of prime factorization which is used for $\pi_{\text{ATPC-Sel}}$ in order to restrict the output of a party to its local view.

5 Bartering Process

In the following, we introduce our novel multi-party protocol, $\pi_{\text{ATPC-Sel}}$, for selecting an actual trade partner constellation from a given public trade partner constellation set and providing each party with its local view of this actual trade partner constellation as output. We define the underlying functionality $\mathcal{F}_{\text{ATPC-Sel}}$ followed by a detailed protocol description (Sect. 5.2) using the building blocks reviewed in Sect. 5.1. Additionally, in Sect. 5.3 we describe how each party can locally compute their part of the actual trade (i.e., determine the actual quantities for the commodities to be traded) based on the actual trade partner constellation, and how the ATPC-selection can be optimized (Sect. 5.4). In the extended version of this paper [15], we provide an example of how $\pi_{\text{ATPC-Sel}}$ can be used for computing an actual trade from a given trade partner constellation set.

5.1 Building Blocks

Definition 7 ($\mathcal{F}_{\text{OE-TPCF}}$: Oblivious (O) Evaluation (E) of a Trade Partner Constellation Formula (TPCF)). *Let P_i hold private input $\mathbf{q}^{(i)}$ ($i \in \mathscr{P}$) as well as a public trade partner constellation formula $\varphi \in \Phi$. Then, functionality $\mathcal{F}_{\text{OE-TPCF}}$ is given by $(E(e)) \leftarrow \mathcal{F}_{\text{OE-TPCF}}(\mathbf{q}^{(1)}, \ldots, \mathbf{q}^{(\iota)}, \varphi)$ where $E(e)$ is an (ι, ι) threshold Paillier ciphertext of $e = 1$ if $[\![\varphi]\!] = 1$ and $e = 0$ otherwise.*

Definition 8 ($\mathcal{F}^{i^*}_{\text{CRS-C}}$: Multi-party Conditional (C) Random (R) Selection (S) with output Check (C)). *Let $P_1, \ldots, P_\iota$ hold m vectors $E(L_i) = (E(l_{i,1}), \ldots, E(l_{i,n}))$ of length n of integers $l_{i,j} \in \mathbb{P}$ ($i \in \mathbb{N}_m$, $j \in \mathbb{N}_n$) encrypted with (ι, ι) threshold Paillier. Let $E(L_{i^*})$ be an encrypted binary indicator vector and $\{E(L_1), \ldots, E(L_m)\} \backslash \{E(L_{i^*})\}$ be the value vectors with $i^* \in \mathbb{N}_m$. Then, functionality $\mathcal{F}^{i^*}_{\text{CRS-C}}$ is given by $((E(o_1), \ldots, E(o_m))) \leftarrow \mathcal{F}^{i^*}_{\text{CRS-C}}((E(L_1), \ldots, E(L_m)))$ with $E(o_i) = Rnd(E(l_{i,j^*}))$ ($i \in \mathbb{N}_m$) where $j^* \leftarrow_\$ \{j \in \mathbb{N}_n : l_{i^*,j} = 1\}$ if there exists at least one $j \in \mathbb{N}_n$ s.t. $l_{i^*,j} > 0$. Otherwise, $\mathcal{F}^{i^*}_{\text{CRS-C}}((E(L_1), \ldots, E(L_m)))$ outputs $(\lambda_1, \ldots, \lambda_m)$ with $\lambda_1 = \ldots = \lambda_m = \lambda$. Note that j^* is fix for all $i \in \mathbb{N}_m$.*

Definition 9 ($\mathcal{F}^\omega_{RSI}$: Two-party secure computation of a Random (R) Sub-Interval (SI)). *Let P_1 hold integer interval I_1 and P_2 hold integer interval I_2 such that $\omega \leq |I_1 \cap I_2|$. Then, functionality $\mathcal{F}^\omega_{RSI}$ is given by $([l_r, u_r]) \leftarrow \mathcal{F}^\omega_{RSI}(I_1, I_2)$ where $[l_r, u_r]$ is a sub-interval drawn uniformly at random from $I_o = I_1 \cap I_2$ s.t. $|[l_r, u_r]| = \omega$.*

In the extended version of this paper, a novel protocol $\pi_{\text{OE-TPCF}}$ implementing $\mathcal{F}_{\text{OE-TPCF}}$ is introduced (see Sect. 5 in [15]). A protocol implementing functionality $\mathcal{F}^{i^*}_{\text{CRS-C}}$ is presented in [14] and further improved in [17]. A two-party protocol implementing functionality $\mathcal{F}^\omega_{RSI}$ is introduced in [5]. All of these protocols have been proven secure in the semi-honest model. In this paper, we exclusively use $\pi^{i^*}_{\text{CRS-C}}$ for $i^* = 1$ and π^ω_{RSI} for $\omega = 0$. Consequently, we will omit these indices in the remainder of this paper.

5.2   Protocol for Selecting an Actual Trade Partner Constellation

Definition 10 ($\mathcal{F}_{\text{ATPC-Sel}}$: Actual Trade Partner Constellation (ATPC) Selection (Sel)). *Let party P_i hold private input $\mathbf{q}^{(i)}$ ($i \in \mathscr{P}$). Furthermore, let $TPCS$ be an arbitrary non-empty set of trade partner constellations which is publicly known. Then, the functionality $\mathcal{F}_{\text{ATPC-Sel}}$ is defined as*

$$\left. \begin{array}{cc} (TPT_*^{(1)}, \ldots, TPT_*^{(\iota)}) & \text{if } PTPCS \neq \emptyset \\ \bot & \text{otherwise} \end{array} \right\} \leftarrow \mathcal{F}_{ATPC\text{-}Sel}(\mathbf{q}^{(1)}, \ldots, \mathbf{q}^{(\iota)}, TPCS)$$

where $(TPT_*^{(1)}, \ldots, TPT_*^{(\iota)}) := ATPC \leftarrow_\$ PTPCS \subseteq TPCS$.

In the following, $TPTS^{(i)}$ refers to the set of trade partner tuples for P_i ($i \in \mathscr{P}$) w.r.t. $TPCS$.

In an ideal world where a trusted third party exists, functionality $\mathcal{F}_{\text{ATPC-Sel}}$ could be computed as follows: Each party P_i ($i \in \mathscr{P}$) sends its private input $\mathbf{q}^{(i)}$ to the trusted third party which additionally is given the public set of trade constellation tuples $TPCS$. With the knowledge of $\mathbf{Q} = \{\mathbf{q}^{(1)}, \ldots, \mathbf{q}^{(\iota)}\}$, the trusted third party locally computes $PTPCS \subseteq TPCS$. For the case that $PTPCS \neq \emptyset$, the trusted third party selects an actual trade partner constellation $ATPC = (TPT_*^{(1)}, \ldots, TPT_*^{(\iota)})$ uniformly at random from $PTPCS$ and sends $TPT_*^{(i)} = (x_*^{(i)}, y_*^{(i)})$ to P_i. Otherwise, the trusted third party returns $\bot$ to all parties. Note that a $(0, 0)$ output for party P_i indicates that P_i is not involved in the actual trade partner constellation while $\bot$ indicates that there exists no potential trade constellation in the given $TPCS$ at all.

In the real world, where no trusted party exists, protocol $\pi_{\text{ATPC-Sel}}$ (see Protocol 1) is executed in order to compute functionality $\mathcal{F}_{\text{ATPC-Sel}}$. Following the intuition provided in Sect. 4, $\pi_{\text{ATPC-Sel}}$ can be split up into the following phases:

1. *Construction Phase*: From the public set of trade partner constellations, $TPCS$, each party individually constructs the set of formulas Φ such that at the end of this phase each party holds the same set Φ.
2. *Evaluation Phase*: Each $\varphi_j \in \Phi$ is obliviously evaluated jointly by all parties P_i ($i \in \mathscr{P}$) by calling $\pi_{\text{OE-TPCF}}(\mathbf{q}^{(1)}, \ldots, \mathbf{q}^{(\iota)}, \varphi_j)$ such that at the end of this phase, each party holds a vector $E(L) = (E(e_1), \ldots, E(e_{|TPCS|}))$ where $e_j = [\![\varphi_j]\!]$ ($j \in \mathbb{N}_{|TPCS|}$).
3. *Mapping Phase*: At the begin of the protocol, each party P_i ($i \in \mathscr{P}$) is given an interval $I^{(i)}$ of positive integers with at least $|TPTS^{(i)}|$ prime numbers such that for each $i, i' \in \mathscr{P}$ ($i \neq i'$), $I^{(i)}$ and $I^{(i')}$ are pairwise disjoint. Each party P_i constructs a secret table mapping each element in $TPTS^{(i)}$ to a unique prime number randomly chosen from $I^{(i)}$. More precisely, each party P_i keeps a set $S^{(i)}$ of already assigned prime numbers from $I^{(i)}$ which is initialized with $\emptyset$. P_i then maps each trade partner tuple $(x^{(i)}, y^{(i)}) \in TPTS^{(i)}$ to a prime number $p_{(x^{(i)}, y^{(i)})}^{(i)} \leftarrow_\$ \mathbf{P}_{I^{(i)}} \setminus S^{(i)}$. Subsequently, $p_{(x^{(i)}, y^{(i)})}$ is added to $S^{(i)}$. Once all parties have established their mapping tables, all

Protocol 1. $\pi_{\text{ATPC-Sel}}$ for obliviously selecting an actual trade partner constellation.

---

1 **Construction Phase**
  1.1 Each party P_i ($i \in \mathscr{P}$) locally constructs the same set Φ from $TPCS$.
2 **Evaluation Phase**
  2.1 For each $\varphi_j \in \Phi$:
    2.1.1 Each party P_i participates in $(E(e_j)) \leftarrow \pi_{\text{OE-TPCF}}(\varphi_j)$
  2.2 Each party P_i sets $E(L) := (E(e_1), \ldots, E(e_{|TPCS|}))$
3 **Mapping Phase**
  3.1 Each party P_i:
    3.1.1 Set $S^{(i)} := \emptyset$
    3.1.2 For each $(x^{(i)}, y^{(i)}) \in TPTS^{(i)}$:
      3.1.2.1 Draw a random prime $p^{(i)}_{(x^{(i)}, y^{(i)})}$ from $\mathbf{P}_{I^{(i)}} \setminus S^{(i)}$
      3.1.2.2 Update $S^{(i)} = S^{(i)} \cup \{p^{(i)}_{(x^{(i)}, y^{(i)})}\}$
  3.2 Party P_ι:
    3.2.1 Set $u^{(\iota)}_j := E(p^{(\iota)}_{TPT^{(\iota)}_j})$ ($\varphi_j \overset{Q}{\sim} TPC_j$)
    3.2.2 Send $(u^{(\iota)}_1, \ldots, u^{(\iota)}_{|TPCS|})$ to $P_{\iota - 1}$
  3.3 Each party $P_{i'}$ (from $i' = \iota - 1$ to 1)
    3.3.1 Compute $u^{(i')}_j := u^{(i'+1)}_j \times_h p^{(i')}_{TPT^{(i')}_j} +_h E(0)$
    3.3.2 Send $(u^{(i')}_1, \ldots, u^{(i')}_{|TPCS|})$ to $P_{i'-1}$
  3.4 Party P_1:
    3.4.1 Set $E(L') := (E(e'_1), \ldots, E(e'_{|TPCS|})) := (u^{(1)}_1, \ldots, u^{(1)}_{|TPCS|})$
    3.4.2 Broadcast $E(L')$
4 **Selection Phase**
  4.1 Each party P_i participates in $((c^*_1, c^*_2)) \leftarrow \pi_{\text{CRS-C}}(E(L), E(L'))$
  4.2 For each party P_i
    4.2.1 If $c^*_1 = c^*_2 = \lambda$:
      4.2.1.1 Skip Steps 5 to 7
      4.2.1.2 Each party P_i outputs $\perp$
5 **Decryption Phase**
  5.1 All parties jointly compute $e^*_2 = D(c^*_2)$
6 **Reverse Mapping Phase**
  6.1 Each Party P_i:
    6.1.1 For each $p^{(i)}_{TPT^{(i)}_j} \in S^{(i)}$
      6.1.1.1 If $p^{(i)}_{TPT^{(i)}_j}$ divides e^*_2 then $TPT^{(i)}_* := TPT^{(i)}_j$ and go to Step 7
7 **Output Phase**
  7.1 Each party P_i outputs $TPT^{(i)}_*$

---

parties engage in the consecutive computation of an encrypted prime number product for each $\varphi_j \in \Phi$. Each party P_i contributes a single prime number $p^{(i)}_{TPT^{(i)}_j}$ to the encrypted prime number product associated with $\varphi_j \in \Phi$:

First, P_ι computes $u_j^{(\iota)} = E(p_{TPT_j^{(\iota)}}^{(\iota)})$ $(j \in \mathbb{N}_{|TPCS|})$ and sends the result to $P_{\iota-1}$. Each party $P_{i'}$ from $i' = \iota - 1$ to 1 then computes $u_j^{(i')} = u_j^{(i'+1)} \times_h p_{TPT_j^{(i')}} +_h E(0)$ and sends the results to $P_{i'-1}$, except P_1 which sets $E(L') := (E(e_1'), \ldots, E(e_{|TPCS|}')) := (u_1^{(1)}, \ldots, u_{|TPCS|}^{(1)})$ and broadcasts $E(L')$. This mapping of trade partner constellations to prime number products is one of the central ideas of this protocol and ensures the security of the protocol.

4. *Selection Phase*: From the previous phases, each φ_j is associated with two values $E(e_j)$ and $E(e_j')$ where $e_j \in \{0,1\}$ indicates whether or not φ_j is satisfied while e_j' is a product of individual prime numbers encoding the trade partner tuples of each party w.r.t. φ_j. In this phase, the parties now jointly compute $\pi_{\text{CRS-C}}$ on the common input $(E(L), E(L'))$ in order to select an entry of $E(L')$ associated with a randomly selected $\varphi_j \in \Phi_{sat}$ for the case that $\Phi_{sat} \neq \emptyset$ (i.e., $PTPCS \neq \emptyset$). Otherwise, in the case that $\Phi_{sat} = \emptyset$ (i.e., $PTPCS = \emptyset$), the parties learn of this fact. In the former case, $\pi_{\text{CRS-C}}$ returns a randomly selected pair $(c_1^*, c_2^*) \in (E(L), E(L'))$ with $c_1^* = E(e_1^*)$ and $c_2^* = E(e_2^*)$. In the latter case where $e_1 = \ldots = e_{|TPCS|} = 0$, $\pi_{\text{CRS-C}}(L, L')$ returns (c_1^*, c_2^*) with $c_1^* = c_2^* = \lambda$ which prompts each party P_i to output $\perp$ and to terminate the protocol. The purpose for this approach is to hide the number of satisfied formulas (for the case that $\Phi_{sat} \neq \emptyset$) as this could otherwise not be simulated given the inputs and outputs of the set of corrupted parties.

5. *Decryption Phase*: Each party learns e_2^* from jointly decrypting c_2^* together with all other parties.

6. *Reverse Mapping Phase*: Each party P_i checks which prime in $S^{(i)}$ divides e_2^*. The unique result $TPT_*^{(i)}$ determines P_i's trade partners w.r.t. $\varphi \overset{Q}{\sim} ATPC$.

7. *Output Phase*: Each party P_i outputs $TPT_*^{(i)}$.

Theorem 1. *Let P_i hold $\mathbf{q}^{(i)}$ $(i \in \mathscr{P})$ and let $TPCS$ be public. Then protocol $\pi_{ATPC\text{-}Sel}$ securely computes functionality $\mathcal{F}_{ATPC\text{-}Sel}$ in the semi-honest model.*

Proof (COD). In order to prove COD, we distinguish two cases: (i) $TPCS \supseteq PTPCS = \emptyset$ and (ii) $TPCS \supseteq PTPCS \neq \emptyset$. For case (i), the output of $\pi_{\text{ATPC-Sel}}$ is fixed; each party outputs $\perp$. For case (ii), we have to show $ATPC = (TPT_*^{(1)}, \ldots, TPT_*^{(\iota)})$ is selected uniformly at random from $PTPCS$.

(i) For the case that $TPCS \supseteq PTPCS = \emptyset$, the Evaluation Phase of $\pi_{\text{ATPC-Sel}}$ returns a vector $E(L) = (E(e_1), \ldots, E(e_{|TPCS|}))$ where $e_1 = \ldots = e_{|TPCS|} = 0$ since there exists no $\varphi \in \Phi$ such that $[\![\varphi]\!] = 1$. This implies that in the Selection Phase of $\pi_{\text{ATPC-Sel}}$, $\pi_{\text{CRS-C}}(E(L), E(L'))$ returns (λ, λ). Then, each party P_i $(i \in \mathscr{P})$ outputs $\perp$ and the protocol terminates.

(ii) For the case that $TPCS \supseteq PTPCS \neq \emptyset$, the Evaluation Phase of $\pi_{\text{ATPC-Sel}}$ computes a vector $E(L) = (E(e_1), \ldots, E(e_{|TPCS|}))$ with $e_j = [\![\varphi_j]\!]$ and L has Hamming weight $|\Phi_{sat}|$. $\pi_{\text{CRS-C}}(E(L), E(L'))$, called in the Selection Phase of $\pi_{\text{ATPC-Sel}}$, returns $(E(e_1^*), E(e_2^*))$ for a random $j \in \mathbb{N}_{|TPCS|}$ such that $e_1^* = e_j' = [\![\varphi_j]\!] = 1$ $(\varphi_j \in \Phi_{sat})$ and $e_2^* = p_{TPT_j^{(1)}}^{(1)} \cdot \ldots \cdot p_{TPT_j^{(\iota)}}^{(\iota)}$. After jointly decrypting $E(e_2^*)$ in the Decryption Phase of $\pi_{\text{ATPC-Sel}}$, each party P_i obtains e_2^* and sets its $TPT_*^{(i)} := TPT_j^{(i)}$ for $p_{TPT_j^{(i)}}^{(i)} \in S^{(i)}$ where $p_{TPT_j^{(i)}}^{(i)}$ divides e_2^*. Overall, it follows that $ATPC \leftarrow_\$ PTPCS \subseteq TPCS$.

(CVD). By separating the different phases of Protocol 1, we sketch a simulator $\mathcal{S}$ which outputs a transcript computationally indistinguishable from $\text{VIEW}_{I_C}^\pi(\widehat{X})$. A detailed description of $\mathcal{S}$ is provided by [15]. Note that the number of messages a party P_i ($i \in \mathscr{P}$) receives when participating in $\pi_{\text{ATPC-Sel}}$ depends on the party's position in the protocol execution and on whether or not $PTPCS = \emptyset$. By applying the modular composition theorem, it suffices for $\mathcal{S}$ to simulate the output of $\pi_{\text{OE-TPCF}}$ and $\pi_{\text{CRS-C}}$ by means of a trusted third party performing the computation of $\mathcal{F}_{\text{OE-TPCF}}$ and $\mathcal{F}_{\text{CRS-C}}$, respectively. In the Evaluation Phase of $\pi_{\text{ATPC-Sel}}$, the joint outputs of the $|TPCS|$ sub-protocol calls of $\pi_{\text{OE-TPCF}}$ are simulated by setting $\langle E(L) \rangle := (\langle E(e_1) \rangle, \ldots, \langle E(e_{|TPCS|}) \rangle)$ where $\langle E(e_j) \rangle \leftarrow_\$ \mathbb{C}$ ($j \in \mathbb{N}_{|TPCS|}$). For each P_c ($c \in I_C = \{i_1, \ldots, i_\kappa\}$), $\mathcal{S}$ simulates $E(L)$ as $\langle E(L) \rangle$. The Mapping Phase can be simulated by performing Steps 3.1–3.3 of Protocol 1 for each party P_i ($i \in \mathscr{P}$). From the simulated mapping tables, $\mathcal{S}$ simulates $(u_1^{(i)}, \ldots, u_{|TPCS|}^{(i)})$ for $P_{c'}$ with $c' \in I_C \setminus \{\iota\}$ (cf. Steps 3.2 and 3.3, Protocol 1) and $E(L')$ for $P_{c''}$ with $c'' \in I_C \setminus \{1\}$ (cf. Step 3.4, Protocol 1). Furthermore, $\mathcal{S}$ computes $\langle e_j' \rangle$ ($j \in \mathbb{N}_{|TPCS|}$) from the simulated mapping tables (where one of these values is used to simulate the Decryption Phase). The simulation of the Selection Phase depends on whether or not $\mathcal{F}(\widehat{X}) = \bot$. For the case that $\mathcal{F}(\widehat{X}) \neq \bot$, the output of $\pi_{\text{CRS-C}}$ is simulated by setting $\langle c_1^* \rangle, \langle c_2^* \rangle \leftarrow_\$ \mathbb{C}$. Otherwise, $\langle c_1^* \rangle = \langle c_2^* \rangle := \lambda$. The Decryption Phase is only executed for the case that $\mathcal{F}(\widehat{X}) \neq \bot$. The output of the decryption protocol D is simulated by setting $\langle e_2^* \rangle := \langle e_j' \rangle$ where $j \in \mathbb{N}_{|TPCS|}$ is chosen such that $\varphi_j \overset{\text{Q}}{\sim} TPC_j$ with $TPT_j^{(i_1)} = TPT_*^{(i_1)}, \ldots, TPT_j^{(i_\kappa)} = TPT_*^{(i_\kappa)}$. Note that otherwise, $\langle e_2^* \rangle$ is not consistent with $\mathcal{F}(\widehat{X})$. Due to the fact that the underlying cryptosystem is semantically secure, it follows that the simulated view is computationally indistinguishable from $\text{VIEW}_{I_C}^\pi$.

Complexity. Let $O_{\text{OE-TPCF}}$, $O_{\text{CRC-C}}$, and O_{Dec} denote the computation, communication, and round complexities of $\pi_{\text{OE-TPCF}}$, $\pi_{\text{CRS-C}}$, $D(\cdot)$, respectively, depending on the context. The computation complexity of $\pi_{\text{ATPC-Sel}}$ is dominated by the sub-protocol calls and $|TPCS|$ homomorphic scalar multiplications and overall is in $\mathcal{O}(|TPCS| + |TPCS| \cdot O_{\text{OE-TPCF}} + O_{\text{CRC-C}} + O_{\text{Dec}})$. The communication complexity of $\pi_{\text{ATPC-Sel}}$ is in $\mathcal{O}(\iota \cdot |TPCS| + |TPCS| \cdot O_{\text{OE-TPCF}} + O_{\text{CRC-C}} + O_{\text{Dec}})$ while the round complexity is in $\mathcal{O}(\iota + |TPCS| \cdot O_{\text{OE-TPCF}} + O_{\text{CRC-C}} + O_{\text{Dec}})$.

5.3 Negotiation of Actual Quantities

In order to complete the (privacy-preserving) bartering process, i.e., for each party to compute its local view of the AT based on the $ATPC$, each party has to negotiate the actual quantities of the commodities to be traded with its trade partner. This can be done either offline without any privacy-preserving protocol or, e.g., by engaging in the two-party protocol π_{RSI} with each one of its trade partners. That is for each $TPT_*^{(i)} = (x_*^{(i)}, y_*^{(i)}) \neq (0,0)$, P_i and $P_{y^{(i)}}$ participate in an execution of $(q_{c_o^{(i)}}^{(i,y^{(i)})}) \leftarrow \pi_{RSI}(Q_d^{(y^{(i)})}, Q_o^{(i)})$ where $q_{c_o^{(i)}}^{(i,y^{(i)})}$ indicates the quantity of $c_o^{(i)}$ that P_i has to send to $P_{y^{(i)}}$. Note that $q_{c_o^{(i)}}^{(i,y^{(i)})}$ is chosen uniformly at random from $Q_d^{(y^{(i)})} \cap Q_o^{(i)}$ which honors the specified quantity ranges of the parties without preferring any one of them. Alternatively, to avoid possible imbalances in regards to quantity selection (for details see [16]), it is possible to shrink the private overlap interval $Q_d^{(y^{(i)})} \cap Q_o^{(i)}$ obliviously around the midpoint of the interval (using a similar approach to the one described in [16]).

5.4   Optimization of ATPC-Selection

Until now, we assumed that $ATPC$ was drawn uniformly at random from the set of potential trade partner constellations $PTPCS$. We now sketch a simple modification of protocol $\pi_{\text{ATPC-Sel}}$ which allows the private selection of an $ATPC$ with maximum *welfare* as optimization criteria, where the welfare $\mathcal{W}(\cdot)$ of a TPC is defined as the number of parties actively involved in the trade: $\mathcal{W}(TPC) :=$ $|\{TPT^{(i)} : i \in \mathscr{P}, TPT^{(i)} \in TPC, TPT^{(i)} \neq (0,0)\}|$.

The first step of our protocol modification is to introduce a prioritization of the $TPCs$ given by $TPCS$: At the end of the Evaluation Phase (Step 2.2 in Protocol 1), the parties locally multiply the evaluation result $E(e_i)$ with $\mathcal{W}(TPC_i)$ ($\forall i \in \mathbb{N}_{|TPCS|}$) resulting in a vector $E(L) = (E(e_1) \times_h \mathcal{W}(TPC_1),$ $\dots, E(e_{|TPCS|}) \times_h \mathcal{W}(TPC_{|TPCS|}))$. The second step of our modification is to replace the protocol call of $\pi_{\text{CRS-C}}$ (Step 4.1, Protocol 1) by a variant of conditional random selection (also introduced in [14]) which supports an integer indicator vector instead of just a binary indicator vector (cf. Definition 8). In the context of Protocol 1, this variant of $\pi_{\text{CRS-C}}$ returns $(c_1^*, c_2^*) := (E(e_{j*}), E(e_{j*}'))$ where $j^* \leftarrow_\$ \{j \in \mathbb{N}_{|TPCS|} : e_j = max(e_1, \dots, e_{|TPCS|})\}$.

Similar optimization criteria (e.g., for each TPC given by $TPCS$ a party individually determines the corresponding utility value and the welfare of a given TPC corresponds to the sum of utility values over all parties) can be integrated into protocol $\pi_{\text{ATPC-Sel}}$ analogously.

Acknowledgments. This work was supported by DFG Award ME 3704/4-1.

References

1. Aïmeur, E., Brassard, G., Mani Onana, F.S.: Blind sales in electronic commerce. In: Proceedings of the 6th International Conference on Electronic Commerce, pp. 148–157. ACM (2004)
2. Canetti, R.: Security and composition of multiparty cryptographic protocols. J. Cryptol. **13**(1), 143–202 (2000)

3. Damgård, I., Jurik, M.: A Generalisation, a Simplification and some applications of paillier's probabilistic public-key system. In: Kim, K. (ed.) PKC 2001. LNCS, vol. 1992, pp. 119–136. Springer, Heidelberg (2001). https://doi.org/10. 1007/3-540-44586-2_9

4. Dwork, C.: Differential privacy. In: Bugliesi, M., Preneel, B., Sassone, V., Wegener, I. (eds.) ICALP 2006. LNCS, vol. 4052, pp. 1–12. Springer, Heidelberg (2006). https://doi.org/10.1007/11787006_1

5. Förg, F., Mayer, D., Wetzel, S., Wüller, S., Meyer, U.: A secure two-party bartering protocol using privacy-preserving interval operations. In: 12th Annual International Conference on Privacy, Security and Trust, pp. 57–66 (2014)

6. Franklin, M., Tsudik, G.: Secure group barter: multi-party fair exchange with semi-trusted neutral parties. In: Hirchfeld, R. (ed.) FC 1998. LNCS, vol. 1465, pp. 90–102. Springer, Heidelberg (1998). https://doi.org/10.1007/BFb0055475

7. Frikken, K., Opyrchal, L.: PBS: private bartering systems. In: Tsudik, G. (ed.) FC 2008. LNCS, vol. 5143, pp. 113–127. Springer, Heidelberg (2008). https://doi.org/ 10.1007/978-3-540-85230-8_9

8. Goldreich, O.: Foundations of Cryptography: Basic Applications, vol. 2. Cambridge University Press, Cambridge (2009)

9. Kannan, S., Morgenstern, J., Rogers, R., Roth, A.: Private pareto optimal exchange. In: Proceedings of the Sixteenth ACM Conference on Economics and Computation, pp. 261–278. ACM (2015)

10. López, N., Núñez, M., Rodríguez, I., Rubio, F.: A multi-agent system for e-barter including transaction and shipping costs. In: Proceedings of the 2003 ACM Symposium on Applied Computing, pp. 587–594. ACM (2003)

11. Nakamoto, S.: Bitcoin: A Peer-to-Peer Electronic Cash System (2008)

12. Nzouonta, J., Silaghi, M.-C., Yokoo, M.: Secure computation for combinatorial auctions and market exchanges. In: Proceedings of the 3rd International Joint Conference on Autonomous Agents and Multiagent Systems, pp. 1398–1399. IEEE Computer Society (2004)

13. Paillier, P.: Public-key cryptosystems based on composite degree residuosity classes. In: Stern, J. (ed.) EUROCRYPT 1999. LNCS, vol. 1592, pp. 223–238. Springer, Heidelberg (1999). https://doi.org/10.1007/3-540-48910-X_16

14. Wüller, S., Meyer, U., Förg, F., Wetzel, S.: Privacy-preserving conditional random selection (extended version). In: 13th Annual Conference on Privacy, Security and Trust, pp. 44–53 (2015)

15. Wüller, S., Meyer, U., Wetzel, S.: Towards privacy-preserving multi-party bartering (extended version). Technical report AIB-2016-10, RWTH Aachen (2016)

16. Wüller, S., Pessin, W., Meyer, U., Wetzel, S.: Privacy-preserving two-party bartering secure against active adversaries. In: 14th Annual Conference on Privacy, Security and Trust, pp. 229–238 (2016)

17. Wüller, S., Mayer, D., Förg, F., Schüppen, S., Assadsolimani, B., Meyer, U., Wetzel, S.: Designing privacy-preserving interval operations based on homomorphic encryption and secret sharing techniques. J. Comput. Secur. 25(1), 59–81 (2017)

Multi-level Access in Searchable Symmetric Encryption

James Alderman, Keith M. Martin, and Sarah Louise Renwick[✉]

Information Security Group, Royal Holloway,
University of London, Egham, Surrey TW20 0EX, UK
{James.Alderman,SarahLouise.Renwick.2012}@live.rhul.ac.uk,
Keith.Martin@rhul.ac.uk

Abstract. Remote storage delivers a cost effective solution for data storage. If data is of a sensitive nature, it should be encrypted prior to outsourcing to ensure confidentiality; however, searching then becomes challenging. Searchable encryption is a well-studied solution to this problem. Many schemes only consider the scenario where users can search over the *entirety* of the encrypted data. In practice, sensitive data is likely to be classified according to an access control policy and different users should have different access rights. It is unlikely that all users have unrestricted access to the entire data set. Current schemes that consider multi-level access to searchable encryption are predominantly based on asymmetric primitives. We investigate *symmetric* solutions to multi-level access in searchable encryption where users have different access privileges to portions of the encrypted data and are not permitted to search over, or learn information about, data for which they are not authorised.

1 Introduction

Searchable encryption (SE) enables a user to search over encrypted data that has been outsourced to a remote server. In some schemes [4,5,9,18–20], the data owner may authorise multiple users to make search queries—in such cases, a querier is either authorised to search over the entirety of the data or not at all, in which case (ideally) no information about the outsourced data should be revealed. In practice, the access control requirements of outsourced data sets are likely to be more fine-grained than this binary 'all or nothing' approach; hence existing schemes do not suffice.

We study the problem of enforcing a *multi-level access control policy (MLA)* in the context of searchable symmetric encryption (SSE). As a notable example of this form of data classification, the UK government uses three levels of data classification: official, secret and top secret [16]. In our model, a user with 'secret'

J. Alderman—Supported by the European Commission under project H2020-644024 "CLARUS" and acknowledges support from BAE Systems Advanced Technology Centre.

S.L. Renwick—Supported by Thales UK and EPSRC under a CASE Award.

M. Brenner et al. (Eds.): FC 2017 Workshops 2017, LNCS 10323, pp. 35–52, 2017.
https://doi.org/10.1007/978-3-319-70278-0_3

clearance should be unable to learn any information about data items classified as 'top secret', such as whether they contain searched keywords or not. This is an example of an information flow policy with a total order of security labels [2].

More precisely, consider a (possibly large) data set which is to be outsourced to an external storage provider, which could be outside of the data owner's trusted zone. Although the provider has a business incentive to provide a storage and search service to the client (and to any other users authorised by the data owner), the provider may attempt to learn information about the sensitive data stored; in short, the storage provider may be *honest-but-curious*. Hence, the data must be encrypted prior to outsourcing, and the search procedure should not reveal unintended information to the storage provider or to other unauthorised entities. Each data item within the data set may be associated with some keywords, over which searches may be performed. Furthermore, each data item may differ in sensitivity and have different access control requirements. The data owner may authorise additional users to search the data set and, again, each user may have different access control clearance and therefore be able to access or search different sets of data items. Let us define a set of security labels $\mathbb{L}$, which forms a totally ordered set $(\mathbb{L}, \leqslant)$ to reflect the inheritance of access rights. Each user u and data item d is assigned one of these labels, denoted $\lambda(u)$ and $\lambda(d)$ respectively. A user u may search a data item d if and only if $\lambda(u) \geqslant \lambda(d)$.

Public-key encryption (PKE), especially functional encryption, has previously been used to achieve MLA in SE [3,11,15,21]. In general, PKE is computationally more intensive than symmetric key encryption (SKE), perhaps making SKE more suitable for practical systems. The enforcement of MLA policies in *symmetric* SE has, up to now, remained relatively unexplored. Kissel and Wang [14] presented a SKE-based scheme in which users are divided into groups that each have a specified dictionary of keywords they may search over. These groups are arranged hierarchically so that each group may also search for all keywords in dictionaries assigned to groups at lower levels in the hierarchy. Although this scheme presents a form of hierarchical access in SSE, users may still search over the entire data set. In most access control scenarios, we are concerned with protecting a data item (i.e. the complete content of a data item), not just a single keyword describing the data item. Furthermore, it may be difficult to correctly administer an access control policy expressed only in terms of authorised keywords; data items may gain their classification level due to semantic meaning regarding their contents (for example, the subject to which they pertain), which may not trivially be captured through the associated keywords. For example, consider two data items containing information about company spending: one providing a public report of company-wide spending, whilst the other pertains specifically to the research department. Whilst both items may be labelled by a keyword such as 'finance', detailed knowledge of research spending may be deemed more sensitive than a generalised report. Simply authorising users to search for keywords, such as 'finance', does not suffice in this instance as not all users that can search the public report should also be able to view the specific report. The access control policy in this case must be managed carefully—perhaps additional, more granular, keywords must be defined e.g. 'finance-public' (leading to an increase in the size of the searchable encryption index and a subsequent loss of efficiency) or a (less efficient) SE scheme that supports 'conjunctive keyword-only access control' would be required such that one can be authorised to search for ('finance' AND 'public') and only data items with *both* keywords would be returned. In this work, we consider the problem of fine-grained classification of data items *directly* and gain a more efficient solution.

In this work, we consider Multi-level Searchable Symmetric Encryption (MLSSE). We begin in Sect. 2 by reviewing background material, before defining our system and security models in Sects. 3.1 and 3.2. In Sect. 3.3, we introduce our instantiation based on the constructions of [9,13], and then show, in Sect. 3.5, how to extend our construction to support a dynamic data set using techniques from [13]. Section 3.6 discusses the efficiency of our scheme. The full security proofs of our constructions are omitted but are available in the full version of our paper [1].

2   Background

We aim to enforce *information flow policies* within searchable encryption, which encompass a wide range of access control policies that are of practical interest, including the Bell-LaPadula model, temporal, role-based and attribute-based access control [8].

Definition 1. *An* information flow policy *is a tuple* $\mathcal{P} = ((\mathbb{L}, \leq), \mathcal{U}, \mathcal{D}, \lambda)$, *where* $(\mathbb{L}, \leq)$ *is a partially ordered set (poset)*[1] *of security labels,* $\mathcal{U}$ *is a set of users,* $\mathcal{D}$ *is a set of objects (data items), and* $\lambda : \mathcal{U} \cup \mathcal{D} \rightarrow \mathbb{L}$ *is a function mapping users and objects to security labels in* $\mathbb{L}$. *We say that* $u \in \mathcal{U}$ *is authorised to read (search) an object* $d \in \mathcal{D}$ *if* $\lambda(d) \leq \lambda(u)$.

In this paper, we will focus on the case where $(\mathbb{L}, \leq)$ is a *total order* (chain) giving a simple hierarchy of security levels and, without loss of generality, we assume that each user and object is assigned to at most one security label. Given a set X, we denote the power set of X, comprising all combinations of elements in X, by 2^X. Throughout this paper we refer to 'security levels' and 'security labels' as *access levels*.

Definition 2. *A* Multi-User Searchable Symmetric Encryption (MSSE) *scheme is a set of six polynomial time algorithms defined as follows:*

- $K_O \xleftarrow{\$} \mathsf{MSSE.KeyGen}(1^k)$: *A probabilistic algorithm run by the data owner that takes a security parameter* $k \in \mathbb{N}$ *and outputs a secret key* K_O.

---

[1] A poset is a set of labels L and a binary order relation $\leq$ on L such that for all x, y and $z \in L$, $x \leq x$ (reflexivity), if $x \leq y$ and $y \leq x$ then $x = y$ (antisymmetry), and if $x \leq y$ and $y \leq z$ then $x \leq z$ (transitivity). If $x \leq y$ then we may write $y \geq x$.

- $(\mathcal{I}_\mathcal{D}, st_O, st_S) \xleftarrow{\$} \mathsf{MSSE.BuildIndex}(K_O, \mathcal{D}, \mathcal{G})$: *A probabilistic algorithm run by the data owner that takes a set of data items $\mathcal{D}$, a set of authorized users $\mathcal{G}$ and the secret key K_O. It outputs an index $\mathcal{I}_\mathcal{D}$, and server and owner states st_S and st_O.*
- $K_u \xleftarrow{\$} \mathsf{MSSE.AddUser}(u, K_O, st_O)$: *A probabilistic algorithm run by the data owner that takes the identity, u, of a user to be enrolled in the system along with the owner's secret key and state. It outputs a secret key for the new user K_u.*
- $T_\omega \leftarrow \mathsf{MSSE.Query}(\omega, K_u)^2$: *A deterministic algorithm run by a user that takes a keyword ω and the user's secret key, and outputs a search token.*
- $R_\omega \leftarrow \mathsf{MSSE.Search}(T_\omega, \mathcal{I}_\mathcal{D}, st_S)$: *A deterministic algorithm run by the server that takes as input a search token, an encrypted index and the server state, and outputs a set R_ω of identifiers of data items containing ω.*
- $(st_O, st_S) \xleftarrow{\$} \mathsf{MSSE.Revoke}(u, K_O, st_O)$: *A probabilistic algorithm run by the data owner that takes a user identity of a user to be revoked along with the data owner's secret key and state. It outputs new server and owner states.*

For a data set $\mathcal{D}$ and keyword $\omega \in \Delta$ (where Δ is a dictionary of possible keywords), let us denote by $\mathcal{D}_\omega$ the expected results of searching for ω in $\mathcal{D}$ (in the plain); informally we say that an MSSE scheme is correct if it also produces the output $\mathcal{D}_\omega$. More formally, a MSSE scheme MSSE is correct if for all $k \in \mathbb{N}$, for all K_O output by $\mathsf{MSSE.KeyGen}(1^k)$, for all $\mathcal{D} \in 2^\Delta$, for all $\mathcal{G} \in 2^\mathcal{U}$, for all $(\mathcal{I}_\mathcal{D}, st_O, st_S)$ output by $\mathsf{MSSE.BuildIndex}(K_O, \mathcal{G}, \mathcal{D})$, for all ω in Δ: $\mathsf{Search}(\mathsf{MSSE.Query}(K_u, \omega), \mathcal{I}_\mathcal{D}, st_S) = \mathcal{D}_\omega$.

Definition 3. *A Broadcast encryption (BE) scheme is a set of four polynomial time algorithms as follows, where $\mathcal{U}$ is the user space of all possible user identities:*

- $(PP, K_{\mathsf{BE}}) \xleftarrow{\$} \mathsf{BE.Keygen}(1^k)$: *A probabilistic algorithm that takes a security parameter k outputs public parameters PP and a master secret key K_{BE}.*
- $C \xleftarrow{\$} \mathsf{BE.Enc}(M, \mathcal{G})$: *A probabilistic algorithm that takes a plaintext M, a set of users $\mathcal{G} \in \mathcal{U}$ authorized to decrypt and produces a ciphertext C.*
- $K_u \xleftarrow{\$} \mathsf{BE.Add}(K_{\mathsf{BE}}, u)$: *A probabilistic algorithm that takes as input the master secret key K_{BE} and a user identifier $u \in \mathcal{U}$, and outputs a user key K_u.*
- $(M \text{ or } \bot) \leftarrow \mathsf{BE.Dec}(C, K_u)$: *A deterministic algorithm that takes a ciphertext C and a secret key K_u and outputs either a plaintext M or a failure symbol $\bot$.*

BE *is correct if $\forall k \in \mathbb{N}$, for all PP and K_{BE} output by $\mathsf{BE.KeyGen}(1^k, m)$, for all M in the plaintext space, all sets of users $\mathcal{G} \in \mathcal{U}$, every K_u output by $\mathsf{BE.Add}(u, K_{\mathsf{BE}})$ and all C output by $\mathsf{BE.Enc}(M, \mathcal{G})$ where $u \in \mathcal{G}$ we have: $M \leftarrow \mathsf{BE.Dec}(C, K_u)$.*

---

[2] This algorithm is sometimes referred to as $\mathsf{MSSE.Trapdoor}$ in the literature, however to maintain consistent notation throughout this paper we refer to it as $\mathsf{MSSE.Query}$.

3 Multi-level Access in Searchable Symmetric Encrytion

A MLSSE scheme permits searching over encrypted data in the symmetric key setting for multiple users that have varying access rights to the set of data items. The access levels are hierarchical (totally ordered), meaning a user may search all data items at their own access level as well as all data items that are classified at lower access levels.

3.1 System Model

Consider a *data owner* O, a *server* S, and a set of m data *users* $\mathcal{U}=\{u_1, ..., u_m\}$. The data owner possesses a set of data items $\mathcal{D}=\{d_1, ..., d_n\}$ which they wish to encrypt and outsource to S whilst authorising other users to search over some data items within $\mathcal{D}$. Each data item $d_i \in \mathcal{D}$ is associated with an identifier id_{d_i}.

To enable searching over the encrypted data, O must upload some encrypted metadata to the server. It first defines a dictionary of keywords, denoted $\Delta = \{\omega_1, ..., \omega_{|\Delta|}\}$, and assigns a set $\delta_{d_i} \subseteq \Delta$ of keywords to each data item $d_i \in \mathcal{D}$. We refer to the set of keywords for all data items as $\delta_{\mathcal{D}} = (\delta_{d_1}, ..., \delta_{d_n})$. The data owner then produces an encrypted *index* $\mathcal{I}_{\mathcal{D}}$ based on $\delta_{\mathcal{D}}$, over which searches will be performed.

O also defines an information flow policy $\mathcal{P}$ with a labelling function λ mapping each user $u_i \in \mathcal{U}$ and data item $d_j \in \mathcal{D}$ to an access level, denoted $\lambda(u_i)$ and $\lambda(d_j)$ respectively, in the totally ordered set $\mathbb{L} = \{a_1, ..., a_l\}$. Access control in our model is enforced at data item level—users are restricted in the data items that they may search, not the keywords they may search for [14]. A user with access level $\lambda(u_i)$ is authorised to search a data item with classification $\lambda(d_j)$ if and only if $\lambda(d_j) \leq \lambda(u_i)$. To search for a keyword $\omega \in \Delta$, a user u_i (with access level $\lambda(u_i)$) generates a search query $T_{\omega, \lambda(u_i)}$. Let $\mathcal{D}_\omega$ be the set of identifiers of all data items assigned the keyword ω, and denote by $\mathcal{D}_{\omega, \lambda(u_i)} \subseteq \mathcal{D}_\omega$ the search results that user u_i is authorised to view; in other words, the set of identifiers of all data items id_{d_j} assigned ω where $\lambda(d_j) \leq \lambda(u_i)$.

To add and revoke users, we use *broadcast encryption* (BE) (Definition 3) as per [9]; a user may only produce a valid search query if they are authorized in the BE scheme.

To ease notation, we define the tuple $d_i{}^{aug} = (d_i, id_i, \delta_{d_i}, \lambda(d_i))$ to completely describe a data item $d_i \in \mathcal{D}$ (being the data itself, the identifier, the associated keywords and the security classification). We denote the information regarding all data items by $\mathcal{D}^{aug} = \{d_1{}^{aug}, ..., d_n{}^{aug}\}$.

We present a *structure only* MLSSE system—we only consider the data structure (index) and do not encrypt the data items themselves; data items may be encrypted separately and retrieved based on the search results, which comprise a set of data item identifiers that fulfil the query. We permit data items to be of any format and the sets of keywords can be arbitrarily chosen from the dictionary—they may not necessarily correspond to the actual content of the data, but could be descriptive attributes of the data item. This may help minimise the risk of a statistical attack on the index as the frequency of a certain word in a document is not necessarily reflected in the set of keywords chosen to index the data item.

Definition 4. *A Multi-level Searchable Symmetric Encryption Scheme (MLSSE) scheme consists of six algorithms defined as follows:*

- $(K_O, k_S, PP) \overset{\$}{\leftarrow} \mathsf{KeyGen}(1^k, S, \mathcal{P})$: *A probabilistic algorithm run by the data owner O that takes the security parameter k, policy $\mathcal{P}$ and the server identity S, and outputs O's secret key K_O, a server key k_S and public parameters PP.*
- $\mathcal{I}_{\mathcal{D}} \overset{\$}{\leftarrow} \mathsf{BuildIndex}(\mathcal{D}^{aug}, K_O, PP)$: *A probabilistic algorithm run by O. It takes the description of the data set $\mathcal{D}^{aug}$ and O's secret key, and outputs the index $\mathcal{I}_{\mathcal{D}}$.*
- $(K_u, PP) \overset{\$}{\leftarrow} \mathsf{AddUser}(u, \lambda(u), K_O, PP)$: *A probabilistic algorithm run by O to enrol a new user into the system. It takes the new user's identity u and access level $\lambda(u)$, and O's key, and outputs a secret key for the new user.*
- $T_{\omega, \lambda(u)} \leftarrow \mathsf{Query}(\omega, K_u)$: *A deterministic algorithm run by a user with access level $\lambda(u)$ to generate a search query. It takes as input a keyword $\omega \in \Delta$ and the user's secret key and outputs a search query $T_{\omega, \lambda(u)}$.*
- $\mathcal{R}_{\omega, \lambda(u)} \leftarrow \mathsf{Search}(T_{\omega, \lambda(u)}, \mathcal{I}_{\mathcal{D}}, k_S)$: *A deterministic algorithm run by S to search the index for data items containing a keyword ω. It takes a search query and the index, and returns the search results $\mathcal{R}_{\omega, \lambda(u_i)}$, comprising either a set $\mathcal{D}_{\omega, \lambda(u)}$ of identifiers of data items d_j containing ω such that for all $\lambda(d_j) \leq \lambda(u)$ (where $\lambda(u)$ is the access level of the user that submitted the search query), or a failure symbol $\perp$.*
- $(K_O, PP) \overset{\$}{\leftarrow} \mathsf{RevokeUser}(u, K_O, PP)$: *A probabilistic algorithm run by O to revoke a user from the system. It takes the user's id, the data owner's and server's secret keys, and outputs updated owner and server keys.*

An MLSSE scheme is correct if for all $k \in \mathbb{N}$, for all K_O, k_S output by $\mathsf{KeyGen}(1^k, S, \mathcal{P})$, for all $\mathcal{D}^{aug}$, for all $\mathcal{I}_{\mathcal{D}}$ output by $\mathsf{BuildIndex}(\mathcal{D}^{aug}, K_O, PP)$, for all $\omega \in \Delta$, for all $u \in \mathcal{U}$, for all K_u output by $\mathsf{AddUser}(u, \lambda(u), K_O, PP)$, $\mathsf{Search}(\mathsf{Query}(\omega, K_u), \mathcal{I}_{\mathcal{D}}, k_S) = \mathcal{D}_{\omega, \lambda(u)}$.

3.2 Security Model

A secure MLSSE scheme would, ideally, reveal no information regarding the data set $\mathcal{D}$ to the server (i.e. a curious server cannot learn information about the data it stores) and reveal no information to users regarding data items that they are not authorised to search. However, most SSE schemes leak additional information to gain efficiency. For example, the search results $\{\mathcal{R}_{\omega_1, \lambda(u)}, ..., \mathcal{R}_{\omega_p, \lambda(u)}\}$ for a set of queries $\{T_{\omega_1, \lambda(u)}, ..., T_{\omega_p, \lambda(u)}\}$ could be revealed. This is referred to as the *access pattern* (Definition 5) and defines the link between a search query and the search results it produces; it may be thought of as a database where each row stores a search query and a corresponding set of identifiers of data items that satisfies the search query.

Most efficient SSE schemes also leak the *search pattern* (Definition 6), which reveals the set of search queries made to the server. In most single-user SSE schemes [6,7,9,10,12,13], search queries are formed deterministically; the server can therefore ascertain whether a search query has been made previously.

Definition 5. *For a sequence of q search queries $\Omega = \{T_{\omega_1, \lambda(u_1)}, ..., T_{\omega_q, \lambda(u_q)}\}$ where for $1 \leq i, j \leq q$: ω_i and ω_j or $\lambda(u_i)$ and $\lambda(u_j)$ are not necessarily distinct for $i \neq j$, the* access pattern *is defined as:*

$$AP(\mathcal{I_D}, \Omega) = \{(T_{\omega_1, \lambda(u_1)}, \mathcal{R}_{\omega_1, \lambda(u_1)}), ..., (T_{\omega_q, \lambda(u_q)}, \mathcal{R}_{\omega_q, \lambda(u_q)})\}.$$

Definition 6. *For a sequence of q search queries $\Omega = \{T_{\omega_1, \lambda(u_1)}, ..., T_{\omega_q, \lambda(u_q)}\}$ where for $1 \leq i, j \leq q$: ω_i and ω_j or $\lambda(u_i)$ and $\lambda(u_j)$ are not necessarily distinct for $i \neq j$, the* search pattern *is defined as a $q \times q$ symmetric binary matrix $SP(\mathcal{I_D}, \Omega)$ such that for $1 \leq i, j \leq q$:*

$$SP(\mathcal{I_D}, \Omega)_{i,j} = 1 \iff T_{\omega_i, \lambda(u_i)} = T_{\omega_j, \lambda(u_j)}.$$

Intuitively, the search pattern reveals when the ith and jth queries are the same, which happens when queries are issued for the same keyword by users with the same access level.

Definition 7. *For an index $\mathcal{I_D}$ we define the* setup leakage *$\mathcal{L}_{Setup}(\mathcal{I_D})$ to be all the information that is leaked by the index $\mathcal{I_D}$.*

Definition 8. *For an index $\mathcal{I_D}$ and set of q search queries $\Omega = (T_{\omega_1, \lambda(u)}, ..., T_{\omega_q, \lambda(u)})$ we define the* query leakage *$\mathcal{L}_{Query}(\mathcal{I_D}, \Omega)$ to be all the information leaked by evaluating the queries in Ω on the index $\mathcal{I_D}$.*

We now formalise the notions of security we require in MLSSE. We use cryptographic games to formalize our notions of security. For each game, a challenger $\mathcal{C}$ instantiates a probabilistic polynomial time (PPT) adversary $\mathcal{A}$ whose inputs are chosen to reflect the information available to a realistic adversary. Our notion of adaptive security is based on that of IND-CKA2 presented in [9]. In the following we represent the dictionary of keywords as Δ, λ defines the mapping function as described in Sect. 3.

Multi-level Access. Our first security notion, in Game 1.1, is that of *multi-level access* which requires that a user, u, cannot receive search results or learn information relating to data items d_i such that $\lambda(u) < \lambda(d_i)$. More specifically, a server colluding with several users cannot learn anything about the index beyond the specified leakage according to the corrupt users' access rights.

We define a *maximal query leakage with access level λ_{max}* on $\mathcal{I_D}$ to be $\mathcal{L}_{Query}(\mathcal{I_D}, \{T_{\omega_i, \lambda_{max}}\}_{\omega_i \in \Delta})$—this is the leakage resulting from every possible keyword search with the maximal access level available, in Game 1.1 we denote this as $\mathcal{L}^{max}(\mathcal{I_D})$.

The challenger sets up the system, including instantiating several global variables (which the challenger can use in the main game and in oracle functions, but which the adversary cannot see): L is a list of users that have been corrupted, λ^{max} is the maximal access level of any corrupted user, and chall is a Boolean flag to show whether the challenge parameters have been generated yet. The adversary is given the security parameter, access control policy, server key and the public parameters, as well as providing access to the following oracles.

The ADDUSER oracle allows the adversary to enrol a user into the system, and the adversary corrupts this user by receiving the user key. If the challenge has not yet been generated, then the challenger adds the requested user to the list L of corrupted users, checks if the maximal access level of corrupted users needs updating, and runs the AddUser algorithm. Otherwise, if the challenge has been generated, the above procedure is carried out only if the maximal query leakage for the new user's access level is equal on both challenge data sets—that is, providing the user key for the queried user cannot allow the adversary to trivially distinguish the two data sets.

The REVOKEUSER oracle first checks that the requested user has indeed been added previously. If so, it removes the user identity from L and checks whether the maximal access level needs changing. It returns the server key resulting from running the RevokeUser algorithm.

The BUILDINDEX oracle simply runs BuildIndex and returns the output to the adversary.

After a polynomial number of queries, the adversary outputs two data sets which must have identical maximal query leakages for the maximal access level of any corrupted user. The adversary cannot choose data sets where a user that it has corrupted could make any query that legitimately distinguishes the data sets since this would count as a trivial win. Whilst this may appear to be a strong assumption, we believe it to be the minimal assumption necessary to avoid trivial wins in the multi-user setting. The main issue is that in the multi-user setting it is necessary to consider the server colluding with a set of users (but not the data owner); as such, the adversary is able to perform the roles of the server and of an authorised user, and therefore may produce arbitrary search queries and perform searches themselves. Thus, the challenger in the game is unable to monitor which searches have been performed and hence cannot determine whether the query leakages of the *actual* queries on both data sets are equal, and instead must rely on the stronger assumption that no possible authorised search query can distinguish the data sets. Note that Van Rompay et al. [17] deal with the multi-user case without this assumption since they deal with single word indexes and have a proxy through which all queries are made.

The challenger sets the challenge flag to true and chooses a random bit b which determines the data set used to form an index. The adversary is given the index and oracle access as described in Game 1.1 and must determine which data set was used.

Definition 9 (*Multi-level Access*). *Let $\mathcal{ML}$ be a multi-level searchable symmetric encryption scheme where $k \in \mathbb{N}$ is the security parameter, $\mathcal{P}$ is an information flow policy, S is the identity of the server and $\mathcal{A}$ a PPT adversary. The advantage of $\mathcal{A}$ is:*

$$Adv_{\mathcal{A}}^{MLA}(\mathcal{ML}, 1^k, \mathcal{P}) = |\Pr[\mathbf{Exp}_{\mathcal{A}}^{MLA}[\mathcal{ML}, 1^k, S, \mathcal{P}] = 1] - \frac{1}{2}|.$$

We say that $\mathcal{ML}$ is $(\mathcal{L}_{Setup}, \mathcal{L}_{Query})$-secure against adaptive chosen keyword attacks in the sense of Game 1.1 if for all $\mathcal{A}$, all $k \in \mathbb{N}$, all S and all $\mathcal{P}$, $Adv_{\mathcal{A}}^{MLA}(\mathcal{ML}, 1^\kappa, S, \mathcal{P}) \leq \mathrm{negl}(k)$ for a negligible function negl.

$\mathbf{Exp}_{\mathcal{A}}^{MLA}[X]$:	Oracle AddUser$(u, \lambda(u), K_O, PP)$
$\lambda^{max} \leftarrow \perp$	if chall $=$ false
chall $\leftarrow$ false	if $\lambda(u) > \lambda^{max}$
$(K_O, K_S, PP) \leftarrow\!\!\$ \mathsf{KeyGen}(1^\kappa, \mathcal{U}, \mathcal{P})$	$\lambda^{max} \leftarrow \lambda(u)$
$(\mathcal{D}_0^{aug}, \mathcal{D}_1^{aug}, st) \leftarrow\!\!\$ \mathcal{A}^O(X, K_S, PP)$	return AddUser$(u, \lambda(u), K_O, PP)$
$\mathcal{I}_{\mathcal{D}_0} \leftarrow\!\!\$ \mathsf{BuildIndex}(\mathcal{D}_0^{aug}, K_O, PP)$	else if $\lambda(u) > \lambda_{max}$
$\mathcal{I}_{\mathcal{D}_1} \leftarrow\!\!\$ \mathsf{BuildIndex}(\mathcal{D}_1^{aug}, K_O, PP)$	return $\perp$
if $\mathcal{L}_{Search}^{\lambda^{max}}(\mathcal{I}_{\mathcal{D}_0}) \neq \mathcal{L}_{Search}^{\lambda^{max}}(\mathcal{I}_{\mathcal{D}_1})$	else return AddUser$(u, \lambda(u), K_O, PP)$
return 0	
chall $\leftarrow$ true	
$b \leftarrow\!\!\$ \{0, 1\}$	
$b' \leftarrow\!\!\$ \mathcal{A}^O(\mathcal{I}_{\mathcal{D}_b}, st)$	
if $b' = b$ return 1	
else return 0	

Game 1.1: The Multi-level Access game

Revocation Security. In MLSSE, as with other multi-user SSE schemes, we need to consider user *revocation* to remove a user's ability to submit valid search queries to the server, and hence receive search results. We capture this in Game 1.2. The adversary is given the public parameters and selects a data set (along with associated access levels, keywords and identifiers). The challenger then creates the index. The adversary is given access to a set of oracles that perform the AddUser$(\cdot, \lambda(\cdot), K_O, PP)$, Search$(\cdot, \mathcal{I}_{\mathcal{D}}, k_S)$ and RevokeUser$(\cdot, K_O, PP)$ functions, where the parameters represented by $\cdot$ are provided by the adversary, and the adversary is given the resulting user keys and search results. Once the adversary has completed his queries, the challenger revokes all users that were queried to the AddUser oracle but were not subsequently queried to the RevokeUser oracle (i.e. all users for which the adversary holds a valid user key). The adversary must then produce a search query T which, when used as input to the Search algorithm, does not produce $\perp$ i.e. the adversary must produce a valid search query even though it does not hold a non-revoked key.

Definition 10 (*Revocation*). Let $\mathcal{ML}$ be a multi-level searchable symmetric encryption scheme where $k \in \mathbb{N}$ is the security parameter, S the server identity, $\mathcal{P}$ is an information flow policy and $\mathcal{A}$ a PPT adversary. We define the advantage of $\mathcal{A}$ in Game 1.2 as:

$$Adv_{\mathcal{A}}^{Revoke}(\mathcal{ML}, 1^\kappa, S, \mathcal{P}) = |\mathbb{P}[\mathbf{Exp}_{\mathcal{A}}^{Revoke}[\mathcal{ML}, 1^\kappa, S, \mathcal{P}] = 1] - \frac{1}{2}|.$$

We say that $\mathcal{ML}$ achieves revocation if for all $\mathcal{A}$, all $k \in \mathbb{N}$, all S and all $\mathcal{P}$,

$$Adv_{\mathcal{A}}^{Revoke}(\mathcal{ML}, 1^\kappa, S, \mathcal{P}) \leq \mathrm{negl}(k).$$

$\mathbf{Exp}_{\mathcal{A}}^{Revoke}[X]$:	Oracle ADDUSER$(u, \lambda(u), K_O, PP)$
$\mathcal{G} \leftarrow \emptyset$	**if** $u \in \mathcal{G}$
$(K_O, K_S, PP) \leftarrow\!\!{}_\$ \mathsf{KeyGen}(1^k, \mathcal{U}, \mathcal{P})$	**return** $\bot$
$(\mathcal{D}^{aug}, st) \leftarrow \mathcal{A}^{\mathcal{O}}(X, PP)$	**else**
$\mathcal{I}_{\mathcal{D}} \leftarrow\!\!{}_\$ \mathsf{BuildIndex}(\mathcal{D}^{aug}, K_O, PP)$	$\mathcal{G} \leftarrow \mathcal{G} \cup u$
$st \leftarrow\!\!{}_\$ \mathcal{A}^{\mathcal{O}}(st)$	**return**
for $u \in \mathcal{G}$	AddUser$(u, \lambda(u), K_O, PP)$
$(K_O, PP) \leftarrow\!\!{}_\$ \mathsf{RevokeUser}(u, K_O, PP)$	Oracle REVOKEUSER(u, K_O, PP)
$T_\omega \leftarrow\!\!{}_\$ \mathcal{A}^{\mathcal{O}}(st, PP)$	
$\mathcal{R} \leftarrow \mathsf{Search}(T_\omega, \mathcal{I}_{\mathcal{D}}, K_S)$	**if** $u \in \mathcal{G}$
if $\mathcal{R} \neq \bot$	$\mathcal{G} \leftarrow \mathcal{G} \backslash u$
return 1	**return**
else	RevokeUser(u, K_O, PP)
return 0	**else**
	if $u \notin \mathcal{G}$
	return
	$\bot$

Game 1.2: The Revocation game

3.3   Construction

Our construction MLSSE is an adaptation of the scheme of Kamara et al. [13], which is based on the construction of the influential inverted index scheme SSE-1 by Curtmola et al. [9].

Informally, MLSSE scheme uses an array $\mathbb{A}$ of linked lists, along with a look-up table $\mathbb{T}$ to index the encrypted data. This produces a sequential search that lends itself well to the hierarchical access rights on the data items that we require. For each keyword $\omega_i \in \Delta$, we define a list L_{ω_i} which stores the identifiers for all data items containing that keyword and is ordered according to the access level of the data items—data items with the highest classification are placed at the beginning of the list, and those with the lowest classification at the end. Each list L_{ω_i} is encrypted and stored in $\mathbb{A}$ as a linked list. During the search phase the look-up table $\mathbb{T}$ is used to point the server to the correct node in the array depending on the information in the search query i.e. which keyword was searched for and what access rights the user that submitted the search query has. This node is decrypted using information in the search query and the node itself, revealing the address of the next node in the linked list. The server may continue to decrypt all other relevant nodes in the linked list, obtaining the set of search results relevant to the user's searched keyword and access level.

The key difference between our scheme and that of [13] is that, rather than pointing to the *beginning* of each linked list, the entry in $\mathbb{T}$ will point to the appropriate position within the linked list according to the access rights of the querier (recall that the list is ordered by access levels). Since it is not possible to move backwards through the encrypted lists, the only search results available are those contained beyond this point in this list—that is, identifiers for those documents containing the keyword and whose classification is at most that of the querier, as required by the information flow policy.

Let BE be an IND-CPA secure broadcast encryption scheme. We define the following pseudorandom functions (PRFs):

$$F : \{0,1\}^k \times \{0,1\}^* \to \{0,1\}^k,$$

$$G : \{0,1\}^k \times \{0,1\}^* \to \{0,1\}^*,$$

$$P : \{0,1\}^k \times \{0,1\}^* \to \{0,1\}^k,$$

$$H : \{0,1\}^* \times \{0,1\}^k \to \{0,1\}^*,$$

and a pseudorandom permutation (PRP):

$$\phi : \{0,1\}^k \times \{0,1\}^* \times \{0,1\}^k \times \{0,1\}^k \to \{0,1\}^k \times \{0,1\}^* \times \{0,1\}^k,$$

$\mathbb{A}$ is a $|\Delta| \times |\mathbb{L}|$ array and $\mathbb{T}$ is a dictionary of size $|\Delta| \cdot |\mathbb{L}|$. We denote the address of a node N in $\mathbb{A}$ as $addr_\mathbb{A}(N)$.

Let λ map users and data items to their relevant access levels as described in Sect. 3.1. We define a function γ which outputs three ordered lists $\mathsf{L}_{\omega_i}, \mathsf{X}_{\omega_i}$ and N_{ω_i} given the set of identifiers $\mathcal{D}^{aug}$ and the array $\mathbb{A}$. We refer to the nth item in a list L_{ω_i} as $\mathsf{L}_i[n]$. The list L_{ω_i} contains identifiers of data items in $\mathcal{D}_{\omega_i}$ ordered from the identifiers with the highest to the lowest access levels, the list N_{ω_i} contains the addresses of $|\mathsf{L}_{\omega_i}|$ nodes chosen randomly from $\mathbb{A}$ and the list X_{ω_i} contains the indices of the identifiers in L_{ω_i} where each access level starts i.e. if we have an ordered list of identifiers $\mathsf{L}_{\omega_i} = (id_1, id_2, id_3, id_4, id_5)$ where:

$$a_1 = \lambda(id_1) = \lambda(id_2) = \lambda(id_3) > \lambda(id_4) = \lambda(id_5) = a_3.$$

We have that $\mathsf{X}_{\omega_i}[3] = 4$, which says that the list of nodes with access level at most a_3 starts at the fourth entry in L_{ω_i}. There is an entry per each access level in X_{ω_i}, even if two access levels have the same starting point in L_{ω_i}; from the example above we can see that $\mathsf{X}_{\omega_i}[2] = \mathsf{X}_{\omega_i}[3] = 4$. If an access level is not authorised to view any data items in $\mathcal{D}_{\omega_i}$ then the entry corresponding to that access level (as well as the entries corresponding to all access levels below it) in X_{ω_i} is set to $\perp$. An identifier of a data item $d_i \in \mathcal{D}_{\omega_i}$ will inherit the access level label of the respective data item, i.e. $\lambda(id_{d_i}) = \lambda(d_i)$.

The KeyGen algorithm initialises the system and generates the keys K_O, k_S, along with the public parameters, PP. The key K_O includes the secret key for the BE scheme and the sets of $|\mathbb{L}|$ keys for each pseudo-random function: F, G and P and the key for the pseudo-random permutation ϕ (referred to as the data owner's state, st_O). The server is enrolled as a user and its secret key is also generated (although it does not receive the necessary keys to form search queries). PP includes the information flow policy $\mathcal{P}$, the authorized user group $\mathcal{G}$, the server state st_S (which is an encryption of the owner state generated using BE) and the public parameters for BE, PP_{BE}.

The BuildIndex algorithm initializes a set $free$ which consists of all nodes in the array $\mathbb{A}$. BuildIndex considers each keyword contained in the dataset in turn. For each keyword ω_i, the function γ generates $\mathsf{L}_{\omega_i}, \mathsf{X}_{\omega_i}$ and N_{ω_i}. The free list is then updated according to which nodes have been chosen by γ. The nodes in the array that form the linked lists consist of the identifier from L_{ω_i} of a data item containing ω_i, the address in the array of the next node in the linked list, the key used to decrypt the following node in the linked list and a random bit string $r_i \in \{0,1\}^k$. The identifier, address of the next node and the key used to decrypt the following node in the linked list are XORed with the output of a PRF H in order to encrypt this information. For the first node in the linked list he input of H is the decryption key for the current node (which corresponds to an access level and keyword and forms part of the search query) along with r_i), hence the information stored in the node can only be decrypted by the server if the server has a search query generated by a user who is authorized to view the data item whose identifier is stored at that node. The decryption key for all subsequent nodes is contained in the previous node of the linked list. BuildIndex then proceeds to create the look-up table $\mathbb{T}$. Unlike prior schemes [9], each user may have a different access level and thus the starting points for search results within the linked lists may vary; a search query made by a user with a higher access level should traverse more of the list than that of a user with lower access rights (the user is authorised to search more data items). Table $\mathbb{T}$ has an entry for each access level/keyword pair containing the address of a node in $\mathbb{A}$, which is the node in the linked list L_{ω_i} from which the user with a specified access level is authorised to decrypt. If an access level is not authorised to view any part of the linked list then the value in $\mathbb{T}$ is set to $\perp$. Finally the index $\mathcal{I}_{\mathcal{D}} = (\mathbb{A}, \mathbb{T})$ is returned.

The AddUser algorithm grants a user u the ability to search the index at a specific access level. The user is added to the set $\mathcal{G}$ of authorized users and a BE key, k_u, is derived for the new user. The new user is given k_u and the secret keys associated with their access level $k_{\lambda(u),1}, k_{\lambda(u),2}$ and $k_{\lambda(u),3}$ and PP is updated.

The RevokeUser algorithm revokes a user's search privileges. A new value for st_O is selected and the user is removed from $\mathcal{G}$. This value is encrypted using BE to form the new server state st_S. The updated versions of K_O and PP are ouput.

The Query algorithm generates a search query for a user u to search for a keyword w. The user first attempts to decrypt the current server state st_S using their secret key k_u; we denote the output of the decryption by st'_O. Note that if u is not authorised then decryption will return $\perp$, if this is the case Query outputs $\perp$. The query itself comprises three parts. The first is the output of the PRF F applied to the keyword ω, keyed with the secret key for F associated with the user's access level $k_{\lambda(u),1}$. This part of the query is used to locate the relevant entry in $\mathbb{T}$. The second part is the output of the PRF G applied to the keyword ω and is used to mask the entry in $\mathbb{T}$ in order to locate the user's relevant the starting position in the linked list corresponding to ω in $\mathbb{A}$. The third part is the output of the PRF P applied to the keyword ω, which is used to decrypt the first relevant node in $\mathbb{A}$ according to the user's access level. The PRP ϕ is applied to the search query, using st'_O as the key.

The Search algorithm finds data item identifiers associated with the searched keyword from the subset of data item identifiers the user is authorized to search. The server decrypts st_S and applies the inverse of the PRP ϕ to the query it received; it parses the result as (τ_1, τ_2, τ_3). The server then looks up entry $\mathbb{T}[\tau_1]$ and if that entry is not equal to $\bot$, the server XORs the value with τ_2 and parses the resulting value as y. The server looks up the node at $\mathbb{A}[y]$, parses the entry as (z_1, z_2), and decrypts it by XORing z_1 with the output of H (which takes as input τ_3 along with z_2).

The server is able to sequentially decrypt the rest of the list stored in $\mathbb{A}$ until they reach a node where the address stored in that node for the next item in the linked list is 0.

3.4   Security

In MLSSE search queries for the same keyword that are produced by users with different access levels are indistinguishable from one another. That is, a search query for a keyword ω from a user u_i with access level $\lambda(u_i)$ is indistinguishable from a search query for ω from a user u_j with access level $\lambda(u_j)$ for $\lambda(u_i) \neq \lambda(u_j)$. This means that from the queries alone an adversary is unable to deduce how many times a certain keyword has been searched for overall, it can only deduce how many times the same keyword has been searched for within each access level. This information leakage is less than that of standard single or multi user SSE schemes such as $[6, 7, 9, 10, 12, 13]$.

In terms of access pattern we also reduce the amount of information leakage compared with standard single user or multi-user SSE schemes. In particular we do not reveal whether a data item contains the keyword ω_i associated with a search query unless the access level of that data item is less than or equal to that of the user u_i that generated the search query, meaning that an adversary cannot see a full set of search results.

However when a search query is paired with the search results it generates (the access pattern, Definition 5) then an adversary may be able to correlate which search queries are for the same keyword by looking at the intersections of the search results. For example if one set of search results is a subset of another set of search results then this may imply that the two search queries used to generate these results are for the same keyword. An adversary may eventually be able to build up a complete set of search results for a particular keyword, which is equivalent to the leakage produced by a search query in a single user SSE scheme. The server does not know, however, how many access levels there are altogether so a server would need to receive all possible search queries before it can ascertain whether or not a set of search results for a particular keyword is complete or not.

The hierarchal relationships between the data item identifiers i.e. which identifiers represent data items at higher access level than others could also be leaked in the same way. If an adversary has ascertained that two sets of search results

$\mathcal{R}_{\omega,a_i} \subset \mathcal{R}_{\omega,a_j}$ represent searches for the same keyword ω, then an adversary will be able to conclude that identifiers in the set $\mathcal{R}_{\omega,a_j} \setminus \mathcal{R}_{\omega,a_i}$ are at a higher access level than those in $\mathcal{R}_{\omega,a_i}$. We note that unless the search results are padded in some way this leakage is inevitable. Padding search results is not standard in SSE schemes as it requires post-processing of the search results by the user hence we do not pad the search results in our system model in order to maintain an efficient scheme.

From this we can see that initially our scheme leaks less information about the search pattern and access pattern than a single user SSE scheme, however over time as more queries are generated the information leakage tends to that of a single user SSE scheme. The information leakage relating to a keyword ω i.e. the access patterns for search queries corresponding to ω only reaches that of a single user SSE scheme once a search query has been generated at each possible access level, our leakage remains lower up until this point.

As a search query for a keyword and access level pair is created deterministically we can think of the search query as a *codeword* for the combination of that keyword and access level. The index usually reveals these codewords as a search is carried out by matching search queries to relevant codewords in the index. A codeword for keyword ω at access level a is denoted $id(\omega, a)$.

We give the specific leakage functions to precisely capture the leakage in MLSSE, where Ω is a set of queries from users in the system that have been evaluated on the encrypted index by the server:

1. $\mathcal{L}_{Setup}(\mathcal{I}_\mathcal{D}) = (|\mathbb{A}|, |\mathbb{T}|, [id(\omega, a)]_{\omega \in \Delta, i \in [|\mathbb{L}|]})$
2. $\mathcal{L}_{Query}(\mathcal{I}_\mathcal{D}, \Omega) = (AP(\mathcal{I}_\mathcal{D}, \Omega), SP(\mathcal{I}_\mathcal{D}, \Omega), [id(\omega, a)]_{\forall T_{\omega,a} \in \Omega}, \Omega)$

Theorem 1. *Given an IND-CPA secure broadcast encryption scheme* BE, *a pseudo-random permutation ϕ, and pseudorandom functions F, G, P, H. Let* MLSSE *be the searchable symmetric encryption scheme with multi-level access defined in Fig. 1. Then* MLSSE *is $(\mathcal{L}_{Setup}, \mathcal{L}_{Query})$-secure in the sense of multi-level access and revocation.*

We provide the intuitions of our security proofs here and refer the reader to the full online version of the paper for the full security proofs [1].

Multi-level access: To show multi-level access we reduce the security to that of the IND-CPA security of a symmetric encryption scheme which encrypts plaintexts by XORing them with the output of a PRF. We assume the possibility of a adversary $\mathcal{A}$ that is able to break the multi-level security of our scheme then we construct a second adversary $\mathcal{A}'$ that is able to use $\mathcal{A}$ as a subroutine in order to break the IND-CPA security of the symmetric encryption scheme with non-negligible probability.

Revocation: In this proof we show that if we assume an adversary $\mathcal{A}$ with non-negligible advantage δ in Game 1.2 then $\mathcal{A}$ can be used as a subroutine by an adversary $\mathcal{A}_{BE}$ to break the security of an IND-CPA secure broadcast encryption scheme BE.

Fig. 1. The MLSSE construction

3.5   Achieving Dynamicity

We can extend MLSSE to support multi-level access on a dynamic data set by adding two new data structures to the index: a deletion table ($\mathbb{T}_d$) and a deletion array ($\mathbb{A}_d$). There are also four additional algorithms: AddToken, Add, DeleteToken, Delete. Array $\mathbb{A}_d$ stores a list of nodes for each data item which point to nodes in $\mathbb{A}$ that would need to be removed if the corresponding data item was deleted. This means that every node in $\mathbb{A}$ will have a corresponding node in $\mathbb{A}_d$, which is called its *dual* node. $\mathbb{T}_d$ is a table with an entry for each data item which points to the start of the corresponding linked list in $\mathbb{A}_d$, given a valid *delete token* for that data item. In addition to these two new structures the index consists of a search array $\mathbb{A}_s$ and a search table $\mathbb{T}_s$ (as in the original construction) and a *free list* that keeps track of all the unused space in $\mathbb{A}_s$.

In the dynamic scheme searching for a keyword is done similarly to the static construction in Sect. 3.3 and follows the concept of linked lists presented by [9].

To add a data item to the index, changes need to be made to $\mathbb{T}_d$, $\mathbb{A}_s$ and $\mathbb{A}_d$. The data owner creates an *add token* using AddToken and sends this to the server. The server then determines the free space available in $\mathbb{A}_s$ using the free list and adds the relevant information to the free nodes and updates the free list. When adding a new data item the relevant nodes cannot be added to the end of each linked list; instead we have to insert in the appropriate place in the linked list according to the access level of the new data item. Information in the add token will allow the server to locate the correct point at which to insert the nodes in each linked list, so instead of the entry in $\mathbb{T}_s$ just pointing to the end node of each linked list this is altered so that it points to the correct node in the linked list according to the access level of the new data item. The respective predecessor of each new node is modified to point to the new node instead of its previous ancestor.

In order to remove a data item, a deletion token is created which allows the server to locate and delete the correct entries in $\mathbb{T}_d$. This, in turn, allows the server to locate and delete the correct entries in $\mathbb{A}_s$. Some nodes will need to be updated in $\mathbb{A}_s$ (as some of the linked lists will have nodes which point to nodes that have been deleted) and this is done using homomorphic encryption.

3.6 Efficiency

In this section we discuss the efficiency of our multi-user, multi-level construction compared with the single-user construction of [13]. As our scheme is static and the scheme of [13] is dynamic, we ignore the structures and algorithms in [13] that apply to the dynamicity, such as the deletion table, the deletion array and algorithms AddToken, Add, DeleteToken, Delete.

The index is composed of a look-up table and a search array. No changes are made to the search array that effect the time needed to generate it or the search time, but the look-up table needs to be augmented by a factor of $|\mathbb{L}|$; this will require more space on the server but does not effect the search time. The size of our index is $\mathcal{O}(\Delta \cdot |\mathbb{L}| + n)$ whereas the size of the index in the single user scheme is $\mathcal{O}(\Delta + n)$.

There search time of our scheme is $\mathcal{O}(|\mathcal{D}_{\omega,a}|)$ where $\mathcal{D}_{\omega,a}$ is the set of data item identifiers satisfying the search query $T_{\omega,a}$. This is equivalent to the search time of [13], however in our scheme the size of $\mathcal{D}_{\omega,a}$ is likely to be smaller, depending on the access level of the user who generated the search query.

The amount of computation required to generate the search queries as well as the size of the search queries is the same in both schemes, they are both constructed by evaluating three PRFs.

We note that in terms of efficiency our construction is very similar to that of [13]. This is also true for the dynamic version of our construction.

4   Conclusion

We have defined a new system, security models and a construction for symmetric solutions to searching on encrypted data in the multi-level setting. Users may search for keywords within a set of encrypted data items, restricting the search to data items they are authorised to view only. Future work will focus on increasing the range of query types beyond that of single keyword equality search and to expand the access control policies to arbitrary information flow policies.

References

1. Alderman, J., Martin, K.M., Renwick, S.L.: Multi-level access in searchable symmetric encryption. IACR Cryptology ePrint Archive, Report 2017/211 (2017)
2. Bell, E., La Padula, L.: Secure computer system: unified exposition and multics interpretation. Technical report, Mitre Corporation (1976)
3. Benaloh, J., Chase, M., Horvitz, E., Lauter, K.E.: Patient controlled encryption: ensuring privacy of electronic medical records. In: Proceedings of the First ACM Cloud Computing Security Workshop, CCSW 2009, pp. 103–114. ACM (2009)
4. Boneh, D., Di Crescenzo, G., Ostrovsky, R., Persiano, G.: Public key encryption with keyword search. In: Cachin, C., Camenisch, J.L. (eds.) EUROCRYPT 2004. LNCS, vol. 3027, pp. 506–522. Springer, Heidelberg (2004). https://doi.org/10.1007/978-3-540-24676-3_30
5. Byun, J.W., Rhee, H.S., Park, H.-A., Lee, D.H.: Off-line keyword guessing attacks on recent keyword search schemes over encrypted data. In: Jonker, W., Petković, M. (eds.) SDM 2006. LNCS, vol. 4165, pp. 75–83. Springer, Heidelberg (2006). https://doi.org/10.1007/11844662_6
6. Chang, Y.-C., Mitzenmacher, M.: Privacy preserving keyword searches on remote encrypted data. In: Ioannidis, J., Keromytis, A., Yung, M. (eds.) ACNS 2005. LNCS, vol. 3531, pp. 442–455. Springer, Heidelberg (2005). https://doi.org/10.1007/11496137_30
7. Chase, M., Kamara, S.: Structured encryption and controlled disclosure. In: Abe, M. (ed.) ASIACRYPT 2010. LNCS, vol. 6477, pp. 577–594. Springer, Heidelberg (2010). https://doi.org/10.1007/978-3-642-17373-8_33
8. Crampton, J.: Cryptographic enforcement of role-based access control. In: Degano, P., Etalle, S., Guttman, J. (eds.) FAST 2010. LNCS, vol. 6561, pp. 191–205. Springer, Heidelberg (2011). https://doi.org/10.1007/978-3-642-19751-2_13
9. Curtmola, R., Garay, J.A., Kamara, S., Ostrovsky, R.: Searchable symmetric encryption: improved definitions and efficient constructions. In: Proceedings of the 13th ACM Conference on Computer and Communications Security, CCS 2006, pp. 79–88. ACM (2006)
10. Goh, E.-J.: Secure indexes. IACR Cryptology ePrint Archive, Report 2003/216 (2003)
11. Kaci, A., Bouabana-Tebibel, T., Challal, Z.: Access control aware search on the cloud computing. In: 2014 International Conference on Advances in Computing, Communications and Informatics, ICACCI 2014, pp. 1258–1264. IEEE (2014)
12. Kamara, S., Papamanthou, C.: Parallel and dynamic searchable symmetric encryption. In: Sadeghi, A.-R. (ed.) FC 2013. LNCS, vol. 7859, pp. 258–274. Springer, Heidelberg (2013). https://doi.org/10.1007/978-3-642-39884-1_22
13. Kamara, S., Papamonthou, C., Roeder, T.: Dynamic searchable symmetric encryption. In: The ACM Conference on Computer and Communications Security, CCS 2012, pp. 965–976. ACM (2012)
14. Kissel, Z.A., Wang, J.: Verifiable symmetric searchable encryption for multiple groups of users. In: Proceedings of the 2013 International Conference on Security and Management, pp. 179–185. CSREA Press (2013)

15. Li, M., Yu, S., Cao, N., Lou, W.: Authorized private keyword search over encrypted data in cloud computing. In: 2011 International Conference on Distributed Computing Systems, ICDCS, pp. 383–392. IEEE Computer Society (2011)
16. Cabinet Office: Goverment security classifications. Technical report (2013)
17. Van Rompay, C., Molva, R., Önen, M.: Multi-user searchable encryption in the cloud. In: Lopez, J., Mitchell, C.J. (eds.) ISC 2015. LNCS, vol. 9290, pp. 299–316. Springer, Cham (2015). https://doi.org/10.1007/978-3-319-23318-5_17
18. Song, D.X., Wagner, D., Perrig, A.: Practical techniques for searches on encrypted data. In: 2000 IEEE Symposium on Security and Privacy, pp. 44–55. IEEE (2000)
19. Sun, W.,Yu, S., Lou, W.: Protecting your right: attribute-based keyword search with fine-grained owner-enforced search authorization in the cloud. In: 2014 IEEE Conference on Computer Communications, INFOCOM 2014, pp. 226–234. IEEE (2014)
20. Sun, W., Yu, S., Lou, W., Hou, T., Li, H.: Protecting your right: verifiable attribute-based keyword search with fine-grainedowner-enforced search authorization in the cloud. IEEE Trans. Parallel Distrib. Syst. **27**(4), 1187–1198 (2016)
21. Yang, Y.: Attribute-based data retrieval with semantic keyword search for e-health cloud. J. Cloud Comput.: Adv. Syst. Appl. **4**, 10 (2015)

Privacy-Preserving Computations of Predictive Medical Models with Minimax Approximation and Non-Adjacent Form

Jung Hee Cheon, Jinhyuck Jeong, Joohee Lee, and Keewoo Lee[(✉)]

Seoul National University (SNU), Seoul, Republic of Korea
{jhcheon,wlsyrlekd,skfro6360,activecondor}@snu.ac.kr

Abstract. In 2014, Bos et al. introduced a cloud service scenario to provide private predictive analyses on encrypted medical data, and gave a proof of concept implementation by utilizing homomorphic encryption (HE) scheme. In their implementation, they needed to approximate an analytic predictive model to a polynomial, using Taylor approximations. However, their approach could not reach a satisfactory compromise so that they just restricted the pool of data to guarantee suitable accuracy. In this paper, we suggest and implement a new efficient approach to provide the service using minimax approximation and Non-Adjacent Form (NAF) encoding. With our method, it is possible to remove the limitation of input range and reduce maximum errors, allowing faster analyses than the previous work. Moreover, we prove that the NAF encoding allows us to use more efficient parameters than the binary encoding used in the previous work or balaced base-B encoding. For comparison with the previous work, we present implementation results using HElib. Our implementation gives a prediction with 7-bit precision (of maximal error 0.0044) for having a heart attack, and makes the prediction in 0.5 s on a single laptop. We also implement the private healthcare service analyzing a Cox Proportional Hazard Model for the first time.

Keywords: Homomorphic encryption · Healthcare · Predictive analysis · Minimax approximation · Non-Adjacent Form · Cloud service

1 Introduction

The cloud computing paradigm provides promising scenarios for user-friendly healthcare services. Patient-to-Cloud healthcare scenario, which enables patients to self-check the hazards of having particular diseases, is one of the clear-eyed scenarios. To protect the crucial medical data, the scenario consists of the following procedures. At first, a user who needs predictive healthcare services feeds personal device with private health data such as age, sex, and ECG, where the device here is meant to be a smart device connected to networks via wireless protocols, e.g. smartphone and smartwatch. The device encrypts the inputs with the secret key stored in it, and sends them to a cloud server. After receiving the

© International Financial Cryptography Association 2017
M. Brenner et al. (Eds.): FC 2017 Workshops 2017, LNCS 10323, pp. 53–74, 2017.
https://doi.org/10.1007/978-3-319-70278-0_4

encrypted data from the device, The cloud server calculates an exposure risk of some disease with a predictive model on the encrypted data and sends the encrypted result back to the device. Then the device decrypts it with the secret key, providing an output to the user on its screen (Fig. 1).

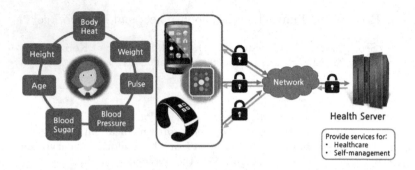

Fig. 1. Patient-to-Cloud scenario

In this scenario, standard encryption schemes have a restriction: it is impossible to perform outsourced computational tasks on the encrypted data. To perform computations for the encrypted data, the data must be decrypted first and some information might be leaked to adversaries. For this obstacle, homomorphic encryption (HE) can be a solution allowing computations on encrypted data without decryption process. Thus, a secure cloud service can be realized by using a secure HE scheme.

Recently, Bos et al. [BLN14] implemented the private healthcare services using a HE scheme. They implemented a privacy-preserving cloud service providing the likelihood to have a heart attack based on the predictive model called Logistic Regression Model (LRM) [Cox58, LRM]. They used a scale-invariant leveled HE scheme which is a practical variant of YASHE [BLLN13] and used Taylor approximations.[1] However, to guarantee the accuracy, the inputs are required to be close to the expanding point 0 as one can see in Sect. 3.1.

In this paper, we suggest and implement another approach to provide a private predictive analysis. We use an optimized polynomial approximation method, called minimax approximation. That is to say, the minimax approximation is the optimal approximation in the sense of supremum norm if the range of input values is a bounded interval. Moreover, we employ the Non-Adjacent Form (NAF) encoding and present a proof that this gives us more efficient parameters theoretically than the binary encoding in [BLN14] or the balanced-base B encoding used in [DGBL+15, CSVW]. As a result, our method allows removing the limitation of input range, reducing maximum errors on overall input range and

---

[1] Since only integer operations (addition and multiplication) are provided by the HE scheme, they needed to approximate the model to a polynomial which can be computed only by addition and multiplication.

providing faster analyses. In our implementation, we use the open library called HElib [HS13,HS14] based on the leveled HE scheme suggested by Brakerski et al. [BGV12]. Our implementation results of private predictive analysis compared with the previous result are summarized in the Table 1. Homomorphic evaluation of desired prediction for having a heart attack based on LRM would take 0.5 s which is about 50 times faster than the previous result (>30 s) using YASHE and degree 7 polynomial. We also put the service based on the Cox Proportional Hazard Model (CPHM) into practice and it permits us to analyze various diseases such as diabetes. For CPHM, it takes 2.2 s to analyze the risk of general cardiovascular disease.

Table 1. Summary of our work, where the security parameter $\lambda = 80$ (In the case of [BLN14], it is probably not 80-bit secure against modern attacks [Alb17].)

Predictive model	Logistic model		Cox model
Approach	BLN14	Our	Our
HE scheme	YASHE	BGV&HElib	BGV&HElib
Encoding method	Binary	NAF	NAF
Approximation method	Taylor	Minimax	Minimax
Degree of polynomial	7	7	5	7
Range of x	[−3.7,2.4]		[−3.6,5.7]
Range for maximum error to be 0.01	[−2.1,2.1]	[−3.7,2.4]	[−3.6,5.7]
Maximum error	1.163	0.0010	0.0044	0.0095
Server time (s)	>30	1.8	0.5	2.2
Client time (s)		1.2	0.5	1.1

Organization. In Sect. 2, first we introduce two predictive models, LRM and CPHM, that we mainly considered. Then we explain how we approximate the models to polynomials in Sect. 3. In Sect. 4, we present our methods to evaluate the approximation with encrypted input values, using HE scheme. We also provide our implementation results in the same section.

Notation. Throughout this paper, we use the following notations.

- We use P_n to denote the set of polynomials with real number coefficients of degree equal or less than n.
- We use $C[a, b]$ to denote the set of continuous functions on $[a, b]$.
- For function $f \in C[a, b]$,

$$\|f\| := max\{|f(x)| : x \in [a, b]\}.$$

2 Models for Predictive Analysis in Healthcare Services

Many mathematical models to perform predictive analysis in healthcare have been suggested and studied for several decades. For example, one can use a statistical technique called regression such as the logistic regression model or some survival model for some disease such as the Cox proportional hazard model [Cox92]. In this section, we bring two such predictive models into focus: the logistic regression model and the Cox proportional hazard model.

2.1   The Logistic Regression Model

The logistic regression model is used to assess severity of a patient or to predict whether a patient will have a given disease based on observed characteristics of the patient (e.g. age, sex, body mass index, results of various blood tests, etc.). For example, Boyd et al. developed the Trauma and Injury Severity Score (TRISS) method [BTC87], which is widely used to predict mortality in injured patients. Some works [BRD+00, KEAS00] used this model to predict mortality in patients with peritonitis, and Blankstein et al. [BWA+05] proposed a predictor of mortality after certain types of heart surgery. Moreover, Tabaei and Herman [TH02] provided a method to use the model for a prediction of incident diabetes. The logistic regression model has been also used to analyze cardiovascular diseases [TCK67, DVP+08, DPMC13, BSJ+05].

To demonstrate logistic regression analysis, previous work [BLN14] used the following model for men[2] [LRM] to predict the possibility to have a heart attack for an individual. We would also adopt this model for our predictive healthcare services. The model is precisely described as follows: for given six inputs consisting of observed characteristics of a patient, age (a), systolic blood pressure (sys), diastolic blood pressure (dia), cholesterol level ($chol$), height (ht, inches), and weight (wt, pounds), the model provides the likelihood in an interval $[0, 1]$ to have a heart attack by calculating

$$L(\mathbf{x}) = \frac{e^{\mathbf{x}}}{e^{\mathbf{x}} + 1},$$

where $\mathbf{x}$ is the sum of the variables weighted by the logistic regression coefficients as

$$\mathbf{x} = 0.072 \cdot a + 0.013 \cdot sys - 0.029 \cdot dia + 0.008 \cdot chol - 0.053 \cdot ht + 0.021 \cdot wt.$$

We note that the range of $\mathbf{x}$ in the regression data is the interval $[-3.755, 2.403]$ [LRM].

2.2   The Cox Proportional Hazard Model

The Cox proportional hazard model suggested by Cox [Cox72] is a well-known procedure for analyzing the time-to-event curve. This model has been the most widely used model over many years in medical research because of its applicability to a wide variety of types of clinical studies [CO84]. For an application, it provides a general methodology for the statistical analysis of relationship between

---

[2] Measured 200 male patients, over an observation period which remains unspecific.

the survival of a patient and several explanatory variables such as age, gender, weight, height, etc. For example, [AYDA+14] estimated the association between treatments and the survival times of breast cancer patients using the Cox model. Moreover, [TS14] also used this model for analyzing the tuberculosis, which is a chronic infectious disease and mainly caused by mycobacterium tuberculosis.

D'Agostino et al. [DVP+08] provided the following models analyzing the risk of general cardiovascular disease (CVD), where the population of interest consists of individuals 30–74 years old and without CVD at the baseline examination. Precisely, the model is described as follows. This model assesses the 10-year risk of general CVD. There are six predictive variables: age (A), cholesterol level ($Chol$), HDL cholesterol level (HDL), systolic blood pressure (SBP), smoker ($S = 1$) or not ($S = 0$), and having diabetes ($D = 1$) or not ($D = 0$). The model is given by[3]

$$C(\mathbf{x}) = 1 - 0.95012^{\exp(\mathbf{x})} \quad \text{for women}$$

where $\mathbf{x}$ is computed from the variables as

$$\mathbf{x} = 2.32888 \cdot \log(A) + 1.20904 \cdot \log(Chol) - 0.70833 \cdot \log(HDL)$$
$$+2.76157 \cdot \log(SBP) + 0.52873 \cdot S + 0.69154 \cdot D - 26.1931.$$

We set the range of the parameters manually as below. We followed the range of parameters which was used in the risk score calculator of Framingham Heart Study website [FHS].

– Age: 30–74
– Cholesterol: 100–405
– HDL: 10–100
– SBP: 90–200

The range of parameters give the range of $\mathbf{x}$ defined above, which is the interval $[-3.6, 5.7]$.

3 Polynomial Approximation of Analytic Functions

In our scenario, two models $L(\mathbf{x})$ and $C(\mathbf{x})$ will be approximated by polynomials, since our HE scheme only allows addition and multiplication of integers. To measure the reliability of outputs, errors will be computed in the sense of supremum norm.

In Sect. 3.1, we analyze the approach of [BLN14] which used the Taylor approximation. Moreover, we assert that using minimax approximation gives optimal error in Sect. 3.2.

---

[3] $C(\mathbf{x}) = 1 - 0.88936^{\exp(\mathbf{x} - 23.9802)}$ for men.

3.1   Taylor Approximation in Previous Works

Bos et al. [BLN14] suggested using Taylor approximation for approximating predictive models to polynomials. For the logistic model $L(\mathbf{x})$ described in the Sect. 2.1, Bos et al. claimed that truncating Taylor series at point 0 after degree 7 gives roughly 2 digits of accuracy. As they suggested, the approximation is very accurate near the expanding point 0. However, considering the range of input described in Sect. 2.1, error may become larger than the claimed accuracy at the end of the interval.

The graph in Fig. 2 plots logistic function and its Taylor approximation polynomial of degree 7 at point 0, along the range of input. In the graph, the approximation is very accurate near the point 0 but the error grows rapidly at the rear of the interval. Maximal errors are given at the two endpoints of the interval: 1.16 at the point -3.7 and 0.04 at the point 2.4. The errors are too large to be ignored, regarding that the result of the prediction model is a probability. To achieve 2 digits of accuracy, it is required to restrict the original interval to the interval $[-2.1, 2.1]$ which is quite smaller than the original one.

The Table 2 shows the maximum error in the interval $[-3.7, 2.4]$ between logistic function and Taylor approximation polynomials for various degrees.[4] As the table shows, increasing degree of approximation polynomial does not guarantee the error to decrease, in the sense of supremum norm. These problems occur because Taylor approximation is a local approximation rather than an approximation specialized for the intervals.

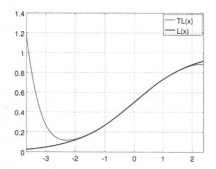

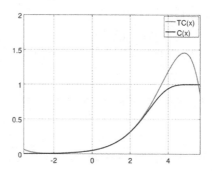

Fig. 2. Taylor approximation of $L(\mathbf{x})$ domain: $[-3.7, 2.4]$

Fig. 3. Taylor approximation of $C(\mathbf{x})$ domain: $[-3.6, 5.7]$

Similar problems occur in the case of Cox model. The graph in Fig. 3 plots $C(\mathbf{x})$ for women, and its Taylor approximation polynomial of degree 7 at point 0, which is the expanding point that gives minimal maximum error. The graph is drawn along the range of input described in Sect. 2.1. It can be seen that

---

[4] We only give errors for odd degree polynomials, since in Taylor expansion of logistic function, constant and odd degree terms only appear. This is because the logistic function is a odd function up to a constant.

approximation is very accurate near the expanding point 0.3 but the error grows rapidly at the rear of the interval as in the case of $L(\mathbf{x})$.

Table 2. Taylor approximation of logistic model

Degree of Taylor polynomial	0	1	3	5	7	9	11	13
Maximum error		0.476	0.449	0.606	0.839	1.163	1.613	2.237	3.103

The Table 3 shows the maximum error in the interval $[-3.6, 5.7]$ between $C(\mathbf{x})$ and its Taylor approximation polynomials for various degrees. In addition, we give ideal expanding points for each degree. As the table shows, increasing degree of approximation polynomial does not guarantee the error to decrease. The maximum errors are at least larger than 0.2 which is 20%. Regarding that the result of the prediction model is a probability, the maximum errors are too large to be practical as the case of the logistic model.

Table 3. Taylor approximation of Cox model

Degree of Taylor polynomial	1	2	3	4	5	6	7	8	9
Expanding point	4.0	0.2	−1.2	−2.5	−3.6	0.6	0.0	−0.6	−1.2
Maximum error	0.3619	0.2707	0.3209	0.3497	0.4844	0.4910	0.4562	0.5227	0.6050

3.2 Remez Therapy: Adopting Minimax Approximation

In this section, we introduce another polynomial approximation called minimax approximation and describe how it settles the problems of Taylor approximation.

Minimax Approximation and Remez Algorithm. In this subsection, we present a brief explanation of minimax approximation and how to find it. For more details, see [Fra65].

Definition 1. *We say that $p \in P_n$ is an n-th minimax approximation of $f \in C[a, b]$ if*

$$\|f - p\| = \inf\{\|f - q\| : q \in P_n\}.$$

The name, minimax approximation, comes from the fact that it minimizes the maximum error over all $q \in P_n$. For the proof of its existence and uniqueness, see [Ach13]. Now, we consider a lemma, which is a key idea lying in the Remez algorithm [Rem34] to find the minimax approximation of a given polynomial. For the proof of this lemma, see [Ach13].

Definition 2. *A function $f \in C[a,b]$ is said to equioscillate on n points of $[a,b]$ if there exists n points $a \leq x_1 < \cdots < x_n \leq b$ such that*

$$|f(x_i)| = \|f\|, \quad i = 1, \cdots, n,$$

and

$$f(x_i) = -f(x_{i+1}), \quad i = 1, \cdots, n-1.$$

Lemma 1 [Ach13]. *Let $f \in C[a,b]$ and $p \in P_n$. Then, p is an n-th minimax approximation for f on $[a,b]$ if and only if $(f-p)$ equioscillates on $n+2$ points of $[a,b]$.*

Now, we briefly describe the Remez algorithm. For given $(n+2)$ nodes, it repeats to interpolate given function with oscillating error and update nodes to make the difference between the maximum error and the oscillating error smaller. It is known that the Remez algorithm always terminates regardless of the initial choice of the set of nodes [NP51], and the rate of convergence is quadratic [Vei60].[5] However, it is recommended to use *Chebyshev nodes* as an initial choice for making the convergence faster. The Chebyshev nodes of degree n for the interval $[a,b]$ is defined by

$$\frac{1}{2}(a+b) + \frac{1}{2}(b-a)\cos\left(\frac{2k-1}{2n}\right), \quad k = 1, \cdots, n.$$

The reason that the Chebyshev nodes are good for initial choice comes from the following lemma which implies the polynomial interpolated at Chebyshev nodes, called Chebyshev approximation, is a near-minimax approximation. For the proof and detailed discussion, see [Riv90].

Lemma 2 [Riv90]. *Let $f \in C[a,b]$ and Mf and Cf be the n-th minimax approximation and the n-th Chebyshev approximation of f, repectively. Then, the following inequality holds.*

$$\|f - Cf\| < \left(2 + \frac{2}{\pi}\ln(n+1)\right)\|f - Mf\|.$$

How Remez Therapy Works. The minimax approximation resolves problems of Taylor approximation mentioned in Sect. 3.1. The graph in Fig. 4 plots logistic function $L(x)$ and its 7-th minimax approximation $ML(x)$ for the interval $[-3.8, 2.5]$. The approximation is accurate throughout the whole interval and the error is much smaller than the Taylor approximation.

The Table 4 shows the maximum error between $L(x)$ and the minimax approximations for various degrees. The even degree coefficient in minimax

---

[5] Let us denote the maximum error between the function and the minimax approximation by e, and the oscillating error of kth iteration by e_k. The rate of convergence being quadratic means $|e - e_k| = O(|e - e_{k+1}|^2)$.

approximation of $L(x)$ for symmetric interval is zero, since the logistic function is an odd function up to a constant. This makes reducing multiplications possible in the implementation. In spite that expanding the interval grows the maximum error, since the multiplication is expensive operation in our scheme it is worth to expand the interval to a symmetric interval. For this reason, We also give the errors of minimax polynomials for the interval $[-3.8, 3.8]$ not only $[-3.8, 2.5]$. As degree of approximation polynomial increases, the error decreases and is small enough to be practical at not too high degree approximation.

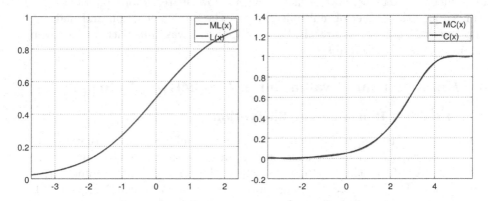

Fig. 4. Minimax approximation of $L(\mathbf{x})$

Fig. 5. Minimax approximation of $C(\mathbf{x})$

Table 4. Maximum errors of the minimax and Taylor approximations for LRM

Degree of approximation polynomial	3	5	7	9	11
Max error of minimax on $[-3.8, 2.5]$	0.0196	0.0039	0.0007	0.0001	0.000
Max error of minimax on $[-3.8, 3.8]$	0.0198	0.0044	0.0010	0.0002	0.0000
Max error of Taylor	0.606	0.839	1.163	1.613	2.237

The minimax approximation also settles problems of Taylor approximation for Cox model. The graph in Fig. 5 plots the function $C(\mathbf{x})$ and its minimax polynomial of degree 7 for the interval $[-3.6, 5.7]$. In the graph, the approximation is accurate throughout the whole interval and the error is much smaller than the Taylor approximation. The Table 5 shows the maximum error in the interval $[-3.6, 5.7]$ between the function $C(\mathbf{x})$ and the minimax polynomials for various degrees. It can be seen that, as degree of approximation polynomial increases, the error decreases and be small enough to be practical at not too high degree approximation.

Table 5. Maximum errors of the minimax and Taylor approximations for CPHM

Degree of approximation polynomial	3	4	5	6	7	8	9
Max error of minimax on $[-3.6, 5.7]$	0.1030	0.0387	0.0386	0.0227	0.0095	0.0091	0.0053
Max error of Taylor		0.3209	0.3497	0.4844	0.4910	0.4562	0.5227	0.6050

The tables suggest that the maximum errors of minimax approximation are much smaller than the maximum errors of Taylor approximation, for same degree of approximation polynomial and also for any observed degree. This allows us to implement a disease prediction model with a low degree approximation, which will reduce the number of multiplications in the implementation and make the implementation faster as a result. We note that this was done without narrowing the interval as [BLN14] did.

4   Homomorphic Evaluation of Predictive Models

4.1   Practical Homomorphic Encryption

Homomorphic Encryption (HE) is a cryptographic primitive that enables homomorphic operations on encrypted data without decryption procedures. Since Gentry [Gen09a, Gen09b] proposed a blueprint of Fully Homomorphic Encryption (FHE), a plenty of work arose in this area [VDGHV10, CMNT11, CNT12, CCK+13, CLT14, CKLY15]. In 2012, Brakerski, Gentry, and Vaikuntanathan [BGV12] suggested practical variant of leveled FHE scheme based on Ring Learning with Errors (RLWE) problem, which can evaluate L-level arithmetic circuits without bootstrapping. Assembling all of the techniques such as SIMD techniques for the ciphertext bits in [SV14] and bootstrappings in [HS15] to the scheme in [BGV12] with reduced error growths [Bra12], IBM researchers published a software library for HE, which is called HElib [HS13, HS14]. This library is well known to be efficient enough to serve the homomorphic evaluation of AES [GHS12] or fast fourier transformations [CSVW]. In our approach, we also used HElib to evaluate the exposure risk of a disease securely with the predictive models in Sect. 2. We remark that we set our parameters not to run bootstrapping in the HElib, since it costs a lot.

We briefly explain the leveled homomorphic encryption scheme of depth L used in HElib here for self-containedness. We set the sequence of moduli for our homomorphic evaluation of depth L by choosing L small primes $p_0, p_1, \cdots, p_{L-1}$ and the t-th modulus in the scheme is defined by $q_t = \prod_{i=0}^{t} p_t$ for $0 \leq t \leq L - 1$. We set the ring $\mathbb{Z}_q$ as $(-q/2, q/2) \cap \mathbb{Z}$. Let $\Phi_M(x)$ be a M-th cyclotomic polynomial of degree $\phi(M) = N$, $\mathbb{A}$ be a polynomial ring divided with an ideal generated by the cyclotomic polynomial, and $\mathbb{A}_q = \mathbb{A}/q\mathbb{A}$ for some integer q, i.e. $\mathbb{A}_q = \mathbb{Z}[x]/(\Phi_M(x), q)$.

- KeyGen(): Sample $s \in \mathbb{A}_2$ of low hamming weight, $a \leftarrow \mathbb{A}_{q_{L-1}}$ randomly, and e from a discrete Gaussian distribution in $\mathbb{A}_{q_{L-1}}$ with a standard deviation $\sigma > 0$. A public key would be $\mathsf{pk} = (a, b = a \cdot s + 2e)_{q_{L-1}} \in \mathbb{A}_{q_{L-1}}^2$ and a secret key is $\mathsf{sk} = s \in \mathbb{A}_{q_{L-1}}$.

- $\mathsf{Enc}_{\mathsf{pk}}(m \in \mathbb{A}_2)$: Choose a small polynomial v with coefficients in $\{-1, 0, 1\}$ and sample Gaussian polynomials e_0, e_1 in the same distribution with that of KeyGen. Let $c_0 = b \cdot v + 2e_0 + m$ and $c_1 = a \cdot v + 2e_1$, where the calculations are held in $\mathbb{A}_{q_{L-1}}$. The ciphertext is $\mathsf{c} = ((c_0\ c_1), L-1, v)$ where v is a noise estimate so that it is polynomial of the value $\phi(m)$.
- $\mathsf{Dec}_{\mathsf{sk}}(\mathsf{c})$: For a ciphertext $\mathsf{c} = ((c_0\ c_1), t, v)$ at level t, setting $m' \leftarrow (c_0 - s \cdot c_1)_{q_t}$, output $m' \mod 2$.
- $\mathsf{Add}(\mathsf{c},\mathsf{c}')$: For two ciphertexts $\mathsf{c} = ((c_0\ c_1), t, v)$ and $\mathsf{c}' = ((c_0'\ c_1'), t', v')$ of plaintexts m and m' respectively, some how matching the level of the ciphertexts, simply calculate

$$\mathsf{c}_{\mathsf{add}} = ((c_0 + c_0'\quad c_1 + c_1'), t'', v + v'),$$

for the new level t''.
- $\mathsf{Mult}(\mathsf{c},\mathsf{c}')$: Given $\mathsf{c} = ((c_0\ c_1), t, v)$ and $\mathsf{c}' = ((c_0'\ c_1'), t', v')$ for m and m' respectively, let $(d_0, d_1, d_2) \leftarrow (c_0 \cdot c_0',\ c_1 \cdot c_0' + c_0 \cdot c_1',\ -c_1 \cdot c_1')$. Managing the noise estimate with some techniques and matching the level of the ciphertexts, the ciphertext corresponding to the message $m \cdot m'$ is

$$\mathsf{c}_{\mathsf{mult}} = \mathsf{SwitchKey}((d_0, d_1, d_2),\ t'',\ v \cdot v')$$

for the new level t'', where $\mathsf{SwitchKey}$ algorithm here basically switches the transformed ciphertext to be decrypted with an original secret key so that it can be decrypted correctly. In this $\mathsf{SwitchKey}$ algorithm, there is an usage of another modulus P which is aimed to boost up the modulus from q_t to $P \cdot q_t$ for time and space efficiency. In other words, the largest modulus used in this library is $P \cdot q_{L-1}$.

We omit all the important details like noise estimating and modulus switching techniques here and just look at how the basic functionality works, so for more details, we recommend to see the Appendix of [GHS09].

4.2   Encoding Strategy

Since the plaintext space of previous homomorphic encryption is a polynomial ring over $\mathbb{Z}_q$, we need encoding and decoding phases for practical use with real numbers in the real world. Proper encoding strategies are needed to guarantee correctness of the results and to not harm the performance of the scheme. In this section, we explain the encoding strategies used in our implementations. For explanation, we divide our encoding phase into two stages: encoding real numbers as integers and encoding integers as polynomials.

Encoding Real Numbers as Integers. Encoding real numbers as integers can be done by the method in [BLN14] as following:

1. For each corresponding factors, give precision by rational numbers where denominators are power of 10.

2. Normalize them into integers by multiplying their denominators.
3. Operate homomorphic computations with scaled integers.
4. After decryption, divide the result with 10^n for appropriate n.

Note that, through this encoding technique, some errors might come up from Step 1 for the real value inputs. Therefore, we should take proper denominator for input values, which make the error of output sufficiently small. In our implementations, we take these parameters such that the error generated in the encoding phase is smaller than the error derived from polynomial approximation. For more details, see Sect. 4.3.

Encoding Integers as Polynomials: Previous Works and Our Approach. Since the plaintext space of BGV scheme is a polynomial ring over $\mathbb{Z}_q$, we need to encode integers as polynomials. Choosing an adequate size of plaintext space would be important in this step because of the following two reasons: 1. After some additions and multiplications, coefficients of the polynomials might be reduced by the modulus q and we cannot decode the polynomial correctly. Hence, we need a sufficiently large modulus for correctness. 2. However, the performance of HE heavily relies on the size of the plaintexts, and the larger the modulus of plaintexts, the worse performance becomes. Moreover, some open source libraries may not support such a large modulus. Especially, HElib only supports modulus of long integers (i.e. up to 2^{32}).

One way to maintain small plaintext modulus is to use Chinese Remainder Theorem (CRT) to split the data into multiple smaller moduli. However, this procedure makes the source code more complicated, and since it requires different keys for different moduli, key management starts to disturb users. Another way is suggested in [DGBL+15] and also studied in [CSVW], which utilizes balanced base-B encoding (Bal-B) to make a profit on the size of plaintexts with respect to those of the usual binary encoding as in [BLN14]. We describe their approach briefly, and then introduce a new method to achieve better results.

Definition 3. *For an odd integer B, the balanced base-B encoding of an integer n is $(n_\ell, \cdots, n_0)_{Bal\text{-}B}$, where $n = \sum_{i=0}^{\ell} n_i B^i$ with $n_i \in \{-\frac{B-1}{2}, \cdots, 0, \cdots, \frac{B-1}{2}\}$.*

Definition 4. *For non-negative integers d and e, define $c_{(d,e)}$ as $\|(1 + x + x^2 + \cdots + x^d)^e\|_\infty$.*

Theorem 1 [MR08]. *If either $e \neq 2$ or $d \in \{1, 2, 3\}$, it satisfies*

$$c_{(d,e)} < \sqrt{\frac{6}{\pi \cdot e \cdot d \cdot (d+2)}} \cdot (d+1)^e,$$

and the bound is tight in the sense that

$$\lim_{e \to \infty} \frac{\sqrt{e} \cdot c_{(d,e)}}{(d+1)^e} = \sqrt{\frac{6}{\pi \cdot e \cdot d \cdot (d+2)}}.$$

Definition 5. *Let L, D, A be nonnegative integers. For a given circuit of inputs in $[-L, L]$ which requires depth D for HE and allows A additions per depth, we define $\mathcal{B}_{\mathcal{E}}(L, D, A)$ by the greatest lower bound of modulus with respect to L, D, and A to guarantee correctness for the circuit, where $\mathcal{E}$ denotes the method used for encoding integers to polynomials.*

Theorem 2 [CSVW]. *Assume there is a circuit we want to compute of depth D with allowed A additions per depth. If $\mathcal{E}$ is standard n-ary encoding or balanced base-B encoding, following equality holds.*

$$\mathcal{B}_{\mathcal{E}}(L, D, A) = c_{(d_{\mathcal{E}}, 2^D)} \cdot m_{\mathcal{E}}^{2^D} \cdot 2^{A(2^{D+1}-2)},$$

where $d_{\mathcal{E}}$ is the maximum number of digits of integers in $[-L, L]$ for $\mathcal{E}$ and $m_{\mathcal{E}}$ is the maximum value of the coefficient for $\mathcal{E}$.[6]

Theorem 2 states that the sufficient bound for correctness can be calculated by the formula, if we are using the standard n-ary encoding or the balanced base-B encoding. Moreover, together with Theorem 1, it can be shown that using balanced base-B encoding decreases the plaintext modulus to achieve correctness by double exponential factor of depth D, compared to the standard binary encoding. However, we still have a problem even if we use balanced base-3 encoding as [CSVW] did since the modulus has to be larger than 2^{32} to guarantee correctness for our models. To improve the result of [CSVW], we suggest using non-adjacent form (NAF) instead of balanced base-3 form.

Definition 6. *The Non-Adjacent Form (NAF) of a integer n is $(n_\ell, \cdots, n_0)_{NAF}$, where $n = \sum_{i=0}^{\ell} n_i 2^i$ with $n_j n_{j-1} = 0$ and $n_j \in \{-1, 0, 1\}$ for all j.*

For example, the NAF of 7 is $(1, 0, 0, -1)_{NAF}$. It is well-known that the NAF of an integer is unique. The following theorem suggests that using NAF is beneficial in general. Second equation says that using NAF instead of balanced base-3 encoding decreases the size of plaintext modulus to achieve correctness by double exponential factor with respect to the depth D. With NAF, we were able to use a plaintext modulus smaller than 2^{32} for the predictive models.

Theorem 3. *Under the same notations as Theorem 2, the followings hold.*

$$- \mathcal{B}_{NAF}(L, D, A) = c_{(d_{NAF}, 2^D)} \cdot 2^{A(2^{D+1}-2)}, \quad d_{NAF} = \left\lceil \frac{\lfloor \log L \rfloor + 1}{2} \right\rceil$$

$$- \frac{\mathcal{B}_{Bal\text{-}3}(L, D, A))}{\mathcal{B}_{NAF}(L, D, A)} = O((\log 4 / \log 3)^{2^D})$$

Proof. See Appendix B.

Below, we present the pseudo-code of computing the NAF of an integer. We note that NAF of an integer can be obtained very efficiently.

---

[6] The detailed formula can be found in [CSVW].

Algorithm 1. Non-Adjacent Form

Input: n
Output: $m = (f_k, \cdots, f_0)_{NAF}$
Set $i=0$
while $n > 0$ **do**
  1. **if** n is odd :
      $f_i \leftarrow 2 - (n \mod 4)$
      $n \leftarrow n - f_i$
    else
      $f_i \leftarrow 0$
  2. $n \leftarrow n/2$
  3. $i \leftarrow i + 1$
return m

4.3   Parameter Selection

In this section, we describe the procedure for parameter selection to guarantee security and correctness. At the end of this section we provide the Table 6 consisting of actual parameters we used for implementations.

– Inputs: security parameter λ, predictive model (e.g. $L(\mathbf{x})$ or $C(\mathbf{x})$), and permissible maximum error with respect to the model.
– Output: L, q, M, P and q_t for $0 \leq t \leq L - 1$.

1. Set the degree D of minimax approximation for a desired maximum error. For our work, it can be done by taking a glance at Tables 4 and 5. For example, if we are concerning $L(\mathbf{x})$ and want to make maximum error be smaller than 0.01, we choose minimax approximation of degree 5. Note that the maximum error will become a bit larger than the error by polynomial approximation, since the error from the encoding process exists.
2. Calculate the suitable input precision R. We need to set the input precision to encode real numbers as integers as described in Sect. 4.2. The more precise the inputs become, the larger modulus should be. As a consequence, extravagant precisions unnecessarily slow down the performance of implementation. Thus we suggest using similar or a bit smaller maximum error precision for encoding relative to the error by polynomial approximation. For example, the maximum error for 5-th minimax approximation of $L(\mathbf{x})$ is 0.0044. To make the error by encoding to be less than 0.0044, we approximate real value inputs to rationals getting 2 digits of accuracy below the decimal point.
3. Set the proper plaintext modulus q which guarantees security and correctness. If one uses NAF for encoding, one can choose proper q by using bound from Theorem 3. However since the bound in Theorem 3 is for the general circuits with certain properties, it may be inefficient. Therefore, we recommend to analyze the circuit with help of the Corollary 1 in Appendix B. In other words, get a tighter upper bound of maximum coefficient of the results using the bound of the corollary. Let b be the bit size of the maximum coefficient of the results. We can use the smaller modulus q than 2^{b+1}, if the error

generated from reducing by modulus is negligible relative to the error by polynomial approximation. For example, since an upper bound for absolute value of coefficients after computations is 2^{24}, we can use modulus $q = 33554467$ for 5-th minimax approximation of $L(\mathbf{x})$.

4. Get proper M with security parameter λ, HElib level L, and modulus q. To obtain the λ-bit security, we set the parameters in HElib so that our scheme is secure against the dual lattice attack by [Alb17] using the estimator [APS15][7]. After finding a proper M, we can use buildModChain function to set the rest of the parameters, q_i and P. For example, using the estimator we can find out that, for modulus $q = 33554467$, level $L = 13$, and security parameter $\lambda = 80$, it is sufficient to use $M = 13217$ for 5-th minimax approximation of $L(\mathbf{x})$.

Table 6. Parameter settings with the security parameter $\lambda = 80$. Column D denotes the degree of minimax approximations, column R denotes the input precision, column b denotes the bit size of maximum coefficient of outputs, and the value $P \cdot q_{L-1}$ is the largest modulus used in the library.

	D	R	b	q	L	$\log_2 q_{L-1}$	$\log_2 P$	M
LRM	5	1	24	33554467	13	27	202	13217
	7	2	36	4294967291	17	370	259	17431
	9	3	45	4294967291	21	448	276	20191
	11	4	49	4294967291	25	539	323	23431
CPHM	4	2	20	1048583	8	194	134	9487
	5	2	26	67108879	12	278	192	13483
	6	2	31	2147483659	14	324	235	15943
	7	3	37	4294967291	16	370	259	17431
	8	3	41	4294967291	16	370	259	17431
	9	3	47	4294967291	21	448	276	20191

4.4 Implementation Results

We give Table 7 so that one can see our performance at a glance and choose the parameters for similar applications. The time results are measured by the mean values of times to compute the wanted output for five independently measured input values. This implementation was performed on a laptop (Intel Core i5-3337U at 1.80 GHz). Since the computations, in our scenario, are performed by cloud server with high performance, one can expect the time results to be much smaller.

---

[7] https://bitbucket.org/malb/lwe-estimator/src.

Table 7. Performance result

	Logistic model				Cox model					
Degree of approximation polynomial	5	7	9	11	4	5	6	7	8	9
Maximum error	0.0044	0.0010	0.0002	0.0000	0.0387	0.0386	0.0227	0.0095	0.0091	0.0053
Encoding & Encryption (ms)	463	1052	1308	1547	333	467	547	1035	1042	1240
Computation (ms)	479	1750	2777	4208	354	708	1099	2188	2630	4209
Decryption & Decoding (ms)	47	114	203	281	32	56	78	110	114	198

5   Conclusion

In this paper, we introduced the minimax approximation method and suggested it as an option for approximation polynomial of medical analyses with predictive models. This selection makes the analyses more efficient and accurate than the case one choose the Taylor approximation method as in [BLN14]. The previous work [BLN14] choose the Taylor approximation method and YASHE scheme as their option. On the other hand, we choose the minimax approximation method and HElib as our option. Additionally, we utilize the Non-Adjacent Form encoding method. As a result, we can evaluate the medical predictive models much faster than [BLN14] with smaller error as one can see in Table 1. Moreover, with minimax approximation, one can perform accurate analyses using Cox proportional hazard models which is impossible with Taylor approximation.

Acknowledgement. This work was supported by Institute for Information & communications Technology Promotion (IITP) grant funded by the Korea government (MSIP) (No. B0717-16-0098). The authors would like to thank Yong Soo Song, Kyoohyung Han, and the anonymous reviewers for valuable comments and suggestions.

A   Approximation Polynomials

In this section, we list the approximation polynomials those have been used in this paper and the implementation.

A.1   Minimax Approximation for Logistic Model

(See Table 8).

Table 8. Coefficients of minimax polynomials for logistic model in $[-3.7, 3.7]$

Degree	0th term	1st term	3rd term	5th term	7th term	9th term	11th term
3	0.50000	0.21969	−0.0070164				
5	0.50000	0.24141	−0.013984	0.00042530			
7	0.50000	0.24771	−0.017996	0.0010405	−0.000026488		
9	0.50000	0.24941	−0.019789	0.0015352	−0.000076288	0.0000016561	
11	0.50000	0.24985	−0.020479	0.0018310	−0.00012735	0.0000054811	−0.00000010362

A.2 Minimax Approximation for Cox Model

(See Table 9).

Table 9. Coefficients of minimax polynomials for Cox model

Degree	0th term	1st term	2nd term	3rd term	4th term	5th term	6th term	7th term	8th term	9th term
3	$3.974e-2$	$1.409e-1$	$3.014e-2$	$-3.882e-3$						
4	$1.348e-2$	$6.502e-2$	$5.143e-2$	$3.997e-3$	$-1.738e-3$					
5	$1.344e-2$	$6.457e-2$	$5.164e-2$	$4.046e-3$	$-1.768e-3$	$3.060e-6$				
6	$3.266e-2$	$2.553e-2$	$4.380e-2$	$1.603e-2$	$-2.232e-3$	$-7.269e-4$	$9.144e-5$			
7	$5.096e-2$	$3.151e-2$	$2.118e-2$	$1.602e-2$	$1.968e-3$	$-1.088e-3$	$-1.068e-4$	$2.689e-5$		
8	$5.258e-2$	$3.225e-2$	$1.828e-2$	$1.639e-2$	$2.621e-3$	$-1.256e-3$	$-1.326e-4$	$3.846e-5$	$-9.284e-7$	
9	$5.511e-2$	$4.706e-2$	$1.048e-2$	$8.302e-3$	$6.069e-3$	$-2.761e-4$	$-6.022e-4$	$2.624e-5$	$1.860e-5$	$-1.754e-6$

B Proof of Theorem 3

For $p \in \mathbb{Z}[x]$, we use $\|p\|_\infty$ to denote the maximum of absolute values of coefficients. We use $\mathbb{Z}_+[x]$ to denote the set of polynomials with coefficients of nonnegative integers. Let $p \in \mathbb{Z}_+[x]$ be a polynomial of degree n defined by $p(x) = \sum_{i=0}^{n} p_i x^i$. Regarding $p_j = 0$ for all $j \geq n + 1$, we define two vector representations of p as follows:

$$R_{std}(p) := (p_0, p_1, p_2, \cdots, p_i, \cdots) \quad \text{and} \quad R_{dec}(p) := (\tilde{p}_0, \tilde{p}_1, \tilde{p}_2, \cdots, \tilde{p}_i, \cdots),$$

where $\{\tilde{p}_i\}$ is the rearrangement of $\{p_i\}$ in decreasing order. $R_{dec}(p)$ is well-defined since p has only finite number of positive terms. For $p, q \in \mathbb{Z}_+[x]$, define a equivalence relation $\sim$ as following.

$$p \sim q \Leftrightarrow R_{dec}(p) = R_{dec}(q)$$

For any polynomial $p(x) = \sum_{i=0}^{n} p_i x^i$, we define $|p| \in \mathbb{Z}_+[x]$ by $|p|(x) = \sum_{i=0}^{n} |p_i| x^i$.

Definition 7 (Λ-shaped). *For $p \in \mathbb{Z}_+[x]$, we give some new definitions below.*

1. *p is Λ-shaped if $R_{std}(p) = (p_0, p_1, p_2, \cdots)$ satisfies the following condition.*
   - *(bisymmetricity) There exists $a \in \mathbb{Z} \cup (\mathbb{Z} + \frac{1}{2})$ such that $p_{\lfloor a+i+\frac{1}{2} \rfloor} = p_{\lceil a-i-\frac{1}{2} \rceil}$ for all $i \leq \lceil a - \frac{1}{2} \rceil$ and $p_i = 0$ for all $i > \lceil a - \frac{1}{2} \rceil$.*
   - *(one-peakness) If $p_i > p_{i+1}$ for some i, then $p_j \geq p_{j+1}$ for all $j \geq i$.*
2. *A polynomial p is potentially Λ-shaped if $p \sim q$ for some Λ-shaped q with nonzero constant term. In this case, we denote this q as $\hat{p}$.*

In other words, $p \in \mathbb{Z}_+[x]$ is Λ-shaped if $R_{std}(p)$ is bisymmetric after erasing some zeros at the end of the sequence and has at most one peak. We present a lemma which asserts that the set of Λ-shaped polynomials in $\mathbb{Z}_+[x]$ is closed for multiplication of polynomials as follows.

Lemma 3. *A finite product of Λ-shaped polynomials is Λ-shaped.*

Proof. It is enough to show for products of two Λ-shaped polynomials. For potentially Λ-shaped polynomials q and r, let $R_{std}^{sym}(\hat{q}) = (\hat{q}_0, \hat{q}_1, \hat{q}_2, \cdots, \hat{q}_n)$ and $R_{std}^{sym}(\hat{r}) = (\hat{r}_0, \hat{r}_1, \hat{r}_2, \cdots, \hat{r}_m)$ be bisymmetric sequences obtained by erasing some zeros at the end of $R_{std}(\hat{q})$ and $R_{std}(\hat{r})$ respectively. Then,

$$R_{std}(\hat{q}\cdot\hat{r}) = \left(\sum_{i+j=0} \hat{q}_i\hat{r}_j, \sum_{i+j=1} \hat{q}_i\hat{r}_j, \cdots, \sum_{i+j=n+m} \hat{q}_i\hat{r}_j, 0, \cdots \right).$$

The *bisymmetricity* holds since

$$\sum_{i+j=k} \hat{q}_i\hat{r}_j = \sum_{i+j=k} \hat{q}_{n-i}\hat{r}_{m-j} = \sum_{i+j=n+m-k} \hat{q}_i\hat{r}_j,$$

and the *one-peakness* comes from

$$\sum_{i+j=k} \hat{q}_i\hat{r}_j \leq \sum_{i+j=k} \hat{q}_{i+1}\hat{r}_j \leq \sum_{i+j=k+1} \hat{q}_i\hat{r}_j \text{ for all } k < \frac{n+m}{2}.$$

$\square$

Definition 8. *Define a partial order $\preceq$ on $\mathbb{Z}_+[x]$ as following. For p and q $\in \mathbb{Z}_+[x]$, let $R_{dec}(p) = (p_0, p_1, p_2, \cdots)$ and $R_{dec}(q) = (q_0, q_1, q_2, \cdots)$.*

$$p \preceq q \iff R_{dec}(q) \text{ majorizes } R_{dec}(p).$$

$$\iff \sum_{i=0}^{\infty} p_i = \sum_{i=0}^{\infty} q_i \text{ and } \sum_{i=0}^{k} p_i \leq \sum_{i=0}^{k} q_i \text{ for all } k \in \mathbb{N}.$$

Lemma 4. *If q and r are potentially Λ-shaped,*

$$p \preceq q \implies pr \preceq \hat{q}\hat{r}.$$

Sketch of Proof. Let $R_{std}(p) = (p_0, p_1, p_2, \cdots)$ and $R_{std}(q) = (q_0, q_1, q_2, \cdots)$. For $R_{std}^{sym}(\hat{q})$ and $R_{std}^{sym}(\hat{r})$, let us recycle the notations used in the proof of the Lemma 3. It is enough to show the following inequality holds for all $t \in \mathbb{N}$ and $K \subset \mathbb{N} \cup \{0\}$ with $|K| = t$, denoting K_{n+m} as $\mathbb{Z} \cap \left[\left\lceil \frac{n+m-t+1}{2} \right\rceil, \left\lfloor \frac{n+m+t}{2} \right\rfloor \right]$ of t elements.

$$\sum_{k \in K} \sum_{i+j=k} p_i r_j \leq \sum_{k \in K_{n+m}} \sum_{i+j=k} \hat{q}_i\hat{r}_j,$$

or equivalently,

$$\sum_{j=0}^{\infty} \left(r_j \sum_{i+j \in K} p_i \right) \leq \sum_{j=0}^{\infty} \left(\hat{r}_j \sum_{i+j \in K_{n+m}} \hat{q}_i \right).$$

Now the proof is completed by the fact that $\left(\sum_{i+j \in K_{n+m}} \hat{q}_i \right)$ majorizes $\left(\sum_{i+j \in K} p_i \right)$ as sequences with index j, which directly comes from the assumption $p \preceq q$.

$\square$

Theorem 4. *If p_i's are potentially Λ-shaped,*

$$\prod_{i=1}^{n} p_i \preceq \prod_{i=1}^{n} \hat{p}_i.$$

Proof. Suppose the theorem is true when $n = k - 1$. Then by Lemmas 3 and 4,

$$\prod_{i=1}^{k} p_i = p_k \cdot \prod_{i=1}^{k-1} p_i \preceq \hat{p_k} \cdot \prod_{i=1}^{k-1} \hat{p}_i = \prod_{i=1}^{k} \hat{p}_i.$$

When $n = 1$, it is trivial. By mathematical induction, the theorem is proved. $\square$

Corollary 1. *If p_i's are binary polynomials,*

$$\left\| \prod_{i=1}^{n} p_i \right\|_{\infty} \leq \left\| \prod_{i=1}^{n} \hat{p}_i \right\|_{\infty}.$$

Proof. Directly follows from Theorem 4 and the fact that every binary polynomial is potentially Λ-shaped. $\square$

Theorem 5. *If a NAF polynomial p lies in P_n, the following inequality holds. Furthermore, the bound is sharp.*

$$\|p^e\|_{\infty} \leq c_{([\frac{n+1}{2}], e)}.$$

Proof. We have

$$\|p^e\|_{\infty} \leq \||p|^e\|_{\infty} \leq \||\hat{p}|^e\|_{\infty} \leq c_{([\frac{n+1}{2}], e)},$$

where the first inequality follows from the triangle inequality and the second inequality comes from Corollary 1. The third inequality follows from the definition of NAF: the number of nonzero terms of NAF polynomial cannot exceed the half of the number of terms. For sharpness, consider the alternating NAF which make the equality holds: $(1010\cdots)_{NAF}$. $\square$

Finally we obtain the first equation of Theorems 3 from Theorem 2 and 5. The second equation is also obtained from simple calculations combining Theorem 2 and the first equation.

References

[Ach13] Achieser, N.I.: Theory of Approximation. Courier Corporation, Chelmsford (2013)

[Alb17] Albrecht, M.R.: On dual lattice attacks against small-secret LWE and parameter choices in HElib and SEAL. Cryptology ePrint Archive, Report 2017/047 (2017). http://eprint.iacr.org/2017/047

[APS15] Albrecht, M.R., Player, R., Scott, S.: On the concrete hardness of learning with errors. J. Math. Cryptol. **9**(3), 169–203 (2015)

[AYDA+14] Abadi, A., Yavari, P., Dehghani-Arani, M., Alavi-Majd, H., Ghasemi, E., Amanpour, F., Bajdik, C.: Cox models survival analysis based on breast cancer treatments. Iran. J. Cancer Prev. **7**(3), 124 (2014)

[BGV12] Brakerski, Z., Gentry, C., Vaikuntanathan, V.: (Leveled) fully homomorphic encryption without bootstrapping. In: Proceedings of the 3rd Innovations in Theoretical Computer Science Conference, pp. 309–325. ACM (2012)

[BLLN13] Bos, J.W., Lauter, K., Loftus, J., Naehrig, M.: Improved security for a ring-based fully homomorphic encryption scheme. In: Stam, M. (ed.) IMACC 2013. LNCS, vol. 8308, pp. 45–64. Springer, Heidelberg (2013). https://doi.org/10.1007/978-3-642-45239-0_4

[BLN14] Bos, J.W., Lauter, K., Naehrig, M.: Private predictive analysis on encrypted medical data. J. Biomed. Inform. **50**, 234–243 (2014)

[Bra12] Brakerski, Z.: Fully homomorphic encryption without modulus switching from classical GapSVP. In: Safavi-Naini, R., Canetti, R. (eds.) CRYPTO 2012. LNCS, vol. 7417, pp. 868–886. Springer, Heidelberg (2012). https://doi.org/10.1007/978-3-642-32009-5_50

[BRD+00] Biondo, S., Ramos, E., Deiros, M., Ragué, J.M., De Oca, J., Moreno, P., Farran, L., Jaurrieta, E.: Prognostic factors for mortality in left colonic peritonitis: a new scoring system. J. Am. Coll. Surg. **191**(6), 635–642 (2000)

[BSJ+05] Boekholdt, S.M., Sacks, F.M., Jukema, J.W., Shepherd, J., Freeman, D.J., McMahon, A.D., Cambien, F., Nicaud, V., De Grooth, G.J., Talmud, P.J., et al.: Cholesteryl ester transfer protein TaqIB variant, high-density lipoprotein cholesterol levels, cardiovascular risk, and efficacy of pravastatin treatment individual patient meta-analysis of 13 677 subjects. Circulation **111**(3), 278–287 (2005)

[BTC87] Boyd, C.R., Tolson, M.A., Copes, W.S.: Evaluating trauma care: the TRISS method. J. Trauma Acute Care Surg. **27**(4), 370–378 (1987)

[BWA+05] Blankstein, R., Ward, R.P., Arnsdorf, M., Jones, B., Lou, Y.-B., Pine, M.: Female gender is an independent predictor of operative mortality after coronary artery bypass graft surgery contemporary analysis of 31 midwestern hospitals. Circulation **112**(9 suppl), I–323 (2005)

[CCK+13] Cheon, J.H., Coron, J.-S., Kim, J., Lee, M.S., Lepoint, T., Tibouchi, M., Yun, A.: Batch fully homomorphic encryption over the integers. In: Johansson, T., Nguyen, P.Q. (eds.) EUROCRYPT 2013. LNCS, vol. 7881, pp. 315–335. Springer, Heidelberg (2013). https://doi.org/10.1007/978-3-642-38348-9_20

[CKLY15] Cheon, J.H., Kim, J., Lee, M.S., Yun, A.: CRT-based fully homomorphic encryption over the integers. Inf. Sci. **310**, 149–162 (2015)

[CLT14] Coron, J.-S., Lepoint, T., Tibouchi, M.: Cryptanalysis of two candidate fixes of multilinear maps over the integers. IACR Cryptology ePrint Archive 2014, p. 975 (2014)

[CMNT11] Coron, J.-S., Mandal, A., Naccache, D., Tibouchi, M.: Fully homomorphic encryption over the integers with shorter public keys. In: Rogaway, P. (ed.) CRYPTO 2011. LNCS, vol. 6841, pp. 487–504. Springer, Heidelberg (2011). https://doi.org/10.1007/978-3-642-22792-9_28

[CNT12] Coron, J.-S., Naccache, D., Tibouchi, M.: Public key compression and modulus switching for fully homomorphic encryption over the integers. In: Pointcheval, D., Johansson, T. (eds.) EUROCRYPT 2012. LNCS, vol. 7237, pp. 446–464. Springer, Heidelberg (2012). https://doi.org/10.1007/978-3-642-29011-4_27

[CO84] Cox, D.R., Oakes, D.: Analysis of Survival Data, vol. 21. CRC Press, Boca Raton (1984)

[Cox58] Cox, D.R.: The regression analysis of binary sequences. J. R. Stat. Soc. Ser. B (Methodol.) **20**(2), 215–242 (1958). JSTOR. www.jstor.org/stable/2983890

[Cox72] Cox, D.R.: Regression models and life-tables. J. R. Stat. Soc. Ser. B **34**(2), 187–220 (1972)

[Cox92] Cox, D.R.: Regression models and life-tables. In: Kotz, S., Johnson, N.L. (eds.) Breakthroughs in Statistics. SSS, pp. 527–541. Springer, New York (1992). https://doi.org/10.1007/978-1-4612-4380-9_37

[CSVW] Costache, A., Smart, N.P., Vivek, S., Waller, A.: Fixed point arithmetic in SHE schemes. Technical report, Cryptology ePrint Archive, Report 2016/250 (2016). http://eprint.iacr.org/2016/250

[DGBL+15] Dowlin, N., Gilad-Bachrach, R., Laine, K., Lauter, K., Naehrig, M., Wernsing, J.: Manual for using homomorphic encryption for bioinformatics. Microsoft Research (2015). http://research.microsoft.com/pubs/258435/ManualHEv2.pdf

[DPMC13] D'Agostino, R.B., Pencina, M.J., Massaro, J.M., Coady, S.: Cardiovascular disease risk assessment: insights from Framingham. Glob. Heart **8**(1), 11–23 (2013)

[DVP+08] D'Agostino, R.B., Vasan, R.S., Pencina, M.J., Wolf, P.A., Cobain, M., Massaro, J.M., Kannel, W.B.: General cardiovascular risk profile for use in primary care the Framingham heart study. Circulation **117**(6), 743–753 (2008)

[FHS] http://www.framinghamheartstudy.org/risk-functions/cardiovascular-disease/10-year-risk.php

[Fra65] Fraser, W.: A survey of methods of computing minimax and near-minimax polynomial approximations for functions of a single independent variable. J. ACM (JACM) **12**(3), 295–314 (1965)

[Gen09a] Gentry, C.: A fully homomorphic encryption scheme. PhD thesis, Stanford University (2009). https://crypto.stanford.edu/craig/

[Gen09b] Gentry, C.: Fully homomorphic encryption using ideal lattices. In: Proceedings of the 41st Annual ACM Symposium on Theory of Computing-STOC 2009, pp. 169–169. ACM Press (2009)

[GHS09] Gentry, C., Halevi, S., Smart, N.P.: Homomorphic evaluation of the AES circuit. Cryptology ePrint Archive, Report 2012/099 (2009). https://eprint.iacr.org/2012/099

[GHS12] Gentry, C., Halevi, S., Smart, N.P.: Homomorphic evaluation of the AES circuit. In: Safavi-Naini, R., Canetti, R. (eds.) CRYPTO 2012. LNCS, vol. 7417, pp. 850–867. Springer, Heidelberg (2012). https://doi.org/10.1007/978-3-642-32009-5_49

[HS13] Halevi, S., Shoup, V.: Design and implementation of a homomorphic-encryption library. IBM Research, Manuscript (2013)

[HS14] Halevi, S., Shoup, V.: Algorithms in HElib. In: Garay, J.A., Gennaro, R. (eds.) CRYPTO 2014. LNCS, vol. 8616, pp. 554–571. Springer, Heidelberg (2014). https://doi.org/10.1007/978-3-662-44371-2_31

[HS15]   Halevi, S., Shoup, V.: Bootstrapping for HElib. In: Oswald, E., Fischlin, M. (eds.) EUROCRYPT 2015. LNCS, vol. 9056, pp. 641–670. Springer, Heidelberg (2015). https://doi.org/10.1007/978-3-662-46800-5_25

[KEAS00]   Kologlu, M., Elker, D., Altun, H., Sayek, I.: Validation of MPI and PIA II in two different groups of patients with secondary peritonitis. Hepatogastroenterology 48(37), 147–151 (2000)

[LRM]   http://www.claudiaflowers.net/rsch8140/logistic_regression_example.htm

[MR08]   Mattner, L., Roos, B.: Maximal probabilities of convolution powers of discrete uniform distributions. Stat. Probab. Lett. 78(17), 2992–2996 (2008)

[NP51]   Novodvorskii, E.P., Pinsker, I.S.: The process of equating maxima. Uspekhi Matematicheskikh Nauk 6(6), 174–181 (1951)

[Rem34]   Remez, E.Y.: Sur le calcul effectif des polynomes d'approximation de tschebyscheff. CR Acad. Sci. Paris 199, 337–340 (1934)

[Riv90]   Rivlin, T.-J.: Chebyshev Polynomials. Wiley, New York (1990)

[SV14]   Smart, N.P., Vercauteren, F.: Fully homomorphic SIMD operations. Des. Codes Crypt. 71(1), 57–81 (2014)

[TCK67]   Truett, J., Cornfield, J., Kannel, W.: A multivariate analysis of the risk of coronary heart disease in Framingham. J. Chronic Dis. 20(7), 511–524 (1967)

[TH02]   Tabaei, B.P., Herman, W.H.: A multivariate logistic regression equation to screen for diabetes development and validation. Diab. Care 25(11), 1999–2003 (2002)

[TS14]   Tolosie, K., Sharma, M.K.: Application of Cox proportional hazards model in case of tuberculosis patients in selected Addis Ababa health centres, Ethiopia. Tuberc. Res. Treat. 2014, 11 p. (2014). https://doi.org/10.1155/2014/536976. Article ID 536976

[VDGHV10]   van Dijk, M., Gentry, C., Halevi, S., Vaikuntanathan, V.: Fully homomorphic encryption over the integers. In: Gilbert, H. (ed.) EUROCRYPT 2010. LNCS, vol. 6110, pp. 24–43. Springer, Heidelberg (2010). https://doi.org/10.1007/978-3-642-13190-5_2

[Vei60]   Veidinger, L.: On the numerical determination of the best approximations in the Chebyshev sense. Numer. Math. 2(1), 99–105 (1960)

Private Outsourced Kriging Interpolation

James Alderman[1], Benjamin R. Curtis[1(✉)], Oriol Farràs[2], Keith M. Martin[1],
and Jordi Ribes-González[2]

[1] Information Security Group, Royal Holloway, University of London, London, UK
{James.Alderman,Benjamin.Curtis.2015,Keith.Martin}@rhul.ac.uk
[2] Universitat Rovira i Virgili, Tarragona, Catalonia, Spain
{oriol.farras,jordi.ribes}@urv.cat

Abstract. Kriging is a spatial interpolation algorithm which provides
the best unbiased linear prediction of an observed phenomena by taking a
weighted average of samples within a neighbourhood. It is widely used in
areas such as geo-statistics where, for example, it may be used to predict
the quality of mineral deposits in a location based on previous sample
measurements. Kriging has been identified as a good candidate process to
be outsourced to a cloud service provider, though outsourcing presents an
issue since measurements and predictions may be highly sensitive. We
present a method for the private outsourcing of Kriging interpolation
using a tailored modification of the Kriging algorithm in combination
with homomorphic encryption, allowing crucial information relating to
measurement values to be hidden from the cloud service provider.

1 Introduction

Cost-effective third-party (cloud) service providers facilitate the outsourcing of
large, potentially sensitive, datasets for both storage *and* processing. In this
paper, we discuss approaches to outsourcing a particular computational process
known as *Kriging* in an efficient and secure fashion.

Kriging [6,7,9,14] is a well-recognized form of linear interpolation that predicts the value z_0^* of some phenomena at an unobserved location (x_0, y_0) in a
two-dimensional region. The quality of a Kriging prediction relies on some *variogram parameters*, which reflect the assumption that measurements taken at
nearby locations are more likely to be 'similar' than measurements taken far
apart. Such parameters must be carefully selected prior to interpolation. The
prediction is then formed as a weighted sum of prior measurements, where measurements taken close to (x_0, y_0) are given a greater weight than those far away.
Kriging was designed with geo-statistical applications in mind (*e.g.* to predict
the best location to mine based on the mineral deposits found at previous boreholes within a region), but has also found applications in a variety of settings
including remote sensing, real-estate appraisal and computer simulations.

Kriging has been identified as a good candidate process to be outsourced,
based on the practical and legislative requirements of industrial users (for
instance, [1,2]). Many users may need access to a Kriging prediction service

© International Financial Cryptography Association 2017
M. Brenner et al. (Eds.): FC 2017 Workshops 2017, LNCS 10323, pp. 75–90, 2017.
https://doi.org/10.1007/978-3-319-70278-0_5

(indeed legal frameworks may require such data to be shared amongst relevant authorities [8]). A secured storage server may be preferable to distributing copies of the entire dataset to each authorised user, especially when datasets are large and/or user devices are constrained. Further, Kriging might need to be performed over data owned by multiple organizations, with an independent cloud service provider performing processing duties on behalf of all concerned parties. Centralized outsourcing also makes sense when remote sensors take frequent measurements and push the results to a central database.

Consider a client C that owns a Kriging dataset (a set of measurements taken at various locations) which it wishes to outsource to an honest-but-curious cloud service provider S. Client C would like to make use of both the storage *and* computational power of S to make a Kriging service on its dataset available to multiple users. Further, other *data generating nodes* may be authorised by C to add/remove data (measurements) to/from the outsourced dataset.

A trivial solution consists of encrypting all data using a symmetric encryption scheme and using the server only for Storage-as-a-Service. To compute a Kriging prediction, all relevant data is retrieved, decrypted and computed on locally. Unfortunately, this solution may not be efficient, particularly if client devices have limited computational power or storage capacity, and require a high bandwidth during queries. This may be an issue if, for example, a surveyor in the field requires an on-line Kriging prediction service; mobile data services may be expensive, intermittently available or slow.

An alternative is to compute the entire Kriging process on encrypted data by encrypting all data using Fully Homomorphic Encryption (FHE)[1]. Unfortunately, Kriging involves several computations that are currently challenging when using FHE, including computing square roots and natural exponentiations. It is possible to outsource the Kriging process and protect *all* information using FHE. However this results in prohibitively high encryption and decryption costs, as well as a large amount of interactivity and local computation, which may diminish the benefits of cloud computing. Preliminary experiments using the SEAL library [4] (admittedly without optimization of code or parameter choices) did not yield promising results when computing a Kriging prediction using a dataset of more than three measurements. Whilst the use of FHE schemes should be explored further in future work, particularly to reflect advances in FHE schemes, we show in this work that such schemes are not strictly required in this setting.

Our proposed solution uses additive homomorphic encryption to outsource Kriging interpolation efficiently. We make a trade-off by protecting only the most sensitive parameters. That is, we protect the prior measurement values in the dataset, the generated Kriging predictions and the variogram parameters chosen by the client. We do not hide locations (of prior measurements or queries), noting that prior measurement locations may well be externally observable (*e.g.* if measurements come from previous mining operations).

---

[1] In fact, it suffices to consider Somewhat Homomorphic Encryption rather than FHE as the functionality is fixed and has a reasonably low multiplicative depth.

Our main contribution is to show that the Kriging process can be adapted such that the sensitive variogram parameters may be 'factored out' from the online computation by S whilst the remainder of the Kriging computation may be performed on *encrypted* measurement values using an additively homomorphic encryption scheme. We thus gain a practical, efficient and secure solution to outsourced, private Kriging. An outline of our protocol is as follows:

1. C uploads an encrypted dataset, comprising n measurements, to S. The cost of this step is $O(n)$ due to encryption of the measurement values.
2. S prepares the Kriging dataset for future queries. This process comprises plaintext operations that are also necessary in an unprotected outsourced Kriging scheme.
3. C makes a query to S requesting a Kriging prediction at a location (x_0, y_0); this is done in plaintext with virtually no cost.
4. S computes the interpolation on encrypted measurements. The cost with respect to an unprotected outsourced Kriging scheme is increased by $O(n)$, due to operations over encrypted data.
5. C decrypts the result.

Cryptographically-secured Kriging was previously studied in a different setting, where a *server* owns a dataset and clients may query the dataset at a previously unsampled location [12]: the queried location and resulting prediction should be private from the server, whilst the dataset held by the server should be private from the client. Two solutions are proposed in [12] which, unlike our solution, support only one variogram model and require high communication complexity, interactivity and local computation. The first is based on creating random 'dummy' queries to hide the queried location, and using an oblivious transfer protocol to hide predictions for all but the legitimate query location. The second solution uses the Paillier encryption scheme in an interactive protocol requiring multiple round-trips between client and server. In [13] collaborative private Kriging was investigated, where users combine their datasets to gain more accurate Kriging predictions.

The remainder of this paper is structured as follows. In Sect. 2 we describe the Kriging interpolation process (additional details may be found in Appendix A). In Sect. 3 we define our system model and analyse the required security properties of each piece of data in our setting. In Sect. 4 we introduce the idea of a *canonical* variogram, which we use in our construction to allow the server to compute a Kriging prediction without relying on the sensitive parameters. Our construction is given in Sect. 5 and we discuss its performance in Sect. 6. Finally in Sect. 7 we conclude the article with some final remarks and outline some potential directions for future work.

2 Kriging Interpolation

This section outlines the background theory of Kriging Interpolation. For more detail, see Appendix A and [6,7,9,14]. There are many variants of Kriging, but we focus on the widely used *Ordinary Kriging* variant.

The Kriging process starts with a set of measurements taken at some locations in a spatial region, and produces predicted measurements at unsampled locations. We denote this spatial region by $R \subset \mathbb{R}^2$ and denote the locations of prior measurements by $P = (r_1, r_2, \ldots, r_n)$, where each $r_i = (x_i, y_i) \in R$. The Euclidean distance between two locations $r_i, r_j \in R$ is denoted by $d(r_i, r_j)$. We refer to the set of taken measurements by $S = (z_1, z_2, \ldots, z_n)$, where z_i is measured at the location $r_i \in P$. The *Kriging dataset* then is the tuple (P, S).

The Kriging process allows a client to query an arbitrary location $r_0 \in R$ in order to receive a prediction z_0^* of the true value z_0 that would be measured at r_0. Informally, Kriging consists of three phases:

1. *Computing the experimental variogram*: one of the underlying assumptions of the Kriging process is that two measurements of a phenomenon will be similar if measured in nearby locations. Using the sampled dataset, one can plot the *experimental variogram* to show the dependence between measurements sampled at locations at certain distances h.
2. *Fitting a variogram model*: unfortunately, the experimental variogram is not usually sufficient to use in the Kriging prediction directly, since there may not be sampled data at every required distance. Therefore, one chooses a parametric *variogram model* and empirically chooses model parameters to fit a curve to the points of the experimental variogram.
3. *Computing the prediction*: using the variogram, one can determine appropriate weights for each measurement (based on the distance between each measurement and the queried location). The Kriging prediction is then computed as a weighted sum of the measured samples.

Let $N(h) = \{(z_i, z_j) : d(r_i, r_j) \in (h - \Delta, h + \Delta)\}$ be the set of all pairs of measurements taken approximately distance h apart[2]. The *experimental variogram* γ^* plots, for every distance h such that $N(h) \neq \emptyset$:

$$\gamma^*(h) = \frac{1}{2N(h)} \sum_{(z_i, z_j) \in N(h)} (z_i - z_j)^2.$$

A suitable variogram function $\gamma : \mathbb{R}^{\geq 0} \to \mathbb{R}$, in phase 2, must satisfy a set of conditions [6,7]; the most commonly used models require that $\gamma(0) = 0$, that $\gamma(h)$ is positive and bounded, and the existence of the limits $\lim_{h \to 0^+} \gamma(h)$ and $\lim_{h \to \infty} \gamma(h)$. These models are parametrized by the following three variables:

- The *nugget effect* η: The limit of $\gamma(h)$ as $h \to 0^+$.
- The *sill* ν: The limit of $\gamma(h)$ as $h \to \infty$.
- The *range* ρ: Controls how fast $\gamma(h)$ approaches ν as h increases.

Typically, one chooses a variogram model from a set of standard parametric variogram models, and then fits the model to the experimental variogram by empirically adjusting the nugget effect, sill and range parameters. A selection of the most common choices of bounded variogram models are, for $h > 0$:

---

[2] The approximation tolerance Δ can be increased when the Kriging dataset does not include enough sample points at a close enough distance.

- The *bounded linear model*: $\gamma(h) = \nu - (\nu - \eta)\left(1 - \frac{h}{\rho}\right)1_{(0,\rho)}(h)$.
- The *exponential variogram model*: $\gamma(h) = \nu - (\nu - \eta)e^{-h/\rho}$.
- The *spherical variogram model*: $\gamma(h) = \nu - (\nu - \eta)\left(1 - \frac{3h}{2\rho} + \frac{h^3}{2\rho^3}\right)1_{(0,\rho)}(h)$.
- The *Gaussian variogram model*: $\gamma(h) = \nu - (\nu - \eta)e^{-h^2/\rho^2}$.

where $1_I(x) = 1$ if $x \in I$, and $1_I(x) = 0$ otherwise.

Let γ be one of the above variogram models instantiated with empirically chosen parameters. To construct the best unbiased linear predictor of the phenomenon at a queried location $r_0 = (x_0, y_0) \in R$, we first form the *Kriging matrix* $K \in \mathbb{R}^{(n+1)\times(n+1)}$ with elements:

- $K_{i,j} = \gamma(d(r_i, r_j))$ for $1 \le i, j \le n$,
- $K_{n+1,i} = K_{i,n+1} = 1$ for $i \ne n + 1$, and
- $K_{n+1,n+1} = 0$.

Next, define a real vector $v \in \mathbb{R}^{n+1}$ with $v_i = \gamma(d(r_0, r_i))$ for $1 \le i \le n$, and $v_{n+1} = 1$. Let $\lambda = (\lambda_i)_{i=1}^{n+1}$ satisfy $K\lambda = v$. The *(Ordinary) Kriging prediction* z_0^* of the measured phenomena at the location r_0 is computed as the weighted sum of the sampled measurements, with the weights defined by λ. That is,

$$z_0^* = \sum_{i=1}^{n} \lambda_i z_i.$$

The set of linear equations defined by K and v are known as the *Normal Equations*. They are derived by imposing that the induced linear predictor is unbiased (by ensuring that the first n weights sum to one; that is $\sum_{i=1}^{n} \lambda_i = 1$) while minimizing the variance of the induced linear predictor [14].

The resulting minimized variance σ_0^{*2} is called the *(Ordinary) Kriging variance*, and it is described by the following expression

$$\sigma_0^{*2} = \lambda_{n+1} + \sum_{i=1}^{n} \lambda_i \gamma(d(r_0, r_i)).$$

The Kriging variance allows the construction of confidence intervals for each prediction and thus describes the error associated to the prediction. For a reference on the computation of confidence intervals in this context, see [7].

We define a variogram function to be *non-degenerate* if $\eta \ne \nu$ *i.e.* if γ is non-constant for $h > 0$. We restrict our attention to non-degenerate variogram functions. It is easy to see that using the degenerate variogram (also called the *nugget effect* variogram [14]) results in the average Kriging predictor $z_0^* = \sum_{i=1}^{n} z_i/n$ at all unsampled locations $r_0 \notin P$, with Kriging variance $\sigma_0^{*2} = n + 1$.

3   Private Outsourced Kriging Interpolation

Consider a system comprising a client $\mathcal{C}$ that owns a Kriging dataset (P, S) along with a choice of variogram γ, a server $\mathcal{S}$ that is willing to perform outsourced

Kriging on behalf of the client, and additional users $\mathcal{U}$ that are authorised by $\mathcal{C}$ to make Kriging queries to $\mathcal{S}$. Furthermore, there may be additional data generating nodes (*e.g* other users or remote sensors *etc.*) that may update the outsourced dataset by producing additional measurement data or removing prior (*e.g* outdated) measurements. The requirements of each entity are as follows:

- The data owner must choose the variogram to be used and upload a Kriging dataset, and should be able to update data and request Kriging predictions.
- Data users may request Kriging predictions and update data.
- Data generating nodes should only be able to update data.
- The server should only be able to perform Kriging predictions, and should do so without learning the data used in the computation. We assume that the server $\mathcal{S}$ is honest-but-curious, i.e. it follows the Kriging protocol (indeed, its business model may depend on doing so) but may attempt to learn information about the outsourced data.

Informally, the protocol runs as follows. The data owner $\mathcal{C}$ chooses the variogram to be used and runs the Outsource algorithm to generate the (protected) dataset to be sent to the server, as well as 'keys' that are issued to authorise entities to update the outsourced dataset or to perform Kriging queries respectively. Upon receipt of the protected data, the server may run the Setup algorithm to process the data and perform any necessary precomputation. After this step, the system is ready to accept queries. The data owner or an authorised data user (in possession of the query key) may request a Kriging prediction at a specified location by running the Query algorithm to generate a query token Q. This is sent to the server who runs the Interpolate algorithm using the processed database to generate an encrypted prediction and an encoding of the Kriging variance (the estimation of the error in the prediction). An entity authorised to perform queries may learn the prediction and variance by running the Decrypt algorithm. To dynamically update the outsourced dataset, an authorised entity (in possession of the update key) may run the AddRequest algorithm on a specified location r' and measurement z', or the DeleteRequest algorithm on a specified location r. These algorithms produce an addition token $\alpha_{r',z'}$ or deletion token δ_r respectively that is sent to the server. Upon receipt of such a token, the server may run the Add or Delete algorithm respectively to update the database accordingly.

For the purposes of this paper, we assume that any user authorised to generate a Kriging query is also permitted to update the dataset. If this should not be the case, then the proposed construction can be easily modified to include a digital signature computed on any addition or deletion token, where the signing key is contained in the update key (and not the query key). The server should be trusted to reject any tokens that do not have a valid signature. Then, only users in possession of the private signature key would be able to update the dataset.

Definition 1. *A private outsourced Kriging interpolation scheme comprises the following algorithms:*

- $(C, UK, QK) \xleftarrow{\$} $ Outsource$(1^\lambda, P, S, \gamma)$: *A probabilistic algorithm run by* $\mathcal{C}$ *which takes as input a security parameter* λ, *the Kriging dataset comprising* *measurement locations P and measurement values S, and the chosen vari-ogram γ. It produces an outsourceable data set C that may be transmitted to the server, an update key UK that may used to update the outsourced dataset, and a query key QK which may be used to form Kriging queries.*

- DB $\leftarrow$ Setup(C): *A deterministic algorithm run by S which takes as input the outsourceable dataset C. This algorithm enables S to perform any necessary processing that will enable it to compute Kriging predictions, and produces a processed outsourced dataset* DB.

- $Q \xleftarrow{\$}$ Query(r_0, QK): *A probabilistic algorithm run by C or a data user in U which takes as input a location $r_0 = (x_0, y_0) \in R$ for which a Kriging prediction should be computed, and the query key QK. It produces a query token Q which is sent to S.*

- $(\tilde{Z}_0, \tilde{\sigma}_0^{*2}) \leftarrow$ Interpolate(Q, DB): *A deterministic algorithm run by S that, given a query token Q and the database DB, returns an encrypted Kriging interpolation $\tilde{Z}_0$ and the partially computed Kriging variance $\tilde{\sigma}_0^{*2}$.*

- $(z_0^*, \sigma_0^{*2}) \leftarrow$ Decrypt($\tilde{Z}_0, \tilde{\sigma}_0^{*2}, QK$): *A deterministic algorithm run by C or a user in U that takes the Kriging results $\tilde{Z}_0$ and $\tilde{\sigma}_0^{*2}$ from the server and the query key QK, and outputs the Kriging prediction z_0^* and the Kriging variance σ_0^{*2} at the queried location.*

- $\alpha_{r', z'} \leftarrow$ AddRequest(r', z', UK): *A deterministic algorithm run by C, a data user in U or a data generating node, which takes a location r', a measurement value z' and the update key UK, and outputs an addition token $\alpha_{r', z'}$.*

- DB$' \leftarrow$ Add(DB, $\alpha_{r', z'}$,): *A deterministic algorithm run by S which takes the current outsourced database DB and an addition token $\alpha_{r', z'}$, and outputs an updated database DB$'$ representing the Kriging dataset $(P \cup \{r'\}, S \cup \{z'\})$.*

- $\delta_r \leftarrow$ DeleteRequest(r, UK): *A deterministic algorithm run by C, a data user in U or a data generating node. The algorithm takes as input a location $r \in P$ and the update key UK and outputs a deletion token δ_r.*

- DB$' \leftarrow$ Delete(DB, δ_r): *A deterministic algorithm by the server which takes as input the current database DB and a deletion token δ_r and outputs an updated database DB$'$ representing the Kriging dataset $(P \setminus \{r\}, S \setminus \{z_r\})$ where $z_r \in S$ is the measurement corresponding to location $r \in P$ in DB.*

We now analyse the security requirements of each component within a Kriging system; Table 1 summarizes the analysis:

- The measurement values $z_i \in S$ are highly sensitive and business-critical and must be protected at all times.
- In the current work, we consider the coordinates $r_i \in P$ of previous measurements to not be sensitive. This is reasonable, since in some applications they may be externally observable, for instance if they are the locations of previous mining activity.
- The queried location r_0 at which a new prediction should be computed may reveal areas of particular interest to the user. The sensitivity of this relies on the setting and individual user requirements. However, in practice, Kriging queries are often made at *every* location within a region to produce a

heat map of a phenomenon, which may limit the sensitivity of individual query locations. Further, the basic assumption of Kriging is that the quality of prediction degrades with distance; thus, the best Kriging results will be obtained when the queried location is broadly within the region of prior (observed) measurements.

- The computed prediction z_0^* is highly sensitive as it may form the basis of future decisions and may be business-critical, and must be protected.
- The choice of variogram model (without the variogram parameters) may reveal something about the overall trend of the spatial dependencies of the measurements. We assume that this is not particularly sensitive information.
- The range parameter ρ of the variogram is a constant scaling of the region R denoting the inter-measurement distance h at which the spatial dependency becomes negligible. For distances $h > \rho$, the variogram approaches the variance of the measurements [14], which is represented by the sill ν.

The nugget effect η reveals the spatial dependency at very small distances. In this work, we assume that the range is not sensitive (as it merely scales the region R), but that information revealed by the nugget and sill may be sensitive. Even in applications where this direct information on the variance and spatial dependency of measurements is deemed non-sensitive, it may be the case that the variogram parameters are commercially sensitive. These parameters must be chosen empirically to best fit the experimental data, a process which may be time-consuming, and the quality of predictions depends on how well the variogram matches the experimental variogram.

Table 1. Data protection offered by our private outsourced Kriging scheme.

Data	r_i	z_i	(x_0, y_0)	z_0^*	γ model	ρ	ν	η
Protection	✗	✓	✗	✓	✗	✗	✓	✓

4   Our Techniques

In this section we introduce the main concept used in our construction, namely the canonical variogram. We then show how to factor out the variogram parameters in the Normal equations which, ultimately, allows us to remove these parameters from the outsourced dataset and use them only to recover the final prediction on the client side.

The crux of our solution for the private outsourcing of Kriging interpolation is to observe how the Kriging solution varies according to the variogram nugget effect η, the sill ν, and range ρ in the non-degenerate case. We define a *canonical* variogram for each variogram model by arbitrarily fixing the parameters $\eta = \rho = 1$ and $\nu = 0$, although our results clearly translate to other choices.

Since the Kriging process is inherently linear, we show how to 'factor out' the sensitive parameters η and ν from the variogram to leave just the canonical variogram. Using this result and an additively homomorphic scheme, an untrusted server can compute a related Kriging prediction and variance without any knowledge of η, ν and the actual measurements. The variogram parameters can then be efficiently re-added by the client locally to compute the final prediction.

Definition 2 (Canonical variogram). *Let $\gamma(h)$ be a non-degenerate variogram function with nugget effect η, sill ν and range ρ. We define its associated canonical variogram as the function $\tilde{\gamma} : \mathbb{R}^{\geq 0} \to \mathbb{R}$ satisfying $\tilde{\gamma}(0) = 0$ and*

$$\tilde{\gamma}(h) = -\frac{1}{\nu - \eta}\gamma(\rho h) + \frac{\nu}{\nu - \eta} \quad \text{for } h > 0. \tag{1}$$

Note that for any non-degenerate variogram function coming from the parametric variogram models defined in Sect. 2, the canonical variogram depends only on the considered model itself and not on any parameters.

Now, given a Kriging dataset (P, S) of n measurements, a query position $r_0 \notin P$ and a variogram function γ with nugget effect η, sill ν and range ρ, let $K\lambda = v$ be the corresponding Normal equations as defined in Sect. 2. Our main result in this stage is that it suffices to consider a canonical version of the Normal equations that depends only on the chosen variogram model, as well as P and the range parameter ρ of γ.

Definition 3. *We define the canonical Normal equations as the linear system obtained from the Normal equations $K\lambda = v$ by replacing*

- *every $r_i \in P$ by r_i/ρ,*
- *the query position r_0 by r_0/ρ,*
- *the variogram $\gamma(h)$ by the canonical variogram $\tilde{\gamma}(h)$,*

and we denote the canonical Normal equations by $\tilde{K}\tilde{\lambda} = \tilde{v}$.

Note that, since the canonical variogram is parameterless, the canonical Normal equations involve only the variogram model and the locations in P scaled by the inverse of the range parameter ρ. We make extensive use of this observation in our construction. Indeed, this observation allows us to take advantage of the linearity of the Kriging predictor, in order to protect the measurements and interpolation value, while hiding the sill and nugget parameters ν, η from the server by storing them locally.

The solution to the canonical Normal equations can be described as follows:

Proposition 1. *Let $K, K' \in \mathbb{R}^{(n+1)\times(n+1)}$ be real matrices, and let $v, v' \in \mathbb{R}^{n+1}$ be real vectors such that:*

- *there exist $a, b \in \mathbb{R}$ such that $K'_{i,j} = aK_{i,j} + b$ and $v'_i = av_i + b$ for all $1 \leq i, j \leq n$,*
- *$K_{i,n+1} = K_{n+1,i} = K'_{i,n+1} = K'_{n+1,i} = v_{n+1} = v'_{n+1} = 1$ for all $1 \leq i \leq n$,*
- *$K_{n+1,n+1} = K'_{n+1,n+1} = 0$.*

Then, if $\lambda \in \mathbb{R}^{n+1}$ satisfies $K\lambda = v$, the vector $\lambda' \in \mathbb{R}^{n+1}$ defined by

$$\lambda'_i = \lambda_i \text{ for all } 1 \leq i \leq n,$$
$$\lambda'_{n+1} = a\lambda_{n+1}$$

satisfies $K'\lambda' = v'$.

Proof. Note that $(K'\lambda')_i = av_i + b\sum_{i=1}^{n}\lambda_i$ for $1 \le i \le n$, and $(K'\lambda')_{n+1} = 1$. Since $\sum_{i=1}^{n}\lambda_i = 1$ (by the last equation of the system $K\lambda = v$), the result follows. □

This result extends an observation by [7], which states that summing a constant to the variogram does not alter the solutions of the Normal equations, and that such a transformation of the variogram may sometimes be necessary in order to obtain a numerically stable Kriging prediction.

We apply this proposition to the Normal equations with $a = -1/(\nu - \eta)$ and $b = \nu/(\nu - \eta)$, and consider the canonical Normal equations. By the definitions of the Kriging prediction and the Kriging variance in Sect. 2, we directly obtain the following Corollary.

Corollary 1. *Let z_0^* and $\tilde{z}_0^*$ be the Kriging predictions computed from the Normal and the canonical Normal equations described above, respectively. Denote by σ_0^{*2} and $\tilde{\sigma}_0^{*2}$ the Kriging variance associated to each of the predictors. Then*

$$\tilde{z}_0^* = z_0^* \quad and \quad \tilde{\sigma}_0^{*2} = -\frac{1}{\nu - \eta}\sigma_0^{*2} + \frac{\nu}{\nu - \eta}.$$

Therefore, in case that the employed variogram is non-degenerate, the Kriging prediction is independent of the sill ν and nugget η parameters of the variogram, whilst the range parameter ρ scales positions. We also see that, when applying a linear transformation to the variogram, the Kriging variance of the obtained Kriging predictor varies according to the same transformation.

5   Our Construction

We now outline the operation of each of the algorithms in Definition 1. Let $\mathcal{H} = (\mathcal{H}.\text{Gen}, \mathcal{H}.\text{Enc}, \mathcal{H}.\text{Dec})$ be an IND-CPA-secure additive homomorphic encryption scheme, such as the Paillier encryption scheme [11]. Then:

- $(C, UK, QK) \xleftarrow{\$} \text{Outsource}(1^\lambda, P, S, \gamma)$: If γ is a degenerate variogram function, halt and return $\perp$; in this case, our protocol fails. However, if γ is degenerate, the variogram is constant (the so-called 'nugget effect model') and models a purely random variable with no spatial correlation. Hence it is particularly easy to compute predictions in this case: the prediction is $z_0^* = \sum z_i/n$ for $r_0 \notin P$ and the variance is $\sigma_0^{*2} = n + 1$. Otherwise, generate a key-pair for the homomorphic encryption scheme:

$$(pk, sk) \xleftarrow{\$} \mathcal{H}.\text{Gen}(1^\lambda).$$

Recall that $P \subseteq \mathbb{R}^2$ is the ordered set of locations $(r_i)_{i=1}^{n}$ and that $S \subseteq \mathbb{R}$ is the ordered set of measurements $(z_i)_{i=1}^{n}$. Recall also that the variogram γ comprises three parameters: the nugget η, the sill ν and the range ρ. Let $\tilde{\gamma}$ be the canonical variogram associated to γ, as defined in Sect. 4. Define

$$UK = (pk, \rho) \text{ and } QK = (sk, \eta, \nu, \rho).$$

To account for the factor of ρ in the input to γ in Eq. 1, compute

$$\tilde{P} = ((x_i/\rho, y_i/\rho))_{i=1}^n.$$

Finally, encrypt each measurement in S and define the ordered set

$$Z = (\mathcal{H}.\text{Enc}_{pk}(z_i))_{i=1}^n.$$

Output $C = (\tilde{P}, Z, \tilde{\gamma})$, along with UK and QK.

- DB $\leftarrow$ Setup(C): Instantiate the matrix $\tilde{K}$ from the canonical Normal equations using positions in $r_i' \in \tilde{P}$ and the canonical variogram function $\tilde{\gamma}$:
  - $\tilde{K}_{i,j} = \tilde{\gamma}(d(r_i', r_j'))$ for $1 \leq i, j \leq n$,
  - $\tilde{K}_{n+1,i} = \tilde{K}_{i,n+1} = 1$ for $i \neq n+1$, and
  - $\tilde{K}_{n+1,n+1} = 0$.
  Return DB $= (\tilde{K}, C)$.

- $Q \xleftarrow{\$}$ Query(r_0, QK): Let $r_0 = (x_0, y_0)$ and, recalling that ρ is contained within QK, return $Q = (x_0/\rho, y_0/\rho)$.

- $(\tilde{Z}_0, \tilde{\sigma_0}^{*2}) \leftarrow$ Interpolate(Q, DB): Recall that $C = (\tilde{P}, Z, \tilde{\gamma})$. If $Q \in \tilde{P}$, then the exact measurement is contained in the outsourced dataset and no prediction is required. Let j be the index such that $Q = r_j$, and return $(Z_j, \perp)$, where $\perp$ is a distinguished symbol denoting that the prediction is exact.

  Otherwise, compute the vector $\tilde{v}$ from the canonical Normal equations using the locations $r_i' \in \tilde{P}$, the query position Q and the canonical variogram $\tilde{\gamma}$:
  - $v_i = \tilde{\gamma}(d(Q, r_i'))$ for $1 \leq i \leq n$, and
  - $v_{n+1} = 1$.

  Compute the solution $\tilde{\lambda}$ to the canonical Normal equation $\tilde{K}\tilde{\lambda} = \tilde{v}$; this step essentially computes the Kriging coefficients λ using the canonical variogram and the scaled locations *without* requiring the parameters of the variogram. Then, using the homomorphic property of the encryption, compute:

$$\tilde{Z}_0 = \sum_{i=1}^n \tilde{\lambda}_i Z_i \text{ and } \tilde{\sigma_0}^{*2} = \tilde{\lambda}_{n+1} + \sum_{i=1}^n \tilde{\lambda}_i \tilde{\gamma}(Q, r_i').$$

  Return the encrypted prediction $\tilde{Z}_0$ and the partially computed Kriging variance (error estimation) $\tilde{\sigma_0}^{*2}$.

- $(z_0^*, \sigma_0^{*2}) \leftarrow$ Decrypt($\tilde{Z}_0, \tilde{\sigma_0}^{*2}, QK$): First decrypt the Kriging prediction:

$$\tilde{z}_0^* = \mathcal{H}.\text{Dec}_{sk}(\tilde{Z}_0),$$

where sk is contained within QK. Then, if $\tilde{\sigma_0}^{*2} = \perp$, set $\sigma_0^{*2} = 0$. Else, compute the Kriging variance

$$\sigma_0^{*2} = \nu - (\nu - \eta)\tilde{\sigma_0}^{*2}.$$

This final step essentially adds back in the parameters of the variogram, which were removed for outsourcing, using the result from Corollary 1.

– $\alpha_{r',z'} \leftarrow$ AddRequest(r', z', UK): Let $r_a = \frac{r'}{\rho}$ and compute the ciphertext

$$Z_a = \mathcal{H}.\mathrm{Enc}_{pk}(z'),$$

where ρ and pk are contained within UK. Output the addition token

$$\alpha_{r',z'} = (r_a, Z_a).$$

– DB$'$ $\leftarrow$ Add(DB, $\alpha_{r',z'}$): Recall that $\alpha_{r',z'} = (r_a, Z_a)$. Compute the updated dataset: if $r_a \in \tilde{P}$ then let j be the index such that $r_j = r_a$ and modify $Z_j \in \mathrm{Z}$ to be Z_a. Otherwise, set $C' = (\tilde{P} \cup \{r_a\}, \mathrm{Z} \cup \{Z_a\}, \tilde{\gamma})$. Return the output of Setup(C').
– $\delta_r \leftarrow$ DeleteRequest(r, UK): Return $\delta_r = r/\rho$.
– DB$'$ $\leftarrow$ Delete(DB, δ_r): If $\delta_r \notin \tilde{P}$, return DB as there is nothing to remove. Otherwise, let j be the index such that $r = r_j$ in $\tilde{P}$. Compute the updated dataset $C' = (\tilde{P} \setminus \{r_j\}, \mathrm{Z} \setminus \{Z_j\}, \tilde{\gamma})$ and return the output of Setup(C').

6   Discussion

The correctness of the scheme is immediate from Corollary 1 as well as the correctness and homomorphic properties of the encryption scheme $\mathcal{H}$. These homomorphic properties enable addition and scalar multiplication of ciphertexts, whilst ensuring that the results decrypt appropriately. Corollary 1 shows that the Kriging prediction, as well as the Kriging variance, can be computed by applying a linear transformation to the result computed using the canonical (parameterless) variogram. Correctness of the updates is apparent because the addition and deletion tokens format the data in the same way as the original dataset. Since the server is trusted to act honestly (but curiously), it shall modify the dataset correctly; the remainder of the update algorithms then simulate a new setup procedure running Setup on a new Kriging dataset from Outsource.

In terms of security, it is easy to see that the measurement values are always in encrypted form whilst outsourced, and that the leakage is bounded by the variogram model as well as both the queried and observed locations (scaled by the inverse of range parameter ρ). Thus, assuming no collusion between the server and users, the data is confidential from the server. Furthermore, the homomorphic and security properties of the encryption scheme permit the computation to be performed on the measurements whilst they are encrypted; at no point during the computation is the data revealed. The security of the encryption scheme requires each ciphertext to be indistinguishable from a random number, whilst the final prediction $\tilde{Z}_0$ computed by the server comprises a weighted sum of such pseudorandom numbers. Thus, $\tilde{Z}_0$ is a valid ciphertext and is indistinguishable from random, and hence the server cannot learn the prediction from this value.

It is also clear that neither the variogram parameters η and ν, nor any values computed from them, are ever revealed to the server. The final parameter of the variogram, the range ρ, is never explicitly given to the server. However, the server does learn the coordinates of measurements scaled by ρ. Hence, the range could be revealed *if* the server has existing knowledge of the measurement locations. Of the three variogram parameters, we believe that the range is the least sensitive— it reveals how quickly the variogram approaches the sill (*i.e* the distance at which the spatial correlation between measurements becomes negligible) but does not reveal anything relating to the measurement values themselves.

Whilst the queried location is revealed in the plain to the server, we note that the mechanism of Tugrul and Polat [12] may easily be used to gain a weak form of secrecy: during the Query algorithm, the party carrying out the query may choose $q - 1$ additional locations from the region, and scale each by ρ. The query token then comprises q scaled locations, randomly permuted. The server must perform Interpolate for each location, and the client may discard all results except the one it is interested in. Unlike [12], we do not require an oblivious transfer protocol since the querier is authorised to learn as many queries on the dataset as it wishes. However, as in [12], the server may guess the location of interest with probability $1/q$ (but cannot learn the prediction at this location).

Data generating nodes cannot learn Kriging predictions as they do not have the decryption key and $\mathcal{H}$ is assumed to be IND-CPA secure.

Regarding the performance evaluation of our scheme, we have implemented our scheme in Python 3.4.3 using the PHE library [3] to provide the Paillier encryption scheme. The implementation is intended as a proof of concept to evaluate the efficiency of the proposed solution. The encryption scheme has not been further optimised beyond that provided by default in the PHE library, and does not use the provided countermeasures to avoid leaking the exponent of floating point numbers. We remark that implementations of Paillier typically manage issues related to fixed-point arithmetic and overflows in a transparent manner; it is not the aim of this article to discuss such issues. All code is executed locally on a t2.micro Amazon EC2 instance with a 2.5 GHz Intel Xeon processor and 1GB memory running Ubuntu 14.04.4; in practice, one would expect the server to have a better specification. All timings are averaged over 30 iterations, each on a new randomly generated dataset.

Figures 1a and b give some simple timing results using our construction; Fig. 1b shows the per-algorithm costs (excluding the update algorithms). The cost of the Outsource algorithm dominates all others (due to the cost of n encryptions); hence, for clarity, Fig. 1a shows the same results with the exclusion of the Outsource algorithm. It can be seen that, with the exception of the (high) one-time cost of Outsource (which may be amortised over many queries), the remaining client-side processes are very efficient. The server must perform quadratic work to perform Setup, but this will be required relatively rarely— during initial setup and when the outsourced dataset is updated. The online workload of the client is very low, whilst the server's online work is linear in the size of the dataset and greater than the client's workload (making outsourcing worthwhile). We believe that these experiments are sufficient to demonstrate the performance and scalability of our solution; to our knowledge, the range of the number of measurements is reasonable compared to what may be used in

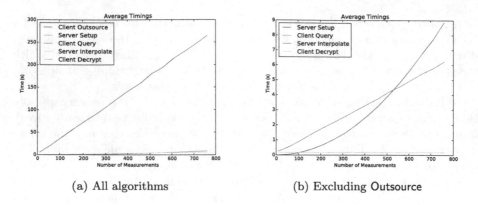

(a) All algorithms   (b) Excluding Outsource

Fig. 1. Graphs showing the timing costs of each algorithm.

practice—for example, the well-known Meuse dataset [5] (often used to illustrate the Kriging process) comprises 155 measurements.

7 Conclusion

The Kriging interpolation technique describes the best unbiased linear prediction of an observed phenomena in a geographical region, based on a set of measurements, and it is widely used in a wide range of applications. In this article we present a construction that allows for Kriging interpolation to be securely outsourced to a cloud service provider, such that the measurement values and sensitive variogram parameters are withheld from the server.

The proposed construction may be extended in several ways. For example, it would be interesting to protect locations. This can be easily achieved if we increased interactivity, communication complexity and client computation in the query process. However, if most computations should be done by the server, it seems necessary to efficiently compute square roots and natural exponentials over encrypted data which, to the best of our knowledge, remains an open problem. Finally, although we have focused on Kriging due to its current practical applications, it would be interesting to consider whether the techniques presented here could be applied in similar problems such as outsourced polynomial curve fitting and regression techniques such as linear or generalized least squares.

Acknowledgements. Oriol Farràs and Jordi Ribes-González were supported by the European Comission through H2020-ICT-2014-1-644024 "CLARUS" and H2020-DS-2015-1-700540 "CANVAS", by the Government of Spain through TIN2014-57364-C2-1-R "SmartGlacis" and TIN2016-80250-R "Sec-MCloud", by the Government of Catalonia through Grant 2014 SGR 537, and by COST Action IC1306. James Alderman was supported by the European Comission through H2020-ICT-2014-1-644024 "CLARUS". Benjamin R. Curtis was supported by the UK EPSRC through EP/K035584/1 "Centre for Doctoral Training in Cyber Security at Royal Holloway".

A   Additional Details on Kriging

In order to apply the Kriging interpolation technique, the observed phenomena is viewed as a realization of a *random field* which satisfies certain properties related to the observed measurements. A random field generalizes the notion of stochastic process, by allowing the underlying parameter to take values other than real numbers. In the case of spatial interpolation, a random field Z is defined as a collection of real-valued random variables $\{Z(r)\}_{r \in R}$, all defined in the same probability space, and indexed by locations r in a fixed region $R \subseteq \mathbb{R}^2$.

Given a set of n samples S taken at positions P, every sample $z_i \in S$ can be viewed as a realization of the random variable $Z(r_i)$, indexed by the position $r_i \in P$ in a random field Z. Given such realizations, a *linear predictor* Z^* of the random field Z is defined as a random field of the form

$$Z^*(r) = \lambda_0 + \sum_{i=1}^{n} \lambda_i Z(r_i), \quad \text{where } \lambda_i \in \mathbb{R}.$$

We say a linear predictor Z^* is *unbiased* if the expectation $\mathbb{E}(Z(r) - Z^*(r)) = 0$ for all $r \in R$. Moreover, we say that a linear predictor Z^* is *best* or *optimal* if, for every location $r \in P$, it minimizes the prediction variance $\mathrm{Var}(Z(r) - Z^*(r))$ among all unbiased linear predictors.

The Kriging interpolation technique aims to find a best unbiased linear predictor for the random field Z derived from a Kriging dataset (P, S). In this sense, note that Kriging deals with the same problem as linear least squares in random fields. However, in order to derive such a predictor from sampled values, additional assumptions are usually made on the *stationarity* of the random field. The most widely applied Kriging process is *Ordinary Kriging*. This form of Kriging stems from two stationarity assumptions. The *second-order stationarity* assumption states that the first and second-order moments of the random variables in the random field are shift invariant:

Definition 4. *A random field Z parametrized by elements of a region $R \subseteq \mathbb{R}^2$ is defined to be* second-order stationary *if the following conditions are satisfied:*

- *The mean $\mathrm{E}(Z(r))$ does not depend on $r \in R$, and*
- *The covariance $\mathrm{Cov}(Z(r), Z(r+h))$ is a function of only the separating vector h for every $r, r + h \in R$.*

The *intrinsic stationarity* assumption considers variance of increments instead of covariance:

Definition 5. *A random field Z parametrized by elements of a region $R \subseteq \mathbb{R}^2$ is defined to be* intrinsic stationary *if the following conditions are satisfied:*

- *The mean $\mathrm{E}(Z(r))$ does not depend on $r \in R$, and*
- *The variance of the increments $\mathrm{Var}(Z(r+h) - Z(r))$ is a function of only the separating vector h for every $r, r + h \in R$.*

Second-order stationarity implies intrinsic stationarity [14] and thus we restrict our attention to the more general intrinsic stationarity assumption. Our techniques are, however, applicable to Ordinary Kriging in general.

The intrinsic stationarity assumption naturally leads to the notion of *theoretical variogram* [7,10] which models the spatial dependency between the random variables $Z(r)$. Given an intrinsic stationary random field Z, the *theoretical variogram* $\hat{\gamma} : R \to \mathbb{R}$ is defined as the function $\hat{\gamma}(h) = \mathrm{Var}(Z(r+h) - Z(r))$. Under the intrinsic assumption, $\hat{\gamma}(h)$ depends only on the norm of h [14]. Hence, we may view $\hat{\gamma}$ as a function defined over positive real numbers.

References

1. CLARUS: User centered privacy and security in the cloud. http://clarussecure.eu. Accessed 11 Dec 2016
2. InGeoCloudS: inspired geo-data cloud services. https://www.ingeoclouds.eu/. Accessed 11 Dec 2016
3. python-paillier: a library for partially homomorphic encryption in python, Data61|CSIRO. https://github.com/NICTA/python-paillier. Accessed 11 Dec 2016
4. SEAL: Simple encrypted arithmetic library, cryptography research group, microsoft research. http://sealcrypto.codeplex.com/. Accessed 11 Dec 2016
5. Burrough, P.A., McDonnell, R., McDonnell, R.A., Lloyd, C.D.: Principles of Geographical Information Systems. Oxford University Press, Oxford (2015)
6. Chilès, J.-P., Delfiner, P.: Multivariate methods. In: Geostatistics: Modeling Spatial Uncertainty, Second Edn., pp. 299–385 (1999)
7. Cressie, N.: Statistics for spatial data. Terra Nova **4**(5), 613–617 (1992)
8. EU Parliament: Directive 2007/2/EC of the European Parliament and of the Council of 14 establishing an infrastructure for spatial information in the European Community (INSPIRE). Off. J. Eur. Union **50**(L108) (2007)
9. Krige, D.: A statistical approach to some basic mine valuation problems on the Witwatersrand. J. South Afr. Inst. Min. Metall. **52**(6), 119–139 (1951)
10. Matheron, G.: Traité de géostatistique appliquée. Mémoires du Bureau de Recherches Géologiques et Minières. Éditions Technip (1962–1963)
11. Paillier, P.: Public-key cryptosystems based on composite degree residuosity classes. In: Stern, J. (ed.) EUROCRYPT 1999. LNCS, vol. 1592, pp. 223–238. Springer, Heidelberg (1999). https://doi.org/10.1007/3-540-48910-X_16
12. Tugrul, B., Polat, H.: Estimating kriging-based predictions with privacy. Int. J. Innov. Comput. Inf. Control (2013, accepted for publication)
13. Tugrul, B., Polat, H.: Privacy-preserving kriging interpolation on partitioned data. Knowl.-Based Syst. **62**, 38–46 (2014)
14. Wackernagel, H.: Multivariate Geostatistics: An Introduction with Applications. Springer Science & Business Media, Berlin (2013)

An Analysis of FV Parameters Impact Towards Its Hardware Acceleration

Joël Cathébras[(✉)], Alexandre Carbon, Renaud Sirdey, and Nicolas Ventroux

CEA, LIST, 91191 Gif-sur-Yvette, France
{joel.cathebras,alexandre.carbon,renaud.sirdey,nicolas.ventroux}@cea.fr

Abstract. The development of cloud computing services is restrained by privacy concerns. Centralized medical services for instance, require a guarantee of confidentiality when using outsourced computation platforms. Fully Homomorphic Encryption is an intuitive solution to address such issue, but until 2009, existing schemes were only able to evaluate a reduced number of operations (Partially Homomorphic Encryption). In 2009, C. Gentry proposed a blueprint to construct FHE schemes from SHE schemes. However, it was not practical due to the huge data size overhead and the exponential noise growth of the initial SHE. Since then, major improvements have been made over SHE schemes and their noise management, and resulting schemes, like BGV and FV, allow to foresee small applications.

Besides scheme improvements, new practical approaches were proposed to bring homomorphic encryption closer to practice. The *IV*-based stream cipher trans-ciphering approach brought by Canteaut et al. in 2015 reduces the on-line latency of the trans-ciphering process to a simple homomorphic addition. The homomorphic evaluation of stream ciphers, that produces the trans-ciphering keystream, could be computed in an off-line phase, resulting in an almost transparent trans-ciphering process from the user point of view. This approach combined with hardware accelerations could bring homomorphic encryption closer to practice.

This paper deals the choice of FV parameters for efficient implementation of this scheme in the light of related works' common approaches. At first sight, using large polynomial degree to reduce the coefficients size seemed to be advantageous, but further observations contradict it. Large polynomial degrees imply larger ciphertexts and more complex implementations, but smaller ones imply more primes to find for CRT polynomial representation. The result of this preliminary work for the choice of an adequate hardware target motivates the choice of small degree polynomials rather than small coefficients for the FV scheme.

Keywords: Homomorphic evaluation · FV parameters · Chinese Remainder Theorem · Number Theorical Transform

1 Introduction

Privacy is one of the main concerns regarding the development of cloud services in the context of applications handling sensible data. The data privacy on remote

© International Financial Cryptography Association 2017
M. Brenner et al. (Eds.): FC 2017 Workshops 2017, LNCS 10323, pp. 91–106, 2017.
https://doi.org/10.1007/978-3-319-70278-0_6

servers is guaranteed with standard cryptography. The issue comes up during the exploitation of these data directly on the outsourced servers. Since 2009 and the thesis of Gentry [15], the concept of fully homomorphic encryption introduced by Rivest et al. in 1978 [22], is not a conjecture any more. Homomorphic encryption schemes guarantee the equivalence of an operation between the clear data and the encrypted data algebraic systems. A fully homomorphic encryption scheme guarantees that an homomorphic equivalent can be found for any function considered over the clear data domain. Homomorphic encryption schemes are emerging along with practical approaches, but the lack of performances of software implementations makes them difficult to use in real life applications. Hardware optimizations for efficient homomorphic encryption should then be explored.

Partial Homomorphic Encryption schemes are able to homomorphically evaluate additions (e.g. Paillier) or multiplications (e.g. RSA). Problems arise to design an homomorphic encryption scheme able to evaluate both additions and multiplications. Indeed, in homomorphic cryptography a noise is added to the encrypted data for security reasons (non-deterministic encryption). If it is possible to construct Somewhat Homomorphic Encryption schemes (that could evaluate both additions and multiplications) the added noise results in a large data size expansion between clear and encrypted data. Moreover, the level of noise grows with operations in the encrypted domain, and especially with multiplications. At a certain level, the decryption primitive does not retrieve the clear data correctly.

Gentry's blueprint to construct FHE schemes is based on the bootstrapping procedure: an SHE scheme that can homomorphically evaluate its own decryption circuit and at least an other operation, becomes a FHE scheme. The first implementations of the bootstrapping procedure were impractical due to the SHE exponential noise growth, their complex decryption circuit, and their large data size expansion [12,24]. Numerous works proposed new schemes introducing different mechanisms from sub-exponential noise growth [4,13] to constant noise growth [3,11]. Despite the improved performances, the bootstrapping procedure is still too complex for them to be practical. Nevertheless these new schemes lead to a compromise: they can evaluate functions with a multiplicative depth under a practical limit (20 to 30) but become impractical beyond it. The FV [11] and BGV [13] schemes are the most accepted today.

In 2013, Gentry et al. proposed a new approach revisiting the bootstrapping procedure to construct FHE schemes [14]. This work is followed by promising results for fast bootstrapping primitives [7,10]. They open interesting perspectives in the definition of efficient FHE systems.

The important data size expansion inherent to homomorphic encryption implies, among other things, an overhead problem in communication costs. To solve this problem, Naehrig et al. [17] proposed a practical approach known as trans-ciphering: the owner encrypts its data under a standard symmetric encryption scheme, without data size expansion, and sends them to the server along with an homomorphic encryption of the symmetric key. Once the server possesses the encrypted data, the decryption function of the symmetric scheme is homomorphically evaluated by the FHE, SHE or L-FHE scheme, resulting in homomorphic encrypted data. This approach has been improved by Canteaut et al. [5]. They proposed the use of lightweight additive IV-based stream ciphers as the underlying symmetric schemes. They have shown that using their approach, the trans-ciphering procedure's performance is then dependent of an intensive off-line computation part, reducing the on-line part of trans-ciphering to a simple homomorphic addition. This approach solves only the upward communication overhead as the trans-ciphering is a one-way procedure. Still, it improves the practicability of homomorphic encryption but performances are still not sufficient for software only implementations. For example, it takes ∼35 min on a mid-end 48-core server to generate 57 homomorphic keystream elements that could handle up to 7 additional ciphertext multiplication levels [5].

The SHE scheme FV [11] handles polynomials with modular integer coefficients (500 to 5000 bits) modulo a fixed degree polynomial which is in practice a cyclotomic polynomial of rather large degree (128 to 32768). Manipulation of such polynomials is expensive, especially during multiplications. This issue is already addressed with the hardware optimization of lattice based cryptography [21]. The opportunity of lattice-based homomorphic encryption helps to extend the previous work to the context of homomorphic encryption, and in particular of homomorphic evaluation [9,19,23].

In lattice-based cryptography, the parameter selection is difficult in practice. To the best of our knowledge, most of works related to the hardware acceleration of homomorphic primitives tend to select previously used parameter sets. We assume it is done for comparison purposes, but the choice of parameters could have a significant impact on the correct exploitation of available hardware resources. It motivates the work presented in this paper which makes an analysis of the FV parameters for adequacy of hardware architecture and algorithm.

In this paper, we exploit the distinction between the application parameters and the implementation parameters of the FV scheme. When the security and multiplicative depth requirements are fixed (application parameters), we still have one degree of freedom to choose the cyclotomic polynomial's degree N and the size of the modulus q. By examining the algorithms of recent hardware acceleration work, both these parameters impact the resulting implementation complexities.

In a first section, the mathematical notations and the FV evaluation primitives are presented. The second section presents the profiling results that motivate focus on polynomial multiplications, and then describes the approaches proposed in hardware optimization studies to implement efficiently these operations. The third section derives from the inter-dependency of FV parameters the impacts of the degree N and the size of the modulus q on the implementation strategy. Finally, the fourth section concludes this paper.

2 Preliminaries on the FV Scheme

This section has two objectives, first to get used to the notations, and second to make the distinction between a ciphertext multiplication and polynomial multiplications occurring in ciphertext multiplication and ciphertext relinearisation. In a first subsection the mathematical representation used in this paper are presented, and the second subsection reminds the FV primitives. The third subsection presents the set of FV parameters that interests us.

2.1 Mathematical Notations

Algebraic Structure: The cyclotomic polynomial of order m is denoted $\Phi_m(X)$ and ϕ is the function. $R_m = \mathbb{Z}[X]/(\Phi_m(X))$ refers to the ring of the polynomial classes of degree less than $N = \phi(m)$ with integer coefficients. In practice, m is selected as power of 2 and it follows that $\Phi_m(X) = X^N + 1$ and $N = m/2$.

Elements of the ring R_m are noted in lowercase bold (e.g. $\mathbf{a} \in R_m$) and their coefficients in indexed lowercase (e.g. $a_i \forall i \in (0, 1, ..., N-1)$). The notation $\mathbf{a}$ is used indifferently for the polynomial or its N-point sequence of coefficients.

For an integer $q > 1$, $\mathbb{Z}_q$ is the set of integers $[-q/2, q/2)$. The unique integer in $\mathbb{Z}_q$ such that $[a]_q = a \bmod q, \forall a \in \mathbb{Z}$ is noted $[a]_q$. By extension, $R_{m,q}$ is the set of polynomials in R_m with coefficients in $\mathbb{Z}_q$. For a polynomial $\mathbf{a} \in R_m$, $[\mathbf{a}]_q$ is the polynomial in $R_{m,q}$ obtained by applying $[\cdot]_q$ to all its coefficients. The notation $[\mathbf{a}]_q$ is used indifferently for the polynomial or its N-point sequence of coefficients.

Plaintext and Ciphertext Spaces: The plaintext space of the FV scheme is defined with respect to an integer $t > 1$, and it is the set of polynomial in $R_{m,t}$ (e.g. $t = 2$).

The ciphertext space is also defined with respect to an integer $q > 1$. A ciphertext is a pair of polynomials in $R_{m,q}$. Let c be a ciphertext, its canonical form is noted $c = (\mathbf{c}_0, \mathbf{c}_1) \in R_{m,q}^2$. After multiplications, ciphertexts are in a non-canonical form that requires a relinearisation procedure. Such ciphertexts are noted $\tilde{c}$ with $\tilde{c} = (\tilde{\mathbf{c}}_0, \tilde{\mathbf{c}}_1, \tilde{\mathbf{c}}_2) \in R_{m,q}^3$.

2.2 FV Primitives

In the context of stream cipher trans-ciphering, both the off-line part and on-line part are based on homomorphic evaluations. During the off-line phase, the homomorphic scheme evaluates the IV-based stream cipher, and during the on-line phase it evaluates the application required by the user. This paper focuses on the FV primitives specific to homomorphic evaluation. A complete presentation of the scheme could be found in the original work [11].

The choice is made to work with the second version of the relinearisation procedure presented in the original work. This version makes the relinearisation primitive close to the ciphertext multiplication primitive. It is motivated by the intuition that if a hardware platform computes ciphertext multiplications efficiently, it conducts also efficient relinearisations.

This relinearisation primitive requires the definition of an integer $p > 1$ (usually $p \geq q^3$) and a relinearisation key which is a pair of polynomials in $R_{m,p\cdot q}$. We note $rlk = (\mathbf{rlk_0}, \mathbf{rlk_1}) \in R^2_{m,p\cdot q}$ the relinearisation key of the FV instance.

Let $a = (\mathbf{a_0}, \mathbf{a_1}) \in R^2_{m,q}$ and $b = (\mathbf{b_0}, \mathbf{b_1}) \in R^2_{m,q}$ be two ciphertexts of the same FV instance. We note by $\times$ (resp. $+$) the polynomial multiplication (resp. addition) over R_m. The scalar multiplication is noted $\cdot$ and the scale-and-center-rounding operation is represented using $\lfloor S \cdot . \rceil$ with S the scaling value. Finally we remind that $[.]_q$ reduces all the polynomial coefficients to the interval $[-q/2, q/2)$.

Figure 1 shows the operation flow of the ciphertext multiplication and the ciphertext relinearisation described in the original paper of Fan and Vercauteren [11] (Sect. 4). In practice the FV multiplication is immediately followed by a relinearisation in order to always handle canonical ciphertexts. It is important to note that polynomial arithmetic takes place in R_m and it is not possible to reduce the coefficients modulo q at will.

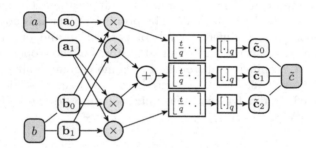

(a) Ciphertext multiplication

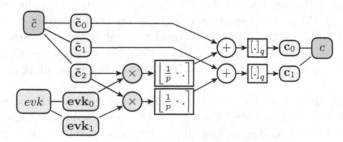

(b) Ciphertext relinearisation

Fig. 1. FV multiplication and relinearisation primitives

2.3   FV Parameters

In this paper an FV instance is a particular set of FV parameters. Four parameters are considered: the security level λ, the multiplicative depth evaluation capability L, the degree of the cyclotomic polynomial N, and the size of the ciphertext's polynomial coefficients T_q. Other parameters are described in the original work [11].

The particular set of parameters (λ, L, N, T_q) has three degrees of freedom: it requires three of them to be fixed to derive the fourth. A distinction is made between the application level parameters (λ, L), and (N, T_q) which are implementation level parameters.

Both the cyclotomic polynomial degree N and the size of the coefficients T_q have an impact on handling the polynomials. The purpose of this paper is to investigate their impact on the hardware optimization strategies explored in related works.

3   Improving Performances of FV Homomorphic Evaluation

According to Amdahl's law, a dedicated hardware solution should cover the most repetitive and compute intensive operations of an application. The identification of their critical operations is usually done by profiling. When it is possible, hardware optimizations exploit different levels of parallelism and/or mathematical simplifications inherent to the underlying algorithms of these operations.

In this section, profiling results of the FV homomorphic evaluation of Trivium from Canteaut et al. [5] are presented. In a second subsection, common approaches for efficient polynomial multiplications are described, highlighting the influence of FV parameters.

3.1   FV Homomorphic Evaluation of Trivium

Using a library implementing the FV scheme [6], the experimentation of Canteaut et al. [5] is reproduced by executing an homomorphic evaluation of Trivium. The Valgrind tool suite [18] is used to identify the ciphertext multiplication operation as the performance bottleneck of homomorphic evaluation with more than 99% of the estimated cycles. The results of the profiling are detailed in Table 1.

The CtxtMult operation is, as explained in the previous section, decomposed into the actual ciphertext multiplication (30.6 %) and the immediately following relinearisation (62.8 %). Digging a bit more into these two steps, it appears that they both rely on the same bottleneck operation, the polynomial multiplications, realized through FFT convolutions. During the whole evaluation of Trivium-12, 76.1% of the estimated cycles are spent in these convolutions.

The ciphertext relinearisation is twice the computation workload of the ciphertext multiplication as the relinearisation key is a pair of polynomials with coefficients four times the size of ciphertext polynomials.

Table 1. Profiling results of an homomorphic evaluation of Trivium-12 with the FV implementation of Canteaut et al. [5]. FV parameters: security 80, multiplicative depth 19, polynomial cyclotomic order 4096 (implies polynomials with 2048 coefficients) modulus q size 2658-bits. The experiment uses Valgrind 3.10.

HE operation	Est. cycles (Million cycles)	% Est
HE Trivium	**13 337 699**	100%
CtxtMult	**13 272 536**	99.5%
- Relinearise	8 381 331	62.8%
- Multiply	4 085 675	30.6%
- Others	805 530	6.1%
CtxtAdd	**50 923**	0.4%
Others	**14 240**	0.1%

This profiling confirms that the critical part of FV homomorphic evaluation is the ciphertext multiplication and relinearisation. Both rely on polynomial multiplication, which is also found in lattice-based cryptography.

3.2 Improving Polynomial Multiplications

Polynomial operations are conducted over R_m, it implies that multi-precision integer operations handle values that could grow up to $N * q^2$ during ciphertext multiplication and up to $N * p * q^2$ during ciphertext relinearisation. In practice, two integers $Q > N * q^2$ and $K > N * p * q^2$ are selected, and the polynomial multiplications are conducted over $R_{m,Q}$ and $R_{m,K}$. The size of modulus q depends on the others FV parameters, but it grows from hundred of bits up to thousand of bits in some FV instances. To tackle the large integer arithmetic, the use of RNS arithmetic through the Chinese Remainders Theorem (CRT) is quite popular for hardware optimisation approaches [8,19,25].

Besides the integer arithmetic, a polynomial multiplication is highly dependent of the degree involved. The naive approach for polynomial multiplication consists in computing the linear convolution product of its coefficients and has a complexity in $O(N^2)$. To reduce this complexity, the NTT based polynomial multiplication is widely used in hardware optimization works [19,21]. A recent work from Migliore et al. [16] proposes the use of the Karatsuba polynomial multiplication algorithm for small multiplicative depth applications.

Chinese Remainder Theorem: To exploit the parallelism brought by CRT, the different modulus q, Q and K are constructed as fixed size primes' products. The number of primes required for each modulus (l_q, l_Q and l_K) depends on Tq and the desired size of these primes T_{primes} (1). By construction of the modulus Q and K, $T_Q = 2 * T_q + \log_2(N)$ and $T_K = 5 * T_q + \log_2(N)$.

$$l_q = \left\lceil \frac{T_q}{T_{\text{primes}}} \right\rceil, \quad l_Q = \left\lceil \frac{2 * T_q + \log_2(N)}{T_{\text{primes}}} \right\rceil, \quad l_K = \left\lceil \frac{5 * T_q + \log_2(N)}{T_{\text{primes}}} \right\rceil . \quad (1)$$

With a direct application of the CRT, the bijections $R_{m,Q} \cong (R_{m,p_0} \times \ldots \times R_{m,p_{l_Q-1}})$ and $R_{m,K} \cong (R_{m,p_0} \times \ldots \times R_{m,p_{l_K-1}})$ allow the addition of parallelism in the polynomial multiplication. The computational cost of switching the polynomial representation from $R_{m,Q}$ (resp. $R_{m,K}$) to the residue system representation, and vice versa, is not taken into account. A recent work from Bajarad et al. [2] proposes a variant of the FV scheme in which polynomials stay all along in Residue Number System representations.

The ciphertext polynomial multiplications are decomposed into l_Q (resp. l_K) independent residue polynomial multiplications during ciphertext multiplication (resp. ciphertext relinearisation). The independence of each residue polynomial multiplication implies a thread level parallelism that could be exploited through distributed computation.

Considering a residue polynomial multiplication as a simple hardware block (B_{RPM}), the latency and the hardware cost of a ciphertext polynomial multiplication block is roughly expressed in function of the number of blocks at disposal ($\#B_{\text{RPM}} \in [1; l_Q]$ (resp. $[1; l_K]$)). Equations (2) and (3) express them for a polynomial multiplication during ciphertext multiplications.

$$Lat_{\text{PolyMult}} = \left\lceil \frac{l_Q}{\#B_{\text{RPM}}} \right\rceil * Lat_{B_{\text{RPM}}} \quad (2)$$

$$HCost_{\text{PolyMult}} = \#B_{\text{RPM}} * HCost_{B_{\text{RPM}}} \quad (3)$$

As a residue polynomial has the size of its coefficients fixed by T_{primes}, the characteristics of a block B_{RPM} are independent of the parameter T_q. It can be already pointed out that when exploiting the RNS arithmetic introduced by the CRT, the parameters T_q and T_{primes} determine the thread level parallelism. The impact of the parameters N and T_{primes} on the hardware blocks B_{RPM} are detailed in the next subsection.

Polynomial Multiplication over $R_{m,pi}$: For high degree polynomials, the NTT-based polynomial multiplication seems to be the most popular approach for hardware optimizations. It computes the convolution product of the polynomial multiplication through Number Theoretical Transforms (Fourier transform on finite fields), and the Cooley-Tukey algorithm reduces the NTT complexity to $O(N \log(N))$. Furthermore, exploiting the negacyclic convolution theorem, the NTT-based multiplication can directly perform polynomial multiplications modulo $\Phi_m(X) = X^N + 1$, avoiding a non-trivial polynomial modular reduction. Nevertheless this approach reduces the choice of the primes p_i, as the existence of an N-point NTT over the residue space $\mathbb{Z}_{p_i}$ must be guaranteed.

As described in [20], the existence of the N-point NTT over R_{m,p_i} is conditioned by the existence of a primitive N-root of unity ω over $\mathbb{Z}_{p_i}$. If one wants to use the negacyclic convolution theorem over $\mathbb{Z}_{p_i}$, he has to find a primitive $2N$-root of unity ψ such that $\psi^2 = \omega \mod p_i$. Furthermore, all the elements of

$\mathbb{Z}_{p_i}$ should be invertible, this property is guaranteed by selecting p_i as a prime. According to [20], all the conditions above are satisfied if a prime p_i can be found such that $2N$ divides $(p_i - 1)$. Then it just remains the selection of appropriate ω and ψ. Efficient prime selection is addressed by the NFLlib developmental team Aguilar-Melchor et al. [1].

During the computation of a residue polynomial multiplication, two forward and one backward N-point NTT are computed ($O(N \log(N))$ complexity). The other operations consist in point-wise coefficient multiplications between N-point sequences ($O(N)$ complexity). It is then reasonable to focus the hardware optimizations on the NTT. We would like now to observe the impact of N on the NTT latency and hardware cost.

The implementation of an NTT with respect to a radix-2 basic block B_{RX2} is now considered. The latency and hardware cost of this block are noted respectively $Lat_{B_{\mathrm{RX2}}}$ and $HCost_{B_{\mathrm{RX2}}}$. An N-point NTT computation, with N a power of two, is composed of $\log_2(N)$ iterations of $N/2$ radix-2 block computations. In this work, it is assumed that an iteration has to finish before the next one can start, and that the radix-2 blocks are re-used from one iteration to another. Let $\#B_{\mathrm{RX2}} \in [1; N/2]$ be the number of radix-2 blocks available for the computation of one iteration of an N-point NTT.

$$Lat_{B_{\mathrm{NTT}}} = \left\lceil \frac{N}{2 * \#B_{\mathrm{RX2}}} \right\rceil * \log_2(N) * Lat_{B_{\mathrm{RX2}}}(T_{\mathrm{primes}}) \tag{4}$$

$$HCost_{B_{\mathrm{NTT}}} = \#B_{\mathrm{RX2}} * HCost_{B_{\mathrm{RX2}}}(T_{\mathrm{primes}}) \tag{5}$$

Now that the impact of N over an NTT computation is known ((4) and (5)), its influence on latency and hardware cost of a residue polynomial multiplication must be expressed. It is done by considering that the N extra modular multiplications required for backward NTT are computed as an N-point wise multiplication. It is reminded that in the negacyclic convolution approach there are already four N-point wise modular multiplications to compute [21].

Equations (6) and (7) express the latency and the hardware cost of a residue polynomial multiplication with respect to an NTT block (B_{NTT}) and a modular multiplier block (B_{MM}). Let $\#B_{\mathrm{MM}} \in [1; N]$ be the number of modular multipliers available for an N-point wise multiplication.

$$Lat_{B_{\mathrm{RPM}}} = 3 * Lat_{B_{\mathrm{NTT}}} + 5 * \left\lceil \frac{N}{\#B_{\mathrm{MM}}} \right\rceil * Lat_{B_{\mathrm{MM}}}(T_{\mathrm{primes}}) \tag{6}$$

$$HCost_{B_{\mathrm{RPM}}} = HCost_{B_{\mathrm{NTT}}} + \#B_{\mathrm{MM}} * HCost_{B_{\mathrm{MM}}}(T_{\mathrm{primes}}) \tag{7}$$

Both the radix-2 and the modular multiplier implementations have their efficiency related to the choice of an efficient modular reduction, but also in the choice of the T_{primes} parameter [1]. From an hardware design point of view, working with small T_{primes} could be interesting to have smaller integer arithmetic to perform.

This section has expressed some high level equations that link the FV parameters and the hardware optimization choices together. The next one describes an analysis of the FV parameters and their impact on the hardware optimization opportunities.

4   FV Parameters and Optimization Opportunities

From an applicative point of view, the security level λ and the multiplicative depth L are the parameters that determine the FV instance. But when λ and L are fixed, there is still freedom in the choice of the cyclotomic polynomial degree N and in the coefficient size T_q of the ciphertext polynomials. As seen in the previous section, the parameter T_q has an impact on thread parallelism, and the parameter N has an impact on the residue polynomial multiplication. This section discusses the impacts of the relation $T_q(N)$ over the hardware optimization strategy.

To generate correct sets of FV parameters, a Sage script [6] implementing the derivation rules from Fan and Vercauteren [11] is used. Some sets of parameters are generated with ranges that one could expect in a stream-cipher transciphering context with Trivium-12 from Canteaut et al. [5]. The security level is selected between 80 and 192 and the multiplicative depth is selected between 16 and 32.

4.1   Scalability over Applicative Level Parameters

Figure 2 shows the impact of the security and the multiplicative depth parameters on the relation $T_q(N)$. The first relation $T_q(N)$ displayed is fixed for security 80 and multiplicative depth 16. Figure 2a represents the influence of the security, and Fig. 2b the multiplicative depth's influence over this relation. We observe that high degree cyclotomic polynomials reduce the influences of λ and L over coefficient sizes.

A direct relation between the latency of a polynomial multiplication during ciphertext multiplication and the size of the modulus q is expressed in Eqs. (1), (2) and (3).

$$Lat_{\text{PolyMult}} = \left\lceil \frac{2 * T_q + \log_2(N)}{T_{\text{primes}} * \#B_{\text{RPM}}} \right\rceil * Lat_{B_{\text{RPM}}} \tag{8}$$

As explained in Sect. 3.2, the latency and the hardware cost of a residue polynomial multiplication block are only dependent of T_{primes} and N. Thus when T_{primes}, N and the hardware target ($\#B_{\text{RPM}}$) are fixed, it seems that small variations of T_q imply small variations of Lat_{PolyMult}. Naturally, it depends also on the constant $Lat_{B_{\text{RPM}}}$. An implementation that chooses to handle large N, has its latency Lat_{PolyMult} less impacted by T_q compare to one that handle smaller N. However, it is necessary to assess the influence of N over $Lat_{B_{\text{RPM}}}$ before concluding that large N reduces application parameter's influences over a given implementation.

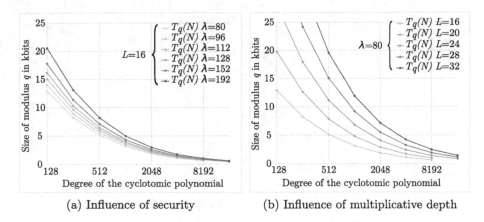

Fig. 2. Influence of λ and L on the relation $T_q(N)$. The size of the modulus q is expressed in kbits.

4.2 Smaller Ciphertexts

The ciphertext size is a high level indicator for memory requirements (storage capacity, access latency...) that directly impact performances. Without considering any parallelism, implementation details or optimized data accesses, a coarse grain relation could be expressed: the smaller the ciphertexts, the better the performances.

Figure 3 shows the impact of the security and multiplicative depth on the ciphertext size, which is directly related to T_q and N, CtxtSize $= 2 * (T_q * N)$. The observation shows that a large degree N increases the influence of security and multiplicative depth over the size of the ciphertexts. This is mildly counterintuitive with the influence of N on the size of the modulus q. It seems now more interesting to select small N, and further discussions confirms it.

4.3 Influence of N on Residue Polynomial Multiplications

The description of the NTT-based polynomial multiplication presents the bottleneck operation as the computation of forward and backward N-point NTT. Equations (4), (6), (5) and (7) have expressed the latency and the hardware cost of a residue polynomial multiplication function of the FV parameter N and the hardware blocks availability $\#B_{\mathrm{RX2}}$, $\#B_{\mathrm{MM}}$.

$$Lat_{B_{\mathrm{RPM}}} = 3 * \left\lceil \frac{N}{2 * \#B_{\mathrm{RX2}}} \right\rceil * \log_2(N) * Lat_{B_{\mathrm{RX2}}} + 5 * \left\lceil \frac{N}{\#B_{\mathrm{MM}}} \right\rceil * Lat_{B_{\mathrm{MM}}} \quad (9)$$

$$HCost_{B_{\mathrm{RPM}}} = \#B_{\mathrm{RX2}} * HCost_{B_{\mathrm{RX2}}} + \#B_{\mathrm{MM}} * HCost_{B_{\mathrm{MM}}} \quad (10)$$

Because N is a power of two, selecting larger N has a major impact on the latency and/or on the hardware implementation cost. In Fig. 4, the theoretical latency and hardware cost function of N is represented, and this for different

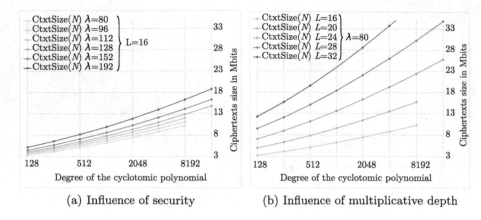

Fig. 3. Influence of λ and L on the ciphertext's size, expressed in Mbits.

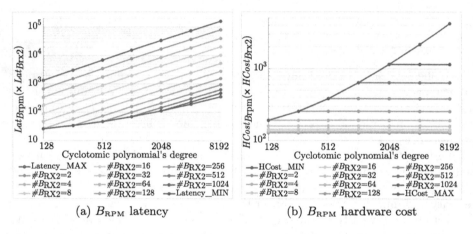

Fig. 4. Influence of the FV parameter N over the latency and the hardware cost of a residue polynomial multiplication, with $\#B_{\mathrm{MM}} = 128$ and for different $\#B_{\mathrm{RX2}}$.

levels of parallelism introduced in a NTT computation. In this representation, the latency and the hardware cost of the N-point wise multiplications are fixed by choosing $\#B_{\mathrm{MM}} = 128$. The latency (resp. the hardware cost) is expressed as multiples of $Lat_{B_{\mathrm{RX2}}}$ (resp. $HCost_{B_{\mathrm{RX2}}}$). For more simplicity $Lat_{B_{\mathrm{RX2}}}$ is considered equivalent to $Lat_{B_{\mathrm{MM}}}$ (resp. $HCost_{B_{\mathrm{RX2}}} \sim HCost_{B_{\mathrm{MM}}}$).

This theoretical experimentation is considered as a best case scenario due to the approximations made in (4), (5), (6) and (7). Indeed the data dependencies in the NTT computations, the storage cost of pre-evaluated factors, and the memory access latencies are not taken into account. In each residue space R_{m,p_i}, $2N$ factors have to be pre-computed for an NTT based negacyclic convolution. Thus doubling N roughly doubles the number of twiddle factors and memory accesses.

As displayed in Fig. 4a and b, and accordingly to Eqs. (9) and (10), choosing larger N linearly increases the latency of a residue polynomial multiplication. Similarly, to guarantee a low latency residue polynomial multiplication for any N, one has to pay an extra hardware cost which linearly increases with N. Nevertheless, N exponentially increases as its value is restricted to be power of two (to have both batching property [24] and nega-cyclic convolution) and naturally, the latency and the hardware cost of a residue polynomial multiplication suffer from this exponentiation.

Considering now that N is fixed, the Eqs. (9) and (10) show that the latency decreases with larger $\#B_{\mathrm{RX2}}$, but the hardware cost similarly increases. his linear behaviour is also reminiscent with $\#B_{\mathrm{RMP}}$ in Eqs. (2) and (3).

4.4   Influence of T_q on Parallelism from the CRT

As described in Subsect. 3.2, the CRT parallelism capability is theoretically enforced by large T_q that increases the number of residue spaces for a fixed prime size T_{primes}. n our context, the considered choices of N, and its implication on T_q, always enable a valuable acceleration when exploiting the CRT parallelism.

Two limitations to the hardware optimization at CRT level are identified. The first one is not considered in this paper and is fixed by the extra computation added by the switches between the CRT representation of a polynomial and its standard representation with coefficients over $R_{m,q}$. he second is the availability of residue spaces for a given size T_{primes}. Indeed, the use of the CRT is conditioned by the existence of l_K primes of size T_{primes}. Moreover, the NTT-based polynomial multiplication brings an additional condition over the choice of those primes to guarantee the existence of the $2N$-NTT in the residue spaces.

The number of required primes l_K is directly dependent of the relation $T_q(N)$ and the size T_{primes} (cf. Eq. 1). The number of primes required to represent a polynomial in $R_{m,q}$ using a residue representation is presented in Fig. 5, and this for different N and size of primes. To conduct the polynomial multiplications over $R_{m,Q}$ (resp. $R_{m,K}$) with the CRT approach, one has to find roughly $l_Q \sim 2 * l_q$ (resp. $l_K \sim 5 * l_q$) primes.

As introduced in Sect. 3.2, the choice of a small T_{primes} is interesting to reduce the latency and the hardware cost of a modular multiplier block, and has a direct impact on the efficiency of a residue polynomial multiplication. But according to the Prime Number Theorem, the number of prime smaller than n is roughly $\pi(n) \sim n/\log(n)$. Finding enough primes with $T_{\mathrm{primes}} \geq 32$, is not an issue, but considering smaller prime sizes, the number of candidates quickly drops down. The GMP library is used to find a maximum number of primes that satisfy the NTT requirement when T_{primes} is 16-bits and 24-bits, the results are shown in Table 2.

The comparison of the number of primes found over 16-bits and 24-bits sizes with the requirements in Fig. 5, shows a limitation in the choice of small T_{primes} to improve the efficiency of basic arithmetic blocks. Nevertheless, as observed in Fig. 5, and even with large N, l_q (and by extension l_Q and l_K) is still large enough to exploit the parallelism bring by CRT.

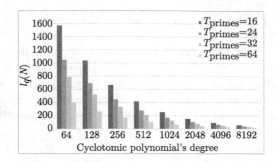

Fig. 5. Influence of N over l_q for $T_{\text{primes}} \in (16, 24, 32, 64)$-bits. Security is fixed at 80 and multiplicative depth at 18.

Table 2. Number of primes allowing N-point NTT transform over $\mathbb{Z}_{p_i}$.

Degree N	128	256	512	1024	2048	4096	8192
16-bits primes	47	24	14	5	3	1	0
24-bits primes	8430	4230	2134	1047	536	260	130

5   Conclusion

In this paper, insights over the choices of FV parameters are provided for efficient hardware resources exploitation for its evaluation primitives. The analysis was conducted in the context of stream-cipher based trans-ciphering using the Trivium cipher. This analysis was also based both on CRT and NTT approaches to conduct the polynomial multiplications over $R_{m,Q}$ (resp. $R_{m,K}$). This choice was motivated by the existing works on hardware optimization of lattice-based cryptography.

The distinction between application level parameters (λ, L) and implementation level parameters (N, T_q) has been expressed. During the analysis some observations have been brought to help in the choice of appropriate FV implementation parameters for a flexible and efficient hardware implementation, regarding the application parameters.

Larger N reduces the impact of security and multiplicative depth over coefficient's size but still increases ciphertext's size. The cyclotomic polynomial degree N, being a power of two, makes the design of efficient NTT-based polynomial multiplications difficult with increasing N. Furthermore, the CRT parallelism is easier to exploit than large polynomial multiplication as explained by Bajard et al. [2]. It implies that all (N, T_q) are not quite the same for a fixed (λ, L), and small degree N should be preferred over small coefficient size T_q.

This analysis was a preliminary study for adequacy of hardware architecture and algorithms underlying the FV evaluations primitives. Despite the motivation of choosing small N, concrete choice of (N, T_q) still depends on the practical limitations of the targeted hardware, and in particular on the memory access bandwidth and the available computing resources.

References

1. Aguilar-Melchor, C., Barrier, J., Guelton, S., Guinet, A., Killijian, M.-O., Lepoint, T.: NFLLIB: NTT-based fast lattice library. In: Sako, K. (ed.) CT-RSA 2016. LNCS, vol. 9610, pp. 341–356. Springer, Cham (2016). https://doi.org/10.1007/978-3-319-29485-8_20

2. Bajard, J.C., Eynard, J., Hasan, A.M., Zucca, V.: A full RNS variant of FV like somewhat homomorphic encryption schemes. In: Avanzi, R., Heys, H. (eds.) SAC 2016. LNCS, vol. 10532, pp. 423–442. Springer, Cham (2017). https://doi.org/10.1007/978-3-319-69453-5_23. http://hal.upmc.fr/hal-01371941

3. Brakerski, Z.: Fully homomorphic encryption without modulus switching from classical GapSVP. In: Safavi-Naini, R., Canetti, R. (eds.) CRYPTO 2012. LNCS, vol. 7417, pp. 868–886. Springer, Heidelberg (2012). https://doi.org/10.1007/978-3-642-32009-5_50

4. Brakerski, Z., Vaikuntanathan, V.: Efficient fully homomorphic encryption from (standard) LWE. In: IEEE ASFC 2011 (2) (2011)

5. Canteaut, A., Carpov, S., Fontaine, C., Lepoint, T., Naya-Plasencia, M., Paillier, P., Sirdey, R.: Stream ciphers: a practical solution for efficient homomorphic-ciphertext compression. In: Peyrin, T. (ed.) FSE 2016. LNCS, vol. 9783, pp. 313–333. Springer, Heidelberg (2016). https://doi.org/10.1007/978-3-662-52993-5_16

6. Carpov, S., Dubrulle, P., Sirdey, R.: Armadillo: a compilation chain for privacy preserving applications. In: Proceedings of the 3rd International Workshop on Security in Cloud Computing. Association for Computing Machinery (ACM) (2015)

7. Chillotti, I., Gama, N., Georgieva, M., Izabachène, M.: Faster fully homomorphic encryption: bootstrapping in less than 0.1 seconds. In: Cheon, J.H., Takagi, T. (eds.) ASIACRYPT 2016. LNCS, vol. 10031, pp. 3–33. Springer, Heidelberg (2016). https://doi.org/10.1007/978-3-662-53887-6_1

8. Dai, W., Doroz, Y., Sunar, B.: Accelerating NTRU based homomorphic encryption using GPUS. In: 2014 IEEE High Performance Extreme Computing Conference (HPEC), pp. 1–6. IEEE (2014)

9. Dai, W., Sunar, B.: cuHE: a homomorphic encryption accelerator library. In: Pasalic, E., Knudsen, L.R. (eds.) BalkanCryptSec 2015. LNCS, vol. 9540, pp. 169–186. Springer, Cham (2016). https://doi.org/10.1007/978-3-319-29172-7_11

10. Ducas, L., Micciancio, D.: FHEW: bootstrapping homomorphic encryption in less than a second. In: Oswald, E., Fischlin, M. (eds.) EUROCRYPT 2015. LNCS, vol. 9056, pp. 617–640. Springer, Heidelberg (2015). https://doi.org/10.1007/978-3-662-46800-5_24

11. Fan, J., Vercauteren, F.: Somewhat practical fully homomorphic encryption. IACR Cryptology ePrint Archive 2012, p. 144 (2012)

12. Gentry, C., Halevi, S.: Implementing gentry's fully-homomorphic encryption scheme. In: Paterson, K.G. (ed.) EUROCRYPT 2011. LNCS, vol. 6632, pp. 129–148. Springer, Heidelberg (2011). https://doi.org/10.1007/978-3-642-20465-4_9

13. Gentry, C., Halevi, S., Smart, N.P.: Homomorphic evaluation of the AES circuit. In: Safavi-Naini, R., Canetti, R. (eds.) CRYPTO 2012. LNCS, vol. 7417, pp. 850–867. Springer, Heidelberg (2012). https://doi.org/10.1007/978-3-642-32009-5_49

14. Gentry, C., Sahai, A., Waters, B.: Homomorphic encryption from learning with errors: conceptually-simpler, asymptotically-faster, attribute-based. In: Canetti, R., Garay, J.A. (eds.) CRYPTO 2013. LNCS, vol. 8042, pp. 75–92. Springer, Heidelberg (2013). https://doi.org/10.1007/978-3-642-40041-4_5

15. Gentry, C., et al.: Fully homomorphic encryption using ideal lattices. In: STOC, vol. 9, pp. 169–178 (2009)

16. Migliore, V., Real, M.M., Lapotre, V., Tisserand, A., Fontaine, C., Gogniat, G.: Hardware/software co-design of an accelerator for FV homomorphic encryption scheme using Karatsuba algorithm. IEEE Trans. Comput. 1 (2016). https://doi.org/10.1109/TC.2016.2645204

17. Naehrig, M., Lauter, K., Vaikuntanathan, V.: Can homomorphic encryption be practical? In: Proceedings of the 3rd ACM workshop on Cloud Computing Security Workshop, pp. 113–124. ACM (2011)

18. Nethercote, N., Walsh, R., Fitzhardinge, J.: Building workload characterization tools with valgrind. In: 2006 IEEE International Symposium on Workload Characterization. Institute of Electrical and Electronics Engineers (IEEE), October 2006

19. Öztürk, E., Doröz, Y., Sunar, B., Savas, E.: Accelerating somewhat homomorphic evaluation using FPGAs. IACR Cryptology ePrint Archive 2015, p. 294 (2015)

20. Pollard, J.M.: The fast fourier transform in a finite field. Math. Comput. 25(114), 365–374 (1971)

21. Pöppelmann, T., Güneysu, T.: Towards practical lattice-based public-key encryption on reconfigurable hardware. In: Lange, T., Lauter, K., Lisoněk, P. (eds.) SAC 2013. LNCS, vol. 8282, pp. 68–85. Springer, Heidelberg (2014). https://doi.org/10.1007/978-3-662-43414-7_4

22. Rivest, R.L., Adleman, L., Dertouzos, M.L.: On data banks and privacy homomorphisms. Found. Secure Comput. 4(11), 169–180 (1978)

23. Sinha Roy, S., Järvinen, K., Vercauteren, F., Dimitrov, V., Verbauwhede, I.: Modular hardware architecture for somewhat homomorphic function evaluation. In: Güneysu, T., Handschuh, H. (eds.) CHES 2015. LNCS, vol. 9293, pp. 164–184. Springer, Heidelberg (2015). https://doi.org/10.1007/978-3-662-48324-4_9

24. Smart, N.P., Vercauteren, F.: Fully homomorphic encryption with relatively small key and ciphertext sizes. In: Nguyen, P.Q., Pointcheval, D. (eds.) PKC 2010. LNCS, vol. 6056, pp. 420–443. Springer, Heidelberg (2010). https://doi.org/10.1007/978-3-642-13013-7_25

25. Wang, W., Chen, Z., Huang, X.: Accelerating leveled fully homomorphic encryption using GPU. In: 2014 IEEE International Symposium on Circuits and Systems (ISCAS), pp. 2800–2803. IEEE (2014)

Controlled Homomorphic Encryption: Definition and Construction

Yvo Desmedt[1,2], Vincenzo Iovino[3(✉)], Giuseppe Persiano[4], and Ivan Visconti[5]

[1] University of Texas at Dallas, Richardson, USA
yvo.desmedt@utdallas.edu
[2] University College London, London, UK
[3] University of Luxembourg, Luxembourg City, Luxembourg
vinciovino@gmail.com
[4] DISA-MIS, University of Salerno, Fisciano, Italy
pino.persiano@unisa.it
[5] DIEM, University of Salerno, Fisciano, Italy
visconti@unisa.it

Abstract. Fully Homomorphic Encryption schemes (FHEs) and Functional Encryption schemes (FUNCTEs) have a tremendousimpact in cryptography both for the natural questions that they address and for the wide range of applications in which they have been (sometimes critically) used.

In this work we put forth the notion of a Controllable Homomorphic Encryption scheme (CHES), a new primitive that includes features of both FHEs and FUNCTEs. In a CHES it is possible (similarly to a FHE) to homomorphically evaluate a ciphertext $\mathsf{Ct} = \mathsf{Enc}(m)$ and a circuit C therefore obtaining $\mathsf{Enc}(C(m))$ but *only* if (similarly to a FUNCTE) a token for C has been received from the owner of the secret key.

We discuss difficulties in constructing a CHES and then show a construction based on any FUNCTE.

As a byproduct our CHES also represents a FUNCTE supporting the re-encryption functionality and in that respect improves existing solutions.

Keywords: Functional   encryption   ·   Non-malleability   ·   Fully homomorphic encryption

1 Introduction

Fully Homomorphic Encryption has received a lot of attention and even was mentioned in the New York Times. We first briefly argue that in many real life applications, Fully Homomorphic Encryption is *not* a very useful primitive. In particular we look at issues involving financial issues and issues that are money related.

For privacy reasons many utility bills and bank statements, sent electronically, are now encrypted. In practice such bills and other documents are based on

© International Financial Cryptography Association 2017
M. Brenner et al. (Eds.): FC 2017 Workshops 2017, LNCS 10323, pp. 107–129, 2017.
https://doi.org/10.1007/978-3-319-70278-0_7

standard sub-documents that have been carefully checked by the legal department of the utility corporation or the bank. The other parts are based on the amount due, or the transactions made by the bank's customer. Obviously, very different type of standard letters, checked by the legal department, are sent to customers who are not paying their bills, and in the worst case a disconnect letter is sent.

To maintain privacy as much as possible the original standard letters should be stored on the corporation's company under encrypted form. So, it seems that Fully Homomorphic Encryption is ideally suited to modify the standard letter to include the name and address of the customer and to also add other encrypted information, e.g., obtained from an electronic utility meter. We now explain why this is a bad idea.

Now that Podesta's (the chairman of the 2016 Hillary Clinton presidential campaign) e-mails were hacked many people have realized how vulnerable systems are. Moreover, similar phishing attacks have been used against large corporations. So, in case the computer used to make encrypted utility bills and bank statements is hacked and Fully Homomorphic Encryption is used, *then the hacker can completely change the letter*! Obviously, the legal department does not want to have potentially very offensive letters to be produced. In the case of manual editing of the standard file, digital signature could be used, but if many parties are authorized, then that would require to keep track of all changes made and to keep the digital signatures for these intermediately produced messages. We now briefly motivate our approach.

In our approach, we will avoid the aforementioned use of digital signatures. Instead, using a new primitive, we will restrict what changes can be made. So, no hacker, even having full control of the computer, will be able to drastically change the encrypted document. The worst that can happen is that the wrong (slightly modified) standard letter will be sent. However, in our system, if the status of the customer is maintained under encrypted form, it will even be impossible that the complete wrong standard letter is sent to the customer. Similar protecting mechanisms can be used such that in case of utility bill, the encrypted data provided by the meter has to be used.

In this paper we put forth the notion of a *controllable homomorphic encryption* scheme (CHES, in short) that blends together the notion of a fully homomorphic encryption scheme [15] (FHE, in short) and of a functional encryption scheme [4,11,17] (FUNCTE, in short). Specifically, like in a FHE, a CHES-ciphertext of plaintext m can be homomorphically transformed into a ciphertext of plaintext $C(m)$, for every efficiently computable function C; on the other hand, like in a FUNCTE, the homomorphic transformation can only be efficiently performed by a party that has a special *token* for function C that is released by the owner of the master secret key. Except for the token for C, no other secret information is needed to homomorphically transform a ciphertext according to function C.

Non-triviality. The following scheme is a straightforward (albeit inefficient) construction of a CHES derived from any standard public key encryption scheme $\mathcal{E}$ = (GenKey, Enc, Dec) and any secure signature scheme $\mathcal{S}$ = (SigKeyGen, Sign, Verify). The public key of the CHES consists of a pair (pk, vk) of a randomly generated public key pk of $\mathcal{E}$ and of a randomly generated verification key vk of $\mathcal{S}$. To encrypt message m, one simply computes an encryption of m with respect to key pk. The token for function C is simply a signature σ_C of C and to homomorphically transform ciphertext ct_0, one simply appends an encryption ct_1 of the pair (C, σ_C) to ct_0. The decryption function takes a pair of ciphertexts (ct_0, ct_1), decrypts both and obtains (m, C, σ_C). If σ_C is a correct signature of C, then the decryption function outputs $C(m)$; otherwise, it outputs $\perp$.

There is a clear drawback in the above construction: the size of the ciphertext depends on the size of the description of the function C. In this paper, to avoid triviality, we require ciphertext size and decryption time to be upper bounded by a polynomial of the security parameter and be independent of the function C. This is the same requirement that makes the construction of a FHE non-trivial [15].

1.1 Contribution

The contribution of this work consists of the following three steps. We introduce and define this new primitive, we discuss some interesting applications, and provide a construction based on any FUNCTE. Our main result is the above last step, indeed we will show a general procedure that builds a CHES starting from a general functional encryption scheme.

Limitations of FUNCTE*s w.r.t.* CHES*s.* At first, one might think that a CHES is just a special case of a functional encryption scheme: the token to transform an encryption of m into an encryption of $C(m)$ is simply a token for the function that first computes $C(m)$ and then re-encrypts the result. Such a direct construction suffers of two major problems.

Probabilistic and re-encryption functionalities. One first problem posed by this simple construction is that randomness must be used to construct the resulting ciphertext and this would require a notion of functional encryption for probabilistic functionalities proposed in two independent works. Alwen *et al.* [2] put forward a definition of randomized functional encryption but they are able to construct it only for very restricted classes of functionalities. In another work, Goyal *et al.* [18] propose functional encryption schemes for randomized functionalities for two different notions of security, both suffering from some limitation. The first one is simulation-based but stated in the *selective* model. This is the best one can hope for simulation-based security since, due to the impossibility result of Agrawal *et al.* [1] and Boneh *et al.* [4], for non-selective security it is necessary to put a bound on the number of queries the adversary can ask (see also Gorbunov *et al.* [17], De Caro *et al.* [10] and De Caro and Iovino [9]). The second definition they propose is indistinguishability-based but is affected by

the severe problem of forbidding the adversary to ask queries for computationally indistinguishable distributions, thus not providing any guarantee of security
in applications where the server is provided with a token for the re-encryption
function. Therefore, for the scope of our applications the solution of Goyal *et al.*
is not satisfactory unless one wants to resort to bounded security (i.e., putting a
bound on the number of ciphertexts and tokens generated by the system) that
represents a strong limitation. Instead, our approach does not suffer from this
problem. In fact, we are able to prove the security of our scheme under a notion
of security that (1) is *not* selective, (2) allows the adversary to ask an unbounded
number of queries and (3) does allow the adversary to request token for the re-
encryption function. We also mention that in the context of verifiable secure
outsourcing of computation, Barbosa and Farshim [3] have studied the concept
Delegatable Homomorphic Encryption (DFE) which is conceptually very similar
to CHES. The security of their construction of a DFE is based on the existence
FUNCTE that are CCA1 secure and on the existence of an FHE (in contrast,
we only require INDCPA secure FUNCTE). As a byproduct our CHES offers a
solution to the problem of providing a FUNCTE supporting the re-encryption
functionality that improves the previous works as discussed above.

Another more serious problem in using functional encryption naively is made
evident by looking at the following example. Suppose an adversary obtains a
token for the increment function $C(m) := m + 1$. Clearly, for every two messages
$m_1 \neq m_2$ the output range of the evaluation of the token for C are disjoint (as one
contains encryptions of $m_1 + 1$ and the other encryptions of $m_2 + 1$). This makes
the security requirement of the functional encryption scheme vacuous. Indeed,
security for functional encryption schemes is only with respect to adversaries that
obtain tokens for which the two challenge plaintexts give the same result and,
quite understandably, no guarantees is given for adversaries that have requested
and obtained tokens for which the two challenge plaintexts give different results[1].
Therefore, if the token for the innocent looking increment function is released,
all security disappears.

Tricks to construct a CHES. We obtain a CHES by solving the two major
problems of the above direct construction of a CHES from a FUNCTE. Concerning the first problem, we will make use of pseudorandom functions in order
to provide to the evaluation process a pseudorandom string to be used for re-
encryption. Concerning the second problem, we exploit the fact that even though
the two output ranges are disjoint they are still indistinguishable. Interestingly,
a similar observation could be used for functional encryption in order to have a
relaxed (and therefore easier to achieve) but still fully meaningful definition.

In sums, our construction considers as starting point the problematic construction described above and will leverage on various techniques in order to
obtain the desired security. Our construction is proved secure against an adversary that receives tokens for circuits of his choice after seeing the challenge

---

[1] Here we only consider game-based notions of security as simulation-based ones suffer
of more serious limitations [1,4,9,10,19].

ciphertext. We leave open the problem of constructing a CHES where the adversary can ask encryption and token queries in any order.

Targeted malleability. In a recent paper, Boneh et al. [5] put forward the notion of targeted malleability that generalizes the notion of non-malleability [12] by ensuring that the malleability of an encryption scheme is limited to a set of *legal* functions $\mathcal{F}$, specified in the public key. We note that, unlike in CHES, in targeted malleability the set $\mathcal{F}$ of legal functions is specified during the key-generation phase and then any party can efficiently homomorphically transform any ciphertext according to any function in $\mathcal{F}$ without receiving any secret information from the owner of the secret key. Thus the two primitives are quite different in scope. Boneh et al. [5] show how to transform any FHE scheme into one that offers targeted malleability based on the existence of succinct non-interactive arguments that are known to exist under non-falsifiable assumptions [20]. We are aware that such assumptions could ease the construction of a CHES but one of our goals is to avoid them.

We also notice that in their construction [5], ciphertexts obtained through homomorphic transformations can themselves be transformed again and this process can be repeated up to a constant number t of times; the value t must be specified during the generation of the public key that grows with t but the length of the ciphertexts is independent of t.

In this work, we do not concentrate on this property and give a construction of CHES in which the mauling procedure can only be applied to ciphertexts output by the encryption procedure. We mention though (and do not elaborate further) that our construction can be modified so that the homomorphic transformation procedure can be applied any constant number of times, starting from a ciphertext generated by the encryption procedure. We stress that in our case this number does not affect the length of the ciphertexts nor the one of the public key.

Application scenarios. The notion of a CHES finds natural applications in the problem of outsourcing computation on private data to an untrusted server.

In the first scenario we consider a user U that has one message m and stores it in encrypted form Ct on an untrusted server S using a CHES. At some later point, U wishes to compute value $C(m)$ and sends a CHES token Tok_C for C (i.e., the token that when applied on a ciphertext for m returns a ciphertext for $C(m)$). The server S applies the token Tok_C to Ct and returns the resulting ciphertext to U. If the server S is honest-but-curious, the above scheme guarantees that U gets the desired result without revealing anything about m (not even the value $C(m)$). The same would work with a FHE. However, a malicious server S could just pick an arbitrary value, encrypt it using the CHES and then return the value to U. Against such a dishonest adversary, we can use the standard trick of adding a MAC as follows. U sends S an encryption Ct of m and of a random value R (i.e., Ct is an encryption of the concatenation of m and R). To compute the value $C(m)$, for some circuit C, U picks an arbitrary value x and generates a token for the circuit that returns an encryption of $C(m)$ and of $F(R, x)$, where F is a pseudo-random family of functions[2]. In other words, the token encrypts $C(m)$ and a MAC of the fact that the right token was used to compute the result. Notice that this simple tweak would *not* give security against malicious servers in the above case based on a FHE and this shows that in some applications CHESs is conceptually stronger than FHEs.

As mentioned before, CHES also represents a FUNCTE supporting the re-encryption functionality and in that respect it improves existing solutions as discussed previously.

2   Definitions

Functional Encryption for Circuits. In this paper we use a special FUNCTE, which we call FE4C, that allows to compute any polynomial size circuit (see [13, 17]). Due to space constraints we defer to Appendix A the definition of FE4C and of its tag-based version and its security notion of IND-CPA Security that we use in our construction.

3   Controllable Homomorphic Encryption

In this section we define the notion of a *Controllable Homomorphic Encryption Scheme* (CHES).

Roughly speaking, in a CHES it is possible to homomorphically create a string that will be decrypted as $C(M)$ on input a ciphertext for M only if one holds a special token for the circuit C. Similarly to the compactness requirement of FHE, we require that the length of the string homomorphically computed be independent of the circuit.

Definition 1. *A* Controllable Homomorphic Encryption Scheme (CHES, in short) *is a tuple* CHE $=$ (CHE.Setup, CHE.KeyGen, CHE.Enc, CHE.HEval, CHE.Dec) *of efficient algorithms with the following syntax and that enjoys the following property of correctness.*

1. CHE.Setup$(1^\lambda, 1^n)$ *on input the* security parameter λ *and* length parameter n, *outputs* public *and* master secret *keys* (Pk, Msk).
2. CHE.KeyGen(Msk, C) *on input master secret key* Msk *for length parameter n and the description of an n-bit input and n-bit output circuit C, outputs token* Tok$_C$ *for circuit C.*
3. CHE.Enc(Pk, M) *on input public key* Pk *with length parameter n and plaintext $M \in \{0,1\}^n$, outputs a ciphertext* Ct.
4. CHE.HEval(Pk, Ct, Tok) *on input public key* Pk *for length parameter n, a ciphertext* Ct *for plaintext $M \in \{0,1\}^n$ and a token* Tok *for circuit C, outputs a string* Ct$'$ *of size independent of C.*

---

[2] The use of a PRF is needed to allow the use of more than one token for the same ciphertext; otherwise, a simple encryption of $C(m)$ concatenated to R would be sufficient.

5. $\mathsf{CHE.Dec}(\mathsf{Msk}, \mathsf{Ct}'')$ *on input the master secret key* Msk *and a string* Ct'' *outputs a string* $M \in \{0,1\}^n \cup \{\bot\}$.

For the correctness we require that $(\mathsf{CHE.Setup}, \mathsf{CHE.Enc}, \mathsf{CHE.Dec})$ *be an encryption scheme, and that there exists a negligible function* μ *such that for all* $n = \mathsf{poly}(\lambda)$, *for all* n-*bit input and* n-*bit output circuits* C, *and all plaintexts* $M \in \{0,1\}^n$ *it holds that:* $\Pr\left[\,\mathsf{CHE.Dec}(\mathsf{Msk}, \mathsf{HEval}(\mathsf{Pk}, \mathsf{Ct}, \mathsf{Tok}_C)) \neq C(M)\,\right] \leq \mu(\lambda)$, *where* $(\mathsf{Pk}, \mathsf{Msk}) \leftarrow \mathsf{Setup}(1^\lambda, 1^n)$, $\mathsf{Tok}_C \leftarrow \mathsf{KeyGen}(\mathsf{Msk}, C)$ *and* $\mathsf{Ct} \leftarrow \mathsf{Enc}(\mathsf{Pk}, M)$.

Composing tokens. In the definition of a CHES, the output of $\mathsf{CHE.HEval}$ is not required to be a valid ciphertext (that is, an output of $\mathsf{CHE.Enc}$) and correctness only requires it to be a valid input for $\mathsf{CHE.Dec}$. This means that the security definition does not necessarily need to tolerate an adversary that receives a token for a circuit C, an encryption of m and then computes an encryption of $C^i(m)$, for any $i > 0$. More in general, the security definition does not have to assume that an adversary is able to compose tokens.

We would like to point out that it is possible to formally define a CHES so that tokens could be composed. The requirement then for a successful adversary would be to output a ciphertext of $C(m_b)$ for a circuit C that is not the composition of the ones for which she received tokens. However efficiently proving such a fact could be difficult as it is a CO-NP statement.

Along these lines, we point out that the concept of targeted malleability as implemented in [5] allows composition of homomorphic transformations for a constant and fixed number of times (this allows to go-around CO-NP) using non-falsifiable knowledge extraction assumptions (these are needed to construct succinct extractable arguments that are needed for compactness). We finally point out that our construction can be modified to allow a constant and fixed number of compositions of homomorphic transformations, even though in the paper we do not elaborate further.

Given the above subtleties, from now on we consider a ciphertext as the output of the encryption function. While the output of the evaluation function is just a string.

3.1   Security of a CHES

As usual in encryption schemes, there are two flavors to measure the security of a CHES. The most interesting flavor is the non-malleable one, since it captures the idea of controlling the capability of mauling a ciphertext. We will therefore continue with the definition of an NM-CPA CHES, and the interested reader can find in Appendix B the notion of IND-CPA CHES, along with some expected implications concerning this notion.

NM-CPA security of a CHES *scheme.* We now consider a security definition for CHES that is the conceptually equivalent to the notion of NM-CPA security of plain encryption schemes. We formalize this notion of security for a CHES

CHE = (CHE.Setup, CHE.KeyGen, CHE.Enc, CHE.HEval, CHE.Dec) by means of games CHES-NMCPA-GAME$_{b,\mathcal{A}}^{\mathsf{CHE}}$, for $b = 0, 1$, between an adversary $\mathcal{A}$ and a challenger $\mathcal{CHE}.\mathcal{C}$.[3] The adversary $\mathcal{A}$ receives a randomly generated public key of CHE and can issue two types of queries to $\mathcal{CHE}.\mathcal{C}$: *encryption queries* and *token queries*. Below we formalize how queries are answered by $\mathcal{CHE}.\mathcal{C}$ and the output of the games.

CHES-NMCPA-GAME$_{b,\mathcal{A}}^{\mathsf{CHE}}(\lambda, n)$

Setup. $\mathcal{CHE}.\mathcal{C}$ computes $(\mathsf{Pk}, \mathsf{Msk}) \leftarrow \mathsf{CHE.Setup}(1^\lambda, 1^n)$ and runs $\mathcal{A}$ on input Pk.

Token Query. $\mathcal{CHE}.\mathcal{C}$ replies to a token query for a circuit C by returning $\mathsf{Tok}^C \leftarrow \mathsf{CHE.KeyGen}(\mathsf{Msk}, C)$.

i-th Encryption Query. $\mathcal{CHE}.\mathcal{C}$ replies to an encryption query (M_0^i, M_1^i) with $M_0^i \neq M_1^i$ and $|M_0^i| = |M_1^i|$, by returning $\mathsf{Ct} \leftarrow \mathsf{CHE.Enc}(\mathsf{Pk}, M_b^i)$.

Output of the Game. Let $(j, \mathsf{Ct}^\star, C)$ be $\mathcal{A}$'s output.

If all the following conditions hold:

1. $\mathcal{A}$ did not issue a token query for circuit C' that coincides with C on M_b^j.

2. $C(M_0^j) \neq C(M_1^j)$.

3. $\mathsf{CHE.Dec}(\mathsf{Msk}, \mathsf{Ct}^\star) = C(M_b^j)$.

4. $\mathsf{Ct}^\star$ is not a ciphertext obtained as a reply to an encryption query.

then the output is $C(M_b^j)$. Otherwise the output of the game is $\perp$.

The above definition captures the fact that the adversary manages to produce (see conditions 3 and 4) a new ciphertext of $C(M_b^j)$ (for otherwise, the adversary could issue encryptions queries for (M_0, M_1) and for $(C(M_0), C(M_1))$ and returns the ciphertext obtained as a reply to this second query; in case of a single ciphertext query, the adversary could set C equal to the identity function and return the ciphertext obtained as a reply to the encryption query (M_0, M_1)). For this to be a meaningful achievement, it must be that the circuit C gives different output for the two challenge plaintexts (see condition 2) (for otherwise, the ciphertext could have been obtained by simply giving in output $C(M_0^j) = C(M_1^j)$). Moreover, it is also required (see condition 1) that the adversary has not asked for a token for a function C' for which $C(M_b^j) = C'(M_b^j)$ (for otherwise, the ciphertext could have been obtained by simply applying the token).

Definition 2. *A CHES CHE is a* NM-CPA *secure CHES if for every PPT adversary $\mathcal{A}$ for all polynomially bounded $n = n(\lambda)$ we have that the following two ensembles are indistinguishable* $\{\text{CHES-NMCPA-GAME}_{0,\mathcal{A}}^{\mathsf{CHE}}(\lambda, n)\}$ *and* $\{\text{CHES-NMCPA-GAME}_{1,\mathcal{A}}^{\mathsf{CHE}}(\lambda, n)\}$. *A CHES CHE is* single-message NM-CPA

---

[3] Note that during the course of this work, we often use the term game when we actually mean a distribution.

secure *if it is* NM-CPA *secure with respect to all PPT adversaries* $\mathcal{A}$ *that ask exactly one encryption query.*

In Appendix C we show that any single-message NM-CPA-secure CHES is also NM-CPA-secure.

4   CHES from Functional Encryption

In this section, we describe an NM-CPA CHES CHE = (CHE.Setup, CHE. KeyGen, CHE.Enc, CHE.HEval, CHE.Dec). We stress that our security proof works only for an adversary that is required to first ask for an encryption query and then can ask for tokens.

In the description of CHE, we let FE = (FE.Setup, FE.Enc, FE.KeyGen, FE.Eval) be an IND-CPA secure non-rerandomizable[4] tag-based FE4C. For a CHES with n-bit plaintexts and security parameter λ, we use an FE for plaintexts of length n, auxiliary message of length $\lambda + 2$. In addition we let $\mathcal{F} = \{F(\cdot, \cdot)\}$ be a pseudorandom family of functions $F(\cdot, \cdot)$ (the first argument is the seed), and PKE = (Setup, Enc, Dec) be a public-key encryption scheme.

For sake of simplicity, we assume that secret keys of PKE with security parameter λ are exactly λ-bit long and that ciphertexts of n-bit messages computed with respect to public key with security parameter λ have length $\ell = \ell(\lambda, n)$. Also, not to overburden notation, we assume that the tag space T_λ of FE coincides with the seed space of F and that they both coincide with $\{0, 1\}^\lambda$. In addition, for an n-bit input and n-bit output circuit C, ℓ-bit string s, and public key FE.Pk of FE, we denote by $C_{s,\mathsf{FE.Pk}}$ the $(n + 2\lambda + 2)$-bit input circuit defined as follows:

- if $t = 0$ then $C_{s,\mathsf{FE.Pk}}(M, r, t, \mathsf{sk}) = \mathsf{FE.Enc}(\mathsf{FE.Pk}, (C(M), 0^\lambda, \perp, 0^\lambda); F(r, C))$,
- if $t = 1$ then $C_{s,\mathsf{FE.Pk}}(M, r, t, \mathsf{sk}) = \mathsf{Dec}(\mathsf{sk}, s)$,
- if $t = \perp$ then $C_{s,\mathsf{FE.Pk}}(M, r, t, \mathsf{sk}) = \perp$,

where $M \in \{0, 1\}^n$, $r, \mathsf{sk} \in \{0, 1\}^\lambda$ and $t \in \{0, 1, \perp\}$.

In what follows, we will drop FE.Pk from $C_{s,\mathsf{FE.Pk}}$ whenever it is clear from the context and simply write C_s.

Circuit C_s takes three types of plaintexts: *regular* plaintexts, corresponding to $t = 0$, which are the outputs of the encryption algorithm; *mauled* plaintexts, corresponding to $t = \perp$, which are outputs of the application of a token; *trapdoor* plaintexts, corresponding to $t = 1$, which are used only in the proof. For ciphertexts carrying regular plaintexts, the circuit C_s outputs a ciphertext for $C(m)$ and this captures the correct application (through the CHE.HEval algorithm) of a token for circuit C to an encrypted message. Notice that in this case the resulting ciphertext carries a mauled plaintext. For ciphertexts carrying mauled plaintexts, the circuit C_s outputs $\perp$ and this captures the (incorrect) application of a token to an already mauled message. For ciphertexts carrying a trapdoor

---

[4] In the proof, we give details of the impact of the transformation of Sect. 2 in case FE is re-randomizable.

plaintexts, C_s outputs a decryption of s with respect to the secret key that is part of the trapdoor plaintext. In the reduction of an adversary for CHE to an adversary for FE, trapdoor plaintexts are very useful because they force C_s to return a value that is independent of the actual input M, and thus can be used to contradict the security of FE (cfr., discussion in the Introduction). To do so the value s used in the generation of the tokens must be carefully chosen so to be indistinguishable from the ones output by algorithm CHE.KeyGen.

Algorithm CHE.Setup($1^\lambda, 1^n$).

1. Run algorithm FE.Setup on input $(1^\lambda, 1^{n+2\lambda+2})$ and obtain (FE.Pk, FE.Msk);
2. run algorithm Setup on input 1^λ and obtain (pk', sk');
3. set Pk = FE.Pk and Msk = (FE.Pk, FE.Msk, pk');
4. return (Pk, Msk).

Algorithm CHE.KeyGen(Msk, C).

1. set $s = $ Enc(pk', FE.Enc(FE.Pk, $(0^n, 0^\lambda, \bot, 0^\lambda)$))); notice that 0^n is the plaintext, $(0^\lambda, \bot)$ constitute the auxiliary message and 0^λ the tag.
2. set Tok = FE.KeyGen(FE.Msk, C_s);
3. return Tok.

Algorithm CHE.Enc(Pk, M).

1. Randomly select tag $r \in \{0,1\}^\lambda$;
2. run algorithm Setup on input 1^λ and obtain (pk, sk);
3. set Ct = FE.Enc(FE.Pk, $(M, r, 0, sk)$); notice that M is the plaintext, $(0, sk)$ is the auxiliary message and r is the tag.
4. return Ct.

Algorithm CHE.HEval(Pk, Ct, Tok) outputs FE.Eval(FE.Pk, Ct, Tok);

Algorithm CHE.Dec(Msk, Ct)

1. Set Tok = FE.KeyGen(FE.Msk, ID) where the circuit ID is defined in the following way: $\mathsf{ID}(x_1, x_2, x_3, x_4) = x_1$.
2. return FE.Eval(FE.Pk, Ct, Tok).

In our construction we are using the r component of a plaintext both as a tag and as the seed of the PRF that gives the randomness of the ciphertext resulting from the application of a token (see the definition of C_s). In case T_λ does not coincide with the seed space of the PRF then we add another value to be used as a seed of a PRF.

The correctness of the scheme follows by the correctness of FE and by the definition of C_s. In the next section we prove the following theorem.

Theorem 1. *Under the assumption of the existence of an* IND-CPA *secure functional encryption scheme for all circuits (*FE4C*), there exists a* NM-CPA *secure* CHES *secure against adversaries that ask all encryption queries before the token queries.*

Constructions of FE4C that are secure (according to Definition 4) when the adversary sees any polynomial number of tokens have recently been given in [6, 13, 14, 22].

4.1   Proof on NM-CPA Security

Here we prove the security of our scheme for adversaries that issues all token queries after the encryption query and issues exactly one encryption query (by Theorem 5 we get security against multi-message adversaries).

Assume that there exists such an adversary $\mathcal{A}$ that breaks the security of CHE for parameters λ and n; that is, there exists a distinguisher $\mathcal{D}$ such that, denoted by $p_b(\lambda, n)$ the probability that $\mathcal{D}$ outputs 1 when its input is sampled according to CHES-NMCPA-GAME$_{b,\mathcal{A}}^{\text{CHE}}(\lambda, n)$, $p_0(\lambda, n) \geq p_1(\lambda, n) + \mu(\lambda)$ for some non-negligible function $\mu(\cdot)$.

Based on $\mathcal{A}$, we build adversary $\mathcal{B}$ for FE for security parameter λ and length parameter $n + 2\lambda + 2$. $\mathcal{B}$ interacts with challenger $\mathcal{FE}.\mathcal{C}$ for FE to which $\mathcal{B}$ can issue encryption and token queries and runs internal copies of $\mathcal{A}$ and $\mathcal{D}$.

Adversary $\mathcal{B}$ tricks adversary $\mathcal{A}$ into believing it is interacting with $\mathcal{CHE}.\mathcal{C}$ by presenting a view that differs indistinguishably by the one offered by $\mathcal{CHE}.\mathcal{C}$ since the challenge ciphertext is trapdoor. Then, from $\mathcal{A}$'s output $\mathcal{B}$ manages to decrypt by obtaining from $\mathcal{FE}.\mathcal{C}$ a token for a function that is equivalent to decryption when applied to $\mathcal{A}$'s output but, nonetheless, gives the same value when applied to a ciphertext for one of the two challenge plaintexts output by $\mathcal{B}$. This therefore allows $\mathcal{B}$ to win in the security game of functional encryption. Next we formally describe how $\mathcal{B}$, $\mathcal{FE}.\mathcal{C}$, $\mathcal{D}$, and $\mathcal{A}$ interact.

Setup. $\mathcal{FE}.\mathcal{C}$ randomly selects $b \leftarrow \{0,1\}$, computes $(\text{FE.Pk}, \text{FE.Sk}) \leftarrow \text{FE.Setup}(1^\lambda, 1^{n+2\lambda+2})$ and runs $\mathcal{B}$ on input FE.Pk.
$\mathcal{B}$ computes $(\text{pk}', \text{sk}') \leftarrow \text{Setup}(1^\lambda)$, sets CHE.Pk = FE.Pk and runs $\mathcal{A}$ on input CHE.Pk.

Encryption query. When $\mathcal{A}$ issues an encryption query for the pair of messages (M_0, M_1), $\mathcal{B}$ proceeds as follows. $\mathcal{B}$ selects random $r_0, r_1 \leftarrow \{0,1\}^\lambda$, sets $m_0 = (M_0, r_0, 1, \text{sk}')$ and $m_1 = (M_1, r_1, 1, \text{sk}')$, and issues encryption query (m_0, m_1) to challenger $\mathcal{FE}.\mathcal{C}$.
We remind the reader that, for $b = 0, 1$, M_b is the plaintext, r_b is the tag and $(1, \text{sk}')$ is the auxiliary message.
Challenger $\mathcal{FE}.\mathcal{C}$ returns $\text{Ct} = \text{FE.Enc}(\text{FE.Pk}, m_b)$ and $\mathcal{B}$ returns ciphertext Ct to $\mathcal{A}$.

Token query. When $\mathcal{A}$ issues a token query for circuit C, $\mathcal{B}$ proceeds as follows. $\mathcal{B}$ sets $m_0^C = (C(M_0), 0^\lambda, \bot, 0^\lambda)$ and $m_1^C = (C(M_1), 0^\lambda, \bot, 0^\lambda)$, issues encryption query (m_0^C, m_1^C) to challenger $\mathcal{FE}.\mathcal{C}$ and receives Ct^C as a reply.
We remind the reader that, for $b = 0, 1$, $C(M_b)$ is the plaintext, 0^λ is the tag and $(\bot, 0^\lambda)$ is the auxiliary message.
$\mathcal{B}$ then sets $s = \text{Enc}(\text{pk}', \text{Ct}^C)$, issues a token query for C_s and receives token Tok^C as a reply. $\mathcal{B}$ returns Tok^C to $\mathcal{A}$.

Output. $\mathcal{A}$ outputs circuit G and $\text{Ct}^\star$ (claimed to be an encryption of $G(M_b)$).
Define circuit $\tilde{\text{ID}}(\cdot, \cdot, \cdot, \cdot)$ as follows:
  - if $(M, r) = (M_0, r_0)$ or $(M, r) = (M_1, r_1)$ then $\tilde{\text{ID}}(M, r, t, \text{sk}) = \bot$,
  - if $t = \bot$ then $\tilde{\text{ID}}(M, r, t, \text{sk}) = \bot$,
  - $\tilde{\text{ID}}(M, r, t, \text{sk}) = M$ otherwise.

$\mathcal{B}$ issues token query for $\tilde{\mathsf{ID}}$ and obtains token $\mathsf{Tok}^{\mathsf{ID}}$ as a reply from $\mathcal{FE}.\mathcal{C}$. $\mathcal{B}$ then computes $\mathsf{Out} = \mathsf{FE.Eval}(\mathsf{FE.Pk}, \mathsf{Ct}^\star, \mathsf{Tok}^{\mathsf{ID}})$. If $\mathcal{D}(\mathsf{Out}) = 1$ then $\mathcal{B}$ outputs 0 as its guess for b; $\mathcal{B}$ outputs 1 otherwise.

This ends the description of $\mathcal{B}$.

Handling re-randomizable FE4C. Before proceeding further, we briefly discuss the impact on algorithm $\mathcal{B}$ of the transformation outlined in Sect. 2 in case the underlying FE4C FE is re-randomizable. We remind the reader that, in order to enforce non-rerandomizability, the encryption algorithm is modified by using a signature verification key as tag and then adding a signature to the ciphertext. Tokens check that the signature that is part of the ciphertext is correct according to the verification key in the plaintext. Thus we modify the encryption algorithm so that one extra slot is used in the plaintext: $(M, r, t, sk, \mathsf{vk})$ where now (M, r) constitute the plaintext, (t, sk) the auxiliary message, and vk the tag. During the setup, algorithm $\mathcal{B}$ picks a pair $(\mathsf{vk}', \mathsf{sgk}')$ and the verification key vk' is used as tag in the ciphertexts returned as replies to encryption queries and the associated signing key sgk' is used to sign the ciphertexts. The function $\tilde{\mathsf{ID}}$ is then modified to return $\bot$ if $(M, r, \mathsf{vk}) = (M_0, r_0, \mathsf{vk}')$ or if $(M, r, \mathsf{vk}) = (M_1, r_1, \mathsf{vk}')$. We omit further details.

We continue the proof by showing that $\mathcal{B}$ is a legitimate adversary for FE. That is, we need to prove that for all the encryption queries (m_0, m_1) issued by $\mathcal{B}$ we have that m_0 and m_1 have the same length; and that, if $\mathcal{B}$ has issued token query for circuit C then for all encryption queries (m_0, m_1) we have that $C(m_0) = C(m_1)$. The first condition is easily seen to be satisfied. Let us verify that the second condition holds. For each token query for circuit C issued by $\mathcal{A}$, $\mathcal{B}$ issues token query for circuit C_s. $\mathcal{B}$, on the other hand, issues encryption queries for $(M_0, r_0, 1, \mathsf{sk}')$ and $(M_1, r_1, 1, \mathsf{sk}')$ while answering $\mathcal{A}$'s challenge query. In this case we have $C_s(M_0, r_0, 1, \mathsf{sk}') = C_s(M_1, r_1, 1, \mathsf{sk}') = \mathsf{Decrypt}(s, \mathsf{sk}')$. $\mathcal{B}$ also issues encryption queries while preparing the answer to $\mathcal{A}$'s token queries. In this case we have that $C_s(C(M_0), 0^\lambda, \bot, 0^\lambda) = C_s(C(M_1), 0^\lambda, \bot, 0^\lambda) = \bot$. A similar reasoning holds for the token query for $\tilde{\mathsf{ID}}$ issued by $\mathcal{B}$ in the output phase.

In the rest of the proof we will show that $\mathcal{A}$'s view in the interaction with $\mathcal{B}$ is indistinguishable from the view of $\mathcal{A}$ in CHES-NMCPA-GAME$^{\mathsf{CHE}}_{b,\mathcal{A}}(\lambda, n)$ (b is the random bit selected by $\mathcal{CHE}.\mathcal{C}$ in the Setup phase). We will then prove that, except with negligible probability, the value x computed by $\mathcal{B}$ is the same as the output of CHES-NMCPA-GAME$^{\mathsf{CHE}}_{b,\mathcal{A}}(\lambda, n)$ and thus the output of the distinguisher $\mathcal{D}$ can be used to correctly guess b. Specifically, we show that, for $\beta = 0, 1$, the view of $\mathcal{A}$ in CHES-NMCPA-GAME$^{\mathsf{CHE}}_{\beta,\mathcal{A}}$ is indistinguishable from the view of $\mathcal{A}$ in the interaction with $\mathcal{B}$ that is in turn interacting with $\mathcal{FE}.\mathcal{C}$ that sets $b = \beta$. We do so by considering a sequence of hybrid experiments and then showing that adjacent hybrid experiments are indistinguishable.

Hybrid H_0^β.

1. **Setup.** Set $(\mathsf{pk}, \mathsf{sk}) \leftarrow \mathsf{Setup}(1^\lambda), (\mathsf{pk}', \mathsf{sk}') \leftarrow \mathsf{Setup}(1^\lambda)$ and $(\mathsf{FE.Pk}, \mathsf{FE.Sk}) \leftarrow$ $\mathsf{FE.Setup}(1^\lambda, 1^{n+2\lambda+2})$. Randomly pick $r, r' \leftarrow \{0,1\}^\lambda$. Run $\mathcal{A}$ on input $\mathsf{CHE.Pk} = \mathsf{FE.Pk}$.
2. **Encryption query.** When $\mathcal{A}$ issues an encryption query for messages (M_0, M_1), return $\mathsf{Ct} = \mathsf{FE.Enc}(\mathsf{FE.Pk}, (M_\beta, r, 0, \mathsf{sk}))$.
3. **Token query.** When $\mathcal{A}$ issues a token query for circuit C, proceed as follows. Pick random $z \in \{0,1\}^\lambda$ and set $s' = \mathsf{FE.Enc}(\mathsf{FE.Pk}, (0^n, 0^\lambda, \perp, 0^\lambda); z)$. Set $s = \mathsf{Enc}(\mathsf{pk}', s')$. Set $\mathsf{Tok} = \mathsf{FE.KeyGen}(\mathsf{FE.Sk}, C_s)$ and return Tok.

For $\beta = 0, 1$, the view of $\mathcal{A}$ in H_0^β is the same as the view of $\mathcal{A}$ is $\mathsf{CHES\text{-}NMCPA\text{-}GAME}_{\beta,\mathcal{A}}^{\mathsf{CHE}}(\lambda, n)$.

Hybrid H_1^β. Hybrid H_1^β differs from H_0^β only in the way value s' is computed in the reply to token query for circuit C. Specifically, s' is computed by using pseudorandom value $F(r', C)$ instead of truly random value z. The formal description of H_1^β follows.

1. **Setup.** Set $(\mathsf{pk}, \mathsf{sk}) \leftarrow \mathsf{Setup}(1^\lambda), (\mathsf{pk}', \mathsf{sk}') \leftarrow \mathsf{Setup}(1^\lambda)$ and $(\mathsf{FE.Pk}, \mathsf{FE.Sk}) \leftarrow$ $\mathsf{FE.Setup}(1^\lambda, 1^{n+2\lambda+2})$. Randomly pick $r, r' \leftarrow \{0,1\}^\lambda$. Run $\mathcal{A}$ on input $\mathsf{CHE.Pk} = \mathsf{FE.Pk}$.
2. **Encryption query.** When $\mathcal{A}$ issues an encryption query for messages (M_0, M_1), return $\mathsf{Ct} = \mathsf{FE.Enc}(\mathsf{FE.Pk}, (M_\beta, r, 0, \mathsf{sk}))$.
3. **Token query.** When $\mathcal{A}$ issues a token query for circuit C, proceed as follows. Set $s' = \mathsf{FE.Enc}(\mathsf{FE.Pk}, (0^n, 0^\lambda, \perp, 0^\lambda); F(r', C))$. Set $s = \mathsf{Enc}(\mathsf{pk}', s')$ and return $\mathsf{Tok} = \mathsf{FE.KeyGen}(\mathsf{FE.Sk}, C_s)$.

Next we show that, by the pseudorandomness of F, the views of $\mathcal{A}$ in H_0^β and H_1^β are indistinguishable, for $\beta = 0, 1$. We do so by constructing an efficient simulator algorithm S that interacts with adversary $\mathcal{A}$ and has access to an oracle $\mathcal{O}$ that can be either random or pseudorandom. Depending on the nature of $\mathcal{O}$, S produces $\mathcal{A}$'s view in H_0^β or in H_1^β. This suffices for proving that $H_0^\beta \approx_c H_1^\beta$. Next we describe S.

1. **Setup.** S sets $(\mathsf{pk}, \mathsf{sk}) \leftarrow \mathsf{Setup}(1^\lambda), (\mathsf{pk}', \mathsf{sk}') \leftarrow \mathsf{Setup}(1^\lambda)$ and $(\mathsf{FE.Pk}, \mathsf{FE.Sk}) \leftarrow \mathsf{FE.Setup}(1^\lambda, 1^{n+2\lambda+2})$. Then S randomly picks $r, r' \leftarrow \{0,1\}^\lambda$. Finally, S runs $\mathcal{A}$ on input $\mathsf{CHE.Pk} = \mathsf{FE.Pk}$.
2. **Encryption query.** When $\mathcal{A}$ issues an encryption query for messages (M_0, M_1), S returns $\mathsf{Ct} = \mathsf{FE.Enc}(\mathsf{FE.Pk}, (M_\beta, r, 0, \mathsf{sk}))$.
3. **Token query.** When $\mathcal{A}$ issues a token query for circuit C, S proceeds as follows. S queries $\mathcal{O}$ on C, obtains z and sets $s' = \mathsf{FE.Enc}(\mathsf{FE.Pk}, (0^n, 0^\lambda, \perp, 0^\lambda); z)$. Finally, S sets $s = \mathsf{Enc}(\mathsf{pk}', s')$ and returns $\mathsf{Tok} = \mathsf{FE.KeyGen}(\mathsf{FE.Sk}, C_s)$.

Suppose the oracle $\mathcal{O}$ is in random mode; that is, all queries are answered with random values. Then it is easy to see that $\mathcal{A}$'s view is exactly the same as in H_0^β. On the other hand, suppose the oracle $\mathcal{O}$ is in pseudorandom mode; that is, $\mathcal{O}$ picks a random r' and, upon receiving C, it replies with $F(r', C)$. Then it is easy to see that $\mathcal{A}$'s view is exactly the same as in H_1^β.

Hybrid H_2^β. Hybrid H_2^β differs from H_1^β again in the randomness used to compute the value s'. Specifically, s' is computed by using as randomness the pseudorandom value $F(r, C)$ instead of $F(r', C)$. The formal description of H_2^β follows.

1. **Setup.** Set $(\mathsf{pk}, \mathsf{sk}) \leftarrow \mathsf{Setup}(1^\lambda)$, $(\mathsf{pk}', \mathsf{sk}') \leftarrow \mathsf{Setup}(1^\lambda)$ and $(\mathsf{FE.Pk}, \mathsf{FE.Sk}) \leftarrow \mathsf{FE.Setup}(1^\lambda, 1^{n+2\lambda+2})$. Randomly pick $r, r' \leftarrow \{0,1\}^\lambda$. Run $\mathcal{A}$ on input $\mathsf{CHE.Pk} = \mathsf{FE.Pk}$.
2. **Encryption query.** When $\mathcal{A}$ issues an encryption query for messages (M_0, M_1), return $\mathsf{Ct} = \mathsf{FE.Enc}(\mathsf{FE.Pk}, (M_\beta, r, 0, \mathsf{sk}))$.
3. **Token query.** When $\mathcal{A}$ issues a token query for circuit C, proceed as follows. Set $s' = \mathsf{FE.Enc}(\mathsf{FE.Pk}, (C(M_\beta), 0^\lambda, \bot, 0^\lambda); F(r, C))$. Set $s = \mathsf{Enc}(\mathsf{pk}', s')$ and return $\mathsf{Tok} = \mathsf{FE.KeyGen}(\mathsf{FE.Sk}, C_s)$.

Next we show that, by the IND-CPA security of encryption scheme Enc, the views of $\mathcal{A}$ in H_1^β and H_2^β are indistinguishable, for $\beta = 0, 1$. We do so by constructing an IND-CPA adversary S for Enc that uses $\mathcal{A}$ as a subroutine and interacts with a challenger $\mathcal{C}$ for Enc. S has the property that if $\mathcal{C}$ answers S's encryption queries for (s'_0, s'_1) by encrypting s'_0 then $\mathcal{A}$'s view is exactly the same as in H_1^β; on the other hand, if $\mathcal{C}$ answers encryption queries by encrypting s'_1 then $\mathcal{A}$'s view is exactly the same as in H_2^β. Thus, if the two views can be distinguished, S can break the IND-CPA security of Enc. Next we describe S.

1. **Setup.** S receives pk' from $\mathcal{C}$ and sets $(\mathsf{pk}, \mathsf{sk}) \leftarrow \mathsf{Setup}(1^\lambda)$. Moreover, S sets $(\mathsf{FE.Pk}, \mathsf{FE.Sk}) \leftarrow \mathsf{FE.Setup}(1^\lambda, 1^{n+2\lambda+2})$ and randomly picks $r, r' \leftarrow \{0,1\}^\lambda$. Finally, S runs $\mathcal{A}$ on input $\mathsf{CHE.Pk} = \mathsf{FE.Pk}$.
2. **Encryption query.** When $\mathcal{A}$ issues an encryption query for messages (M_0, M_1), S returns $\mathsf{Ct} = \mathsf{FE.Enc}(\mathsf{FE.Pk}, (M_\beta, r, 0, \mathsf{sk}))$.
3. **Token query.** When $\mathcal{A}$ issues a token query for circuit C, S proceeds as follows. S sets $s'_0 = \mathsf{FE.Enc}(\mathsf{FE.Pk}, (0^n, 0^\lambda, \bot, 0^\lambda); F(r', C))$, $s'_1 = \mathsf{FE.Enc}(\mathsf{FE.Pk}, (C(M_\beta), 0^\lambda, \bot, 0^\lambda); F(r, C))$ and issues an encryption query to $\mathcal{C}$ obtaining s. Finally, S returns $\mathsf{Tok} = \mathsf{FE.KeyGen}(\mathsf{FE.Sk}, C_s)$.

Hybrid H_3^β. Hybrid H_3^β differs from H_2^β in the way $\mathcal{A}$'s encryption queries are answered. Specifically, Ct is a ciphertext of $(M_\beta, r', 1, \mathsf{sk}')$ instead of $(M_\beta, r, 0, \mathsf{sk})$. The formal description of H_3^β follows.

1. **Setup.** Set $(\mathsf{pk}, \mathsf{sk}) \leftarrow \mathsf{Setup}(1^\lambda)$, $(\mathsf{pk}', \mathsf{sk}') \leftarrow \mathsf{Setup}(1^\lambda)$ and $(\mathsf{FE.Pk}, \mathsf{FE.Sk}) \leftarrow \mathsf{FE.Setup}(1^\lambda, 1^{n+2\lambda+2})$. Randomly pick $r, r' \leftarrow \{0,1\}^\lambda$. Run $\mathcal{A}$ on input $\mathsf{CHE.Pk} = \mathsf{FE.Pk}$.
2. **Encryption query.** When $\mathcal{A}$ issues an encryption query for messages (M_0, M_1), return $\mathsf{Ct} = \mathsf{FE.Enc}(\mathsf{FE.Pk}, (M_\beta, r', 1, \mathsf{sk}'))$.

3. **Token query.** When $\mathcal{A}$ issues a token query for circuit C, proceed as follows. Set $s' = \mathsf{FE.Enc}(\mathsf{FE.Pk}, (C(M_\beta), 0^\lambda, \bot, 0^\lambda); F(r, C))$. Set $s = \mathsf{Enc}(\mathsf{pk}', s')$ and return $\mathsf{Tok} = \mathsf{FE.KeyGen}(\mathsf{FE.Sk}, C_s)$.

Next we show that, by the IND-CPA security of functional encryption scheme FE, the views of $\mathcal{A}$ in H_2^β and H_3^β are indistinguishable, for $\beta = 0, 1$. We do so by constructing an IND-CPA adversary S for FE that uses $\mathcal{A}$ as a subroutine and interacts with a challenger $\mathcal{FE.C}$ for FE. S has the property that if $\mathcal{FE.C}$ answers S's encryption query for (m_0', m_1') by encrypting m_0' then $\mathcal{A}$'s view is exactly the same as in H_2^β; on the other hand, if $\mathcal{FE.C}$ answers encryption queries by encrypting m_1' then $\mathcal{A}$'s view is exactly the same as in H_3^β. Thus, if the two views can be distinguished, S can break the IND-CPA security of FE. Next we describe S.

1. **Setup.** S receives $\mathsf{FE.Pk}$ from $\mathcal{FE.C}$ and sets $(\mathsf{pk}, \mathsf{sk}) \leftarrow \mathsf{Setup}(1^\lambda)$, $(\mathsf{pk}', \mathsf{sk}') \leftarrow \mathsf{Setup}(1^\lambda)$. Moreover, S randomly picks $r, r' \leftarrow \{0, 1\}^\lambda$ and runs $\mathcal{A}$ on input $\mathsf{CHE.Pk} = \mathsf{FE.Pk}$.
2. **Encryption query.** When $\mathcal{A}$ issues an encryption query for messages (M_0, M_1), S sets

$$m_0 = (M_\beta, r, 0, \mathsf{sk}) \text{ and } m_1 = (M_\beta, r', 1, \mathsf{sk}')$$

   issues encryption query (m_0, m_1) to $\mathcal{FE.C}$, obtains Ct and returns it to $\mathcal{A}$.
3. **Token query.** When $\mathcal{A}$ issues a token query for circuit C, S proceeds as follows. S sets $s' = \mathsf{FE.Enc}(\mathsf{FE.Pk}, (C(M_\beta), 0^\lambda, \bot, 0^\lambda); F(r, C))$, $s = \mathsf{Enc}(\mathsf{pk}', s')$ and issues an encryption query to $\mathcal{FE.C}$ for a token for circuit C_s. Finally, S returns the token Tok received from $\mathcal{FE.C}$ to $\mathcal{A}$.

Firstly, we verify that S is a legal adversary for IND-CPA of FE. Indeed, S issues one encryption query for m_0 and m_1 and for all circuits C_s for which S asks for a token it holds that

$$C_s(m_0) = C_s(m_1) = \mathsf{FE.Enc}(\mathsf{FE.Pk}, (C(M_\beta), 0^n, \bot, 0^n); F(r, c)).$$

Clearly, if $\mathcal{FE.C}$ returns an encryption of m_0 then $\mathcal{A}$'s view is exactly as in H_2^β; if $\mathcal{FE.C}$ returns an encryption of m_1 then $\mathcal{A}$'s view is exactly as in H_3^β.

Hybrid H_4^β. Hybrid H_4^β differs from H_3^β for the randomness used to compute s'. Specifically, in H_3^β, $F(r, C)$ is used as randomness for computing s' whereas in H_4^β true randomness is used. The formal description of H_4^β follows.

1. **Setup.** Set $(\mathsf{pk}, \mathsf{sk}) \leftarrow \mathsf{Setup}(1^\lambda)$, $(\mathsf{pk}', \mathsf{sk}') \leftarrow \mathsf{Setup}(1^\lambda)$ and $(\mathsf{FE.Pk}, \mathsf{FE.Sk}) \leftarrow \mathsf{FE.Setup}(1^\lambda, 1^{n+2\lambda+2})$. Randomly pick $r, r' \leftarrow \{0, 1\}^\lambda$. Run $\mathcal{A}$ on input $\mathsf{CHE.Pk} = \mathsf{FE.Pk}$.
2. **Encryption query.** When $\mathcal{A}$ issues an encryption query for messages (M_0, M_1), return $\mathsf{Ct} = \mathsf{FE.Enc}(\mathsf{FE.Pk}, (M_\beta, r', 1, \mathsf{sk}'))$.

3. **Token query.** When $\mathcal{A}$ issues a token query for circuit C, proceed as follows. Randomly pick $z \leftarrow \{0,1\}^{\lambda}$ and set $s' = \mathsf{FE.Enc}(\mathsf{FE.Pk}, (C(M_{\beta}), 0^{\lambda}, \bot, 0^{\lambda}); z)$. Set $s = \mathsf{Enc}(\mathsf{pk}', s')$ and return $\mathsf{Tok} = \mathsf{FE.KeyGen}(\mathsf{FE.Sk}, C_s)$.

Notice that, for $\beta = 0, 1$, the view of $\mathcal{A}$ in H_4^{β} coincides with the view of $\mathcal{A}$ while interacting with $\mathcal{B}$. Moreover, by the pseudorandomness of F, H_3^{β} and H_4^{β} are indistinguishable.

$\mathcal{B}$'s *success probability.* Finally, we show that the probability that $\mathcal{B}$ correctly guesses b is at least $1/2 + \mu(\lambda)$ for a non-negligible function μ.

All it is left to show is that the string Out computed by $\mathcal{B}$ and then fed as input to $\mathcal{D}$ is indistinguishable from the output of $\mathsf{CHES\text{-}NMCPA\text{-}GAME}_{b,\mathcal{A}}^{\mathsf{CHE}}$. This is necessary since $\mathcal{B}$ does not have access to Msk and uses a token for function $\tilde{\mathsf{ID}}$ instead. However, observe that $\tilde{\mathsf{ID}}$ differs from the decryption function when the plaintext associated with $\mathsf{Ct}^{\star}$ is of the form $(M_b, r_b, t, \mathsf{sk})$ or $(M_{1-b}, r_{1-b}, t, \mathsf{sk})$ for some t and sk. In the first case, this means that $\mathcal{A}$ has managed to re-randomize a ciphertext for FE since it has produced a different ciphertext with the same plaintext M_b and the same tag r_b as the plaintext received from the encryption query. This, by hypothesis, occurs only with negligible probability. For the second case, observe that r_{1-b} is a random λ-bit string that is independent from $\mathcal{A}$'s view and thus the probability that $\mathcal{A}$ produces a ciphertext carrying r_{1-b} is negligible. We can thus conclude that the input provided by $\mathcal{A}$ to $\mathcal{D}$ is indistinguishable from its input in $\mathsf{CHES\text{-}NMCPA\text{-}GAME}$. Therefore, by the hypothesis on $\mathcal{D}$ we can conclude that $\mathcal{B}$ breaks the IND-CPA security of FE.

5   Conclusions and Future Work

In this work we have put forth the notion of a CHES, a new primitive that includes features of both FHEs and FUNCTEs. The proposed CHES construction requires rather strong assumptions. We leave as open problem the possibility of achieving CHES from weaker assumptions or proving that the existence of CHES is equivalent to, e.g., iO.

Acknowledgements. Vincenzo Iovino is supported by a FNR CORE grant (no. FNR11299247) of the Luxembourg National Research Fund. Part of this work was done while Vincenzo Iovino was at the University of Warsaw and was supported by the WELCOME/2010-4/2 grant funded within the framework of the EU Innovative Economy Operational Programme. Ivan Visconti was supported in part by "GNCS - INdAM" and EU COST Action IC1306.

A   Syntax and Security of Functional Encryption for Circuits

Definition 3 (FE4C: Functional Encryption Scheme for Circuits). *A Functional Encryption scheme for Circuits is a tuple* $\mathsf{FE} = (\mathsf{FE.Setup}, \mathsf{FE.KeyGen}, \mathsf{FE.Enc}, \mathsf{FE.Eval})$ *of 4 efficient algorithms with the following syntax:*

1. FE.Setup($1^\lambda, 1^n$) *outputs* public *and* master secret *keys* (Pk, Msk) *for* security parameter λ *and* length parameter n.
2. FE.KeyGen(Msk, C), *on input a master secret key* Msk *for length parameter* n *and an n-bit input and n-bit output circuit* C, *outputs* token Tok_C.
3. FE.Enc(Pk, M), *on input public key* Pk *for length parameter* n *and* plaintext $M \in \{0,1\}^n$, *outputs* ciphertext Ct.
4. FE.Eval(Pk, Ct, Tok) *outputs* $B \in \{0,1\}^n \cup \{\perp\}$.

For the correctness *condition we require that for all n-bit input and n-bit output circuits C, all $M \in \{0,1\}^n$, and for* (Pk, Msk) $\leftarrow$ Setup($1^\lambda, 1^n$), Tok $\leftarrow$ KeyGen(Msk, C) *and* Ct $\leftarrow$ Enc(Pk, M), *the probability that* Eval(Pk, Ct, Tok) $\neq C(M)$ *is negligible in λ.*

We formalize security for a FE4C FE by means of the following game FE-INDCPA-GAME between a challenger $\mathcal{FE}.\mathcal{C}$ and an adversary $\mathcal{A}$ that can issue two types of queries to $\mathcal{FE}.\mathcal{C}$, *encryption queries* and *token queries*. The definition is essentially the one in [4].

FE-INDCPA-GAME^{F}E$_\mathcal{A}(\lambda, n)$

Setup. $\mathcal{FE}.\mathcal{C}$ generates (Pk, Msk) $\leftarrow$ FE.Setup($1^\lambda, 1^n$), selects random $b \in \{0,1\}$ and runs $\mathcal{A}$ on input Pk.

Token Query. $\mathcal{FE}.\mathcal{C}$ on input an n-bit input n-bit output circuit C, computes and returns Tok $\leftarrow$ FE.KeyGen(Msk, C).

Encryption Query. $\mathcal{FE}.\mathcal{C}$, on input a pair (m_0, m_1) of plaintexts, answers by computing and returning FE.Enc(Pk, m_b).

Output of the Game. Let b' the output of $\mathcal{A}$. Then the game outputs 1 if and only if
1. $b = b'$;
2. for all encryption queries (m_0, m_1), it holds that m_0 and m_1 are of the same length;
3. for all token queries C and for all encryption queries (m_0, m_1), it holds that $C(m_0) = C(m_1)$.

Definition 4. *We say that a FE4C FE is* IND-CPA *secure if for all PPT adversaries $\mathcal{A}$ there exists a negligible function μ such that*

$$\text{Prob}[\text{FE-INDCPA-GAME}^{\text{FE}}_\mathcal{A}(\lambda) = 1] \leq 1/2 + \mu(\lambda).$$

Tag-Based Non-rerandomizable Functional Encryption. In our main construction we use a special type of FE4C in which ciphertexts cannot be rerandomized. More precisely, we consider *tag-based* FE4C in which the encryption algorithm for n-bit plaintext m and security parameter λ takes two extra arguments: a *tag* τ from the set T_λ of λ-bit tags and an *auxiliary message* of length n_1. It is easy to see how any FE4C can be modified to accommodate tags and auxiliary messages at the expenses of increasing the length parameter n. In a *non-rerandomizable tag-based* FE4C, given a ciphertext for an adversarially chosen plaintext m and auxiliary message aux and a random tag τ, no adversary can produce another ciphertext for the same plaintext m and the same tag. Specifically, we consider the following security game between a challenger $\mathcal{FE.C}$ and and adversary $\mathcal{A}$ that can issue one single encryption query.

$\mathrm{RERANDOM}_{\mathcal{A}}^{\mathsf{TFE}}(\lambda, n, n_1)$

Setup. $\mathcal{FE.C}$ generates $(\mathsf{Pk}, \mathsf{Msk}) \leftarrow$ $\mathsf{TFE.Setup}(1^\lambda, 1^n, 1^{n_1})$ and runs $\mathcal{A}$ on input Pk.

Token Query. $\mathcal{FE.C}$ on input an $(n + n_1 + \lambda)$-bit input $(n + n_1 + \lambda)$-bit output circuit C, computes and returns $\mathsf{Tok} \leftarrow \mathsf{TFE.KeyGen}(\mathsf{Msk}, C)$.

Encryption Query. $\mathcal{FE.C}$, on input plaintext m and auxiliary message aux, picks a random tag τ from the set T_λ of tags of length λ and returns a ciphertext $\mathsf{Ct} = \mathsf{TFE.Enc}(\mathsf{Pk}, m, \mathsf{aux}, \tau)$ with tag τ.

Output of the Game. Let $\mathsf{Ct}^\star$ the output of $\mathcal{A}$. Then the game outputs 1 if and only if
1. $\mathsf{Ct}^\star \neq \mathsf{Ct}$;
2. $\mathsf{TFE.Dec}(\mathsf{Msk}, \mathsf{Ct}^\star) = (m', \mathsf{aux}', \tau')$ with $m' = m$ and $\tau = \tau'$;

We say that a tag-based FE4C TFE is non-rerandomizable if for all PPT adversaries $\mathcal{A}$ and for n and n_1 polynomially bounded in λ there exists a negligible function μ such that

$$\mathrm{Prob}[\mathrm{RERANDOM}_{\mathcal{A}}^{\mathsf{TFE}}(\lambda, n, n_1) = 1] \leq \mu(\lambda).$$

It is easy to see that any tag-based FE4C can be transformed into a non-rerandomizable one by using a secure signature scheme. More precisely, we define the encryption algorithm $\mathsf{TFE.Enc}$ that encrypts plaintext m and aux, to pick a random pair of $(\mathsf{vk}, \mathsf{sgk})$ of verification and signing key for a secure signature scheme $(\mathsf{SigKeyGen}, \mathsf{Sign}, \mathsf{Verify})$ and m, aux are encrypted using vk as tag obtaining Ct. Finally, a signature σ_{Ct} of Ct is computed using the signing key sgk and the resulting ciphertext consists of the pair $(\mathsf{Ct}, \sigma_{\mathsf{Ct}})$. Tokens for function C on ciphertext $(\mathsf{Ct}, \sigma_{\mathsf{Ct}})$ first verify σ_{Ct} and, if successful, proceed to compute $C(m, \mathsf{aux})$. We observe that $\mathcal{A}$ either changes the verification key (and thus changes the tag) or keeps the same verification key but then it has to sign a new ciphertext or compute a new signature (which would violate the security of the signature scheme).

B   IND-CPA CHES

IND-CPA security of a CHES We formalize the notion of security equivalent to IND-CPA for a CHES CHE = (CHE.Setup, CHE.KeyGen, CHE.Enc, CHE.HEval, CHE.Dec) by means of game CHES-INDCPA-GAME between an adversary $\mathcal{A}$ and a challenger $\mathcal{CHE.C}$. The adversary $\mathcal{A}$ receives a randomly generated public key of CHE and can issue two types of queries to $\mathcal{CHE.C}$: *encryption queries* and *token queries*. Below we formalize how queries are answered by $\mathcal{CHE.C}$ and what it means for $\mathcal{A}$ to win the game.

CHES-INDCPA-GAME$_{\mathcal{A}}^{\mathsf{CHE}}(\lambda, n)$

Setup. $\mathcal{CHE.C}$ computes (Pk, Msk) ← CHE.Setup($1^\lambda, 1^n$), selects a random $b \in \{0, 1\}$ and runs $\mathcal{A}$ on input Pk.

Token Query. $\mathcal{CHE.C}$ replies to a token query for a circuit C by returning Tok^C ← CHE.KeyGen(Msk, C).

i-th Encryption Query. $\mathcal{CHE.C}$ replies to encryption query (M_0^i, M_1^i) with $|M_0^i| = |M_1^i|$, by returning Ct ← CHE.Enc(Pk, M_b^i).

Output of the Game. Let b' be $\mathcal{A}$'s output. Return 1 (meaning that $\mathcal{A}$ has won) iff $b = b'$.

Definition 5. *A* CHES CHE *is* IND-CPA *secure if for every PPT adversary $\mathcal{A}$, there exists a negligible function $\mu(\cdot)$ such that* $\Pr\left[\text{CHES-INDCPA-GAME}_{\mathcal{A}}^{\mathsf{CHE}}(\lambda, n) = 1\right] \leq 1/2 + \mu(\lambda)$.

A CHES CHE *is* single-message IND-CPA *secure if it is IND-CPA secure for all PPT adversaries $\mathcal{A}$ asking exactly one encryption query.*

B.1   Implications

IND-CPA CHES *from LWE* Noticing that any fully homomorphic encryption scheme [16] is also an IND-CPA CHES, we have that the results of [7,8] prove the following theorem.

Theorem 2. *Assuming LWE, there exists an* IND-CPA-*secure* CHES.

NM-CPA CHES $\Rightarrow$ *IND-CPA* CHES Here we show the natural implication that every NM-CPA CHES is also an IND-CPA CHES.

Theorem 3. *Any* NM-CPA-*secure* CHES *is also* IND-CPA-*secure.*

Proof. The proof is by contradiction. Assume there exists a PPT adversary $\mathcal{A}$ IND-CPA that is able to guess the challenge bit with probability at least $1/2 + \mathsf{nneg}(\lambda)$, for some non-negligible function $\mathsf{nneg}(\cdot)$ and consider the following adversary $\mathcal{A}'$. $\mathcal{A}'$ interacts with a challenger for NM-CPA, runs an internal copy of $\mathcal{A}$ and uses the challenger to answer $\mathcal{A}$'s queries. When $\mathcal{A}$ outputs b, $\mathcal{A}'$ outputs with the triple $(1, ct^*, C^*)$, where ct^* is an encryption of $C^*(M_b^1)$ and C^* is a circuit that satisfies the condition of the definition. Specifically, $C^*(m) = m + i$ where i is the smallest integer for which C^* satisfies the condition of the definition (that is $C^*(M_0^1) \neq C^*(M_1^1)$ and none of the tokens asked by $\mathcal{A}$ coincides with C^* on messages M_0^1 and M_1^1). Since the number of token queries is polynomially bounded, the circuit C^* can be efficiently found.

IND-CPA: *single message vs many messages* Here we show that in order to prove the IND-CPA and NM-CPA security of a construction for a CHES, it is sufficient to concentrate on the case of an adversary that asks for one encryption query only. Indeed, we prove that any single-message IND-CPA-secure CHES is also IND-CPA and similarly for NM-CPA security.

Theorem 4. *Any single-message IND-CPA-secure CHES is also IND-CPA.*

Proof. Consider a single-message IND-CPA CHES CHE and suppose by contradiction that there exists an adversary $\mathcal{A}$ against its (many-message) IND-CPA security that succeeds with probability $1/2 + \mathsf{nneg}(\lambda)$ for some non-negligible function $\mathsf{nneg}(\cdot)$. We construct an adversary $\mathcal{A}'$ against the single-message IND-CPA security of CHE as follows. $\mathcal{A}'$ behaves as a proxy between the challenger of single-message IND-CPA and $\mathcal{A}$ except for encryption queries and answers. Specifically, $\mathcal{A}'$ selects a random bit b' and a random index j' in $\{1, \ldots, q\}$, where q is an upper bound on the number of queries of $\mathcal{A}$ and will behave as a proxy between $\mathcal{A}$ and the challenger for all token queries and for j'-th encryption query; for the remaining encryption queries (M_0^i, M_1^i) instead, $\mathcal{A}'$ replies by computing an encryption of $M_{b'}^i$. Finally, $\mathcal{A}'$ outputs the same bit that $\mathcal{A}$ outputs.

Observe that the success probability of $\mathcal{A}$ is equal to $1/2(S_0 + S_1)$, where we let S_b denote the success probability of $\mathcal{A}$ when the challenger chooses bit b. Therefore we have that $1/2(S_0 + S_1) \geq 1/2 + \mathsf{nneg}(\lambda)$.

Now consider the probability that $\mathcal{A}$ outputs the same bit b chosen by the challenger but in an experiment where for a randomly chosen challenge ciphertext the value $\bar{b}$ is used instead of b, and let us denote such a probability by T_b. Notice that, for $b = 0, 1$, $T_b \geq S_b - \mu(\lambda)$ for some negligible function μ, for otherwise we can trivially break the single-message IND-CPA security of CHE.

Noticing that with probability $1/2$ it holds that $b = b'$, we have that the success probability of $\mathcal{A}'$ is $S_0 + S_1$ with probability $1/2$, and $T_0 + T_1$ with probability $1/2$.

Summing up, the success probability of $\mathcal{A}'$ can be computed as follows: $\frac{S_0 + S_1 + T_0 + T_1}{2} \geq 1/2 + \mathsf{nneg}'(\lambda)$ for some non-negligible function nneg'.

C   Single-Message vs Multi-Message NM-CPA CHES

Theorem 5. *Any single-message NM-CPA-secure CHES is also NM-CPA-secure.*

Proof. Let CHE be a single-message NM-CPA-secure CHES. Assume by contradiction that there exists a successful adversary $\mathcal{A}$ for NM-CPA security and an efficient distinguisher $\mathcal{D}$ that distinguishes

$$\text{CHES-NMCPA-GAME}_{0,\mathcal{A}}^{\text{CHE}}(\lambda, n) \text{ and } \text{CHES-NMCPA-GAME}_{1,\mathcal{A}}^{\text{CHE}}(\lambda, n).$$

We now reduce $\mathcal{A}$ to an adversary $\mathcal{A}'$ for single-message NM-CPA security of CHES. The reduction is similar to the one given in [21]. Let $q > 1$ be an upper bound on the the number of encryption queries made by $\mathcal{A}$. Consider the game $\text{CHES-NMCPA-GAME}_{J,\mathcal{A}}^{\text{CHE}}(\lambda, n)$ indexed by vector $J = (b_1, \ldots, b_q)$ that specifies that the j-th encryption query is answered by encrypting $M_{b_j}^j$. For $j = 0, \ldots, q$, we define vector $J_j = (1, \ldots, 1, 0, 0, \ldots, 0)$ as the vector whose first j components are 1 and the remaining components are 0. We can now run hybrid arguments since $\text{CHES-NMCPA-GAME}_{0,\mathcal{A}}^{\text{CHE}}(\lambda, n)$ corresponds to $\text{CHES-NMCPA-GAME}_{J_0,\mathcal{A}}^{\text{CHE}}(\lambda, n)$ and

$\text{CHES-NMCPA-GAME}_{1,\mathcal{A}}^{\text{CHE}}(\lambda, n)$ corresponds   to   CHES-NMCPA-$\text{GAME}_{J_q,\mathcal{A}}^{\text{CHE}}(\lambda, n)$. Since $\mathcal{D}$ distinguishes

$$\text{CHES-NMCPA-GAME}_{J_0,\mathcal{A}}^{\text{CHE}}(\lambda, n) \text{ and } \text{CHES-NMCPA-GAME}_{J_q,\mathcal{A}}^{\text{CHE}}(\lambda, n),$$

there exists $j \in \{0, \ldots, q - 1\}$ such that $\mathcal{D}$ distinguishes between

$$\text{CHES-NMCPA-GAME}_{J_j,\mathcal{A}}^{\text{CHE}}(\lambda, n) \text{ and } \text{CHES-NMCPA-GAME}_{J_{j+1},\mathcal{A}}^{\text{CHE}}(\lambda, n).$$

We can therefore use $\mathcal{D}$ along with adversary $\mathcal{A}$ to contradict single-message NM-CPA security of CHE as follows. $\mathcal{A}'$ behaves as proxy between the challenger and $\mathcal{A}$ for the token queries. Instead encryption queries are handled as follows. $\mathcal{A}'$ selects a random $j' \in \{0, \ldots, q - 1\}$ and forwards to the challenger the j'-th encryption query $(M_0^{j'}, M_1^{j'})$ received from $\mathcal{A}$, and forwards to $\mathcal{A}$ the corresponding answer received from the challenger. Instead, for all remaining encryption queries (M_0^i, M_1^i), $\mathcal{A}'$ answers on its own by sending an encryption of M_1^i when $i < j'$ and of M_0^i when $i > j'$.

Assume $j = j'$. Notice that when the challenger encrypts M_0^j, the above game corresponds to

$$\text{CHES-NMCPA-GAME}_{J_j,\mathcal{A}}^{\text{CHE}}(\lambda, n)$$

while when the challenger encrypts M_1^j, the above game corresponds to

$$\text{CHES-NMCPA-GAME}_{J_{j+1},\mathcal{A}}^{\text{CHE}}(\lambda, n).$$

By conditioning on the event that $j = j'$ we conclude observing that therefore $\mathcal{D}$ distinguishes $\text{CHES-NMCPA-GAME}_{0,\mathcal{A}'}^{\text{CHE}}(\lambda', n)$ from CHES-NMCPA-$\text{GAME}_{1,\mathcal{A}'}^{\text{CHE}}(\lambda, n)$.

References

1. Agrawal, S., Gorbunov, S., Vaikuntanathan, V., Wee, H.: Functional encryption: new perspectives and lower bounds. In: Canetti, R., Garay, J.A. (eds.) CRYPTO 2013. LNCS, vol. 8043, pp. 500–518. Springer, Heidelberg (2013). https://doi.org/10.1007/978-3-642-40084-1_28

2. Alwen, J., Barbosa, M., Farshim, P., Gennaro, R., Gordon, S.D., Tessaro, S., Wilson, D.A.: On the relationship between functional encryption, obfuscation, and fully homomorphic encryption. In: Stam, M. (ed.) IMACC 2013. LNCS, vol. 8308, pp. 65–84. Springer, Heidelberg (2013). https://doi.org/10.1007/978-3-642-45239-0_5

3. Barbosa, M., Farshim, P.: Delegatable homomorphic encryption with applications to secure outsourcing of computation. In: Dunkelman, O. (ed.) CT-RSA 2012. LNCS, vol. 7178, pp. 296–312. Springer, Heidelberg (2012). https://doi.org/10.1007/978-3-642-27954-6_19

4. Boneh, D., Sahai, A., Waters, B.: Functional encryption: definitions and challenges. In: Ishai, Y. (ed.) TCC 2011. LNCS, vol. 6597, pp. 253–273. Springer, Heidelberg (2011). https://doi.org/10.1007/978-3-642-19571-6_16

5. Boneh, D., Segev, G., Waters, B.: Targeted malleability: homomorphic encryption for restricted computations. In: ITCS, pp. 350–366 (2012)

6. Boyle, E., Chung, K.-M., Pass, R.: On extractability obfuscation. In: Lindell, Y. (ed.) TCC 2014. LNCS, vol. 8349, pp. 52–73. Springer, Heidelberg (2014). https://doi.org/10.1007/978-3-642-54242-8_3

7. Brakerski, Z., Gentry, C., Vaikuntanathan, V.: (Leveled) fully homomorphic encryption without bootstrapping. In: ITCS, pp. 309–325 (2012)

8. Brakerski, Z., Vaikuntanathan, V.: Efficient fully homomorphic encryption from (Standard) LWE. In: FOCS, pp. 97–106 (2011)

9. De Caro, A., Iovino, V.: On the power of rewinding simulators in functional encryption. Des. Codes Crypt. **84**, 1–27 (2016)

10. De Caro, A., Iovino, V., Jain, A., O'Neill, A., Paneth, O., Persiano, G.: On the achievability of simulation-based security for functional encryption. In: Canetti, R., Garay, J.A. (eds.) CRYPTO 2013. LNCS, vol. 8043, pp. 519–535. Springer, Heidelberg (2013). https://doi.org/10.1007/978-3-642-40084-1_29

11. Desmedt, Y.: Computer security by redefining what a computer is. In: Proceedings on the 1992–1993 Workshop on New Security Paradigms, NSPW 1992–1993, pp. 160–166. ACM, New York (1993)

12. Dolev, D., Dwork, C., Naor, M.: Non-malleable cryptography. In: 23rd Annual ACM Symposium on Theory of Computing, New Orleans, Louisiana, USA, 6–8 May 1991, pp. 542–552. ACM Press (1991)

13. Garg, S., Gentry, C., Halevi, S., Raykova, M., Sahai, A., Waters, B.: Candidate indistinguishability obfuscation and functional encryption for all circuits. In: 54th Annual IEEE Symposium on Foundations of Computer Science, FOCS 2013, Berkeley, CA, USA, October 26–29 2013, pp. 40–49. IEEE Computer Society (2013)

14. Garg, S., Gentry, C., Halevi, S., Zhandry, M.: Functional encryption without obfuscation. In: Kushilevitz, E., Malkin, T. (eds.) TCC 2016. LNCS, vol. 9563, pp. 480–511. Springer, Heidelberg (2016). https://doi.org/10.1007/978-3-662-49099-0_18

15. Gentry, C.: A fully homomorphic encryption scheme. Ph.D. thesis, Stanford University (2009). crypto.stanford.edu/craig

16. Gentry, C.: Fully homomorphic encryption using ideal lattices. In: Mitzenmacher, M. (ed.) 41st Annual ACM Symposium on Theory of Computing, Bethesda, Maryland, USA, 31 May–2 June 2009, pp. 169–178. ACM Press (2009)

17. Gorbunov, S., Vaikuntanathan, V., Wee, H.: Functional encryption with bounded collusions via multi-party computation. In: Safavi-Naini, R., Canetti, R. (eds.) CRYPTO 2012. LNCS, vol. 7417, pp. 162–179. Springer, Heidelberg (2012). https://doi.org/10.1007/978-3-642-32009-5_11
18. Goyal, V., Jain, A., Koppula, V., Sahai, A.: Functional encryption for randomized functionalities. In: Dodis, Y., Nielsen, J.B. (eds.) TCC 2015. LNCS, vol. 9015, pp. 325–351. Springer, Heidelberg (2015). https://doi.org/10.1007/978-3-662-46497-7_13
19. Iovino, V., Żebroski, K.: Simulation-based secure functional encryption in the random oracle model. In: Lauter, K., Rodríguez-Henríquez, F. (eds.) LATINCRYPT 2015. LNCS, vol. 9230, pp. 21–39. Springer, Cham (2015). https://doi.org/10.1007/978-3-319-22174-8_2
20. Naor, M.: On cryptographic assumptions and challenges. In: Boneh, D. (ed.) CRYPTO 2003. LNCS, vol. 2729, pp. 96–109. Springer, Heidelberg (2003). https://doi.org/10.1007/978-3-540-45146-4_6
21. Pass, R., Shelat, A., Vaikuntanathan, V.: Construction of a non-malleable encryption scheme from any semantically secure one. In: Dwork, C. (ed.) CRYPTO 2006. LNCS, vol. 4117, pp. 271–289. Springer, Heidelberg (2006). https://doi.org/10.1007/11818175_16
22. Waters, B.: A punctured programming approach to adaptively secure functional encryption. In: Gennaro, R., Robshaw, M. (eds.) CRYPTO 2015. LNCS, vol. 9216, pp. 678–697. Springer, Heidelberg (2015). https://doi.org/10.1007/978-3-662-48000-7_33

Bitcoin and Blockchain Research

ValueShuffle: Mixing Confidential Transactions for Comprehensive Transaction Privacy in Bitcoin

Tim Ruffing[1]([✉]) and Pedro Moreno-Sanchez[2]

[1] Saarland University, Saarbrücken, Germany
tim.ruffing@mmci.uni-saarland.de
[2] Purdue University, West Lafayette, USA
pmorenos@purdue.edu

Abstract. The public nature of the blockchain has been shown to be a severe threat for the privacy of Bitcoin users. Even worse, since funds can be tracked and tainted, no two coins are equal, and fungibility, a fundamental property required in every currency, is at risk. With these threats in mind, several privacy-enhancing technologies have been proposed to improve transaction privacy in Bitcoin. However, they either require a deep redesign of the currency, breaking many currently deployed features, or they address only specific privacy issues and consequently provide only very limited guarantees when deployed separately.

The goal of this work is to overcome this trade-off. Building on CoinJoin, we design ValueShuffle, the first coin mixing protocol compatible with Confidential Transactions, a proposed enhancement to the Bitcoin protocol to hide payment values in the blockchain. ValueShuffle ensures the anonymity of mixing participants as well as the confidentiality of their payment values even against other possibly malicious mixing participants. By combining CoinJoin with Confidential Transactions and additionally Stealth Addresses, ValueShuffle provides *comprehensive privacy* (payer anonymity, payee anonymity, and payment value privacy) without breaking with fundamental design principles or features of the current Bitcoin system. Assuming that Confidential Transactions will be integrated in the Bitcoin protocol, ValueShuffle makes it possible to mix funds of different value as well as to mix and spend funds in the same transaction, which overcomes the two main limitations of previous coin mixing protocols.

1 Introduction

In Bitcoin's initial design, privacy plays only a minor role. The initial perception of Bitcoin providing some built-in anonymity has been refuted by a vast set of academic works [2,3,19,24,25,32,37] showing many different privacy weaknesses with the current Bitcoin protocol. This state of affairs has led to a plethora of privacy-enhancing technologies [3–5,7,16,17,26,34,35,39,42] aiming at overcoming these shortcomings without breaking with the fundamental design of Bitcoin.

© International Financial Cryptography Association 2017
M. Brenner et al. (Eds.): FC 2017 Workshops 2017, LNCS 10323, pp. 133–154, 2017.
https://doi.org/10.1007/978-3-319-70278-0_8

However, all of these approaches offer only partial solutions, focusing typically on just one aspect of privacy (payer anonymity, payee anonymity or payment value privacy). For instance, Confidential Transactions (CT) [22], a proposed enhancement to the Bitcoin protocol, which is currently evaluated and tested in the Elements Alpha sidechain [12] and could be implemented in Bitcoin as a soft-fork, defines a transaction format that ensures payment value privacy in the blockchain. Stealth Addresses (SA) [38] is a mechanism for payers to generate unique one-time addresses for improved payee anonymity.

For payer anonymity, the most prevalent approach retaining compatibility with Bitcoin is coin mixing. In a coin mixing protocol, a group of users exchange their coins with each other, effectively hiding the relations between funds and owners. Such functionality can be achieved in practice for example by jointly generating a multi-input multi-output CoinJoin [21] transaction, which enables the users to atomically transfer their funds from potentially tainted inputs to fresh untainted output addresses. Since such a transaction must be signed by each involved user to be valid, theft of funds can easily be avoided. Additionally, if users exchange their output accounts by means of an anonymous broadcast protocol [10,33,34], inputs cannot be linked to outputs even by malicious users in the mixing, and such malicious users cannot prevent the honest users from successfully completing the protocol.

To achieve comprehensive privacy, it is necessary to combine all the three aforementioned partial privacy solutions (CT, SA, and mixing) into one solution, but this poses a challenge. SA or other means to generate one-time addresses can be easily combined with coin mixing, but while CT has in fact been designed with CoinJoin mixing in mind, it is not clear that the trust models of CT and P2P coin mixing can be made compatible. The design of CT assumes that a transaction is created by just one user, whereas in P2P coin mixing it is a group of mutually distrusting users who jointly must create a CoinJoin transaction. This leads to the following question:

> Can we design a P2P coin mixing protocol that enables a group of mutually distrusting users to create a CoinJoin confidential transaction, without revealing the relation between inputs and outputs or their payment values to each other?

1.1   ValueShuffle: Mixing Confidential Transactions

In this work, we answer this question affirmatively. We design ValueShuffle, the first coin mixing protocol compatible with CT. ValueShuffle is an extension of the P2P coin mixing protocol CoinShuffle++ [34], which is the result of instantiating the efficient message mixing protocol DiceMix [34] in the setting of CoinJoin-based coin mixing. Since ValueShuffle successfully combines coin mixing, SA and the CT proposal, the resulting currency provides comprehensive privacy, i.e., payer anonymity, payee anonymity and value privacy. Since it builds upon CoinJoin, ValueShuffle inherits a variety of features crucial to its practical deployment in the Bitcoin ecosystem, e.g., compatibility with Bitcoin scripts and compatibility with blockchain pruning.

Exploiting Synergies. By combining coin mixing with SA and CT, we exploit important synergies which make P2P coin mixing both more efficient and more practical, thereby releasing the full potential of coin mixing. We achieve that goal by overcoming the two main limitations of current coin mixing approaches.

First, all forms of coin mixing have been heavily restricted to mixing funds of the same value, because otherwise it is trivial for an observer to link inputs and outputs together just based on their monetary value, independently of how the mixing is organized. Adding value privacy to coin mixing removes this restriction entirely but comes with the challenge of proving to the network that no money is created in the mixing, since payment values are no longer in clear.

Second, current P2P coin mixing protocols [34] suffer from the problem that users are required to mix their funds (in a CoinJoin transaction) by sending them to a fresh address of their own first, which removes the trace to the owner. Only afterwards can users spend the mixed funds to a payee in a second transaction.[1]

This two-step process renders mixing expensive for users, who pay additional fees and need to wait longer, and for the entire Bitcoin network, which has to process essentially twice the amount of transaction data. As a result, privacy comes at a large expense. This is highly undesirable and creates a conflict between privacy and efficiency.

In ValueShuffle, instead, we rely on SA and CT to enable users to send their funds directly to the expected receivers in the CoinJoin transaction, which is arguably the most desirable mode of use of CoinJoin.

1.2   Features of ValueShuffle

The combination of the three privacy-enhancing technologies ValueShuffle, SA, and CT achieves the following main features.

Comprehensive Privacy. The combination of technologies provides the privacy guarantees of interest in Bitcoin. In particular, ValueShuffle ensures that no attacker observing the blockchain or the network, or even participating in the protocol, can link inputs and outputs of the CoinJoin transaction created in an execution of ValueShuffle. That implies that given an output of this transaction, the payer's input address cannot be identified among the honest input addresses in the mixing (payer anonymity). Additionally, SA provides one-time addresses for receiving payments, preventing linkage to the intended payee (payee anonymity), and CT provides value privacy.

Single Transaction. ValueShuffle can be used to transfer funds to payees directly without any form of premixing as required by current P2P coin mixing solutions,

---

[1] This is due to a fundamental restriction [34] of P2P mixing protocols; they can only handle freshly generated messages, which can be discarded if the protocol is disrupted, e.g., Bitcoin addresses of their own generated in the beginning of the protocol. As a result, paying to a payee directly is not possible, because that would require using a fixed amount or a fixed address as a message.

and without requiring interaction with the payee. As a result, private payments can be performed with just one single transaction on the blockchain.

DoS Resistance. ValueShuffle succeeds in the presence of denial-of-service attacks by disruptive users aiming to prevent honest users from completing the mixing. While disruptive users can delay the protocol, they cannot stop it. Since ValueShuffle is based on the efficient CoinShuffle++ protocol [34], it terminates in only $4 + 2f$ communication rounds in the presence of f disruptive users.

Anonymous Channel Not Strictly Required. For providing unlinkability of inputs and outputs in a CoinJoin transaction, ValueShuffle does not rely on any external anonymous channel such as the Tor network [11]. (However, to avoid an observer being able to link inputs of the CoinJoin transaction with network-level identifiers such as IP addresses, using an external means of anonymous communication is highly recommended.)

Features Inherited from CoinJoin. Since ValueShuffle is based on the CoinJoin paradigm, it additionally inherits all of its practical advantages.

Theft Resistance. Since honest users will check the final CoinJoin transaction before signing it, no money can be stolen from them.

Script Compatibility. While ValueShuffle does not keep the scripts confidential, it is compatible with transaction outputs that use complex scripts, e.g., advanced smart contracts, and provides meaningful privacy guarantees for them.

No Overhead for the Network. Unlike ring signatures, as for example deployed in Monero [28], which require a signature of size proportional to the anonymity set, our approach—while requiring interaction between users—provides anonymity without putting an additional burden in terms of blockchain space or verification time on the Bitcoin network.

Reduced Fees and Space Requirements. Taking this one step further, CoinJoin makes Bitcoin in fact more efficient, assuming the availability of Schnorr signatures [36], which are planned to be deployed in Bitcoin Core in the future [6]. The introduction of Schnorr signatures will enable aggregate signatures using an interactive two-round protocol among the users in a CoinJoin [41], reducing the number of signatures from n to 1, where n is the number of users. This protocol can easily be integrated in ValueShuffle, and since we can exploit concurrency, the resulting protocol will have the same number of rounds as the non-interactive variant $(4f + 2)$. This enhancement greatly reduces the size of transactions, thereby providing large savings in terms of blockchain space, verification time, and transaction fees as compared to n individual confidential transactions.

Incentive for Privacy. Due to the reduced fees, users save money by performing privacy-preserving transactions. This provides an unprecedented incentive for deployment and use of privacy-enhancing technologies in Bitcoin.

Compatibility with Pruning. Unlike in Zerocash [4] or Monero [28], using Coin-Join it can be publicly observed which transaction outputs are unspent. While this releases some information to the public, it allows pruning spent outputs from the set of (potentially) unspent transaction outputs. Pruning helps to mitigate the scaling issues of Bitcoin.

Overlay Design. The unlinkability provided by ValueShuffle through the use of CoinJoin is built as a separate layer on top of Bitcoin, which avoids additional complexity and risk in the underlying Bitcoin protocol.

2   Related Work

A variety of privacy solutions have been proposed so far in the literature, based on different paradigms.

Coin Mixing. CoinShuffle [33] and its successor CoinShuffle++ [34] use P2P mixing to create a CoinJoin [21] transaction. This approach has the advantage that theft is excluded by the design; however, efforts are required to ensure termination even with malicious users. ValueShuffle is an extension of CoinShuffle++; both easily scale up to anonymity sets of moderate size (e.g., 50 users).

Another line of research defines mixing using an intermediary tumbler [7, 16,17,39]. Notably, TumbleBit is the first such protocol that does not require users to trust in the tumbler for privacy or security of funds. An immediate advantage of mixing with a tumbler is that it scales better to larger anonymity sets. For instance, TumbleBit has been tested with an anonymity set of 800 users. However, a normal payment using TumbleBit needs at least two sequential Bitcoin transactions. ValueShuffle instead needs only one transaction to perform a payment. To enable more efficient mixing, TumbleBit also supports mixing based on payment channels with the tumbler.

Xim [5] uses announcements on the blockchain to pool users for mixing, thereby avoiding that a single party such as the bulletin board in P2P mixing or the tumbler can deny service to honest users and simplify Sybil attacks reducing the effective anonymity set of other honest users. However, Xim supports only two-party mixing, and thus many mixing transactions are required to achieve even an anonymity set of moderate size.

Apart from their differences in terms of requirements (e.g., number of transactions or trust assumptions), all coin mixing protocols proposed thus far are not compatible with CT and thus share the common drawback inherent to coin mixing with plain amounts: payments must transfer the same amount of funds, as otherwise unlinkability of input and output accounts is trivially broken.

CryptoNote. The CryptoNote [35] design is the closest to our work in terms of provided privacy guarantees. CryptoNote relies on ring signatures to provide anonymity for the sender of a transaction. An extension of CryptoNote is fully compatible with CT [27] and has been implemented in the cryptocurrency Monero [28]. In contrast to ValueShuffle, an online mixing protocol is not required, and a sufficient anonymity set can be created using funds of users currently offline.

However, CryptoNote's use of ring signatures comes with two important drawbacks for scalability. First, CryptoNote essentially performs mixing on the blockchain and requires each transaction to contain a ring signature of size $O(n)$, where n is the size of the anonymity set. Storing the ring signatures requires a lot of precious space in the blockchain, and verifying them puts a large burden on all nodes in the currency network. In contrast, ValueShuffle performs the actual mixing off-chain and stores only the result on the blockchain.

Second, CryptoNote is not compatible with pruning, a feature supported, e.g., by the Bitcoin Core client [29]. Pruning reduces the storage requirements of nodes drastically by deleting old blocks and spent transactions once verified. This is impossible in CryptoNote because its use of ring signatures prevents clients from determining whether an transaction output has been spent and can be pruned. A CoinJoin-based approach such as ValueShuffle does not have this problem and is compatible with pruning.

From a high-level point of view, ValueShuffle moves the overhead of providing payer anonymity from the blockchain and thus the whole Bitcoin network to only the users actively involved in a single mixing.

Mimblewimble. Mimblewimble [18,31] is a design for a cryptocurrency with confidential transactions that can be aggregated non-interactively and even across blocks. This has tremendous benefits for the scalability of the underlying blockchain. However, such aggregation alone does not ensure input-output unlinkability against parties who perform the aggregation, e.g., the miners. Furthermore, Mimblewimble is not compatible with smart contracts due to the lack of script support. In contrast, ValueShuffle seamlessly supports scripts as currently implemented in Bitcoin.

Zerocoin and Zerocash. Zerocoin [26] and its follow-up work Zerocash [4], whose implementation Zcash has recently been deployed, are cryptocurrency protocols that provide anonymity by design. Although these solutions provide strong privacy guarantees, it is not clear whether Zcash will see widespread adoption, in particular given its reliance on a trusted setup and non-falsifiable cryptographic assumptions [14] due to the use of zkSNARKS. Moreover, since it is not possible to observe which outputs have been spent already, blockchain pruning is not possible in Zerocoin and Zerocash.

3   Building Blocks

We describe the three building blocks of ValueShuffle, namely peer-to-peer mixing, Confidential Transactions, and Stealth Addresses.

3.1   Peer-to-Peer Mixing

A peer-to-peer (P2P) mixing protocol [10,33,34] allows a set of untrusted users to simultaneously broadcast their messages without requiring any trusted third party. The protocol ensures *sender anonymity*, i.e., an attacker controlling the network and some of the participating users cannot associate a message to its corresponding honest sender. In this work, we use DiceMix [34] (as in CoinShuffle++), which relies on Dining Cryptographers networks (DC-nets) [9] to achieve anonymity. Before the DC-net can be run, DiceMix runs a key exchangeto establish pairwise symmetric keys.

DoS Resistance. Disruptive users, whose goal is to prevent honest users from mixing, will be exposed and excluded in DiceMix. To this end, users broadcast the ephemeral secret key used in the key exchange of a failed protocol run. Then at least one malicious user is identified by replaying the expected computations, allowing the honest users to start a new run excluding the malicious user.

Eventually only honest users remain, and the protocol terminates.

Freshness of Messages. A P2P mixing protocol requires mixed messages to be fresh and to have sufficient entropy [34]. Freshness enables the protocol to sacrifice anonymity in failed runs in order to identify malicious users. As the messages will be discarded and no transaction will be performed, this does not hurt privacy at this point. Freshness is then required to ensure that a message from a particular user used in a failed run (with sacrificed anonymity) cannot be linked to a message from the same user used in the final successful run, in which a transaction will be performed and anonymity must be ensured.

3.2   Confidential Transactions

Confidential Transactions (CT) [15,22] is a cryptographic extension to Bitcoin that allows a single user to perform a transaction such that none of the monetary values in the inputs or outputs are revealed, thereby guaranteeing *value privacy*. Nevertheless, the balance property, i.e., no new coins are generated in the transaction, remains publicly verifiable.

This is mainly achieved by hiding the values using additively homomorphic commitments, i.e., $\mathsf{Com}(x, r) \oplus \mathsf{Com}(x', r') = \mathsf{Com}(x + x', r + r')$. As an example, assume a user has an input value x_1 and two output values x_2 and x_3. She can commit to x_1, x_2, and x_3, as $c_i := \mathsf{Com}(x_i, r_i)$, where r_i is chosen uniformly at random. Then, she computes $r_\Delta = r_1 + r_2 - r_3$ and adds this value in clear to the transaction. Ignoring fees, a verifier can then verify the balance property by checking whether $c_1 \oplus c_2 = c_3 \oplus \mathsf{Com}(0, -r_\Delta)$.

In fact, the current design of CT avoids adding r_Δ explicitly by choosing the randomness values such that always $r_\Delta = 0$. Our description of ValueShuffle is not compatible with this optimization, because it is not clear how to support it without adding communication rounds to the protocol. In practice, CT uses Pedersen commitments [30] and range proofs based on borromean ring signatures [23].

To ensure that commitments do not contain negative or too-large values that could overflow, a non-interactive zero-knowledge *range proof* is added to every commitment, proving that the value is in a certain range. (Also other components, e.g., an ephemeral public key, are added. To simplify presentation, we assume throughout the paper that these other components are part of the range proof.)

Monetary values are in fact represented not as integers but as floating point numbers with a public exponent, and only the mantissa is hidden in the commitment; this is to support large values efficiently. However, in this work we assume ordinary integers, i.e., we assume that the exponent is effectively not used (i.e., it is always 0), which will be necessary to ensure anonymity.

3.3 One-Time Addresses

Users performing transactions via ValueShuffle require a sufficient supply of fresh unlinkable addresses of the payee. This will make it possible to discard a recipient address used in a failed run of DiceMix. In this case, a fresh address can be used for the following run, satisfying the freshness requirement of messages mixed using DiceMix. (If there are n users in the mixing, DiceMix will require at most $n - 1$ addresses.) Several methods are available. First, the payee can post a stealth address, which enables any payer to derive fresh addresses. Second, the payee can send a BIP32 public key [40] to the payer, which enables the payer to derive fresh addresses. The necessary derivation index can be derived from public information, e.g., a hash of the value commitment. Third, the payee can simply send enough fresh addresses to the payer.

The method based on stealth addresses provides the strongest privacy guarantees. A stealth address is a public long-term address of a payee, which enables a payer to derive an arbitrary number of unlinkable addresses owned by the payee. A payment using a stealth address does not require any direct communication between payer and payee, and thus provides strong payer anonymity when used together with coin mixing: not even the payee can identify the payer, which is a useful property for anonymous donations, for example.

Nevertheless, ValueShuffle is oblivious of the method to generate fresh addresses; we only require that the payee has access to some method, and we refer the reader to the respective descriptions of the individual methods for details.

4   ValueShuffle

In this section, we overview ValueShuffle, the first P2P coin mixing protocol compatible with CT. We detail the protocol and the security analysis in Sect. 5.

Bootstrapping and Communication Model. A suitable bootstrapping mechanism is required for finding users. A malicious bootstrapping mechanism can hinder payer anonymity, as it can prevent honest users from participating in the protocol. Although this is a realistic threat, we consider prevention of such attacks orthogonal to our work.

Since ValueShuffle is an extension of CoinShuffle++, which uses DiceMix to mix Bitcoin addresses of the users, we rely on the same communication model as CoinShuffle++ and DiceMix. For completeness, we sketch this model here. We assume that users communicate with each other via a (broadcast) bulletin board, e.g., an IRC server echoing messages from one user to the others. Moreover, we assume the bounded synchronous communication setting, where a message from a user is available to all others at the end of a round and absence of a message from a user indicates that the user did not send any message. We stress that privacy is guaranteed even against a fully malicious bulletin board; the bulletin board is purely a means of communication.

4.1 Security and Privacy Features

ValueShuffle provides the following security and privacy guarantees.

Unlinkability: Given an output and two inputs belonging to honest users in the CoinJoin transaction created by the protocol, the attacker is not able to tell which of the two inputs pays to the output.
CT Compatibility: The protocol generates a CoinJoin transaction without compromising the individual value privacy of honest users provided by CT.
Theft Resistance: Funds of each honest user are either transferred to the payee as intended or remain with the honest user.
Termination: The protocol terminates for the honest users.

Threat Model. We consider an attacker that controls f malicious users. We do not put restrictions on f. However, for unlinkability we need $f < n - 1$, where n is the set of unexcluded users, to ensure there is a meaningful anonymity set.

The attacker additionally controls the bulletin board, which enables him to block messages from honest users. Only for the termination property, we assume that the bulletin board is honest, because otherwise, all communication could be blocked by the attacker and termination is impossible to ensure.

4.2 Challenges and Our Solutions

To combine coin mixing with CT and one-time addresses, we need to overcome the following challenges. For the sake of explanation, we assume that each user has only one input and one output in the transaction, and that there is no transaction fee. The full protocol does not have these limitations.

Basic Design. From a high-level point of view, the users in an execution of ValueShuffle run DiceMix to mix not only their output addresses (as done in Coin-Shuffle++) but their *output triples*, i.e., triples consisting of output address (or script), CT value commitment, and corresponding range proof. If DiceMix runs successfully, then it will pass a set of anonymized triples to an application-defined *confirmation* mechanism, which confirms the result of the mixing. As in CoinShuffle++, the confirmation mechanism in ValueShuffle is the collective signing of the CoinJoin transaction, either by collecting a plain list of signatures or by performing an interactive protocol to create an aggregate Schnorr signature [41].

Handling Disruption. If a run of DiceMix fails, it must be possible to identify at least one disruptive user to be excluded in a subsequent run of the protocol. This will eventually guarantee termination. Crucially, DiceMix requires the confirmation mechanism to output at least one such user if confirmation itself is disrupted. The confirmation mechanism can assume that the result of the mixing is correct, i.e., it contains the messages of all honest users. Given that assumption, identifying a disruptive user is straightforward: a user that refuses to sign the final CoinJoin transaction, or provides wrong signatures (or wrong partial signatures in the case of Schnorr aggregate signatures) is obviously disruptive.

Freshness of Mixed Output Triples. Recall that DiceMix requires mixed messages (i.e., the output triples in our case) to be fresh [34] and have sufficient entropy to ensure anonymity. This is exactly where we are able to exploit one-time addresses and CT. In particular, the payer is able to create fresh unlinkable output triples: We assume that the payer has a method to create fresh unlinkable output addresses all belonging to same payee, so the address component of the output triple is fresh. Moreover, the payer uses CT and since the commitment scheme and the range proof are randomized, the payer is able to generate many fresh unlinkable value commitments and range proofs. So all three components of the output triple can be freshly generated.

Only by combining one-time addresses and CT, we are able to guarantee anonymity if users are mixing and performing actual payments in the same transaction. Previous P2P coin mixing protocols such as CoinShuffle++ [34] require users to mix funds to a fresh output address of their own, because using the fixed address of the recipient or even using the plain monetary value in the mixing is not possible if anonymity and termination are desired [34].

Multiple-Payer CT. In the original design'of CT, the single payer can easily craft the randomness for the commitments to input and output values in the transaction such that anyone can verify its correctness (see Sect. 3.2). However, in a mixing transaction with several payers, a naive construction of such a verifiable transaction would require that users reveal to each other the randomnesses used in the commitments, thereby compromising the hiding property of the commitments.

To overcome this issue, the users can run a secure sum protocol to jointly compute the sum r_Δ of their random values, i.e., $r_\Delta = \sum_i r_i - r_i'$, where r_i denotes the randomness in the commitment to the input value of user i, and r_i' denotes the randomness in the commitment to the output value of the same user i. As a sum, r_Δ does not reveal which user contributed which summand to r_Δ. Now all users can add r_Δ as an explicit public randomness value to the transaction, and the overall transaction is valid again, which can be publicly verified by checking whether $\bigoplus c_i = \bigoplus c_i' \oplus \mathsf{Com}(0, -r_\Delta)$.

The value r_Δ can be obtained with a standard secure sum protocol based on additive secret sharing, where every user i broadcasts her value $r_i - r_i'$ blinded by multiple pads, each one shared with one other user. The messages from all users are then combined so that shared keys cancel out and the sum r_Δ is obtained. This mechanism is in essence equivalent to a DC-net as already used in DiceMix.

Handling Disruption of the Secure Sum Protocol. Malicious users can disrupt not only the mixing of output triples but also the secure sum protocol by creating an output value commitment that does not match the value of the input commitment, which can be detected when creating the CoinJoin transaction.

Similar to sacrificing anonymity in the DC-net used for mixing output triples, we can sacrifice anonymity in the DC-net used as a secure sum protocol. This reveals for every user i what she claims is $r_i - r'_i$. Using the verification equation of CT, all honest users can easily check the balance property of every user i individually, i.e., check whether user i's output commitments are consistent with her input commitments. Note that this approach does not reveal the random values used for the input commitments or the output commitments of user i, which would also reveal her intended payment value.

Combining P2P Mixing and Secure Sum. Since both DiceMix and the secure sum protocol are similar in structure (they both rely on DC-nets after all), we can optimize their combination. First, we can rely on a single key exchange and derive independent subkeys for the P2P mixing and the secure sum protocol. This means that if one of the two protocols is aborted, then the other must be aborted as well, because the same ephemeral secret is used for the key exchange and must be revealed. This is not a problem because the proper result of one of the two protocols does not yield a valid mixing transaction, and the users have to restart from scratch by generating a fresh output triple anyway.

Mixing Long Messages in DiceMix. While DiceMix in its current form is practical for small messages m (e.g., $|m| = 160$ bits as used by CoinShuffle++), it is prohibitively slow for messages of the size we require; we need $|m| \approx 20\,000$ bits to mix the quite large range proofs necessary in CT. The most expensive computation step is a polynomial factorization and requires each message to be an element of a finite field and consequently the finite field must have a size of about $2^{|m|}$.

To overcome this issue, we split m into several chunks, i.e., $m = m_1 \| \ldots \| m_\ell$ and mix those chunks in different parallel runs of the essential mixing step in DiceMix. The challenge that arises is to recombine the messages again, because the mixing ensures that it is not possible to know which chunks belong together (i.e., to the same user). Our solution is to prefix every m_i for $1 < i \le \ell$ with

$F(m_1)$, where F is a collision-resistant hash function, so that every user mixes: $m_1' = m_1$ and $m_i' = F(m_1) \| m_i$ for $1 < i \leq \ell$. This arrangement allows for a trade-off between computation and communication required for mixing: bigger chunks reduce the number of parallel mixing instances required but demand higher computation costs for the polynomial factorization.

Supporting Arbitrary Scripts. So far we have discussed only output addresses, which are essentially hashes, but not about their type. While mixing works fine with ordinary pay-to-pubkey-hash (P2PKH) hashes, we require pay-to-script-hash (P2SH) hashes [1][2] to support arbitrary scripts. However, it is not possible to mix P2PKH and P2SH hashes in the same mixing, because this would require adding the address type explicitly to the mixing message, which breaks anonymity: in case of a disruption, it becomes clear which inputs go a P2PKH address and which inputs go to a P2SH address. To support P2PKH and P2SH together, we can instead perform P2PKH transactions nested in P2SH.[3] For simplicity, we will ignore this issue and assume addresses in the remainder of the paper.

4.3   Overview of ValueShuffle

We assume that every user i is represented by a triple $in_i = (c_i = \mathsf{Com}(x_i, r_i), \pi_i, vk_i)$, where c_i denotes the commitment to the input value x_i using randomness r_i, π_i denotes a range proof for c_i, and vk_i denotes a Bitcoin address owned by the user i. For ease of explanation, we assume here that every user has only one input triple and that there are no fees in place.

From a high-level perspective, an execution of ValueShuffle consists of *runs*, and each run of ValueShuffle consists of four phases as follows.

1. Output Generation. Every user i locally generates her output triple $out_i = (c_i' = \mathsf{Com}(x_i', r_i'), \pi_i', addr_i')$, where c_i' is a CT-style commitment, π_i' is the corresponding range proof, and $addr_i'$ is a fresh one-time address of the receiver. Note that users can have several output triples (including change outputs), but for simplicity we restrict our attention to only one output here.

2. Mixing and Secure Sum. Users run in parallel a P2P mixing protocol to mix their output triples out_i and a secure sum protocol to privately compute the sum $r_\Delta = \sum_i r_i' - r_i$. Finally, input and output messages can be combined to deterministically form a (still unsigned) CoinJoin transaction by adding the explicit random value r_Δ.

---

[2] In P2PKH, funds are sent to a public key specified by its hash, and the user who wants to spend the resulting output is responsible for showing the public key. P2SH is a generalization: In P2SH, funds are sent to a script specified by its hash, and the user who wants to spend the resulting output is responsible for providing the script.

[3] Such nesting has also been proposed in the context of Segregated Witness [20].

3. Check. Users check validity of the resulting CoinJoin transaction, i.e., they check whether all range proofs π_i' verify with respect to commitments c_i', and check whether the overall balance of the intended transaction is correct, i.e., whether $\bigoplus_i c_i = \bigoplus_i c_i' + \mathsf{Com}(0, -r_\Delta)$. Also, every user verifies that her output triple is part of the mixing result, i.e., no coins are stolen by the transaction.

4a. Confirm. If all checks pass, the transaction is valid and users are required to sign it. While every user checked only that her output is present, DiceMix guarantees that this suffices to ensure that the outputs of all users are present. Thus if some honest user reached this point, she can be sure that users refusing to sign the transaction are disruptive. If this happens, they will be excluded and a new run of the protocol is started.

4b. Blame. If any of the aforementioned checks fail, a blame phase is performed to detect at least one malicious user. Every user i broadcasts the secrets she used for the mixing and secure sum protocols, thereby revealing the value $r_i - r_i'$, which suffices to check that user i committed the same value in the input and output addresses (and therefore no coins were created). Now every other user j can recompute the mixing and secure sum steps of user i and detect whether she faithfully followed the protocol specification. The thereby exposed malicious user is then excluded from the protocol and a new run is started.

4.4 Performance

To reduce the number of necessary communication rounds, DiceMix is able to start a subsequent run even if the current run has not yet failed, and thus even if it is not yet clear who will be the disruptor to be excluded in the subsequent run [34]. ValueShuffle is able to exploit this mechanism as well and as a result, ValueShuffle terminates in $4 + 2f$ rounds in the presence of f disrupting users (instead of $4 + 4f$ rounds without this feature).

5   ValueShuffle: Full Protocol Description

In this section we specify ValueShuffle fully. We start by describing the building blocks that the protocol relies on.

Digital Signatures. We require a digital signature scheme (KeyGen, Sign, Verify) unforgeable under chosen-message attacks (UF-CMA). The algorithm KeyGen returns a private signing key sk and the corresponding public verification key vk. On input message m, $\mathsf{Sign}(sk, m)$ returns σ, a signature on message m using signing key sk. The verification algorithm $\mathsf{Verify}(pk, \sigma, m)$ outputs *true* iff σ is a valid signature for m under the verification key vk.

Non-interactive Key Exchange. We require a non-interactive key exchange (NIKE) mechanism (NIKE.KeyGen, NIKE.SharedKey) secure in the CKS model [8, 13]. Algorithm NIKE.KeyGen(id) outputs a public key npk and a secret key nsk, given a party identifier id. Algorithm NIKE.SharedKey($id_1, id_2, nsk_1, npk_2, sid$) outputs a shared key for the two parties and a session id sid, such that for all session ids sid, all parties id_1, id_2, and all corresponding key pairs (npk_1, nsk_1) and (npk_2, nsk_2), we have NIKE.SharedKey($id_1, id_2, nsk_1, npk_2, sid$) = NIKE.SharedKey($id_2, id_1, nsk_2, npk_1, sid$). We require an algorithm NIKE.ValidatePK(npk), which outputs *true* iff npk is a public key in the output space of NIKE.KeyGen, and we require an algorithm NIKE.ValidateKeys(npk, nsk) which outputs *true* iff nsk is a secret key for the public key npk.

Static Diffie-Hellman key exchange satisfies these requirements [8], given a suitable key derivation algorithm such as NIKE.SharedKey(id_1, id_2, x, g^y) := K($(g^{xy}, \{id_1, id_2\}, sid)$) for a hash function K modeled as a random oracle.

Hash Functions. We require hash functions H, G, and F modeled as random oracles.

Confidential Transactions. Confidential Transactions (CT) relies on a non-interactive commitment scheme (Com, Open), which uses public parameters we keep implicit, and a range proof (RPCreate, RPVerify). Algorithm Com(m, r) uses the randomness $r \in \mathcal{R}$ to output a commitment c of message m. Algorithm Open($param, c, m, r$) returns *true* iff c is a valid commitment of message m with randomness r. Informally, a commitment scheme is *hiding*, i.e., the commitment c reveals nothing about m; and *binding*, i.e., no attacker can produce a commitment that it can open to two different messages $m' \neq m$. CT requires an additively homomorphic commitment scheme, i.e., there is an efficient operation $\oplus$ on commitments such that Com(m_1, r_1) $\oplus$ Com(m_2, r_2) = Com($m_1 + m_2, r_1 + r_2$). In practice, CT uses Pedersen commitments [30].

In a range proof scheme, the algorithm π := RPCreate(m, r) creates a proof π that c = Com(m, r) is a commitment of a value in a valid range. The algorithm b := RPVerify(π, c) returns *true* iff π is a valid range proof for c. We refer the reader to the CT draft [15, 22] for details.

Confirmation. The confirmation subprotocol CONFIRMTx() uses CoinJoin to perform the actual mixing. The algorithm CoinJoinTx() creates a CoinJoin transaction, and the algorithm Submit($tx, \sigma[\,]$) submits transaction tx including the corresponding signatures $\sigma[\,]$ to the Bitcoin network.

Our implementation of CONFIRMTx() produces a CoinJoin transaction with one signature from each user. As noted above, alternative schemes are possible, e.g., the two-round aggregate Schnorr signature protocol [41] can be used to sign the transaction if Schnorr signatures will available in Bitcoin. In that case, it is possible to pre-perform the first round of the two-round protocol (in parallel to the main part of ValueShuffle), because this round does not depend on the output of the mixing, such that CONFIRMTX() effectively still takes only one round, and the full protocol still takes only $4 + 2f$ rounds.

Conventions and Notation for Pseudocode. We use arrays written as ARR$[i]$, where i is the index. We denote the full array (all its elements) as ARR$[\,]$.

Message x is broadcast using "**broadcast** x". The command "**receive** X$[p]$ **from all** $p \in P$ **where** $X(\mathrm{X}[p])$ **missing** $C(P_{off})$" attempts to receive a message from all users $p \in P$. The first message X$[p]$ from user p that fulfills predicate $X(\mathrm{X}[p])$ is accepted and stored as X$[p]$; all further messages from p are ignored. When a timeout is reached, the command C is executed, which has access to a set $P_{off} \subseteq P$ of users that did not send a (valid) message.

Regarding concurrency, a thread that runs a procedure P($args$) is started using "$t :=$ **fork** P($args$)", where t is a handle for the thread. A thread t can either be joined using "$r :=$ **joint** t", where r is its return value, or it can be aborted using "**abort** t". A thread can wait for a notification and receive a value from another thread using "**wait**". The notifying thread uses "**notify** t **of** v" to notify thread t of some value v.

Setup. We assume that funds that should be used as input in ValueShuffle can only be spent by providing signatures, i.e., they are associated with a verification key that can also be used in ValueShuffle. Furthermore, for ease of explanation we assume here that every user has only one input. However, ValueShuffle can easily be adapted to overcome this restriction: If a user has more than one input, she can simply sign her messages using all signing keys corresponding to all verification keys, and the code for checking the balance can be adapted to consider the homomorphic combination of several input commitments.

As a result of these assumptions, every user in the beginning knows an unspent transaction output UTXO$[p]$, its corresponding CT commitment C$[p]$ and verification key VK$[p]$ for every other user p.

Furthermore, every user has her corresponding secrets, i.e., the value x and randomness r such that $c = \mathsf{Com}(x, r)$, the secret key sk corresponding to vk, and every user has a set *Payments* with recipients and corresponding amounts (including a change address if necessary), describing the payments she wants to perform. We assume that every user wants to perform the same number of payments and that the transaction fee *fee* is evenly split among the users.

Full Pseudocode. Here we describe the full protocol in pseudocode. We assume that the reader is familiar with the details of DiceMix and CoinShuffle++ [34] to understand the code. For better readability, our essential changes to CoinShuffle++, which result in ValueShuffle, are printed in blue.

```
 1: procedure ValueShuffle(P, my, VK[], sk, UTXO[], C[], r, Payments, sid)
 2:     sid := (sid, P, VK[])
 3:     if my ∈ P then
 4:         fail "cannot run protocol with myself"
 5:     return Run(P, my, VK[], sk, sid, 0)

 6: procedure Run(P, my, VK[], sk, sid, run)
 7:     if P = ∅ then
 8:         fail "no honest users"
 9:     ▷ Exchange pairwise keys
10:     (NPK[my], NSK[my]) := NIKE.KeyGen(my)
11:     sidPre := H((sidPre, sid, run))
12:     broadcast (KE, NPK[my], Sign(sk, (NPK[my], sidPre)))
13:     receive (KE, NPK[p], σ[p]) from all p ∈ P
14:         where NIKE.ValidatePK(NPK[p])
                 ∧ Verify(VK[p], σ[p], (NPK[p], sidPre))
15:     missing P_off do
16:         P := P \ P_off                                    ▷ Exclude offline users
17:     sid' := H((sid', sid, P ∪ {my}, NPK[], run))
18:     K[] := DC-Keys(P, NPK[], my, NSK[my], sid'))
19:     ▷ Generate fresh outputs to mix
20:     (myOut, myr) := GenOutputs(Payments)
21:     DC[my][][][] := DC-Mix(P, my, K[], myOut)
22:     SumDC[my] := myr + DC-Slot-Pad(P, my, K[], sum)
23:     P_ex := ∅                         ▷ Malicious (or offline) users for later exclusion
24:     ▷ Commit to DC-net vector
25:     Com[my] := H((CM, DC[my][][][], SumDC[my]))
26:     broadcast (CM, Com[my], Sign(sk, (Com[my], sid')))
27:     receive (CM, Com[p], σ[p]) from all p ∈ P
28:         where Verify(VK[p], σ[p], (Com[p], sid'))
29:     missing P_off do                                ▷ Store offline users for exclusion
30:         P_ex := P_ex ∪ P_off
31:     if run > 0 then
32:         ▷ Wait for prev. run to notify us of malicious users
33:         P_exPrev := wait
34:         P_ex := P_ex ∪ P_exPrev
35:     ▷ Collect shared keys with excluded users
36:     for all p ∈ P_ex do
37:         K_ex[my][p] := K[p]
38:     ▷ Start next run (in case this one fails)
39:     P := P \ P_ex
40:     next := fork Run(P, my, VK[], sk, sid, run + 1)
41:     ▷ Open commitments and keys with excluded users
42:     broadcast (DC, DC[my][][][], SumDC[my], K_ex[my][], Sign(sk, K_ex[my][]))
43:     receive (DC, DC[p][][][], SumDC[p], K_ex[p][], σ[p]) from all p ∈ P
44:         where H((CM, DC[p][][][], SumDC[p])) = Com[p]
                 ∧ {p' : K_ex[p][p'] ≠ ⊥} = P_ex
                 ∧ Verify(VK[p], K_ex[p][], σ[p])
45:     missing P_off do                                  ▷ Abort and rely on next run
46:         return Result-Of-Next-Run(P_off, next)
47:     Out := DC-Mix-Res(P ∪ {my}, DC[][][][], P_ex, K_ex[][])
48:     r_Δ := DC-Slot-Open(P ∪ {my}, SumDC[], sum, P_ex, K_ex[][])
49:     ▷ Check if our output is contained in the result
50:     (balanced, Out_mal) := VerifyResult(i, P, Out, C[], r_Δ)
51:     if myOut ⊆ Out ∧ balanced ∧ Out_mal = ∅ then
52:         P_mal := ConfirmTx(i, P, Out, my, VK[], sk, UTXO[], sid)
53:         if P_mal = ∅ then                                              ▷ Success?
54:             abort next
55:             return m
56:     else
57:         broadcast (SK, NSK[my])                                ▷ Reveal secret key
```

```
58:         receive (SK, NSK[p]) from all p ∈ P
59:            where NIKE.ValidateKeys(NPK[p], NSK[p])
60:         missing P_off do                                      ▷ Abort and rely on next run
61:            return RESULT-OF-NEXT-RUN(P_off, next)
62:         ▷ Determine malicious users using the secret keys
63:         P_mal := BLM(P, NPK[], my, NSK[], DC[][][][], sid', P_ex, K_ex[][], Out_mal, C[])
64:      return RESULT-OF-NEXT-RUN(P_mal, next)

65: procedure DC-MIX(P, my, K[], myM)
66:      o := 1
67:      for all m ∈ myM do
68:         ▷ Split message into chunks and prefix those
69:         C[1] ‖ rem := m                                   ▷ C[1] must be long enough to be unpredictable
70:         C[2] ‖ ... ‖ C[n] := rem             ▷ ∀j ∈ {2, ..., n}. |C[j]| = |C[1]| − |F(C[1])|
71:         for j := 2, ..., n do
72:            C[j] := F(C[1]) ‖ C[j]
73:         ▷ Create power sums in individual slots
74:         for j := 1, ..., n do
75:            for i := 1, ..., |P| + 1 do
76:               DCMY[o][j][i] := C[j]^i + DC-SLOT-PAD(P, my, K[], (o, j, i))
77:         o := o + 1
78:      return DCMY[][][]

79: procedure DC-MIX-RES(P_all, DCMIX[][][], P_ex, K_ex[][])
80:      n := |DCMIX[1]|
81:      for j := 1, ..., n do
82:         for s := 1, ..., |P_all| do
83:            M*[s] := DC-SLOT-OPEN(P_all, DCMIX[][j][], s, P_ex, K_ex[][])
84:         ▷ Solve equation system for array M[] of messages
85:         M[j][] := Solve(∀s ∈ {1, ..., |P_all|}. M*[s] = ∑_{i=1}^{|P_all|} M[i]^s)
86:      ▷ Recombine messages
87:      M := ∅
88:      for i := 1, ..., |P_all| do
89:         m := M[1][i]
90:         for j := 2, ..., n do
91:            S := {(i, m*) : h ‖ m* = M[j][i] ∧ h = F(M[1][i])}
92:            ▷ Unique match?
93:            if ∃i, m*. S = {(i, m*)} then
94:               m := m ‖ m*
95:            else
96:               continue (outer loop)                      ▷ Invalid encoding, ignore message
97:         M := M ∪ {m}
98:      return M

99: procedure DC-SLOT-PAD(P, my, K[], s)
100:      return ∑_{p∈P} sgn(my − p) · G((K[p], s))                ▷ in 𝔽

101: procedure DC-SLOT-OPEN(P_all, DC[][], s, P_ex, K_ex[][])
102:      ▷ Pads cancel out for honest users
103:      m* := ∑_{p∈P_all} DC[p][s]                             ▷ in 𝔽
104:      ▷ Remove pads for excluded users
105:      m* := m* − ∑_{p∈P_all} DC-SLOT-PAD(P_ex, p, K_ex[p][], s)
106:      return m*

107: procedure DC-KEYS(P, NPK[], my, nsk, sid')
108:      for all p ∈ P do
109:         K[p] := NIKE.SharedKey(my, p, nsk, NPK[p], sid')
110:      return K[]

111: procedure BLM(P, NPK[], my, NSK[], DC[][][][], sid', P_ex, K_ex[][], Out_mal, C[])
112:      P_mal := ∅
113:      for all p ∈ P do
114:         P' := (P ∪ {my} ∪ P_ex) \ {p}
115:         K'[] := DC-KEYS(P', NPK[], p, NSK[p], sid')
116:         ▷ Reconstruct purported message m' of p
117:         for o := 1, ..., |DC[my]| do
118:            m' := DC[p][o][1][1] − DC-SLOT-PAD(P', p, K'[], (o, 1, 1))
119:            for j := 2, ..., |(DC[p][o]| do
120:               m* ‖ h := DC[p][o][j][1] − DC-SLOT-PAD(P', p, K'[], (o, j, 1))
```

```
121:              m' := m' ∥ m*
122:              Out' := Out' ∪ {m'}
123:          ▷ Replay DC-net messages of p
124:          DC'[][][] := DC-Mix(P', p, K'[], Out')
125:          if DC'[][][] ≠ DC[p][][][] then          ▷ Exclude inconsistent p
126:              P_mal := P_mal ∪ {p}
127:          ▷ Verify that p has sent valid range proofs
128:          if Out' ∩ Out_mal ≠ ∅ then
129:              P_mal := P_mal ∪ {p}
130:          ▷ Reconstruct randomness r' of p
131:          r' := SumDC[p] − DC-Slot-Pad(P', p, K'[], sum)
132:          ▷ Verify that the balance of p is correct
133:          if C[p] = (⊕_{(c,π,addr)∈Out'} c) ⊕ Com(fee/|P|, −r') then
134:              P_mal := P_mal ∪ {p}
135:          ▷ Verify that p has published correct symmetric keys
136:          for all p_ex ∈ P_ex do
137:              if K_ex[p][p_ex] ≠ K'[p_ex] then
138:                  P_mal := P_mal ∪ {p}
139:      return P_mal

140: procedure Result-Of-Next-Run(P_exNext, next)
141:      ▷ Hand over to next run and notify of users to exclude
142:      notify next of P_exNext
143:      ▷ Return result of next run
144:      result := join next
145:      return result

146: procedure VerifyResult(i, P, Out, C[], r_Δ)
147:      Out_mal := ∅
148:      ▷ Verify range proofs
149:      for all out ∈ Out do
150:          (c, π, addr) := out
151:          if RPVerify(π, c) then
152:              Out_mal := Out_mal ∪ {out}
153:      ▷ Check balance
154:      balanced := (⊕_{p∈P} C[p] = (⊕_{(c,π,addr)∈Out} c) ⊕ Com(fee, −r_Δ))
155:      return (balanced, Out_mal)

156: procedure GenOutputs(Payments)
157:      myr := 0
158:      myOut := ∅
159:      for all (recipient, amount) ∈ Payments do
160:          r ←$ R                    ▷ Fresh random value; implicitly stored in wallet
161:          c := Com(amount, r)
162:          π := RPCreate(amount, r)
163:          myr := myr + r
164:          addr := FreshRecipientAddress(recipient)
165:          myOut := myOut ∪ {(c, π, addr)}
166:      return (myr, myOut)

167: procedure ConfirmTx(i, P, my, VK[], sk, UTXO[], Out, sid)
168:      tx := CoinJoinTx(UTXO[], Out)
169:      σ[my] := Sign(sk, tx)
170:      broadcast σ[my]
171:      receive σ[] from all p ∈ P
172:          where Verify(VK[p], σ[p], tx)
173:      missing P_off do                    ▷ Users refusing to sign are malicious
174:          return P_off
175:      Submit(tx, σ[])
176:      return ∅                            ▷ Success!
```

5.1   Security Analysis

We argue briefly why ValueShuffle achieves the desired security and privacy properties.

Unlinkability. Unlinkability follows from sender anonymity in DiceMix [34]: Whenever some honest user i signs the CoinJoin transaction, the confirmation phase has been reached. In this case, because output triples are freshly generated for each run, DiceMix guarantees that the honest users form a proper DC-net. This in turn ensures that the attacker cannot distinguish whether an output triple of user i belongs to i or some other honest user j. Note that the relation between user and output triple can be revealed in the blame phase, but then a CoinJoin transaction with the current output triple will never be signed, so it is safe to reveal the relation. Instead, the output triple will be discarded and a further run will be started, using a fresh output triple, which is unlinkable to the discarded output triples. We refer the reader to DiceMix [34] for a detailed discussion. The only difference from DiceMix is that ValueShuffle runs two proper DC-nets in parallel.

CT Compatibility. ValueShuffle does not impair the privacy guarantees provided by CT. The only CT secrets belonging to a user i that ValueShuffle uses (and actually reveals in the blame phase) is her value $r - \sum_k r'_k$, where k ranges over her output triples. Since r and all r'_k are random, this sum does not reveal anything about the individual r and r'_k values and thus does not affect the hiding property of the input commitment or any of the individual output commitments.

Termination. DiceMix itself provides termination, and we have to argue that our extensions do not affect this property. This mainly boils down to ensuring that a malicious user can be detected in each protocol run.

   If one of the DC-nets for mixing the output triples is disrupted, then a malicious user will be identified. This follows from the termination of DiceMix and the observation that each message chunk is unpredictable. If the DC-net for computing r_Δ is disrupted, then the blame phase will sacrifice anonymity for this run (discarding the output triples), and the malicious user will be identified by checking her individual balance property, i.e., whether just her set of inputs and outputs are balanced, as done in the blame phase. If a wrong range proof is provided, then the blame phase will sacrifice anonymity for this run (discarding the output triples), and the malicious user can be identified by checking who provided the wrong range proof. In all other cases, the transaction will be valid by construction, so users refusing to sign it are malicious (or offline) and thus can be excluded from further runs.

   By construction, and since the bulletin board is honest (which we assume for termination, as otherwise it is impossible to achieve), all honest users agree on the set of users to exclude and thus on the set of remaining users in the subsequential run of the protocol. We refer the reader to DiceMix [34] for details of termination.

Theft Resistance. The protocol must ensure that no honest user incurs money loss (ignoring transaction fees). ValueShuffle ensures theft resistance since the mixing of output triples and randomness does not involve the transfer of funds. Before the CoinJoin transaction is formed, every honest user checks that her output address and the corresponding committed value is included and only then signs the transaction. As a CoinJoin transaction becomes valid only when every user has signed the transaction (and thus confirmed that her funds are not stolen), ValueShuffle provides theft resistance.

Acknowledgements. We thank Pieter Wuille for pointing out a mistake in a preprint, and we thank the anonymous reviewers for their very helpful comments. This work was supported by the German Ministry for Education and Research (BMBF) through funding for the German Universities Excellence Initiative.

References

1. Andresen, G.: Pay to script hash, BIP 16. https://github.com/bitcoin/bips/blob/master/bip-0016.mediawiki
2. Androulaki, E., Karame, G.O., Roeschlin, M., Scherer, T., Capkun, S.: Evaluating user privacy in Bitcoin. In: Sadeghi, A.-R. (ed.) FC 2013. LNCS, vol. 7859, pp. 34–51. Springer, Heidelberg (2013). https://doi.org/10.1007/978-3-642-39884-1_4
3. Barber, S., Boyen, X., Shi, E., Uzun, E.: Bitter to better—how to make Bitcoin a better currency. In: Keromytis, A.D. (ed.) FC 2012. LNCS, vol. 7397, pp. 399–414. Springer, Heidelberg (2012). https://doi.org/10.1007/978-3-642-32946-3_29
4. Ben-Sasson, E., Chiesa, A., Garman, C., Green, M., Miers, I., Tromer, E., Virza, M.: Zerocash: decentralized anonymous payments from Bitcoin. In: S&P 2014 (2014)
5. Bissias, G., Ozisik, A.P., Levine, B.N., Liberatore, M.: Sybil-resistant mixing for Bitcoin. In: WPES 2014 (2014)
6. Bitcoin Core: Segregated witness: the next steps. https://bitcoincore.org/en/2016/06/24/segwit-next-steps/#schnorr-signatures
7. Bonneau, J., Narayanan, A., Miller, A., Clark, J., Kroll, J.A., Felten, E.W.: Mixcoin: anonymity for Bitcoin with accountable mixes. In: Christin, N., Safavi-Naini, R. (eds.) FC 2014. LNCS, vol. 8437, pp. 486–504. Springer, Heidelberg (2014). https://doi.org/10.1007/978-3-662-45472-5_31
8. Cash, D., Kiltz, E., Shoup, V.: The twin Diffie-Hellman problem and applications. J. Cryptol. **22**(4), 470–504 (2009)
9. Chaum, D.: The dining cryptographers problem: unconditional sender and recipient untraceability. J. Cryptol. **1**(1), 65–75 (1988)
10. Corrigan-Gibbs, H., Ford, B.: Dissent: accountable anonymous group messaging. In: CCS 2010 (2010)
11. Dingledine, R., Mathewson, N., Syverson, P.: Tor: the second-generation onion router. In: USENIX Security 2004 (2004)
12. Elements Project: Alpha sidechain. https://www.elementsproject.org/sidechains/alpha/
13. Freire, E.S.V., Hofheinz, D., Kiltz, E., Paterson, K.G.: Non-interactive key exchange. In: Kurosawa, K., Hanaoka, G. (eds.) PKC 2013. LNCS, vol. 7778, pp. 254–271. Springer, Heidelberg (2013). https://doi.org/10.1007/978-3-642-36362-7_17
14. Gentry, C., Wichs, D.: Separating succinct non-interactive arguments from all falsifiable assumptions. In: STOC 2011 (2011)
15. Gibson, A.: An investigation into Confidential Transactions (2016). http://diyhpl.us/~bryan/papers2/bitcoin/An%20investigation%20into%20Confidential%20Transactions%20-%20Adam%20Gibson%20-%202016.pdf
16. Heilman, E., Alshenibr, L., Baldimtsi, F., Scafuro, A., Goldberg, S.: TumbleBit: an untrusted Bitcoin-compatible anonymous payment hub. In: NDSS 2017 (2017)

17. Heilman, E., Baldimtsi, F., Goldberg, S.: Blindly signed contracts: anonymous on-blockchain and off-blockchain Bitcoin transactions. In: Clark, J., Meiklejohn, S., Ryan, P.Y.A., Wallach, D., Brenner, M., Rohloff, K. (eds.) FC 2016. LNCS, vol. 9604, pp. 43–60. Springer, Heidelberg (2016). https://doi.org/10.1007/978-3-662-53357-4_4

18. Jedusor, T.E.: Mimblewimble. https://scalingbitcoin.org/papers/mimblewimble.txt

19. Koshy, P., Koshy, D., McDaniel, P.: An analysis of anonymity in Bitcoin using P2P network traffic. In: Christin, N., Safavi-Naini, R. (eds.) FC 2014. LNCS, vol. 8437, pp. 469–485. Springer, Heidelberg (2014). https://doi.org/10.1007/978-3-662-45472-5_30

20. Lombrozo, E., Lau, J., Wuille, P.: Segregated witness (consensus layer), BIP 141. https://github.com/bitcoin/bips/blob/master/bip-0141.mediawiki#p2wpkh-nested-in-bip16-p2sh

21. Maxwell, G.: CoinJoin: Bitcoin privacy for the real world. Post on Bitcoin Forum (2013). https://bitcointalk.org/index.php?topic=279249

22. Maxwell, G.: Confidential transactions (2015). https://people.xiph.org/~greg/confidential_values.txt

23. Maxwell, G., Poelstra, A.: Borromean ring signatures (2015). https://github.com/Blockstream/borromean_paper/raw/master/borromean_draft_0.01_9ade1e49.pdf

24. Meiklejohn, S., Orlandi, C.: Privacy-enhancing overlays in Bitcoin. In: Brenner, M., Christin, N., Johnson, B., Rohloff, K. (eds.) FC 2015. LNCS, vol. 8976, pp. 127–141. Springer, Heidelberg (2015). https://doi.org/10.1007/978-3-662-48051-9_10

25. Meiklejohn, S., Pomarole, M., Jordan, G., Levchenko, K., McCoy, D., Voelker, G.M., Savage, S.: A fistful of bitcoins: characterizing payments among men with no names. In: IMC 2013 (2013)

26. Miers, I., Garman, C., Green, M., Rubin, A.D.: Zerocoin: anonymous distributed e-cash from Bitcoin. In: S&P 2013 (2013)

27. Noether, S., Mackenzie, A.: Ring confidential transactions. Ledger (2016). http://www.ledgerjournal.org/ojs/index.php/ledger/article/view/34

28. Noether, S.: Review of CryptoNote white paper. https://downloads.getmonero.org/whitepaper_review.pdf

29. OmegaStarScream: Bitcoin Core & pruning mode. Bitcoin Forum. https://bitcointalk.org/index.php?topic=1599458.0

30. Pedersen, T.P.: Non-interactive and information-theoretic secure verifiable secret sharing. In: Feigenbaum, J. (ed.) CRYPTO 1991. LNCS, vol. 576, pp. 129–140. Springer, Heidelberg (1992). https://doi.org/10.1007/3-540-46766-1_9

31. Poelstra, A.: Mimblewimble. http://diyhpl.us/~bryan/papers2/bitcoin/mimblewimble-andytoshi-INCOMPLETE-DRAFT-2016-10-06-001.pdf

32. Reid, F., Harrigan, M.: An analysis of anonymity in the bitcoin system. In: Altshuler, Y., Elovici, Y., Cremers, A., Aharony, N., Pentland, A. (eds.) Security and Privacy in Social Networks. Springer, New York (2013). https://doi.org/10.1007/978-1-4614-4139-7_10

33. Ruffing, T., Moreno-Sanchez, P., Kate, A.: CoinShuffle: practical decentralized coin mixing for bitcoin. In: Kutyłowski, M., Vaidya, J. (eds.) ESORICS 2014. LNCS, vol. 8713, pp. 345–364. Springer, Cham (2014). https://doi.org/10.1007/978-3-319-11212-1_20

34. Ruffing, T., Moreno-Sanchez, P., Kate, A.: P2P mixing and unlinkable Bitcoin transactions. In: NDSS 2017 (2017)

35. van Saberhagen, N.: CryptoNote (2013). https://cryptonote.org/whitepaper.pdf

36. Schnorr, C.P.: Efficient signature generation by smart cards. J. Cryptol. **4**(3), 161–174 (1991)
37. Spagnuolo, M., Maggi, F., Zanero, S.: BitIodine: extracting intelligence from the Bitcoin network. In: Christin, N., Safavi-Naini, R. (eds.) FC 2014. LNCS, vol. 8437, pp. 457–468. Springer, Heidelberg (2014). https://doi.org/10.1007/978-3-662-45472-5_29
38. Todd, P.: Stealth addresses. Post on Bitcoin development mailing list. https://www.mail-archive.com/bitcoin-development@lists.sourceforge.net/msg03613.html
39. Valenta, L., Rowan, B.: Blindcoin: blinded, accountable mixes for Bitcoin. In: Brenner, M., Christin, N., Johnson, B., Rohloff, K. (eds.) FC 2015. LNCS, vol. 8976, pp. 112–126. Springer, Heidelberg (2015). https://doi.org/10.1007/978-3-662-48051-9_9
40. Wuille, P.: Hierarchical deterministic wallets, BIP 32. https://github.com/bitcoin/bips/blob/master/bip-0032.mediawiki
41. Wuille, P.: Schnorr-SHA256 module in libsecp256k1. https://github.com/sipa/secp256k1/blob/968e2f415a5e764d159ee03e95815ea11460854e/src/modules/schnorr/schnorr.md
42. Ziegeldorf, J.H., Grossmann, F., Henze, M., Inden, N., Wehrle, K.: CoinParty: Secure multi-party mixing of bitcoins. In: CODASPY 2015 (2015)

Could Network Information Facilitate Address Clustering in Bitcoin?

Till Neudecker$^{(\boxtimes)}$ and Hannes Hartenstein

Institute of Telematics, Karlsruhe Institute of Technology, Karlsruhe, Germany
{till.neudecker,hannes.hartenstein}@kit.edu

Abstract. Address clustering tries to break the privacy of bitcoin users by linking all addresses created by an individual user, based on information available from the blockchain. As an alternative information source, observations of the underlying peer-to-peer network have also been used to attack the privacy of users. In this paper, we assess whether combining blockchain and network information may facilitate the clustering process. For this purpose, we apply all applicable clustering heuristics that are known to us to current blockchain information and associate the resulting clusters with IP address information extracted from observing the message flooding process of the bitcoin network. The results indicate that only a small share of clusters (less than 8%) were conspicuously associated with a single IP address. Also, only a small number of IP addresses showed a conspicuous association with a single cluster.

1 Introduction

The electronic currency system bitcoin [13] allows users to transfer money using pseudonyms represented by public keys (*addresses*). As all transactions in bitcoin are stored in a public blockchain, it is common practice to create new addresses for each transaction. This aims at ensuring the privacy of participants by making the linkage of several addresses difficult. Previous research (e.g., [16]), however, proposed heuristics for the clustering of addresses and showed that it is possible to link several addresses to one user. It was also shown that it can be possible to establish a link between one of a user's addresses and information from additional sources that reveals the user's identity. In the worst case, this knowledge can be used to learn about all financial transactions of an identifiable user.

Before becoming part of the blockchain, transactions are broadcasted through a public peer-to-peer (P2P) network. By joining and observing that network, additional information about the issuer of a transaction might be gained. Several works indicate that such linking is possible (e.g., [6]). However, with users using dynamically assigned IP addresses, operating from clients behind NAT routers or using wallet services, it is not clear whether information obtained by participating in the network and observing the normal message flow could be used in deanonymization of bitcoin users.

One fundamental challenge is that neither for a blockchain based clustering nor for the extracted network based information a ground truth validation can

© International Financial Cryptography Association 2017
M. Brenner et al. (Eds.): FC 2017 Workshops 2017, LNCS 10323, pp. 155–169, 2017.
https://doi.org/10.1007/978-3-319-70278-0_9

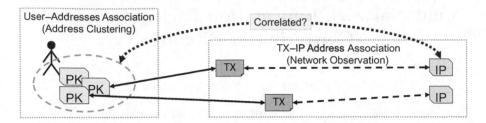

Fig. 1. High-level overview of the used approach: addresses are clustered using known heuristics; transactions are assigned to IP addresses based on network observations and to clusters based on their content. We then check whether single clusters are conspicuously often associated to a single IP address, and whether single IP addresses are conspicuously often associated to a single cluster.

be performed (with a few exceptions). Therefore, we analyze whether clusters created using known heuristics are correlated to IP addresses associated to transactions based on network observations (cf. Fig. 1). As both approaches operate on disjoint data (blockchain vs. network) but aim at indicating the same outcome (addresses controlled by one user), a correlation would likely mean that both approaches in fact approximate the desired outcome.

The contributions of this paper are twofold:

- We review all published heuristics known to us and apply them to the current blockchain state in a comparable and reproducible manner.
- We show that although for the majority of users no correlation between network information and the clustering performed on blockchain data could be found, a small number of participants exhibit correlations that might make them susceptible to network based deanonymization attacks.

2 Related Work

The anonymity of users in bitcoin has been analyzed in several ways in the past. The fact that all transactions are publicly available facilitated clustering approaches with the goal to group addresses by the controlling user. We will review all published heuristics known to us in detail in Sect. 4 and briefly sketch related work here. The first analysis was performed by Reid and Harrigan [16] and already made use of the most commonly used heuristic. Meiklejohn et al. [10] proposed additional heuristics based on the behavior of standard clients.

Blockchain information has not only been used for clustering but also for large scale analysis of the distribution of wealth, common transaction patterns, behavior analysis, etc. [17], and for an evaluation of user privacy [1]. More recently, Nick was able to use ground truth data of consumer wallets due to a bug in a client implementation [15]. This work also proposes a heuristic specific to the behavior of consumers in bitcoin. Reasons for the effectiveness of clustering have been given by Harrigan et al. [5], e.g., the incremental growth of clusters.

Network based information has also been used previously. It was shown that the topology of the bitcoin peer-to-peer network can be inferred by using marker IP addresses [2], by exploiting flaws in the bitcoin reference client implementation [12], or by observing the information propagation through the network [14]. Furthermore, the observation of anomalous relaying behavior has been used to map bitcoin addresses to IP addresses [7]. It was also shown that the creation time of transactions can be used to infer the user's time zone [4]. Biryukov and Pustogarov [3] performed a man in the middle attack on clients using Tor by becoming the only possible Tor exit node by banning all other exit nodes in the bitcoin network. This also enabled them to link IP addresses to bitcoin addresses.

3   Fundamentals

The two main data objects in bitcoin are *transactions* and *blocks*. Transactions are used to transfer bitcoins between users. Blocks are created in the process of mining and contain a set of accepted transactions that the bitcoin network has agreed on to be valid. We will exclude the details of mining here. Transactions specify inputs and outputs, i.e., sources and destinations of the money flow. With the exception of coinbase transactions, inputs refer to an output of another, previous transaction. These inputs are then spending the output. Obviously, one output must not be spent more than once.

Transactions: All accepted transactions form the transaction graph. The transaction graph is constructed by using all accepted transactions as vertices and by adding one edge from every output to the input that is spending the output. The transaction graph is a directed, acyclic, append-only graph, which represents the current ownership of bitcoins. Intuitively, ownership of bitcoins is the right to spend them. Technically, ownership of bitcoins equals the possession of a private key that corresponds to a public key, which is defined in the output of a transaction. Hence, in order to create a valid transaction, a user must be able to sign the transaction spending an input using the private key corresponding to the public key defined in the spent output. The public keys are also called *addresses*, as they specify where the money is sent to.

For the definition of the heuristics used in clustering, we will use the following notation, which loosely follows the notation used in [10]: Let $t \in T$ be a transaction. Let $\mathcal{P}$ be the set of all addresses specified in all transactions in T. Let the set inputs$(t) \subseteq \mathcal{P}$ include all addresses referenced by the inputs of a transaction t and the set outputs$(t) \subseteq \mathcal{P}$ include all addresses contained in the outputs of a transaction t. Let $o_j(t) \in$ outputs(t) be the j-th output $(j \leq |\text{outputs}(t)|)$, and let $i_j(t) \in$ inputs(t) be the j-th input $(j \leq |\text{inputs}(t)|)$.

Each user can create a practically unlimited number of distinct public/private key pairs and use each of them only for one transaction. Hence, each address can be seen as a pseudonym of the user. The goal of address clustering is to partition the set of addresses into subsets (*clusters*), so that each subset contains the addresses under the control of one user.

Network Information: After a transaction is created it needs to be broadcasted through the bitcoin P2P network in order to reach all participants. Especially miners need to receive the transaction, check its correctness, and include the transaction in an upcoming block. The bitcoin P2P network currently consists of 4,200–5,700 reachable peers[1] and an unknown number of unreachable peers.

In order to publish a transaction on the network, the user has to either run one of the reachable peers or connect to one of the reachable peers and transmit the transaction. When a new transaction arrives at a peer, the peer checks the correctness of the transaction and rebroadcasts the transaction to all of its neighbors. Therefore, the transaction gets flooded through the whole network. For rebroadcasting, the bitcoin reference client *bitcoind*, which is used by the vast majority of network peers, implements a mechanism called *trickling*: Transactions are not immediately rebroadcasted to all neighbors, but are randomly delayed according to a Poisson distribution.

4   Clustering Based on Blockchain Information

Several heuristics for address clustering in bitcoin have been proposed. We will first briefly describe the general procedure for clustering, which uses one or more heuristics, and then describe and discuss the used heuristics.

4.1   Clustering Procedure and Heuristics

The clustering procedure computes a partition $\Pi = \{C_1, C_2, ..., C_n\}$ of the set of all addresses $\mathcal{P}$ with $C_1, ..., C_n$ denoting the resulting clusters. For this, it processes all transactions in their temporal sequence. For each transaction t, all selected heuristics compute a partition $\Pi_t = \{\Pi_t^1, ..., \Pi_t^m\}$ of all input and output addresses of t (outputs(t) $\cup$ inputs(t)). This transaction specific partition Π_t encodes which addresses used in the transaction are controlled by one user (i.e., those addresses being in one Π_t^i).

The heuristics are applied in a predefined order, each heuristic further altering Π_t. Π_t is then used to update Π: First, all clusters Π_t^i are added to P. Then each added cluster Π_t^i is merged with all existing clusters in Π that contain any of the addresses in Π_t^i. This transitively connects all addresses controlled by one user (according to the applied heuristics).

Heuristic 1 (H1): Multi-Input. If a transaction spends more than one input, the transaction needs to be signed using the private keys corresponding to the public keys from *all* inputs. Assuming that the transaction was created by a

---

[1] According to our measurements (http://dsn.tm.kit.edu/bitcoin), there are $\approx$4,200 peers reachable via IPv4 and an additional $\approx$1,500 peers reachable via IPv6. As we do not know how many peers are dual-stacked (reachable via IPv4 *and* IPv6), we cannot directly determine the exact number of reachable peers.

single user, that user controls all addresses that are input to the transaction. This heuristic was first used in [10,16].

For a transaction t the partition determined by this heuristic is

$$\Pi_t = \{\text{inputs}(t), \{o_1(t)\}, ..., \{o_{|\text{outputs}(t)|}(t)\}\}.$$

This heuristic is always applied first and is used for all our clusterings. This heuristic only produces false positives (i.e., clustering addresses that are not controlled by the same user into the same cluster), if the assumptions are not correct. This can be either the case if users give services access to their private key (e.g., Mt.Gox) or if transactions are assembled by multiple users in a decentralized fashion (e.g., CoinJoin [9]).

Heuristic 2 (H2): Change Address. One output of a transaction can only be spent in its entirety. Hence, if Alice controls an unspent output worth 2 BTC and wants to pay Bob 1 BTC, Alice creates a transaction claiming the 2 BTC as an input with two outputs: One output of 1 BTC to Bob's address and one output of 1 BTC to a *change address* [10] under the control of Alice (assuming no transaction fees). Since the change address as well as the addresses of the inputs (cf. *H1*) are all controlled by Alice, they should be clustered together. The challenge is to identify which output is the change address and which output is the address of the payee, which should be in a different cluster. Meiklejohn et al. [10] proposed the following heuristic to identify the change address: An output $o_j(t)$ is the change address if these four conditions are met:

1. This is the first appearance of the address $o_j(t)$.
2. The transaction t is not a coin generation.
3. There is no address within the outputs, which also appears on the input side (self-change address).
4. Condition 1 is only met for $o_j(t)$ and not also for some $o_k(t)$ with $j \neq k$.

For a transaction t the partition determined by this heuristic (based on Π_t from *H1*) is

$$\Pi_t = \{\text{inputs}(t) \cup \{o_j(t)\}, \{o_1(t)\}, ..., \{o_{j-1}(t)\}, \{o_{j+1}(t)\}, ..., \{o_{|\text{outputs}(t)|}(t)\}\}.$$

The rationale behind this heuristic is that the standard bitcoin client creates a new key pair for change addresses and only uses these addresses once when the received change is spent again. Ancient version of the client used to send change to an address that was also used as input (self-change address).

Obviously, this heuristic can lead to false positives and false negatives. In a transaction with two outputs, which have not appeared before, it is not possible to determine the change address (cond. 4), although there might be one. Also, a transaction could spend money to two payees without any change and the heuristic could mistake one of the payees addresses for the change address.

Heuristic 2 Exceptions. In order to capture changing wallet behavior, two exceptions to Heuristic 2 have been proposed in [10]. There is no change address in a transaction t if there is an output that...

- had already received exactly one input (**H2a**)
- had been used in a self-change transaction before (**H2b**)

These exceptions captured common behavior in 2013, however, it is not clear whether the exceptions are useful anymore.

We now define an additional exception to heuristic $H2$ that makes use of blockchain information that is newer than the current processed transaction t. The behavior for change addresses is that they are only used once. In $H2$ we demand that, in order to qualify as a change address, an address must not occur before t. However, with **H2c** we demand that the address also does not occur in later transactions (except for one occurrence as an input).

Value Based (HV): Optimal Change. If a transaction has only one output, whose value is smaller than any of its inputs, this output address is likely the change address. This heuristic is based on the behavior of bitcoin clients to minimize the transaction size, i.e., the number of inputs and outputs. If the change was larger than any input, the input could be omitted and the change could be reduced by this input. This heuristic was used in [15].

Consumer Based: Redeeming Transaction. Nick [15] proposed a heuristic that uses properties of the redeeming transaction of a possible change output (i.e., the transaction with the change output as an input). For a change address it requires that the redeeming transaction has at most two outputs. The heuristic was used specifically for clustering consumer wallets that show this characteristic. As we cannot distinguish between consumer wallets and other wallets, we omit this heuristic from further analysis.

Cluster Growth (HG). In [5] it has been shown that clusters normally grow in steady, but small steps. Especially the merger of two already large clusters by a new transaction is unlikely and might hint at a false positive from one of the applied heuristics. This observation can be formulated as a heuristic that can be applied after other heuristics have already established a transaction specific partition.

HG$_k$: If updating Π with Π_t would cause the largest affected partition in Π to grow by more than a constant number of k addresses, then set

$$\Pi_t = \{\{i_1(t)\}, ..., \{i_{|\text{inputs}(t)|}\}, \{o_1(t)\}, ..., \{o_{|\text{outputs}(t)|}(t)\}\}.$$

Discussion. To our knowledge, we list all heuristics that were published. However, there is a whole class of heuristics that we barely cover. Most described heuristics only consider single transactions. However, heuristics could use the whole transactions graph and base their decisions on any property derived from the graph. The consumer based heuristic and the Cluster Growth heuristic use simple transaction graph information, but much more sophisticated methods, e.g., facilitating metrics such as connectivity or centrality are possible.

Furthermore, we acknowledge that a lot of manual effort can be put into a better clustering by carefully inspecting special cases, modeling specific behavior and manually merging or splitting clusters. For the sake of comparability, we chose not to do any manual intervention in our clustering process.

4.2   Results

We will now compare the results of the clustering process with different combinations of heuristics. The clustering was performed at block 440,349. Using machines equipped with a Xeon E7-8837 and 512 GB memory, one run of our implementation[2] of the clustering process took about 30 min to complete. Prior to clustering we generated the transaction graph as a pointer-based data structure. This data structure is then read to memory by the clustering process, which is run completely in-memory and requires no further hard disk accesses.

Table 1 lists a comparison of key properties of the resulting clusterings for the heuristics *H1*, all discussed variants of *H2*, *HV*, and several variants of *HG*. Details on the distribution of cluster sizes are given in the Appendix. Applying only heuristic *H1* results in a clustering with 88 m clusters. Additionally applying *H2* causes more clusters to be merged, hence resulting in fewer, but bigger, clusters. Additionally applying variants of *HG*, however, causes fewer clusters to be merged, hence resulting in more, but smaller, clusters.

The different variants of heuristic *H2* lead to 46 m to 63 m clusters. The three exceptions to *H2* cause fewer clusters to be merged than by applying *H1* and

Table 1. Comparison of all heuristics. Total number of addresses: 196,963,722, total number of transactions: 172,868,721.

Heuristics	# Cluster	$\varnothing$Size	Max size	#clusters w/size 1
H1	88 m	2.24	12 m	65 m
H1+H2	46 m	4.25	92 m	29 m
H1+H2a	51 m	3.89	87 m	32 m
H1+H2b	63 m	3.10	66 m	40 m
H1+H2c	48 m	4.13	85 m	30 m
H1+HV	72 m	2.71	76 m	62 m
H1+HG_{10}	146 m	1.34	0.1 m	123 m
H1+HG_{100}	121 m	1.62	0.25 m	97 m
H1+HG_{1000}	108 m	1.83	1 m	84 m
H1+HG_{10000}	104 m	1.88	8 m	81 m

---

[2] https://github.com/tillneu/bitcoin-clusterer.

H2 only. The strongest effect on the resulting clusters has *H2b*, which reduces the average cluster size from 4.25 for *H2* to 3.1 addresses per cluster for *H2b*.

The value based heuristic *HV* has only a small effect on the average cluster size (grows to 2.71 addresses per cluster) but a large effect on the size of the largest cluster (from 12 m to 76 m). A possible explanation for the result is that a disproportionately large share of transactions that originated from that super-cluster have a combination of input and output values that makes *HV* applicable to them, thus merging more addresses into the super-cluster.

A small choice of the parameter k for the heuristic *HG* causes fewer clusters to be merged as the threshold is easily exceeded. This causes the average cluster size to decrease down to 1.34 addresses per cluster for HG_{10}. Notably, there are only minor changes in the number of clusters with a size of 10 to 100,000 addresses (cf. Appendix). Most likely, transactions that cause a false positive in *H1* are less likely to occur in these medium sized clusters.

In all variants the largest identified cluster contains between 100,000 and 92 m addresses. This cluster contains among others the addresses of the former exchange Mt.Gox. The existence of this super-cluster was also discussed in [5]. The size of that cluster is substantially increased by application of variants of *H2* and *HV*, whereas the application of *HG* can limit the growth of that cluster.

5 Network Information

We will now explain how network based information was acquired and how that information is compared to the blockchain information based clustering results. The main idea is to associate IP addresses to transactions based on observations on the bitcoin P2P network and then use the previously established linking between clusters and transactions in order to determine the correlation between clusters and IP addresses.

5.1 Association of Transactions and IP Addresses

In order to observe transactions being flooded through the network, we deployed two monitor peers that maintain connections to all reachable peers in the network and log for each transaction, when it is received from each peer in the network. For each transaction there is one peer (*originator*) which first sent the transaction to our monitor peer. We want to associate one IP address to each transaction. However, we cannot conclude that the first peer we received a transaction from has really first brought the transaction to the network, nor can we conclude that the peer generated the transaction. First, the user could connect to any reachable peer in the network, send the transaction to that peer and leave the network afterwards. Secondly, due to trickling, the transaction can be sent to other network peers, which might forward the transaction to our monitor peers before we receive the transaction from the creating peer. Therefore, we apply several heuristics that aim at reducing the number of obviously false mappings:

- If both monitor peers first received a transaction from different peers, we discard both possible originators.
- If the time difference at which the transaction is received from the originator by both monitor peers differs by $\geq$100 ms, the originator is discarded.
- The subsequent receptions of the transaction from other peers must not be faster than what the speed of light in fiber allows. By using GeoIP services[3], we can approximate the location of the other network peers and establish a lower bound on the time it takes for a transaction to be transmitted from the originator to our monitor peer *via* any other network peer. If we receive a transaction faster than that lower bound, we discard the originator.

During the monitored period between block 366,000 (2015-07-19) and block 440,349 (2016-11-24), 96,520,958 transactions were added to the blockchain. For 9,934,056 of these transactions ($\approx$10%), we identified an originator IP address using the heuristics described above. In total, 79,079 unique IP addresses appeared as originators. This leads to an average of about 125 transactions per IP address. However, the number of transactions associated per IP address follows a heavy tailed distribution. Figure 2 shows the distribution of how many transactions were associated with each IP address. Most IP addresses were an originator address only for a small number of transactions. However, two IP addresses were originators for more than 65,000 transactions. Interestingly, both of these IP addresses (one of which IPv4 and one IPv6) are in IP ranges assigned to the same hosting provider.

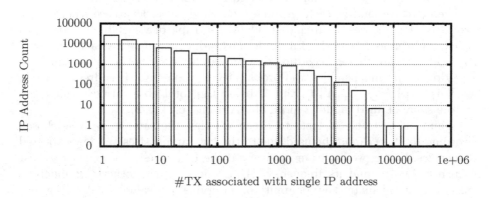

Fig. 2. Histogram of the number of unique transactions associated per IP address. Read as: *There are 10,000 IP addresses, each of which are associated to 4 to 8 transactions.*

Although we are able to associate IP addresses to transactions, we do not know whether the mapped IP addresses in fact identify the user that issued the transaction and simply regard the IP address as a piece of information that might be linked to the user. In order to analyze that linking, we will now compare the results from the clustering based on the transaction graph to the collected IP address information.

---

[3] http://dev.maxmind.com/geoip/.

5.2 Methodology

We will now introduce the notation used for the association of clusters with IP address information. For the association between transactions and clusters we use the following notation: Let $c(t)$ describe the cluster that issued a transaction t according to $H1$. Let the set of transactions issued by a cluster C be $T_C := \{t \in T : c(t) = C\}$. For the association between transactions and IP addresses as described in Sect. 5.1 we use the following notation: Let $\mathcal{A}$ be the set of all observed IP addresses. Let $a(t) \in \mathcal{A}$ describe the IP address of the originator (if any) of a transaction t. Finally, we define the tuple of all IP addresses associated with a cluster C as $A_C = (a(t) : t \in T_C)$. A_C is defined as a tuple because single IP addresses can occur multiple times in A_C and we are interested in that count.

The main question now is whether there is a correlation between clusters and IP addresses or whether for each transaction the originator is simply a random IP address. Both, IP addresses and clusters, are nominal variables that cannot be ranked in any way. Standard statistical methods (e.g., [11]) would suggest to fill a contingency table with all observed IP addresses as one dimension and all clusters as the other dimension. Then, for each tuple (IP address, Cluster) the expected frequency and the observed frequency could be compared. However, a problem with the data is that the contingency table is very sparsely populated. In order to perform the chi squared test, no more than 20% of the expected frequencies should be less than 5 and all individual expected frequencies should be 1 or greater [18], which is not the case for our data. Even if the frequencies were sufficient, the large sample size would cause biased results [8].

Therefore, we analyze each cluster C separately in order to see whether the associated IP addresses A_C are independent. The tuple of associated IP addresses A_C can be seen as the result of a random experiment, where for each cluster C $|A_C|$ addresses are chosen according to a probability distribution. If clusters and IP addresses are independent, the probability to choose an IP address A would be $P(A) = |A| / \sum_{A' \in \mathcal{A}} |A'|$ (with $|A|$ being the total observation count of A, i.e., the share of an IP address in all observations, cf. Fig. 2).

Again, most statistical tests to check whether the sample A_C was chosen according to $P(A)$ cannot be used due to the low sample sizes and low expected frequencies. Hence, we limit our analysis to the IP address $\hat{A}$ that occurs most frequently in A_C, and its frequency $|\hat{A}_C|$. Under the hypothesis of independence, we can calculate the probability of observing any value for $|\hat{A}_C|$. Figure 3 shows the probability distribution $P_i(X = |\hat{A}_C|)$ that describes the probability of observing a specific value for $|\hat{A}_C|$, assuming independence of IP addresses and clusters. For large values of $|A_C|$, the distribution can be approximated with the binomial distribution with p being the probability of the most likely IP address ($p \approx 0.02$ for our data). For a cluster C, we reject the independence hypothesis if the probability of observing the most frequent IP address $\hat{A}_C$ at least $|\hat{A}_C|$ times is less than 1%, according to P_i. We then add this cluster to the set of conspicuous clusters $C^+ = \{C : P_i(X \geq |\hat{A}_C|) < 1\%\}$. The chosen significance level implies that about 1% of the clusters in C^+ actually are not conspicuous.

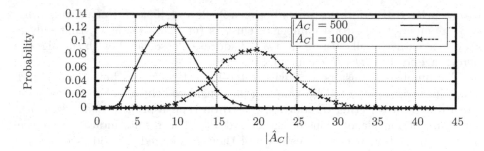

Fig. 3. Probability distribution $P_i(X = |\hat{A}_C|)$ for $|A_C| = 500$ and $1{,}000$ transactions, respectively, assuming independence and given the empirical IP address counts (cf. Fig. 2). Values numerically approximated.

Obviously, in addition to checking for each cluster whether the associated IP addresses were randomly chosen, we can also check for each IP address whether the associated clusters are randomly chosen. This analysis has been also performed using the same method as described above for the opposite direction with T_A denoting the set of transactions associated with an IP address A and $\mathcal{A}^+$ the set of conspicuous IP addresses according to the hypothesis testing.

5.3   Results and Discussion

From our data we selected all clusters with at least two IP addresses associated ($|A_C| \geq 2$), determined $|\hat{A}_C|$ for these clusters, and calculated the set of conspicuous clusters C^+. Table 2 shows the number of clusters with at least two associated IP addresses ($|\{C : |A_C| \geq 2\}|$) and the number of conspicuous clusters $|C^+|$ for various heuristics. The number of clusters with at least

Table 2. Comparison of the number of clusters with at least two associated IP addresses ($|\{C : |A_C| \geq 2\}|$) and the number and share of conspicuous clusters (C^+), and the share of conspicuous IP addresses ($\mathcal{A}^+$) for various heuristics.

Heuristics	$\|\{C : \|A_C\| \geq 2\}\|$	$\|C^+\|$	$\frac{\|C^+\|}{\|\{C:\|A_C\|\geq 2\}\|}$	$\frac{\|\mathcal{A}^+\|}{\|\{A:\|T_A\|\geq 2\}\|}$
H1	282,950	14,879	5.26%	18.7%
H1+H2	398,802	32,623	8.18%	6.2%
H1+H2a	387,696	32,026	8.26%	6.2%
H1+H2b	456,063	35,138	7.70%	6.5%
H1+H2c	452,189	35,602	7.87%	6.7%
H1+HV	296,132	14,736	4.97%	6.9%
H1+HG_{10}	299,140	15,537	5.19%	16.7%
H1+HG_{100}	300,927	15,755	5.23%	19.6%
H1+HG_{1000}	301,775	16,434	5.45%	20.2%
H1+HG_{10000}	308,900	18,788	6.08%	19.7%

two associated IP addresses varies between 283k and 456k clusters. Comparing these numbers to the total number of clusters (cf. Table 1) shows, that only a small percentage of all clusters has two IP addresses associated, with the highest percentage for the *H1+H2c* combination.

The number of clusters $|C^+|$ with a too-large $|\hat{A}_C|$ varies between 15k and 35k, which corresponds to 5% to 8.3% of the considered clusters. For comparison, when randomly selecting IP addresses based on their a-priori probability $P(a)$, the share of conspicuous clusters is around 1%. The results indicate that the highest correlation between clusters and their associated IP addresses exists, when clustering using variants of *H2*. For the value based heuristic, the growth based heuristic, and the base heuristic *H1*, fewer conspicuous clusters were found.

Table 2 also shows the share of conspicuous IP addresses $\mathcal{A}^+$ among those IP addresses with at least two associated transactions. The share varies between 6.2% and 20.2% with the smallest percentages for clusterings with variants of *H2*. This is caused by the extremely large super cluster that is created by these heuristics (cf. Table 1): The probability to randomly select that cluster very often (assuming independence) rises with the number of transactions associated with that cluster. Therefore, the independence hypothesis gets accepted for more IP addresses.

Only for a small share of clusters and IP addresses, a correlation between clusters and network information could be shown. At least for these clusters, information obtained by observing the network could also be used in a constructive way during the clustering process. For example, the set of candidate clusters for a transaction could be reduced based on networking information. Also, the information could be used for tie breaking when having multiple change address candidates.

For the majority of clusters and IP addresses, we did not observe any correlation to network information. This could mean that there is no correlation, or that the used method did not reveal a correlation. For example, a more powerful observer with more monitoring nodes could be able to associate IP addresses to transactions more precisely. Furthermore, the statistical analysis used here only reveals certain correlations between a cluster and a single IP address.

6   Conclusion

In this paper we performed address clustering in bitcoin according to published heuristics, compared the resulting clusters to IP address information obtained from observations in the bitcoin P2P network, and showed that only a small share of clusters was conspicuously associated with a single IP address, and that only a small number of IP addresses showed a conspicuous association with a single cluster.

Our results indicate that for the vast majority of users network information cannot facilitate address clustering easily. However, a small number of participants exhibit correlations that might make them susceptible to network based deanonymization attacks. A more precise network observation or better clustering heuristics might reveal further correlations that could not be observed with our approach. A next step could be to identify the anomalous behavior that caused the revealed correlations. Since this would require an in-depth analysis of single entities on the network, we decided not to carry out such an analysis without ensuring the user's privacy. We emphasize that for ethical reasons no further attempt at linking the conspicuous IP addresses or clusters to other available information was performed.

In future work, a privacy preserving method for identifying the causes of the correlation should be developed. Such an analysis could point to possible improvements in the P2P protocol or specific client implementations. Furthermore, the used heuristic for extracting the originator from the network observation could be improved to consider IP address changes over time or the aggregation of IP addresses by provider or location. Finally, the statistical analysis might benefit from more advanced methods to establish sharper bounds on possible correlations.

Acknowledgement. This work was supported by the German Federal Ministry of Education and Research (BMBF) within the project $KASTEL\_IoE$ in the Competence Center for Applied Security Technology ($KASTEL$). The authors acknowledge the use of the InstitutsCluster II at the Steinbuch Centre for Computing, and would like to thank the anonymous reviewers for their valuable comments and suggestions.

Appendix

Figures 4 and 5 show a comparison of the resulting cluster sizes for all discussed clustering heuristics and various parameterizations of the growth based heuristic HG. For all heuristics, the cluster sizes roughly follow a power-law distribution.

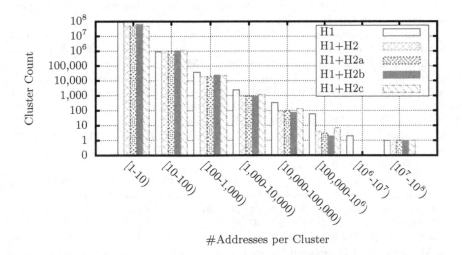

Fig. 4. Histogram of the number of clusters for various sizes (i.e., number of addresses per cluster).

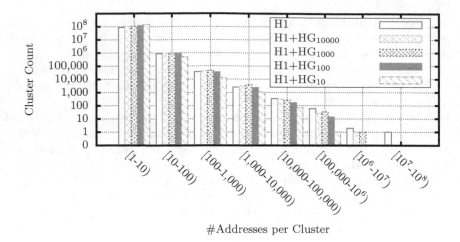

Fig. 5. Histogram of the number of clusters for various sizes (i.e., number of addresses per cluster).

References

1. Androulaki, E., Karame, G.O., Roeschlin, M., Scherer, T., Capkun, S.: Evaluating user privacy in bitcoin. In: Sadeghi, A.-R. (ed.) FC 2013. LNCS, vol. 7859, pp. 34–51. Springer, Heidelberg (2013). https://doi.org/10.1007/978-3-642-39884-1_4
2. Biryukov, A., Khovratovich, D., Pustogarov, I.: Deanonymisation of clients in bitcoin P2P network. In: Proceedings of the 2014 ACM SIGSAC Conference on Computer and Communications Security. ACM (2014)
3. Biryukov, A., Pustogarov, I.: Bitcoin over tor isn't a good idea. arXiv preprint arXiv:1410.6079 (2014)
4. DuPont, J., Squicciarini, A.C.: Toward de-anonymizing bitcoin by mapping users location. In: Proceedings of the 5th ACM Conference on Data and Application Security and Privacy, pp. 139–141. ACM (2015)
5. Harrigan, M., Fretter, C.: The unreasonable effectiveness of address clustering. arXiv preprint arXiv:1605.06369 (2016)
6. Kaminsky, D.: Black ops of TCP/IP. Black Hat USA (2011)
7. Koshy, P., Koshy, D., McDaniel, P.: An analysis of anonymity in bitcoin using P2P network traffic. In: Christin, N., Safavi-Naini, R. (eds.) FC 2014. LNCS, vol. 8437, pp. 469–485. Springer, Heidelberg (2014). https://doi.org/10.1007/978-3-662-45472-5_30
8. Lin, M., Lucas Jr., H.C., Shmueli, G.: Research commentary-too big to fail: large samples and the p-value problem. Inf. Syst. Res. **24**(4), 906–917 (2013)
9. Maxwell, G.: Coinjoin: Bitcoin privacy for the real world (2013). https://bitcointalk.org/index.php?topic=279249. Accessed 27 Sep 2016
10. Meiklejohn, S., Pomarole, M., Jordan, G., Levchenko, K., McCoy, D., Voelker, G.M., Savage, S.: A fistful of bitcoins: characterizing payments among men with no names. In: Proceedings of the 2013 Conference on Internet Measurement Conference, pp. 127–140. ACM (2013)
11. Mendenhall, W., Beaver, R.J., Beaver, B.M.: Introduction to Probability and Statistics. Cengage Learning (2012)

12. Miller, A., Litton, J., Pachulski, A., Gupta, N., Levin, D., Spring, N., Bhattacharjee, B.: Discovering Bitcoin's Public Topology and Influential Nodes (2015)
13. Nakamoto, S.: Bitcoin: a peer-to-peer electronic cash system, p. 1 (2012), p. 28 (2008)
14. Neudecker, T., Andelfinger, P., Hartenstein, H.: Timing analysis for inferring the topology of the bitcoin peer-to-peer network. In: 2016 International IEEE Conference on Advanced and Trusted Computing (ATC), pp. 358–367, July 2016
15. Nick, J.D.: Data-Driven De-Anonymization in Bitcoin. Master's thesis, ETH-Zürich (2015)
16. Reid, F., Harrigan, M.: An analysis of anonymity in the bitcoin system. In: Altshuler, Y., Elovici, Y., Cremers, A., Aharony, N., Pentland, A. (eds.) Security and Privacy in Social Networks, pp. 197–223. Springer, New York (2013). https://doi.org/10.1007/978-1-4614-4139-7_10
17. Ron, D., Shamir, A.: Quantitative analysis of the full bitcoin transaction graph. In: Sadeghi, A.-R. (ed.) FC 2013. LNCS, vol. 7859, pp. 6–24. Springer, Heidelberg (2013). https://doi.org/10.1007/978-3-642-39884-1_2
18. Yates, D., Moore, D., McCabe, G.: The Practice of Statistics. WH Freeman and Company, New York (1996)

Switch Commitments: A Safety Switch for Confidential Transactions

Tim Ruffing[1(✉)] and Giulio Malavolta[2]

[1] Saarland University, Saarbrücken, Germany
tim.ruffing@mmci.uni-saarland.de
[2] Friedrich-Alexander University, Erlangen-Nürnberg, Germany
malavolta@cs.fau.de

Abstract. Cryptographic agility is the ability to switch to larger cryptographic parameters or different algorithms in the case of security doubts. This very desirable property of cryptographic systems is inherently difficult to achieve in cryptocurrencies due to their permanent state in the blockchain: for example, if it turns out that the employed signature scheme is insecure, a switch to a different scheme can only protect the outputs of future transactions but cannot fix transaction outputs already recorded in the blockchain, exposing owners of the corresponding money to risk of theft. This situation is even worse with Confidential Transactions, a recent privacy-enhancing proposal to hide transacted monetary amounts in homomorphic commitments. If an attacker manages to break the computational binding property of a commitment, he can create money out of thin air, jeopardizing the security of the entire currency. The obvious solution is to use statistically or perfectly binding commitment schemes but they come with performance drawbacks due to the need for less efficient range proofs.

In this paper, our aim is to overcome this dilemma. We introduce *switch commitments*, which constitute a cryptographic middle ground between computationally binding and statistically binding commitments. The key property of this novel primitive is the possibility to switch existing commitments, e.g., recorded in the blockchain, from computational bindingness to statistical bindingness if doubts in the underlying hardness assumption arise. This switch trades off efficiency for security. We provide a practical and simple construction of switch commitments by proving that ElGamal commitments with a restricted message space are secure switch commitments. The combination of switch commitments and statistically sound range proofs yields an instantiation of Confidential Transactions that can be switched to be resilient against post-quantum attackers trying to inflate the currency.

1 Introduction

The security of Bitcoin relies on cryptographic hardness assumptions, e.g., the hardness of computing discrete logarithms on the `secp256k1` [3] elliptic curve. Advances in solving the discrete logarithm problem can lead to uncertainty about whether currently deployed key sizes or algorithms are still safe.

© International Financial Cryptography Association 2017
M. Brenner et al. (Eds.): FC 2017 Workshops 2017, LNCS 10323, pp. 170–181, 2017.
https://doi.org/10.1007/978-3-319-70278-0_10

In this situation, the obvious step is to obsolete current parameters, and switch to larger parameters or even entirely different algorithms in the system. Since Bitcoin relies on the hardness of the discrete logarithm problem for unforgeability of ECDSA signatures, this just ensures security of future transactions but cannot fix already performed transactions: the current unspent transaction outputs in the blockchain are still protected by the obsolete cryptographic parameters.

While this is a very unfortunate situation, because users' funds are at risk of theft, it is then the responsibility of users to spend these outputs to fresh addresses of their own, thereby creating new unspent outputs protected by new keys and possibly new cryptographic algorithms. (After this step, the attacker can still break old signing keys. However, then consensus will ensure that the old outputs are already spent and thus the signing keys are worthless.) To sum up, individual users may lose their money if they fail to perform this safety measure, but the security of the Bitcoin system as a whole is unaffected.

However, the situation will be much worse in a cryptocurrency with Confidential Transactions (CT) [6,9]. CT is a privacy-enhancing technology thas has been proposed as an extension to Bitcoin. The proposal is currently tested and evaluated in the Elements Alpha sidechain [4]; moreover, it has been successfully deployed in the cryptocurrency Monero [11].

The purpose of CT is to hide the monetary amounts in transactions by replacing plain amounts by commitments to the amounts. Since the commitment scheme used is additively homomorphic, the creator of a transaction can easily prove to the network that a transaction is *balanced*, i.e., the sum of its outputs is not more money than the sum of its inputs. The proof essentially opens the commitment to the homomorphic sum of the inputs minus the outputs to zero, which does not reveal the individual monetary amounts of the inputs and outputs in the transaction. To be sound, a non-interactive zero-knowledge proof is added to each commitment to show that the committed value is in a certain range. These so-called *range proofs* ensure that the computation of the sum does not overflow.

The current CT proposal relies on Pedersen commitments on an elliptic curve computed as $c = g^m h^r$, where m is the message, r is a random value, and g and h are public generators of the elliptic curve group. Pedersen commitments are only computationally binding under the assumption that computing discrete logarithms is hard. Thus, if an attacker manages to break one discrete logarithm with current parameters, the balance property of the currency breaks down with catastrophic consequences: Knowledge of $\log_g h$ enables the attacker to open each of his commitments, no matter what amount it is supposed to commit to, to an arbitrary amount of money. That is, the attacker can effectively create an arbitrary amount of money, limited only by the maximum amount of money that can be transferred in a transaction. Even worse, this attack will go unnoticed due to the hiding property of the commitments. As a consequence, if the attacker manages to compute a single discrete logarithm, not only is the individual security of funds threatened, but the entire currency is doomed.

As a consequence, the situation is much worse with CT than without CT, when there is doubt in the hardness of the selected parameters. With CT, the only safe way out is to introduce new parameters or algorithms and force users to spend unspent transaction outputs using the obsolete parameters *before some hard deadline T*. After time T, such obsolete outputs will not be spendable anymore, i.e., the corresponding funds will expire, effectively destroying money. This is clearly highly undesirable and it is not clear at all if such a change will be accepted by miners.

2   Switch Commitments

The obvious way to overcome all of the aforementioned issues is to use a commitment scheme that is statistically binding, i.e., it is binding even for a computationally unrestricted attacker. For instance, just adding g^r turns a computationally binding Pedersen commitment into a statistically binding ElGamal commitment.[1]

However, this modification requires efficient range proofs particularly suited to the new commitment scheme and, as a consequence, precludes the use of the highly optimized range proofs [8,13] developed for Pedersen commitments.

Instead, we aim for a solution compatible with the efficient range proofs. Our tool to achieve this goal is a novel security notion between computational and statistical bindingness. We introduce *switch commitments*, which are commitments with a *partial* and a *full* verification algorithm and special binding properties as follows.

- The commitment is computationally binding when partially verified.
- The commitment is statistically binding when fully verified.
- The commitment is *everlastingly binding*. This novel property captures the essence of switch commitments. It states that if the commitment is created by a computationally bounded attacker, and can be opened to some message when partially verified, then later even a computationally unbounded attacker can open the commitment to a different message when fully verified.

These properties enable verifiers to use the commitment scheme in a computationally binding or a statistically binding way, depending on the verification algorithm used. In particular, everlasting bindingness ensures that it is possible to start with partial verification and then *switch* to full verification, even for already existing commitments, e.g., commitments stored in the blockchain.

We prove that an ElGamal commitment $(g^m h^r, g^r)$ with a message space of polynomial size is a homomorphic switch commitment where the partial verification algorithm ignores the element g^r and verifies only the Pedersen commitment $g^m h^r$. Since the message space of commitments used in CT is restricted to integers in a fixed range to avoid overflow anyway, this switch commitment scheme is an optimal choice if a trade-off between security and performance is desired.

---

[1] The ElGamal commitment is actually even perfectly binding. We stick to the more general statistical property in this work.

2.1   Usage in Confidential Transactions

A switch commitment scheme can be used in CT as follows: When performing a transaction now, the network relies only on the partial verification to ensure that the transaction is balanced, i.e., the transaction does not generate money out of thin air. In particular, creators of transactions are forced to prove that they can open the commitments to messages such that no money will be created and the partial verification algorithm accepts the openings. While this means that the balance property holds only computationally, it is sufficient to use range proofs that cover only partial verification, i.e., the creator of the commitment must only demonstrate that he can open the commitment to a value in range when the opening is partially verified. Applied to ElGamal commitments, this effectively means that it suffices for the range proof to cover only the first element, which is a Pedersen commitment. This is more efficient because the most efficient known range proofs systems rely on Pedersen commitments.

In the future, if there is serious doubt about the cryptographic strength of the used commitment scheme or its parameters, a soft-fork can require confidential transactions created after some time T to be fully verified. Then, creators of transactions are forced to prove that they can open commitments only to values such that no money will be created, and that the full verification algorithm will accept this opening. This means that further transactions are required to provide proofs of the balance property with respect to full verification. In other words, no attacker can spend an already existing output with more money than it is supposed to contain, even if this output was created by the attacker before T (when the attacker was assumed to be computationally bounded). These proofs of the balance property require range proofs, which are potentially less efficient than range proofs which only cover partial verification. As a result, this switch to different range proofs trades off efficiency for security.

Efficiency Comparison of Known Range Proof Systems. Assume we would like to prove that the committed value m is in the range $[0, b^n]$. We further assume that we rely on elliptic curves, so group and field elements are of roughly the same size. For Pedersen commitments, the smallest known range proof has been proposed by Back and Maxwell [13] and needs $bn+1$ elements. For ElGamal commitments, the smallest known range proof has been proposed by Andreev [1] and needs $(b+1)n+1$ elements. Consequently, range proofs for Pedersen commitments are more efficient.

Soundness of the Range Proofs. All discussed range proofs for ElGamal commitments are constructed using the Fiat-Shamir transform. They are sound *even if the attacker is able to compute discrete logarithms*, and a recent result of Unruh [15] shows that their soundness holds up in a post-quantum world. That is, an instantiation of CT using ElGamal commitments and one of the aforementioned range proof systems is secure against post-quantum attackers trying to break the balance property.

We note that, even though the soundness of the aforementioned proofs is unconditional in the random oracle model, the soundness only holds against computationally bounded attackers due to the hash function in the Fiat-Shamir transform. This means that even the usage of switch commitments in CT can only protect against further advances in the discrete logarithm problem but not against a failure of the hash function used in the Fiat-Shamir transform. Consequently, larger parameters are necessary for the post-quantum soundness of the range proofs as compared to classical security.

Hidingness of the Commitments. Note that switch commitments can only be computationally hiding, so the privacy of individual commitments cannot be guaranteed if we assume that the underlying problem is not hard anymore. However, giving up privacy is arguably better than putting the security of the entire currency at risk.

Observe that a soft-fork is a possible way to perform the switch, but it is not strictly necessary. In the time until the soft-fork is deployed (or if the fork cannot be agreed upon), recipients could alternatively just force the new rules by refusing to accept payments via non-statistically secure outputs created after time T (and any of their child transaction outputs in the transaction graph), effectively rendering the funds worthless.

3   Preliminaries

In this section we introduce the notation and the cryptographic primitives that we will use throughout our work. We denote by $\lambda \in \mathbb{N}$ the security parameter and by $\mathsf{poly}(\lambda)$ any function that is bounded by a polynomial in λ. We denote any function that is *negligible* in the security parameter with $\mathsf{negl}(\lambda)$. We say that an algorithm is ppt if its running time is bounded by some function $\mathsf{poly}(\lambda)$. Given a set S, we denote by $x \leftarrow S$ that x is uniformly sampled from S.

3.1   Commitments

A commitment scheme [12] is a two-phase protocol between a sender and a receiver. In the first phase, the sender commits to a message m with a string com. In the second phase, the sender reveals the opening information op and the message m to the receiver, who can check whether com was indeed a valid commitment on m. All algorithms have access to a public random string crs generated by a trusted setup party.

A commitment scheme is *computationally hiding* if commitment itself does not reveal information about the message to a computationally bounded attacker.

Definition 1 (Computationally Hiding). *A commitment scheme with commitment algorithm* Commit *is computationally hiding if there exists a negligible function* $\mathsf{negl}(\lambda)$ *such that for all* ppt *attackers* $\mathcal{A}$, *for a randomly sampled* crs $\leftarrow$ Setup(1^λ), *and for all pairs of messages* (m_0, m_1), *we have that*

$$\Pr\left[\mathcal{A}(\mathsf{crs}, \mathsf{com}) = b \mid b \leftarrow \{0,1\}; \mathsf{com} \leftarrow \mathsf{Commit}(\mathsf{crs}, m_b)\right] \leq \frac{1}{2} + \mathsf{negl}(\lambda).$$

A commitment scheme is *binding* if no sender is able to output openings (op, op′) for the same commitment com such that they open it to two different values. We consider binding against computationally bounded and unbounded attackers.

Definition 2 (Computationally and Statistically Binding). *A verification algorithm* Verify *is computationally binding if there exists a negligible function* negl(λ) *such that for all* ppt *attackers* $\mathcal{A}$ *and for a randomly sampled* crs ← Setup(1^λ), *we have that*

$$\Pr\left[\begin{matrix} \text{Verify}(\text{crs}, \text{com}, \text{op}, m) = 1 \\ \wedge\ \text{Verify}(\text{crs}, \text{com}, \text{op}', m') = 1 \\ \wedge\ m \neq m' \end{matrix} \,\middle|\, (\text{com}, \text{op}, m, \text{op}', m') \leftarrow \mathcal{A}(\text{crs})\right] \leq \text{negl}(\lambda).$$

Statistical bindingness is defined identically except that $\mathcal{A}$ *is computationally unbounded.*

3.2 Hardness Assumptions

Here we formally describe the computational hardness assumptions that we need for the security of our construction. First, we introduce the discrete logarithm assumption.

Definition 3 (Discrete Logarithm Assumption). *Let* $\mathcal{G}$ *be a multiplicative cyclic group of order p proportional to the security parameter* λ *and let g be a generator of* $\mathcal{G}$. *We say that the* discrete logarithm *problem is hard if, for a random integer* $x \in \mathbb{Z}_p$ *and for all* ppt *attackers* $\mathcal{A}$, *there exists a negligible function* negl(λ) *such that*

$$\Pr\left[\mathcal{A}(\mathcal{G}, g, g^x) = x\right] \leq \text{negl}(\lambda).$$

Second, we formalize the computational Diffie-Hellman problem and the inverse computational Diffie-Hellman problem. These problems are known to be equivalent [2].

Definition 4 (Computational Diffie-Hellman Assumption). *Let* $\mathcal{G}$ *be a multiplicative cyclic group of order p proportional to the security parameter* λ *and let g be a generator of* $\mathcal{G}$. *We say that the* computational Diffie-Hellman *problem is hard if, for two random integers* $x, y \in \mathbb{Z}_p$ *and for all* ppt *attackers* $\mathcal{A}$, *there exists a negligible function* negl(λ) *such that*

$$\Pr\left[\mathcal{A}(\mathcal{G}, g, g^x, g^y) = g^{xy}\right] \leq \text{negl}(\lambda).$$

Definition 5 (Inverse Computational Diffie-Hellman Assumption). *Let* $\mathcal{G}$ *be a multiplicative cyclic group of order p proportional to the security parameter* λ *and let g be a generator of* $\mathcal{G}$. *We say that the* inverse computational Diffie-Hellman *problem is hard if, for a random integer* $x \in \mathbb{Z}_p$ *and for all* ppt *attackers* $\mathcal{A}$, *there exists a negligible function* negl(λ) *such that*

$$\Pr\left[\mathcal{A}(\mathcal{G}, g, g^x) = g^{x^{-1}}\right] \leq \text{negl}(\lambda),$$

where x^{-1} *denotes the multiplicative inverse of x.*

Finally, we formalize the decisional Diffie-Hellman problem.

Definition 6 (Decisional Diffie-Hellman Assumption). *Let $\mathcal{G}$ be a multiplicative cyclic group of order p proportional to the security parameter λ and let g be a generator of $\mathcal{G}$. We say that the decisional Diffie-Hellman problem is hard if, for three random integers $x, y, z \in \mathbb{Z}_p$ and for all ppt attackers $\mathcal{A}$, there exists a negligible function $\mathsf{negl}(\lambda)$ such that:*

$$\Pr\left[\mathcal{A}(\mathcal{G}, g, g^x, g^y, h) = b \mid b \leftarrow \{0,1\}; h = \begin{cases} g^{xy} & \text{if } b = 0 \\ g^z & \text{if } b = 1 \end{cases}\right] \leq \frac{1}{2} + \mathsf{negl}(\lambda).$$

4   Problem Description

The main ingredient of CT [6,9] is homomorphic Pedersen commitments [12]. Given a group $\mathcal{G}$ of prime order p, and two generators g and h, a Pedersen commitment on a message m consists of a single group element computed as $g^m h^r$, for some $r \in \mathbb{Z}_p$ chosen uniformly at random. The opening information is the tuple (m, r) and the verifier can check the validity of a given commitment by simply recomputing it. Commitments are homomorphic due to $g^m h^r \cdot g^{m'} h^{r'} = g^{m+m'} h^{r+r'}$. It is easy to see that the commitment scheme is information-theoretically hiding, and that it is computationally binding under the discrete logarithm assumption.

Loosely speaking, a confidential transaction contains a collection of commitments, whose messages add up to zero, and a publicly verifiable proof that this is the case, which is essentially just opening of the homomorphic sum commitment to zero. Additionally, each commitment comes with a range proof that demonstrates that the committed integer value lies within a certain range $[0, d]$, where d is some fixed value that determines the maximum number of currency units allowed in a single transaction output.[2] We remark that, for the specific case of Pedersen commitments, there exist efficient computationally sound range proofs based on borromean ring signatures [8] and optimizations [13].

4.1   Attacker Model

We consider an attacker whose goal is to break the binding property of a commitment by computing a commitment c over a certain value m for a confidential transaction and later on perform a transaction opening c to some $m' \neq m$ (or just proving that he knows how to open c to $m' \neq m$). Clearly this implies that the attacker was able to create money if $m' > m$.

---

[2] In fact, the value supported by CT is expressed by a floating point number, with the exponent being public and only the mantissa hidden in the commitment [6,9]. We ignore the public exponent in our description, because it does not affect our treatment. The valid range of values for the mantissa is $[0, 2^{32} - 1]$, i.e., $d = 2^{32} - 1$ satoshis (currency units).

If we consider an attacker that is computationally bounded at the time of the generation of a commitment, but later on *unbounded*, then it is easy to see that the current implementation of confidential transactions is no longer secure: An attacker could honestly compute a commitment to some small value m as $c = g^m h^r$ and then later on open it to any value $m' > m$ by computing $x = \log_g h$ and $r' = (m - m')/x + r$. It is easy to see that (m', r') is a valid opening for c.

Such a scenario may appear artificial at first glance, but one must consider that system parameters are chosen based on an estimation of the progress of the field, and therefore it is possible that unexpected developments of algorithms or new technologies render current choices for key lengths obsolete. Among others, the advent of quantum computers would imply an immediate breakdown of all systems based on discrete logarithm-related assumptions. Therefore we believe that considering an attacker that is computationally bounded only *during* the execution of the protocol constitutes a problem of practical relevance. We note that a similar model has already been considered for privacy properties in the context of electronic voting [10], multi-party computation [14], and encryption in the bounded storage model [7].

4.2   Switch Commitments

Here we extend the notion of a commitment scheme to support the *switching* functionality and we formally introduce the security definitions for our primitive.

Definition 7 (Switch Commitment Scheme). *A* switch commitment scheme (Commit, Verify^{part}, Verify^{full}) *consists of four* ppt *algorithms as follows:*

- crs $\leftarrow$ Setup(1^λ): *Given the security parameter λ, the setup algorithm* Setup *outputs a public random string* crs.
- (com, op) $\leftarrow$ Commit(crs, m): *Given the public random string* crs, *and a message m, the commitment algorithm* Commit *outputs a commitment* com *and opening information* op.
- $b \leftarrow$ Verify^{part}(crs, com, op, m): *Given the public random string* crs, *a message m, a commitment* com *and opening information* op, *the partial verification algorithm* Verify^{part} *outputs 1 iff* op *is a valid partial opening for commitment* com *on message m.*
- $b \leftarrow$ Verify^{full}(crs, com, op, m): *Given the public random string* crs, *a message m, a commitment* com *and opening information* op, *the full verification algorithm* Verify^{full} *outputs 1 iff* op *is a valid full opening for commitment* com *on message m.*

A switch commitment essentially defines two commitment schemes, namely a scheme with the partial verification algorithm and a scheme with the full verification algorithm. We require that both schemes fulfill standard security notions.

Definition 8 (Standard Security Properties). *For security of a switch commitment scheme* (Setup, Commit, Verify^{part}, Verify^{full}), *we require that*

- *the commitment algorithm* Commit *is computationally hiding,*
- *the verification algorithm* Verify^{part} *is computationally binding, and*
- *the verification algorithm* Verify^{full} *is statistically binding.*

Following our the attacker model as described in Sect. 4.1, we further require that even an unbounded attacker cannot open an old commitment (from the time when the attacker was still bounded) to a different message than it was created for. The novel security property is crucial for the intended application. In the following we formally define the notion of *everlasting bindingness* for a switch commitment scheme.

Definition 9 (Everlastingly Binding). *A switch commitment scheme* (Setup, Commit, Verify^{part}, Verify^{full}) *is everlastingly binding if there exists a negligible function* negl(λ) *such that for all attackers* $\mathcal{A} = (\mathcal{A}_0, \mathcal{A}_1)$, *where* $\mathcal{A}_0$ *is ppt (and* $\mathcal{A}_1$ *is not computationally bounded), and for a randomly sampled* crs $\leftarrow$ Setup(1^λ), *we have that*

$$
\Pr \left[
\begin{array}{c}
\text{Verify}^{part}\,(\text{crs}, \text{com}, \text{op}, m) = 1 \\
\wedge\ \text{Verify}^{full}\,(\text{crs}, \text{com}, \text{op}', m') = 1 \\
\wedge\ m \neq m' \\
\hline
(\text{com}, m, \text{op}, state) \leftarrow \mathcal{A}_0(\text{crs}); \\
(m', \text{op}') \leftarrow \mathcal{A}_1(\text{crs}, state)
\end{array}
\right] \leq \text{negl}(\lambda).
$$

5   Construction

In the following we describe our construction for a switch commitment scheme with efficient range proof. Our scheme is essentially a combination of a Pedersen and ElGamal commitment scheme with restricted message space. The commitment algorithm outputs an ElGamal commitment $(g^x h^r, g^r)$ and the full verification algorithm recomputes the commitment to verify it. However, the partial verification algorithm verifies only the Pedersen commitment $g^x h^r$. This makes it possible to use efficient range proofs optimized for Pedersen commitments.

It is crucial for the security of our construction that the message space is restricted to a size polynomial in the security parameter and the verification algorithm rejects messages not in the space. In the proof of everlasting bindingness, the reduction guesses a message in a commitment, and thus the reduction incurs a loss proportional to the size of the message space. Slightly increased parameters are necessary to compensate for this loss of security.

Note that that the message space of the commitments used in CT is already is restricted to integers in the range $[0, d]$ for a fixed non-negative integer d that is a parameter of the system and determines the maximum value of a transaction.

With the application in CT in mind, we describe the scheme for concreteness with this message space. We however stress that any other restriction of the message space is possible, as long as the message space has polynomial size in the security parameter.

- Setup($1^\lambda, d$): Initialize a multiplicative cyclic group $\mathcal{G}$ of order p, for some prime p of size proportional to λ. Sample random g and h in $\mathcal{G}$ and output crs $= (\mathcal{G}, g, h, d)$.
- Commit(crs, m): Parse crs as $(\mathcal{G}, g, h, d)$ and sample $r \in \mathbb{Z}_p$. Return com $= (g^m h^r, g^r)$, and op $= r$.
- Verify^{part} (crs, com, op, m): Parse crs as $(\mathcal{G}, g, h, d)$, com as (c, ℓ), and op as r. If $c = g^m h^r$ and $m \leq d$, then return 1. Return 0 otherwise.
- Verify^{full} (crs, com, op, m): Parse crs as $(\mathcal{G}, g, h, d)$, com as (c, ℓ), and op as r. If $c = g^m h^r$, $\ell = g^r$, and $m \leq d$, then return 1. Return 0 otherwise.

Avoiding Trusted Setup. We have chosen a description in the standard model to stress that the construction does not require random oracles. However, it is possible to avoid a trusted setup in the random oracle model by setting $h = H(g)$, for a hash function H. This is essentially what has been proposed in the draft of CT.

Homomorphic Property. Since the commitment algorithm is identical to the one of ElGamal commitments, the commitments are homomorphic due to $g^m h^r \cdot g^{m'} h^{r'} = g^{m+m'} h^{r+r'}$ and $g^r \cdot g^{r'} = g^{r+r'}$.

5.1   Security Analysis

Here, we formally argue about the security of the construction described above.

Claim 1 (Standard Security Properties). *The construction fulfills the standard security properties. In particular, commitments are computationally hiding under the decisional Diffie-Hellman assumption, the commitment scheme with the partial verification algorithm is computationally binding under the discrete logarithm assumption, and the scheme with the full verification algorithm is statistically binding.*

Proof. The construction is computationally hiding under the decisional Diffie-Hellman assumption, because the commitment algorithm is identical to the one for ElGamal commitments. For binding, recall that ElGamal commitments are perfectly (and thus statistically) binding, and that Pedersen commitments are computationally binding under the discrete logarithm assumption. We refer the reader to ElGamal [5] and Pedersen [12] for detailed discussions.   □

Theorem 2 (Everlastingly Binding). *The construction is everlastingly binding under the computational Diffie-Hellman assumption.*

Proof. We prove that the construction is everlastingly binding under the inverse computational Diffie-Hellman assumption, which is known to be equivalent to the (standard) computational Diffie-Hellman assumption [2]. Assume towards contradiction that there exists an attacker $(\mathcal{A}_0, \mathcal{A}_1)$ such that $\mathcal{A}_0$ is ppt and

$$\Pr \left[\begin{array}{c} \mathsf{Verify}^{\mathsf{part}}\,(\mathsf{crs},\mathsf{com},\mathsf{op},m) = 1 \\ \wedge\ \mathsf{Verify}^{\mathsf{full}}\,(\mathsf{crs},\mathsf{com},\mathsf{op}',m') = 1 \\ \wedge\ m \neq m' \\ \hline (\mathsf{com},m,\mathsf{op},\mathit{state}) \leftarrow \mathcal{A}_0(\mathsf{crs}); \\ (m',\mathsf{op}') \leftarrow \mathcal{A}_1(\mathsf{crs},\mathit{state}) \end{array} \right] \geq \epsilon(\lambda).$$

for some non-negligible function $\epsilon(\lambda)$. We construct the following reduction $\mathcal{R}$ against the inverse computational Diffie-Hellman assumption.

$\mathcal{R}(1^\lambda, \mathcal{G}, g, h)$: On input the group description $\mathcal{G}$, the generator g and a random element h, the reduction sets $\mathsf{crs} = (\mathcal{G}, g, h, d)$ for a fixed d. Then it runs $\mathcal{A}_0$ in input crs, which outputs $(\mathsf{com} = (c, \ell), m = w, \mathsf{op} = v)$, at some point of the execution. Finally, the reduction samples a random $d' \leq d$ and returns to the challenger

$$I = \left(\frac{\ell}{g^v} \right)^{(w-d')^{-1}}.$$

The reduction is efficient since it only executes $\mathcal{A}_0$, which is ppt; note that the reduction never executes $\mathcal{A}_1$. Let us denote w as m^{part} and v as r^{part}. By assumption, $\mathcal{A}_1$ will be able to open the commitment to some value m^{full} such that $m^{\mathsf{full}} \neq m^{\mathsf{part}}$ and $m^{\mathsf{full}} \leq d$ with probability at least $\epsilon(\lambda)$. Assume that the reduction guesses such a value m^{full} when selecting d' (note that this happens with probability at least $1/d$); then we have that $d' = m^{\mathsf{full}}$. Now we observe that

$$I = \left(\frac{\ell}{g^v} \right)^{(w-d')^{-1}} = \left(\frac{g^{r^{\mathsf{full}}}}{g^{r^{\mathsf{part}}}} \right)^{(m^{\mathsf{part}} - m^{\mathsf{full}})^{-1}}.$$

Since $g^{m^{\mathsf{full}}} h^{r^{\mathsf{full}}} = c$ (by the winning conditions of the game) or equivalently

$$g^{r^{\mathsf{full}}} = \left(\frac{c}{g^{m^{\mathsf{full}}}} \right)^{x^{-1}},$$

we have

$$I = \left(\frac{\left(\frac{c}{g^{m^{\mathsf{full}}}} \right)^{x^{-1}}}{g^{r^{\mathsf{part}}}} \right)^{(m^{\mathsf{part}} - m^{\mathsf{full}})^{-1}}.$$

Since also $g^{m^{\mathsf{part}}} h^{r^{\mathsf{part}}} = c$, it holds that

$$I = \left(\frac{\left(\frac{g^{m^{\mathsf{part}}} h^{r^{\mathsf{part}}}}{g^{m^{\mathsf{full}}}} \right)^{x^{-1}}}{g^{r^{\mathsf{part}}}} \right)^{(m^{\mathsf{part}} - m^{\mathsf{full}})^{-1}} = \left(\frac{\left(\frac{g^{m^{\mathsf{part}} + x r^{\mathsf{part}}}}{g^{m^{\mathsf{full}}}} \right)^{x^{-1}}}{g^{r^{\mathsf{part}}}} \right)^{(m^{\mathsf{part}} - m^{\mathsf{full}})^{-1}}$$

$$= \left(\frac{g^{(m^{\mathsf{part}} - m^{\mathsf{full}})x^{-1} + r^{\mathsf{part}}}}{g^{r^{\mathsf{part}}}} \right)^{(m^{\mathsf{part}} - m^{\mathsf{full}})^{-1}} = g^{x^{-1}}.$$

As argued above, this happens with probability at least $\frac{\epsilon(\lambda)}{d}$, which is non-negligible. This represents a contradiction to the computational inverse Diffie-Hellman assumption and concludes the proof.   □

Acknowledgements. We thank the anonymous reviewers for their helpful comments and suggestions. This work was supported by the German Ministry for Education and Research (BMBF) through funding for the Center for IT-Security, Privacy and Accountability (CISPA) and the German Universities Excellence Initiative.

References

1. Andreev, O.: Confidential Assets (2017). https://github.com/chain/chain/blob/confidential-spec/docs/protocol/specifications/ca.md#value-range-proof, http://www.webcitation.org/6qUEe3dKc
2. Bao, F., Deng, R.H., Zhu, H.F.: Variations of Diffie-Hellman problem. In: Qing, S., Gollmann, D., Zhou, J. (eds.) ICICS 2003. LNCS, vol. 2836, pp. 301–312. Springer, Heidelberg (2003). https://doi.org/10.1007/978-3-540-39927-8_28
3. Certicom Research: Sec 1: Elliptic curve cryptography. http://www.secg.org/download/aid-780/sec1-v2.pdf
4. Elements Project: Alpha sidechain. https://www.elementsproject.org/sidechains/alpha/
5. ElGamal, T.: A public key cryptosystem and a signature scheme based on discrete logarithms. In: Blakley, G.R., Chaum, D. (eds.) CRYPTO 1984. LNCS, vol. 196, pp. 10–18. Springer, Heidelberg (1985). https://doi.org/10.1007/3-540-39568-7_2
6. Gibson, A.: An investigation into confidential transactions (2016). http://diyhpl.us/~bryan/papers2/bitcoin/An%20investigation%20into%20Confidential%20Transactions%20-%20Adam%20Gibson%20-%202016.pdf, http://www.webcitation.org/6qUF8XYmP
7. Harnik, D., Naor, M.: On everlasting security in the hybrid bounded storage model. In: ICALP 2006 (2006)
8. Maxwell, G., Poelstra, A.: Borromean ring signatures (2015). https://github.com/Blockstream/borromean_paper/raw/master/borromean_draft_0.01_9ade1e49.pdf, http://www.webcitation.org/6qUFVS2Ux
9. Maxwell, G.: Confidential transactions (2015). https://people.xiph.org/~greg/confidential_values.txt, http://www.webcitation.org/6qUFGwJah
10. Moran, T., Naor, M.: Receipt-free universally-verifiable voting with everlasting privacy. In: Dwork, C. (ed.) CRYPTO 2006. LNCS, vol. 4117, pp. 373–392. Springer, Heidelberg (2006). https://doi.org/10.1007/11818175_22
11. Noether, S., Mackenzie, A.: Ring confidential transactions. Ledger (2016). http://www.ledgerjournal.org/ojs/index.php/ledger/article/view/34
12. Pedersen, T.P.: Non-interactive and information-theoretic secure verifiable secret sharing. In: Feigenbaum, J. (ed.) CRYPTO 1991. LNCS, vol. 576, pp. 129–140. Springer, Heidelberg (1992). https://doi.org/10.1007/3-540-46766-1_9
13. Poelstra, A., Back, A., Friedenbach, M., Maxwell, G., Wuille, P.: Confidential assets. In: BITCOIN 2017. Springer, Cham (2017). https://fc17.ifca.ai/bitcoin/papers/bitcoin17-final41.pdf
14. Unruh, D.: Everlasting multi-party computation. In: Canetti, R., Garay, J.A. (eds.) CRYPTO 2013. LNCS, vol. 8043, pp. 380–397. Springer, Heidelberg (2013). https://doi.org/10.1007/978-3-642-40084-1_22
15. Unruh, D.: Post-quantum security of Fiat-Shamir. Cryptology ePrint Archive, Report 2017/398 (2017). https://eprint.iacr.org/2017/398

(Short Paper) PieceWork: Generalized Outsourcing Control for Proofs of Work

Philip Daian[1(✉)], Ittay Eyal[1], Ari Juels[2], and Emin Gün Sirer[1]

[1] Department of Computer Science, Cornell University, Ithaca, USA
phil@cs.cornell.edu, ittay.eyal@cornell.edu, egs@systems.cs.cornell.edu
[2] Jacobs Technion-Cornell Institute, Cornell Tech, New York, USA
juels@cornell.edu

Abstract. Most prominent cryptocurrencies utilize proof of work (PoW) to secure their operation, yet PoW suffers from two key undesirable properties. First, the work done is generally wasted, not useful for anything but the gleaned security of the cryptocurrency. Second, PoW is naturally outsourceable, leading to inegalitarian concentration of power in the hands of few so-called pools that command large portions of the system's computation power.

We introduce a general approach to constructing PoW called *Piece-Work* that tackles both issues. In essence, PieceWork allows for a configurable fraction of PoW computation to be outsourced to workers. Its controlled outsourcing allows for reusing the work towards additional goals such as spam prevention and DoS mitigation, thereby reducing PoW waste. Meanwhile, PieceWork can be tuned to prevent excessive outsourcing. Doing so causes pool operation to be significantly more costly than today. This disincentivizes aggregation of work in mining pools.

1 Introduction

Distributed cryptocurrencies such as Bitcoin [16] rely on the equivalence "computation = money." To generate a batch of coins, clients in a distributed cryptocurrency system perform an operation called *mining*. Mining requires solving a computationally intensive problem involving repeated cryptographic hashing. Such problem and its solution is called a Proof of Work (PoW) [9].

As currently designed, nearly all PoWs suffer from one of two drawbacks (or both, as in Bitcoin). First, due to the computationally intensive nature of PoWs, miners of popular cryptocurrencies such as Bitcoin and Ethereum require massive computing hardware and consume natural resources such as electricity. As mining serves no purpose other than maintaining blockchain security, these resources are otherwise wasted. Second, the cost advantages of special-purpose mining equipment and a desire to reduce the variance of mining rewards incentivize the concentration of mining effort in large *mining pools*. Such concentration of power in the hands of a small number of entities erodes the egalitarian founding principles of most decentralized cryptocurrencies, starting with Bitcoin.

© International Financial Cryptography Association 2017
M. Brenner et al. (Eds.): FC 2017 Workshops 2017, LNCS 10323, pp. 182–190, 2017.
https://doi.org/10.1007/978-3-319-70278-0_11

There are several proposed solutions to first problem of costly and difficult-to-repurpose PoWs. Primecoin [12] is an alt-coin in which mining involves discovery of long sequences of prime numbers. The Primecoin PoW achieves a secondary goal beyond blockchain security, but the economic value of its byproduct remains unclear. In Permacoin [14], the mining process is replaced by proofs-of-retrievability [11], which prove that miners are storing a large corpus of data [14]. Permacoin, however, recoups only a small fraction of wasted resource, and does not recycle computational resources. Indeed, despite such efforts, the Bitcoin FAQ[1] continues to claim that, "To provide security for the Bitcoin network, the calculations involved need to have some very specific features. These features are incompatible with leveraging the computation for other purposes". Note that this claim is distinct from the marginal cost argument in [21], which claims any scheme achieving more efficiency than proof of work is impossible for equal security. This claim is refuted by [6], with further experimentation in PieceWork and elsewhere serving to validate or refute these opposing hypotheses.

To address the problem of mining centralization, some work has explored the idea of preventing PoW outsourcing. Examples include Nonoutsourceable Scratch-Off Puzzles [15], 2 Phase-Proof of Work (2P-PoW) [8], and Sign to Mine [23]. The idea behind these schemes is to base mining on the use of a private key that controls mining revenue. Thus outsourcing in, e.g., a mining pool would expose the outsourcer to theft.

Other areas of work on proof of work outsourcing involve studying solutions to attacks on outsourcing work proofs. In such attacks, an unscrupulous worker that finds a full PoW solution might choose not to submit it to the outsourcer, a problem called *withholding*. Workers can, in many cases, act in this way to harm an outsourcer's overall profit at little to no cost to themselves, as they are still getting compensated for partial solutions. (Another, blockchain-level form of this attack is known as the block withholding attack [4, 7].)

Our Contribution: PieceWork

We introduce *PieceWork*, a generalized scheme for restructuring standard hash-based PoWs that addresses the two drawbacks of existing PoWs described above. As we explain, PieceWork encompasses a number of existing PoW construction ideas, particularly from [8,9]. PieceWork decomposes a PoW into two sequential exponentially distributed computational problems called *puzzles*. In PieceWork, a PoW consists of a k_{in}-bit hard *inner* puzzle and a k_{out}-bit-hard *outer* puzzle. We call this modification *two-stage hashing* [8].

Inner puzzles are *outsourceable* as small units of work called *puzzlets*. A miner can delegate puzzlet-solving safely to other, potentially untrusted workers. Puzzlets in PieceWork are also *reusable*, meaning that they can serve *useful goals beyond blockchain security*. These include spam deterrence [1,5], denial-of-service mitigation [10], MicroMint coin generation [9,20], Tor relay payments [3], and more. The value of these puzzlets is derived from potential applications, creating a HashCash-like scheme in which verifiers can simultaneously mint Bitcoin.

---

[1] Referenced 11 Dec. 2016 at https://en.bitcoin.it/wiki/FAQ.

Our puzzlets are based on the computation recycling ideas ("breadpudding protocols") in [9]. That work predated Bitcoin, though, and thus didn't address distributed cryptocurrencies and problems such as withholding [19], a significant barrier preventing the reuse of work in PoW currencies today.

In contrast, outer puzzles can be *non-outsourceable*, i.e., solved safely only by the miner receiving the mining reward for a given PieceWork PoW. For example, by leveraging the mechanism 2P-PoW, PieceWork can cause outsourcing of outer puzzles to result in exposure to theft of mining rewards. Verifiers of the proof of work must check both inner and outer puzzle solutions.

PieceWork permits tuning of k_{in} and k_{out}, and thus the amount of permissible outsourcing in a cryptocurrency. Through gradual adjustments to k_{in} and k_{out}, PieceWork thus also supports graceful *migration from outsourceable to non-outsourceable work*. By inducing changes slightly over time, PieceWork can enable a mining community to adjust its equipment and organization over time.

In summary, our contributions in introducing PieceWork are as follows:

- *Unified PoW outsourcing framework:* PieceWork offers a unified PoW construction that incorporates a number of previously proposed ideas on safe (withholding-resistant) outsourcing, reusable PoW work, tunable outsourcing, and prevention of outsourcing in mining pools. PieceWork adapts these ideas, some predating Bitcoin, to modern cryptocurrencies and specifies them precisely, as some proposed ideas include unspecified details.
- *PoW reuse:* By offering concrete examples of computation reuse in PieceWork, we show that PoWs can both enforce blockchain security and serve practical and economically valuable secondary goals—refuting the Bitcoin Wiki claim to the contrary.
- *Novel technical extensions:* PieceWork includes novel technical extensions to previous ideas, including double-harvesting.

2   PieceWork: Two-Stage Hashing, Puzzles, and Puzzlets

We now present details of how existing PoWs are modified in PieceWork.

2.1   Background: Hash-Based PoWs

Most PoWs in distributed cryptocurrencies adhere to the same general structure as that in Bitcoin, which we focus on for concreteness. Our description here and of PieceWork thus generalize to other cryptocurrencies (e.g., Ethereum).

The Bitcoin PoWs involves finding a valid solution n to the following problem:

$$\text{SHA-256}^2\{v \parallel B_l \parallel \text{MR}(\text{TR}_1, \ldots, \text{TR}_n) \parallel T \parallel n\}$$
$$\leq target,$$

where v is a (software) version number, B_l denotes the last generated block, $TR_1, \ldots TR_n$ is a set of valid transactions not yet confirmed, $MR(x)$ denotes the root of the Merkle tree over transactions x, T is the current Unix timestamp,

n is a nonce in the space N, and *target* is a 256-bit value that determines the difficulty of the mining operation. It is updated according to the generation times of the last 2016 blocks.

We may abstract away the details of the mining problem by defining

$$X = v \parallel B_l \parallel \mathrm{MR}(\mathrm{TR}_1, \ldots, \mathrm{TR}_n) \parallel T.$$

to be the collection of inputs specific to a block. We let $H(\cdot)$ represent the hashing operation $\mathtt{SHA\text{-}256}^2$ and, for brevity, let $Z = target$.

A Bitcoin mining operation then involves, for block value X, the discovery of an input ("nonce") $n \in N$ for which $H(X, n) \leq Z$. We refer to this hash-inversion problem as the "Bitcoin puzzle", designed to achieve several properties essential to the Bitcoin system described in [14]: predictable effort, fast verification, and precomputation resistance.

2.2 Basic PieceWork Scheme

PieceWork relies on a hierarchical form of hashing that we call two-stage hashing. In PieceWork, we partition the hash function H into a pair F_{in} and F_{out} of sequentially composed functions that we refer to as the "inner" and "outer" puzzles. A global puzzle is then of the following form:

$$H(X, n) = F_{out}(X, F_{in}(X, n; s)).$$

and is considered valid when the inner and outer puzzles evaluate to below the respective targets. Here, s is an extra input used for the purposes of puzzlet recycling and discussed in detail in Sect. 3.

We refer to the inner function as a *puzzlet*. A valid solution to a puzzlet is a pair (n, s) that satisfies $I = F_{in}(X, n; s) \leq Z_{in}$.

A solution (n, s) to a puzzlet is also a solution to the global puzzle if it satisfies the additional condition $F_{out}(X, I) \leq Z_{out}$.

Both F_{in} and F_{out} must have the additional desired conditions of being cheap to compute, with output independently identically distributed across instances. The former condition allows for the fast verification required in the global scheme, and the latter allows for an exponential block generation curve that can be tuned predictably by adjusting the target. In general, we focus on hash functions or functions that hash the results of a constant-time function to achieve the latter. This includes the double-SHA256 scheme currently in Bitcoin.

In PieceWork, an outsourcer provides a puzzlet to a worker with a specified value of s (selection explained in Sect. 3). Thus a puzzlet P takes the form:

$$P = (X, Z_{in}, s).$$

The task of the worker is to find an n such that (n, s) solves a puzzlet. The expected computation of the worker is R/Z_{in} executions of F_{in} (where R is the size of the hash function range). The outsourcer can, however, quickly check the correctness of a solution (n, s) to P. Each solution to P represents one or more potentially valid preimages for F_{out} for the outsourcer to try. On average, the outsourcer must try R/Z_{out} inputs to F_{out} to find a solution to the global puzzle.

Tunability. Tuning inner and outer puzzles to any desired difficulty is straight-forward. By setting Z_{in} and Z_{out}, an expected number of hash iterations $2^{k_{in}}$ and $2^{k_{out}}$ can be enforced for inner and outer puzzles respectively. Such tunability is a feature of 2P-PoW [8], and thus PieceWork can support the migration from higly outsourceable to outsourcing resistant mining proposed there.

Non-outsourceability of outer puzzles. By choosing F_{out} appropriately, it is possible to make outer puzzles non-outsourceable, as outlined in Sect. 3.2.

2.3 Full PieceWork Scheme: Adding Withholding Resistance

Bitcoin puzzles in their current form are in fact already outsourceable. Mining pools can outsource a block solution puzzles to miners (workers in our scheme), and reward these miners for *partial proofs of work*, or solutions to the block problem that satisfy some weaker target than the global difficulty target.

Block withholding arises when a worker *can determine whether her work constitutes a full PoW solution.* In the basic version of PieceWork specified above, a worker can determine whether puzzlet I represents a global puzzle solution. She can then choose to withhold it from the outsourcer. A solution to this problem is to conceal from a worker whether or not her solution to an outsourced puzzle represents a full PoW solution. In PieceWork, such concealment is possible with a slight enhancement to the basic PieceWork scheme as follows:

$$PW(X, n) = F_{out}(X, F_{in}(X, n; s, r_{in}), r_{out}), \tag{1}$$

where r_{out} is a secret value generated by the outsourcer and $r_{in} = H(r_{out})$ for some suitable hash function H. Thus a puzzlet takes the form:

$$P = (X, Z_{in}, s, r_{in}). \tag{2}$$

Note that the dependence between r_{in} and r_{out} is important: If r_{in} were selectable by the outsourcer independently of r_{out}, the outsourcer could, for a single puzzlet solution I, solve for a valid r_{out}, and, with $1/Z_{out}$ work on expectation, easily find a global puzzle solution. Lastly, this scheme relies on the outsourcer compensating workers for only solved puzzlets, procluding "puzzlet pools" (who could withhold full puzzlet solutions). The variance of workers and other concrete parameters of this scheme are deferred to future work.

Withholding was called out as urgent on the Bitcoin developer mailing list in 2015 [19]. The mailing list post on block withholding mentions a "two-stage target mechanism" that may perhaps resemble our scheme; we were able to find one public reference to the details such a scheme in [22]. That solution suffers from potential rounding bias, lacks a full specification, and postdates a scheme developed by Back to solve similar withholding problems in original implementations of HashCash [2].

3   Applying PieceWork

We now explain how puzzlets in PieceWork can be used to recycle computation. Then we show how PieceWork may be used to prevent outsourcing.

3.1   Outsourceable Puzzlet Applications

A puzzlet solution has an easily quantifiable expected value for an outsourcer in PieceWork. Suppose that V is the value generated by a successfully mined block. Then the expected value of a puzzlet solution is V/Z. Their value is probabilistic, much like micropayments in [13], but may be made non-probabilistic by an outsourcer joining a traditional mining pool.

By judicious setting of s, outsourceable puzzlets can be used to perform useful computations in other domains. Interactive applications with short timeouts are preferred, allowing for a high probability that a puzzlet will be applicable to the current latest Bitcoin block. In this section, we describe some sample applications and effective choices for s that accomplish these goals.

Spam deterrence. Dwork and Naor [5] proposed a scheme in which the sender of a piece of e-mail attaches the solution to a puzzlet. A receiver only accepts e-mail with a valid puzzlet solution. Puzzlets are receiver-specific in this scheme, so a would-be spammer incurs the high cost of solving puzzles for a large number of receivers. Dwork and Naor's puzzle construction was complicated, but can be easily replaced with a hash-based PoW, as in [1].

As a receiver of e-mail cannot easily transmit a newly generated, block-specific value s to a sender *before the sender transmits e-mail*, we propose that $s = H(\text{Digest}\|\text{Header})$ for some CRHF H.

DoS deterrence. "Client puzzles" are hash-function inversion puzzles that a client must solve to receive a resource from a server, such as a TCP or TLS connection [10, 18] or DNS query information. This scheme helps deter DoS attacks, as it would require an attacker to solve many puzzles.

We can set $s = H(\text{Client IP}\|\text{fresh})$, with the freshness parameter being a shared random variable to prevent stale puzzle recycling.

MicroMint. Rivest and Shamir [20] proposed a digital cash system called MicroMint, in which coins are minted via hash collisions. MicroMint mimics the economics of a real, physical mint, where there is a high base cost for design of coinage, the purchase of machinery, etc. The incremental cost of producing coins, though, is small. Similarly, MicroMint requires many hashes to find the first coinworthy collision. Subsequent collisions accumulate quickly thereafter.

Jakobsson and Juels [9] showed how the problem of computing a hash image can be made moderately hard so that the problem serves as a puzzlet. Their scheme can be easily instantiated in PieceWork. In this case, s is the hash of a secret minting key and an unique puzzlet index. (See [9] for details; some slight modifications to the original scheme are required for PieceWork.)

MicroMint outsourcing in PieceWork can be *combined* with outsourcing for DoS resistance, i.e., a worker can simultaneously help produce MicroMint coins *and* aid in DoS prevention. We call this idea *double-harvesting*.

Tor Relay Payments. Biryukov and Pustogarov [3] proposed mining outsourcing as a means for clients to pay relays in Tor. Their scheme suffers in current schemes like Bitcoin from the withholding problem, and therefore would benefit from PieceWork. In one variant, a relay runs its own mining pool. In a second variant, a relay itself serves as a worker in a mining pool and further outsources work. This latter application motivates a three-phase variant of PieceWork.

3.2   Non-Outsourceable Puzzlet Applications

An existing approach to outsourcing resistance represented by 2P-PoW and Sign to Mine, outlined informally in [8,23] respectively, can easily be plugged into the inner puzzles of PieceWork. These schemes involve puzzles based on the application of a digital signature, rather than a hash function. The proposal is that the private key for the puzzle should be identical to that for spending mining rewards. In our scheme, this would prevent outsourcers from pooling worker resources. In PieceWork, the outer function may be defined as, e.g.:

$$F_{out} = H(SIG_{privkey}(X, F_{in}(X, n; s, r_{in}), r_{out})), \tag{3}$$

with the inner function representing the standard Bitcoin block solution, optionally at a lower reuseable difficulty. There are a few provisos. First, we emphasize that such nonoutsourceability is heuristic, and not accompanied by formal guarantees in the sense of "weak" outsourceability in [15]. It is possible in principle digital signing can be securely outsourced—meaning that a "helper" can substantially reduce the computation a signer needs to perform in computing a signature without the helper learning the private key. In practice, however, there is no known effective scheme for outsourcing computation in ordinary signature schemes such as RSA and discrete-log-based schemes, e.g., ECDSA [17]. Thus, signing-based puzzles may be heuristically assumed to prevent outsourcing.

Second, it has been argued (including in the comments of [8]) that, rather than disincentivizing large pools, such a scheme could support outsourcing in which workers place money in escrow that they forfeit should they steal mining rewards. We omit discussion of this argument here, but note that escrow schemes are complicated to implement and would disincentivize many workers, given that escrow amounts would need to match block reward amounts.

4   Conclusion

We have shown that computation in Bitcoin and similar cryptocurrencies need not be wasted, and outlined how a configurable percentage of this computation can be repurposed for protection against e-mail spam, denial of service, and other micropayment-style applications. We have established in PieceWork a framework for defining our puzzles, and unified 2-Phase-PoW, Sign To Mine, and tunably outsourceable two-stage puzzles that counter block withholding under a single model. We hope this will help future efforts in the outsourceable cryptocurrency computation space more effectively and rigorously define their schemes.

Acknowledgments. This work is funded in part by NSF grants CNS-1330599, CNS-1514163, CNS-1564102, CNS-1561209, and CNS-1518779, ARO grant W911NF-16-1-0145, and IC3 sponsorship from Chain, IBM, and Intel.

References

1. Back, A.: Hashcash - a denial of service counter-measure. http://www.hashcash. org/papers/hashcash.pdf (2002)
2. Back, A.: Hashcash-amortizable publicly auditable cost functions. Early draft of paper (2000)
3. Biryukov, A., Pustogarov, I.: Proof-of-work as anonymous micropayment: rewarding a Tor relay. In: Böhme, R., Okamoto, T. (eds.) FC 2015. LNCS, vol. 8975, pp. 445–455. Springer, Heidelberg (2015). https://doi.org/10.1007/ 978-3-662-47854-7_27
4. Courtois, N.T., Bahack, L.: On subversive miner strategies and block withholding attack in Bitcoin digital currency. arXiv preprint arXiv:1402.1718 (2014)
5. Dwork, C., Naor, M.: Pricing via processing or combatting junk mail. In: Brickell, E.F. (ed.) CRYPTO 1992. LNCS, vol. 740, pp. 139–147. Springer, Heidelberg (1993). https://doi.org/10.1007/3-540-48071-4_10
6. Ethereum Proof of Stake FAQ (2017). https://github.com/ethereum/wiki/wiki/ Proof-of-Stake-FAQ. Accessed 28 Feb 2017
7. Eyal, I.: The miner's dilemma. In: 2015 IEEE Symposium on Security and Privacy, pp. 89–103. IEEE (2015)
8. Eyal, I., Sirer, E.G.: How to disincentivize large bitcoin mining pools. http://hack ingdistributed.com/2014/06/18/how-to-disincentivize-large-bitcoin-mining-pools/ (2014). Accessed 05 Nov 2016
9. Jakobsson, M., Juels, A.: Proofs of work and bread pudding protocols (extended abstract). In: Preneel, B. (ed.) Secure Information Networks. ITI-FIP, vol. 23, pp. 258–272. Springer, Boston, MA (1999). https://doi.org/10.1007/ 978-0-387-35568-9_18
10. Juels, A., Brainard, J.: Client puzzles: a cryptographic countermeasure against connection depletion attacks. In: NDSS, pp. 151–165 (1999)
11. Juels Jr., A., Burton, S.K.: PORs: proofs of retrievability for large files. In: ACM CCS, pp. 584–597 (2007)
12. King, S.: Primecoin: cryptocurrency with prime number proof-of-work (2013)
13. Micali, S., Rivest, R.L.: Micropayments revisited. In: Preneel, B. (ed.) CT-RSA 2002. LNCS, vol. 2271, pp. 149–163. Springer, Heidelberg (2002). https://doi.org/ 10.1007/3-540-45760-7_11
14. Miller, A., Juels, A., Shi, E., Parno, B., Katz, J.: Permacoin: repurposing bitcoin work for data preservation. In: 2014 IEEE Symposium on Security and Privacy, pp. 475–490. IEEE (2014)
15. Miller, A., Kosba, A., Katz, J., Shi, E.: Nonoutsourceable scratch-off puzzles to discourage bitcoin mining coalitions. In: Proceedings of the 22nd ACM SIGSAC Conference on Computer and Communications Security, pp. 680–691. ACM (2015)
16. Nakamoto, S.: Bitcoin: a peer-to-peer electronic cash system. (2008). http:// bitcoin.org/bitcoin.pdf
17. Nguyen, P., Stern, J.: The Béguin-Quisquater server-aided RSA protocol from Crypto'95 is not secure. In: Ohta, K., Pei, D. (eds.) ASIACRYPT 1998. LNCS, vol. 1514, pp. 372–379. Springer, Heidelberg (1998). https://doi.org/10.1007/ 3-540-49649-1_29
18. Nygren, E., Erb, S., Biryukov, A., Khovratovic, D.: TLS client puzzles extension. IETF Internet-Draft (2016). Expires 30 Dec 2016
19. Priest, C.: [bitcoin-dev] we need to fix the block withholding attack. https://lists. linuxfoundation.org/pipermail/bitcoin-dev/2015-December/012059.html   (2015). Accessed 05 Nov 2016

20. Rivest, R.L., Shamir, A.: PayWord and MicroMint: two simple micropayment schemes. In: Lomas, M. (ed.) Security Protocols 1996. LNCS, vol. 1189, pp. 69–87. Springer, Heidelberg (1997). https://doi.org/10.1007/3-540-62494-5_6
21. Sztorc, P.: Nothing is cheaper than proof of work (2016). http://www.truthcoin. info/blog/pow-cheapest/. Accessed 01 Nov 2016
22. Todd, P.: Re: [bitcoin-dev] we need to fix the block withholding attack (2015). https://lists.linuxfoundation.org/pipermail/bitcoin-dev/2015-December/ 012069.html. Accessed 05 Nov 2016
23. ziftrCOIN: a cryptocurrency to enable commerces. (2014). https://d19y4lldx7po3t. cloudfront.net/assets/docs/ziftrcoin-whitepaper-120614.pdf. Accessed 05 Nov 2016

Enhancing Bitcoin Transactions with Covenants

Russell O'Connor$^{(\boxtimes)}$ and Marta Piekarska

Blockstream, Montréal, Canada
{roconnor,marta}@blockstream.com

Abstract. Covenants are Bitcoin Script programs that restrict how funds are allowed to be spent. In previous work [9], Möser et al. implemented covenants with a new Script operation that allows one to programmatically query the transaction. In this paper, we show that covenants can be implemented with a new CHECKSIGFROMSTACK operation that verifies a signature for a message passed as an argument. When the same public key and signature is used together with CHECKSIG, one can recover transaction data, which then allows one to enforce a covenant. To illustrate our technique, we reimplement Möser et al.'s vault construction for securing funds against key compromise. We use Elements Alpha, a sidechain whose Script language has the needed operations.

1 Introduction

To spend funds in Bitcoin, one has to provide an input to satisfy a predicate that is associated with the funds. This predicate is programmed in a language called Script [11]. A typical predicate requires a digital signature for a public key that is fixed by the particular program. However, more complex predicates are possible.

Predicates restrict who is authorized to make a transaction. Recent extensions to the Script language, such as CHECKSEQUENCEVERIFY [3], allow predicates to restrict when a transaction is authorized. However, there is no way to restrict what transactions are authorized. Once someone has the authorization to spend funds, they may send the funds anywhere they wish.

A way to limit how funds may be spent, including specifying how much must be spent and to what addresses, is by the introduction of covenants. Covenants may be recursive by requiring transactions to be spent to outputs that contain the same covenant. State can be stored and updated in these scripts allowing one to build smart contracts that execute a state machine through a series of transactions.

It is believed that it is impossible to introduce covenants in Bitcoin as Script does not contain operations that allow reading of the transaction data. The only way to interact with the transaction data is by use of CHECKSIG that verifies a digital signature for a message built from the transaction data. Thus, some have proposed to extend Script to support covenants by adding new operations to interact directly with the transaction data [9].

© International Financial Cryptography Association 2017
M. Brenner et al. (Eds.): FC 2017 Workshops 2017, LNCS 10323, pp. 191–198, 2017.
https://doi.org/10.1007/978-3-319-70278-0_12

This paper introduces a novel approach to the problem. We show that it is possible to implement covenants in Bitcoin by adding purely computational operations that do not access the transaction data. Instead, we leverage the existing CHECKSIG operation to recover the signed message data that is built from the transaction data. Then it is easy to add conditions that restrict what transaction data is acceptable for one's particular covenant.

To illustrate how this works, we implement Möser et al.'s covenant for vault transactions [9] in Elements Alpha, a Bitcoin sidechain that includes our needed extensions to Script.

The rest of the paper is organized as follows. In the next section, we introduce the basics required to understand how covenants work. Next, in Sect. 3, we talk about the Elements Alpha sidechain that we used for implementation of our solution. Section 4 describes the covenants and how they work in Elements Alpha. In Sect. 5, a classical use case is presented: Möser et al.'s vault covenant. Related work is discussed in Sect. 6, and we conclude in Sect. 7.

2 Background

In this section we discuss how Bitcoin Transactions work and what Script is.

2.1 Bitcoin Transactions

A Bitcoin transaction contains a series of inputs and outputs. The data for each output contains its Bitcoin value and a predicate written in Script called the *scriptPubKey*. The data for each input contains an *outpoint*, which references a previous transaction's output, and a *scriptSig*, which is the input for that output's predicate. The sum of the output values must be equal to no more than the sum of the values of the outpoints referenced by the inputs. Any difference between the two sums counts as fee that Bitcoin miners may collect for adding the transaction to the blockchain.

2.2 Script

Script is a Forth-like, stack based language for defining predicates. Its operations manipulate a stack of byte arrays. Input for a Script program, the scriptSig, gives the initial state of the stack. Execution is successful when all of the program's operations complete and the resulting stack has a non-zero value on top.

Script is a deliberately limited language; it has conditionals but no looping (or recursion) operations. This means that the language is not Turing complete. These limitations facilitate static analysis of its programs. For example, only a limited number of expensive, digital signature verification operations are allowed per transaction, and this limit is statically checked by counting the number of the operations appearing in the program.

The CHECKSIG and CHECKSIGVERIFY operations perform a digital signature verification of a *signed hash*. A signed hash is a double SHA-256 hash of *signed data* generated from the transaction data. The signed data is determined by a *SigHash type* which is specified by a byte that is appended to the digital signature. For the most common SigHash type, SIGHASH_ALL, the signed data consists of the transaction data with the scriptSigs replaced by the byte 0x00. The exception being the input corresponding program being executed. There the scriptSig is replaced with the scriptPubKey of its outpoint, which is the script-PubKey being executed. Later we use this exception to implement recursive covenants.

Other SigHash types produce variants of this signed data. We will be using one that allows us to discard all but the first input and output of the transaction data.

3   Elements Sidechain

Elements Alpha [1] is a fork of the Bitcoin codebase that implements a sidechain on Bitcoin's testnet [2]. Instead of mining, a federation of signers produces one block per minute. Coins are not minted by new blocks; instead they enter the sidechain through a pegging process. The user sends testnet coins to a multi-signature scriptPubKey controlled by the federation. Once confirmed, the same value of coins are unlocked on the Elements Alpha sidechain. Elements Alpha's coins can be redeemed on Bitcoin's testnet later by locking the coins on the sidechain. Once locked, the federation will release the same value of coins on Bitcoin's testnet.

Elements Alpha lets us explore new features for Bitcoin without putting the main network at risk. For example, Segregated Witness [6,7], Confidential Transactions [8] as well as the new Script operations were all developed in Elements Alpha. In particular, the inputs in Element Alpha's signed data include their Bitcoin value. We will now show how these new Script operations let us implement covenants.

4   Covenants in Elements Alpha

New operations in Elements Alpha's Script include: CHECKSIGFROMSTACK, CHECKSIGFROMSTACKVERIFY and CAT. Interestingly, the CAT operation used to exist in Bitcoin Script, but it was disabled [10].

The two CHECKSIGFROMSTACK operations are similar to the CHECKSIG operations except they perform a digital signature verification of the SHA-256 hash of a messaged passed on the stack. These operations have several applications including secure multi-party computation [5]. For the purposes of covenants, CHECKSIGFROMSTACK is used in conjunction with CHECKSIG to recover the signed data.

After a successful CHECKSIG operation, the digital signature and public key together form a commitment to the signed data. If the same public key and signature are used in a successful CHECKSIGFROMSTACK operation, it provides a cryptographic guarantee that the message passed to the CHECKSIGFROMSTACK operation is identical to the signed data.

4.1   Recovering Signed Data

In order to present a clear example of how our solution is realized, let us take the following stack:

> *signature*
> *pubkey*
> *message*

In the Script program presented in Listing 1.1, the first line duplicates the signature and public key, and then it appends the byte 0x01 to the end of the signature, which is the flag for SIGHASH_ALL type. In the next line, a CHECK-SIGVERIFY is executed using the signature and the public key. If it is successful, it means that the signature and public key form a commitment to the signed data for the SIGHASH_ALL SigHash type. This leaves the original three items on the stack. Next, the program computes the SHA-256 hash of message data. Finally, a successful CHECKSIGFROMSTACKVERIFY ensures that the message is identical to the signed data from the CHECKSIGVERIFY operation on the second line. This leaves only the message on the stack which has been proven identical to the signed data.

```
1   2DUP 1 CAT
2   SWAP CHECKSIGVERIFY
3   2 PICK SHA256
4   ROT CHECKSIGFROMSTACKVERIFY
```

Listing 1.1. Elements Alpha Script to verify that *message* is the signed data

Further operations can be added to enforce that the transaction data contained in the signed data satisfies whatever policy the user desires to enforce.

The signed data recovery process only relies on the *integrity* property of digital signatures. In essence, we are treating the *signature-pubkey* pair as a cryptographic hash of message data. The three inputs, *signature*, *pubkey*, and *message*, can be provided in the scriptSig by the person creating the transaction. In the next section, we will show how to apply this technique to build a practical covenant.

5   The Möser-Eyal-Sirer Vault

In this section, we recreate the Möser-Eyal-Sirer Vault in Elements Alpha. Möser, Eyal, and Sirer described an implementation of covenants using a new operation, CHECKOUTPUTVERIFY, that directly verifies if a transaction output matches a given pattern [9]. Using this operation, they developed covenants to implement a smart contract for a vault to help secure funds against malicious transfers.

In their scheme, funds held in the vault can only be withdrawn through a two transaction process. The first transaction's output has a time-lock. This introduces a fixed delay, called the *unvaulting period*, before the second transaction can send the funds to the destination. The purpose of the time-lock is to provide an opportunity for the fund's owner to detect transfers made by a malicious party who may have obtained the vault's private keys. During the unvaulting period, the user has an option to use a rescue private key, kept offline, to create a transaction that overrides the destination address of the withdrawal. This override starts another unvaulting period, during which further overrides can be made. This design ensures that even if the malicious party gets the rescue private key, they still won't be able to profit because the owner and the malicious party end up locked in an endless battle of repeatedly resetting the target script. Given the no-win scenario, hopefully the malicious party realizes that there is no point in attacking in the first place.

Our implementation of the vault smart contract is composed of two Script programs [12]. The first program is the *main vault script*. It holds funds in the vault and its covenant forces that the funds are sent to a scriptPubKey containing a vault loop script, which is the second half of the smart contract. The *vault loop script* uses CHECKSEQUENCEVERIFY to enforce the unvaulting period after which its covenant forces that the funds are sent to a destination that was set by the main vault script's input. Alternatively, the vault loop script allows the funds to be sent, at any time, to another instance of vault loop script containing a new destination address when authorized by a rescue key. In this sense, the vault loop script is recursive.

5.1   Main Vault Script

The main vault script reconstructs the signed data from pieces provided by the scriptSig and from fixed constants. Table 1 summarizes the reconstructed signed data. The items in italics are provided by the scriptSig while the other items are fixed by the main vault script. The CHECKSIG/CHECKSIGFROMSTACK technique described in Sect. 4 verifies that the reconstructed signed data matches the actual signed data. For the public key, we require either the wallet or rescue key to be used. This way, the CHECKSIG is used for both covenant enforcement and verifying the transaction is authorized.

The same *value* parameter is used in both the input and output of the signed data to ensure the entire vault's funds are moved together. We use the SIGHASH_SINGLE type to generate signed data that excludes all but the first input and first output. This allows other inputs to cover the transaction fees.

Table 1. Summary of recovered signed data for the main vault script. Items in italics are data provided by the scriptSig input.

input 1	*outpoint*
	value
script	*main-vault-script*
output 1	*value*
scriptPubKey	PUSH *target*
	vault-loop-script
SigHash type	SIGHASH_SINGLE

The output's scriptPubKey begins by pushing a *target* value, and it is followed by the vault loop script. The *target* value is the initial "state" for the vault loop script. It determines the scriptPubKey of the fund's destination. The next section will describe how vault loop script works.

5.2 Vault Loop Script

There are two different ways to redeem the vault loop script. The primary method is to wait out the unvaulting period and then send the funds to the target destination. The secondary method is to use the rescue key to send the funds to another copy of the vault loop script with a new target script.

Table 2 summarizes the standard redemption's signed data. We allow any public key to be used for the covenant enforcement because redemption doesn't require authorization. Instead, we rely on the covenant to restrict the transaction's output to the target script that is fixed by the script's "state", and we use a time-lock to enforce the unvaulting period.

At any time, the owner may change the destination of the vault loop by redeeming it with a rescue transaction that replaces the "state" with a *new-target*. Table 3 summarizes the signed data for the rescue transaction. In this case, we require that the rescue public key is use to enforce covenant as this also verifies that the transaction is authorized.

Table 2. Summary of signed data for the standard redemption of funds for the vault loop script.

input 1	*outpoint*
	value
script	PUSH target
	vault-loop-script
output 1	*value*
scriptPubKey	target
SigHash type	SIGHASH_SINGLE

Table 3. Summary of signed data for rescue of funds for the vault loop script.

input 1	*outpoint*
	value
script	PUSH target
	vault-loop-script
output 1	*value*
scriptPubKey	PUSH *new-target*
	vault-loop-script
SigHash type	SIGHASH_SINGLE

Because the signed data includes the script being executed, we can enforce the input and output scripts are the same. It is an example of building a recursive smart contract composed of Scripts, even though the Script language itself does not allow loops or recursion.

6 Related Work

In this section we compare our solution for covenants with Möser et al.'s solution [9]. Their solution proposes adding a CHECKOUTPUTVERIFY operation to Script. Given an output index, a value, and a script pattern, CHECKOUT-PUTVERIFY verifies that the transaction's output at the given index has the given value and its scriptPubKey matches the given pattern. Their script pattern relies on a few ad hoc placeholders including PUBKEY, PUBKEYHASH, and PATTERN. The PUBKEY and PUBKEYHASH placeholders provide places where "state" variables can be changed. The PATTERN placeholder is replaced with an instance of the script itself, allowing one to construct recursive covenants without resorting to building Quines.

Our solution does not require patterns. Using CAT, we can assemble arbitrary scripts from some parts taken from inputs and other parts that are fixed. Instead of having a PATTERN placeholder or using Quines, we take advantage of the fact that the input script is part of the signed data to build recursive covenants. We can copy only part of the input script to the output script, leaving the rest of the script to store the updateable "state" of a smart contract.

That said, our solution comes at significant cost. The CHECKSIGFROM-STACK operation is as expensive as CHECKSIG, which is by far the most expensive operation in the Script language. Also, CHECKOUTPUTVERIFY is designed to be easily soft-forked in, while our solution depends on CAT, which would require a new Segregated Witness Script version to enable it.

The next section will discuss how the implications of this work is more about the inevitability of covenants rather than about our solution being practical.

7   Conclusion

In this paper we presented a way to implement covenants, which can limit how funds may be spent, including specifying how much must be spent and to what addresses. To present a specific use case, we implemented the Möser-Eyal-Sirer vault in Elements Alpha. It would be possible to adapt it to create vaults and other covenants for similar blockchains. In particular, if CAT and CHECKSIGFROMSTACKVERIFY were added to Bitcoin's Script language then the implementation presented here could be introduced in Bitcoin.

It is important to observe that CAT and CHECKSIGFROMSTACK are pure functions in the sense that they are functions whose outputs are computable solely from their stack arguments. This paper demonstrates we can recover the signed data without the needing operations that access the signed data beyond the existing CHECKSIG operation. The fact is that the main thing stopping signed data recovery in Bitcoin's Script today is that it is *infeasible* to implement CHECKSIGFROMSTACK with the existing operations, rather that it being inexpressible. Any new operations that would make it feasible to implement CHECKSIGFROMSTACK would enable covenants. For example, adding primitive elliptic curve and finite field operations for the Secp256-k1 curve [4] would likely be sufficient for implementing CHECKSIGFROMSTACK.

We see that Bitcoin's CHECKSIG operation fails to abstract away the signed data, even if abstraction was the intention. Rather than forcing users to go through an expensive CHECKSIGFROMSTACK to gain access to the transaction data embedded in the signed data, it would be better and cheaper for everyone involved to provide operations to directly access the transaction data.

References

1. Back, A.: Announcing sidechain elements: open source code and developer sidechains for advancing Bitcoin (2015). https://blockstream.com/2015/06/08/714/
2. Back, A., Corallo, M., Dashjr, L., Friedenbach, M., Maxwell, G., Miller, A., Poelstra, A., Timón, J., Wuille, P.: Enabling Blockchain innovations with pegged sidechains (2014). https://www.blockstream.com/sidechains.pdf
3. BtcDrak, Friedenbach, M., Lombrozo, E.: BIP112: Checksequenceverify. Bitcoin Improvement Proposal (2015). https://github.com/bitcoin/bips/blob/master/bip-0112.mediawiki
4. Certicom Research: Standards for Efficient Cryptography 2: Recommended Elliptic Curve Domain Parameters. Standard SEC2, Certicom Corp., Mississauga, ON, USA, September 2000
5. Kumaresan, R., Bentov, I.: Amortizing secure computation with penalties. In: Proceedings of the 2016 ACM SIGSAC Conference on Computer and Communications Security, CCS 2016, pp. 418–429. ACM, New York (2016), http://doi.acm.org/10.1145/2976749.2978424
6. Lombrozo, E., Lau, J., Wuille, P.: BIP141: segregated witness (consensus layer). Bitcoin Improvement Proposal (2015). https://github.com/bitcoin/bips/blob/master/bip-0141.mediawiki
7. Lombrozo, E., Wuille, P.: BIP144: segregated witness (peer services). Bitcoin Improvement Proposal (2016). https://github.com/bitcoin/bips/blob/master/bip-0144.mediawiki
8. Maxwell, G.: Confidential transactions (2015). https://people.xiph.org/~greg/confidential_values.txt
9. Möser, M., Eyal, I., Gün Sirer, E.: Bitcoin covenants. In: Clark, J., Meiklejohn, S., Ryan, P.Y.A., Wallach, D., Brenner, M., Rohloff, K. (eds.) FC 2016. LNCS, vol. 9604, pp. 126–141. Springer, Heidelberg (2016). https://doi.org/10.1007/978-3-662-53357-4_9
10. Nakamoto, S.: Misc changes, August 2010. https://github.com/bitcoin/bitcoin/commit/4bd188c4383d6e614e18f79dc337fbabe8464c82, https://bitcoin.svn.sourceforge.net/svnroot/bitcoin/trunk@131
11. Nakamoto, S.: Re: Transactions and Scripts: DUP HASH160 ... EQUALVERIFY CHECKSIG, June 2010. https://bitcointalk.org/index.php?topic=195.msg1611#msg1611
12. O'Connor, R.: Covenants in Elements Alpha, November 2016. https://blockstream.com/2016/11/02/covenants-in-elements-alpha.html

Decentralized Prediction Market Without Arbiters

Iddo Bentov[1]([⊠]), Alex Mizrahi[2], and Meni Rosenfeld[3]

[1] Cornell University, Ithaca, USA
iddobentov@cornell.edu
[2] chromawallet.com, Stockholm, Sweden
alex.mizrahi@gmail.com
[3] Israeli Bitcoin Association, Tel Aviv, Israel
meni@bitcoin.org.il

Abstract. We consider a prediction market in which all aspects are controlled by market forces, in particular the correct outcomes of events are decided by the market itself rather than by trusted arbiters. This kind of a decentralized prediction market can sustain betting on events whose outcome may remain unresolved for a long or even unlimited time period, and can facilitate trades among participants who are spread across diverse geographical locations, may wish to remain anonymous and/or avoid burdensome identification procedures, and are distrustful of each other. We describe how a cryptocurrency such as Bitcoin can be enhanced to accommodate a truly decentralized prediction market, by employing an innovative variant of the *Colored Coins* concept. We examine the game-theoretic properties of our design, and offer extensions that enable other financial instruments as well as real-time exchange.

1 Introduction

A prediction market (PM) enables its participants to continuously place bets on the outcome of uncertain future events. As the PM is transparent and provides price discovery, each participant can take into consideration the current market price for outcomes of events, and attempt to make informed decisions regarding whether to buy or sell shares in such outcomes. Another use of PMs is in hedging positions. An individual may buy a prediction not because she believes that the event will happen, but because it would have a negative effect on her. She thus reduces her risk by betting on the event, anticorrelating with her current position. Further, PMs function as a useful forecasting tool even for non-participants, because predictions that are made when traders risk their own money have proven to be more accurate than polls and other methods [2].

The decentralized structure of the Bitcoin [17] network implies that its soundness does not require reliance on trusted parties, and that its participants can operate anonymously [13–16] if they take appropriate precautions. By utilizing *Colored Coins* [20] protocols, a decentralized stock exchange and other financial services can be integrated with Bitcoin. Similarly, "meta"-protocols such as the

© International Financial Cryptography Association 2017
M. Brenner et al. (Eds.): FC 2017 Workshops 2017, LNCS 10323, pp. 199–217, 2017.
https://doi.org/10.1007/978-3-319-70278-0_13

Counterparty [11] and Omni [18] layers[1] can provide more advanced financial services. Thus, one may regard it to be of interest to explore whether a decentralized PM can also be deployed on top of Bitcoin.

At first glance, it may seem that a decentralized exchange of assets poses less of a challenge than a decentralized PM. This is because the relevant aspects when trading an asset are just whether the issuer of the specific asset is reputable, and whether the trading platform is secure. Some assets may not require any reliance on reputation, e.g. an asset that gives ownership rights over a digital art item (including the right to present it at a gallery), which can then be traded in an atomic fashion. By contrast, even though a PM only deals with digital information, a fully decentralized PM requires a broad agreement regarding the outcomes of events.

Indeed, the work of [7] constructs a PM via a cryptocurrency of the Bitcoin mold, but it relies on trusted arbiters to decide the correct outcome of events. An alternative presented in [7] is to let the "miners" who perform the *Proof of Work* computations register their votes on the outcomes of events in the blocks that they solve. However, this alternative raises significant concerns, which stem from the fact that miners in a decentralized cryptocurrency can operate anonymously. Consider, for example, an obscure event that is relevant only to a small village. Some faction of this village can try to bribe miners to vote for their preferred outcome. Ideally, miners would be disincentivized from voting incorrectly as it entails the risk of losing the block reward in case their solved block is rejected by honest miners. For this to happen, honest miners would need to parse every obscure event description and keep up with the real-world outcomes of such events, which is impractical. Hence, choosing a trusted entity as arbiter in accord with hierarchical certification (cf. [7, Sect. 5.3]) is probably a better option for a PM of this kind.

One may ask why it is of value to decentralize all the aspects of a PM. Some of the possible reasons are as follows:

- For arbiters, credibility is inversely correlated with susceptibility. An anonymous arbiter is probably untrustworthy, while a well-known arbiter can be pressured by hostile elements to not resolve an event correctly.
- Eliminating the need for arbiters makes it easier to bet on events that extend over a very long time period (e.g., "Texas will secede from the U.S. before the year 2030"), or even events with unbounded time (e.g., "The State of Jefferson will be created out of California and Oregon before Texas secedes from the U.S."). It is desirable to let the market assign probabilities to such outcomes in a continuous fashion while relevant occurrences in the world unfold, without running the risk that a designated arbiter will not be alive or no longer be (the *only* one) in possession of her secret signing key at the time when the outcome is resolved.
- Anonymous traders may make predictions on interesting events that a traditional PM does not tend to accommodate. For example, "Street gang #1

---

[1] Each of them reached a market cap greater than $20 million in 2014, see http://coinmarketcap.com/.

will win the turf war in which they swore to expel street gang #2 from region x before the year 2018". Market participants might not be able to agree in advance on a trustworthy arbiter for this event, even though the outcome can be agreed upon by impartial observers and hence suitable to be decided by a decentralized PM.

- Reputable arbiters may expect to be compensated for the service that they provide, in part because they need to take precautions to secure their secret signing key. This implies that market participants will need to pay fees that go to the trusted arbiters, on top of the fees that are paid to the miners.
- In case the designated arbiter makes the wrong call for an event resolution, her decision becomes irreversible according to the protocol rules of a semi-decentralized PM [7]. Thus, shares of the winning outcome that are still in circulation are unfortunately worthless. This stands in contrast to a fully decentralized PM, in which market forces will re-adjust the value of the shares as the mistaken outcome becomes known.[2]

These reasons add to the obvious observation that designated arbiters may be malicious or willing to be bribed. For instance, a corrupt arbiter may stonewall and refuse to sign the correct resolution of an event until she receives extra money on the side. The corrupt arbiter may also stock up on cheap shares of an unlikely outcome, then rule in favor of that outcome and in effect steal money from other traders.

In Sect. 3 we discuss the conditions under which our fully decentralized PM scheme is likely to work well, and conditions under which a PM with trusted arbiters may be more appropriate.

1.1 Prediction Markets with Anonymous Participants

An anonymous marketplace with or without trusted arbiters can facilitate insider trading and other kinds of fraud that are less probable in non-anonymous setting.

E.g., a goalkeeper can secretly buy shares that predict that her team will lose a soccer game, then concede goals on purpose and profit. Still, even in a non-anonymous PM the goalkeeper may ask someone else to buy the shares and later divvy up the profits between them, hence the issue boils down to the observation that an anonymous marketplace allows fraudsters to operate with less friction.

Therefore, it is safer to bet on events whose significance is likely greater than their trade volume, particularly in the case of a PM with anonymous participants.

See for example [9] for further discussion and analysis of outside incentives.

1.2 Related Work

The work of [7] presents a cryptocurrency protocol for a PM that is decentralized in the sense that anyone can inject liquidity for betting on new or existing events,

---

[2] An example of a mistaken ruling is the 2012 Iowa caucus incident at https://en. wikipedia.org/wiki/Intrade#Disputes.

but centralized in the sense that it depends on trusted arbiters to decide the outcomes of events. Moreover, [7] presents a decentralized matching platform for PM trading directly on the cryptocurrency network. In Appendix A we outline how it is also possible to construct a trading platform that is suitable for real-time trades.

The Truthcoin [22] and Augur [19] projects attempt to build a different variant of a decentralized PM, where holders of tradeable "reputation" cryptocurrency take over the role of trusted arbiters in deciding outcomes of events. This is done via quite intricate voting methods in which all holders of these reputation coins may cast their votes for each event resolution, voters who agree with the majority earn fees, and voters who end up in the minority may suffer a loss. One aspect that neither *Truthcoin* nor *Augur* try to decentralize is the initial issuance of reputation coins by means of an auction or an IPO (cf. [6, Sect. 4] and [8, Sect. V.B]). By contrast, in our PM protocol the outcomes of events are decided by market forces rather than by votes, hence there is no need for an IPO that would potentially enrich the parties that initiate the PM system.

2   Mechanism

The *Colored Coins* concept [20] allows Bitcoin to support non-fungible assets rather than only fungible coins. This means that "tagged" or "colored" coins can be sent and received on the Bitcoin network. Thus, if Alice has a portfolio of $\{(5, \texttt{red}), (6, \texttt{blue})\}$ coins, she can send $(1.9, \texttt{red})$ coins to Bob's address and have $\{(3.1, \texttt{red}), (6, \texttt{blue})\}$ coins remaining.

The PM system that we hereby construct is based on Bitcoin, with all assets colored according to the fixed form $(\texttt{amount}, \texttt{bet}, \texttt{history})$. Initially, the system has uncolored assets $(\texttt{amount}, \perp, \emptyset)$, that can be used in exactly the same way as ordinary bitcoins. For example, if Bob has $(9, \perp, \emptyset)$ coins, he can send $(1.2, \perp, \emptyset)$ coins to Alice's address and have $(7.8, \perp, \emptyset)$ coins left.

To allow everyone to participate in the PM in a fully decentralized fashion, we define three types of special transactions, as follows.

Creating a prediction pair. Anyone can execute a special *outcome-split* transaction that transforms her $(\texttt{amount}, \perp, \texttt{history})$ asset to

$$\{(\texttt{amount}, \texttt{Yes:eid}, \texttt{history}), (\texttt{amount}, \texttt{No:eid}, \texttt{history})\},$$

where $\texttt{eid}$ is some particular event-id that is derived via

$$\texttt{eid} = \texttt{hash}(\text{"Textual description of an event"}).$$

We assume that $\texttt{hash}()$ is a cryptographic hash function. These split Yes/No shares can now be transferred as is the case with colored coins. E.g., Alice may split $(m, \perp, \emptyset)$ using event-id $\texttt{eid}_0$, then send $(2/3 \cdot m, \texttt{Yes:eid}_0, \emptyset)$ shares to Bob, and remain with $\{(1/3 \cdot m, \texttt{Yes:eid}_0, \emptyset), (m, \texttt{No:eid}_0, \emptyset)\}$ shares in her possession.

Redeeming a prediction pair. Anyone in possession of $(\texttt{amount},\texttt{Yes}\!:\!\texttt{eid},h_1)$ shares and $(\texttt{amount},\texttt{No}\!:\!\texttt{eid},h_2)$ shares is allowed to execute a special *outcome-combine* transaction that transforms these shares to $(\texttt{amount},\bot,h_1\cup h_2)$.

Hence, no matter what are the current market value of $(\texttt{amount},\texttt{Yes}\!:\!\texttt{eid},\emptyset)$ and $(\texttt{amount},\texttt{No}\!:\!\texttt{eid},\emptyset)$ separately, their combination is always worth $(\texttt{amount},\bot,\emptyset)$ ordinary coins.

Forcing an encumbered history. Anyone can execute a special *outcome-force* transaction that transforms her $(\texttt{amount},\texttt{Yes}\!:\!\texttt{eid},\texttt{history})$ asset to $(\texttt{amount},\bot,\texttt{history}\cup\{\texttt{Yes}\!:\!\texttt{eid}\})$.

Likewise, anyone can transform her $(\texttt{amount},\texttt{No}\!:\!\texttt{eid},\texttt{history})$ asset to $(\texttt{amount},\bot,\texttt{history}\cup\{\texttt{No}\!:\!\texttt{eid}\})$.

Let us elaborate on these mechanisms by providing several examples. See the accompanying Fig. 1 for an illustration.

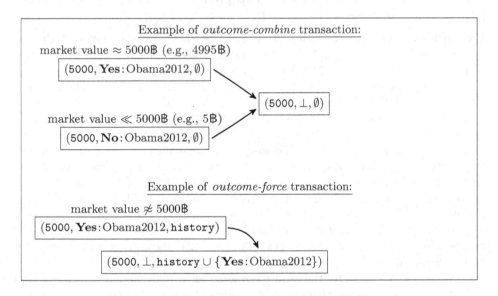

Fig. 1. Special transactions for event resolution.

Exemplary scenario 1. During 2011, Alice believes that President Obama will win the 2012 presidential election. She computes $\texttt{Obama2012}=\texttt{hash}(\text{"Barack Obama will win re-election in 2012"})$ and executes *output-split* to transform $(5000,\bot,\emptyset)$ ordinary coins that she possesses to

$$\{(5000,\texttt{Yes}\!:\!\texttt{Obama2012},\emptyset),(5000,\texttt{No}\!:\!\texttt{Obama2012},\emptyset)\}.$$

Suppose that the market believes that President Obama has 70% probability to win re-election. Alice trades her $(5000,\texttt{No}\!:\!\texttt{Obama2012},\emptyset)$ shares for $(1500,\bot,\emptyset)$ ordinary coins, since $^{30}/_{100}\cdot 5000=1500$. After President Obama wins re-election, the market price of $\texttt{No}\!:\!\texttt{Obama2012}$ plummets to 0.001 coins per share.

Hence, Alice buys $(5000, \texttt{No:Obama2012}, \emptyset)$ shares for 5 coins, and then uses the $(5000, \texttt{Yes:Obama2012}, \emptyset)$ shares that she kept to execute *outcome-combine* and earn 5000 coins back. Alice's total gain is $1500 - 5 = 1495$ coins.

Exemplary scenario 2. During 2011, Alice wishes to risk her entire wealth of 5000 coins by betting in favor of President Obama's re-election. The market assigns 70% probability to this event. Alice trades her $(5000, \perp, \emptyset)$ coins for $(7142.8, \texttt{Yes:Obama2012}, \emptyset)$ shares on the market, since $7142.8 \cdot 70/100 \approx 5000$. After President Obama wins re-election, the market price of $\texttt{Yes:Obama2012}$ rises to 0.999 coins per share, hence Alice sells her $(7142.8, \texttt{Yes:Obama2012}, \emptyset)$ shares for $(7135.7, \perp, \emptyset)$ coins. Alice's total gain is $7135.7 - 5000 = 2135.7$ coins.

The difference between scenarios 1 and 2 demonstrates that traders who provide the initial liquidity to the market need to commit more funds than the traders who join later, thus it can be reasonable for early traders to expect a small premium over the market price. This premium can be materialized in the form of a slightly wider bid-ask spread.

Exemplary scenario 3. During 2011, Alice wishes to bet in favor of President Obama's re-election, and executes *output-split* to transform her $(1000, \perp, \emptyset)$ coins to $(1000, \texttt{Yes:Obama2012}, \emptyset)$ shares and $(1000, \texttt{No:Obama2012}, \emptyset)$ shares. The market believes that the price of a $\texttt{No:Obama2012}$ share is $30/100$ coins. Hence, Alice sells her $(1000, \texttt{No:Obama2012}, \emptyset)$ shares for $(300, \perp, \emptyset)$ coins. After President Obama wins re-election, Alice wishes to buy $(1000, \texttt{No:Obama2012}, \emptyset)$ shares in order to execute *outcome-combine*, but traders who hold these shares demand an unreasonable high price of $20/100$ coins per $\texttt{No:Obama2012}$ share. Alice declines to pay such an excessive price, and instead executes an *outcome-force* transaction to transform her $(1000, \texttt{Yes:Obama2012}, \emptyset)$ shares to $(1000, \perp, \{\texttt{Yes:Obama2012}\})$ coins with encumbered history. Thus, Alice presumes that since all reasonable people should agree that President Obama won in 2012, she will be able to pay with these encumbered coins at the grocery store, etc. For instance, a store may accept Alice's payment of $(803, \perp, \{\texttt{Yes:Obama2012}\})$ for an item that normally costs 800 coins.

As scenario 3 alludes to, the intuitive reason for supporting an *outcome-force* operation is that it serves as a deterrent against traders who would demand an excessive price for their losing shares, by offering an alternative that removes the dependence on such misbehaving traders. The game-theoretic implications of *outcome-force* are examined with more details in Sect. 3. Let us note that misbehaving traders can pose problems even with a trusted arbiter who may not decide the outcome until a future date, which implies that unless the traders who hold the losing shares act reasonably, the winning shares would be neither interest-baring nor spendable for a possibly long time period (cf. [7, Sect. 4.2]).

It is likely that traders will prefer to buy the losing shares for cheap and execute *outcome-combine* to obtain coins with a clean history, rather than execute *outcome-force* and encumber the history of their coins, because nobody wants to run the risk of having unrecognized coins that get declined when they attempt to make payments. Still, some users of the currency might wish to resort to reputable oracles to fetch and thereby recognize widely agreed upon versions of encumbered history. This can be helped via protocol support for hashing event-ids into a single set-id according to a canonical order, so that a set-id can be re-hashed into a larger set when its preimage (that consists of event-ids) is given.

Therefore, when the PM functions properly (as in scenarios 1 and 2), the price of an $(1, \text{Yes:eid}, \emptyset)$ share can be interpreted as the probability that the market assigns to the event, since the cost of a losing share will be close to 0.

Another question is why it is needed to execute *outcome-force* instead of simply keeping the winning shares and using them as currency. The reason is that such shares would have to be transacted separately rather than joined with the ordinary coins that the user holds, which entails extra complexity and is not scalable. Also, such shares cannot be used to place bets on a new event, unless they first get converted to a usable format via either *outcome-force* or *outcome-combine*.

Finally, let us note that this PM system relies on a softfork (or hardfork if desired) of the Bitcoin protocol, due to two reasons. First, when colored coins are implemented as an optional layer on top of Bitcoin, miners are oblivious to it, and hence there may not be widespread agreement regarding the coloring rules. Additionally, in optional colored coins layers it is typically the case that one can always "uncolor" a colored coin, which implies that colored coins that exist in the Bitcoin system are always worth at least as much as their uncolored amount. In any case, a protocol fork is needed for a more efficient tagging-based colored coins support (cf. [5,20]), and our reference colored coins implementation with split/combine/encumber operations demonstrates that the overhead for a decentralized PM is minor [10].

3 Analysis

We are interested in analyzing what will be the prediction share price when each type of share is traded in the open market. We assume that a pair of "+" share and "−" share can always be exchanged for 1 BTC. In this abstract model, we further assume that due to agreement about which prediction was correct, a "+" share will be worth p BTC even if it is never combined with a "−" share, while a "−" share will be worthless without the possibility to combine it.

The parameter p can be regarded as the probability that the Bitcoin miners and full nodes will form a new consensus rule (by means of a softfork) that cleanses the encumbered coins corresponding to the prediction, thus transforming them into unencumbered coins. For example, the majority of miners will probably agree that it is reasonable to cleanse the aforementioned Obama2012 event if many such encumbered coins are in circulation. However, in case the miners are unreasonable an wish to regard another candidate as the winner of the 2012 elections (contrary to what the rest of the population thinks), our analysis will unfortunately reflect that by assigning the higher value to what ought to have been "−" shares. Notice that if the event description has some ambiguity, then even reasonable actors may fail to reach consensus. For example, an unambiguous event description for the U.S. presidential election in 2000 could have been "Al Gore will be inaugurated as the 43rd President of the United States".

Let us note that there exists a significant difference between letting miners have the power to vote on outcomes of all events in the blocks that they solve, and the above possibility of miners reaching consensus to cleanse the shares of an old event that are still in circulation. The problematic nature of the first method is discussed in Sect. 1. By contrast, the second method is a deliberate process that can be done in phases where in an initial phase the miners express willingness to support the supposedly benign fork, and in a latter phase the fork becomes operational. This method of deliberation to reach consensus has already been deployed in Bitcoin several times, in particular for the benevolent P2SH [1] and CLTV [23] forks. Therefore, in the case of well-known events for which there is wide agreement on the outcome among the general population, the decision to cleanse "+" shares can be a suitable candidate for a protocol fork.

It can also be appropriate to regard the probability p as corresponding to other conditions that are easier to meet, for example that a quorum of reputable oracles (that payment processors can utilize as in Sect. 2) consider "+" shares to be indistinguishable from unencumbered coins. The downside of such a condition is that it relies on a system with some centralized elements, rather than a fully decentralized system.

Other possibilities include deciding the outcome via an algorithm that was not yet known at the time when the prediction was made, or via measurements that rely on physical data and thus cannot be scripted in the cryptocurrency.

Let us stress that the most basic condition is that a user simply consults with herself before accepting an encumbered coin as payment, since popular event descriptions (e.g., "Barack Obama will win re-election in 2012") can be easy enough to consider. Therefore, $p > 0$ should hold even without reliance on extra mechanisms such a miners' fork or reputable oracles, though such mechanisms can help in making p larger.

Generally, the parameter p can thus be considered to be the expected price of a "+" share, where the expectation is taken over all the events that can influence the worth of the "+" shares.

Hence, this is essentially a situation known in game theory as the "glove game" [3]. A common method of analyzing cooperative games like this is the Shapley value [3,21], which essentially gives a stable evaluation of each participant's assets. A coalition of k players with a "+" share and ℓ players with a "−" share has a total value of $pk + (1 - p)\min(k, \ell)$; so if there are m "+" players and n "−" players, the Shapley value of a "−" player is given by:

$$v_- = \frac{1-p}{(m+n)!} \sum_{i=1}^{m+n} \sum_{j=0}^{\lfloor i/2 \rfloor - 1} (m+n-i)!(i-1)! \binom{n-1}{j}\binom{m}{i-j-1}.$$

And the shapley value of a "+" player is

$$v_+ = \frac{mp - nv_- + (1-p)\min(m,n)}{m}.$$

For example, if $p = 1/10$, $m = 30$ and $n = 25$, then $v_- = 0.670012$ and $v_+ = 0.329988$. As we see in this case, "−" shares actually have the higher value, because the oversupply of "+" shares implies that the holders of those shares have less bargaining power, and $p = 1/10$ is too small to compensate for that. By contrast, $p = 3/4, m = 30, n = 25$ result in $v_- = 0.186114$ and $v_+ = 0.813886$.

There is an economics phenomenon of destroying assets (often food) in order to increase the price of the stock that was kept. While counterintuitive, there are market conditions in which this can actually increase the overall profit. It is interesting to consider whether a similar phenomenon can happen here. Let us note that with Bitcoin and similar cryptocurrencies, players can indeed destroy assets that they control in a publicly verifiable way, by sending an unspent output to a script that always returns `False`.

In normal circumstances this should not happen. If a player chooses to "burn" some of her coins, this will increase the Shapley value of her remaining coins – but not so much that her total value will increase. This is because the Shapley value, in a way, considers all possible negotiation tactics of the different players, and if there was a way to gain from burning coins, it should already be accounted for in the original Shapley value.

But this can happen in the case of incomplete information and erroneous assumptions by the players. For example, assume there are 100 "+" shares and 100 "−" shares, with $p = 0$. Most players assume that there are 200 players with 1 share each; they base their trading activity on this assumption, and this results in a market value equal to the Shapley value for this game. However, unbeknownst to them, there is actually a single player in possession of all 100 "+" shares. If she decides to visibly burn some shares and keep only m, and the market reacts naively by calculating the Shapley value for a new game with a reduced number of players, her total value as a function of the coins she keeps is given in Fig. 2.

We can see that as this player starts burning shares, the rise in the value of each is steep enough to increase her total value. She will get the optimal value of 70.5882 if she keeps only 84 shares. Thus, in case this player had less than 84 shares to begin with, it would be disadvantageous for her to burn shares.

Notice that the benefit in burning "+" shares depends on the parameter p. This can be seen by noting that the value of each "+" share is given by $v_+ = p \cdot 1 + (1 - p) \cdot s_+$, where s_+ is the Shapley value for a "+" share in a game with $p = 0$. To see that the equality holds, consider the event

$E_+ = \{$player with "+" completes a pair in a random permutation of players$\}$.

According to the definition of the Shapley value (see also Fig. 3), we have

$$s_+ = \Pr(E_+)$$
$$v_+ = \Pr(E_+) \cdot 1 + (1 - \Pr(E_+)) \cdot p = p \cdot 1 + (1 - p) \cdot s_+.$$

Therefore, destroying all but x shares implies a revenue of $x \cdot (p \cdot 1 + (1-p) \cdot s_+(x))$, i.e., with s_+ as a function of x. We can thus see that as p tends towards 1, the destruction of "+" shares becomes counterproductive.

On the other hand, the decision to burn "−" shares is unaffected by p. The reason for this is that each "−" share is worth $v_- = p \cdot 0 + (1 - p) \cdot s_-$, with

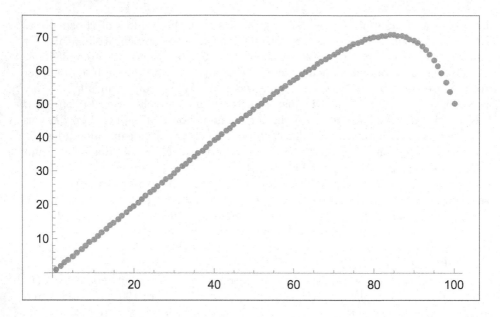

Fig. 2. Total value after the destruction of shares.

"+"	"+"	"−"	"+"	"−"	"+"	"+"	"−"	"+"	"+"
0	0	1	1	2	p	$2p$	$1+p$	$1+2p$	$1+3p$

Fig. 3. Incremental value of coalitions in glove games with $p = 0$ and $p > 0$.

s_- being the Shapley value for "−" in a game with $p = 0$. The rationale for this equality is the same as in the case of v_+ above. As we can thus see, burning all but x of the "−" shares implies a revenue of $x \cdot (1 - p) \cdot s_-(x)$, and the maximum of this expression does not depend on p.

Figure 4 demonstrates the total value that a player with m shares can obtain by not revealing that she possesses the entire supply of the "+" shares. Thus, as in the previous example we assume that there are m individual players who possess one "−" share each, and a single player with all of the m "+" shares. In this figure,

$$m = 100 \text{ corresponds to } m(p + s_+(m)(1 - p)) = 100\left(p + \frac{1}{2}(1 - p)\right) = 50(1 + p),$$

$p = 0$ corresponds to Fig. 2,

$p = 1$ corresponds to $m(p + s_+(m)(1 - p)) = m$,

and all other values in the range $p \in [0, 1], m \in [0, 100]$ are plotted.

One may ask whether burning fungible coins (e.g., ordinary bitcoins) could also be profitable for an individual player. Since the value function in this case is different than in the glove game, the answer is always no. To see this, assume that there are n coins in total that are worth C/n each. Consider a player who possesses m coins, hence her total value is $m \cdot C/n$. In case this player burns x coins, each coin would now be worth (at most) $\frac{C}{n-x}$, and the total value of this player would be $\frac{m-x}{n-x} \cdot C$. Since $m < n \Rightarrow \frac{m-x}{n-x} < \frac{m}{n}$, it follows that burning ordinary coins is always unprofitable.

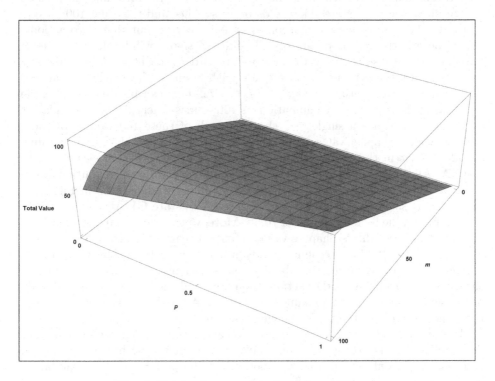

Fig. 4. Total value as a function of p and the m.

It is also appropriate to consider whether a player who possesses a large amount of "+" shares can gain an advantage by simply announcing that she controls this entire amount, instead of burning some of her shares. From the technical aspect, such an announcement can be done in Bitcoin and other cryptocurrencies: the player who possesses this amount of "+" shares can publish one common message that is signed with all of the secret keys that control these "+" shares, and thereby prove that these shares have a common owner.

However, due to the fact that the Shapley value takes into account all the possible strategies of the players, such an announcement would in fact have a detrimental effect from the point of view of this player.

To demonstrate, let us consider the same setting that Fig. 2 describes. Thus, we assume that $p = 0$, that a single player named Alice has all of the 100 "+" shares, and that the 100 "−" shares are held by 100 individual players. Alice will earn the value of $s_+(100) \cdot 100 = 50$ if she trades her shares on the open market. For a comparison between announcement of ownership and burning of shares, we first note that the diagram in Fig. 5 is commutative, i.e., the state **D** can be reached from the initial state **A** by traversing through either state **B** or state **C**. That is to say, Alice can first burn some amount of shares and then announce ownership over the remaining shares, or announce ownership over all of her 100 shares and then burn that same amount of shares, and both cases will result in the same state. This holds because Alice and the other 100 players will have the exact same information after Alice carries out these two actions, hence the resulting Shapley value of "+" and "−" shares will be the same. Next, note that the transition from state **A** to state **B** does not affect Alice's Shapley value, because the symmetric glove game with a single player who has all the "+" shares also gives the values $s_+ = s_- = 1/2$. This can be seen for example by viewing the game as a combination of 100 games where Alice plays against only one player with a single "−" share in each of these 100 games. In these games, Alice's Shapley value is $1/2$, and due to linearity of the Shapley value, it follows that in the original game Alice's Shapley value is $100 \cdot 1/2 = 50$. In state **A**, Alice's Shapley value is also 50, which follows from the definition of the Shapley value and symmetry. On the other hand, as we have seen in Fig. 2, by first burning shares (i.e., traversing from state **A** to state **C**), Alice can increase her Shapley value to an optimum of 70.58. Moreover, we note that the edge **B** → **D** only decreases Alice's Shapley value. This is because the strategies that the Shapley value takes into account already include the action of burning shares: if Alice does not settle for the Shapley value and instead defects by burning shares or performing any other action, then her resulting Shapley value will only decrease. In summary, the announcement of the **A** → **B** edge is ineffective, and the announcement of the **C** → **D** edge is detrimental.

Hence, this reasoning serves as an indication that in our anonymous and decentralized PM setting, burning shares (by a player with a large enough amount) is the only action that can potentially be preferable to bargaining in accordance with the Shapley value.

Let us note that there are also other concepts in analysing cooperative games with side payments, such as the core [12]. However, the Shapley value represents an evaluation that is reached from repeated bargaining among the players, as is indeed the case in an open marketplace, and hence its use is reasonable to in the context of our analysis.

It is desired that the decentralized PM will operate in a way that is advantageous towards players who made the correct prediction. Given the above analysis, this becomes more probable in accord with either of the following properties:

1. The parameter p is larger (the closer that p is to 1, the better).
2. The distribution of players who hold "−" shares is more decentralized.

The second property refers to a condition in which there are many players with a relatively small portion of all the "−" shares, while no single player holds a relatively very large portion of the "−" shares.

We can thus conclude that betting on popular events such as presidential elections is more likely to work well in a fully decentralized PM, in comparison

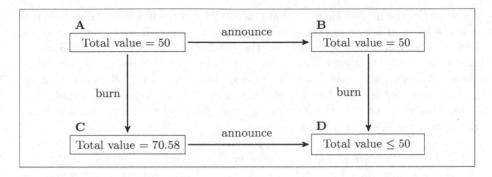

Fig. 5. Announcement of ownership vis-a-vis burning of shares.

to betting on obscure events. It may be preferable to use a semi-decentralized PM with trusted arbiters when betting on events with less popularity, though Sect. 1.1 should then be taken into account.

4   Extensions

We present here add-ons that complement the core PM mechanism of Sect. 2

4.1   Continuous Outcomes

An event description can specify a non-discrete outcome, for instance $e_1 = $ hash ("The percentage of votes in favor of staying in the European Union in the referendum in country x on January 1, 2018"). After say 45% voted in favor in this referendum, the Yes:e_1 and No:e_1 shares should have a market price of $\frac{45}{100}$ and $\frac{55}{100}$ coins per share, respectively.

However, if one opts to encumber e.g. 10 shares of Yes:e_1 to pay for groceries, then the merchant would need to recognize that this 10 amount is worth 4.5 unencumbered coins, which requires payment processors of higher complexity.

4.2   Non-binary Outcomes

Section 4.1 can be generalized to a non-binary fixed amount of outcomes, by extending the protocol to support an *outcome-split*(N) transaction that utilizes the extra parameter N to transforms (amount, $\perp$, history) to

$$\{(\text{amount}, 1:\text{eid}, \text{history}), \ldots, (\text{amount}, \text{N}:\text{eid}, \text{history})\}.$$

For instance, Alice can compute $e_2 = $ hash("Percentages for top 24 contestants in American Idol season 99: 1=band, 2=girl, 3=boy, 4=other"), and invoke *outcome-split*(4) to transform her $(60, \perp, \emptyset)$ coins to

$$\{(60, 1:e_2, \emptyset), (60, 2:e_2, \emptyset), (60, 3:e_2, \emptyset), (60, 4:e_2, \emptyset)\}.$$

Suppose that the market believes that the top 24 will be divided equally between bands, girls, and boys, and Alice believes that the percentage of bands will be much greater than 33%. Alice sells on the market $(60, 2\!:\!e_2, \emptyset)$ and $(60, 3\!:\!e_2, \emptyset)$ for $1/3 \cdot 60 = 20$ coins each. If it later turns out that 50% in the top 24 were bands, 25% were girls, and 25% were boys, then Alice buys 60 shares of $2\!:\!e_2$ and $3\!:\!e_2$ on the market for $1/4 \cdot 60 = 15$ coins each, and executes *outcome-combine*(4) together with the $(60.1\!:\!e_2, \emptyset)$ and $(60, 4\!:\!e_2, \emptyset)$ shares that she kept. Alice's profit is $2(20 - 15) = 10$ coins.

Suppose instead that no boy has reached the top 24, but holders of $3\!:\!e_2$ shares demand a price significantly greater than 0 for their supposedly worthless assets. Alice thus buys $(60, 2\!:\!e_2, \emptyset)$ shares, and executes *outcome-force* to transform $\{(60, 1\!:\!e_2, \emptyset), (60, 2\!:\!e_2, \emptyset), (60, 4\!:\!e_2, \emptyset)\}$ to the encumbered coins $(60, \bot, \{(1\!:\!e_2, 2\!:\!e_2, 4\!:\!e_2)\})$, which can be regarded to have the same meaning as in Sect. 2.

4.3   Capped Contracts for Difference

A contract for difference (CFD) is used for betting on the future value of an asset. In decentralized setting, if a certain stock is currently valued at say \$200, Alice places a bet that its value in one year will be \$290, and the rest of the market places bets that predict (on average) that its value in one year will be \$210, then Alice should profit in case the stock's value in a year will be greater than \$250, as $210 + \frac{290 - 210}{2} = 250$. This can be thought of as a generalization of Sect. 4.2 in which traders place bets on multiple outcomes $\{\ldots, 199, 200, 201, \ldots\}$, but it is infeasible to use the mechanisms of Sect. 4.2 because the range of possible outcomes is continuous and large.

When we consider some CFD of an asset x where x is traded for example on NYSE, it may make sense to employ the services of NYSE as a trusted arbiter. However, the centralized nature of this approach carries the same implications as described in Sect. 1. Consider, for example, a CFD for the BTC/USD exchange rate according to one or several predefined Bitcoin exchanges. These exchanges may collapse, or their secret signing keys may leak due to carelessness or malice, etc. By contrast, a decentralized PM can accommodate a CFD for the fair market price of BTC/USD in a way that is resilient to such potential hazards.

The basic prediction mechanism of Sect. 2 is already enough to support a simple capped CFD variant. To demonstrate this, let us use the following event-id for a capped CFD of an asset x whose price on January 1, 2016 is \$30: $e_3 = \mathtt{hash}($"Starting from January 1, 2016, the price of asset x will reach \$40 before reaching \$20"$)$.

As in the Black-Scholes model [4], by assuming as an approximation that market movements are caused by a large number of traders which are independent and indistinguishable from random, we have that this CFD instrument behaves locally like Brownian motion and thus its price is linear. That is, the price that market participants would assign to $\mathtt{Yes}\!:\!e_3$ shares is $c/20 - 1$, and the price assigned to $\mathtt{No}\!:\!e_3$ shares is $2 - c/20$, where $20 < c < 40$ is the current price of the asset x. See Fig. 6 for an illustration.

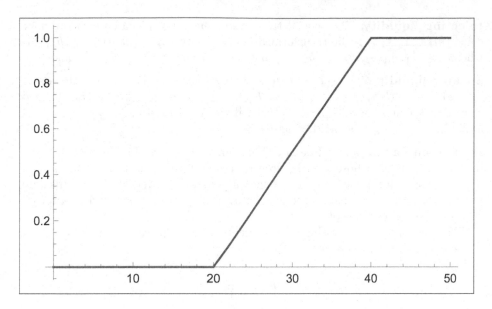

Fig. 6. Capped CFD price function.

Let us note that it is possible to define capped variants of other financial instruments in a similar fashion, e.g., put and call options. In decentralized setting, all such instruments are inherently capped because one cannot earn more than the coins that were used to create an asset (see also Sect. 4.4). By contrast, standard CFDs and put/call options are uncapped.

A significant drawback of capped CFDs of this form is that holders of shares corresponding to event-id e_3 cannot use shares of say e_4=hash("Starting from January 1, 2016, the price of asset x will reach \$50 before reaching \$10") for *outcome-combine* operations, which implies that such CFDs will probably not enjoy a market with high liquidity.

4.4   Vector CFDs

We now define and explore *vector* CFDs, which can potentially increase the available market liquidity.

Vector CFDs utilize colored coins of the form (`amount`, `eid`, `V`, `J`, `history`), such that $V = (b_1, w_1, b_2, w_2, \ldots, b_k, w_k)$ with $\sum_{i=1}^{k} w_i = 1$, and $J \in \{1, 2, \ldots, k\}$. The `eid`, `V`, `J`, fields generalize the `i:eid` field of Sect. 4.2. The event-id should conform with a format of the type `eid = hash(baseline asset`x`)`, where x specifies the identity of an asset such that the market participants wish to place bets on the future price of x.

Variants of the special transactions of the PM system of Sect. 2 are also used for vector CFDs, as follows.

Injecting liquidity. The special transaction *outcome-split* allows m ordinary coins $(m, \perp, \perp, \perp, h)$ to be transformed into k assets $\{z_j = (m, \mathsf{eid}, v, j, h)\}_{j=1}^k$, where $v = (b_1, w_1, b_2, w_2, \ldots, b_k, w_k)$ and the constraint $\sum_{i=1}^k w_i = 1$ holds.

Soaking liquidity. The special transaction *outcome-combine* allows the assets $\{(m, \mathsf{eid}, v_i = (b_{i,1}, w_{i,1}, b_{i,2}, w_{i,2}, \ldots, b_{i,k_i}, w_{i,k_i}), j_i, h_i)\}_{i=1}^t$ to be transformed to ordinary coins $(m, \perp, \perp, \perp, \cup_{i=1}^t \{h_i\})$, if the constraints $s_1 = s_2 = \cdots = s_t$ and $\sum_{i=1}^t w_{i,j_i} b_{i,j_i} = s_1$ hold, where $s_i \triangleq \sum_{q=1}^{k_i} w_{i,q} b_{i,q}$.

Forcing an encumbered history. This can be supported as in Sect. 4.2, i.e., by having weights whose sum is close to 1 and V, J fields that define a sum $\sum_{i=1}^t w_{i,j_i} b_{i,j_i}$ that is close to the market value of x. However, forcing of this kind would require $\mathsf{eid} = \mathsf{hash}(\text{baseline asset} x \text{at date} y)$, with y specifying a future date for the target price of x.

The formula for assessing the current market price of an asset $z = (m, \mathsf{eid}, v, j, \emptyset)$ can be given as

$$\mathrm{price}(z) = m \cdot \frac{1}{k-1} \cdot (1 - \frac{d_j}{s}),$$

where $\mathsf{eid} = \mathsf{hash}(\text{baseline asset} x)$, c is the current market value of x, $v = (b_1, w_1, b_2, w_2, \ldots, b_k, w_k)$, $d_i = w_i \cdot |b_i - c|$, and $s = \sum_{i=1}^k d_i$.

Notice that after an initial *outcome-split* of m ordinary coins, it holds that $\sum_{i=1}^k \mathrm{price}(z_i) = m$, as it should.

Also note that with this price formula, a fully accurate prediction $b_i = c$ implies earnings of $\frac{m}{k-1}$ ordinary coins.

Using the same denotations, an alternative price formula can be given as

$$\mathrm{price}'(z) = \max(0, m \cdot (1 - (k-1)\frac{d_i}{s})).$$

Here $\sum_{i=1}^k \mathrm{price}'(z_i) = m$ only when $\forall i : 1 - (k-1)\frac{d_i}{s} \geq 0$, because this formula does not allow the price of an individual share to be negative. This means that someone who holds a share with $1 - (k-1)\frac{d_i}{s} < 0$ has made a very poor bet, but this share is not completely worthless and should be sold on the market for a low price, as it can facilitate an *outcome-combine* transaction.

The upside of the price' formula is that it amplifies the rewards for accurate predictions. In particular, a fully accurate prediction $b_i = c$ results in a maximal earnings of m ordinary coins. This also serves as a demonstration that vector CFDs are capped, as it is impossible to earn more than the initial m coins that were used to create the asset.

In fact, there are infinitely many possible price formulas, since the price is driven by the market, as opposed to being enforced at the protocol level. Thus, it is up to the market participants to pick their preferred price as they see fit, in accordance with the law of supply and demand.

As example, suppose Alice transforms 500 coins to $\{z_j = (500, \mathsf{e}_5, v, j, \emptyset)\}_{j=1}^3$ with $\mathsf{e}_5 = \mathsf{hash}(\text{baseline asset } x)$ and $v = (75, 1/3, 100, 1/3, 125, 1/3)$. Let us assume that x is currently valued at \$200. Bob predicts that the value of x

will fall dramatically, and buys z_1 from Alice for price(z_1) = 145.8333 coins. Later, x falls to \$110. Bob sells z_1 to Alice for price(z_1) = 104.1666 coins. Alice now executes *outcome-combine* to recover her 500 coins. Hence, Alice collected Bob's loss of 145.8333 − 104.1666 = 41.666 coins. If x fell further so that its value was closer to \$75 than \$125, Bob would have profited.

Now, in case Carol transforms e.g. 400 coins to $\{z'_j = (400, \mathsf{e}_5, v', j, \emptyset)\}_{j=1}^4$ with $v' = (150, 1/2, 40, 1/4, 50, 1/8, 70, 1/8)$, these shares can take part in the same market with Alice and Bob. For instance, if z_1 is divided into $(100, \mathsf{e}_5, v, 1, \emptyset)$ and $(400, \mathsf{e}_5, v, 1, \emptyset)$, then the latter can be combined with z'_1 to produce 400 ordinary coins.

5   Conclusion

The trust that participants need to extend to different forms of financial services is a spectrum. For a decentralized currency system such as Bitcoin, one can argue that little or no trust is needed. Since the financial instruments that are traded in a prediction market represent only digital information, we motivated and presented a construction for a decentralized prediction market that requires essentially the same level of trust as that of Bitcoin. While our construction readily generalizes to additional financial instruments such as CFDs, other kinds of financial services may require a higher degree of trust.

A   Real-Time Semi-decentralized Order Book

In [7], a fully decentralized order book mechanism is presented. As discussed in [7, Sect. 6.1], this kind of a decentralized trading platform can work well by letting miners keep the surplus of the spread. However, it is inherently the case that decentralized platforms cannot achieve instant trades when responsiveness to real-time price fluctuations is desired, and that dishonest and self-interested participants can manipulate the market by placing orders and then reneging instead of fulfilling them. Therefore, in the case of a highly liquid PM, a fully decentralized order book might not be the best option for traders.

To complement the construction of [7], we outline an order book mechanism that is semi-decentralized in the sense that traders rely on a supposedly reputable trusted third party (TTP) to execute in real-time the orders that they place, and in case the TTP becomes corrupt they will regain their original assets. That is to say that a corrupt TTP can prevent trades from taking place, but cannot steal the traded assets and disappear.

The basic idea is to let traders deposit assets into a multisignature script that can be spent either by both the trader and the TTP, or by the trader alone but only after a specified time (cf. [23]). Trades are executed off-chain so that the TTP co-signs every transaction and can thus disallow double-spending by malicious traders. Each traded output uses a multisignature script of the above form, so traders are ultimately in control of their assets. From time to time, the TTP publishes the state to the decentralized Bitcoin network, in order to make the off-chain history irreversible.

References

1. Andresen, G.: Pay to Script Hash (2012). https://github.com/bitcoin/bips/blob/master/bip-0016.mediawiki
2. Arrow, K.J., Forsythe, R., Gorham, M., Hahn, R., Hanson, R., Ledyard, J.O., Levmore, S., Litan, R., Milgrom, P., Nelson, F.D., Neumann, G.R., Ottaviani, M., Schelling, T.C., Shiller, R.J., Smith, V.L., Snowberg, E., Sunstein, C.R., Tetlock, P.C., Tetlock, P.E., Varian, H.R., Wolfers, J., Zitzewitz, E.: The promise of prediction markets. Science **320**(5878), 877 (2008)
3. Aumann, R.: The Shapley Value. http://www.ma.huji.ac.il/raumann/pdf/The%20Shapley%20Value.pdf
4. Black, F., Scholes, M.: The pricing of options and corporate liabilities. J. Polit. Econ. **81**(3), 637–654 (1973)
5. Bentov, I.: The effect of colored coins on Bitcoin security (2015). http://blog.chromaway.com/2015/11/the-effect-of-colored-coins-on-bitcoin.html
6. Bentov, I., Gabizon, A., Mizrahi, A.: Cryptocurrencies without proof of work. In: Clark, J., Meiklejohn, S., Ryan, P.Y.A., Wallach, D., Brenner, M., Rohloff, K. (eds.) FC 2016. LNCS, vol. 9604, pp. 142–157. Springer, Heidelberg (2016). https://doi.org/10.1007/978-3-662-53357-4_10
7. Bonneau, J., Clark, J., Felten, E., Kroll, J., Miller, A., Narayanan, A.: On decentralizing prediction markets and order books. In: 13th Workshop on the Economics of Information Security (WEIS) (2014)
8. Bonneau, J., Clark, J., Felten, E., Kroll, J., Miller, A., Narayanan, A.: SoK: research perspectives and challenges for Bitcoin and cryptocurrencies. In: 36th IEEE Symposium on Security and Privacy (S&P) (2015)
9. Chen, Y., Gao, X., Goldstein, R., Kash, I.: Market manipulation with outside incentives. In: Proceedings of the Twenty-Fifth AAAI Conference on Artificial Intelligence (2011). https://www.aaai.org/ocs/index.php/AAAI/AAAI11/paper/viewFile/3747/3948
10. ColorCoin github repository. https://github.com/baldmaster/ColorCoin/blob/master/Src/Prediction.hs
11. Counterparty. http://counterparty.io/
12. Gillies, D.: Solutions to general non-zero-sum games. Contrib. Theory Games **4**(40), 47–85 (1959)
13. Heilman, E., Baldimtsi, F., Goldberg, S.: Blindly signed contracts: anonymous on-blockchain and off-blockchain Bitcoin transactions. In: Clark, J., Meiklejohn, S., Ryan, P.Y.A., Wallach, D., Brenner, M., Rohloff, K. (eds.) FC 2016. LNCS, vol. 9604, pp. 43–60. Springer, Heidelberg (2016). https://doi.org/10.1007/978-3-662-53357-4_4
14. Heilman, E., Alshenibr, L., Foteini, B., Scafuro, A., Goldberg, S.: TumbleBit: an untrusted Bitcoin-compatible anonymous payment hub (2016). https://eprint.iacr.org/2016/575
15. Ruffing, T., Moreno-Sanchez, P., Kate, A.: CoinShuffle: practical decentralized coin mixing for Bitcoin. In: Kutyłowski, M., Vaidya, J. (eds.) ESORICS 2014 Part II. LNCS, vol. 8713, pp. 345–364. Springer, Cham (2014). https://doi.org/10.1007/978-3-319-11212-1_20
16. Kate, A., Moreno-Sanchez, P., Ruffing, T.: P2P mixing and unlinkable Bitcoin transactions (2016). http://eprint.iacr.org/2016/824
17. Nakamoto, S.: Bitcoin: a peer-to-peer electronic cash system (2008). https://bitcoin.org/bitcoin.pdf

18. Omni Layer. http://www.omnilayer.org/
19. Peterson, J., Krug, J.: Augur: a decentralized, open-source platform for prediction markets 2015. https://arxiv.org/abs/1501.01042
20. Rosenfeld, M.: Colored Coins (2013). https://bitcoil.co.il/files/Colored%20Coins.pdf, https://bitcoil.co.il/BitcoinX.pdf
21. Shapley, L.: A value for n-person games. Contrib. Theory Games II Ann. Math. Stud. **2**(28), 307–317 (1953)
22. Sztorc, P.: Truthcoin: trustless, decentralized, censorship-proof, incentive-compatible, scalable cryptocurrency prediction marketplace (2014). http://www.truthcoin.info/papers/truthcoin-whitepaper.pdf
23. Todd, P.: Checklocktimeverify (2014). https://github.com/bitcoin/bips/blob/master/bip-0065.mediawiki

An Analysis of Bitcoin OP_RETURN Metadata

Massimo Bartoletti[(✉)] and Livio Pompianu

Università degli Studi di Cagliari, Cagliari, Italy
{bart,livio.pompianu}@unica.it

Abstract. The Bitcoin protocol allows to save arbitrary data on the blockchain through a special instruction of the scripting language, called OP_RETURN. A growing number of protocols exploit this feature to extend the range of applications of the Bitcoin blockchain beyond transfer of currency. A point of debate in the Bitcoin community is whether loading data through OP_RETURN can negatively affect the performance of the Bitcoin network with respect to its primary goal. This paper is an empirical study of the usage of OP_RETURN over the years. We identify several protocols based on OP_RETURN, which we classify by their application domain. We measure the evolution in time of the usage of each protocol, the distribution of OP_RETURN transactions by application domain, and their space consumption.

1 Introduction

Bitcoin was the first decentralized digital currency to be created, and now it is the most widely used, with a market capitalization of ∼20 billions USD[1]. Technically, the Bitcoin network is a peer to peer system, where users can securely transfer currency without the intermediation of a trusted authority. Transactions of currency are gathered in blocks, that are added to a public data structure called *blockchain*. The consensus algorithm of Bitcoin guarantees that, for an attacker to be able to alter an existing block, she must control the majority of the computational resources of the network [37]. Hence, attacks aiming at incrementing one's balance, e.g. by deleting transactions that certify payments to other users, are infeasible in practice. This security property is often rephrased by saying that the blockchain can be seen as an *immutable* data structure.

Although the main goal of Bitcoin is to transfer digital currency, the immutability and openness of its blockchain have inspired the development of new protocols, which "piggy-back" metadata on transactions in order to implement a variety of applications beyond cryptocurrency. For instance, some protocols allow to certify the existence of a document (e.g., [21, 29, 33]), while some others allow to track the ownership of a digital or a physical asset (e.g., [16, 24, 25]). Many of these protocols save metadata on the blockchain by using an instruction called OP_RETURN, which is part of the Bitcoin scripting language.

A debate about the scalability of Bitcoin has been taking place over the last few years [2, 30, 31]. In particular, users argue over whether the blockchain should

---

[1] Source: coinmarketcap.com, accessed on February 28th, 2017.

© International Financial Cryptography Association 2017
M. Brenner et al. (Eds.): FC 2017 Workshops 2017, LNCS 10323, pp. 218–230, 2017.
https://doi.org/10.1007/978-3-319-70278-0_14

allow for storing spurious data, not inherent to currency transfers. Although many recent works analyse the Bitcoin blockchain [35,38,39,41,42], as well as some services related to OP_RETURN [6,22,26,32], many relevant questions are still open. What is the impact of the data attached to OP_RETURN on the size of the blockchain? Which kinds of blockchain-based applications are exploiting the OP_RETURN instruction, and how?

Contributions. We analyse the usage of OP_RETURN throughout the Bitcoin blockchain, collecting a total of 1,887,708 OP_RETURN transactions. We investigate to which protocols OP_RETURN transactions belong, identifying 22 distinct protocols (associated to 51% of these transactions). We find that 15% of this total are *empty* transactions, which attach no metadata to OP_RETURN. By studing the usage of OP_RETURN over time, we identify several transaction peaks related to empty transactions, and we show that they are mainly caused by stress tests and spam attacks happened in summer 2015. We classify protocols according to their application domain, and we study the numerical proportion of these applications. Finally, we measure the size of OP_RETURN metadata, and the proportion between the size of OP_RETURN transactions and the overall size of the transactions in the blockchain. To the best of our knowledge, ours is the widest investigation about the usage of OP_RETURN. All our analyses are supported by a tool we have developed. The sources of our tool, as well as the experimental data, are available at [5].

2   Background on Bitcoin

Bitcoin [40] is a decentralized infrastructure to exchange virtual currency—the *bitcoins*. The transfers of currency, called *transactions*, are the basic elements of the system. The transactions are recorded on a public, append-only data structure, called *blockchain*. To illustrate how Bitcoin works, we consider two transactions T_0 and T_1 of the following form:

T_0
in: $\cdots$
in-script: $\cdots$
out-script(T, σ): $ver_k(T, \sigma)$
value: v_0

T_1
in: T_0
in-script: $sig_k(\bullet)$
out-script$(\cdots)$: $\cdots$
value: v_1

The transaction T_0 contains a value v_0 bitcoins. Anyone can *redeem* the amount of bitcoins in T_0 by putting on the blockchain a transaction (e.g., T_1), whose in field contains the identifier of T_0 (the hash of the whole transaction, displayed as T_0 in the figure) and whose in-script contains values making the out-script[2] of T_0, a programmable boolean function, evaluate to true. When this happens, the value of T_0 is transferred to the new transaction T_1, and T_0 becomes unredeemable. A subsequent transaction can then redeem T_1 likewise.

---

[2] in-script/out-script are called scriptPubKey/scriptSig in the Bitcoin wiki.

In the transaction T_0 above, the out-script just checks the digital signature σ on the redeeming transaction T w.r.t. a given key k. We denote with $ver_k(T, \sigma)$ the signature verification, and with $sig_k(\bullet)$ the signature of the enclosing transaction (T_1 in our example), including all the parts of the transaction but its in-script (obviously, because it contains the signature itself).

Now, assume that T_0 is redeemable on the blockchain when someone tries to append T_1. The Bitcoin network accepts the redeem if (i) $v_1 \leq v_0$, and (ii) the out-script of T_0, applied to T_1 and to the signature $sig_k(\bullet)$, evaluates true.

The previous example is a special case of a Bitcoin transaction: the general form is displayed in Fig. 1a. First, there can be multiple inputs and outputs (denoted with array notation in the figure), and each output has its own out-script and value. Since each output can be redeemed independently, in fields must specify which one they are redeeming ($T_0[n_0]$ in the figure). A transaction with multiple inputs redeems *all* the (outputs of) transactions in its in fields, providing a suitable in-script for each of them. To be valid, the sum of the values of all the inputs must be greater or equal to the sum of the values of all outputs. The *Unspent Transaction Output* (in short, UTXO) is the set of redeemable outputs of all transactions included in the blockchain. To be valid, a transaction must only use elements of the UTXO as inputs.

T
in[0]: $T_0[n_0]$
in-script[0]: $\cdots$
$\vdots$
out-script[0](T_0', w_0): $\cdots$
value[0]: v_0
$\vdots$
lockTime: s

T
in[0]: ...
in-script[0]: ...
$\vdots$
out-script[0](...): OP_RETURN "$EW\,Hello!$"
value[0]: 0
$\vdots$

(a) General form of transactions.   (b) An OP_RETURN transaction.

Fig. 1. (a) General form of transactions and (b) An OP RETURN transaction.

In its general form, the out-script is a program in a non Turing-complete scripting language, which features a limited set of logic, arithmetic, and cryptographic operators. The lockTime field specifies the earliest moment in time when the transaction can appear on the blockchain.

Writing Metadata in Transactions. Bitcoin transactions do not provide a field where one can save arbitrary data. Nevertheless, users have devised various creative ways to encode data in transactions. A first method is to abuse the standard *Pay-to-PubkeyHash* script[3], which implements the signature verification ver_k seen before (actually, the script does not contain the public key k, but its

---

[3] en.bitcoin.it/wiki/Transaction#Pay-to-PubkeyHash.

hash $h = H(k)$). To make the script evaluate to true, the redeeming transaction T has to provide the signature σ and a public key k such that $H(k) = h$ and $ver_k(T, \sigma)$. One can store an arbitrary message m (a few bytes long) within the out-script, by writing m in place of the hash h. Since computing a value k such that $H(k) = m$ (i.e., a preimage of m) and a signature σ such that $ver_k(T, \sigma)$ are computationally hard operations, outputs crafted in this way are unspendable in practice. However, these outputs are not easily distinguishable from the spendable ones, hence the nodes of the Bitcoin network must keep them in their UTXO set [3]. Since this set is usually stored in RAM for efficiency concerns [28], this practice negatively affects the memory consumption of nodes [35].

The OP_RETURN instruction allows to save metadata on the blockchain, as shown in Fig. 1b[4]. However, unlike *Pay-to-PubkeyHash*, an out-script containing OP_RETURN always evaluates to false, hence the output is provably unspendable, and its transaction can be safely removed from the UTXO. In this way, OP_RETURN overcomes the UTXO consumption issue highlighted above. Although the OP_RETURN instruction has been part of the scripting language since the first releases of Bitcoin, originally it was considered *non-standard* by nodes, so transactions containing OP_RETURN were difficult to reliably get mined. In March 2014 [12], OP_RETURN became standard, meaning that all nodes started to relay unconfirmed OP_RETURN transactions[5]. The limit for storing data in an OP_RETURN was originally planned to be 80 bytes, but the first official client supporting the instruction, i.e.the release 0.9.0 [12], allowed only 40 bytes. This animated a long debate [7,8,17,18]. From the release 0.10.0 [9] nodes could choose whether to accept or not OP_RETURN transactions, and set a maximum for their size. The release 0.11.0 [10] extended the data limit to 80 bytes, and the release 0.12.0 [11] to a maximum of 83 bytes.

3   Methodology for Classifying OP_RETURN Transactions

We discuss our methodology for identifying protocols that use OP_RETURN.

We gather all the OP_RETURN transactions from the origin block up to the block number 453,200 (added on 2017/02/15). We end up with a set of 1,887,708 OP_RETURN transactions. For each of them, we save the following data in a database: (i) the hash of the transaction; (ii) the hash of the enclosing block; (iii) the timestamp of the block; (iv) the metadata attached to the OP_RETURN.

Next, we detect to which protocols the OP_RETURN transactions belong. Usually, a protocol is identified by the first few bytes of metadata attached to the OP_RETURN, but the exact number of bytes may vary from protocol to protocol. Hence, we associate OP_RETURN transactions to protocols as follows:

---

[4] Hash: d84f8cf06829c7202038731e5444411adc63a6d4cbf8d4361b86698abad3a68a.

[5] Regarding the use of OP_RETURN, the release notes of Bitcoin Core version 0.9.0 state that: *"This change is not an endorsement of storing data in the blockchain."* At the same time, some Bitcoin explorers, (e.g. blockchain.info, blockexplorer.com, smartbit.com) allow to inspect data encoded in OP_RETURN scripts.

1. we search the web for known associations between identifiers and protocols;
2. we accordingly classify the OP_RETURN transactions that begin with one of the identifiers obtained at step 1;
3. on the remaining *unknown transactions*, we perform a frequency analysis of the first few bytes of metadata, to discover new protocol identifiers.

In more details, in the first step we query Google to obtain public identifier/protocol bindings. For instance, the query *"Bitcoin OP_RETURN"*, returns ~26,500 results, and we manually inspect the first few pages of them. Note that a protocol can be associated with more than one identifier (e.g., Stampery, Blockstore [34], Remembr, CryptoCopyright), or even do not have any identifier. In this way we obtain 22 protocols associated to 33 identifiers; further, we find 3 protocols that do not use any identifier (Counterparty, Diploma [19], Chainpoint [14]).

The second step is performed by our tool: it associates 970,374 transactions to a protocol (~51% of the total OP_RETURN transactions). The other transactions are classified either as *empty* or *unknown*. Empty transactions have no data attached to the OP_RETURN instruction (296,491 transactions, ~15% of the total); unknown transactions have no known identifier (620,843 transactions, ~32% of the total).

The final step analyses unknown transactions, attempting to discover new protocol identifiers. Since identifiers may have different lengths, we gather the first D bytes of unknown transactions, for D ranging from 1 to 12, and we perform a frequency analysis of these strings. This analysis does not reveal relevant statistical anomalies (roughly, the strings are uniformly distributed), hence this step does not yield any new identifier. Algorithm 1 details this search, which is executed with the following parameters: $D = 12$, $\delta = 2$, $N = 100$.

Algorithm 1. Detect protocol identifiers

---

unknownTx ← *set of all unknown transactions*
Codes ← ∅
for i ← 1 to D do
   H ← *new hash table from protocol identifiers to number of occurrences*
   for all tx ∈ unknownTx do
      code ← tx.substring(i)   ▷ first i characters of tx
      if (H.contains(code)) then
         H.code ← H(code)+1 else H.code ← 1
      end if
   end for
   expectedOccurrences ← unknownTx.size() / pow(16,i)
   for all h ∈ H do
      if (h.occurrences > expectedOccurrences * δ and h.occurrences > N) then
         Codes ← Codes ∪ {h.code}
      end if
   end for
end for
return Codes

---

4   Qualitative Analysis of OP_RETURN Transactions

We now classify the protocols obtained in Sect. 3, associating each protocol to a *category* that describes its intended application domain. To this purpose, we manually inspect the web pages of each protocol.

Assets gathers protocols that exploit the immutability of the blockchain to certify ownership, exchange, and eventually the value of real-world assets. Metadata in transactions are used to specify e.g. the value of the asset, the amount of the asset transferred, the new owner, *etc.*

Document notary includes protocols for certifying the ownership and timestamp of a document. A user can publish the hash of a document in a transaction, and in this way he can prove its existence and integrity. Similarly, signatures can be used to certify ownership.

Digital arts includes protocols for declaring access right and copy rights on digital arts files, like e.g. photos or music.

Other includes protocols whose goals differ from the ones above. For instance, *Eternity Wall* [20] allows users to store short text messages on the blockchain; *Blockstore* [13] is a generic key-value store, on top of which more complex protocols can be implemented[6].

Empty includes protocols that do not attach any data to OP_RETURN.

Unknown includes protocols for which we have not been able to detect an identifier (possibly, because they do not use any).

We report our classification of protocols in the first two columns of Table 1. Due to the OP_RETURN space limit, long pieces of metadata require to be split in many transactions, and higher fees. Hence, *assets* protocols usually feature complex rules, have space-efficient representations of data, and often propose off-chain solutions [15]. We distinguish document notary protocols from digital arts protocols for the following reason. Most document notary applications do not require users to provide their documents to the application, and the main purpose of the protocol (certifying ownership) can be fulfilled also when the application is no longer live. Instead, digital arts application usually need to gather user documents, and require interactions with users, e.g. they often play the role of broker between producers and consumers.

5   Quantitative Analysis of OP_RETURN Transactions

Table 1 shows some statistics about OP_RETURN transactions. The first column indicates the protocol categories, introduced in Sect. 4. The second and third columns show, respectively, the protocol names and the associated identifiers. The fourth column shows the date in which the protocol generated the first transaction. Since transactions do not have a "date" field, we infer dates from

---

[6] Hereafter we aggregate all the protocols built upon *Blockstore*, by identifying them with *Blockstore* itself.

Table 1. Statistics about OP_RETURN protocols.

Category	Protocol	Identifiers	First trans.	Tot. trans.	Tot. size	Avg. size
Assets	Colu	CC	2015/07/09	237,479	4,290,388	18.0
	CoinSpark	SPK	2014/07/02	28,026	956,904	34.1
	OpenAssets	OA	2014/05/03	133,570	1,728,350	12.9
	Omni	omni	2015/08/10	105,979	2,132,565	20.1
	Counterparty	N/A	N/A	N/A	N/A	N/A
	Total	-	-	**505,054**	**9,108,207**	**18.0**
Document notary	Factom	Factom!!, FACTOM00, Fa, FA	2014/04/11	74,159	2,966,234	40.0
	Stampery	S1, S2, S3, S4, S5	2015/03/09	74,249	2,627,540	35.4
	Proof of Existence	DOCPROOF	2014/04/21	5,262	210,433	40.0
	Blocksign	BS	2014/08/04	1,460	55,192	37.8
	CryptoCopyright	CryptoTests-, CryptoProof-	2014/08/02	46	1,840	40
	Stampd	STAMPD##	2015/01/03	473	18,867	39.9
	BitProof	BITPROOF	2015/02/25	758	30,320	40
	ProveBit	ProveBit	2015/04/05	57	2,280	40
	Remembr	RMBd, RMBe	2015/08/25	28	1,128	40.3
	OriginalMy	ORIGMY	2015/07/12	126	4,788	38
	LaPreuve	LaPreuve	2014/12/07	67	2,623	39.1
	Nicosia	UNicDC	2014/09/12	20	684	34.2
	Chainpoint	N/A	N/A	N/A	N/A	N/A
	Diploma	N/A	N/A	N/A	N/A	N/A
	Total	-	-	**156,705**	**5,921,929**	**37.8**
Digital arts	Monegraph	MG	2015/06/28	63,278	2,317,151	36.6
	Blockai	0 × 1f00	2015/01/09	527	34,225	64.9
	Ascribe	ASCRIBE	2014/12/19	40,859	847,641	20.7
	Total	-	-	**104,664**	**3,199,017**	**30.6**
Other	Eternity Wall	EW	2015/06/24	3,715	160,191	43.1
	Blockstore	id, 0 × 5888, 0 × 5808	2014/12/10	191,907	5,494,174	28.6
	SmartBit	SB.D	2015/11/24	8,329	299,844	36
	Total	-	-	**203,951**	**5,954,209**	**29.2**
Empty	**Total**	-	2014/03/20	**296,491**	**0**	**0**
Unknown	**Total**	-	2014/03/12	**620,843**	**20,023,345**	**32.3**
TOTAL	-	-	2014/03/12	**1,887,708**	**44,206,707**	**23.4**

the timestamp of the block containing the transaction. The next two columns count the total number of transactions, and the total size (in bytes) of the OP_RETURN data contained therein. To compute the size we only consider the metadata, i.e. we do not count neither the OP_RETURN instruction nor the other fields of the transaction. The last column shows the average size of the transaction metadata.

5.1 Overall Statistics

We detect 1,887,708 OP_RETURN transactions, distributed into 98,233 blocks, by scanning the blockchain until block number 453,200. Overall, OP_RETURN transactions constitute ∼0.96% of the total transactions in the blockchain, and ∼1.16% of the portion of the blockchain from 2014/03/12 (when the first

OP_RETURN transaction appeared). Although the former measurement considers 7 years of transactions while the latter only considers the last 3 years, we note that the values are very close. We explain this fact by observing that the daily number of transactions rapidly increased since July 2014.

5.2   Transaction Peaks

Figures 2a and b display the number of OP_RETURN transactions per week, from 2014/03 (date of the first OP_RETURN transaction) to 2017/02 (end of our extraction). In the graph we note several peaks, that we explain as follows:

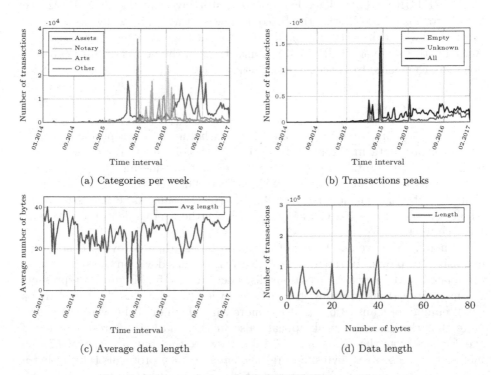

(a) Categories per week

(b) Transactions peaks

(c) Average data length

(d) Data length

Fig. 2. Usage and size of OP_RETURN transactions.

1. ~100,000 transactions from 2015/07/08 to 2015/08/05. This peak is mainly composed of two different peaks of *empty* transactions: the july peak (~36,900 transactions from 2015/07/08 to 2015/07/10) and the august peak (~29,200 transactions from 2015-08-01 to 2015-08-03). Both peaks seem to be caused by a spam campaign that resulted in a DoS attack on Bitcoin which happened in the same period, as reported in [35].
2. ~300,000 transactions from 2015/09/09 to 2015/09/23. This second peak is the highest and longest-lasting one. As before, it is mainly caused by *empty* transactions (~223,000), although here we also observe a component of

unknown and *blockstore* transactions (~35,000 each). The work [35] detects a spike also in this period, precisely around 2015/09/13, where an anonymous group performed a stress-test on the network with a *money drop*. This involves a public release of private keys, with the aim to cause a big race which would cause a large number of *double-spend* transactions.

3. ~50,000 transactions from 2016/03/02 to 2016/03/09. The last peak is due to the sum of two different peaks: *unknown* (about 18,000) and *stampery* (about 23,000) transactions. We conjecture that this peak is caused by the testing and bootstrap of protocols.

We observe that the Bitcoin blockchain has also other peaks, not related to OP_RETURN transactions. For instance, starting from the 2015/05/22 and for a duration of 100 blocks, the Bitcoin network was targeted by a stress test [4], during which the network was flooded with a huge number of transactions. Actually, the usage of OP_RETURN transactions in the period of this peak does not seem to diverge from their normal usage.

5.3   Space Consumption

A debated topic in the Bitcoin community is whether it is acceptable or not to save arbitrary data in the blockchain. The sixth column in Table 1 shows, for each protocol, the total size of metadata (i.e., not considering the bytes of the instructions OP_RETURN and PUSH_DATA). The last row of Table 1 shows that the total size of metadata is ~42 MB (in the same date, the size of the whole blockchain is ~102 GB). Figure 2c shows the average length of the data for each week.

Generally, the average length of metadata is less than 40 bytes, despite the extension to 80 bytes introduced on 2015/07/12. Peaks down on the same period are related to the *empty* transactions discussed in Sect. 5.2. Figure 2d represents the number of transactions with a given data length: also this chart confirms a small number of transactions that use more than the half of the available space. Note that the discussed peak appears also in this chart, in correspondence of the 0 value. From the last column of Table 1 we see that only the size of *Blockai* metadata is close to 80 bytes. Several *document notary* protocols take 40 bytes on average: this depends from their identifiers, composed of 16 bytes, and from the size of the hash they save. Generally, *document notary* protocols carry longer data than the other protocols.

We now evaluate the minimum space consumption of the OP_RETURN transactions on the whole blockchain. First, we observe that an *empty* transaction with one input and one output has a total size of 156 bytes. From Table 1 we see that OP_RETURN transaction carry ~23.4 bytes of metadata, on average. Hence, we approximate the average size of OP_RETURN transaction as ~179.4 bytes, and so an approximation of the space consumption of all the OP_RETURN transactions is ~323 MB.

Finally, we estimate the ratio between the total size of OP_RETURN transactions and the size of all the transactions on the blockchain. The block header has size 97 bytes at most. Hence, removing the size of the headers of our 453,200 extracted blocks (~42 MB) from the total size of the blockchain at 2017/02/15, we obtain ~102 GB of transactions. From this we conclude that OP_RETURN transactions consume ~0.3% of the total space on the blockchain.

5.4   Distribution of Protocols by Category

Figure 3 displays how the OP_RETURN transactions are distributed in the categories identified in Sect. 4. We note a relevant component of *empty* and *unknown* transactions. Although *assets* protocols produce the highest number of transactions, the most numerous category is *document notary*.

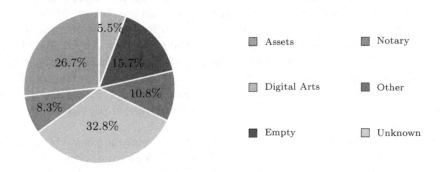

Fig. 3. Distribution of transactions by category.

Figure 2a and the fourth column of Table 1 suggest that, originally, the protocols using OP_RETURN were in the categories *assets* and *notary*, while the other use cases were introduced subsequently (indeed, the *other* category was not inhabited before the end of 2014).

Empty transactions use OP_RETURN without any data attached, so they are not associated to any protocol. We evaluate that ~96% of these transactions are related to the transaction peaks discussed in Sect. 5.2. Since those peaks happened in the same period of the stress tests and spam campaign discussed in [35], we conjecture that *empty* transactions are related to those events[7].

The *unknown* category contains ~33% of the OP_RETURN transactions. We identify 3 protocols [14,19,36] that write OP_RETURN data only as *unknown* transactions. We also identify one protocol [23] that besides using an identifier for saving document hashes, allows to save text messages without any identifier.

6   Conclusions

Our analysis shows an increasing interest in the OP_RETURN instruction. While in the first year of existence of OP_RETURN transactions (from March 2014)

---

[7] To verify this conjecture we would need to compare the transaction identifiers of our *empty* transactions with the identifiers of [35], which are not available online.

only a few hundreds of these transactions were appended per week, their usage has been steadily increasing since March 2015. In the last weeks of our experiments (February 2017) we counted ∼25,000 new OP_RETURN transactions per week, on average. Overall, we estimate that OP_RETURN transactions constitute ∼1% of the transactions in the blockchain, and use ∼0.3% of its space.

Besides using OP_RETURN and *Pay-to-PubkeyHash* as shown in Sect. 2, there are other techniques to save metadata on the Bitcoin blockchain. With a slightly different flavour, the "sign-to-contract" and "pay-to-contract" [1, 27] allow to prove that, if a certain transaction is redeemed, then a certain value was known at the time it was put on the blockchain. A benefit of these techniques is that they do not affect the size of transactions. Comparing different methods to store metadata on Bitcoin would be an interesting topic for future research.

Although the official Bitcoin documentation discourages the use of the blockchain to store arbitrary data[8], the trend seems to be a growth in the number of blockchain-based applications that embed their metadata in OP_RETURN transactions. We think that the main motivation for not using cheaper and more efficient storage is the perceived sense of security and persistence of the Bitcoin blockchain. If this trend will be confirmed, the specific needs of these applications could affect the future evolution of the Bitcoin protocol.

Related Work. Besides ours, other projects aim at analysing metadata in the Bitcoin blockchain. For instance, blockchainarchaeology.com collects files hidden in the blockchain. These files are usually split into several parts, stored e.g. on different output scripts in a transaction. Various techniques are used to detect how the files were encoded (e.g. by binary grep on the PNG pattern) and to reconstruct them. The Bitcoin wiki [6] provides a list of protocols using OP_RETURN, together with their identifiers. Excluding those protocol identifiers that, at time of writing, are not used yet in any OP_RETURN transaction, the collection in [6] is strictly included in ours. The website opreturn.org shows charts about OP_RETURN transactions over time, organised by protocol, and statistics about their usage on the last week and over the last two years. The website smartbit.com recognises some OP_RETURN identifiers and shows related statistics. Finally, the website kaiko.com sells data about Bitcoin, including data related to OP_RETURN transactions.

Acknowledgments. The authors thank the anonymous reviewers of BITCOIN 2017 for their insightful comments on a preliminary version of this paper. This work is partially supported by Aut. Reg. of Sardinia P.I.A. 2013 "NOMAD".

---

[8] The release notes of Bitcoin Core version 0.9.0 state that: *"Storing arbitrary data in the blockchain is still a bad idea; it is less costly and far more efficient to store non-currency data elsewhere."*.

References

1. Alternatives to opreturn. http://bitcoin.stackexchange.com/questions/37206/alternatives-to-op-return-to-store-data-in-bitcoin-blockchain. Accessed 15 Feb 2017
2. Bicoin scalability. https://en.bitcoin.it/wiki/Scalability_FAQ. Accessed 15 Dec 2016
3. Bitcoin core dev update 5 transaction fees embedded data. http://www.coindesk.com/bitcoin-core-dev-update-5-transaction-fees-embedded-data/. Accessed 15 Dec 2016
4. Bitcoin network survives surprise stress test. http://www.coindesk.com/bitcoin-network-survives-stress-test/. Accessed 15 Dec 2016
5. Bitcoin OPRETURN explorer. https://github.com/BitcoinOpReturn/. Accessed 15 Dec 2016
6. Bitcoin OP_RETURN wiki page. https://en.bitcoin.it/wiki/OP_RETURN. Accessed 15 Dec 2016
7. Bitcoin pull request 5075. https://github.com/bitcoin/bitcoin/pull/5075. Accessed 15 Dec 2016
8. Bitcoin pull request 5286. https://github.com/bitcoin/bitcoin/pull/5286. Accessed 15 Dec 2016
9. Bitcoin release 0.10.0. https://bitcoin.org/en/release/v0.10.0. Accessed 15 Dec 2016
10. Bitcoin release 0.11.0. https://bitcoin.org/en/release/v0.11.0. Accessed 15 Dec 2016
11. Bitcoin release 0.12.0. https://bitcoin.org/en/release/v0.12.0. Accessed 15 Dec 2016
12. Bitcoin release 0.9.0. https://bitcoin.org/en/release/v0.9.0. Accessed 15 Dec 2016
13. Blockstore website. https://github.com/blockstack/blockchain-id/wiki/Blockstore. Accessed 15 Dec 2016
14. Chainpoint website. http://www.chainpoint.org/. Accessed 15 Dec 2016
15. Colu protocol, torrents. https://github.com/Colored-Coins/Colored-Coins-Protocol-Specification/wiki/Metadata\#torrents. Accessed 15 Dec 2016
16. Colu website. https://www.colu.com/. Accessed 15 Dec 2016
17. Counterparty open letter and plea to the Bitcoin core development team. http://counterparty.io/news/an-open-letter-and-plea-to-the-bitcoin-core-development-team/. Accessed 15 Dec 2016
18. Developers battle over bitcoin block chain. http://www.coindesk.com/developers-battle-bitcoin-block-chain/. Accessed 15 Dec 2016
19. Diploma website. http://diploma.report/. Accessed 15 Dec 2016
20. Eternity wall website. https://eternitywall.it/. Accessed 15 Dec 2016
21. Factom website. https://www.factom.com/. Accessed 15 Dec 2016
22. Kaiko data store. https://www.kaiko.com/. Accessed 15 Dec 2016
23. La preuve website. http://lapreuve.eu/explication.html. Accessed 15 Dec 2016
24. Omni website. http://www.omnilayer.org/. Accessed 15 Dec 2016
25. Open assets website. https://github.com/OpenAssets/. Accessed 15 Dec 2016
26. opreturn.org. http://opreturn.org/. Accessed 15 Dec 2016
27. Pay-to-contract and sign-to-contract. https://bitcointalk.org/index.php?topic=915828.msg10056796#msg10056796. Accessed 15 Feb 2017
28. Peter Todd delayed txo commitments. https://petertodd.org/2016/delayed-txo-commitments. Accessed 15 Dec 2016

29. Proof of existence website. https://proofofexistence.com/. Accessed 15 Dec 2016
30. Scalability debate ever end. https://www.cryptocoinsnews.com/will-bitcoin-scalab ility-debate-ever-end/. Accessed 30 Nov 2016
31. Scaling debate in Reddit. http://www.coindesk.com/viabtc-ceo-sparks-bitcoin-sca ling-debate-reddit-ama/. Accessed 15 Dec 2016
32. Smartbit OP_RETURN statistics. https://www.smartbit.com.au/op-returns. Accessed 15 Dec 2016
33. Stampery website. https://stampery.com/. Accessed 15 Dec 2016
34. Ali, M., Nelson, J., Shea, R., Freedman, M.J.: Blockstack: a global naming and storage system secured by blockchains. In: USENIX Annual Technical Conference (2016)
35. Baqer, K., Huang, D.Y., McCoy, D., Weaver, N.: Stressing out: Bitcoin "stress testing". In: Clark, J., Meiklejohn, S., Ryan, P.Y.A., Wallach, D., Brenner, M., Rohloff, K. (eds.) FC 2016. LNCS, vol. 9604, pp. 3–18. Springer, Heidelberg (2016). https://doi.org/10.1007/978-3-662-53357-4_1
36. Dermody, R., Krellenstein, A., Slama, O., Wagner, E.: Counterparty: protocol specification (2014). http://counterparty.io/docs/protocol_specification/. Accessed 15 Dec 2016
37. Garay, J., Kiayias, A., Leonardos, N.: The Bitcoin backbone protocol: analysis and applications. In: Oswald, E., Fischlin, M. (eds.) EUROCRYPT 2015. LNCS, vol. 9057, pp. 281–310. Springer, Heidelberg (2015). https://doi.org/10.1007/978-3-662-46803-6_10
38. Lischke, M., Fabian, B.: Analyzing the Bitcoin network: the first four years. Future Internet 8(1), 7 (2016)
39. Möser, M., Böhme, R.: Trends, tips, tolls: a longitudinal study of Bitcoin transaction fees. In: Brenner, M., Christin, N., Johnson, B., Rohloff, K. (eds.) FC 2015. LNCS, vol. 8976, pp. 19–33. Springer, Heidelberg (2015). https://doi.org/10.1007/978-3-662-48051-9_2
40. Nakamoto, S.: Bitcoin: a peer-to-peer electronic cash system (2008). https://bitcoin.org/bitcoin.pdf
41. Reid, F., Harrigan, M.: An analysis of anonymity in the Bitcoin system. In: Altshuler, Y., Elovici, Y., Cremers, A., Aharony, N., Pentland, A. (eds.) Security and Privacy in Social Networks, pp. 197–223. Springer, New York (2013). https://doi.org/10.1007/978-1-4614-4139-7_10
42. Ron, D., Shamir, A.: Quantitative analysis of the full Bitcoin transaction graph. In: Sadeghi, A.-R. (ed.) FC 2013. LNCS, vol. 7859, pp. 6–24. Springer, Heidelberg (2013). https://doi.org/10.1007/978-3-642-39884-1_2

Constant-Deposit Multiparty Lotteries on Bitcoin

Massimo Bartoletti[1]([⊠]) and Roberto Zunino[2]

[1] Università degli Studi di Cagliari, Cagliari, Italy
bart@unica.it
[2] Università degli Studi di Trento, Trento, Italy

Abstract. An active research trend is to exploit the consensus mechanism of cryptocurrencies to secure the execution of distributed applications. In particular, some recent works have proposed fair lotteries which work on Bitcoin. These protocols, however, require a deposit from each player which grows quadratically with the number of players. We propose a fair lottery on Bitcoin which only requires a constant deposit.

1 Introduction

Recent research on blockchain technologies studies how to extend the applications of cryptocurrencies from simple transfers of money to complex financial transactions. The goal is to make financial agreements or "smart contracts" [24] between mutually distrusting participants, and automatically enforce them via the consensus mechanism of the cryptocurrency, without relying on a trusted third party. In particular, some works propose to run smart contracts on top of existing cryptocurrencies (mostly, on Bitcoin). Many of these approaches, e.g. [1,6,8,16–18], implement *fair* computations, where a set of players contribute to compute a function without revealing their inputs; fairness, studied in various forms, guarantees e.g. that any player that aborts after learning the output pays a penalty to all players that did not learn the output. Other works implement decentralised authorization systems [10], and contracts which allow users to make statements, penalising those which make conflicting ones [22].

A particular kind of smart contract is the one which implements a lottery among a set a players. Intuitively, this is an application where each one of N players puts their bets in a pot, and a winner—uniformly chosen among the players—gets the whole pot. Secure protocols for multiparty lotteries on Bitcoin have been recently proposed by [2,4,5,8]. These protocols enjoy a *fairness* property, which roughly guarantees that: (i) each honest player will have (on average) a non-negative payoff, even in the presence of adversaries who play against; (ii) when all the players are honest, the protocol behaves as an ideal lottery: one player wins the whole pot, while all the others lose their bets.

To obtain the result, these protocols require that, to bet e.g. 1 coin, each one of the N players must block a *deposit* of $O(N^2)$ coins throughout the whole

© International Financial Cryptography Association 2017
M. Brenner et al. (Eds.): FC 2017 Workshops 2017, LNCS 10323, pp. 231–247, 2017.
https://doi.org/10.1007/978-3-319-70278-0_15

protocol[1]. Since the deposit grows quadratically with N, these protocols are only practical for a small number of players. In this paper we address this issue.

Contributions. We propose a fair protocol for multiparty lotteries, whose deposit does *not depend* on the number N of players. More specifically, our protocol is fair for any choice of the deposit value (including zero), and for any adversarial strategy. Furthermore, if the deposit value is positive, an adversary who tries to attack the protocol with the goal of altering the payoff of honest players, can only lose money on average. Our protocol is based on a *single-elimination tournament*, i.e. a tree of $N-1$ two-player matches where the loser of each match is eliminated. Overall, a complete run of the protocol requires $O(N)$ transactions on-chain and $O(\log N)$ time (assuming that the time to put transactions on the Bitcoin ledger dominates the time required for communications and local computations). Our protocol has been implemented as an Ethereum smart contract; an implementation on Bitcoin would require a variant of the mechanism for verifying the signature of transactions, to allow the malleability of input fields.

An extended version of this paper is available online at [7].

2   Statically Signing Chains of Transactions

The current signature mechanism of Bitcoin is known to be unsuitable for signing *chains* of transactions before they are put on the ledger[2]. Consider e.g. two players, a and b, and three transactions, T_0, T_1 and T_2, made as follows.

– transaction T_1 has T_0 as input, while T_2 has T_1 as input: hence the three transactions form a chain.
– the out-scripts of T_0 and T_1 require signatures by both players a and b.

The players want to put the chain of transactions on the ledger, assuming that T_0 is already there. Intuitively, the players have two possible ways of proceeding:

dynamic signing: both players sign T_1 and put it on the ledger. After that, they both sign T_2 and put it on the ledger.
static signing: a signs both T_1 and T_2 *before* these transactions are on the ledger, and sends her signatures to b. Then, b adds his own signatures, and puts both T_1 and T_2, one after the other, on the ledger.

Without the *segregated witnesses* feature [19], only dynamic signing is feasible. Of course, in static signing, the addition of b's signature to the in-script of T_1 alters its in-script.[3] Note that this will not invalidate a's signature of T_1 (because the signature does not consider the in-script), so T_1 can still be put on

---

[1] Concurrently and independently of our work, [20] proposes a lottery protocol for Bitcoin that requires zero deposit.
[2] See https://en.bitcoin.it/wiki/Transaction_Malleability.
[3] in-script and out-script are respectively referred as scriptPubKey and scriptSig in the Bitcoin documentation.

the ledger. However, altering the in-script changes the *hash* of T_1, which is used in T_2.in to refer to the previous transaction. Because of this, a's signature of T_2 is no longer valid, hence b can not put T_2 on the ledger.

A possible solution to this problem is to allow *partial* signatures, which e.g. neglect the in part of transactions, as already done for the in-script part. Indeed, even if T_2.in (i.e., the hash of T_1) is modified, the (partial) signature in T_2.in-script is still valid, because it neglects the in part. More in general, we define below a signature scheme for Bitcoin transactions, allowing users to choose which parts M of the transaction to include in the signature. In this way, once the transaction is signed, anyone can modify the parts not in M without invalidating the signature. The ability of modifying transactions while preserving their signatures is called *transaction malleability*: while in some circumstances it can cause security vulnerabilities [3], if used in a controlled manner it can extend the range of applications built upon Bitcoin [1]. Note that the unsigned parts of a transaction can be freely altered by adversaries; therefore, designing a secure protocol must take into account for this possibility. E.g., in the previous static signing example, b can alter T_2.in so to refer to some $T \neq T_1$ whose out-script can be satisfied by a's signature. In this way T becomes unredeemable. To protect against this attack, a could use a fresh key in T_1.out-script, so that nothing else can be redeemed by her signature.

We anticipate that our lottery protocol does not require the whole flexibility of the signature mechanism outlined below, but it only relies on the malleability of the in and in-script fields. While the malleability of in-script is already allowed by the segregated witnesses release, that of in fields would require support from the signature verification mechanism (e.g., a new signature flag or opcode).

Signature scheme for transaction malleability. Let

$$M \subseteq \{\text{in}[n], \text{in-script}[n], \text{value}[n], \text{out-script}[n], \text{lockTime} \mid n \geq 0\}$$

and denote with $M(T)$ the bitstring obtained by concatenating the parts of the transaction T mentioned in M. We then define:

$$\mathbf{sig}_k^M(T) = (sig_k(M(T)), M) \qquad \mathbf{ver}_k(T, (y, M)) = ver_k(M(T), y)$$

Hereafter, we use σ as a meta-variable for the *partial signatures* $(sig_k(\ldots), M)$, and $\boldsymbol{\sigma}$ for arrays of such pairs (we will always use the same convention for arrays). When $\boldsymbol{k}$ and $\boldsymbol{\sigma}$ have the same size n, we define:

$$\mathbf{sig}_{\boldsymbol{k}}^M(T) = (\mathbf{sig}_{\boldsymbol{k}[0]}^M(T), \ldots, \mathbf{sig}_{\boldsymbol{k}[n-1]}^M(T)) \qquad \mathbf{ver}_{\boldsymbol{k}}(T, \boldsymbol{\sigma}) = \bigwedge_i \mathbf{ver}_{\boldsymbol{k}[i]}(T, \boldsymbol{\sigma}[i])$$

Transaction templates. The mechanism shown above allows to statically sign chains of transactions; further, we can also use it to statically sign chains of the form $T_0\,T_1(y)\,T_2$, where the transaction $T_1(y)$ depends on a parameter y such that (i) y is unknown at signing time (it will only be known later on), and (ii) y only affects those parts of $T_1(y)$ not included in the partial signatures. Under these assumptions, instantiating y in a later moment will *not* invalidate any signature. More importantly, while there might be a large number of values for y (and so, a large number of chains that can be put on the ledger), only one partial static signature of T_1 is needed (as well as for T_0 and T_2).

Parametric descriptions like the chain above are useful when designing complex protocols, where the actual chain (or graph) of transactions to be put on the ledger depend on events known after signatures have already been computed. We now introduce a general notation for expressing transactions with parameters and variants, which hereafter we name *transaction templates*. Our notation shows all the possible forms of the malleable transaction parts which are used in a protocol. Further, we will show how to statically sign such transactions (in all their forms). We anticipate that, for our lottery protocol, the number of possible transactions is large, while the number of needed static signatures is small.

Hereafter, we fix $M = \{\mathsf{value}[n], \mathsf{out\text{-}script}[n], \mathsf{lockTime} \mid n \geq 0\}$ in our signature scheme, so making the in and in-script fields malleable.[4]

The general form of transaction templates $\mathsf{t}, \mathsf{t}', \ldots$ is shown on the right. The template $\mathsf{t}(\mathbf{x})$ is parametrized over an array of values $\mathbf{x}$, in a given domain. Further, for its in and in-script fields, the template describes a few *variants*, each of which may take some additional parameters $\mathbf{y}$. Note that out-scripts may only refer to the template parameters $\mathbf{x}$, while in and in-scripts may also refer to their own variant parameters $\mathbf{y}$. Further, the in field refers to another template. A template $\mathsf{t}(\mathbf{x})$ can be instantiated to a transaction $\mathsf{T} = \mathsf{t}(\mathbf{x}).Variant^i \langle \mathbf{y}^i \rangle$, by choosing the variant i and the parameters. Here, $\mathsf{T}.\mathsf{in}$ is set to any redeemable transaction on the ledger which is an instantiation of the template in the in field of t.

$\mathsf{t}(\mathbf{x})$
$Variant^1 \langle \mathbf{y}^1 \rangle$
$\mathsf{in}[0]: \mathsf{t}_0^1(\mathbf{x}_0^1)[n_0^1]$ $\mathsf{in\text{-}script}[0]: \mathbf{W}_0^1$
$\vdots$
$\vdots$
$\mathsf{out\text{-}script}[0](\mathsf{T}_0', \mathbf{w}_0): \mathsf{OS}_0$ $\mathsf{value}[0]: v_0$
$\vdots$
$\mathsf{lockTime}: s$

The procedure for signing transaction templates is detailed in [7].

3   The Tournament Protocol

We introduce our lottery protocol for $N = 2^L$ players; each player is represented by a bit-string in $\mathcal{P} = \{0,1\}^L$, ranged over by $a, b, \ldots$. We assume that each player bets $1\math{B}$ in the lottery, and blocks a deposit of $d\math{B}$, for an arbitrary $d \geq 0$. Our protocol is based on a single-elimination tournament, where matches are organised as a complete binary tree of L levels. The tournament involves $N - 1$

---

[4] Note that only the transactions related to our protocol need to use this form of malleability. Instead, signers of transactions unrelated to the protocol can simply choose non-malleable signatures, unless they are prepared to defend against malleability-related attacks. For instance, if T and T' are standard transactions on the ledger with the same out-script, when T is redeemed by T_1 with a malleable in field, an adversary can also make T' redeemed, by putting on the ledger a copy of T_1 where the in field is changed to point to T'.

two-player matches: the winners of the matches at level $\ell \in 1..L - 1$ play at the next level $\ell - 1$; the winner of the match at level 0 wins the whole $N\cancel{B}$ stake.

Let $\Pi = \{\{0,1\}^n \mid n \leq L\}$ (i.e., sequences of n bits) be the set of tree *paths*. Intuitively, for every path in $\Pi \setminus \mathcal{P}$ we have a two-player match. For any two paths $\pi, \pi' \in \Pi$, we write $\pi \sqsubseteq \pi'$ when π is a prefix of π' ($\sqsubset$ for proper prefixes).

Key pairs and secrets. Our protocol requires players to exchange a certain number of Bitcoin transactions, together with their signatures. To this purpose, each player p generates all the following key pairs for every $a, b \in \mathcal{P}$ and for every π:

$$K_p(Bet_p),\ K_p(Collect),\ K_p(Init, a)$$

$$K_p(Win, \pi, a),\ K_p(WinTO, \pi, a) \qquad\qquad\qquad \epsilon \neq \pi \sqsubseteq a$$

$$K_p(Turn1, \pi, a, b),\ K_p(Turn1TO, \pi, a, b),\ K_p(Turn2TO, \pi, a, b) \quad \pi \sqsubset a, b$$

$$K_p(Turn2, \pi, a) \qquad\qquad\qquad\qquad\qquad\qquad\qquad\qquad \pi \sqsubset a$$

$$K_p(Timeout1, \pi, a, b),\ K_p(Timeout2, \pi, a, b) \qquad\qquad\quad \pi \sqsubset a, b$$

The first component in each key pair above (e.g., *Collect*) is a distinct label. Note that each player generates $O(N^2)$ key pairs. We assume that the private part of a key pair $K_p(\cdots)$ is kept secret by p, while the public part is communicated to the other players. For each set of key pairs $K_p(X, \cdots)$, we denote with $\mathbf{K}(X, \cdots)$ the set of key pairs $\{K_p(X, \cdots) \mid p \in \mathcal{P}\}$. We denote with ϵ the empty sequence.

The outcome of a match is randomly determined with a "coin toss" protocol, as in [2]. Intuitively, the players generate two random secrets, and exchange their hashes; then, they reveal the secrets: the winner is determined by a function of the two secrets (i.e., the parity of the sum of the lengths of the two secrets). Since a player may be involved in L distinct matches, we assume that each p generates L secrets (i.e., long random sequences of bits), one for each $\pi \sqsubset p$. The secret of p at level π is denoted by s_p^{π}; its public hash $H(s_p^{\pi})$ is denoted by h_p^{π}.

Overview of the protocol. Our protocol uses a number of transactions, the templates of which are in Fig. 1. The protocol is organised in three phases:

initialization: the players exchange the public data, e.g. the static signatures and hashed secrets. Then, they collect all the bets, and put on the ledger the transactions for the leaves of the tournament tree.

execution: this phase is organised in L *rounds*, one for each level of the tree. In each round ℓ, exactly 2^ℓ two-player matches are played, by the winners of the previous round. The possible executions of a single round are depicted in Fig. 3. The winner of the last round collects the whole stake.

garbage collection: this allows players to recover from some potential interference, to be discussed in the proof of Theorem 5.

We now comment the protocol in Fig. 2. We denote the duration of each round with $\tau_{Round} = 6\,\tau_{Ledger}$, following Fig. 3. The transaction templates of Fig. 1 define some timelocks, which depend on a time τ_1 (chosen in the initialization phase), corresponding to the start of the execution phase.

Win(π, a) with $\epsilon \neq \pi \sqsubseteq a$
certifies that a has won all the rounds until π (included)
Timeout1 $\langle b \rangle$
in: Timeout1(π, b, a)
in-script: $\mathbf{sig}_{\mathbf{K}(Timeout1, \pi, b, a)}(\bullet)$
Timeout2 $\langle b \rangle$
in: Timeout2(π, a, b)
in-script: $\mathbf{sig}_{\mathbf{K}(Timeout2, \pi, a, b)}(\bullet)$
Turn2fst $\langle b, \hat{s}_a, \hat{s}_b \rangle$
in: Turn2(π, a, b)
in-script: $\hat{s}_a, \hat{s}_b, \mathbf{sig}_{\mathbf{K}(Turn2, \pi, a)}(\bullet)$
Turn2snd $\langle b, \hat{s}_a, \hat{s}_b \rangle$
in: Turn2(π, b, a)
in-script: $\hat{s}_b, \hat{s}_a, \mathbf{sig}_{\mathbf{K}(Turn2, \pi, a)}(\bullet)$
out-script(T, σ): $\mathbf{ver}_{\mathbf{K}(Win, \pi, a)}(\mathsf{T}, \sigma)$ $\qquad\qquad \vee \; \mathbf{ver}_{\mathbf{K}(WinTO, \pi, a)}(\mathsf{T}, \sigma)$
value: $(1 + d)\, 2^{L - |\pi|}\, \math!B$

Init
certifies that all players have placed their bets (and deposits)
$\forall p \in \mathcal{P} : \left\{ \begin{array}{l} \mathsf{in}[p]:\ \mathsf{Bet}_p \\ \mathsf{in\text{-}script}[p]:\ \mathbf{sig}_{K_p(Bet_p)}(\bullet) \end{array} \right.$
$\forall p \in \mathcal{P} : \left\{ \begin{array}{l} \mathsf{out\text{-}script}[p](\mathsf{T}, \sigma):\ \mathbf{ver}_{\mathbf{K}(Init, p)}(\mathsf{T}, \sigma) \\ \mathsf{value}[p]:\ 1 + d\, \math!B \end{array} \right.$
Win(a, a) (leaf)
contains the bet (and deposit) of a at the first round
in: Init$[a]$
in-script: $\mathbf{sig}_{\mathbf{K}(Init, a)}(\bullet)$
out-script(T, σ): $\mathbf{ver}_{\mathbf{K}(Win, a, a)}(\mathsf{T}, \sigma)$
value: $1 + d\, \math!B$
Win(ϵ, a) (root)
certifies that a has won the lottery
(Variants as for Win(π, a))
out-script$[a](\mathsf{T}, \sigma)$: $\mathbf{ver}_{K_a(Collect)}(\mathsf{T}, \sigma)$
value$[a]$: $N + d\, \math!B$
$\forall p \neq a : \left\{ \begin{array}{l} \mathsf{out\text{-}script}[p](\mathsf{T}, \sigma):\ \mathbf{ver}_{K_p(Collect)}(\mathsf{T}, \sigma) \\ \mathsf{value}[p]:\ d\, \math!B \end{array} \right.$

Turn1(π, a, b) with $\pi \sqsubseteq a, b$
certifies that a and b are playing in match π, where it is a's turn to reveal her secret
in$[0]$: Win$(\pi 0, a)$
in-script$[0]$: $\mathbf{sig}_{\mathbf{K}(Win, \pi 0, a)}(\bullet)$
in$[1]$: Win$(\pi 1, b)$
in-script$[1]$: $\mathbf{sig}_{\mathbf{K}(Win, \pi 1, b)}(\bullet)$
out-script$(\mathsf{T}, \hat{s}_a, \sigma)$: $\big(H(\hat{s}_a) = h_a^\pi \wedge \mathbf{ver}_{\mathbf{K}(Turn1, \pi, a, b)}(\mathsf{T}, \sigma) \big)$ $\qquad \vee \; \mathbf{ver}_{\mathbf{K}(Turn1TO, \pi, a, b)}(\mathsf{T}, \sigma)$
value: $(1 + d)\, 2^{L - |\pi|}\, \math!B$

Turn2(π, a, b) with $\pi \sqsubseteq a, b$
certifies that a and b are playing in match π, where a has revealed her secret, and now it is b's turn
Secret $\langle \hat{s}_a \rangle$
in: Turn1(π, a, b)
in-script: $\hat{s}_a, \mathbf{sig}_{\mathbf{K}(Turn1, \pi, a, b)}(\bullet)$
out-script$(\mathsf{T}, \hat{s}_a, \hat{s}_b, \sigma)$: $\big(H(\hat{s}_a) = h_a^\pi \wedge H(\hat{s}_b) = h_b^\pi$ $\qquad \wedge \mathbf{ver}_{\mathbf{K}(Turn2, \pi, winner(a, b, \hat{s}_a, \hat{s}_b))}(\mathsf{T}, \sigma) \big)$ $\qquad \vee \; \mathbf{ver}_{\mathbf{K}(Turn2TO, \pi, a, b)}(\mathsf{T}, \sigma)$
value: $(1 + d)\, 2^{L - |\pi|}\, \math!B$

Timeout1(π, a, b) with $\pi \sqsubseteq a, b$
certifies that a lost against b in match π because she did not reveal her secret in time
in: Turn1(π, a, b)
in-script: $\bot, \mathbf{sig}_{\mathbf{K}(Turn1TO, \pi, a, b)}(\bullet)$
out-script(T, σ): $\mathbf{ver}_{\mathbf{K}(Timeout1, \pi, a, b)}(\mathsf{T}, \sigma)$
value: $(1 + d)\, 2^{L - |\pi|}\, \math!B$
lockTime: $\tau_1 + (L - |\pi| - 1)\tau_{Round} + 2\tau_{Ledger}$

Timeout2(π, a, b) with $\pi \sqsubseteq a, b$
certifies that b lost against a in match π because she did not reveal her secret in time
in: Turn2(π, a, b)
in-script: $\bot, \bot, \mathbf{sig}_{\mathbf{K}(Turn2TO, \pi, a, b)}(\bullet)$
out-script(T, σ): $\mathbf{ver}_{\mathbf{K}(Timeout2, \pi, a, b)}(\mathsf{T}, \sigma)$
value: $(1 + d)\, 2^{L - |\pi|}\, \math!B$
lockTime: $\tau_1 + (L - |\pi| - 1)\tau_{Round} + 4\tau_{Ledger}$

CollectOrphanWin(π, a) with $\epsilon \neq \pi \sqsubseteq a$
certifies that a was prevented by an adversary to participate in the rounds after π, but she can collect her winnings so far (see ?? for details)
in: Win(π, a)
in-script: $\mathbf{sig}_{\mathbf{K}(WinTO, \pi, a)}(\bullet)$
out-script$[a](\mathsf{T}, \sigma)$: $\mathbf{ver}_{K_a(Collect)}(\mathsf{T}, \sigma)$
value$[a]$: $2^{L - |\pi|} + d\, \math!B$
$\forall p$ with $a \neq p \sqsubseteq \pi : \left\{ \begin{array}{l} \mathsf{out\text{-}script}[p](\mathsf{T}, \sigma):\ \mathbf{ver}_{K_p(Collect)}(\mathsf{T}, \sigma) \\ \mathsf{value}[p]:\ d\, \math!B \end{array} \right.$
lockTime: $\tau_1 + (L - |\pi|)\tau_{Round} + \tau_{Ledger}$

Fig. 1. Transaction templates for the lottery protocol.

Precondition: for all players p, the ledger contains a transaction Bet_p with value $(1 + d)\mathrm{\dot{B}}$, and redeemable with key $K_p(Bet_p)$.

Initialization phase:

1. each player p generates all the key pairs and the secrets s_p^π as in Section 3, and broadcasts to the other players the public keys and hashes $h_p^\pi = H(s_p^\pi)$;
2. if $h_p^\pi = h_{p'}^{\pi'}$ for some $(p, \pi) \neq (p', \pi')$, the players abort;
3. choose the time τ_1 large enough to fall after the initialization phase;
4. each player signs all the transactions templates in Figure 1 except for Init, and broadcasts the signatures;
5. each player verifies the signatures received by the others; if some signature is not valid or missing, the player aborts the protocol;
6. each player p signs Init, and sends the signature to the first player;
7. the first player puts the (signed) transaction Init on the ledger;
8. if Init does not appear within one τ_{Ledger}, then each p redeems Bet_p and aborts;
9. the players put the signed transactions $\mathsf{Win}(p, p)$ on the ledger, for all $p \in \mathcal{P}$.

Execution phase:

for each level $\ell = L..1$:

    for each π such that $|\pi| = \ell - 1$, in parallel, a two-player match is played:

10. let a and b be such that $\mathsf{Win}(\pi 0, a)$ and $\mathsf{Win}(\pi 1, b)$ are on the ledger;
11. the players put $\mathsf{Turn1}(\pi, a, b)$ on the ledger;
12. player a puts $\mathsf{Turn2}(\pi, a, b).Secret\langle s_a^\pi \rangle$ on the ledger;
13. the players wait until either $\mathsf{Turn2}(\pi, a, b)$ is confirmed, or $\mathsf{Timeout1}(\pi, a, b)$ is enabled. In the second case, they put $\mathsf{Timeout1}(\pi, a, b)$ on the ledger; once it is confirmed, they put $\mathsf{Win}(\pi, b).Timeout1\langle a \rangle$ on the ledger, and terminate the match at π;
14. player b computes $w = winner(a, b, s_a^\pi, s_b^\pi)$, the winner of the match at π;
    - if $w = a$, player b puts $\mathsf{Win}(\pi, a).Turn2fst\langle b, s_a^\pi, s_b^\pi \rangle$ on the ledger.
    - if $w = b$, player b puts $\mathsf{Win}(\pi, b).Turn2snd\langle a, s_a^\pi, s_b^\pi \rangle$ on the ledger.
15. the players wait until either $\mathsf{Win}(\pi, c)$ is confirmed (for some $c \in \{a, b\}$) , or $\mathsf{Timeout2}(\pi, a, b)$ is enabled. In the second case, they put $\mathsf{Timeout2}(\pi, a, b)$ on the ledger; once confirmed, they put $\mathsf{Win}(\pi, a).Timeout2\langle b \rangle$ on the ledger.

Garbage collection phase: if there is some unredeemed $\mathsf{Win}(\pi, p)$ with $\pi \neq \epsilon$, then the players put $\mathsf{CollectOrphanWin}(\pi, p)$ on the ledger.

Fig. 2. Tournament lottery protocol.

Initialization phase. In step 1, all the players generate the signatures and secrets, and exchange the related public data. Step 2 is needed to prevent attacks where a player does not compute a hash from her own secret, but replays the hash of another player. In step 3 we choose the time τ_1 to be large enough so that the initialization can be completed within τ_1. In steps 4–5 the players exchange all the static signatures needed in the execution phase. Each player p contributes his own part of the signature, using his own keys $K_p(\ldots)$. Steps 6–8 collect the bets from the transactions Bet_p in a single transaction Init. If Init is not confirmed

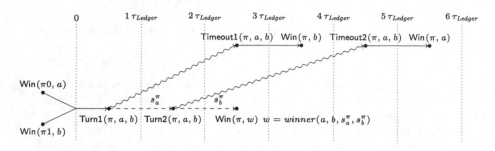

Fig. 3. Graph of the transactions in a tournament round. An edge from transaction T to T′ means that T′ redeems T. Solid edges mean that any player can redeem; wavy edges mean that any player can redeem, but only after a timeout. Dashed edges mean that only the player who knows the secret on the label can redeem.

on the ledger, e.g. because some player has already redeemed his bet, then all the other players redeem their original bets. In this way, they ensure that Init can no longer appear on the ledger, hence the protocol is aborted. Step 8 also prevents an attack where Init is maliciously delayed so to make honest players lose. Finally, step 9 sets up the first level of the tournament, by splitting the stake in the Init among all the leaves of the tree, i.e. $\mathsf{Win}(p, p)$.

To choose τ_1, note that the initialization phase requires:

- at steps 1–6, to generate all the needed $O(N^3)$ signatures and NL secrets, and share the related public parts. This costs $O(N^3)$ time.
- at step 7, to put on the ledger the transaction Init. This costs $1\ \tau_{Ledger}$.
- after that, at step 9, to put all the transactions $\mathsf{Win}(p, p)$. This costs $1\ \tau_{Ledger}$, because it can be done in parallel.

Therefore, we choose τ_1 such that $\tau_1 \geq \mathsf{currentTime} + O(N^3) + 2\tau_{Ledger}$.

Execution phase. In this phase, the players play against each other. We recommend the reader to examine Fig. 3 for an overview of how matches are played. Matches correspond to the nodes of the tournament tree, and so they are indexed by tree paths π. The match at π involves the winners of the two matches $\pi 0$ and $\pi 1$ of the previous round (i.e., the children of π). These winners are, respectively, the players a and b in the transactions $\mathsf{Win}(\pi 0, a)$ and $\mathsf{Win}(\pi 1, b)$ which are on the ledger at the start of the match (step 10). The goal of steps 10–15 is to put on the ledger a transaction $\mathsf{Win}(\pi, w)$, where w is the winner at π.

Step 11 starts by redeeming both $\mathsf{Win}(\pi 0, a)$ and $\mathsf{Win}(\pi 1, b)$ through the transaction $\mathsf{Turn1}(\pi, a, b)$. Note that any player (not only a and b) can perform this step, since everyone has the required signatures. At step 12, player a is expected to reveal her secret s_a^π; otherwise, after a certain deadline, the other players can make a lose. If a chooses to reveal her secret, she must put on the ledger the transaction $\mathsf{Turn2}(\pi, a, b)$, which redeems $\mathsf{Turn1}(\pi, a, b)$, through an input script containing s_a^π. Otherwise, after $1\tau_{Ledger}$, the timelock on $\mathsf{Timeout1}(\pi, a, b)$ expires, allowing any other player to put $\mathsf{Timeout1}(\pi, a, b)$ on the ledger at step 13. After that, $\mathsf{Win}(\pi, b)$ can be put on the ledger by any player, so making a lose the match. At step 14, it is the turn of player b to reveal his secret s_b^π; otherwise, similarly to the previous steps, the other players can make b lose after some time. If b chooses to reveal his secret, he must first compute the winner w of the match—this is possible because b knows both secrets s_a^π and s_b^π. Then, he must put $\mathsf{Win}(\pi, w)$ on the ledger, which redeems $\mathsf{Turn2}(\pi, a, b)$, through an input script containing s_b^π. Otherwise, after $1\tau_{Ledger}$, the timelock on $\mathsf{Timeout2}(\pi, a, b)$ expires, allowing any other player to put $\mathsf{Timeout2}(\pi, a, b)$ on the ledger at step 13. After that, $\mathsf{Win}(\pi, a)$ can be put on the ledger by any player, so making b lose the match.

After the last round of the execution phase, the tournament protocol is over. At this point, there is exactly one transaction $\mathsf{Win}(\epsilon, a)$ on the ledger, for some a. This transaction can be redeemed by a at any time, by putting on the ledger a transaction with in-script $\mathsf{sig}_{K_a(Collect)}(\bullet)$. Note that only a has the private key needed for this signature. In this way a can obtain the whole stake of $N\mathring{\mathtt{B}}$.

Garbage collection phase. As discussed in the proof of Theorem 5, a dishonest player can try to cheat by forging Win transactions. When this happens, some legit Win transactions are left orphan on the ledger: garbage collection allows the players who contributed to these transactions to redeem their money back. In this way the protocol remains secure, as established later on by Theorem 5.

4   Security of the Tournament Protocol

We assume that all the algorithms used by the players run in PPTIME with respect to a security parameter η. A function $f : \mathbb{N} \to \mathbb{R}$ is said to be *negligible* iff, for some constant $c \in \mathbb{N}$, the inequation $|f(\eta)| \le \eta^{-c}$ holds asymptotically. We assume that all the cryptographic primitives (e.g., digital signatures, hash functions) are secure, up-to a negligible probability of attack.

We assume that Bitcoin works as a robust public transaction ledger, where every player can append valid transactions (which are confirmed in τ_{Ledger}), while invalid transactions cannot appear. Recent results [13] show that, in a backbone Bitcoin protocol, this assumption holds when the honest miners hold the majority of the hashing power (despite the negative results in [11]). For simplicity, we assume that transactions require no fees. All our results hold even when there is only one honest player.

Basic properties. Consider an arbitrary lottery protocol with N players, where each player bets a certain amount *bet* of bitcoins to have the chance to win $N \cdot bet$. A *run* is a pair (β, λ), where β is the state of the blockchain when the protocol starts, and λ is the timed sequence of public events occurred in a (possibly partial) protocol execution. The component λ includes, e.g., the exchanged signatures and the transactions put on the ledger after β. Each player a uses a *strategy* Σ_a to choose which events to perform at any time in a run of the protocol. Roughly, $\Sigma_a(1^\eta, \beta, \lambda)$ is a PPTIME algorithm which can observe the whole past (β, λ), and choose the next moves (not necessarily those prescribed by the protocol). We further allow Σ_a to access the local state of a, including her private information. A strategy Σ_a is *honest* when it follows the protocol; a player is honest when she uses an honest strategy. A run is *maximal* for a when she has performed all the enabled actions prescribed by Σ_a.

We say that a transaction is *freely redeemable by* a when (i) a can use her knowledge (including private information) to compute the needed witness, and (ii) a can freely choose the output script of the redeeming transaction. The *wealth* of a after a certain run (β, λ), denoted by $wealth(a, \beta, \lambda)$, is the amount of bitcoins freely redeemable at that time by a, but not by any other player.

Lottery protocols usually require players to block a *deposit* of bitcoins throughout their execution (beyond the bet). Technically, we define the deposit of a as the minimum amount of bitcoins $wealth(a, \beta, \epsilon) - bet$ such that, starting from β, a can always perform a maximal run of the protocol (using an honest strategy), regardless of the behaviour of the other players. Then, we say that a lottery protocol is *d-deposit* if d is the maximum of the deposits of all players. Note that, by definition, it must be $d \geq 0$: otherwise, should a lose the lottery, there would not be enough bitcoins to pay the other players.

The following Theorem 1 states that the tournament protocol requires *constant* $d\cancel{B}$ deposit; note instead that the protocols in [2,4,5,8] require $O(N^2)\cancel{B}$ deposit.

Theorem 1. *The tournament protocol is d-deposit.*

Lemma 1. *For each level $\ell = L..1$ of the execution phase:*

1. *for every π such that $|\pi| = \ell$, the ledger contains a transaction $\mathsf{Win}(\pi, a)$ with value $(1 + d)\, 2^{(L-\ell)}\cancel{B}$, for some a;*
2. *the round starts within time $\tau_1 + (L - \ell) \cdot \tau_{Round}$.*

Theorem 2 exploits Lemma 1 to establish an upper bound to the completion time of our protocol. Note that a single honest player a is enough to guarantee termination: indeed, even if the other players do not cooperate, a can always put all the required transactions on the ledger, after the respective timeouts.

Theorem 2. *Assume that at least one player is honest, while the others can be adversaries with arbitrary strategies. Then:*

1. *after τ_1, either Init is on the ledger, or the protocol is aborted without any honest players losing their wealth;*
2. *after Init is on the ledger, a transaction $\mathsf{Win}(\epsilon, p)$ is put on the ledger within $6\,L\,\tau_{Ledger}$, for some p (who is the winner of the lottery).*

Payoff distribution. We now quantify the payoff of each player in a *single* run of the protocol where all the players are honest. The *payoff* of a player at a given point of an execution is the wealth difference between that point and the beginning of the protocol. Formally, given a run (β, λ) for a, this amounts to:

$$\Phi(a, \beta, \lambda) = wealth(a, \beta, \lambda) - wealth(a, \beta, \epsilon)$$

Then, Theorem 3 states that, once the Init transaction has been put on the ledger, there are only two possible outcomes of the protocol: either a player loses $1\mbox{Ƀ}$ (her bet), or she wins $N - 1\mbox{Ƀ}$ (the bets of all the other players).

Theorem 3. *If all players are honest, then, for all players a and for all maximal runs (β, λ) of a such that $\mathsf{Init} \in \lambda$, we have $\varPhi(a, \beta, \lambda) \in \{-1\mbox{Ƀ}, N - 1\mbox{Ƀ}\}$.*

Theorem 4 below describes the probability distribution of the payoff of an honest player in contexts where the other players are adversaries. In particular, we will assume that adversaries follow *rational* strategies which, on average, will not make them lose money (but for a negligible amount). In order to define rational strategies, we introduce an auxiliary notion. Given a set of strategies $\mathbf{\Sigma}$ for all players and a blockchain state β, we denote with $\mathrm{E}_{\varPhi}(a, \mathbf{\Sigma}, \beta, \eta)$ the *expected payoff* of a over all the runs (β, λ) which are maximal for each player p using $\mathbf{\Sigma}[p]$. Then, we say that player a is *rational in* $\mathbf{\Sigma}$ iff for all β, there exists a negligible f such that, for all η, $\mathrm{E}_{\varPhi}(a, \mathbf{\Sigma}, \beta, \eta) \geq f(\eta)$.

Theorem 4 states that the expected payoff of each player p in a given set of honest players $\mathcal{H}$ is either -1 or $N - 1$ with probabilities, respectively, $N-1/N$ or $1/N$, up-to a negligible error. This holds when either all the players are honest (and the deposit is arbitrary, potentially zero), or the adversaries are rational and the deposit is greater than zero.

Theorem 4. *Let $\mathcal{H} \subseteq \mathcal{P}$ be a set of players, and let $\mathbf{\Sigma}$ be such that $\mathbf{\Sigma}[a]$ is honest for all $a \in \mathcal{H}$. If (i)$\mathcal{H} = \mathcal{P}$, or (ii) $d > 0$ and $\mathbf{\Sigma}[b]$ is rational for all $b \in \mathcal{P} \setminus \mathcal{H}$, then the payoff of each $p \in \mathcal{H}$ is distributed as follows, for all β:*

$$
Pr(\varPhi(p, \beta, \lambda) = v \mid \mathsf{Init} \in \lambda \ maximal) = \begin{cases} \frac{N-1}{N} + f_1(\eta) & \text{if } v = -1 \\ \frac{1}{N} + f_2(\eta) & \text{if } v = N - 1 \\ f_3(\eta) & \text{otherwise} \end{cases}
$$

where f_1, f_2, f_3 are negligible functions, and λ is a random variable, sampled so that (β, λ) is maximal with respect to $\mathbf{\Sigma}$.

In the presence of adversaries (i.e., $\mathcal{H} \neq \mathcal{P}$), the hypothesis (ii) is necessary. Indeed, if adversaries are not rational, they can simply increase the payoff of honest players by giving them money, or voluntarily losing by timeout. Instead, if $d = 0$, a rational adversary can interfere with the protocol and cause the payoff distribution to differ from the one given by Theorem 4. Remarkably, we will show in Theorem 5 that even if the adversary can alter the payoff *distribution*, she can not diminish the payoff *average*, which is at least negligible in all cases. Hence, the protocol is still secure.

Honest strategies are rational. Theorem 5 below establishes that, even in the case of adversaries with *arbitrary* strategies, for any value of the deposit (including zero), our lottery protocol is secure, i.e. a player which follows the protocol does not lose money, on average.

Theorem 5. *Honest strategies are rational in any set of strategies* Σ.

Proof (Sketch). Without loss of generality, assume that only one player, say a, is honest, while the other $N - 1$ players are adversaries, with arbitrary (not necessarily rational) strategies Σ. We need to prove that the average payoff of a is nonnegative, up to a negligible quantity. Before Init is put on the ledger, a can redeem her bet, so her payoff is zero. Hence, we only need to consider the case where Init has been put on the ledger. Hereafter, we inductively define *proper* transactions as follows: T is proper either if T = Init, or all the inputs of T are proper. Note that, in a run of the protocol where all the players are honest, all the transactions put on the ledger are proper.

We start by studying the possible attack strategies, which determine how adversaries put new transactions on the ledger, and how they redeem existing transactions. Adversaries can move their wealth through transactions unrelated to the protocol. Further, they can put on the ledger any transaction obtained by instantiating some transaction template of the protocol. In doing that, they can exploit the malleability of in fields, and make them redeem some previous transaction unrelated to the protocol, consuming part of their wealth in the process. This results in an improper transaction. Its presence on the ledger is not a problem per se, unless it can be exploited to interfere with a proper protocol transaction—e.g., by preventing it to be redeemed, and causing the tournament behavior to diverge from the protocol. So, we now turn our attention to how proper transactions can be redeemed.

We first note that each out script of the protocol transactions (except for the *final* transactions $\mathsf{Win}(\epsilon, p)$ and $\mathsf{CollectOrphanWin}(\pi, p)$) requires a signature from every player, including the honest a. Hence, adversaries can only redeem those transactions through the signatures exchanged during the initialization phase, i.e. using some instantiation of the protocol templates. Further, every transaction template uses its own public keys, so when a protocol transaction T is redeemed by T′, then (exactly) one of the following cases applies:

(a) T is Init and T′ is a leaf $\mathsf{Win}(p, p)$, or
(b) T has an outgoing edge to T′, according to Fig. 3, or
(c) T is $\mathsf{Win}(\pi, p)$ with $\pi \neq \epsilon$, and T′ is $\mathsf{CollectOrphanWin}(\pi, p)$, or
(d) T is a final transaction.

For example, if T is a Turn1, then T′ must provide a signature made with the keys of Turn1 or Turn1TO. So, as per item (b), T′ can only be redeemed by Turn2 or Timeout1. By the above reasoning, and by carefully inspecting the protocol (Fig. 2) and the used transactions (Fig. 1), we see that improper transactions can not interfere with the protocol steps where a proper transaction T is redeemed by a *single-input* template instantiation T′. Indeed, when such redemption happens, T′ must be a proper protocol transaction as well. However, this reasoning does *not* extend to the case where the redeeming transaction T′ has *multiple* inputs. In our protocol, this is only possible when T′ is a Turn1. Indeed, consider the case when a proper $\mathsf{T_0} = \mathsf{Win}(0\pi, b)$ is on the ledger, as well as a proper $\mathsf{T_1} = \mathsf{Win}(1\pi, a)$. If $\mathsf{T_0}$ is redeemed by Turn1 (as per item (b)), however, we have no guarantees that such Turn1 is redeeming both T_0 and T_1—because it is possible that Turn1 is instead redeeming the proper T_0 together with an improper transaction $\mathsf{Win}(1\pi, m)$, which was forged by the adversaries. When this interference happens, the protocol continues with an improper Turn1, and T_1 is left on the ledger as an "orphan". Therefore, player a will not be able to participate in the current match. Note that, since Turn1 is the only multiple-input protocol transaction, this interference can only happen at the *start* of a match. After a match is started, the honest player a has at least $1/2$ probability to win the match, since a will always respect deadlines (so to avoid losing the match by timeout), and she chose her secret s_π^a in a uniformly random way during initialization. So, either the adversaries lose by timeout, or reveal their secrets and the match proceeds in a fair way.

We can now estimate the average payoff of the honest player a, by tracking her composite bet throughout the tournament rounds (i.e., the sum gained by a so far, that she must invest in further rounds). We start by noting that, at the beginning of each round, at least one of the following must hold:

1. a has lost a previous match.
2. there is an unspent $T = \mathsf{Win}(\pi, a)$ on the ledger, and the adversaries *do not* interfere: hence, T is redeemed by Turn1, and a participates in the match. In this case, a has at least $1/2$ probability to double her composite bet.
3. there is an unspent $T = \mathsf{Win}(\pi, a)$ on the ledger, and the adversaries *do* interfere: so, T is not redeemed (unlike its sibling Win), and a cannot participate in the match. The transaction T is left "orphan" on the ledger; after $1\,\tau_{Ledger}$, player a can collect the composite bet she earned so far, by putting $\mathsf{CollectOrphanWin}(\pi, a)$ on the ledger. In this way a can redeem her current composite bet.

Since a is honest, she will reveal her secret for a match only *after* Turn1 has been put on the ledger (i.e., when adversaries can no longer interfere in the match). Note that the adversaries do not know the match result when they have to choose whether to interfere or not. Therefore, the whole tournament is similar to a game where a tosses L fair coins in sequence, doubling up her bet every time she wins the flip, and losing the whole stake at the first loss. Her opponent can choose to stop her before any of the coin tosses, but in such case she is allowed to collect what she won so far. Since this coin game is fair, also the average payoff of a in the tournament protocol is nonnegative.   □

5   Related Work

Several lottery protocols have been investigated outside the cryptocurrency setting, e.g. by [12,14,15,21,23]. In the last few years, some authors have proposed protocols that work on Bitcoin or similar cryptocurrencies.

Concurrently and independently of our work, Miller and Bentov [20] proposed a lottery protocol, that similarly to ours exploits a tournament tree and requires zero deposit. Two variants of the protocol are presented: the first one only relies on the SegWit feature [19], while the second one proposes a new signature verification opcode, called MULTIINPUT. The first variant requires players to statically sign a tree of $O(2^N)$ transactions. To reduce this overhead, our protocol relies on a more flexible signature verification scheme, that allows malleability of in fields, resulting in $O(N)$ transactions. This malleability introduces the interference issues discussed in Sect. 4. Such interferences do not make our protocol insecure, because the average payoff of honest players is non-negative, even for $d = 0$ (Theorem 5), thanks to the garbage collection phase. However, such interferences are still undesirable, because adversaries can prevent honest players from completing the tournament. The second variant of the protocol in [20] achieves $O(N)$ transactions and avoids interferences through a "controlled" malleability of in fields. This is obtained through the new MULTIINPUT opcode, which allows to malleate in fields (to achieve $O(N)$ transactions), but only within a pre-specified set (to avoid interferences).

Table 1 summarises the comparison between our protocol and [20] (MB), and also with the protocols in [2] (ADMM), [8] (BK). We also consider a variant of ours and [2], called "2 players iterated", which implement an N-players lottery by running $N-1$ instances of a two-players protocol. Similarly to our tournament protocol, these instances are composed in a tree: only the winners of a level can play at the next one, and the winner of the root collects all the bets. In the iterated versions, the initialization phase is performed for *every* match (using independent keys/secrets), while in the non-iterated version the initialization is done only once, at the beginning.

Table 1. Comparison of cryptocurrency-based lottery protocols.

	ADMM [2] N players	ADMM [2] 2 players iter.	BK [8] N players	MB [20] v1	MB [20] v2 N players	Tournament N players	Tournament 2 players iter.
Deposit	$N(N-1)$	N	$O(N^2)$	0	0	$d \geq 0$	$d \geq 0$
Completion time	$4\,\tau_{Ledger}$	$4\,L\,\tau_{Ledger}$	$O(N)$	$O(L)$	$4\,L\,\tau_{Ledger}$	$(2+6\,L)\,\tau_{Ledger}$	$7\,L\,\tau_{Ledger}$
Off-chain trans	$O(N^2)$	$O(N)$	—	$O(2^N)$	$O(N^2)$	$O(N^2)$	$O(N)$
On-chain trans	$O(N)$	$O(N)$	$O(N^2)$	$O(N^2)$	$O(N)$	$O(N)$	$O(N)$
All-or-nothing	Yes	No	Yes	Yes	Yes	Yes, if $d > 0$	No
Bitcoin features				SegWit	SegWit MULTIINPUT	SegWit in-malleability	SegWit in-malleability

The first row in Table 1 quantifies the deposit: this is constant ($d \geq 0$) in our protocol, zero in [20], while in the others it grows with the number of players. More specifically, the deposit is $O(N^2)$ in [8] and in the non-iterated version of [2], while in the iterated version it is N: intuitively, an N-deposit at the last round is needed to guarantee that the final winner can collect the whole N stake.

The second row quantifies the completion time of the protocol, excluding the communication and computation time (which is marginal in practice, compared to the time required to put transactions on the ledger). Only the non-iterated version of [2] requires constant time; in [8] the time is linear in N, while in the other protocols the time is proportional to $L = \log N$.

The number of off-chain and on-chain transactions required by each protocol is shown in the third and fourth rows. Not that all protocols require a linear number of on-chain transactions, except for [8] and the first version of [20], which require $O(N^2)$ transactions.

The fifth row describes whether a protocol has an ideal behaviour, where only one player wins the whole stake, while the others lose their bets. More specifically, we call a protocol "all-or-nothing" if, assuming rational adversaries, the payoff of honest players is either -1 or $N - 1$. The iterated versions of the protocols are not "all-or-nothing": indeed, a rational adversary can simply stop playing after winning a match, collecting the partial winnings and making impossible for any other player to obtain the whole $N\text{B}$ stake (hence forcing some honest player to gain $-1 < v < N - 1\text{B}$). Instead, our (non-iterated) protocol is "all-of-nothing" when $d > 0$ (Theorem 4).

The last row describes which Bitcoin features a protocol requires to be actually implemented. All protocols make use of non-standard transactions, which are currently handled by a small fraction of the miners. Note that some recent works [6] address the issue of implementing complex protocols on Bitcoin by using only standard transactions. Both our protocol and the ones in [8,20] also rely on the SegWit feature [19]. Additionally, our protocol requires the malleability of in-fields, as discussed in Sect. 2, while the second version of the protocol in [20] requires the `MULTIINPUT` opcode. This opcode would also allow to avoid the interferences outlined in the proof of Theorem 5. The protocol in [8] assumes resilience to malleability attacks, which can be obtained through [19].

The work [16] proposes a general model for secure multiparty computations on cryptocurrencies, which goes beyond the features provided by Bitcoin. Applying this model to lotteries, we would obtain a protocol where the deposit grows linearly in the number of dishonest players. This approach might also allow for reducing the number of rounds from $\log N$ to a constant number.

6   Conclusions

We have presented a lottery protocol based on Bitcoin, where N players can place a bet, and one of them, uniformly chosen, wins all the bets. Our protocol is parametric w.r.t. the deposit $d \geq 0$ that the players have to block throughout the protocol. For any value of d, our protocol ensures that honest players have a negligible average payoff, even in the presence of arbitrary adversaries (Theorem 5). Further, for $d > 0$, the payoff is distributed like an ideal lottery (Theorem 4): that is, the winner gets the sum of all the bets with probability close to $1/N$, while the other players lose their bets with probability close to $N-1/N$. This holds unless the adversaries follow strategies which (on average) make them lose money, and make honest players gain money. According to the terminology in [2], our protocol implements a *fair* lottery.

Although our protocol has been crafted for Bitcoin, the underlying ideas can be used to implement fair lotteries on other frameworks for smart contracts. This could allow to relax the rationality assumption of Theorem 4 when the deposit is zero. For instance, the implementations in Ethereum [9] of Miller and Bentov[5] and of Atzei[6] follow the structure of rounds of the tournament protocol.

Acknowledgments. The authors thank Patrick McCorry, Andrew Miller, and Iddo Bentov for their comments on a preliminary version of this paper. This work is partially supported by Aut. Reg. of Sardinia P.I.A. 2013 "NOMAD".

References

1. Andrychowicz, M., Dziembowski, S., Malinowski, D., Mazurek, Ł.: Fair two-party computations via Bitcoin deposits. In: Böhme, R., Brenner, M., Moore, T., Smith, M. (eds.) FC 2014. LNCS, vol. 8438, pp. 105–121. Springer, Heidelberg (2014). https://doi.org/10.1007/978-3-662-44774-1_8
2. Andrychowicz, M., Dziembowski, S., Malinowski, D., Mazurek, Ł.: Secure multi-party computations on Bitcoin. In: IEEE S&P, pp. 443–458 (2014)
3. Andrychowicz, M., Dziembowski, S., Malinowski, D., Mazurek, Ł.: On the malleability of Bitcoin transactions. In: Brenner, M., Christin, N., Johnson, B., Rohloff, K. (eds.) FC 2015. LNCS, vol. 8976, pp. 1–18. Springer, Heidelberg (2015). https://doi.org/10.1007/978-3-662-48051-9_1
4. Andrychowicz, M., Dziembowski, S., Malinowski, D., Mazurek, Ł.: Secure multi-party computations on Bitcoin. Commun. ACM **59**(4), 76–84 (2016)
5. Back, A., Bentov, I.: Note on fair coin toss via Bitcoin. http://www.cs.technion.ac.il/~idddo/cointossBitcoin.pdf (2013)
6. Banasik, W., Dziembowski, S., Malinowski, D.: Efficient zero-knowledge contingent payments in cryptocurrencies without scripts. In: Askoxylakis, I., Ioannidis, S., Katsikas, S., Meadows, C. (eds.) ESORICS 2016. LNCS, vol. 9879, pp. 261–280. Springer, Cham (2016). https://doi.org/10.1007/978-3-319-45741-3_14
7. Bartoletti, M., Zunino, R.: Constant-deposit multiparty lotteries on Bitcoin. IACR Cryptology ePrint Archive, 2016/955 (2016). http://eprint.iacr.org/2016/955
8. Bentov, I., Kumaresan, R.: How to use Bitcoin to design fair protocols. In: Garay, J.A., Gennaro, R. (eds.) CRYPTO 2014. LNCS, vol. 8617, pp. 421–439. Springer, Heidelberg (2014). https://doi.org/10.1007/978-3-662-44381-1_24
9. Buterin, V.: Ethereum: a next generation smart contract and decentralized application platform (2013). https://github.com/ethereum/wiki/wiki/White-Paper
10. Crary, K., Sullivan, M.J.: Peer-to-peer affine commitment using Bitcoin. In: ACM Conference on Programming Language Design and Implementation, pp. 479–488 (2015)
11. Eyal, I., Sirer, E.G.: Majority is not enough: Bitcoin mining is vulnerable. In: Christin, N., Safavi-Naini, R. (eds.) FC 2014. LNCS, vol. 8437, pp. 436–454. Springer, Heidelberg (2014). https://doi.org/10.1007/978-3-662-45472-5_28
12. Fouque, P.-A., Poupard, G., Stern, J.: Sharing decryption in the context of voting or lotteries. In: Frankel, Y. (ed.) FC 2000. LNCS, vol. 1962, pp. 90–104. Springer, Heidelberg (2001). https://doi.org/10.1007/3-540-45472-1_7
13. Garay, J., Kiayias, A., Leonardos, N.: The Bitcoin backbone protocol: analysis and applications. In: Oswald, E., Fischlin, M. (eds.) EUROCRYPT 2015. LNCS, vol. 9057, pp. 281–310. Springer, Heidelberg (2015). https://doi.org/10.1007/978-3-662-46803-6_10

---

[5] https://github.com/amiller/zero-collateral-lottery
[6] https://github.com/natzei/constant-deposit-lottery

14. Goldschlag, D.M., Stubblebine, S.G.: Publicly verifiable lotteries: applications of delaying functions. In: Hirchfeld, R. (ed.) FC 1998. LNCS, vol. 1465, pp. 214–226. Springer, Heidelberg (1998). https://doi.org/10.1007/BFb0055485
15. Goldschlag, D.M., Stubblebine, S.G., Syverson, P.F.: Temporarily hidden bit commitment and lottery applications. Int. J. Inf. Secur. **9**(1), 33–50 (2010)
16. Kiayias, A., Zhou, H.-S., Zikas, V.: Fair and robust multi-party computation using a global transaction ledger. In: Fischlin, M., Coron, J.-S. (eds.) EUROCRYPT 2016. LNCS, vol. 9666, pp. 705–734. Springer, Heidelberg (2016). https://doi.org/10.1007/978-3-662-49896-5_25
17. Kumaresan, R., Bentov, I.: How to use Bitcoin to incentivize correct computations. In: ACM CCS, pp. 30–41 (2014)
18. Kumaresan, R., Moran, T., Bentov, I.: How to use Bitcoin to play decentralized poker. In: ACM CCS, pp. 195–206 (2015)
19. Lombrozo, E., Lau, J., Wuille, P.: Segregated witness (consensus layer), BIP 141. https://github.com/bitcoin/bips/blob/master/bip-0141.mediawiki
20. Miller, A., Bentov, I.: Zero-collateral lotteries in Bitcoin and Ethereum (2014). http://arxiv.org/abs/1612.05390
21. Rivest, R.L.: Electronic lottery tickets as micropayments. In: Hirschfeld, R. (ed.) FC 1997. LNCS, vol. 1318, pp. 307–314. Springer, Heidelberg (1997). https://doi.org/10.1007/3-540-63594-7_87
22. Ruffing, T., Kate, A., Schröder, D.: Liar, liar, coins on fire!: penalizing equivocation by loss of Bitcoins. In: ACM CCS, pp. 219–230 (2015)
23. Syverson, P.F.: Weakly secret bit commitment: applications to lotteries and fair exchange. In: IEEE CSFW, pp. 2–13 (1998)
24. Szabo, N.: Formalizing and securing relationships on public networks. First Monday **2**(9) (1997)

Exchange Pattern Mining in the Bitcoin Transaction Directed Hypergraph

Stephen Ranshous[1(✉)], Cliff A. Joslyn[2], Sean Kreyling[2], Kathleen Nowak[4],
Nagiza F. Samatova[1,3], Curtis L. West[2], and Samuel Winters[2]

[1] North Carolina State University, Raleigh, USA
smransho@ncsu.edu, samatova@csc.ncsu.edu
[2] Pacific Northwest National Laboratory, Seattle, WA, USA
{cliff.joslyn,sean.kreyling,curtis.west,
samuel.winters}@pnnl.gov
[3] Oak Ridge National Laboratory, Oak Ridge, USA
[4] Pacific Northwest National Laboratory, Richland, USA
katy.nowak@pnnl.gov

Abstract. Bitcoin exchanges operate between digital and fiat currency networks, thus providing an opportunity to connect real-world identities to pseudonymous addresses, an important task for anti-money laundering efforts. We seek to characterize, understand, and identify patterns centered around exchanges in the context of a directed hypergraph model for Bitcoin transactions. We introduce the idea of motifs in directed hypergraphs, considering a particular 2-motif as a potential laundering pattern. We identify distinct statistical properties of exchange addresses related to the acquisition and spending of bitcoin. We then leverage this to build classification models to learn a set of discriminating features, and are able to predict if an address is owned by an exchange with $> 80\%$ accuracy using purely structural features of the graph. Applying this classifier to the 2-motif patterns reveals a preponderance of inter-exchange activity, while not necessarily significant laundering patterns.

Keywords: Bitcoin · Exchanges · Transaction graph · Directed hypergraph · Motif · Classification

1 Introduction

Bitcoin's decentralization makes it difficult to regulate and investigate by law enforcement. This represents a vulnerability in government anti-money laundering (AML) efforts [4]. Conventional AML efforts focus on the Know-Your-Customer (KYC) process, in which banks and other financial services must verify the identity of their customers, monitor transactions, and report suspicious behavior to government entities. As such, government AML and KYC efforts utilize perfect knowledge of identity but incomplete knowledge of financial transactions, which remains in the control of the banks [12,13]. In contrast, law enforcement generally has no knowledge about bitcoin user identities to use

© International Financial Cryptography Association 2017
M. Brenner et al. (Eds.): FC 2017 Workshops 2017, LNCS 10323, pp. 248–263, 2017.
https://doi.org/10.1007/978-3-319-70278-0_16

in detecting anomalous behavior, but access to the blockchain grants complete knowledge of transactions. This motivates the desire to detect money laundering through techniques that do not rely on identity information, such as transaction or user patterns. In particular, patterns centered around exchanges are important, as they provide arguably the most important link between Bitcoin and fiat currency networks. Moreover, exchanges are navigating evolving legal precedent to be AML compliant [1,2]. In 2015, FinCEN fined Ripple Labs in the first act of civil enforcement against a Virtual Currency Exchange for failing to implement a proper AML program [17].

We model Bitcoin transactions as a directed hypergraph (dirhypergraph), which naturally represents the multi-way relation between addresses and transactions (Sect. 2). This is distinguished from previous analyses [15,16] which use graph models with strictly binary edges, whether at the address or tx level. We define motifs in dirhypergraphs as small sub-graph patterns, and introduce a small 2-motif involving exchanges which we call "short thick bands" (STB) as a *potential* laundering pattern. We identify several patterns in the behavior of exchange-owned addresses that differ from non-exchange addresses (Sect. 3). For example, where regular addresses are likely to be sinks [16], simply accumulating bitcoin, exchange addresses typically keep a near-zero balance. Third, we explore the possibility of applying machine learning techniques to classify latent attributes of addresses (Sect. 4). In particular, we focus on whether or not it is possible to predict whether a given address is owned by an exchange or not, and the role of both labeled and putative exchanges in STB patterns. Finally, we seek to understand whether the pattern of exchange use in STBs reveals potential laundering activity, but conclude that what can be identified is a preponderance of inter-exchange activity.

2   Bitcoin Transaction Motifs in a Directed Hypergraph

Bitcoin transactions have a natural graphical structure, one form of which is shown on the left of Fig. 1. Vertices are transactions $E_0, \ldots E_3$, while arcs model inputs and outputs labeled by the Bitcoin address $a_1, \ldots, a_6$, weighted by the quantity. We note some common activities such as change making and aggregation. Coinbase

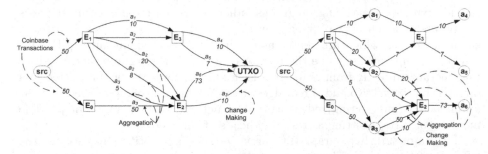

Fig. 1. (Left) Bitcoin transactions as a labeled multigraph. (Right) Bitcoin transactions as a bipartite multigraph. (Color figure online)

transactions are indicated by the vertex SRC in blue, while unspent transaction outputs (UTXOs) are combined into a single sink vertex.

But in analytical tasks, such as detecting money laundering, it is perhaps more important to focus on addresses (arc labels a_i) than the transactions E_j. And while discouraged in Bitcoin, reuse of addresses is legal and somewhat common. To treat addresses as "first class objects" we create new vertices for each unique address, producing the bipartite graph structure on the right of Fig. 1. Square vertices are transactions E_j, while the circles are addresses a_i (addresses currently with an UTXO are red). Input arcs from addresses to transactions are now distinguishable from output arcs from transactions to addresses, and address reuse can create looping structures, such as shown in change-making back into a_3 as an output of E_2.

We consolidate by combining quantities on multi-arcs, producing the directed hypergraph [3,5] in Fig. 2. Dirhypergraphs are characterized as directed bipartite graphs with two kinds of vertices, with connections only between vertices of different types, but possibly multiple inputs from and outputs to each. For us, transaction (square) vertices act as directed hyperarcs. Where an arc in a graph connects a single tail vertex to a single head vertex, hyperarcs connect multiple input (tail) addresses to multiple output (head) addresses (round vertices).

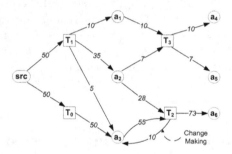

Fig. 2. Bitcoin transactions as a directed hypergraph.

Hypergraphs and directed hypergraphs are well known in math and computer science, and can provide significant advantages over regular graphical structures when data are complex, with multiple inputs and outputs as in our case due to address reuse. Identifying subgraphs indicating potential laundering suggests the potential significance of hypergraph motifs. In network analysis, motifs are small subgraphs which are represented with statistical significance [11]. Our research group appears to be the first to consider dirhypergraph motifs, which we generalize directly from graph motifs. Figure 3 shows all the undirected and directed motifs for two and three edges/arcs. A k-motif is one possible way that k connected (intersecting) edges can be structured, with a range of possible numbers of vertices sitting as tails and heads of the k edges.

The simplest dirhypergraph Bitcoin pattern is the 2-motif,[1] illustrated on the left side of Fig. 4 as a dirhypergraph pattern. As in Fig. 2, the two transactions

---

[1] Terminologically, we can call these hypermotifs or hypergraph motifs, but for simplicity here we will just call them motifs.

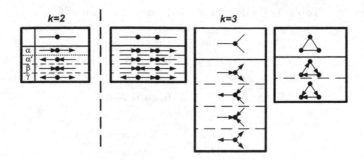

Fig. 3. Graph motifs: (Far Left) The single undirected graph 2-motif (above) with its three directed motifs α, β, and γ (below), including the two isomorphic α, α' patterns. (Right) The three undirected 3-motifs and their directed versions.

E_1, E_2 are square vertices, and addresses circles (circle color will be addressed below). Note that any particular address can sit on either the tails (inputs) or heads (outputs) of any transaction, and indeed, more than one transaction.

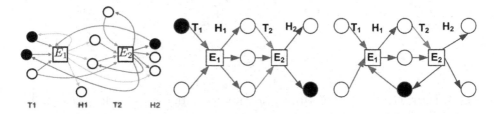

Fig. 4. A 2-motif in a dirhypergraph: Two transactions E_1, E_2 with sets of tail and head vertices T_1, H_1, T_2, H_2 respectively. (Left) Generic. (Center) A linear STB. (Right) A circular STB. (Color figure online)

Formalizing 2-motifs, assume a non-empty finite set of vertices $A = \{a_i\}$ and two hyperarcs $E_j = \langle T_j, H_j \rangle, j = 1, 2$, with tails and heads $T_j, H_j \subseteq A$ (nonempty). The set $M = \{E_1, E_2\}$ is a 2-motif if there is at least one pair of tails and heads in each hyperarc which intersect, that is, if $\bigcup_{X, Y \in \{H, T\}} X_1 \cap Y_2 \neq \emptyset$. The potential intersections are detailed in Table 1. For example, an address sits on a γ pattern if it is in both T_1 (the blue vertices in Fig. 4) and T_2 (the green), that is, in the tails of (inputs to) both transactions (e.g. the lowest left address in Fig. 4). The analogous graph pattern γ is shown in Fig. 3, with the two edges pointed outward. Note that in comparison with Fig. 3, here we also allow self-loops identified in the L_1, L_2 patterns.

The left of Fig. 5 is an abstraction of a 2-motif, where each circular vertex represents one of the patterns in Table 1, standing in for the entire *set* of addresses

Table 1. Participation of addresses in a 2-motif.

Pattern	Condition	Description
α	$H_1 \cap T_2 \neq \emptyset$	Forward 2-chain
α'	$T_1 \cap H_2 \neq \emptyset$	Reverse 2-chain
β	$H_1 \cap H_2 \neq \emptyset$	Inward 2-star
γ	$T_1 \cap T_2 \neq \emptyset$	Outward 2-star
L_1	$T_1 \cap H_1 \neq \emptyset$	Self-loop on E_1
L_2	$T_2 \cap H_2 \neq \emptyset$	Self-loop on E_2

playing that role.[2] The right is the same abstraction, but now with the counts of the number of addresses in each role for transactions between Jan 12 2015 and April 21 2015.[3]

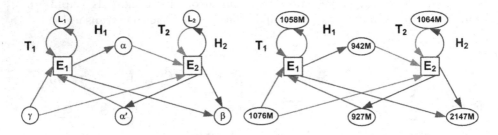

Fig. 5. (Left) Generic 2-motif. (Right) Instantiated with counts for days 2200-2299.

Beyond just identifying dirhypergraph motifs, we are interested in motifs which may or may not involve certain addresses, in our case, exchanges, and their distribution within certain kinds of patterns. In Fig. 4, exchanges are shown as black addresses. A **short thick band (STB)** is then a pattern where a quantity of Bitcoin is purchased from fiat currency, held for a while as Bitcoin, and then converted back to fiat currency. When an STB moves Bitcoin from one exchange address to a different one, we can call it **linear**; and when it returns it to the same exchange address, **circular**. More specifically, STBs are 2-motifs where:

- Two transactions intersect in an α or α' chain only;
- An exchange is included in both an input of the first and an output of the last transaction; but
- No exchange is an intermediate address in the transaction.

---

[2] We include addresses in *exactly* one intersection, ignoring addresses in *only* a tail or head of one of the transactions, and also addresses in *more than two* intersections.

[3] Note the similarities of the counts for α and α', on the one hand, and L_1 and L_2, on the other, due to isomorphism with respect to the ordering of E_1 and E_2.

STBs could exist for many reasons, including financial speculation, simple user convenience, repeated purchases, remuneration, remittance, or fund management. Our interest is considering the hypothesis that STBs could be used as a potential laundering pattern. Moreover, we recognize that as a laundering pattern, it would not be very extensive. In this work we are begining with the simplest possible such pattern.

To formalize STBs, call a motif "pure" if only one pattern from Table 1 is present (this is *not* the case in the left side of Fig. 4), and otherwise "mixed". Then denote $e(a \in A)$ to mean that a is an exchange, and $e(X \subseteq A)$ to mean that X has an exchange: $\exists a \in X, e(a)$. We then can define an STB as follows.

Definition 1 (STB). *A 2-hypermotif $M = \{E_1, E_2\}$ is a* **linear STB** *if one and only one of the following holds:*

1. *It is a pure α 2-motif with $e(T_1) \wedge e(H_2) \wedge \neg e(H_1 \cap T_2)$; or*
2. *It is a pure α' 2-motif with $e(H_1) \wedge e(T_2) \wedge \neg e(T_1 \cap H_2)$.*

M is a **circular STB** *if one and only one of the following holds:*

1. *It is a mixed linear α and α' 2-motif with $e(T_1 \cap H_2) \wedge \neg e(H_1 \cap T_2)$; or*
2. *It is a mixed linear α' and α 2-motif with $e(H_1 \cap T_2) \wedge \neg e(T_1 \cap H_2)$.*

Note that no STB can have a self-loop. But because of the α, α' isomorphism noted above, it is sufficient to assume that a linear STB is a pure α pattern, and a circular STB is a mixed α, α' pattern, with

$$e(T_1) \wedge e(H_2) \wedge \neg e(H_1 \cap T_2), \quad e(T_1 \cap H_2) \wedge \neg e(H_1 \cap T_2)$$

respectively. Figure 4 shows a linear (center) and circular (right) STB.

3   Descriptive Statistics

Given the nature of exchanges, and their primary function of converting between bitcoin and other currencies (including fiat and other alt coins), we question whether exchange addresses exhibit a different type of behavior from address owned by regular users of the network.

We downloaded the Bitcoin blockchain data using the Bitcoin Core Client,[4] and built a custom parser to convert the raw data into the dirhypergraph structure described in Sect. 2. We used data from the first transaction in the network up to April 22 2015, encompassing 72.7M unique addresses (vertices), involved in at least one of 66.3M transactions (hyperarcs) in our dirhypergraph. Addresses known to be exchanges were drawn from the WalletExplorer listing,[5] call these "labeled". Some exchanges are associated with several wallets ("current", "output", "old"). The full list we use is shown in Appendix A. While labeled addresses

---

[4] https://bitcoin.org/en/download.
[5] https://www.walletexplorer.com, accessed January 16 2016.

are presumed to be actual exchanges, the number of exchange addresses which are not listed as such is hard to judge for many reasons. At least, the WalletExplorer listings began on April 23 2011, while we know that exchanges have been around since 2010. Additionally, Mt. Gox, a substantial contributor over that time, was not included. There are still 2.44M labeled addresses (3.36 % of the total addresses), and 6.76M transactions involving an exchange (10.2 % of total transactions). Daily activity is summarized in Fig. 6, with addresses involved in several transactions in a single day counted once.

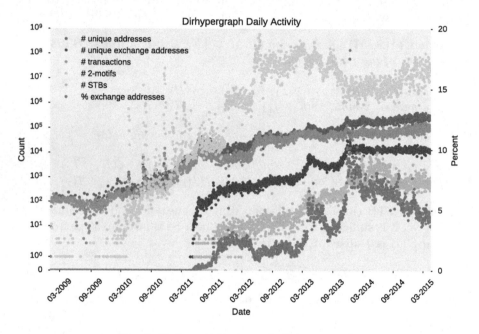

Fig. 6. Daily activity in each dirhypergraph.

Since our dirhypergraph presents as a bipartite graph of addresses and transactions, the in-degree of an address is actually the number of transactions on which an address serves as an output, and *vice versa* for out-degree. While the in- and out-degree distributions for both address types follow a power law, with the distributions having no significant difference using a 2-sample KS test, Table 2 shows several interesting aspects. Where 4.7% of unlabeled addresses are sinks – simply accumulating bitcoin and never redistributing it, resulting in an out-degree of zero – this drops to < 0.1% for labeled addresses. Also labeled addresses are more likely to have equal and positive in- and out-degrees. This behavior for labeled addresses is consistent with the use and function of exchanges, and for unlabeled addresses it is consistent with previous results [16], although to a much lesser extent. We attribute the decline in the proportion of sink addresses to the general growth of Bitcoin, but more importantly the sustained *trading phase* [6] it has been in, dwarfing activity in the *initial phase*.

Table 2. Comparing labeled and unlabeled address' degrees and weights.

Query	Labeled		Unlabeled	
In-degree > 0, out-degree = 0	2, 123	0.087%	3, 297, 725	4.696%
In-degree > 0, out-degree > 0	2, 435, 472	99.91%	66, 914, 170	95.29%
In-degree = out-degree > 0	2, 356, 530	96.67%	64, 305, 459	91.58%
In-weight > 0, out-weight = 0	2, 123	0.087%	3, 297, 195	4.696%
In-weight > 0, out-weight > 0	2, 435, 472	99.91%	66, 914, 166	95.29%
In-weight = out-weight > 0	2, 421, 944	99.35%	65, 658, 855	93.51%

Figure 7 shows the cumulative distribution of weights in bitcoin (BTC), total on the left and average on the right. Unlabeled addresses have a much better separation between the in- and out-weight, suggesting that nonexchange addresses tend to keep a positive balance of bitcoin while exchanges keep zero, or near-zero, balances. The majority of exchange addresses have both an average and total transaction weight between 0.01 and 0.1 BTC, shown by the large jump in the figure. Roughly 50% of labeled addresses sit in this bucket, compared to about 30% of unlabeled addresses.

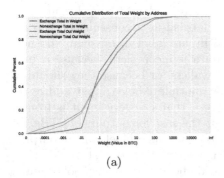   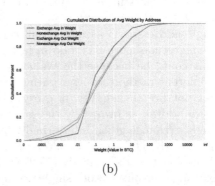

(a)   (b)

Fig. 7. Cumulative percent of addresses with total (left) or average (right) input and output weights.

We next examine 2-motifs, STBs, and how exchanges are involved in them. If there are m transactions in a day, then there are at most $\binom{m}{2}$ possible 2-motifs. Of our 40.0B 2-motifs, 10.3B are pure linear α or α' patterns, just 42.4M of which involve exchanges. 741K of those are STBs, including 727K linear and 13.4K circular. The volume of 2-motifs precludes the opportunity to do a comparison between STBs and non-STB 2-motifs, so instead we focus on just STBs.

The number and proportion of addresses that are labeled as exchanges on the inputs and outputs is shown in Fig. 8.[6] The number of labeled input addresses

---

[6] Recall that this is at the address level, and each exchange has a set of addresses they own. The frequency of each exchange (e.g. BTC-e.com) in STBs is shown in Fig. 10 in the Appendix, and is highly correlated with the number of addresses each exchange has, see Fig. 11.

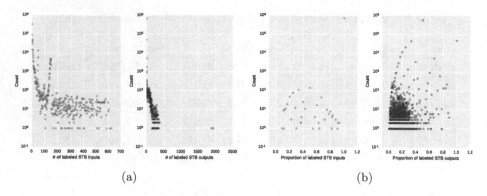

Fig. 8. Counts (left) and proportions (right) of labeled addresses on the inputs and outputs of STBs.

ranges from 1 to 635, while output addresses range from 1 to 1937. However, when the two clear outlier STBs are removed, the max number shrinks to 376.

According to the well known heuristic in Bitcoin to group all addresses that are inputs into the same transaction as being owned by the same entity [10,14,16], the expected proportion of labeled inputs should be 1, because if a single address is labeled, then all others are labeled as a consequence. Orders of magnitude more STBs do in fact have all inputs labeled, but many do not. This could be because the WalletExplorer data is incomplete, because it uses a different method for aggregating exchange wallets, or because they should in fact not be labeled. Yet, in every STB with multiple labeled input addresses, every address is owned by the same exchange – that is, every input is from a single exchange label. Interestingly, this *is not* the case for outputs of STBs. Of the 739.8K STBs, 63.4K (8.57%) have multiple exchange labels in the outputs ("multi-out STBs"), 48.1K (75.9%) of which have exactly two labels. Multiple exchanges on outputs of a single transaction could be due to mining pool payouts, but on outputs of STBs it is more likely indicative of inter-exchange activity.

4 Classifying and Labeling Exchange Addresses

While exchange addresses comprise a small percent of the Bitcoin network, they are of growing importance outside of the Bitcoin world, as they provide potentially the only avenue for connecting real-world people with pseudonymous Bitcoin addresses. Being able to identify exchanges in the network is then a critical task, as it enables one to connect transactions or addresses of interest to the point at which they enter or exit the Bitcoin network.

We can leverage the different characteristics of exchange and non-exchange addresses to construct a machine learning model to classify an address as an exchange or not. In these experiments we use data from September 29 2011, roughly 100 days after exchanges first appear in our data, until April 22 2015. For every address we extract a set of features that numerically characterizes it, e.g. out-degree, total in-weight. Addresses are then assigned a class label corresponding to whether or not they are labeled as an exchange. The goal of the model is to learn a set of features and weights that can accurately discriminate between the two classes. Given the immense class imbalance (far fewer exchange addresses), we randomly sample an equal number of labeled and unlabeled addresses for training and testing the model. To account for the random sampling, 10 independent trials are run, and average results are reported.

Five different classifiers' results are summarized in Table 3.[7] AdaBoost and random forests perform the best, and are far superior to the remaining three, both yielding an F1 score of over 0.99. In the case of random forests, on average only 2,587 out of 972,866 test addresses were incorrectly predicted, falsely classifying 1,190 non-exchanges as exchanges, and 1,397 exchanges as non-exchanges. Moreover, the incredibly low variance of these models indicates they are much more robust than the others, performing well across all random samples.

Table 3. Results for exchange address classification. All results shown are *mean+-std* over the 10 runs.

Model	F1	Recall	Precision
Random forest	0.9973 +− (0.0001)	0.9976 +− (0.0001)	0.9971 +− (0.0001)
AdaBoost	0.9944 +− (0.0001)	0.9974 +− (0.0001)	0.9915 +− (0.0003)
Linear SVM	0.8291 +− (0.0833)	0.8396 +− (0.1514)	0.8573 +− (0.1209)
Perceptron	0.2075 +− (0.3029)	0.3034 +− (0.4557)	0.2210 +− (0.2053)
Logistic regression	0.0014 +− (0.0001)	0.0007 +− (0.0001)	0.2755 +− (0.0304)

Equally important, or perhaps even more important, than achieving such a high accuracy is understanding what it is about exchange addresses that facilitates the result. One way to quantify this is looking at the "feature importance" values that are calculated by the classifier. The top 5 features and their importance in the random forest model are: (1) # sibling exchanges (0.613); (2) # successor exchanges (0.184); (3) # predecessor exchanges (0.072); (4) # siblings total (0.044); (5) total out-weight (0.015).[8] It is not surprising that, by far, the most important feature is the number of exchange siblings. Figure 9a shows the substantial difference in the distributions for exchange siblings. Again, according to the common address group heuristic, if you are siblings with numerous exchange addresses then it is likely you are also an exchange address. Moreover, it is likely that you are an exchange address owned by the same exchange that your siblings are (c.f. Sect. 3). From a network science perspective, homophily [9] tells us that vertices of one type tend to interact with vertices of the same type.

---

[7] All experiments were run using Python 2.7 and the scikit-learn and numpy packages.

[8] For an address a, siblings are addresses that have been a co-input or co-output, successors are addresses that have been an output when a was an input, and predecessors are addresses that were an input when a was an output.

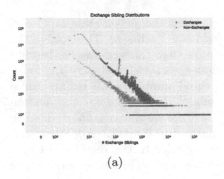
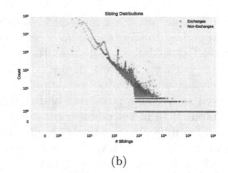

(a)   (b)

Fig. 9. Distribution of how many exchange addresses siblings (left) or total siblings (right) each address has. These distributions were drawn from a random sample of 100 K exchanges and 100 K non-exchanges.

Incorporating features related to the exchange labels clearly produces high quality results. However, it may restrict the capability of our model, failing to generalize well to new data which is not labeled, or handling incomplete labeling as we have in our dataset. To test this a second set of experiments is performed, identical to those described above except all features related to exchange labels are removed. Table 4 summarizes the new results.

Table 4. Results for exchange vertex classification when features related to exchanges are removed. All results shown are *mean+-std* over the 10 runs.

Model	F1	Recall	Precision
Random forest	0.8200 +− (0.0004)	0.8218 +− (0.0006)	0.8183 +− (0.0004)
AdaBoost	0.7941 +− (0.0012)	0.8264 +− (0.0033)	0.7643 +− (0.0018)
Linear SVM	0.3052 +− (0.2619)	0.3488 +− (0.3775)	0.5179 +− (0.1710)
Perceptron	0.1349 +− (0.2683)	0.1998 +− (0.3989)	0.1849 +− (0.1886)
Logistic regression	0.0014 +− (0.0001)	0.0007 +− (0.0001)	0.3056 +− (0.0266)

Removal of the exchange features has an obvious negative impact on the accuracy of the classifiers. Random forest F1 score drops to 0.82 (a decrease of about .18), with the average number of incorrectly classified addresses increasing from 2587 (0.266%) to 175956 (18.086%). Similar to the runs that included exchange features, the average variance for the random forest classifier was very low. With the removal of exchange related features, structural features rose in importance. The new top 5 features and weights are: (1) # siblings (0.255); (2) total out-weight (0.232); (3) total in-weight (0.217); (4) # successors (0.092); (5) # predecessors (0.082). The former fourth and fifth ranked features are now the top two, and in conjunction with the total in-weight represent the majority of the discriminatory power. The top three now have a very equal share of importance, indicating that the model relies on information from each of them instead of a single dominating feature. Figure 9 shows the distribution of the number of siblings for both exchange and non-exchange addresses. The distributions for less than 100 siblings are easily separable, but become much more intertwined when considering addresses with 100 or more siblings.

As we note in Sect. 3, the list of exchange addresses we have is incomplete. However, it is impossible to know exactly how incomplete the list is – whether we have 10% of the exchange addresses or 90%. A natural next question, then, is to try to classify all of the unlabeled addresses using our models constructed in the previous experiments.

All unlabeled addresses not used in training the classifiers were run through both random forest models and predicted as an exchange address or not (Table 5). The two classifiers yielded drastically different results. Using exchange label features, a mere 0.28% of the unlabeled addresses were labeled as exchanges. Conversely, 18.17% of the addresses were labeled as exchanges using the purely structural features. If instead of omitting the training addresses from the results we include them, the percent predicted raise to 3.98% and 21.87%. As 3.36% of the addresses are labeled from our ground truth data, this result is expected.

It is likely that 18% is a much better estimate for the true exchange address percent than 0.28%. The absence of Mt. Gox (among others) from our label data, and its historical dominance in Bitcoin, indicates that we are missing a large number of exchange addresses. Moreover, the extremely high accuracy combined with the extremely low prediction of unlabeled addresses of the first model suggests that the first classifier overfit the training data, exploiting the label features and becoming too reliant. Structural features, which we have perfect knowledge of for all addresses, are much more reliable and generalizable.

Table 5. Percent of addresses classified as exchanges.

	With label features	Without label features
All addresses	3.98%	21.87%
Unlabeled addresses	0.28%	18.17%
Middle addresses 1-out STBs	1.34%	48.35%
Middle addresses multi-out STBs	0.68%	52.09%

Our initial proposition of STBs as a laundering pattern stems from a user activity view of the network: a user receives bitcoin from an exchange, then converts it back into fiat currency, with the hope of obfuscating any money trail. From this perspective, addresses in the middle of an STB – which by definition cannot be labeled as an exchange – should be *less likely* to be predicted as an exchange than a randomly chosen unlabeled address. But (see Table 5) addresses in the middle of an STB are 2-3x *more likely* to be classified as an exchange than an a random unlabeled address. This directly contradicts our hypothesis, and instead is highly suggestive of lots of inter-exchange activity taking place. Self-churn [10] i.e. change-making is likely why an exchange address would be in the middle of what would otherwise be an STB. For example, an exchange E_1 sends bitcoin to one of its customers, making change for itself with the excess bitcoin in the transaction, and then another exchange E_2 buys bitcoin from E_1, creating a 2-motif with exchanges on the input, middle, and output.

5   Conclusions and Future Work

In this work we make a first attempt at statistical and machine learning approaches that may be of interest in identifying laundering patterns, latent attribute classification, and discriminatory analysis. Directed hypergraphs are a sound model for transactions, and exchanges exhibit several patterns that are distinct from general address behaviors, as also shown in previous work. Our machine learning models are capable of labeling addresses as being owned by exchanges or not with very high accuracy, even when restricted to purely structural features. STBs are proposed as a potential laundering pattern, and shown to have a high degree of filtering when compared to the number of general 2-motifs in the network. Finally, we showed that middle vertices in STBs are much more likely to be classified as an exchange, indicating that there is a large amount of inter-exchange activity taking place.

Obvious areas of improvement include a much better label set, including Mt. Gox and generally being of higher fidelity. Similarly, an obvious area of expansion is to move beyond 2-motifs to 3-motifs, and consider triangular and other patterns involving three transactions. We have began the mathematical exploration of the 3-motif in directed hypergraphs, and it is somewhat complicated combinatorially, but manageable. While we use learning to label an address as an exchange or not, the general tasks of latent attribute learning and discriminatory feature analysis impose no such constraint. A variety of customary labels may be of interest [10] – "mining pool", "wallet", "exchange", "vendor", "gambling" – in addition to your own personal labels – "suspicious", "country X". It is also not necessary to constrain the analysis to a single label at a time, but instead use multi-class classification models to predict from a set of labels. Moreover, instead of using a supervised learning approach where we assume our label sets are complete, we could explore methods such as PU Learning [7,8], which account for imperfect data.

In addition to expanding the possible labels, the structure of interest could be expanded as well. Instead of looking at single addresses, transactions, or chains of transactions that form a higher level pattern, could be considered. For example, Möser et al. [12] show that some mixing services leave a distinct transactional pattern as a result of their mixing algorithms. Models for identifying similar patterns could be constructed using the hand curated transactions found in [12].

Acknowledgements. This material is based on work supported in part by the Department of Energy National Nuclear Security Administration under Award Number(s) DE-NA0002576. It is also supported in part under the Laboratory Directed Research and Development Program at the Pacific Northwest National Laboratory, a multi-program national laboratory operated by Battelle for the U.S. Department of Energy.

A   Exchanges Used

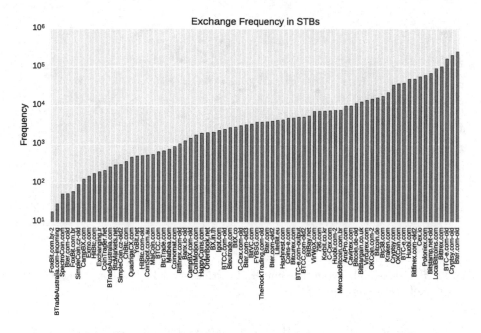

Fig. 10. Frequency of exchanges in STBs.

B   Features Used

An address' feature matrix is composed of the following features, extracted from each day of the data and then aggregated. Features prefixed with "*" are those removed in the second experiment, where exchange label based features are removed.

1. *total_bitcoin_received* – How much BTC the address received from transaction outputs over the full time window.
2. *total_bitcoin_spent* – How much BTC the address spent as transaction inputs over the full time window.
3. *bitcoin_balance* – Total bitcoin received minus total bitcoin spent.
4. *num_predecessors* – How many unique addresses have been an input to transactions where this address was an output.
5. *num_transaction_outputs* – How many times this address has been used in a transaction output.
6. *num_successors* – How many unique addresses have been an output in transactions where this address was an input.

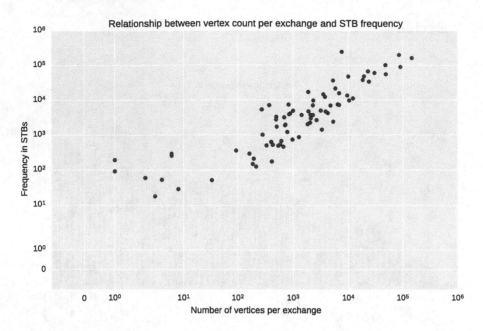

Fig. 11. Relationship between the number of vertices owned by each exchange and the frequency of that exchange in STBs.

7. *num_transaction_inputs* – How many times this address has been used as a transaction input.
8. *num_siblings* – How many unique addresses have been co-inputs or co-outputs with this address.
9. **num_predecessor_exchanges* – How many unique exchange addresses have been an input to transactions where this address was an output.
10. **num_successor_exchanges* – How many unique exchange addresses have been an output in transactions where this address was an input.
11. **num_sibling_exchanges* – How many unique exchange addresses have been co-inputs or co-outputs with this address.
12. *num_gamma_patterns* – How many times this address is part of a γ pattern.
13. *num_beta_patterns* – How many times this address is part of a β pattern.
14. *num_L1_patterns* – How many times this address is part of an L_1 pattern.
15. *num_L2_patterns* – How many times this address is part of an L_2 pattern.
16. *num_alpha_patterns* – How many times this address is part of a α pattern.
17. *num_alphaprime_patterns* – How many times this address is part of a α' pattern.
18. *reciprocity* – How many of this addresses successors are also predecessors.
19. *anti_reciprocity* – How many of this addresses predecessors are also successors.

We focused on local features that are fast to compute. Examples of more expensive but potentially very useful features are explained in [13], e.g. peeling chains or coinbase transactions.

References

1. Anti-money laundering programs for money services businesses, 31 C.F.R. §1022.210
2. Compliance and exemptions, and summons authority, 31 U.S.C. §5318
3. Ausiello, G., Franciosa, P.G., Frigioni, D.: Directed hypergraphs: problems, algorithmic results, and a novel decremental approach. ICTCS 2001. LNCS, vol. 2202, pp. 312–328. Springer, Heidelberg (2001). https://doi.org/10.1007/3-540-45446-2_20
4. FATF: Virtual currencies key definitions and potential AML/CFT risks. Technical report (2014)
5. Gallo, G., Longo, G., Pallottino, S.: Directed hypergraphs and applications. Discret. Appl. Math. **42**, 177–201 (1993)
6. Kondor, D., Pósfai, M., Csabai, I., Vattay, G.: Do the rich get richer? an empirical analysis of the bitcoin transaction network. PloS one **9**(2), e86197 (2014)
7. Li, X.-L., Liu, B.: Learning from positive and unlabeled examples with different data distributions. In: Gama, J., Camacho, R., Brazdil, P.B., Jorge, A.M., Torgo, L. (eds.) ECML 2005. LNCS, vol. 3720, pp. 218–229. Springer, Heidelberg (2005). https://doi.org/10.1007/11564096_24
8. Liu, B., Lee, W.S., Yu, P.S., Li, X.: Partially supervised classification of text documents. In: ICML, vol. 2, pp. 387–394. Citeseer (2002)
9. McPherson, M., Smith-Lovin, L., Cook, J.M.: Birds of a feather: homophily in social networks. Ann. Rev. sociol. **27**, 415–444 (2001)
10. Meiklejohn, S., Pomarole, M., Jordan, G., Levchenko, K., McCoy, D., Voelker, G.M., Savage, S.: A fistful of bitcoins: characterizing payments among men with no names. In: Proceedings of the 2013 conference on Internet measurement conference. pp. 127–140. ACM (2013)
11. Milo, R., Shen-Orr, S., Itzkovitz, S., Kashtan, N., Chklovskil, D., Alon, U.: Network motifs: simlpe building blocks of complex networks. Science **298**, 824–827 (2002)
12. Möser, M., Böhme, R., Breuker, D.: An inquiry into money launder tools in the bitcoin ecosystem. In: eCrime Researchers Summit, 6–24. Springer, Heidelberg (2013)
13. Möser, M., Böhme, R., Breuker, D.: Towards risk scoring of bitcoin transactions. In: Böhme, R., Brenner, M., Moore, T., Smith, M. (eds.) FC 2014. LNCS, vol. 8438, pp. 16–32. Springer, Heidelberg (2014). https://doi.org/10.1007/978-3-662-44774-1_2
14. Ober, M., Katzenbeisser, S., Hamacher, K.: Structure and anonymity of the bitcoin transaction graph. Future Internet **5**(2), 237–250 (2013)
15. Reid, F., Harrigan, M.: An analysis of anonymity in the bitcoin system. In: Altshuler, Y., Elovici, Y., Cremers, A., Aharony, N., Pentland, A. (eds.) Security and Privacy in Social Networks, pp. 197–223. Springer, New York (2013)
16. Ron, D., Shamir, A.: Quantitative analysis of the full bitcoin transaction graph. In: Sadeghi, A.-R. (ed.) FC 2013. LNCS, vol. 7859, pp. 6–24. Springer, Heidelberg (2013). https://doi.org/10.1007/978-3-642-39884-1_2
17. U.S. Department of the Treasury, FinCEN: FinCEN fines ripple labs Inc.: First Civil Enforcement Action Against A Virtual Currency Exchanger. May 2015. https://www.fincen.gov/news/news-releases/fincen-fines-ripple-labs-inc-first-civil-enforcement-action-against-virtual

Incentivizing Blockchain Forks via Whale Transactions

Kevin Liao[1]([✉]) and Jonathan Katz[2]

[1] Arizona State University, Chandler, USA
kevinliao@asu.edu
[2] University of Maryland, College Park, USA
jkatz@cs.umd.edu

Abstract. Bitcoin's core innovation is its solution to double-spending, called Nakamoto consensus. This provides a probabilistic guarantee that transactions will not be reversed or redirected, presuming that it is improbable for an attacker to obtain a majority of mining power in the network. However, this guarantee can be undermined when miners are assumed to be rational, and hence venal. Accordingly, we present the *whale attack*, in which a minority attacker increases her chances of double-spending by incentivizing miners to subvert the consensus protocol and to collude via *whale transactions*, which are bribery transactions carrying anomalously large fees. We analyze the expected cost to carry out the attack with success probability 1, and simulate the attack under realistic system parameters. Our results show that double-spend attacks, conventionally thought to be impractical for minority attackers, can actually be financially feasible and worthwhile under the whale attack. Perhaps more importantly, this work demonstrates that rationality should not underestimated when evaluating the security of cryptocurrencies.

1 Introduction

Decentralized cryptocurrencies have precipitated considerable interest in recent years. Bitcoin [1], the first empirical success of its kind, has laid the foundation for subsequent decentralized cryptocurrencies through its innovative solution to double-spending, a long-standing failure mode of digital currencies that allows an attacker to spend a given set of coins more than once. This solution, known as Nakamoto consensus, provides a high assurance that coins will not be double-spent, barring if an attacker obtains an improbable amount of resources. However, this tenuous assumption has induced notions of a looming crisis in the Bitcoin community, which casts serious doubt on the security of cryptocurrencies as currently prescribed.

In general, the security of a digital currency is congruous with the irreversibility of its transactions. More concretely, when users send coins to vendors in exchange for merchandise, vendors expect that once the purchased merchandise has been disbursed, the transaction will not be reversed or redirected elsewhere. Double-spending undermines this desideratum, in that if an attacker issues two

M. Brenner et al. (Eds.): FC 2017 Workshops 2017, LNCS 10323, pp. 264–279, 2017.
https://doi.org/10.1007/978-3-319-70278-0_17

conflicting transactions using the same set of coins, say, one to the vendor and one to herself, eventually one of these transactions will be invalidated. If the vendor unknowingly disburses the merchandise, under the impression that it has been paid for, and the paying transaction is invalidated, then the vendor is left empty-handed.

In this regard, Nakamoto consensus offers a probabilistic guarantee that a transaction will not be reversed. The protocol is as follows. Participants in the Bitcoin network, known as miners, compete to solve a computationally expensive proof-of-work puzzle. The miner who solves this puzzle is permitted to add a block of newly confirmed transactions to the blockchain, a distributed public ledger serializing all transactions ever issued. In remuneration, the miner is rewarded with newly minted bitcoins and (more importantly for this work), any embedded transaction fees, which are gratuities left by payers. The new block and its proof-of-work are then broadcast to the network, and upon verification, miners will add the block to their corresponding blockchains and repeat the mining process atop their updated ledgers. Since mining is performed concurrently, it may be the case that conflicting versions of the blockchain form, known as branches. In the prescribed protocol, miners resolve this by mining on the longest branch, as measured by the total expense of mining power. During this process, the shorter branch will be orphaned and any conflicting transactions will be invalidated.

Although transactions invalidated during branch selection enables the possibility of double-spending, as transactions gain more confirmations, in other words, when new blocks are added atop their respective blocks, the probability that a conflicting longer branch forms decreases exponentially. Thus, a transaction with six confirmations is well-accepted by the community to be secure against double-spending.

The main caveat of this probabilistic guarantee is that it assumes no single mining entity wields a majority of mining power in the network. Otherwise the system ceases to be decentralized—a majority miner can unilaterally control the blockchain and can thus double-spend at will. Bitcoin's security guarantees have been proven [2] only in accordance with this assumption, namely that a majority of miners (as measured by their mining powers) behave honestly by adhering to the prescribed protocol. The question then arises of whether or not these security guarantees hold when miners are, instead, assumed to behave rationally, in other words, they are incentivized by maximizing their profits.

Our Contributions. We consider a minority attacker, henceforth referred to as Alice, who attempts to double-spend against a vendor, henceforth referred to as Bob, within a rational network. From a cost perspective, double-spend attacks require a large proportion of mining power that may be improbable to attain singly. Auspiciously, Alice can amplify her own mining power by incentivizing rational miners into subverting the prescribed protocol.

Accordingly, we present a bribery attack called the *whale attack*, which was inspired by a peculiar (perhaps erroneous) bitcoin transaction,[1] in which the payer issued a transaction carrying an exorbitant transaction fee of 291 bitcoins. The current recommended transaction fee for a no-delay transaction is 6.0×10^{-7} bitcoins per byte, so at the current median transaction size of 257 bytes, this would only amount to a transaction fee of 1.542×10^{-4} bitcoins (from https://bitcoinfees.21.co, accessed September 1, 2016). We henceforth generalize transactions carrying anomalously large transaction fees as *whale transactions*, and we study the implications of these transactions on mining consensus. In particular, we are interested in the capabilities of whale transactions to incentivize rational and transaction-fee sensitive miners into colluding towards a double-spend attack.

Informally, the whale attack is as follows. To initiate the double-spend, Alice first mines a block. However, instead of broadcasting it to the network, she surreptitiously mines atop this block by herself, thereby forming her private branch. She then uses the same set of bitcoins to pay Bob on the original branch, while issuing a conflicting transaction to herself on her private branch. Upon receiving Alice's transaction, Bob will wait six confirmations, as per conventional wisdom and for concreteness, before sending the purchased merchandise.

For the attack to succeed, Alice's private branch must keep up with and overtake the original branch after at least six confirmations have been reached. Consider that in a traditional double-spend attack, that is, without bribing other miners into colluding, the probability that Alice succeeds is quite low since she wields a minority of mining power in the network. Alternatively, suppose Alice proceeds as described, but once six confirmations have been reached, if Alice's private branch is shorter than the original branch, she publishes her branch to the network and issues whale transactions, which are redeemable only by mining on her branch.

Assuming the network is rational, miners will choose to *whale mine* on Alice's branch if doing so is more profitable than honest mining. Whether whale mining is more profitable depends on the whale transactions' fees given the risk of mining on a shorter branch and the forgone block rewards should the attack fail. As more miners switch to whale mining, the probability that the double-spend succeeds increases. If a majority of mining power comes to whale mine, then the attack is guaranteed to succeed. Finally, once Alice's branch overtakes the original branch in length, Alice's transaction to Bob is invalidated, and Bob is left empty-handed.

The main contributions of this work are the following:

1. We introduce and formalize the whale attack, which demonstrates that rationality should not be underestimated when evaluating the security of cryptocurrencies.
2. We establish informal upper bounds on the expected cost to carry out the whale attack with success probability 1.

---

[1] cc455ae816e6cdafdb58d54e35d4f46d860047458eacf1c7405dc634631c570d.

3. We simulate the whale attack, mirroring the actual Bitcoin network, as a proof of concept for attack's feasibility, even when the attacker wields a modest amount of mining power and capital.

1.1 Related Work

There is a growing body of research examining incentive compatibility in Bitcoin. A number of recent works study the implications of block withholding, that is, delaying the broadcast of newly mined blocks. Rosenfeld [3] and Eyal [4] analyze block withholding attacks, in which an infiltrating miner discards full proofs-of-work, thereby sabotaging the victim pool's expected rewards. Eyal and Sirer [5] develop the selfish mining attack, in which an attacker surreptitiously forks the blockchain and withholds blocks in attempt to later orphan the original branch, thereby wasting computations by honest miners. Nayak et al. [6] and Sapirshtein et al. [7] further analyze and optimize the space of selfish mining strategies.

More closely related to this work are bribery attacks. Bonneau [8] presents various bribery attacks, in which an attacker temporarily rents mining power rather than traditionally buying mining hardware. For example, an attacker pays miners out-of-band, in other words, outside of Bitcoin, to mine on a chosen branch. Alternatively, an attacker sends bribery money to a set of scripted addresses, located in-band on the attacker's branch, that can be claimed by mining the next block(s). Our attack differs from the former, in that whale transactions are trustless and can be issued anonymously, and compares to the latter, but instead disburses bribery money through transaction fees, which are inherent to the protocol.

Teutsch et al. [9] present another bribery attack, in which an attacker casts proof-of-work puzzles as Ethereum smart contracts, called script puzzles, to serve as an additional mining revenue source. Thus, rational miners may increase their profits by apportioning their mining powers between puzzle-solving and Bitcoin mining, thereby reducing mining power in the Bitcoin network. Our attack differs from the script puzzle attack, in that miners are purveyed a single source of revenue, namely the block rewards on the longest branch.

More broadly, there is also a growing interest in the interrelationship between transaction fees and Bitcoin's long-term health. Möser and Böhme [10] perform a longitudinal analysis of transaction fees and examine the externalities that influence these fees. Kroll et al. [11], Houy [12], and Kaşkaloğlu [13] consider the economics of Bitcoin mining and discuss potential changes to transaction fees and their policies in the long-term. Carlsten et al. [14] develop a new attack strategy and revisit the selfish mining attack in the context of a transaction-fee regime.

2 Model

We adapt the model used by Rosenfeld [15] and updated by Sompolinsky and Zohar [16] to consider double-spending under the whale attack.

We assume that the distribution of mining power in the network remains constant. An attacker Alice controls a fraction α of the mining power, where $\alpha < 0.5$, since otherwise she could double-spend by herself at will. The remaining network consists of k mining entities controlling a fraction $\beta = 1-\alpha$ of the mining power. Thus, each mining entity i controls a fraction β_i such that $\sum_{i=1}^{k} \beta_i = \beta$.

Miners mine blocks according to a Poisson process with rate λ, which also remains constant. Further, the propagation of new blocks to the network is instantaneous. Thus, the passage of time is a discrete-time process marked by block creation events on either of the original branch or Alice's branch. The reward for mining a block on the original branch is 1; the reward for mining a block on Alice's branch is $\delta + 1$, where δ is the block reward premium offered by the whale transaction. Throughout the rest of this paper, when we refer to the value of whale transactions, we are referring to the transaction fee δ.

Following each block creation event, each mining entity, including Alice, makes a new rational decision that will be pursued until the next block creation event. More specifically, Alice makes a rational decision for whether to continue the attack or reset the attack. Similarly, once whale transactions are underway, each mining entity i makes a binary rational decision for $\gamma_i \in \{0, 1\}$ of whether to honest mine ($\gamma_i = 0$) or whale mine ($\gamma_i = 1$).

At this point, the remaining network β can be further divided into two partitions: whale miners and honest miners. More formally, a fraction $q = \alpha + \sum_{i=1}^{k} \gamma_i \cdot \beta_i$ of the mining power is devoted to whale mining, in other words, extending Alice's branch. On the other hand, a fraction $p = \sum_{i=1}^{k}(1 - \gamma_i) \cdot \beta_i = 1 - q$ of the mining power is devoted to honest mining, in other words, extending the original branch.

The whale attack is carried out in two phases: the *pre-mining* phase and the *race* phase. An algorithm for the attack is fully specified in Appendix A.

Pre-mining Phase. In this phase, Alice surreptitiously forks the blockchain, issues a pair of conflicting double-spend transactions (tx_B to Bob and tx_A to herself), and then singly mines on her private branch until tx_B has reached n confirmations, at which point Bob will disburse the merchandise. Note that Alice will neither reveal her private branch nor issue whale transactions before Bob disburses the merchandise, since either action could dissuade Bob from doing so.

To initiate the attack, while Alice need only mine one block to begin her private branch, Sompolinsky and Zohar present the *pre-mining* [16] strategy, by which Alice could, in theory, mine $n + 1$ blocks prior to double-spending. Thus, the attack would succeed with probability 1. Since this may take a long time to achieve (depending on the desired n), the assumption is that Alice can freely choose when to purchase merchandise from Bob. While we aver that this is a plausible assumption in practice, Alice can alternatively pre-mine fewer blocks to carry out the attack with a lower success probability. Regardless, Sompolinsky and Zohar also point out that Alice can employ selfish mining strategies [5] to gain while pre-mining.

Suppose Alice aims to pre-mine $l \in \mathbb{N} : 1 \leq l \leq n + 1$ blocks more than the original branch before issuing tx_B. Alice embeds tx_A in the first block she mines ahead of the original branch, which marks the start of a new "attempt." In any attempt, if the original branch overtakes Alice's branch in length, she accepts the original branch and resets to a new attempt. Otherwise, if Alice successfully pre-mines l blocks more than the original branch, she issues tx_B on the original branch.

Then, overloading Sompolinsky's and Zohar's definition of pre-mining, Alice also singly mines m blocks on her private branch while waiting for tx_B to reach n confirmations. In accordance with Rosenfeld's analysis [15], the probability for a given value of m is

$$P(m) = \binom{m + n - 1}{m} \alpha^m \beta^n. \tag{1}$$

Finally, once Bob disburses the merchandise, Alice publishes her heretofore private branch containing $m + l$ pre-mined blocks. If $m + l \leq n$, in other words, Alice's branch is shorter than the original branch, then the attack transitions to the race phase.

Race Phase. In this phase, Alice's branch and the original branch enter into a race. However, instead of continuing to singly mine on her branch, Alice issues whale transactions (tx_W) on her branch, which offer a δ percentage increase over the normal block reward. Although Alice can choose from several payout strategies, we assume that she issues a new tx_W in each block on her branch until the attack succeeds. This allows for a more consistent proportion of whale mining power in the network, since mining entities persistently contend for tx_W fees throughout the race phase (see Sect. 3 for more details about our assumptions).

The race phase can be modeled as a biased random walk. The initial state is $z = n - (m + l)$, where z is the lead of the original branch. In each block creation step, z increases by 1 with probability p and z decreases by 1 with probability q, where p and q are the mining powers devoted to honest mining and whale mining, respectively. Again, in accordance with Rosenfeld's analysis [15], the probability that z reaches the absorbing state -1, in other words, Alice's branch becomes longer than the original branch, as a function of p, q, and z is

$$a_z = min(q/p, 1)^{max(z+1,0)} = \begin{cases} 1 & \text{if } z < 0 \text{ or } q > p \\ (q/p)^{z+1} & \text{if } z \geq 0 \text{ and } q \leq p. \end{cases} \tag{2}$$

As z increases, the probability that the attack succeeds decreases and the attack may become intractable. For this reason, Alice can choose to cut off the attack when z reaches z_{lim}. This is then analagous to the Gambler's Ruin problem.

While it would be interesting to analyze the cost of the attack given various success probabilities, we are more interested in the expected cost to carry out the whale attack with success probability 1. This allows us to determine if the whale attack is worthwhile, without having to make any assumptions about Alice's risk tolerance or the liquidity of the purhased merchandise should the attack fail.

2.1 Assumptions

We make a number of simplifying assumptions and explain their rationales here, as well as enroute of the analysis (Sect. 3). Granted, these assumptions may differ in practice and could dramatically change (in most cases reduce) the cost of the attack. However, we believe that an informal upper bound on the cost of a successful attack is enough to substantiate whether or not the whale attack is worthwhile in practice. That being stated, we also leave these assumptions as points of discussion in Sect. 4.

1. *Mining entities consider at least their own mining power and Alice's mining power when making rational decisions.* We make minimal assumptions about the sophistication of mining entities in evaluating their profits. We simply assume that each mining entity considers its own mining power and Alice's mining power. This serves to establish an upper bound on the cost, since by underestimating whale mining power, the cost of the attack is overestimated. Additionally, this simplifies matters, since if some miner A finds it profitable to whale mine, then some other miner B might find it profitable to whale miner under the assumption A whale mines, and so on with the other pools. Thus, this assumption precludes such a "cascading" effect, which is difficult to model.
2. *Mining entities are not "sticky."* When mining entities mine a whale block, they will not simply "stick" to whale mining for the remainder of the attack. Instead, they continue to make new rational decisions following each block event, without taking into consideration their prior earnings. This memory-lessness property, again, simplifies matters.
3. *Mining entities will choose the more profitable (even marginally) mining strategy.* We later determine strict lower bounds for the value of whale transactions δ that will incentivize some subset of rational pools to whale mine. As long as δ is marginally sufficient, these pools will choose to whale mine.
4. *Whale mining power is kept constant throughout the race phase.* Instead of keeping the values of whale transactions constant throughout the attack, Alice keeps whale mining power constant by issuing appropriate whale transactions in each block on her branch. Although alternative strategies exist, such as keeping δ constant, this strategy allows her to better predict the number of blocks it will take for the attack to succeed, since the race phase can then be modeled as a steady state stochastic process.
5. *Alice issues whale transactions in every block on her branch until the attack succeeds.* Since mining entities always make new rational decisions following each block event, Alice issues whale transactions until her branch is longer than the original branch. This implies that she never cuts off the attack ($z_{lim} = \infty$) and that her budget is unbounded. Since this is a strong assumption, we are only interested in scenarios where whale mining power constitutes a majority of mining power in the network.

3   Analysis

We now establish informal upper bounds on the expected cost to carry out the whale attack with success probability 1. Since Alice's profit is contingent on the value of the double-spend being greater than the sum of the whale transactions, the main questions we are trying to answer are "How large do whale transactions need to be?" and "How many whale transactions are needed?"

3.1   How Large Do Whale Transactions Need to Be?

The first step in evaluating the cost of the whale attack is to determine what values of whale transactions δ are appropriate for incentivizing a desired proportion of the network to whale mine. To do this, we examine the decision problem faced by a rational mining entity m.

Suppose m has mining power β_m and decides to honest mine ($\gamma_m = 0$). This means that m receives block rewards only if the whale attack fails. From Eq. 2, the probability that the whale attack fails is equal to $1 - a_z = 1 - min(q/p, 1)^{max(z+1,0)}$. Recall that whale mining power $q = \alpha + \sum_{i=1}^{k} \gamma_i \cdot \beta_i$. Since Alice singly whale mines, $q = \alpha$. Then, honest mining power p is simply equal to $1 - q = \beta$. Conditioned on the whale attack failing, m receives block rewards with probability β_m/p. It follows that m's profit when honest mining is given by

$$\pi_m(\alpha, \beta_m, \gamma_m = 0, \delta = 0, z) = \frac{(1 - a_z) \cdot \beta_m}{p} = \frac{\left(1 - \left(\frac{\alpha}{\beta}\right)^{z+1}\right) \cdot \beta_m}{\beta}. \tag{3}$$

On the other hand, suppose m decides to whale mine ($\gamma_m = 1$). This means that m receives block rewards only if the whale attack succeeds. The probability that the whale attack succeeds is $a_z = min(q/p, 1)^{max(z+1,0)}$, where $q = \alpha + \beta_m$ and $p = 1 - q = \beta - \beta_m$. Conditioned on the whale attack succeeding, m receives block rewards with probability β_m/q. Recall that the normal block reward is 1 and the whale block reward is $\delta + 1$. It follows that m's profit when whale mining is given by

$$\pi_m(\alpha, \beta_m, \gamma_m = 1, \delta, z) = \frac{a_z \cdot \beta_m}{q} \cdot (\delta + 1) = \frac{\left(\frac{\alpha+\beta_m}{\beta-\beta_m}\right)^{z+1} \cdot \beta_m}{\alpha + \beta_m} \cdot (\delta + 1). \tag{4}$$

By rationality, m will choose $\gamma_i \in \{0, 1\}$ that maximizes its profit π_m. Clearly, as long as $\pi_m(\alpha, \beta_m, \gamma_m = 1, \delta, z) > \pi_m(\alpha, \beta_m, \gamma_m = 0, \delta = 0, z)$, in other words, Eq. 4 is greater than Eq. 3, then m will choose to whale mine. We can then solve for δ to determine what values of whale transactions make whale mining more profitable.

$$\delta > \frac{\left(1 - \left(\frac{\alpha}{\beta}\right)^{z+1}\right)}{\beta} \cdot \frac{\alpha + \beta_m}{\left(\frac{\alpha+\beta_m}{\beta-\beta_m}\right)^{z+1}} - 1, \tag{5}$$

which is equivalent to

$$\delta > \frac{\text{Pr}[\text{whale attack fails} \mid \gamma_m = 0]}{\text{Pr}[\text{honest block} \mid \gamma_m = 0]} \cdot \frac{\text{Pr}[\text{whale block} \mid \gamma_m = 1]}{\text{Pr}[\text{whale attack succeeds} \mid \gamma_m = 1]} - 1.$$

The table in Appendix B provides values for δ, as functions of α and β_m.

We now point out several insights from Eq. 5 and Appendix B. First, we see that, in terms of cost, larger mining entities are more easily bribed into whale mining. In fact, as z approaches -1, m may choose to whale mine regardless of whether or not there are whale transactions on Alice's branch. An intuitive explanation for this is that, from m's perspective in accordance with Assumption 1, it earns a larger proportion of the block rewards on Alice's branch as long as honest mining power is greater than whale mining power. Thus, as the whale attack becomes more likely to succeed, the expected profit in whale mining for a larger proportion of the block reward becomes greater than that of honest mining and being left empty-handed should the whale attack succeed.

Second, if we convert Eq. 5 into a function $f(\alpha)$ and we differentiate with respect to α, we see that $f(\alpha)$ is strictly decreasing in the interval $\alpha \in [0, 0.5)$. This insight is rather straightforward and tells us that increasing Alice's mining power α will decrease the cost of the whale attack. Similarly, if we convert Eq. 5 into a function $f(\beta_m)$, and differentiate with respect to β_m, we see that $f(\beta_m)$ is strictly decreasing in the interval $\beta_m \in [0, 0.5)$. This means that if whale mining is profitable for m, then whale mining is profitable for all mining entities with mining power greater than or equal to β_m.

Now, it becomes more clear why Assumption 1 induces an "upper bound" on the cost. By the latter insights, if it is profitable for m to whale mine, then mining entities larger than m will also whale mine. From m's perspective, considering that larger entities will whale mine has the same effect as if Alice were to increase her mining power, which we already know decreases δ. Regardless, this does not affect m's decision, since whale mining remains the rational strategy.

3.2   How Many Whale Transactions Are Needed?

The next step in evaluating the cost of the whale attack is to determine how many whale transactions are expected to guarantee that the attack succeeds. Referring back to our assumptions, Alice will keep whale mining power constant by issuing appropriate whale transactions δ in each block, and she will continue doing so until her branch is longer than the original branch. Setting aside the assumption that Alice never cuts off the attack for a moment (Assumption 5), the race phase we propose in Sect. 2, in which Alice chooses a finite cutoff for the attack z_{lim}, is analogous to the Gambler's Ruin problem.

To recap, the initial state in the race phase is the lead of the original branch over Alice's branch z. Then, z decreases by 1 with probability q, which is the proportion of whale mining power, and increases by 1 with probability $p = 1 - q$, which is the proportion of honest mining power. Alice's goal is to reach the absorbing state $z = -1$, before reaching the absorbing state $z = z_{lim}$, at which point she becomes ruined. Although, if Alice becomes ruined, the only costs incurred are the forgone block rewards she could have received mining honestly, not the whale transactions.

Alternatively, we can define the initial state as z_{lim} and the absorbing states as 0 and $S = z_{lim} + z + 1$. Thus, we can calculate the expected number of steps (block creation events) before we hit an absorbing state using

$$E(z_{lim}, z) = \begin{cases} \frac{z_{lim}}{1-2q} - \frac{S}{1-2q} \cdot \frac{(\frac{p}{q})^{z_{lim}} - 1}{(\frac{p}{q})^{S} - 1} & \text{if } p \neq 0.5 \\ z_{lim} \cdot (z+1) & \text{if } p = 0.5. \end{cases} \tag{6}$$

Then, extending this back to Assumption 5, which stipulates that Alice never cuts off the attack until it succeeds, is simple.

$$\lim_{z_{lim} \to \infty} E(z_{lim}, z) = \begin{cases} \frac{z+1}{2q-1} & \text{if } p \neq 0.5 \\ \infty & \text{if } p = 0.5. \end{cases} \tag{7}$$

The expected number of whale transactions is then

$$\frac{\lim_{z_{lim} \to \infty} E(z_{lim}, z)}{2} + z + 1, \tag{8}$$

since Alice only issues whale transactions in blocks on her own branch.

Now that we have established an informal upper bound on appropriate values for whale transactions and have calculated the number of whale transactions expected, the ultimate question we are trying to answer is "How much does the whale attack cost?" Given the complexity of posing an analytical result for this question, we determine the cost of the attack by simulation. Before we detail our simulations, here are a number of considerations on the cost of the attack.

First, consider that Alice reclaims her own whale transactions with probability $\frac{\alpha}{q}$, which is reflected in our simulations. Second, to interpret our results, recall that δ is a lower bound on the value of whale transactions for whale mining to be more profitable. Thus, the cost of the attack is marginally more than the sum of the whale transactions in our simulations. Finally, recognize that the whale attack being profitable is different from it being rational. The whale attack is rationally worthwhile for Alice only if the difference between the double-spend tx_B and the cost of the attack is greater than what Alice would have earned simply by honest mining. However, do consider that Alice reaps all of the block rewards from her $m + l$ pre-mined blocks.

3.3   Simulation

We model the snapshot of the Bitcoin network shown in Appendix C and we represent Alice by the largest pool in the network ($\alpha = 0.188$). As aforementioned, we are interested in the expected cost to carry out the attack with success probability 1, so we only consider cases in which the whale mining power $q > 0.5$. For example, we run simulations issuing appropriate δs, such that all pools as large as BTCC Pool will whale mine, to get $q = 0.532$. Similarly, we run simulations issuing appropriate δs, such that pools as large as BW.COM will whale mine, to get $q = 0.670$, and so on. The table in Appendix D presents the cost of the whale attack in terms of δ under different parameters of q and z.

4   Discussion

Our simulations return a number of interesting results. Immediately, we can see the impact that pre-mining has on the cost of the whale attack. As Sompolinsky and Zohar have mentioned, while the l blocks pre-mined before even issuing tx_B may take a long time, as long as Alice controls the timing of the attack and employs selfish mining strategies, mining these l blocks need not be costly [16]. Then, once tx_B has been issued, Alice can mine m more blocks on top of the l guaranteed blocks before tx_B reaches n confirmations to further reduce costs.

Next, we see that centralization of mining increases the venality of the network. As shown in Sect. 3.1, larger pools are more easily bribed than smaller pools. In our simulation, the three largest pools, which includes Alice, already combine for a majority of whale mining power. Since $q = 0.532$ is only slightly above a majority, the cost of the attack is exorbitant. However, simply adding the fourth largest pool for $q = 0.670$ dramatically reduces the cost of the attack. Observing the table in Appendix D for $z = 6$, we see that Alice's cheapest option is to aim for $q = 0.764$. Attempting to bribe the smaller pools, which would allow z to converge faster, would not be cost efficient. Now, consider if mining was completely decentralized, and the largest pools wielded less than 0.01 of the mining power—the whale attack would be incredibly costly in our model.

Finally, consider that Alice only wields $\alpha = 0.188$ of the mining power in our simulations. In the past, mining pools have enjoyed much larger shares of mining power, even exceeding a majority on several occasions. Observing the table in Appendix B, we can see that a larger attacker could dramatically reduce the cost of the attack. Thus, we aver that $\alpha = 0.188$ is modest in comparison, and even so, the whale attack need not require an intractable amount of capital. Taking this a step further, our assumptions from Sect. 3, already induce an upper bound on the cost. We address these assumptions below, and discuss how they might differ in practice.

Assumption 1. We briefly discussed this in Sect. 3, but a more sophisticated mining entity who considers the decisions of other mining entities could dramatically lower the necessary δ for whale mining to be rational. In practice, cooperative mining entities would achieve similar effects, since they could certainly account for each other's mining power when evaluating the profits.

Assumption 2. In practice, if a mining entity mines a large whale block, it would likely be in its best interest to "stick" to whale mining. Consider that it may even be rational to issue their own smaller whale transactions to ensure the success of Alice's branch. From Alice's perspective, the best case (other than if she were to reclaim every whale transaction) would be to have different mining entities each mine a single whale block. If these entities combine for a majority of whale mining power, it is probable that further whale transactions would not be needed at all. Our model assumes the worst case, in which some negligibly sized mining entity miraculously receives $\frac{1-\alpha}{q}$ of the rewards, thus rendering the other mining entities "unsticky."

Assumption 3. In practice, a marginal profit for whale mining over honest mining may not be sufficient, and we would need to consider the "cost of deviation."

Assumption 4. In practice, it is not necessary for Alice to keep whale mining power consistent, especially if Alice does not require that the whale attack succeed with probability 1. Perhaps if the purchased merchandise is quite liquid, having the attack fail with nonzero probability would not be a tremendous setback.

Assumption 5. As we mentioned before in addressing Assumption 2, there are cases in which it would not be necessary to issue whale transactions until the attack is completed. Additionally, Alice might also choose a finite cutoff for z_{lim}, since continuing the whale attack would not be rational if the attack unluckily takes longer than expected.

Our work is primarily a proof-of-concept for the whale attack being feasible for a minority attacker, and we leave open the challenges of modeling the cost of the attack more precisely and exploring the strategy space when combining the whale attack with other mining attacks.

5   Conclusion

Cryptocurrencies fail to fit into established theoretical frameworks for secure distributed systems. Instead, their security relies on the assumption that a majority of miners, as measured by their computational resources, will behave honestly. In this regard, researchers have uncovered many deviant mining strategies, which reveal evident security gaps in a rational setting. In this work, we presented the whale attack, in which a minority attacker increases her chances of double-spending by incentivizing rational miners into colluding. Moreover, we demonstrated that such an attack is feasible, even when the attacker wields a modest amount of mining power and capital. While Nakamoto consensus has been a stopgap to the issue of double-spending, we showed that as currently prescribed, it is by no means a panacea.

Acknowledgments. We thank Elijah Soriah and Andrew Miller for their valuable feedback, and the faculty and students of the CAAR REU program for the wonderful experience. This work is funded by NSF Research Experience for Undergraduates (REU) Grant CNS-1560193.

A   Whale Attack Algorithm

Algorithm 1. Whale Attack

1: **procedure** RESET
2:     $original\_branch \leftarrow$ longest branch
3:     $Alice\_branch \leftarrow$ longest branch
4:     $l\_count \leftarrow 0$ $\triangleright\ len(Alice\_branch) - len(original\_branch)$.
5:     Issue tx_A on $Alice\_branch$.
6:     Mine at head of $Alice\_branch$.

7: **procedure** PRE-MINE(l, n)
8:     RESET
9:     **while** $l\_count < l$ **do**
10:         $new\_block \leftarrow$ LISTEN $\triangleright$ LISTEN for block creation event.
11:         **if** new_block on $Alice\_branch$ **then**
12:             $l\_count \leftarrow l\_count + 1$
13:         **else if** $l\_count = 0$ **then** $\triangleright\ len(Alice\_branch) < len(original\_branch)$.
14:             RESET
15:         **else** $\triangleright\ len(Alice\_branch) \geq len(original\_branch)$.
16:             $l\_count \leftarrow l\_count - 1$
17:     Issue tx_B on $original\_branch$.
18:     $n\_count \leftarrow 0$
19:     $m \leftarrow 0$

20:     **while** $n\_count < n$ **do**
21:         $new\_block \leftarrow$ LISTEN
22:         **if** new_block on $Alice\_branch$ **then**
23:             $m \leftarrow m + 1$
24:         **else**
25:             $n\_count \leftarrow n\_count + 1$
26:     Publish $Alice\_branch$.
27:     **if** $m + l \leq n$ **then** $\triangleright\ len(Alice\_branch) \leq len(original\_branch)$.
28:         RACE $(n - (m + l))$

29: **procedure** RACE(z)
30:     Issue new tx_W on $Alice\_branch$.
31:     **while** $z > -1$ **do**
32:         $new\_block \leftarrow$ LISTEN
33:         **if** new_block on $Alice\_branch$ **then**
34:             $z \leftarrow z - 1$
35:             Issue $tx_W j$ on $Alice\_branch$.
36:         **else if** $z = z_{lim} - 1$ **then** $\triangleright$ Cut off attack.
37:             RESET
38:         **else**
39:             $z \leftarrow z + 1$

B   Full Table for Sufficient Values of Whale Transactions

See Tables 1, 2 and 3.

Table 1. The value of δ (whale attack premium) that makes whale mining more profitable than honest mining, as a function of the lead of the original branch at the start of the race phase z, Alice's mining power α (rows), and m's mining power β_m (columns). For $z = 0$, δ is always equal to 0.

	0.00	0.05	0.10	0.15	0.20	0.25	0.30	0.35	0.40	0.45
$z = 6$										
0.05	47045879.95	503469.42	29624.20	3448.26	574.53	117.91	27.07	6.19	0.93	0
0.10	531439.89	31270.04	3639.89	606.50	124.52	28.63	6.59	1.04	0	0
0.15	33109.34	3854.04	642.23	131.90	30.37	7.04	1.16	0	0	0
0.20	4094.75	682.40	140.20	32.33	7.54	1.29	0	0	0	0
0.25	727.67	149.56	34.54	8.11	1.44	0	0	0	0	0
0.30	159.96	37.00	8.74	1.61	0	0	0	0	0	0
0.35	39.49	9.38	1.78	0	0	0	0	0	0	0
0.40	9.72	1.88	0	0	0	0	0	0	0	0
0.45	1.52	0	0	0	0	0	0	0	0	0
$z = 5$										
0.05	2476097.95	55940.16	5226.98	861.32	190.84	49.96	14.12	3.80	0.58	0
0.10	59047.89	5517.41	909.22	201.50	52.79	14.95	4.06	0.67	0	0
0.15	5841.86	962.74	213.41	55.96	15.89	4.36	0.76	0	0	0
0.20	1022.75	226.76	59.50	16.95	4.69	0.87	0	0	0	0
0.25	241.67	63.47	18.12	5.07	1.00	0	0	0	0	0
0.30	67.74	19.39	5.47	1.13	0	0	0	0	0	0
0.35	20.55	5.84	1.25	0	0	0	0	0	0	0
0.40	5.93	1.28	0	0	0	0	0	0	0	0
0.45	0.91	0	0	0	0	0	0	0	0	0
$z = 4$										
0.05	130319.95	6214.68	921.58	214.58	62.95	20.84	7.14	2.20	0.29	0
0.10	6559.89	972.82	226.55	66.50	22.05	7.59	2.37	0.36	0	0
0.15	1029.95	239.90	70.46	23.41	8.09	2.57	0.44	0	0	0
0.20	254.75	74.86	24.91	8.66	2.79	0.53	0	0	0	0
0.25	79.67	26.55	9.27	3.03	0.63	0	0	0	0	0
0.30	28.21	9.89	3.28	0.73	0	0	0	0	0	0
0.35	10.36	3.46	0.80	0	0	0	0	0	0	0
0.40	3.40	0.78	0	0	0	0	0	0	0	0
0.45	0.41	0	0	0	0	0	0	0	0	0
$z = 3$										
0.05	6857.95	689.63	161.81	52.89	20.32	8.36	3.38	1.13	0.06	0
0.10	727.89	170.83	55.88	21.50	8.88	3.63	1.25	0.12	0	0
0.15	180.79	59.18	22.80	9.45	3.89	1.38	0.18	0	0	0
0.20	62.75	24.21	10.07	4.18	1.52	0.25	0	0	0	0
0.25	25.67	10.71	4.48	1.67	0.32	0	0	0	0	0
0.30	11.28	4.75	1.80	0.39	0	0	0	0	0	0
0.35	4.87	1.85	0.42	0	0	0	0	0	0	0
0.40	1.71	0.34	0	0	0	0	0	0	0	0
0.45	0.01	0	0	0	0	0	0	0	0	0
$z = 2$										
0.05	359.95	75.72	27.73	12.47	6.10	3.01	1.36	0.42	0	0
0.10	79.89	29.29	13.20	6.49	3.23	1.49	0.50	0	0	0
0.15	30.93	13.98	6.90	3.46	1.62	0.58	0	0	0	0
0.20	14.75	7.31	3.69	1.76	0.66	0.01	0	0	0	0
0.25	7.67	3.89	1.88	0.73	0.05	0	0	0	0	0
0.30	4.02	1.95	0.78	0.08	0	0	0	0	0	0
0.35	1.91	0.75	0.07	0	0	0	0	0	0	0
0.40	0.58	0	0	0	0	0	0	0	0	0
0.45	0	0	0	0	0	0	0	0	0	0
$z = 1$										
0.05	17.95	7.50	4.06	2.36	1.36	0.71	0.27	0	0	0
0.10	7.89	4.29	2.51	1.47	0.79	0.32	0	0	0	0
0.15	4.49	2.65	1.56	0.86	0.38	0.03	0	0	0	0
0.20	2.75	1.64	0.91	0.41	0.05	0	0	0	0	0
0.25	1.67	0.94	0.43	0.07	0	0	0	0	0	0
0.30	0.90	0.41	0.05	0	0	0	0	0	0	0
0.35	0.32	0	0	0	0	0	0	0	0	0
0.40	0	0	0	0	0	0	0	0	0	0
0.45	0	0	0	0	0	0	0	0	0	0

C   Bitcoin Mining Distribution Snapshot

Table 2. Distribution of mining power among the ten largest pools (95% of the network) from July 30-August 2, 2016 (Source: https://blockchain.info/pools).

AntPool	F2Pool	BTCC Pool	BW.COM	BitFury
18.8%	18.2%	16.2%	13.8%	9.4%
HaoBTC	SlushPool	ViaBTC	BitClub Net	Kano CKPool
6.4%	5.9%	4.4%	3.7%	3.1%

D   Simulated Cost of Whale Attack

Table 3. The simulated attack cost (sum of δs) under different parameters of the whale mining power q and the lead of the original branch at the start of the race phase z. The values shown are averages across 10^6 simulations for each pair of q and z.

q	6	5	4	3	2	1	0
0.532	2.93e+23	3.09e+22	8.03e+21	1.10e+22	2.57e+24	2.50e+21	4.40e+20
0.670	999.79	464.74	307.71	267.72	56.09	17.64	3.63
0.764	768.09	291.86	109.89	40.16	12.73	2.48	0
0.828	1265.14	417.85	135.80	42.32	11.60	1.65	0
0.887	1205.00	390.63	123.93	37.23	9.46	1.00	0
0.931	1806.67	540.75	159.34	44.66	10.69	1.12	0
0.968	2178.58	628.13	178.19	48.29	11.23	1.15	0
0.999	2598.64	723.92	198.92	52.33	11.89	1.22	0

References

1. Nakamoto, S.: Bitcoin: a peer-to-peer electronic cash system (2008)
2. Garay, J., Kiayias, A., Leonardos, N.: The bitcoin backbone protocol: analysis and applications. In: Oswald, E., Fischlin, M. (eds.) EUROCRYPT 2015. LNCS, vol. 9057, pp. 281–310. Springer, Heidelberg (2015). https://doi.org/10.1007/978-3-662-46803-6_10
3. Rosenfeld, M.: Analysis of bitcoin pooled mining reward systems. arXiv preprint. arXiv:1112.4980 (2011)
4. Eyal, I.: The miner's dilemma. In: 2015 IEEE Symposium on Security and Privacy, pp. 89–103. IEEE (2015)

5. Eyal, I., Sirer, E.G.: Majority is not enough: bitcoin mining is vulnerable. In: Christin, N., Safavi-Naini, R. (eds.) FC 2014. LNCS, vol. 8437, pp. 436–454. Springer, Heidelberg (2014). https://doi.org/10.1007/978-3-662-45472-5_28
6. Nayak, K., Kumar, S., Miller, A., Shi, E.: Stubborn mining: generalizing selfish mining and combining with an eclipse attack. In: 2016 IEEE European Symposium on Security and Privacy (EuroS&P), pp. 305–320. IEEE (2016)
7. Sapirshtein, A., Sompolinsky, Y., Zohar, A.: Optimal selfish mining strategies in bitcoin. arXiv preprint. arXiv:1507.06183 (2015)
8. Bonneau, J.: Why buy when you can rent? Bribery attacks on bitcoin-style consensus. In: Clark, J., Meiklejohn, S., Ryan, P.Y.A., Wallach, D., Brenner, M., Rohloff, K. (eds.) FC 2016. LNCS, vol. 9604, pp. 19–26. Springer, Heidelberg (2016). https://doi.org/10.1007/978-3-662-53357-4_2
9. Teutsch, J., Jain, S., Saxena, P.: When cryptocurrencies mine their own business. In: Grossklags, J., Preneel, B. (eds.) FC 2016. LNCS, vol. 9603, pp. 499–514. Springer, Heidelberg (2017). https://doi.org/10.1007/978-3-662-54970-4_29
10. Möser, M., Böhme, R.: Trends, tips, tolls: a longitudinal study of bitcoin transaction fees. In: Brenner, M., Christin, N., Johnson, B., Rohloff, K. (eds.) FC 2015. LNCS, vol. 8976, pp. 19–33. Springer, Heidelberg (2015). https://doi.org/10.1007/978-3-662-48051-9_2
11. Kroll, J.A., Davey, I.C., Felten, E.W.: The economics of bitcoin mining, or bitcoin in the presence of adversaries. In: Proceedings of WEIS, vol. 2013. Citeseer (2013)
12. Houy, N.: The economics of bitcoin transaction fees. In: GATE WP, vol. 1407 (2014)
13. Kaskaloglu, K.: Near zero bitcoin transaction fees cannot last forever (2014)
14. Carlsten, M., Kalodner, H., Weinberg, S.M., Narayanan, A.: On the instability of bitcoin without the block reward. In: ACM Conference on Computer and Communications Security (2016)
15. Rosenfeld, M.: Analysis of hashrate-based double spending. arXiv preprint. arXiv:1402.2009 (2014)
16. Sompolinsky, Y., Zohar, A.: Bitcoin's security model revisited. arXiv preprint. arXiv:1605.09193 (2016)

Mixing Coins of Different Quality:
A Game-Theoretic Approach

Svetlana Abramova[1,2]($\boxtimes$), Pascal Schöttle[1], and Rainer Böhme[1,2]

[1] University of Innsbruck, Innsbruck, Austria
{svetlana.abramova,pascal.schoettle,rainer.boehme}@uibk.ac.at
[2] University of Münster, Münster, Germany

Abstract. Cryptocoins based on public distributed ledgers can differ in their quality due to different subjective values users assign to coins depending on the unique transaction history of each coin. We apply game theory to study how qualitative differentiation between coins will affect the behavior of users interested in improving their anonymity through mixing services. We present two stylized models of mixing with perfect and imperfect information and analyze them for three distinct quality propagation policies: poison, haircut, and seniority. In the game of perfect information, mixing coins of high quality remains feasible under certain conditions, while imperfect information eventually leads to a mixing market where only coins of the lowest quality are mixed.

Keywords: Bitcoin · Anonymity · Blacklisting · Policy · Game theory

1 Introduction

While public distributed ledgers serve as an essential backbone of many cryptocurrencies, they inherently act as a source of differentiation of coins by quality. Indeed, each individual unspent transaction output has its unique history recorded with cryptographic integrity protection in the public distributed ledger. Having the entire history publicly available makes cryptocoins non-fungible, that means distinguishable from each other in terms of the perceived quality. Coins generated in the genesis block or passed through credible exchanges might be more attractive to someone over coins whose transaction history contains patterns suggesting dubious activities in the past [17].

The traceability offered by public distributed ledgers has called the anonymity of financial transactions into question. For example, the most popular cryptocurrency, Bitcoin, was initially spoken of as a truly anonymous payment method. However, many studies [4,16,23,24] have shown that the public blockchain infringes user privacy. In efforts to impede simple blockchain analyses, privacy-concerned users can cooperate with each other and mix their payments in a single transaction instead of sending multiple individual transactions. Many cryptocurrency protocols support such collective transactions, to which we refer here as *mixing transactions*. In general, mixing can be thought of as a privacy-enhancing overlay [15], which makes money flows more difficult to trace [33].

© International Financial Cryptography Association 2017
M. Brenner et al. (Eds.): FC 2017 Workshops 2017, LNCS 10323, pp. 280–297, 2017.
https://doi.org/10.1007/978-3-319-70278-0_18

If the history of transactions matters to users, mixing coins of good and bad quality in one single transaction bears the risk that good coins are exchanged for worse ones. A simple example of this would be a multi-input transaction, some inputs of which can be traced back to darknet markets or ransomware payments. Such a transaction may come under scrutiny of law enforcement as a payment possibly made by or to a criminal. Moreover, in the name of preventing financial crime, regulators may enforce transaction blacklisting. Although blacklisting is not explicitly implemented today, its ideas are already present in the Bitcoin system in various forms. For example, some wallet providers and exchanges allegedly denied or delayed transactions which tried to spend stolen funds or could be linked to darknet markets [5,12]. So, blacklists are one possible source of qualitative differentiation between coins.

Whenever coin quality matters, each downstream transaction must not lead to the loss of information about the quality of newly generated outputs. Rather, we must assume that some sort of a quality propagation policy is in place to allow for situations when coins of different quality are combined in one transaction. If qualitative differentiation between coins becomes common practice and a specific policy takes effect, users will always have to account for the risk of receiving coins of lower quality. As this risk is especially amplified in the context of mixing, it is of particular interest to analyze how participants of mixing services will behave in these circumstances. Will they be willing to engage in mixing and, if yes, under what conditions? Will the market for mixing services persist after all?

Contributions. We apply game theory to study this scenario and formalize the game of mixing coins of different quality. Besides addressing the quality propagation effect, the model captures two main factors behind users' intentions to mix: privacy enhancement and financial compensation. While distinct propagation policies have been proposed in the literature, they are of limited value to both practice and research if their system-wide implications are not theoretically analyzed. To this end, we make several relevant contributions. Specifically, we devise a variant of the game for each policy and solve it under two regimes of perfect and imperfect information. This allows us to discuss the policy implications from the design perspective of distributed ledger protocols and simultaneously provide theoretical support for arguments brought into the debate around fungibility and privacy.

The remainder of the paper is organized as follows. Using Bitcoin as a prominent example, we begin with preliminaries on cryptocurrencies, mixing transactions and propagation policies in Sect. 2. Then, in Sects. 3 and 4, we present and theoretically analyze the game for each introduced policy. The practical implications are discussed in Sect. 5. We briefly review related work in Sect. 6 and conclude with limitations and future research in Sect. 7.

2 Preliminaries

We use Bitcoin as running example, noting that the problem definition and solution approaches generalize to most cryptocurrencies known to date [7].

Bitcoin is a decentralized system that maintains a public, append-only ledger of confirmed transactions (known as the "*blockchain*") through collective efforts of a peer-to-peer network running a probabilistic consensus protocol [21]. Bitcoin addresses generated from public keys serve as account identifiers, whereas the knowledge of private keys indicates ownership of accounts and control over the coins in them. As no real-world identity is required to generate key pairs, each user may autonomously create an arbitrary number of Bitcoin addresses.

The blockchain stores a log of all valid transactions ever made in Bitcoin. A transaction is a digital record that consists of a list of inputs – references to existing addresses in the blockchain with a positive balance, and a list of outputs – addresses to which specified numbers of bitcoins are sent. Bitcoin is designed in a way that the total value of the inputs has to be spent in the outputs of a transaction. Otherwise, the difference is considered as a fee and paid to special nodes in the network (miners), who validate transactions and ensure a consistent and manipulation-resistant state of the blockchain.

2.1   Coin Mixing

A common thread of criticism of Bitcoin is the lack of full anonymity of payments [16]. With blockchain exploration tools at hand, one can browse through the complete transaction history and trace money flows back to their origins. Furthermore, experimental analyses of the limits of anonymity in Bitcoin [4,16,23,24] show that some users can be deanoynmized by applying appropriate heuristic techniques and consulting external information. Once a real name behind an address is found, the user's privacy might be jeopardized, as the blockchain allows a passive observer to look up other linked transactions [6]. Besides avoiding the re-use of public addresses, individuals seeking for greater anonymity may use available *mixing services.*

The concept of mixing coins of different users is fairly straightforward. Here, it refers to combining inputs and outputs of multiple parties in a single transaction. The current implementation of the protocol enables to build such collaborative transactions as it requires separate signatures for each public key specified in the transaction's inputs. With a sufficient number of participants engaged in a mixing transaction, it becomes harder to trace money flows by finding the connections between sending and receiving addresses. By extension, it gets even more difficult if mixing is done repeatedly. Nevertheless, individual values of inputs and outputs may still reveal enough information for a successful untangling of the transaction's inner flows [33].

The idea of and practical need for mixing has given rise to the emergence of special services and marketplaces designed to match supply and demand of anonymous transactions [17]. Here, we limit our focus on *CoinJoin*, as one specific example present in the Bitcoin system. In its simplest case, a CoinJoin transaction aggregates two or more inputs from two different users and contains at least two outputs of equal value. So, a blockchain observer cannot directly link these two outputs to the sending Bitcoin addresses. The larger the number of participants, the greater the anonymity of a CoinJoin transaction. However,

users interested in anonymity suffer from the necessity of finding other partners who are willing to participate in mixing at the same time. This limitation
explains the presence of special mixing services and platforms [17], where individuals supply their bitcoins for use in mixing transactions in exchange for a
small mixing fee.

2.2 Sources of Qualitative Differentiation

In addition to applications like colored coins [25] or possible cross-chain mixing
in the future, black- and whitelisting are potential sources of qualitative differentiation between coins. For the sake of intuitive illustration, we nonjudgementally
refer to blacklisting in this paper in order to model coins of different quality.

Although not fully implemented today, potential blacklisting of criminal
transactions as well as the issue of fungibility are subjects of intense interest
and ongoing debates. Since each output has an accessible and cryptographically
verifiable history of ownership, Bitcoin is not fungible. Also, the market participants' convention to treat bitcoins as if they were fungible has been repeatedly
called into question. Statements published on Bitcointalk.org and relevant sub-
reddit threads [5,30] illustrate this point:

*"Looking to buy an old 50 BTC block. Where to buy? I'll pay in bitcoin.
No FIAT/Alt coin. Willing to pay premium."*

blockCollector, Nov 11, 2015

*"BitPay is blacklisting certain bitcoins & rejecting customers. I'm certain
others are doing it too. Fungibility is most pressing issue IMO."*

TraderSteve, Sep 25, 2015

These examples support the conjecture underlying this work that coins differ
in their quality. Transaction blacklisting followed by the devaluation of marked
bitcoins has been suggested as a conceivable means of fighting financial crime
[19,20]. In practice, this may be realized by enforcing the centralized actors
(e.g., exchange services or wallet providers) or, alternatively, miners to consult
blacklists and disregard those transactions that try to reclaim funds from criminal proceeds. The notorious story of a recently exploited vulnerability in the
Decentralized Autonomous Organization (DAO), an Ethereum-based program,
has clearly demonstrated the doubtfulness and disagreement in the community
regarding how issues related to illicit use should be resolved and who would bear
the burden of doing it [27].

Several obstacles impede the effectiveness of blacklisting as a policy tool.
First, perpetrators can disguise the origins of money by resending their dirty
coins through as many fake addresses as they need. Therefore, the application of
blacklisting has to propagate through the entire transaction graph, rooted at the
offending transaction. Second, as law enforcement takes time, ordinary users will
inevitably face a risk of receiving allegedly clean coins that might be blacklisted
by authorities later [20]. These facts call for a detailed elaboration of blacklisting
propagation mechanisms and their effects on the ultimate quality of coins. This
is especially crucial in case of multi-input transactions comprising of both high-
and low-quality inputs.

2.3   Quality Propagation Policies

We consider three basic propagation techniques, termed as the **poison, haircut** and **seniority policies** [20], and assume that there is a consensus on one specific policy, implemented in the client software. To demonstrate the application of a propagation mechanism in each case, let us use an example of the transaction graph depicted in Fig. 1. The transaction of interest Z references outputs of the two preceding transactions X and Y. Suppose, the transaction X is discovered to be a ransom payment and, consequently, all of its outputs are added to the blacklist. Under the **poison policy**, every output of the transaction that has at least one blacklisted predecessor is invalidated completely. Consequently, all outputs of Z will be blacklisted.

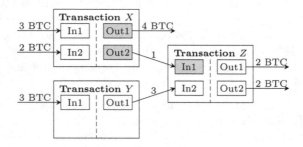

Fig. 1. Example of the transaction subgraph in Bitcoin. Gray areas indicate that both outputs of the transaction X are blacklisted.

The less drastic **haircut policy** dictates to devalue *all* outputs of a transaction proportionally to the total amount of blacklisted coins in its inputs. Thus, each output will contain an identical fraction of blacklisted coins, which is calculated as the fraction of the collective blacklisted value in the total transaction's input. Referring back to our example, both outputs of Z will have a partial devaluation of their nominal worth (25%, to be precise). As Bitcoin is divisible down to the smallest unit of one *satoshi* (worth 10^{-8} BTC), the haircut policy requires a special rule regulating blacklisting of minimum values and preventing money laundering through multiple tiny outputs. Such rule may dictate, for example, that the blacklisted value is rounded up to the full satoshi. (We ignore this quantization effect in the rest of this paper.)

Under the **seniority policy**, the output order and amounts determine how incoming blacklisted coins will be redistributed. Let us assume for simplicity that blacklisted coins are propagated in the order of the output list in a transaction (i.e., from top to bottom). Since the transaction X has one blacklisted input of the value 1 BTC, its first output of nominal value 2 BTC will be devalued by half. Similarly to the haircut policy and in contrast to the poison policy, the seniority regime does not change the total sum of blacklisted coins.

3   Model

Of particular interest for our study is to examine for each policy how users behave if coins of different qualities can hypothetically be mixed in one transaction. For that, we present two game-theoretic models of mixing, one with *perfect and complete* information and one with *imperfect and complete* information. A game of perfect information assumes that each player is aware of the prior actions chosen by other players, whereas imperfect information implies uncertainty regarding at least one move of another player. Complete information means that all players know all players' action sets and payoff functions [29, p. 136].

Two rational players A and B consider to transfer coins in a joint mixing transaction. Player A is a *privacy seeker* who initiates a mixing transaction, and B is a *privacy provider* who helps to establish a (minimum) anonymity set by participating in this transaction. Each player is endowed with an unlimited number of coins (i.e., transaction outputs) of different quality $q \in [0, 1]$. Coins with $q = 1$ are not on the blacklist and referred to as "good" or "clean" (e.g., coins passed through trusted exchanges), whereas coins with $q \neq 1$ are blacklisted or "bad" coins that can be linked to criminal activities. The term $(1 - q)$ can be alternatively interpreted as a fraction of the coin that has been devalued according to the applied policy.

The privacy seeker A desires more anonymity through mixing and pays player B the mixing fee $c \ll 1$ as a reward for joining a transaction. We assume that the fee for anonymity is payed out within the mixing transaction itself. Besides this financial compensation, player B also benefits from anonymity, as the mixing transaction anonymizes the identities of all participants. Player A selects $(1 + c)$ coins of quality q_a, while player B chooses one coin of quality q_b. So, the move of player i is the choice of q_i. In addition, the players have the outside strategy not to engage in mixing at all, as both need to sign a mixing transaction before it can be broadcasted to the network. Note that we explicitly disregard transaction fees payed to miners and assume that each player transfers funds to (possibly multiple) destination addresses *under her control*. Thus, players A and B own afterwards funds of 1 and $(1 + c)$ nominal value, respectively. The quality of these funds may however change once a specific quality propagation policy takes effect. We use the notation q_a' and q_b' to denote the respective post-transaction quality factors.

In the presence of qualitative differentiation and everything else being constant, a rational player always tries to maximize her own utility, which corresponds in our setting to the maximization of the value of coins at disposal. The utility of each player is therefore measured in units of good coins and expressed by three relevant components: (1) the subjective value of anonymity the player attributes to a mixing transaction; (2) the post-transaction value of the funds held by the player; (3) the compensation fee paid by the privacy seeker A to the privacy provider B. We first define each component and later specify the payoff function of each player formally.

In reality, the perceived anonymity of an individual mixing transaction depends on multiple aspects (e.g., the number of participants, the number of inputs and outputs and their exact quantities, repeated mixing etc.). Since transaction parties value anonymity differently and it is not trivial to quantify it, we express the benefit of (somewhat more) anonymity by a relative unit gain equal to one good coin. Suppose, without loss of generality,[1] that player A gains one unit of anonymity, whereas player B gains some level $\tau_b \in [0, 1]$. $\tau_b = 1$ indicates that both players value anonymity of a mixing transaction equally; $\tau_b = 0.5$ means that player B values it half as much as player A; $\tau_b = 0$ means that player B receives no benefit in terms of improved anonymity from mixing. Note that the gain in anonymity is discounted by the post-transaction qualities q_a' and q_b'. There is less value in having bad coins anonymized. Moreover, this avoids corner cases where players have incentives to mix at the risk of receiving bad coins.

The post-transaction qualities endogenously follow from the choice variables q_a and q_b and the applied quality propagation policy. Unlike the seniority policy, the poison and haircut policies allow us to formally define q_a' and q_b' as a function of the pre-transaction quality factors q_a and q_b. Under the poison policy, all coins are either good ($q_i = 1$) or bad ($q_i = 0$). Table 1 specifies the values of q_a' and q_b' for all possible combinations of q_a and q_b. Under the haircut policy, the levels of q_a' and q_b' are equal and, besides the choice variables q_a and q_b, depend on the parameter c. Since the fee (of quality q_a) is transferred in the mixing transaction, it influences the total transaction amount as well as the total level of blacklisted coins in the inputs.

Table 1. Post-transaction quality factors

Policy	q_a	q_b	q_a'	q_b'
	1	1	1	1
Poison	1	0	0	0
	0	1	0	0
	0	0	0	0
Haircut	$q_a \in [0,1]$	$q_b \in [0,1]$	$\frac{q_a \cdot (1+c) + q_b}{2+c}$	$\frac{q_a \cdot (1+c) + q_b}{2+c}$

With regard to the last component of the payoff function, the mixing fee has to be discounted by q_a in the payoff of player A and by q_b' in the payoff of player B in order to measure its value relatively to one clean coin. Thus, the players' payoffs π_i after successful mixing is given as follows:

$$\pi_A = 1 \cdot q_a' + 1 \cdot q_a' - c \cdot q_a = 2 \cdot q_a' - c \cdot q_a; \tag{1}$$
$$\pi_B = \tau_b \cdot q_b' + 1 \cdot q_b' + c \cdot q_b' = (\tau_b + 1 + c) \cdot q_b'. \tag{2}$$

---

[1] Otherwise, switch players A and B.

If one of the players disagrees to mix and chooses the outside option, the payoffs are as follows:

$$\pi_{A\perp} = 1 \cdot q_a + c \cdot q_a = (1 + c) \cdot q_a; \tag{3}$$

$$\pi_{B\perp} = 1 \cdot q_b. \tag{4}$$

4 Results

We first present the game of perfect and complete information for tractability and as a benchmark, before we consider the game of imperfect (and complete) information, in which the players choose coin qualities q_i simultaneously.

4.1 Perfect Information: Sequential Game

The model of perfect information assumes q_a and q_b to be common knowledge. This means that blacklists have to be public and always up-to-date, e.g., law enforcement agencies immediately discover and blacklist offending transactions. With public blacklists, each player can check the quality of the other player's coin before signing and broadcasting a mixing transaction to the network.

Figure 2 shows an extensive form of the sequential game by taking the poison policy as an example. The presented sequence of moves can be extended to the other two regimes, too, by considering a larger set of actions available to both players. Player A initiates the game by committing to the quality of her inputs q_a and the fee level c. Being informed about that choice, player B decides whether to mix with A or not. If B prefers to dismiss, the game is over. Otherwise, player B chooses the coin of a particular quality q_b and notifies A about it. Player A learns about the choice of B and makes the final move of the game. Reciprocally, if A rejects to mix with B, both players exit with the payoffs defined in Eqs. (3) and (4). Otherwise, players form a mixing transaction and get the payoffs as prescribed by (1) and (2). Under the seniority policy, players may additionally negotiate the order and amounts of transaction outputs until they reach a consensus or someone rejects to partner with.

Poison Policy. We apply a backward induction procedure in order to analyze the game and find subgame perfect Nash equilibria. As the game is of perfect information, there are seven subgames in total, labeled Γ_1 through Γ_7 in Fig. 2. Under backward induction, the subgames Γ_4–Γ_7 are solved first. In subgame Γ_4, player A agrees to mix the clean coin if $c \leq 0.5$ and exits otherwise. In subgame Γ_5, player A always exits due to the undesirable propagation of blacklisting. In subgames Γ_6 and Γ_7, player A is indifferent between the two available choices. Taking the respective equilibrium for each of the subgames Γ_4–Γ_7 and going backward in the game tree, we can see that the game has many subgame perfect Nash equilibria[2], all of which contain either the path:

$$(q_a = 1, q_b = 1 \text{ and mix})$$

---

[2] Note that the game of perfect information under the poison regime has even more Nash equilibria. However, these are not subgame perfect.

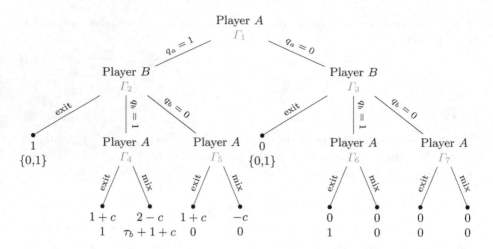

Fig. 2. Poison policy: game of perfect information in extensive form.

if $c \leq 0.5$; or otherwise the path:

$$(q_a = 1, q_b = 1 \text{ and exit}).$$

So, both players mix clean coins if $c \leq 0.5$, but player A refuses to pay a too high fee for anonymity.

Haircut Policy. The haircut policy implies the presence of coins of any quality in the range of $[0, 1]$. Player A signs a mixing transaction if the payoff after mixing π_A is greater or equal than the payoff without mixing $\pi_{A\perp}$:

$$2 \cdot \frac{q_a \cdot (1 + c) + q_b}{2 + c} - c \cdot q_a \geq (1 + c) \cdot q_a,$$

$$\frac{q_a}{q_b} \leq \frac{2}{2 \cdot c^2 + 3 \cdot c}, \quad q_b \neq 0, \ c \neq 0. \tag{5}$$

Analogously for player B:

$$(\tau_b + 1 + c) \cdot \frac{q_a \cdot (1 + c) + q_b}{2 + c} \geq 1 \cdot q_b,$$

$$\frac{q_a}{q_b} \geq \frac{(1 - \tau_b)}{(1 + c) \cdot (1 + c + \tau_b)}, \quad q_b \neq 0. \tag{6}$$

Players A and B agree to mix with each other if both inequalities (5) and (6) hold. Figure 3 shows the corresponding game outcomes over the space defined by the quality ratio q_a/q_b and the fee c for three distinct values of $\tau_b \in \{0, 0.5, 1\}$. Region S_1 depicts all combinations of the model parameters which result in successful mixing for $\tau_b = 0$, regions $S1 \cup S2$ depict the same for $\tau_b = 0.5$;

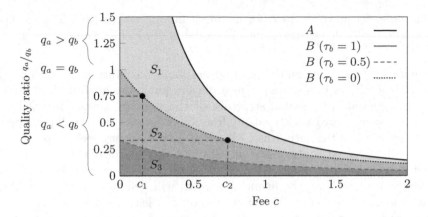

Fig. 3. Haircut policy: existence of equilibrium solutions in the game of perfect information as a function of the fee c and the quality ratio q_a/q_b for three different values of $\tau_b \in [0, 0.5, 1]$. (Color figure online)

regions $S1 \cup S2 \cup S3$ apply to $\tau_b = 1$. In the corner case $q_b = 0$, mixing happens only if player A wishes to mix a bad coin, too.

If player B values transaction anonymity as much as player A, i.e., $\tau_b = 1$, B is willing to partner with A regardless of the fee level c or player A's coin quality q_a. This is due to the fact that even in the worst possible case for player B ($q_a = 0$, $q_b = 1$, and $c = 0$), the degradation in the coin quality ($q_b' = 0.5$) is fully compensated by the gain in anonymity $\tau_b \cdot q_b' = 0.5$. Thus, the space of successful game outcomes in $S1 \cup S2 \cup S3$ is limited only by inequality (5), which corresponds to the uppermost line in Fig. 3. Since the payoff of B is directly proportional to the quality factor of her coin, it is in her best interest to offer the good coin $q_b = 1$ for mixing. Therefore, the Nash equilibria in case $\tau_b = 1$ correspond to the set of action profiles $\{(q_a, q_b) \mid 0 < q_a \leq 1, q_b = 1\}$. If player B values anonymity half as much as player A, i.e., $\tau_b = 0.5$, her best response is defined by the *dashed (green)* line. If A does not offer any fee, B chooses the coin of quality q_b, which is three times higher than q_a. If player A wishes to mix with the coin of higher quality, i.e., $q_b > 3q_a$, she has to compensate player B by offering a strictly positive fee. The exact level of c for a desirable quality ratio can be derived from inequality (6). If player B does not value the anonymity of a mixing transaction, i.e., $\tau_b = 0$, and there is no financial compensation c, she will supply the coin of the same quality ($q_a = q_b$).

In reality, however, the search cost associated with finding another transaction party with exactly the same quality level may be prohibitive. Similarly to conventional trading and payment markets [9], search frictions can be overcome by offering compensation to the enabling party with (slightly) better coins. If B does not have a coin of the required quality and can mix a coin of higher quality instead, she will agree to participate in the mixing transaction in exchange for a higher fee. The greater the difference in the quality of the coins of players A and

B, the more A has to pay to B for joining a mixing transaction. This explains the monotonically decreasing shape of inequality (6) in Fig. 3 when $\tau_b < 1$.

Seniority Policy. This policy grants users more flexibility in controlling the effect of blacklisting propagation. Since players know the quality of all inputs, they can negotiate an internal structure of the mixing transaction until it is designed in such a way that low-quality fractions of inputs of both players appear at the beginning of the output list. Player A, as the privacy-seeking party, may also be willing to list some of her outputs first and sacrifice at the expense of gained anonymity up to half of the clean portion of her coins. Player B, who is interested in receiving the financial reward, will demand to list her address for the incoming fee c at the bottom of the output list. These order constraints may however leak sufficient information for successful matching of the relations between inputs and outputs of a mixing transaction. A passive observer of the blockchain may look up available blacklist data and, knowing the exact transacting amounts, may succeed in deanonymizing the mixing transaction.

The seniority policy can be reduced to the haircut policy if the players agree to split up blacklisted coins equally by randomly alternating the order of their outputs for the sake of anonymity. However, the players can be better off in terms of anonymity while maintaining the quality distribution if they adhere to one constant value for all (blacklisted and clean) transaction outputs. They can divide their input funds into multiple outputs of the same amount and randomize the order of their outputs within the upper subset of blacklisted outputs (*the blacklisted bin*) and the lower subset of clean outputs (*the clean bin*). This way, the attacker is left with a 50:50% chance of correctly differentiating between the output of A and the output of B, whereas the players can preserve the original quality of their funds. The easiest, however impracticable solution would be to use one satoshi as the size of each output. In order to reduce the number of outputs by orders of magnitude, the players can express q_a and q_b as rational numbers in the standard form and use a reciprocal of the least common divisor of the denominators as constant value for all outputs.

Let us demonstrate one numerical example with $q_a = 3/4$ and $q_b = 1/2$ (the mixing fee is disregarded). Following the above logic, each player splits up her coin into four different outputs of the nominal value 0.25. The blacklisted bin will consist of one output of player A and two outputs of player B. The clean bin contains three outputs of player A and two outputs of player B. The order of the outputs within each bin must be random in order to get anonymity. As a result, the post-transaction quality factors q_a' and q_b' do not change and the players still enjoy transaction anonymity. Figure 4 in Appendix A illustrates this example (along with two other specific cases).

4.2 Imperfect Information: Simultaneous-Move Game

Since law enforcement agencies are unable to detect and mark illegal transactions in real time, there is always a risk that already confirmed transactions may get blacklisted later. Due to this time delay, users have to deal with the uncertainty about the quality of inputs when forming and signing a transaction. While they have more information about the origins and nature of their own coins (compared to passive observers of the public blockchain), they cannot know for sure qualities of all other inputs. We model this more realistic case of mixing in a simultaneous-move game, in which players A and B choose q_a and q_b simultaneously.

Poison Policy. Since all circulated coins are either good ($q_i = 1$) or bad ($q_i = 0$), players have only two possible strategies, which enables us to represent the model in normal form (see Table 2). The resulting payoffs are calculated by substituting the pre- and post-transaction quality factors (given in Table 1) in the payoff functions (1) and (2).

Table 2. Poison policy: game of imperfect information in normal form

		Player B	
		$q_b = 1$	$q_b = 0$
Player A	$q_a = 1$	$2 - c,\ \tau_b + 1 + c$	$-c,\ 0$
	$q_a = 0$	$0,\ 0$	$0,\ 0$

The presented model has two pure-strategy Nash equilibria ($q_a = 1, q_b = 1$) and ($q_a = 0, q_b = 0$). Note that the latter Nash equilibrium is weak, as player B gets the same payoff by changing her strategy to $q_b = 1$. Although the action profile ($q_a = 0, q_b = 0$) is a Nash equilibrium, it does not correspond to the social optimum of the game: the sum of the payoffs of both players reaches its maximum when ($q_a = 1, q_b = 1$). Similarly to Akerlof's classic market for lemons [3], the poison policy leads to a market failure because of adverse selection. Without knowing the true quality of coins, nobody is willing to mix good coins at the risk of encountering bad coins at least in one input of the mixing transaction.

Haircut Policy. Over time, the haircut policy results in the circulation of coins of varying qualities. In the absence of an ability to perfectly differentiate coins by quality, users of mixing services will make decisions based on their expectations about the average quality of all coins observed in the mixing market. Substituting q_a and q_b with the expected average quality $\bar{q}$ in inequalities (5) and (6), respectively, the necessary conditions for players A and B to participate in the mixing transaction are as follows:

$$q_a \leq \frac{2 \cdot \bar{q}}{2 \cdot c^2 + 3 \cdot c}, \quad c \neq 0; \tag{7}$$

$$q_b \leq \frac{(\tau_b + 1 + c)(1 + c)}{1 - \tau_b} \cdot \bar{q}, \quad \tau_b \neq 1. \tag{8}$$

If player B values anonymity highly ($\tau_b = 1$), the mixing transaction happens regardless of the expected average quality and the fee level. The more interesting scenario is, however, when player B is solely motivated by the financial reward ($\tau_b = 0$). In this case, inequality (8) takes the form $q_b \leq (1 + c)^2 \cdot \overline{q}$. If player A does not pay a fee, player B has no incentive to supply a coin of quality better than the average quality $\overline{q}$. Otherwise, the fee incentivizes the privacy provider B to offer the coin of marginally higher quality.

It is reasonable to expect that criminals, who know with certainty which of their funds originate from illicit transactions, may engage in mixing for the purpose of money laundering. They have an incentive to supply coins of the worst quality in the hope of getting better ones. As other players can anticipate this behavior, the expected quality factor declines. This further drives owners of better coins out of the market and fuels the race to the bottom of $\overline{q}$, eventually leading to the presence of only bad coins in the mixing market. Consequently, there will be no equilibrium outcome with a strictly positive payoff for both players, and, given the absence of credible signaling mechanisms, the market for mixing coins of (marginally) good quality will not exist.

Seniority Policy. Given the uncertainty regarding q_i, each player will prefer her addresses to be included at the bottom of the output list. Since the seniority policy can be reduced to the haircut regime, the above reasoning and solution can be applied here, too. Facing the risk of getting coins of worse quality, the players will prefer to mix rather bad coins than good ones.

It might seem at first glance that the seniority police allows for a modification of the model to a signaling game, because the output order can convey information and it is linked to payoff. In general, signaling games model strategic settings of incomplete information in which players can observe the actions of their opponents (*signals*) to make inferences about hidden information [28]. A fundamental principle is that signals must be costly to produce, or have costly consequences. This is what differentiates signals from "cheap talk" and guarantees their reliability. To enable mixing in more situations, players must be able to signal that they are committed to supply coins of high quality. A corresponding output order must be more costly to sign for players with bad coins than for players with good coins. However, as owners of bad coins have, in the strong sense, nothing to lose, the only possible signal is that of supplying low quality coins, which unfortunately does not lead to more mixing equilibria.

5   Discussion

This work is an attempt to conceptualize a formal model of the interplay of users in the presence of qualitative differentiation between cryptocoins. Although we motivate the game by taking the illustrative example of mixing services and blacklisting, the model (of imperfect information) can be generalized to a more common case where an individual user needs to decide whether to combine own coins of potentially different qualities in one multi-input transaction.

The regime of perfect information suggests a sequential game. It is applicable if blacklists are timely and public. Under these assumptions, mixing services persist. The poison policy dictates users to mix clean coins (if at all), while the haircut and seniority policies provides certain conditions under which users are also willing to mix coins of varying qualities. Moreover, the seniority policy can (approximately) be reduced to the haircut policy.

The regime of imperfect information suggests a simultaneous-move game. It leads to the failure of the market for mixing of (marginally) good coins under the poison policy, and our preliminary results let us conjecture that the outcome applies to the haircut and seniority policies as well. (We plan to refine the analysis in a revised version of this work.) With uncertainty about a coin's quality and in the presence of criminals interested in using mixers for money laundering, owners of good coins have no incentive to seek anonymity at the risk of mixing with bad coins. In this regard, blacklisting can be viewed as an effective economic mechanism to make mixers less attractive or even to dry them out.

6 Related Work

Our work is related to blacklisting content (or content providers), and therefore to Internet censorship. It also connects to anonymity online. Both are contentious topics; the former more than the latter.

Governments, Internet intermediaries, and organizational network administrators use many kinds of filtering techniques to intentionally limit or block access to online content, resources, or services [1]. Among them, blacklists of malware-infected or phishing sites are perhaps the best known and socially most accepted example. Although many empirical studies exist on the effectiveness, coverage, and sharing of phishing blacklists [26,31,32], there is a limited number of works examining them from a formal viewpoint. Edwards et al. [11] present a simple Markov model to study how malware infections might be contained through blacklisting, while Hofmeyr et al. [14] model potential policy interventions for controlling malware. They analyze the trade-off between prevented harm and collateral damage caused by blocking legitimate traffic.

Blacklisting has been put forward in the context of anonymous communication systems, such as Tor, JAP, or Mixminion, too. In [13], the authors formally define anonymous blacklisting systems and specify their security and privacy features. Such systems should allow users to authenticate anonymously with a service provider, while enabling the service provider to revoke access from abusive users without knowing their identities.

Decentralized anonymity infrastructures (namely, mix-nets [10]) are also studied from an economic perspective. Since anonymity can be obtained only within an anonymity set [22], the authors of [2] explore with a game-theoretic approach economic incentives of users to participate in message anonymization services. The also suggest several possible mechanisms to avoid the problem of public good with free riding.

In the growing literature on cryptocurrencies, the most closely related works can be classified into those that concern the implications of blacklisting and transaction risk scoring [20], and those that conduct various kinds of blockchain analyses in order to examine the (lack of) anonymity in the Bitcoin network [4,16,18,23,24]. Our paper draws on the ideas initially set out in [20], which discusses the potential use of blacklisting in Bitcoin and introduces the propagation policies. It is also inspired by works on the design [8] and use of centralized and decentralized mixing services [18], as well as efforts to detect and break mixing schemes [33].

7   Concluding Remarks

This paper tackles the issue of non-fungibility of decentralized currencies and discusses its potential implications on the behavior of users. Specifically, it proposes a game-theoretic model of mixing coins of different quality under the regimes of perfect and imperfect information and analyzes three variants of it, one for each of three propagation policies. It finds the optimal strategies of players in the game of perfect information, and confirms that a Nash equilibrium in case of imperfect information is to mix bad coins only. Although the current operation of distributed ledgers is closer to the regime of imperfect information, we can still observe the existence of mixers. This is despite a surge of startups specializing in blockchain intelligence, allegedly to supply critical intermediaries, such as exchanges, with private blacklists. We conjecture that this discrepancy between theory and practice is due to several reasons, chiefly limited scope, lack of enforcement, or lack of reliability of existing blacklists. Alternative explanations include very high valuations of anonymity by some users, or simply nativity paired with luck of escaping negative experience.

There are several potential avenues for more rigorous and general models of mixing. First, the measurement of anonymity needs to be refined by taking other relevant transaction features into account. Second, the model needs to generalize to multiple players who choose inputs of arbitrary nominal value, but are constrained in terms of quality. Third, future research should elaborate more on market mechanisms for the survival of mixing services, e.g., by designing possible sanctions for the use of bad coins. The model can also be advanced by taking miner fees and the size of transactions into account. Finally, future work could examine whether it is possible to enforce side payments of the mixing fee without compromising the anonymity of any of the participants, and how this changes the game and its solutions.

Acknowledgments. The authors are grateful to Daniel G. Arce for his insightful comments on an earlier version of this paper. The authors are responsible for all remaining errors and omissions. This work was funded by the German Bundesministerium für Bildung und Forschung (BMBF) under grant agreement No. 13N13505 and by Archimedes Privatstiftung, Innsbruck, Austria.

A   Appendix

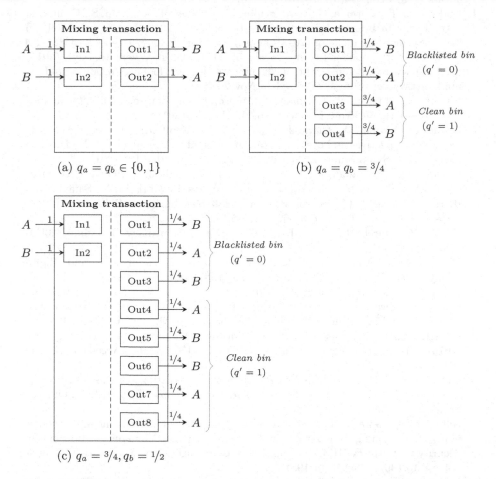

Fig. 4. Seniority policy: examples of mixing transactions in the perfect information regime: (a) shows the case when both coins are either good or bad (2 outputs); (b) – when both coins are of the same quality $q \in (0, 1)$ (4 outputs); (c) – when coins are of different quality (the number of outputs equals two times the least common divisor of the denominators of q_a and q_b expressed as rational numbers). The mixing fee is disregarded in these examples ($c = 0$).

References

1. Aceto, G., Pescapé, A.: Internet censorship detection: a survey. Comput. Netw. **83**, 381–421 (2015)
2. Acquisti, A., Dingledine, R., Syverson, P.: On the economics of anonymity. In: Wright, R.N. (ed.) FC 2003. LNCS, vol. 2742, pp. 84–102. Springer, Heidelberg (2003). https://doi.org/10.1007/978-3-540-45126-6_7

3. Akerlof, G.A.: The market for "Lemon": quality uncertainty and the market mechanism. Q. J. Econ. **84**(3), 161–167 (1970)
4. Androulaki, E., Karame, G.O., Roeschlin, M., Scherer, T., Capkun, S.: Evaluating user privacy in bitcoin. In: Sadeghi, A.-R. (ed.) FC 2013. LNCS, vol. 7859, pp. 34–51. Springer, Heidelberg (2013). https://doi.org/10.1007/978-3-642-39884-1_4
5. blockCollector: Looking to buy an old 50 BTC block. Where to buy? (2015). https://www.reddit.com/r/Bitcoin/comments/3sg8vm/looking_to_buy_an_old_50_btc_block_where_to_buy/. Accessed 14 Nov 2016
6. Böhme, R., Christin, N., Edelman, B., Moore, T.: Bitcoin: economics, technology, and governance. J. Econ. Perspect. **29**(2), 213–238 (2015)
7. Bonneau, J., Miller, A., Clark, J., Narayanan, A., Kroll, J.A., Felten, E.W.: SoK: research perspectives and challenges for bitcoin and cryptocurrencies. In: Proceedings of IEEE Symposium on Security and Privacy, pp. 104–121 (2015)
8. Bonneau, J., Narayanan, A., Miller, A., Clark, J., Kroll, J.A., Felten, E.W.: Mixcoin: anonymity for bitcoin with accountable mixes. In: Christin, N., Safavi-Naini, R. (eds.) FC 2014. LNCS, vol. 8437, pp. 486–504. Springer, Heidelberg (2014). https://doi.org/10.1007/978-3-662-45472-5_31
9. Chacko, G., Jurek, J., Stafford, E.: The price of immediacy. J. Financ. **63**(3), 1253–1290 (2008)
10. Chaum, D.L.: Untraceable electronic mail, return addresses, and digital pseudonyms. Commun. ACM **24**(2), 84–90 (1981)
11. Edwards, B., Moore, T., Stelle, G., Hofmeyr, S., Forrest, S.: Beyond the blacklist: modeling malware spread and the effect of interventions. In: Proceedings of 2012 Workshop on New Security Paradigms, pp. 53–66. ACM, New York (2012)
12. ExpertNeeded: Blockchain analysis help needed. Major money laundering case. (2016). https://bitcointalk.org/index.php?topic=1568048.0/. Accessed 14 Nov 2016
13. Henry, R., Goldberg, I.: Formalizing anonymous blacklisting systems. In: Proceedings of IEEE Symposium on Security and Privacy, pp. 81–95. IEEE Computer Society, Washington, DC (2011)
14. Hofmeyr, S., Moore, T., Forrest, S., Edwards, B., Stelle, G.: Modeling internet-scale policies for cleaning up malware. In: Schneier, B. (ed.) Economics of Information Security and Privacy III. LNCS, pp. 149–170. Springer, New York (2013). https://doi.org/10.1007/978-1-4614-1981-5_7
15. Meiklejohn, S., Orlandi, C.: Privacy-enhancing overlays in bitcoin. In: Brenner, M., Christin, N., Johnson, B., Rohloff, K. (eds.) FC 2015. LNCS, vol. 8976, pp. 127–141. Springer, Heidelberg (2015). https://doi.org/10.1007/978-3-662-48051-9_10
16. Meiklejohn, S., Pomarole, M., Jordan, G., Levchenko, K., McCoy, D., Voelker, G.M., Savage, S.: A fistful of bitcoins: characterizing payments among men with no names. In: Proceedings of 2013 Conference on Internet Measurement Conference, pp. 127–140. ACM, New York (2013)
17. Möser, M., Böhme, R.: Join me on a market for anonymity. In: Proceedings of 15th Annual Workshop on the Economics of Information Security, Berkeley, CA, USA (2016)
18. Möser, M., Böhme, R.: Anonymous alone? Measuring bitcoin's second-generation anonymization techniques. In: IEEE Security & Privacy on the Blockchain (IEEE S&B), Paris, France (2017)
19. Möser, M., Böhme, R., Breuker, D.: An inquiry into money laundering tools in the bitcoin ecosystem. In: APWG eCrime Researchers Summit (ECRIME), San Francisco, CA, USA, pp. 1–14 (2013)

20. Möser, M., Böhme, R., Breuker, D.: Towards risk scoring of bitcoin transactions. In: Böhme, R., Brenner, M., Moore, T., Smith, M. (eds.) FC 2014. LNCS, vol. 8438, pp. 16–32. Springer, Heidelberg (2014). https://doi.org/10.1007/978-3-662-44774-1_2
21. Nakamoto, S.: Bitcoin: a peer-to-peer electronic cash system (2008). http://www.bitcoin.org/bitcoin.pdf. Accessed 14 Nov 2016
22. Pfitzmann, A., Hansen, M.: Anonymity, unlinkability, unobservability, pseudonymity, and identity management - a consolidated proposal for terminology, Technical report (2005)
23. Reid, F., Harrigan, M.: An analysis of anonymity in the bitcoin system. In: Altshuler, Y., Elovici, Y., Cremers, B.A., Aharony, N., Pentland, A. (eds.) Security and Privacy in Social Networks, pp. 197–223. Springer, New York (2013)
24. Ron, D., Shamir, A.: Quantitative analysis of the full bitcoin transaction graph. In: Sadeghi, A.-R. (ed.) FC 2013. LNCS, vol. 7859, pp. 6–24. Springer, Heidelberg (2013). https://doi.org/10.1007/978-3-642-39884-1_2
25. Rosenfeld, M.: Overview of colored coins (2015). https://bitcoil.co.il/BitcoinX.pdf. Accessed 14 Nov 2016
26. Sheng, S., Wardman, B., Warner, G., Cranor, L.F., Hong, J., Zhang, C.: An empirical analysis of phishing blacklists. In: Proceedings of 6th Conference on Email and Anti-Spam, CEAS 2009 (2009)
27. Siegel, D.: Understanding the DAO hack for journalists (2016). https://medium.com/@pullnews/understanding-the-dao-hack-for-journalists-2312dd43e993. Accessed 14 Nov 2016
28. Spence, M.: Job market signaling. Q. J. Econ. **87**(3), 355–374 (1973)
29. Tadelis, S.: Game Theory: An Introduction. Princeton University Press, Princeton (2013)
30. TraderSteve: Bitpay is blacklisting certain bitcoins & rejecting customers. (2015). https://www.reddit.com/r/Bitcoin/comments/3mea6b/bitpay_is_blacklisting_certain_bitcoins_rejecting/. Accessed 14 Nov 2016
31. Tsalis, N., Virvilis, N., Mylonas, A., Apostolopoulos, T., Gritzalis, D.: Browser blacklists: the utopia of phishing protection. In: Obaidat, M.S., Holzinger, A., Filipe, J. (eds.) ICETE 2014. CCIS, vol. 554, pp. 278–293. Springer, Cham (2015). https://doi.org/10.1007/978-3-319-25915-4_15
32. Vasek, M., Weeden, M., Moore, T.: Measuring the impact of sharing abuse data with web hosting providers. In: Proceedings of 2016 ACM on Workshop on Information Sharing and Collaborative Security, WISCS 2016, pp. 71–80. ACM, New York (2016)
33. Yanovich, Y., Mischenko, P., Ostrovskiy, A.: Shared send untangling in bitcoin. In: Working Paper, Bitfury Group Limited (2016). http://bitfury.com/content/5-white-papers-research/bitfury_whitepaper_shared_send_untangling_in_bitcoin_8_24_2016.pdf. Accessed 14 Nov 2016

Smart Contracts Make Bitcoin Mining Pools Vulnerable

Yaron Velner[1], Jason Teutsch[2], and Loi Luu[3(✉)]

[1] The Hebrew University of Jerusalem, Jerusalem, Israel
[2] TrueBit Foundation, Tel Aviv, Israel
[3] School of Computing, National University of Singapore, Singapore, Singapore
loiluu@comp.nus.edu.sg

Abstract. Despite their incentive structure flaws, mining pools account for more than 95% of Bitcoin's computation power. This paper introduces an attack against mining pools in which a malicious party pays pool members to withhold their solutions from their pool operator. We show that an adversary with a tiny amount of computing power and capital can execute this attack. Smart contracts enforce the malicious party's payments, and therefore miners need neither trust the attacker's intentions nor his ability to pay. Assuming pool members are rational, an adversary with a single mining ASIC can, in theory, destroy all big mining pools without losing any money (and even make some profit).

1 Introduction

Bitcoin and emerging cryptocurrencies offer trustless platforms for users to transact and run decentralized applications. Each cryptocurrency maintains a peer-to-peer distributed *ledger* of prior transactions that records all activities in the network. Network participants run a consensus protocol called Nakamoto consensus to agree on the state of the ledger [1]. In every epoch, Nakamoto consensus probabilistically elects a leader who demonstrates a solution to a computational "proof-of-work" puzzle [1]. The leader proposes and broadcasts a *block* which includes set of new transactions to be appended to the ledger. He then receives a reward (12.5 Bitcoin, or 12,000 USD as of Jan. 1, 2017) if his block is *valid*, or accepted by the network.

Pooled Mining. Finding a valid solution to a Bitcoin proof-of-work puzzle, or "mining," is a probabilistic process which requires massive computational resources. Solo miners with modest computational power experience extremely high income variance. For example, even a state of the art AntMiner S9 mining hardware[1] mines only one Bitcoin block per year on average. To reduce income variance, miners often join their computational resources through "mining pools" and share the corresponding block rewards. In a mining pool, a designated pool

---

[1] https://www.bitmaintech.com/productDetail.htm?pid=00020160529072433755530Dc JIoK0654.

© International Financial Cryptography Association 2017
M. Brenner et al. (Eds.): FC 2017 Workshops 2017, LNCS 10323, pp. 298–316, 2017.
https://doi.org/10.1007/978-3-319-70278-0_19

"operator" distributes *share tasks*, each which has a positive probability of yielding a valid block. Thus larger pools expect to find blocks more frequently than smaller ones. When a miner's submitted solution yields a valid block, the pool operator submits it to the network, obtains the block reward, and divides it fairly among all pool members in proportion to their contributed computation power.

Pools Reward Model Vulnerability. Pools are susceptible to the classical *block withholding* attack [2] where a miner sends only partial proof-of-work to the pool manager and discards full proof-of-work. As the structure of the block header is determined by the pool operator, an attacker cannot claim the block reward for himself. On the surface, block withholding attacks might not seem profitable, however, miners outside the victim pool may benefit from block withholding. Dropped blocks increase outside miners' computation power relative to the rest of the network [3], and in the long run, outside miners will mine more blocks (see formal analysis in Sect. 3).

The Attack. Smart contracts are unstoppable programs that live on Ethereum's blockchain [4] and have their own executable code and internal states, including storage for variable values and currency balance. In this paper we introduce smart contracts that reward pool miners who withhold blocks. We analyze attacks comprised by such smart contracts under the assumption that miners are rational and aim to maximize their short-term profits (we analyze the miners' incentives in Sect. 3). We show that when the attack is targeted towards big mining pools who employ the "pay-per-share" scheme, the attack is profitable even for an attacker running a single hardware unit. Moreover, such an attacker could in theory drain all revenue and profit from a big pool. We note that in practice, pool operators that witness significant decrease in their revenues may have to close their operations before being drained out of all revenues and profits. Hence a successful deployment of our attack would undermine the entire pooled mining model.

The use of smart contracts is crucial in order for the attack to be successful. Indeed, it is unlikely that miners would collaborate with such an attack unless their payment is guaranteed. Moreover, rewarding via smart contracts makes it possible for the attacker to remain anonymous and prevents other parties from targeting and shutting him down (e.g., with a denial of service attack).

Contributions. The contributions of our paper are as follows:

- We show how to mathematically prove that a block has been withheld and implement an Ethereum smart contract that rewards block withholding (Sect. 4).
- We show that, under mild assumptions, the smart contract could be implemented with Bitcoin transactions (Appendix A) and we show how one can use an Ethereum smart contract to enforce these assumptions (Appendix B). Bitcoin contracts are more desirable as they save the need to run a full Ethereum node.

– We show how the attacker can form a pool of block withholders in order to reduce the withholders variance, and we analyze the incentives for withholders to withhold a proof of block withholding (Sect. 5).

Comparison with Classical Block Withholding Attacks. Block withholding attacks have been known almost from the beginning of Bitcoin [2]. In recent years it has become apparent that miners can profit from mining for two pools while withholding their full solutions in one of them [3,5,6]. However, the profit from such an attack is relatively small, and an attacker would have to control a lot of computation power (e.g., over 1% of Bitcoin's computation power) in order to cause significant losses (e.g., over 5% decrease in revenues) for large pools (e.g., see [3]).

In this work we propose to pay other miners to withhold blocks. In Sect. 3 we show that an attacker with only 0.0000002% of Bitcoin's computation power can reduce the revenue of a big pool to zero without any financial losses on his side. In fact the theoretical outcome of our attack (if miners are fully rational) is equivalent to a classical block withholding attack in which a miner rents Bitcoin's entire hash power and withholds all the blocks that he finds.

Other Cryptocurrencies. In this paper we focus on attacks on Bitcoin mining pools. Nevertheless, in principle, smart contracts undermine the pooled mining model of all cryptocurrencies. However some cryptocurrencies, e.g., Ethereum, might be currently resilient to such an attack due to some technical issues that we describe in Sect. 4.

2   Background

2.1   Mining and Pool Mining

Bitcoin and popular cryptocurrencies like Ethereum [4] and Zcash [7] maintain a global ledger between all participants in the networks. The network participants run a consensus protocol called Nakamoto consensus to reach agreement on the state of the shared ledger [1]. At a high level, Nakamoto consensus works by probabilistically electing a leader in every 10 min epoch. The leader will then propose a set of additions (*e.g.*, transactions) to the ledger; other participants "apply" these additions after verifying that these changes are valid. Then the next epoch begins. As of this writing, the election happens via a *mining* process in which network participants have to solve computationally hard puzzles (i.e., proof-of-work) which probabilistically yields one solution per 10 min (epoch time in Bitcoin) on average. Technically, network participants, or miners, have to find a valid `nonce` satisfying the following condition:

$$\text{sha256}(\text{sha256}(\text{Block Template} \;||\; \texttt{Nonce})) \leq D \qquad (1)$$

in which "Block Template" includes the miner's proposed changes to the ledger, and D is a global parameter which indicates the difficulty of finding a valid solution.

Solving a proof-of-work (PoW) puzzle, or finding a valid block, requires an enormous amount of computation. For example, at the time of writing, D is a 256-bit integer with approximately 80 leading zero bits. Thus finding a valid PoW solution requires on average 2^{80} sha256 calculations. A normal workstation which can perform a million sha256 calculations per second will expect to spend millions of years to find a PoW solution. Thus, often miners join forces and form *mining pools* to solve PoW puzzles together. The idea of pooled mining is to ask everyone in the pool to find solutions (or *shares*) to easier PoW puzzles where each share has some probability of being a valid solution for the main PoW puzzle. Specifically, pool members find all `nonce` so that the result of the hash in Eq. 1 is less than d, where d is much larger than D. A solution of such puzzles is called a share, and will have a probability D/d being less than D, i.e., being the valid solution for the main puzzle. For example, if d were set to have 60 leading zero bits, then a share would have a probability 2^{-20} of being a valid solution for the main PoW puzzle.

In pooled mining, a pool *operator*, or pool *manager*, keeps track of how many shares each miner submits. If a share is indeed a valid PoW solution, the pool operator broadcasts the block to the network and receives a block reward (12.5 bitcoin and the transaction fee as of this writing). This reward is then distributed to miners in the pools based on their contributions (i.e. number of shares). By joining pools, miners receive more frequent and stable reward, thus significantly reducing their income variance compared to mining separately (or *solo* mining). Note that in pooled mining, the pool operator prepares the block template in Eq. 1, so even if a miner broadcasts a valid block himself, the reward still goes to the pool.

Formal Definitions and Notations. Bitcoin's block consists of a *block header* and a list of transactions[2]. Table 1 depicts the block header format, which consists of 80 bytes.

Table 1. Header of a Bitcoin block

Field size (bytes)	Name	Data type
4	version	int32_t
32	prev_block	char[32]
32	merkle_root	char[32]
4	timestamp	uint32_t
4	bits	uint32_t
4	nonce	uint32_t

A block is said to be a *valid extension* of the blockchain if (i) its difficulty matches the network difficulty, i.e., the sha256(sha256(block header)) $< D$; and

---

[2] https://en.bitcoin.it/wiki/Block_hashing_algorithm

(ii) the previous block hash field in the block header corresponds to a valid block in the blockchain; and (iii) the transactions of the block are valid. A publicly known block that is a valid extension but does not reside on the longest chain is called an *orphan block* or *stale block*.

A block is a *full solution* (or *valid solution*) if its header matches the difficulty D. A block is a *partial* solution if its header matches the difficulty of the pool share difficulty d. The *hash power* (or *hash rate*) of a miner (or a group of miners) is the relative fraction of computation power he possesses relative to the entire Bitcoin network.

2.2 Smart Contracts

Bitcoin transactions are deemed valid only if their linked script condition holds. While Bitcoin scripts have limited expressiveness, emerging cryptocurrencies support expressive scripts that have enabled the development of a variety of powerful decentralized applications. Bitcoin's scripts are stateless, that is, they do not maintain any internal states, and their behavior depends only on their input.

The Ethereum cryptocurrency introduced smart contracts in which the contract code is a "Turing-complete" program [8]. In addition to being more expressive, Ethereum smart contracts can also maintain internal states which are shared among transactions. For example, a smart contract can record the number of different addresses in all transactions sent to its address. Users interact with a contract, i.e. modify the contract state, by sending transactions with payloads (i.e. input data) to the contract address.

3   Block Withholding Incentives

In this section, we analyze the incentives for an attacker to pay pool miners for dropping blocks. We recall that the actual block is worthless for the attacker, as the destination of the block rewards is fixed as the pool's address. Hence the attacker only benefits from reducing the effective hash rate of the entire network. In order to maintain a consistent block rate (*e.g.*, one block per 10 min in Bitcoin), the network periodically adjusts the difficulty of hashing puzzle based on the number of miners participating. In Bitcoin this adjustment happens once every 2018 blocks.

To formally analyze the incentives, we denote the fraction of the network's hash rate controlled by the attacker as α ($0 \leq \alpha \leq 1$), the block reward by r, and a miner's reward for submitting a full solution to the pool by $s \cdot r$.

We first calculate the attacker's expected net revenue increase from purchasing β fraction of the blocks. In the absence of an attack, the attacker's expected revenue is $\alpha \cdot r$ per block epoch. When β fraction of the network's valid blocks are discarded, the attacker's effective hash rate is $a = \alpha/(1 - \beta)$, and hence his expected revenue is $a \cdot r$. Thus the attacker's extra revenue from purchasing the blocks is

$$a \cdot r - \alpha \cdot r = \frac{\alpha\beta \cdot r}{1 - \beta}. \tag{2}$$

This quantity represents the attacker's block purchasing budget.

On the other hand, in order to incentivize a pool member to withhold a block, the attacker would have to offer at least the equivalent of the member's reward for finding a full solution. As β fraction the miners do not submit their blocks to the network, in the long run network difficulty decreases by a multiplicative factor of $(1 - \beta)$. Hence per block epoch those miners would collectively expect to find $\beta/(1 - \beta)$ valid blocks and would expect to be paid

$$\frac{\beta \cdot s \cdot r}{1 - \beta} \tag{3}$$

for this work by the pool manager. Comparing the quantities (2) and (3), we see that the attacker and participating pool members both profit when

$$\alpha > s. \tag{4}$$

We now analyze the share rewards of miners. The two most popular share rewards schemes are the *pay-per-share* (PPS) and *pay-per-last-N-shares* (PPLNS) [9]. In addition, some pools offer bonus payments for miners who submit full solutions.

PPS. In the pay-per-share scheme, every pool miner receives a reward for every share (whether it constitutes a block or only a partial solution) he submits. Initially, the miner sets a share difficulty d and receives $(r \cdot d)/D$ reward for every submitted share, where D is the difficulty level of the Bitcoin network. As of November 1, 2016,[3]

$$D \geq 253,618,246,641\text{Gig}.$$

A pool member can set his own share difficulty for each of his ASIC hardwares, however the recommended upper bound is currently $d \leq 4,096$ Gig[4],[5]. Hence, in PPS

$$s = \frac{d}{D} \approx 2 \cdot 10^{-8}, \tag{5}$$

and a rational miner would, at the current block reward rate, agree to withhold his blocks for $r \cdot s \approx (12.5 \text{ BTC}) \cdot s = 2.5 \cdot 10^{-7}$ BTC, which, as of November 1, 2016, is less than 0.02 cents of a USD[6]. In practice, the attacker likely has to pay more than 0.02 cents in order to motivate pool members to divert their standing loyalties away from pool managers and to compensate them for the risk that the pool manager will run out funds and will not be able to pay them for their

---

[3] https://blockchain.info/charts/difficulty.
[4] https://slushpool.com/help/#!/first-aid/troubleshooting.
[5] Our analysis is valid even for much larger difficulty levels.
[6] http://www.coindesk.com/price/.

previously submitted shares. To aid in overcoming this inertia, we introduce block withholding pools in Sect. 5. Combining Eqs. (4) and (5) we find that the attacker could make a profit if his mining power fraction is at least $1/50,000,000$ of the network (0.000002%). This mining power is currently equivalent to 4 TH/s mining power, which is obtainable by modern ASICs[7]. Moreover, a miner with N ASICs could offer a reward that is N times higher and still make a profit. We note that all the large mining pools work in the PPS model[8]. Hence, all of them are potentially vulnerable to such an attack.

PPLNS. In the pay-per-last-N-shares model, at a high level overview, all miners share the mining rewards proportionally to their relative hash power. In this model, block shares and standard shares equally count towards proof-of-work, however withholding a block would lower the total revenues of the pool and inevitably also the rewards of the single miner. Hence, the effective block reward for a pool member is $s = \gamma$ where γ is the miner's hash power divided by the entire pool's hash power[9]. Hence, the attacker would profit only if $\alpha > \gamma$. We speculate that in most common cases, $\gamma \gg 1/50,000,000$ and thus the price of the attack is more expensive in the PPLNS model (see Table 2 as an example). Nevertheless, the attack could still be profitable for big miners who possess a percent or more of the entire network's hash power. An instantiation of our mathematical analysis can be derived from P2Pool's publicly available statistics[10], which present the hash power of every miner in the pool. Table 2

Table 2. The revenue losses that an attacker can cause a pool while making the attack profitable for himself. Attacker power is in percentages of the entire Bitcoin network hash power. Pool loses are in percentages of the total pool revenue. For example, an attack with 0.1% hash power (i.e., 0.001 fraction of entire Bitcoin's hash power) can cause pools' revenues to decrease by 10%. The results are based on miners' hash power distribution in P2Pool. The third column describe the daily costs that an attacker would have to bare if he also pays for orphan blocks, under the assumption of $12,000 block reward (see Sect. 4.3 for more details).

Attacker hash power	Pool revenue loses	Orphan blocks daily costs
0.1%	10%	$4
2%	22%	$80
4%	32%	$160
6%	37%	$240
13%	70%	$520

---

[7] https://www.bitmaintech.com/.

[8] https://en.bitcoin.it/wiki/Comparison_of_mining_pools.

[9] The miner would also get the standard share reward, however, these are typically smaller by a factor of over 10^9.

[10] http://p2pool.org/stats/.

shows the damages that an attacker could cause P2Pool, under the assumptions that P2Pool employs a pure PPLNS scheme and its miners are rational.

Finally, some pools try to prevent block withholding by giving special bonuses for miners who submit full solutions. These rewards must be limited to a few percent of a block reward, as higher bonuses would significantly increase the variance of payouts to pool members (*e.g.*, in P2Pool the bonus is 0.5%). If a pool offers p fraction of a block reward as a special bonus, then $s = p \cdot r$ and an attack is profitable only if $\alpha > p$, that is, only if the attacker hash power is greater than p.

Remark 1. Our calculations hold also in the extreme case where $\beta = 1 - \alpha$, i.e., when all the network but the attacker are withholding their blocks. However, in reality, if the attacker managed to attract a non-negligible fraction of miners, then PPS pools will go bankrupt and PPLNS pools will suffer from massive abandonment rate, as it would become more profitable to mine solo. Hence, the plausible outcome of a successful attack is a change in the pool mining model (i.e., shift towards solo mining or private pools).

4   Proving Block Withholding

The attacker in Sect. 3 pays a *withholder* to refrain from broadcasting a valid block to the blockchain. In order to convince the attacker that a block has been withheld, the withholder has to prove that (i) he found a valid block; and (ii) he (or his pool operator) did not submit it to the rest of the network. We observe that even for the task of block verification, namely, to verify that 80 bytes data consists of a valid block header, one would have to store the entire blockchain inside a smart contract, and ask for a 1 MB block's transactions data as a witness for the validity of the block. This approach is infeasible as in February 2016 it cost \$76,000 to store 1 GB of data on the Ethereum blockchain[11] (Bitcoin's blockchain size currently exceeds 100 GB[12]).

Thus, we relax the requirement for block withholding proof and ask for a *proof-of-stale-work*. Proof-of stale-work proves that a miner is performing sha256 operations over some data without an intention of submitting full solutions to the blockchain. When the withholder allocates his mining equipment for stale work, the effective hash power of the network is reduced (see Sect. 4).

In the next two subsections we present two different approaches for proving stale work. The non-interactive approach requires only a single submission from the withholder whereas the interactive approach requires the attacker to respond to the withholder submission. The non-interactive scheme makes use of Ethereum's expressive scripting language. Under the non-interactive scheme the withholder can, in a single step, submit his proof-of-stale-work to an Ethereum smart contract and get paid for it in ether without trusting the attacker or vice

---

[11] http://ethereum.stackexchange.com/questions/872/what-is-the-cost-to-store-1kb-10kb-100kb-worth-of-data-into-the-ethereum-block.

[12] https://blockchain.info/charts/blocks-size.

versa. The more complex interactive scheme, while implementable in Bitcoin's limited scripting language, leaves the attacker more vulnerable to the withholders.

In Sect. 4.3 we discuss how to mitigate the submission of orphan blocks.

4.1 Non-interactive Proof

A *non-interactive proof-of-stale-work* is a tuple (b_1, b_2, b_2', b_3), where:

- b_1, b_2, b_2', b_3 are block headers; and
- b_2 and b_2' both extend b_1; and
- b_3 extends only b_2.

Intuitively, b_2' is the withheld block, and the fact that b_3 extends b_2 implies that b_2 is in the blockchain. Formally, in order to prove stale work, we consider two distinct cases:

- In the first case the miner who found b_2' never intended to submit it to the blockchain. In this case, the proof trivially follows.
- In the second case, the miner did submit it to the blockchain. In this case, the network had no incentive to find an extension for b_2 and therefore the withholder would have to spend effort in computing b_3[13]. In this case, the withholder did stale work to find b_3, and the proof follows.

While it is possible to implement this scheme as an Ethereum smart contract (see Fig. 1), one cannot implement it in the current Bitcoin script language as Bitcoin's parsing functionality is currently disabled[14]. Indeed Bitcoin transactions cannot even extract the previous block hash out of a block header.

Remark 2. It is possible to target the attack towards a specific pool. The block header contains some information on the destination account of the block reward and it is possible to extract it if the withholder provides the leftmost branch of the block transaction Merkle tree. The connection between the account and the pool operator is typically public information. Hence the attacker could reward only blocks that are associated with certain accounts.

4.2 Interactive Proof

Let us recall that the header for a valid block, after two composed invocations of sha256, has many leading zeros. The data B in the first step below corresponds to a single $sha256(b'')$ for some valid block header b'' (i.e., $sha256(sha256(b''))$ matches the difficulty level).

---

[13] To prevent cases where it would be profitable to find b_3 for the purposes of selfish mining, we could ask for a chain of blocks that extend b_2 rather than only a single block.

[14] https://en.bitcoin.it/wiki/Script.

```
1 function verifyProofOfStaleWork( bytes b1, bytes b2, bytes b2_, bytes b3 ) returns(bool) {
2         uint prevB2    = 0;
3         uint prevB2_   = 0;
4         uint prevB3    = 0;
5         for( uint index = 4 ; index < 32 ; index++ ) {
6             prevB2 = b2[ index ] | ( prevB2 * 256 );
7             prevB2Prime = b2_[ index ] | ( prevB2_ * 256 );
8             prevB3 = b3[ index ] | ( prevB3 * 256 );
9         }
10        if( prevB2 != prevB2_ ) return false;
11        if( prevB2 != sha256(sha256(b1))) return false;
12        if( prevB3 != sha256(sha256(b2))) return false;
13        if( b2 == b2_ ) return false;
14        uint lowestDifficulty = sha256(sha256(b1))  | sha256(sha256(b2)) |
15                                sha256(sha256(b2_)) | sha256(sha256(b3));
16        if( lowestDifficulty > difficulty ) return false;
17
18      if( prevSubmissions[b2_] ) return false;
19      prevSubmissions[b2_] = true;
20
21        return true;
22    }
```

Fig. 1. Solidity code that verifies proof-of-stale-work.

- Initially, the withholder submits a 32-byte of data B with sha256(B) that matches Bitcoin difficulty level (i.e., has enough leading zeros).
- The attacker has time period T to find a block header b' such that sha256(b') = B.
- The attacker pays if and only if he did not find b' after time period T.

If the valid block b'' was submitted to the blockchain[15], then the attacker could easily come up with $b' = b''$ say after $T = 1\ day$. Otherwise, finding the pre-image of sha256 is computationally infeasible, and the attacker would not be able to find b' in the time period T.

Formally, we first claim that finding B requires roughly the same amount of work as finding a valid block header. Indeed, although technically only half of the sha256 operations are required in order to find B (as in block mining one would have to compute the sha256 function twice for every candidate byte stream), we conjecture that using the existing mining ASICs it is faster to find a block header and take B as its sha256, rather than specifically looking only for B. Given the claim and the impossibility of finding a sha256 pre-image, it is straightforward that if the withholder did the stale work, then he will get paid, and his work was not stale, then he will not get paid.

The interactive scheme requires a script language that can (i) compute sha256; (ii) make 32-byte integer comparison; and (iii) store state (to store the withholder submission). Out of the three, only the first is possible with Bitcoin script language. In Appendix A we show how to perform this scheme over Bitcoin with several off-chain operations, and in Appendix B we show how to use Ethereum smart contracts to force correctness of the off-chain operations.

---

[15] We make the assumption that orphan blocks are also publicly visible, e.g., see https://blockchain.info/orphaned-blocks.

4.3   Mitigating Orphan Blocks

The approaches in Sects. 4.1 and 4.2 are not resilient against submission of orphan blocks. Indeed neither protocol can distinguish orphaned blocks from withheld blocks. In this section we focus on the practical implications (e.g., attacker's losses) that orphan blocks introduce, and suggest practical ways to mitigate them.

We first focus on the expected losses of the attacker due to orphan blocks. In the 365 days between March 2016 and March 2017, 129 orphan blocks were recorded[16]. Hence, in our analysis we assume 0.35 orphan blocks occur every day (on average). Hence, ignoring orphan blocks will cost an attacker $0.35sr$ per day. The third column in Table 2 illustrates the daily loses of an attacker who attacks P2Pool. Our analysis suggests that an attacker who could afford to pay for orphan blocks will bear losses of $4 per day while decreasing the victim pool's revenue by 10% (which might be enough to make all miners leave the pool). However, the costs could rise to $520 per day if the attacker wishes to reduce the victim pool's revenue by 70%. In order to evaluate the total costs of an attack, one would have to speculate on the number of days a pool could successfully survive such an attack. We leave this empirical evaluation to future research. We note that in networks with lower block intervals like Ethereum who operates with the GHOST [10] protocol, the rate of stale blocks is much higher. However, in Ethereum, stale blocks are rewarded and are also included in the blockchain (as so called *uncle* blocks). Hence, for Ethereum, our schemes should be adjusted to verify that the blockchain does not contain the submitted block as an uncle block. Finally, we conjecture that Bitcoin's low orphan block rate might be the result of a highly centralized miner network, and if the network were truly decentralized more orphans would occur.

We now suggest practical ways to mitigate the attacker's losses.

The non-interactive scheme of Sect. 4.1 could reject orphan blocks by requiring that the timestamps of b_2 and b_2' differ by at least one minute. The publicly available orphaned blocks statistic in[17] for the period of January till March 2017 suggests that in practice Sybil blocks (i.e., the orphan block and the accepted block) timestamp differ by at most 40 s. Hence our restriction will prevent the submission of orphan blocks but might also deter withholders from withholding their blocks, as the smart contract will not accept a real block mined in the following minute. For this purpose the attacker should increase the offered reward sr by a factor of $q = e^{0.1} \approx 1.105$. Now the withholder will receive qsr provided that no additional block was mined in the following minute (and the probability that 0 blocks are mined in a single minute is $e^{-0.1}$), and will receive nothing if an additional block was mined. Hence, the expected reward is still sr, and our theoretical mathematical analysis from Sect. 3 still holds. A further empirical study is needed to evaluate the motivation of big pools to skew their timestamps as a means to mitigate against this attack and to gauge the withholders' reaction to increased reward variance.

---

[16] https://blockchain.info/charts/n-orphaned-blocks?timespan=1year.
[17] https://blockchain.info/orphaned-blocks.

The interactive scheme of Sect. 4.2 can mitigate orphaned blocks either by assuming that the attacker is always aware of orphaned blocks (e.g., via public blockchain explorers like blockchain.info or by becoming a peer of all major pools), or by giving incentives to the rest of the network to report that a submitted block is an orphaned block. The latter solution would require the submitter to deposit some collateral along with his submission of B. If a preimage of B is submitted by a peer in the network, then half of the collateral is given to this peer (and other half is slashed). An empirical experiment is needed to evaluate the number of orphaned blocks that are not presented in blockchain.info, the effect of collateral (and collateral size) on the willingness of withholders to participate, and peers' motivation to report preimages.

5   Block Withholders Pool

We discuss two factors that could deter a miner from participating in the withholding scheme from Sect. 4.

- *Ethical and long-run considerations.* Participating as a withholder might violate some agreements with the pool operator. In addition, if such attacks were to become common, miners might face the risk that all pools would cease to operate. In the absence of pools, miners' income variance would become undesirably high.
- *Complicated setup for a rare chance to profit.* On the one hand, collaborating with the attacker requires the withholder to install a special patch for his mining software. On the other hand, a miner could only withhold a block after he finds at least one valid block, which is not even a once in a lifetime event for most small miners. Even if the attacker offers high reward, most small miners would likely not be willing to make the effort and update their software for an event that is unlikely to happen.

In this section, we describe how to mitigate the second issue by forming a pool of block withholders, which reduce the variance of the reward and incentives small miners to participate in the attack. Intuitively, in a *withholders pool* miners submit proof-of-work shares to demonstrate their hash power and share attacker rewards for withholding blocks. The withholders pool distributes block withholding rewards among miners in proportion to their relative hash power.

In order to make the scheme profitable, the block withholder pool's proof-of-work should correlate with the work the miners do for their legitimate pool operator. Otherwise the additional proof-of-work would lead to financial losses. In classical mining pool models, shares must include the pool operator's data in order to ensure that profit from valid blocks gets distributed among pool members. By analogy, in order to ensure fair reward distribution in a withholder pool, the attacker, who distributes all withholding rewards, must serve as the operator. To be precise, the attacker should form exactly one withholding pool and declare that all rewards are routed via that pool. As the attacker may not be trusted, he should form a smart contract that collects proof-of-work and distributes the reward once a proof of block withholding is submitted (as described in Sect. 4).

Ironically, such withholder pool is vulnerable to a *block-withholding-withholding attack*, where miners could avoid submitting the withholding proof to the attacker and instead submit them to their legitimate pool operator. Thus the attacker's payments to withholder pool members must suffice not only to convince miners to install the mining software patch for dropping valid blocks but must also directly and fairly compensate pool members who actually perform withholding. The payment to the member who performs a withholding must exceed what he would have received for submitting his same share to the legitimate pool operator instead. Moreover, the attacker must distribute additional funds to the remaining pool members via some PPLNS scheme in order to motivate miners to install the software patch which includes instructions for diverting valid blocks. In short, while running a withholding pool increases chances that miners will participate in an attack, it also increases the attacker's execution costs.

6   Related Work

Recent literature has pointed incentive structure flaws in pooled mining [3,11] as well as Nakamoto consensus itself [12–14]. In many of these instances, as in this work, the attacker benefits by withholding publication of a live block. References [3,5,6] showed that a miner who mines in multiple pools simultaneously and withholds publication in one of them can, on average, increase his expected net mining profit while decreasing the revenues of the attacked pool. However, in all of these works the attacker must have substantial mining power in order to make a significant attack. For example, a miner who wishes to attack a big pool like F2Pool (for example), which currently posses 20% for the network hash power[18], should initially possess 6.7% [3] hash power in order to not lose money during the attack. In our work, in theory, a mining power of 0.000002% is enough to cause losses to the victim pool. On the other hand, our attack requires cooperation of other parties and guarantees success only if the other parties are rational with respect to their short-term revenues.

Recently Luu *et al.* propose a new efficient decentralized pooled mining protocol using Ethereum smart contracts [15]. Such a protocol, if deployed at a cryptocurrency's protocol level as the network's only mining pool, could prevent block withholding attacks against pooled miners.

Teutsch et al. recently proposed to attack blockchain miners by paying them to use their mining equipment for non-mining purposes (i.e., to solve non-blockchain PoW puzzles) [14]. Bonneau suggested to bribe miners [16] or equivalently rent their equipment, and instruct them how to mine. In both of these options, the attacker benefits by working on a private chain whose length eventually exceeds the public chain's length and thus collects all block mining

---

[18] https://en.bitcoin.it/wiki/Comparison_of_mining_pools.

rewards for himself. However the initial mining power to make the first such attack profitable in Bitcoin is 38.2% [14], while the latter attack relies on exotic rationality assumptions. Our attack is inspired by these attacks as it conceptually pays pool miners to perform certain work (i.e., stale work). It exploits the fact that the pool operator pays for most of the miners' work, and thus we can construct a profitable attack with very small initial hash power. On the other hand, the above attacks directly affect the core blockchain protocol and demonstrate vulnerabilities in Nakamoto consensus itself. Our attack affects only the pool mining protocol, which is not part of Nakamoto consensus.

Sometimes by sheer luck a miner who controls a significant portion of the network's mining power can win two or more blocks in rapid succession. In this case the miner can, on average, increase his profit by withholding a block as the basis for a longer private chain and mining on top of it. Just before the public chain catches up to the private one, the attacker releases his block, making the private chain both public and valid, and wasting the efforts of other miners who were mining on top of the former public chain. This attack is known as selfish mining [12], and has been recently optimized [17] and combined [18] with the network-layer eclipse attack [19].

Finally, we note that not all exploitable incentive structure flaws found in Nakamoto consensus necessarily manifest themselves as block withholding attacks. Miners who benefited from the recent denial-of-service attacks in Ethereum [20] made use of a "verifier's dilemma" [13] to waste others' time, while publishing their own blocks quickly.

Acknowledgments. We thank our shepherd, Iddo Bentov, for useful discussions and the anonymous reviewers of an earlier draft of this paper for helpful feedback.

A   Bitcoin Implementation

In this section, we refine the interactive protocol from Sect. 4.2 for use in Bitcoin. The security of our Bitcoin protocol relies on the following two assumptions which we will later relax in Appendix B:

- The attacker always wants to attack. That is, he is always willing to pay a predefined amount for a valid proof of block withholding.
- The withholder is willing to withhold the block in return for a Bitcoin zero-confirmation payment.

The first assumption is reasonable as the attack is profitable. However, it is not trivial, as malicious parties could dishonestly declare their intentions to make such an attack but never collaborate with the withholder. Such behavior might be expected, e.g., by pool operators who wish to undermine trust between attackers and withholders. The second assumption could be justified as zero confirmation double spending is not trivial to perform [21]. Our protocol would allow the withholder to wait for a short period of time before deciding on his actions. In this period of time the transaction would propagate to the majority of the network, and the odds for double spending could be evaluated and bounded from above, e.g., via [22]. If odds are, for example, less than 50%, then it is enough to double the offered reward in order to incentivize the withholder. In Sect. B we will introduce Ethereum smart contracts that enforce our assumptions. That is, the contracts would compensate the withholder (in ether currency) if the attacker does not collaborate with the protocol or performs double spending.

We are now ready to introduce the protocol.

- Initially, the withholder submits (off-chain) a 32-byte chunk of data b and his Bitcoin public key.
- The attacker computes sha256(b) and rejects the submission if: (i) the difficulty level is not sufficient; or (ii) sha256(b) corresponds to a block in the public blockchain; or (iii) b was already submitted in the past.
- (Otherwise) The attacker signs and sends the withholder a Bitcoin transaction t such that:
  - The attacker can redeem t with an input string b' that satisfies sha256(b') = b.
  - The withholder can redeem t after T block epochs (provided that it was not already redeemed).
- The withholder submits t to the network, waits for it to propagate, withholds his block, and redeems t after T block epochs.

The correctness of the scheme follows by our two assumptions and by the arguments of the correctness proof of the protocol in Sect. 4.2. We note that in the last phase of the protocol, the withholder cannot afford to wait for a block confirmation. Indeed, a block confirmation occurs only after a new block is mined, and when this happens the withholder's block becomes worthless as he can no longer submit it to his pool operator[19].

An implementation of transaction t as a Bitcoin script is illustrated bellow.

Implementation with bitcoin script. Transaction t locking script is:

```
1 OP_IF
2     OP_HASH256
3     <b>
4     OP_EQUALVERIFY
5     <buyer_public_key>
6 OP_ELSE
7     <time_lock> OP_CHECKLOCKTIMEVERIFY OP_DROP
8     <seller_public_key>
9 OP_ENDIF
10 OP_CHECKSIG
```

The buyer can redeem t with this unlocking script:

```
1 <signature>
2 <b'>
3 OP_1
```

The seller can redeem t after sufficient enough time with this unlocking script:

```
1 <signature>
2 OP_0
```

---

[19] E.g., see line 110 in https://raw.githubusercontent.com/slush0/stratum-mining/38637575c8c253aba18f95dffd25c49ca6d0434b/lib/block_template.py.

We note that in order to make these transaction standard we use pay to script hash transactions[20].

B   Ethereum Contracts as Insurance

In this section, we describe two Ethereum smart contracts that eliminates the need for the assumptions we made in Appendix A. The contracts provides the following guarantee:

> The withholder is either payed the promised amount in bitcoin or payed disproportional high value in ether currency.

Such guarantee should mitigate any concern from the withholder side, even if he has strong preference towards bitcoin payments. Indeed, either he gets payed with bitcoin or he receive high ether payment that compensates for his bitcoin preference.

We first describe how to mitigate the assumption that the attacker always wants to attack, and then describe an Ethereum insurance contract against Bitcoin double-spending. For the rest of the section we assume that 1,000 ether (approximately 10,000 USD as of January 3, 2017[21]) are enough to compensate for any preference towards Bitcoin payment.

B.1   Forcing the Attacker to Attack

In this section we describe how an Ethereum contract (published by the attacker) can enforce the attacker to honestly execute his part in the protocol. We recall that the attacker's role in the protocol is to publish a signed transaction t when a valid block withholding witness b is submitted, i.e., when a never before submitted block header with sufficient difficulty is submitted. The contract has four functions, namely, **depositCollateral**, **submitWitness**, **submitTx** and **seizeCollateral**.

- **depositCollateral**: in this function the attacker deposits 1,000 ether.
- **submitWitness**: in this function the withholder submits the witness b and his Bitcoin public key. The function checks that b was never submitted before and its difficulty is sufficient (i.e., sha256(b) is small enough), and records the current time.
- **submitTx**: in this function the attacker submits a signed transaction t and the contract verifies that the transaction is properly signed in the format as described in Appendix A.
- **seizeCollateral**: in this function the withholder can withdraw the 1,000 ether if the attacker did not respond in time (or responded with invalid transaction).

---

[20] https://en.bitcoin.it/wiki/Pay_to_script_hash.
[21] https://www.coingecko.com/en/price_charts/ethereum/usd.

See Fig. 2 for partial implementation of the contract. Intuitively, this contract enforces the attacker to post a signed Bitcoin transaction to the Ethereum blockchain (within a given time period T). Once published, the withholder can post it to the Bitcoin network and claim his payment in bitcoin currency. If the attacker decides not to post the transaction, then the withholder collects the collateral that serves as a compensation for the block withholding and for getting paid in ether.

```
1    function submitWitness( bytes b, uint publicKey ) {
2        if( sha256(b) < difficulty ) {
3            witnessSubmissionTime = now;
4            withholderPublicKey = publicKey;
5        }
6    }
7
8    function submitTx( bytes t ) {
9        if( isSigned( t, attackerPublicKey ) && isInRightFormat(t, b, withholderPublicKey ) ) {
10           txSubmitted = true;
11       }
12   }
13
14   function seizeCollateral( ) {
15       if( ! txSubmitted && ( witnessSubmissionTime + T < now ) ) {
16           msg.sender.send(1000 ether);
17       }
18   }
```

Fig. 2. Solidity code that force the attacker to attack.

We note that the contract can serve as an insurance only when the balance is sufficient (i.e., when a collateral is deposited). Hence, the withholder should check the balance before participating in the scheme[22].

B.2   Insurance Against Double-Spending

In this section, we introduce an Ethereum contract that serves as an insurance against Bitcoin double-spending scenarios. We use it to mitigate the zero-confirmation assumption for our Bitcoin implementation of the block withholding attack. The contract provides insurance for up to N simultaneous, double-spending operations of a single Bitcoin address. Formally, we say that a transaction tx is double-spent by address a if tx is signed by a and there exists another signed transaction tx' such that tx and tx' share at least one common input and differ by at least one output[23].

The contract is illustrated in Fig. 3. In **createInsurance** function the owner of the bitcoin account deposits 1,000 ether for every insured double-spending operation. In the **claimCompensation** function, the victim submits the witness for double-spending and unlocking script for the controversial output, as a

---

[22] To mitigate the incentive for the attacker to seize the collaterals and give it to a Sybil identity, we can change the contract so it would give only half of the collateral and the other half would be destroyed (e.g., would be sent to address 0x000...000).

[23] A naive approach that only search for common inputs and check that $tx \neq tx'$ would fail due to Bitcoin's transaction malleability issue [23].

```
1   function createInsurance( uint publicKey, uint N ) {
2       # check if there are enough funds
3       if( msg.value != N * 1000 ether ) throw;
4       insuredAccount = publicKey;
5   }
6
7   function claimCompensation( bytes tx, bytes txPrime, uint inputIndex,
8                               uint outputIndex, bytes unlockScript ) {
9       if( isSigned( tx, insuredAccount ) && isSigned( txPrime, insuredAccount) )
10          if( inputTx(tx, inputIndex) in txPrime )
11              if( outputTx( tx, outputIndex ) not in txPrime )
12                  if( runBTCScript( outputTx( tx, outputIndex ), unlockScript ) )
13                      msg.sender.send( 1000 ether );
14  }
```

Fig. 3. Insurance for bitcoin double-spending.

witness for being eligible for compensation. To prevent a Sybil attack, where the owner of the insured account claim N compensation units to himself, we could halve the compensation and destroy the remaining 500 ether.

References

1. Nakamoto, S.: Bitcoin: a peer-to-peer electronic cash system (2009). bitcoin.org
2. Rosenfeld, M.: Analysis of bitcoin pooled mining reward systems. CoRR, abs/1112.4980 (2011)
3. Luu, L., Saha, R., Parameshwaran, I., Saxena, P., Hobor, A.: On power splitting games in distributed computation: the case of bitcoin pooled mining. In: 2015 IEEE 28th Computer Security Foundations Symposium, pp. 397–411, July 2015
4. Ethereum Foundation: Ethereum's White paper (2014). https://github.com/ethereum/wiki/wiki/White-Paper
5. Courtois, N.T., Bahack, L.: On subversive miner strategies and block withholding attack in bitcoin digital currency. CoRR, abs/1402.1718 (2014)
6. Eyal, I.: The miner's dilemma. In: SP (2015)
7. Sasson, E.B., Chiesa, A., Garman, C., Green, M., Miers, I., Tromer, E., Virza, M.: Zerocash: decentralized anonymous payments from Bitcoin. In: Proceedings of 2014 IEEE Symposium on Security and Privacy, SP 2014 (2014)
8. Wood, G., Ethereum: a secure decentralised generalised transaction ledger (2014). http://gavwood.com/paper.pdf
9. Bitcoin Wiki: Pool mining's payout schemes. https://en.bitcoin.it/wiki/Comparison_of_mining_pools
10. Sompolinsky, Y., Zohar, A.: Secure high-rate transaction processing in Bitcoin. In: Financial Cryptography and Data Security - 19th International Conference, FC 2015, San Juan, Puerto Rico, 26–30 January 2015, Revised Selected Papers, pp. 507–527, 2015
11. Eyal, I.: The miner's dilemma. In: IEEE Symposium on Security and Privacy (SP 2015), pp. 89–103, May 2015
12. Eyal, I., Sirer, E.G.: Majority is not enough: bitcoin mining is vulnerable. In: Christin, N., Safavi-Naini, R. (eds.) FC 2014. LNCS, vol. 8437, pp. 436–454. Springer, Heidelberg (2014). https://doi.org/10.1007/978-3-662-45472-5_28
13. Luu, L., Teutsch, J., Kulkarni, R., Saxena, P.: Demystifying incentives in the consensus computer. In: Proceedings of 22nd ACM SIGSAC Conference on Computer and Communications Security (CCS 2015), pp. 706–719. ACM, New York (2015)

14. Teutsch, J., Jain, S., Saxena, P.: When cryptocurrencies mine their own business. To appear in Financial Cryptography and Data Security (FC 2016) (2016)
15. Luu, L., Velner, Y., Teutsch, J., Saxena, P.: Smartpool: practical decentralized pooled mining. To appear in USENIX Security Symposium (2017)
16. Bonneau, J.: Why buy when you can rent? Bribery attacks on bitcoin-style consensus. In: Clark, J., Meiklejohn, S., Ryan, P.Y.A., Wallach, D., Brenner, M., Rohloff, K. (eds.) FC 2016. LNCS, vol. 9604, pp. 19–26. Springer, Heidelberg (2016). https://doi.org/10.1007/978-3-662-53357-4_2
17. Sapirshtein, A., Sompolinsky, Y., Zohar, A.: Optimal selfish mining strategies in bitcoin. To appear in Financial Cryptography and Data Security (FC 2016) (2016)
18. Nayak, K., Kumar, S., Miller, A., Shi, E.: Stubborn mining: generalizing selfish mining and combining with an eclipse attack. In: 2016 IEEE European Symposium on Security and Privacy (EuroS&P), pp. 305–320, March 2016
19. Heilman, E., Kendler, A., Zohar, A., Goldberg, S.: Eclipse attacks on bitcoin's peer-to-peer network. In: 24th USENIX Security Symposium (USENIX 2015), pp. 129–144. USENIX Association, Washington, D.C., August 2015
20. https://www.reddit.com/r/ethereum/comments/55xh2w/i_thikn_the_attacker_is_this_miner_today_he_made/
21. Karame, G., Androulaki, E. and Capkun, S.: Two bitcoins at the price of one? Double-spending attacks on fast payments in bitcoin. IACR Cryptology ePrint Archive 2012:248 (2012)
22. blockcypher.com: Confidence factor. http://dev.blockcypher.com/#confidence-factor
23. Bitcoin Wiki: Transaction malleability. https://en.bitcoin.it/wiki/Transaction_Malleability

BatchVote: Voting Rules Designed for Auditability

Ronald L. Rivest[1]([✉]), Philip B. Stark[2], and Zara Perumal[3]

[1] MIT CSAIL, Cambridge, USA
rivest@mit.edu
[2] Department of Statistics, University of California Berkeley, Berkeley, USA
stark@stat.berkeley.edu
[3] MIT, Cambridge, USA
zperumal@mit.edu

Abstract. We propose a family of novel social choice functions. Our goal is to explore social choice functions for which **ease of auditing** is a primary design goal, instead of being ignored or left as a puzzle to solve later.

Our proposal, "**BatchVote**," creates a social choice function f from an arbitrary "inner" social choice function g, such as instant-runoff voting (IRV), and an integer B, the number of batches.

We aim to preserve flexibility by allowing g to be arbitrary, while providing the ease of auditing of a plurality election.

To compute the winner of an election of n votes, the social choice function f partitions the votes into B batches of roughly the same size, pseudorandomly. The social choice function g is applied to each batch. The election winner, according to f, is the weighted plurality winner for the B outcomes, where the weight of each batch is the number of votes it contains. The social choice function f may be viewed as an "interpolation" between plurality (which is easily auditable) and g (which need not be).

Auditing is simple by design: we can view f as being a (weighted) plurality election by B "*supervoters*," where the bth supervoter's vote is determined by applying g to the votes in batch b, and the weight of her vote is the number of votes in her batch. Since plurality elections are easy to audit, the election output can be audited by checking a random sample of "supervotes" against the corresponding paper records.

1 Introduction and Motivation

Designing or selecting a social choice function for elections requires making trade-offs among desirable properties—it is well known that many desirable properties are incompatible. Ease of auditability does not seem to be among the properties that have been considered when selecting a social choice function. In this paper we elevate ease of auditing to be a first-level design criterion, and propose a specific framework, called BatchVote, for ensuring ease of auditing while blending in desirable properties from another social choice function.

© International Financial Cryptography Association 2017
M. Brenner et al. (Eds.): FC 2017 Workshops 2017, LNCS 10323, pp. 317–333, 2017.
https://doi.org/10.1007/978-3-319-70278-0_20

The paper is organized as follows: Sect. 2 provides terminology, notation, and orientation. Then Sect. 3 overviews of the BatchVote method, giving its design philosophy and major characteristics. Section 4 takes a deeper look at the properties of BatchVote, and then Sect. 5 shows how a BatchVote election may be audited with a risk-limiting audit, based on known risk-limiting audit methods for plurality elections. Simulated auditing results are given in Sect. 6. Section 7 presents some variants of BatchVote.

2   Preliminaries

Outcomes, Ballots, Votes, Profiles. We assume that the election is designed to select an outcome from a pre-determined set $\mathcal{C}$ of C alternatives (or candidates). Each of n voters casts a single ballot. A ballot may have an arbitrary format and semantics. The **profile** of cast ballots is

$$P = \{v_1, v_2, \ldots, v_n\},$$

listing the vote v_j cast by voter j, for $j = 1, \ldots, n$. The profile is best viewed as a sequence or a multiset, since it may contain repeated items (identical ballots). A **vote** need not be a valid vote (e.g., it might be an undervote or an overvote according to the inner social choice function; see below).

Social Choice Functions. A **voting rule** or **social choice function** g maps profiles to a single outcome (one of the alternatives). For any profile P, $g(P)$ is the *winner* or *outcome* for the profile P.

We require a social choice function g to be deterministic, so g must break any ties that occur. We therefore allow g to take a second random input K. Here K is the *seed* for a (pseudo-)random number generator used to break ties. Thus $f(P, K)$ is deterministic. We omit f's second argument K when it is understood from context. We assume that g does not depend on the order of the votes, that is, g applied to every permutation of P must give the same result $c \in \mathcal{C}$.

One may choose a social choice function because of its mathematical properties. For example, Tideman's "ranked-pairs method" [25] has many desirable properties [28], as does the Schulze method [13]. But not all otherwise-desirable social choice functions are readily auditable. Indeed, for both Tideman's ranked-pairs method and Schulze's method there is no known efficient method for performing a risk-limiting audit.

Post-election Audits. Confidence in an election outcome can be derived from a **post-election audit**. We assume that voters cast votes on **paper ballots**, and that voters had the opportunity to check that their ballots reflected their choices before casting the ballots. These paper ballots were scanned and those data were electronically aggregated to provide the initial or **reported outcome** w for the election.

The paper ballots represent the "ground truth" for the election; a full and correct count of the paper ballots should give (essentially by definition) the **actual (or true) outcome** t for the election. A "compliance audit" can provide assurance that the paper trail has integrity (see Benaloh et al. [1], Lindeman and Stark [8], and Stark and Wagner [15]).

To check the election outcome, rather than recount all the ballots by hand, it is usually more efficient to audit using a statistical method based on hand examination of a sample of the paper ballots, a method first proposed by Johnson [6]. Such a **statistical (post-election) audit** can give statistical assurance that the reported outcome is indeed equal to the actual outcome, often after examining only a relatively small sample of the paper ballots. If the reported outcome is incorrect, the audit may need to examine many ballots, or even all of them, before concluding that the reported outcome was incorrect.

Stark [16] introduced a particular kind of statistical audit—a **risk-limiting (post-election) audit** (or **RLA**). What distinguishes an RLA is that if the reported outcome is incorrect, a RLA has a large, pre-specified chance of correcting it. Lindeman and Stark provide a "gentle introduction" to RLAs [8]. Lindeman et al. [7], Norden et al. [10], and the Risk-Limiting Audit Working Group [2] give general overviews of post-election audits. Stark and Wagner [15] promulgate "evidence-based elections," which include not only a risk-limiting audit but also ensure that the evidence trail has integrity.

A variety of statistical methods for providing RLAs have been developed [3,5,9,11,12,14,19–22,24]; some of these methods form the foundation of our approach for auditing BatchVote. There are online tools to help conduct risk-limiting audits [23].

3   BatchVote

This section gives an overview of the BatchVote design philosophy, gives details of the method, and provides an analysis of its efficiency.

3.1   Design Philosophy

BatchVote derives a new social choice function f from a pre-existing social choice function g. Roughly speaking, f divides the n ballots into B "batches," applies g to each batch, then defines the overall election outcome as the (weighted) plurality result of the B batch-level outcomes.

When B is very large, most batches contain at most a single ballot, and f behaves like plurality voting. But when B is equal to one, f and g are identical. In between, BatchVote acts like a blend or "interpolation" between plurality and g. Thus, $f(P)$ is not generally equal to $g(P)$, but f may inherit some desirable features of g.

For instance, g could be a preferential voting method that allows voters to express their preferences in more detail than simple plurality voting permits.

Preferential voting methods are notoriously difficult to audit [24,29]; for many preferential voting methods no efficient risk-limiting audit method is known.

But g is, at the top level, just (weighted) plurality, for which efficient risk-limiting auditing methods are well-known (see, for example [8]).

3.2   The BatchVote Method

BatchVote determines the election outcome as follows, given an "inner social choice function" g and the set $\mathcal{C}$ of candidates.

1. Collect the n cast votes (including invalid votes) and assign each a unique "ballot ID."
2. Select λ, the desired average batch size, and calculate the resulting number of batches $B = n/\lambda$.
3. Determine the "random election seed" K, using a public dice-rolling ceremony or similar means.
4. Distribute votes to batches in a deterministic manner, based on the election seed and the ballot IDs.
5. Compute the winner of each batch, using the social choice function g.
6. Compute the overall winner using a weighted plurality method to combine the batch-level outcomes, where the weight of a batch is the number of votes (including invalid votes) it contains.

Details are given in the following subsections. See Fig. 1 for an illustration.

3.3   Inner Social Choice Function g

BatchVote can use *any* social choice function as its "inner social choice function" g; g affects basic properties of the election, such whether ballots allow choices to be ranked in some way.

BatchVote is most interesting when g has desirable properties from a social choice perspective, but is difficult to audit for the entire profile of cast ballots. That includes many preferential voting methods. Applying g to small batches of votes, then combining the results with (weighted) plurality, may give many of the benefits of g while being easy to audit.

When BatchVote is used with inner social choice function g, we call the result "**Batch$g$**." For example, methods **BatchApproval**, **BatchIRV**, **BatchRankedPairs**, or **BatchSchulze** are special cases of BatchVote.

3.4   Choosing λ

The average batch size λ is a free parameter of the BatchVote. There is no "right" choice for λ, but different choices result in different social choice functions f, and different auditing workloads. We recommend as a default $\lambda = 10C$, but other values might be preferable, depending on how much one wants f to act like g (choose λ large) or like plurality (choose λ small).

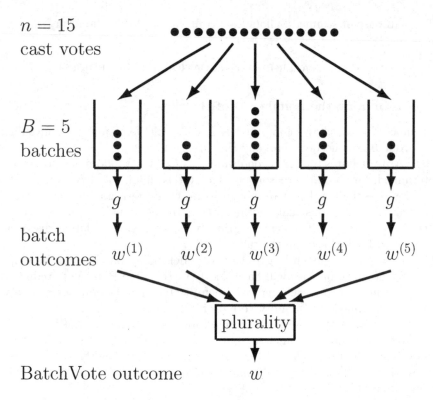

$n = 15$
cast votes

$B = 5$
batches

batch
outcomes

BatchVote outcome

Fig. 1. The BatchVote method. The n cast votes are divided pseudorandomly into B batches. The social choice function g is applied separately to each batch. The overall BatchVote outcome is the weighted plurality result of the batch outcomes. The weight of batch b is the number of votes in batch b, including invalid votes.

3.5 Ballot IDs

In BatchVote, each ballot has a unique "ballot ID" that determines which batch the ballot is placed in. The batch a ballot is placed in does not depend on the choices made on that ballot, on other ballots, or on the number of ballots cast.

Ballot IDs are assigned by a process that does not know how ballot IDs will determine which batch a ballot will be in. In BatchVote, this isolation is accomplished by drawing a random seed K *after* all of the ballot IDs are assigned. The seed, together with the ballot IDs, determines the batch assignments.

The ballot IDs may be arbitrary strings of characters; they may be numeric, alphanumeric, or contain special characters. They may or may not contain information about where the paper ballot is located. Each ballot should have a unique ballot ID.

The ballot ID may be printed on the ballot itself when the ballot is scanned. Some optical scanners can perform this sort of operation. Some states, such as Texas, require that each ballot be "numbered."

The database of scanned ballots then contains triples of the form (assuming a single race):

(BALLOT-ID, PAPER-BALLOT-LOCATION, VOTER-CHOICES).

3.6   Determining the Number B of Batches

The number B of batches is computed as $B = N/\lambda$. (We assume for convenience that no rounding is needed here, and that B is an integer.)

BatchVote requires that B be determined *before* the random election seed K is determined, for the same reason that ballot IDs should be determined before the random election seed is determined: to prevent "gerrymandering." Once B is determined, it remains fixed, even if the number of ballots in the election changes somewhat (e.g. if a box of previously unconsidered ballots is discovered and approved for inclusion in the tally).

If B is very large (much larger than N), then many batches will be empty, and most nonempty batches will have size 1. In this case BatchVote reduces to plurality voting (because the weight of an empty batch is the empty set, however one defines g applied to an empty vote profile).

We remark that the use of a cryptographic hash function makes it harder for an adversary who can somehow control the seed (but not the ballots themselves) to manipulate the election, in much the same spirit as the suggestions of Faliszewski et al. [4] on the use of computational complexity to protect elections from manipulation.

3.7   Random Seed K

BatchVote uses a random "seed" K to help determine which batch a ballot is placed in. The seed K is also used to help break ties.

The seed K may be determined by a dice-rolling ceremony after all votes are cast. This gives a result unpredictable to an adversary. The ceremony is performed *after* all cast ballots have been collected, to prevent an adversary from manipulating the ballot IDs.

If K were predictable, an adversary who can assign ballot IDs might be able to effect the equivalent of "gerrymandering"—giving his own candidate an advantage in many batches, while the opponent gets an advantage in a few.

Our proposed process of generating a random seed *after* the votes are assigned ballot IDs prevents this sort of "gerrymandering."

3.8   Mapping Ballot IDs to Batches

We propose a method based on the use of a "cryptographic hash function" (specifically, SHA256) to compute the assignment of ballots to batches.

The batch number is determined by the hash of the random seed K concatenated with the ballot ID, modulo B. (The fact that 2^{256} is not an exact multiple of B is ignorable here.)

This pseudorandom method is effectively indistinguishable from a truly random mapping, for someone with a feasible amount of computational power who doesn't know the key K. We thus treat this mapping as a random mapping of ballot IDs to batches.

Appendix A gives details of our proposal.

3.9   Variability of Batch Sizes

The sizes of batches in BatchVote can vary. If we treat the output of the pseudorandom procedure as independent, identically distributed variables uniformly distributed on $\{1, \ldots, B\}$, the sizes $\{N^{(b)}\}_{b=1}^{B}$ of the batches are random variables with a multinomial joint distribution corresponding to N draws and equal category probabilities $1/B$. The marginal distribution of the number of ballots in batch b is binomial $\mathrm{BIN}(N, 1/B)$; the chance that batch b will contain k ballots is $\binom{N}{k}(1/B)^{k}(1 - 1/B)^{N-k}$.

BatchVote accommodates the variability in batch sizes by *giving each batch a weight equal to its size* in the final plurality election. Empty batches are ignored. A ballot in a batch of size k has an effective weight of $(1/k) * k = 1$: hence, each voter in the contest has the same effective "weight" in determining the outcome. BatchVote is somewhat similar to the U.S. Electoral College, where the number of electoral votes a state gets depends upon that state's population—although not in direct proportion.

Section 7 discusses other ways of dividing ballots into batches that we considered.

3.10   Applying g to Each Batch

The application of social choice function g to each batch is straightforward, assuming that g is applicable to a batch of any size.

The social choice function g may need to resolve ties. As some batches may be small, ties may be fairly common. Lack of space precludes giving full details of our proposal, but, roughly speaking, when g is applied to batch b it is supplied a "tie-breaking seed" K_b derived pseudorandomly from K and batch index b (for instance, by hashing the concatenation of K and b).

Appendix B provides a concrete example of how this might be done.

3.11   Efficiency

The time required for BatchVote to compute the election outcome is the time taken to assign ballots into batches, plus the time taken to compute each batch outcome using g, plus the time taken to compute the weighted plurality overall result. Depending on how the work of calculating g scales with the number of ballots g is applied to, this can be faster or slower than computing g for the original full ballot profile. We do not expect computing f to be burdensome in practice.

4   Properties

4.1   BatchVote-Specific Properties

Fairness to Voters. Because each batch has weight equal to the number of votes it contains, BatchVote is fair to voters—each voter is treated equally. Moreover, every ballot has the same chance of ending up in each batch.

4.2   General Properties

What properties does f inherit from g and from Plurality, since it is a blend of the two systems?

Clearly, for BatchVote to have some property regardless of the batch size, *both* Plurality and g must have that property, since when B is large BatchVote becomes Plurality, and when $B = 1$, BatchVote is g. Wikipedia provides a nice list of voting system properties[1].

Unfortunately, Plurality itself has few of those properties. We mention two properties here.

Ballot Format. Obviously, the ballot format for f is identical to the ballot format for g.

Monotonicity. A social choice function is monotonic if increasing a voter's preference for a candidate can only help that candidate. If g is monotone, then so is f.

BatchPlurality versus Plurality. BatchPlurality is similar to plurality: there is a precinct level tabulation and reporting of precinct-level results to a central tabulation that aggregates those results. However, with BatchPlurality, precincts do not report the candidate counts, just the winner for the precinct and the overall number of voters. Thus BatchPlurality is closer to how the Electoral College works.

5   Auditing

Efficient post-election audits can be derived from Wald's sequential tests of statistical hypotheses [26,27].

5.1   Ballot-Polling Audits

The ballot-polling post-election audit studied here is a simple modification of the ballot-polling audit method introduced by Lindeman et al. [9].

---

[1] https://en.wikipedia.org/wiki/Voting_system.

Consider a pair of candidates (w, ℓ) where w is a reported winner and ℓ is a reported loser. Candidate w really beat candidate ℓ in the batch plurality contest if $\sum_{b:t^{(b)}=w} N^{(b)} > \sum_{b:t^{(b)}=\ell} N^{(b)}$, i.e., if

$$p_{w\ell} \equiv \frac{\sum_{b:t^{(b)}=w} N^{(b)}}{\sum_{b:t^{(b)}=w} N^{(b)} + \sum_{b:t^{(b)}=\ell} N^{(b)}} > 1/2. \tag{1}$$

Suppose we draw a random batch $\mathbb{B}$ such that $\Pr\{\mathbb{B} = b\} = N^{(b)}/N$. Condition on the event that the true winner of batch $\mathbb{B}$ is either w or ℓ. Then the (conditional) probability that the true winner of the batch is w is $p_{w\ell}$. Wald's sequential probability ratio test [26] can test the hypothesis that $p_{w\ell} \leq 1/2$ against the alternative that $p_{w\ell} = \frac{\sum_{b:w^{(b)}=w} N^{(b)}}{\sum_{b:w^{(b)}=w} N^{(b)} + \sum_{b:w^{(b)}=\ell} N^{(b)}}$, the reported fraction of the weighted votes for either w or ℓ that are reported votes for w.

5.2 Comparison Audits

This section describes a comparison audit for BatchVote.

We have a weighted plurality contest with B batches ("voters" in the weighted contest). Batch b contains $N^{(b)}$ ballots. Let $N \equiv \sum_b N^{(b)}$ be the total number of ballots cast.

Let $\mathcal{C}$ denote the set of possible election outcomes. (Here $\mathcal{C}$ stands for "candidates," although an outcome might involve more than one candidate winning). Let $w^{(b)}$ be the reported outcome (reported winner) for batch b and let $t^{(b)}$ denote the actual (true) outcome for batch b (the outcome that a manual audit of the batch would show).

The total reported weighted vote for outcome c is

$$R_c \equiv \sum_{b:w^{(b)}=c} N^{(b)}. \tag{2}$$

The reported winner of the contest is $w \equiv \arg\max_c R_c$ (assuming no ties). Similarly, the actual (true) winner of the contest is $t \equiv \arg\max_c A_c$. The reported losers are the candidates $\mathcal{L} \equiv \{\ell \in \mathcal{C} : \ell \neq w\}$.

To simplify the notation, define

$$R_c^{(b)} \equiv \begin{cases} N^{(b)}, & \text{if } w^{(b)} = c \\ 0, & \text{else.} \end{cases} \tag{3}$$

That is, $R_c^{(b)}$ is the number of ballots in batch b if batch b was reported to have voted for outcome c, and is zero if batch b was reported to have voted for any other outcome. Thus

$$R_c = \sum_b R_c^{(b)}. \tag{4}$$

For $\ell \in \mathcal{L}$, define the *reported pairwise margins*:

$$R_{w\ell} \equiv R_w - R_\ell. \tag{5}$$

This will be positive for all $\ell \in \mathcal{L}$ if and only if w is the reported winner w.

The total *actual* weighted vote for candidate c is

$$A_c \equiv \sum_{b:t^{(b)}=c} N^{(b)}. \tag{6}$$

Define

$$A_c^{(b)} \equiv \begin{cases} N^{(b)}, & \text{if } t^{(b)} = c \\ 0, & \text{else,} \end{cases} \tag{7}$$

so

$$A_c = \sum_b A_c^{(b)}. \tag{8}$$

The true winner is w if $A_w > A_\ell$ for all $\ell \in \mathcal{L}$ that is, if the *actual pairwise margins*

$$A_{w\ell} \equiv A_w - A_\ell > 0, \quad \forall \ell \in \mathcal{L}. \tag{9}$$

We now give a simple auditing procedure based a sufficient condition for the true winner to be w, couched in terms of a single scalar.

$$\begin{aligned} A_{w\ell} &= A_w - A_\ell \\ &= \sum_b A_w^{(b)} - \sum_b A_\ell^{(b)} \\ &= R_{w\ell} - \sum_b \left((A_\ell^{(b)} - A_w^{(b)}) - (R_\ell^{(b)} - R_w^{(b)}) \right). \end{aligned} \tag{10}$$

The correct outcome is w if and only if for all $\ell \neq w$,

$$R_{w\ell} - A_{w\ell} = \sum_b \left[(A_\ell^{(b)} - A_w^{(b)}) - (R_\ell^{(b)} - R_w^{(b)}) \right] < R_{w\ell}. \tag{11}$$

Define

$$\gamma^{(b)} \equiv \max_{\ell \neq w} \frac{(A_\ell^{(b)} - A_w^{(b)}) - (R_\ell^{(b)} - R_w^{(b)})}{N^{(b)} R_{w\ell}}. \tag{12}$$

If

$$\sum_b \gamma^{(b)} N^{(b)} < 1, \tag{13}$$

then for all $\ell \neq w$,

$$\sum_b (A_\ell^{(b)} - A_w^{(b)}) - (R_\ell^{(b)} - R_w^{(b)}) < R_{w\ell}, \tag{14}$$

i.e., w is the true winner.

Select a batch $\mathbb{B}$ at random, with probability $N^{(b)}/N$ of selecting batch b. If batch b is selected, it can be tallied by hand, revealing $A_c^{(b)}$ for all c; then $\gamma^{(b)}$ can be calculated. Let $X = \gamma^{\mathbb{B}}$, the value of γ for the randomly selected batch. Then

$$\mathbb{E}X = \sum_b \gamma^{(b)} \Pr\{\mathbb{B} = b\} = \frac{1}{N} \sum_b \gamma^{(b)} N^{(b)}. \tag{15}$$

Hence, w is the true winner if $\mathbb{E}X < 1/N$. A sequential test of the hypothesis $\mathbb{E}X \geq 1/N$ can be used to construct a risk-limiting audit with risk limit α: continue to audit until either that hypothesis is rejected at significance level α or there has been a full hand count.

5.3   Masking of Errors

In the presence of no errors, the BatchX method can be viewed as paying a penalty of a factor of λ compared to doing an audit of X on the entire set of ballots. Of course, this statement only makes sense when there is a know method to audit X, which is not true for all social choice functions.

A factor that acts in the other direction is that errors (discrepancies discovered between paper ballots and their electronic counterparts) may be masked in BatchX, as changing a ballot in a batch to its correct value may have no effect on the batch outcome.

6   Experimental Results

Code implementing BatchAudit is available on GitHub.[2] We have experimented with synthetic data sets and data sets from real elections.[3]

Figure 2 shows BatchBorda applied to data from the Burlington, Vermont, 2009 Mayoral Race, which had 8980 voters. For $\lambda \gtrsim 0.8$, the BatchBorda and Borda methods give the same outcome.

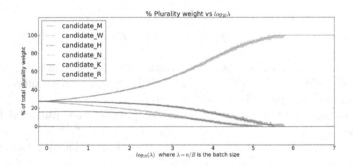

Fig. 2. Batch size vs Outcome for BatchBorda for the Burlington, VT, 2009 Mayoral Race data.

Figure 3 shows BatchRankedPairs applied to data from the Burlington, Vermont, 2009 Mayoral Race, which had 8980 voters. For $\lambda \gtrsim 3.74$, the BatchRankedPairs and RankedPairs methods gave the same outcome.

---

[2] The GitHub repo is https://github.com/ron-rivest/2016-batchvote-code. This is currently private, but will be made public.

[3] Real data sets available at: http://rangevoting.org/TidemanData.html.

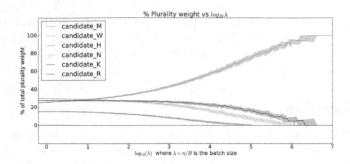

Fig. 3. Batch size vs Outcome for BatchRankedPairs for the Burlington, VT, 2009 Mayoral Race data.

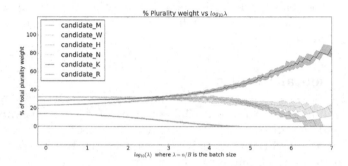

Fig. 4. Batch size vs Outcome for BatchIRV for the Burlington, VT, 2009 Mayoral Race data.

Similar results (with a variety of crossover points) were obtained for other real data sets).

Figure 4 shows BatchIRV applied to data from the Burlington, VT, 2009 Mayoral Race, which had 8980 voters. F $\lambda \gtrsim 2.82$, the BatchRankedPairs and RankedPairs methods gave the same outcome.

Similar results (with a variety of crossover points) were obtained for other real data sets).

We also estimated audit workloads versus λ; see Fig. 5. The number of batches that need to be examined for a risk limit of $\alpha = 0.05$ is about $6/m^2$ for a ballot-polling audit and about $6/m$ for a comparison audit, where m is the margin between the top two candidates. The estimated audit workload is then λ times larger, since auditing a batch requires looking at about λ ballots. Note that the workload peaks when the winner changes. Our recommendation for choosing $\lambda = 10C$ is an attempt to choose a point a bit to the right of the winner-crossover peak, if it exists.

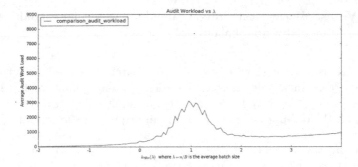

Fig. 5. Comparison audit workload estimate for BatchRankedPairs for the Burlington, VT, 2009 Mayoral Race data.

7 Variants

This section describes possible variations of BatchVote.

Replication. One might replicate each ballot T times, for some $T > 1$, giving extra flexibility to the process of allocating ballots to batches.

Fixed-Size Batches. We explored a number of ways of forcing every batch to have very nearly the same size. For example, one could require all batches to have a fixed size λ (an integer). (Using a replication factor $T = \lambda$ may help.) However, no alternative method seemed sufficiently simple and "random"; we prefer the proposed BatchVote method for its simplicity.

Using Replications and All Subsets of Size λ. BatchVote is sensitive to the random seed K. For a close election, a different value of K might yield a different election outcome. This is not surprising, as K controls tie-breaking.

However, K also controls the placement of ballots in batches, and one might prefer to have a social choice function that is somehow insensitive to the allocation of ballots to batches.

One could consider *all* subsets of size λ, and apply plurality to their batch-level results. However, such an approach is computationally infeasible when N and B are even modestly large.

MajorityThenBatch or CondorcetThenBatch. First check to see if there is a majority or Condorcet winner. If so, then proclaim that candidate to be the winner. Else, proceed with the BatchVote method. (This is a common approach for forcing a voting system to be Majoritarian or Condorcet.) How to audit such combined systems is an open question.

Write-in Votes. We can treat write-in candidates as regular candidates; deriving the list of candidates from ballots cast.

Multiple Races. How should one use the BatchVote method when there are multiple races in an election? In our description so far, we have implicitly assumed that there is only one race being audited. See Stark [18,20] and Benaloh et al. [1] for approaches to auditing multiple contests simultaneously.

Acknowledgments. Ronald L. Rivest gratefully acknowledges support for his work on this project received from the Center for Science of Information (CSoI), an NSF Science and Technology Center, under grant agreement CCF-0939370, and from the Department of Statistics, University of California, Berkeley, which hosted his sabbatical visit when this work began.

Appendix A. Possible Details of Batch Assignment Method

We illustrate the proposed procedure with an example. Suppose the random seed K is the string of 24 decimal digits

$$K = 067541877022641091953584$$

and suppose that a ballot has the 37-character ballot ID

$$\text{ID} = \text{2016-11-08-maricopa-az-1562-7631-5515.}$$

Then the batch to which this ballot is assigned is starting with the concatenation of these two strings—that is:

$$K||ID = \text{067541877022641091953584} \text{2016-11-08-maricopa-az-1562-7631-5515.}$$

Applying SHA256 to this byte string yields the hexadecimal result

db5d8603dcf6e4e122e7b0ff231d4069cb4626f45ab1686cb1b6dd9d424480d9

which, when interpreted as a base-16 integer, yields

99221755554920309225844359348330608520995333449296550547451312649783275192537

(decimal). Finally, we take the result modulo B, the number of batches, and add one. Suppose $B = 10000$. Then the batch number for this ballot is

$$2538 \ .$$

Because the result is obtained modulo B, plus one, the batches are numbered 1 to B, inclusive.

Appendix B. Guidelines for Breaking Ties

We provide each of the B invocations of g with its own random number seed to use in tie-breaking. Suppose the overall election-random seed is

$$067541877022641091953584.$$

Suppose we wish to provide the 15th invocation of g with its own tie-breaking seed. Then the tie-breaking seed $K^{(b)}$ provided will be

$$K^{(b)} = \texttt{067541877022641091953584:batch:15}.$$

That is, the overall election seed, followed by "$\texttt{:batch:}$", followed by the batch number b in decimal, for $b = 1, 2, \dots, B$. This seed can be concatenated with other values within g to break ties, and then SHA256 may be applied to the result.

Of course, the specification of g needs to clearly specify how ties are to be broken, given the tie-breaking seed $K^{(b)}$. (We have, for example, python code that illustrates this for various social choice functions g.)

Each instance of g receives a different tie-breaking seed $K^{(b)}$, to remove the possibility of obviously correlated tie-breaking between the various batches. Although the seeds for different batches are related, they are nonetheless different, and the pseudo-random character of SHA256 makes it computationally infeasible to find statistical correlations in their tie-breaking use.

Notation

This note summarizes notational conventions we use in this paper.

B Number of batches.
b A particular batch. $b = 1, 2, \dots, B$.
$\mathcal{C}$ The set of candidates.
C Number of candidates (possible election outcomes.
c A particular candidate. (Also w, ℓ sometimes, for winner, loser.)
n Number of cast votes.
T Replication factor; how many times each vote is replicated.
N Number of ballots being tabulated; $N = nT$.
$N^{(b)}$ Number of ballots in batch b (so $\sum_b N^{(b)} = N$).
λ Average batch size ($\lambda = N/B$).
R_c Total reported tabulation in favor of candidate c. (i.e. electronic tabulation)
A_c Total actual tabulation in favor of candidate c (i.e. paper ballot tabulation)
$R_c^{(b)}$ Reported tabulation for candidate c in batch b (Either $N^{(b)}$ or 0).
$A_c^{(b)}$ Actual tabulation for candidate c in batch b. (Either $N^{(b)}$ or 0).
$R_{w\ell}$ Reported margin of candidate w over candidate ℓ ($R_{w\ell} = R_w - R_\ell$).
$A_{w\ell}$ Actual margin of candidate w over candidate ℓ ($A_{w\ell} = A_w - A_\ell$).

$R_{w\ell}^{(b)}, A_{w\ell}^{(b)}$ Margins particularized to batch b.
$t^{(b)}$ True winner of batch b.
$w^{(b)}$ Reported winner of batch b.
K Random number seed for the election.
$K^{(b)}$ Random number seed for batch b.
$\mathbb{B}$ A randomly selected batch, with $\Pr\{\mathbb{B} = b\} = N^{(b)}/N$.

References

1. Benaloh, J., Jones, D., Lazarus, E., Lindeman, M., Stark, P.B.: SOBA: secrecy-preserving observable ballot-level audit. In: Proceedings of 2011 Electronic Voting Technology Workshop/Workshop on Trustworthy Elections (EVT/WOTE 2011), (2011). http://static.usenix.org/events/evtwote11/tech/final_files/Benaloh.pdf
2. Bretschneider, J., Flaherty, S., Goodman, S., Halvorson, M., Johnston, R., Lindeman, M., Rivest, R.L., Smith, P., Stark, P.B.: Risk-limiting post-election audits: why and how? (ver. 1.1), October 2012. http://people.csail.mit.edu/rivest/pubs.html#RLAWG12
3. Checkoway, S., Sarwate, A., Shacham, H.: Single-ballot risk-limiting audits using convex optimization. In: Jones, D., Quisquater, J.-J., Rescorla, E. (eds.) Proceedings of 2010 EVT/WOTE Conference. USENIX/ACCURATE/IAVoSS, August 2010
4. Faliszewski, P., Hemaspaandra, E., Hemaspaandra, L.A.: Using complexity to protect elections. CACM **53**(11), 74–82 (2010)
5. Hall, J.L., Miratrix, L.W., Stark, P.B., Briones, M., Ginnold, E., Oakley, F., Peaden, M., Pellerin, G., Stanionis, T., Webber. T.: Implementing risk-limiting post-election audits in California. In: Proceedings of 2009 Electronic Voting Technology Workshop/Workshop on Trustworthy Elections (EVT/WOTE 2009, Montreal, Canada). USENIX, August 2009. http://www.usenix.org/event/evtwote09/tech/full_papers/hall.pdf
6. Johnson, K.: Election verification by statistical audit of voter-verified paper ballots. http://ssrn.com/abstract=640943. Accessed 31 Oct 2004
7. Lindeman, M., Halvorseon, M., Smith, P., Garland, L., Addona, V., McCrea, D.: Principle and best practices for post-election audits (2008). www.electionaudits.org/files/best%20practices%20final_0.pdf
8. Lindeman, M., Stark, P.B.: A gentle introduction to risk-limiting audits. IEEE Secur. Priv. **10**, 42–49 (2012)
9. Lindeman, M., Stark, P.B., Yates, V.S.: BRAVO: ballot-polling risk-limiting audits to verify outcomes. In: Halderman, A., Pereira, O. (eds.) Proceedings of 2012 EVT/WOTE Conference (2012)
10. Norden, L., Burstein, A., Hall, J.L., Chen, M.: Post-election audits: restoring trust in elections. Technical report, Brennan Center for Justice and Samuelson Law, Technology & Public Policy Clinic (2007)
11. California Secretary of State. Post-election risk-limiting audit pilot program (2011–2013). http://www.sos.ca.gov/elections/voting-systems/oversight/post-election-auditing-regulations-and-reports/post-election-risk-limiting-audit-pilot-program/
12. Sarwate, A.D., Checkoway, S., Shacham, H.: Risk-limiting audits and the margin of victory in nonplurality elections. Polit. Policy **3**(3), 29–64 (2013)

13. Schulze, M.: A new monotonic, clone-independent, reversal symmetric, and condorcet-consistent single-winner election method. Soc. Choice Welf. **36**(2), 267–303 (2011)
14. Stark, P.B.: Risk-limiting vote-tabulation audits: the importance of cluster size. Chance **23**(3), 9–12 (2010)
15. Stark, P.B., Wagner, D.A.: Evidence-based elections. IEEE Secur. Priv. **10**(05), 33–41 (2012)
16. Stark, P.B.: Conservative statistical post-election audits. Ann. Appl. Stat. **2**, 550–581 (2008)
17. Stark, P.B.: A sharper discrepancy measure for post-election audits. Ann. Appl. Stat. **2**, 982–985 (2008)
18. Stark, P.B.: Auditing a collection of races simultaneously (2009). https://arxiv.org/abs/0905.1422v1
19. Stark, P.B.: CAST: canvass audits by sampling and testing. IEEE Trans. Inf. Forensics Secur. **4**(4), 708–717 (2009)
20. Stark, P.B.: Efficient post-election audits of multiple contests: 2009 California tests. In: 2009 Conference on Empirical Legal Studies (2009). http://ssrn.com/abstracts=1443314
21. Stark, P.B.: Risk-limiting post-election audits: P-values from common probability inequalities. IEEE Trans. Inf. Forensics Secur. **4**, 1005–1014 (2009)
22. Stark, P.B.: Super-simple simultaneous single-ballot risk-limiting audits. In: Proceedings of 2010 EVT/WOTE Workshop (2010). http://www.usenix.org/events/evtwote10/tech/full_papers/Stark.pdf
23. Stark, P.B.: Tools for comparison risk-limiting election audits (2015). http://www.stat.berkeley.edu/~stark/Vote/auditTools.htm
24. Stark, P.B., Teague, V.: Verifiable European elections: risk-limiting audits for D'Hondt and its relatives. USENIX J. Elect. Technol. Syst. (JETS) **1**(3), 18–39 (2014)
25. Tideman, T.N.: Independence of clones as a criterion for voting rules. Soc. Choice Welf. **4**(3), 185–206 (1987)
26. Wald, A.: Sequential tests of statistical hypotheses. Ann. Math. Stat. **16**(2), 117–186 (1945)
27. Wald, A.: Sequential Analysis. Dover, Mineola (2004)
28. Wikipedia: Voting system. https://en.wikipedia.org/wiki/Voting_system
29. Xia, L.: Computing the margin of victory for various voting rules. In: Proceedings of 13th ACM Conference on Electronic Commerce (EC-2012) (2012)

Advances in Secure Electronic Voting Schemes

Existential Assertions for Voting Protocols

R. Ramanujam[1], Vaishnavi Sundararajan[2], and S.P. Suresh[2(✉)]

[1] The Institute of Mathematical Sciences, IV Cross Road, CIT Campus, Taramani,
Chennai 600113, Tamil Nadu, India
jam@imsc.res.in
[2] Chennai Mathematical Institute and UMI ReLaX, H1, SIPCOT IT Park, Siruseri,
Kelambakkam, Chennai 603103, India
{vaishnavi,spsuresh}@cmi.ac.in

Abstract. In [21], we extended the Dolev-Yao model with assertions.
We build on that work and add existential abstraction to the language,
which allows us to translate common constructs used in voting protocols
into proof properties. We also give an equivalence-based definition of
anonymity in this model, and prove anonymity for the FOO protocol.

1 Anonymity

Formal verification of security protocols often involves the analysis of a property
where the relationship between an agent and a message sent by him/her needs
to be kept secret. This property, called "anonymity", is a version of the general
unlinkability property, and one of much interest. There can be multiple examples
of such anonymity requirements, including healthcare records, online shopping
history, and movie ratings [20]. Electronic voting protocols are a prime example
of a field where ensuring and verifying anonymity is crucial.

It is interesting to see how protocols are modelled symbolically for the analysis of such properties. In the Dolev-Yao model [10], one often requires special
operators in order to capture certain behaviour. Many voting schemes employ
an operation known as a *blind signature* [8]. A blind signature is one where
the underlying object can be hidden (via a blinding factor), the now-hidden
object signed, and then the blind removed to have the signature percolate down
to the underlying object. The FOO voting protocol given in [11] crucially uses
blind signatures in order to obtain a signature on an encrypted object. [7] shows
that the derivability problem for protocols involving blind signatures becomes
DEXPTIME-hard. Protocols which do not use blind signatures often use homomorphic encryption or mix nets, which also make the modelling and verification
quite complex [17].

We thank the anonymous referees for their helpful comments. We would also like
to thank Prof. Steve Kremer (INRIA Nancy and LORIA) for insights which helped
crystallize some of the main ideas in this paper.

V. Sundararajan—Supported by a TCS Research Fellowship, and partially by a
grant from the Infosys Foundation.

S.P. Suresh—Partially supported by a grant from the Infosys Foundation.

© International Financial Cryptography Association 2017
M. Brenner et al. (Eds.): FC 2017 Workshops 2017, LNCS 10323, pp. 337–352, 2017.
https://doi.org/10.1007/978-3-319-70278-0_21

Note that in most common models, terms are the only objects communicated. A "certificate" of an agent's validity – which is an intrinsically different object from a term containing an agent's vote, for example – is also modelled as a term in the term algebra. [4,5], for example, augment the Dolev-Yao term syntax with an extra primitive ZK (a "zero-knowledge term"), which can be used to create a term that codes up a zero-knowledge proof. However, no direct logical inference is possible with these proof terms, and therefore, it is difficult to reason about what further knowledge agents can obtain using them. In [21], we proposed a departure from this paradigm, using *assertions* as a further abstraction that can be used for modelling protocols. Assertions, which code up certificates and have a separate proof system, can be sent by agents in addition to terms. The assertion algebra allows designers to model protocols involving certification in a more explicatory manner (by maintaining terms and certificates as separate objects). It also allows analysts to capture any increase in agents' knowledge achieved by deduction at the level of certificates.

So what are these assertions and how do they behave? Assertions include statements about various terms appearing in the protocol. These include instances of application-specific predicates and equalities between two different symbolic terms. Assertions can also be combined using the usual propositional connectives *and* ($\land$) and *or* ($\lor$). They also include a *says* operator, which works as an ownership mechanism for assertions, and disallows other agents from forwarding such an assertion in their own name. Perhaps the most crucial (and useful) addition to the assertion language here (over the system in [21]) is the existential quantifier. This allows us to quantify out any term from an assertion, thereby effectively hiding the actual term about which that assertion is made. Since existential assertions thus hide the private data used to generate a certificate, while revealing some partial information, they seem especially useful for capturing blinding (and similar operations with this goal) in voting protocols.

1.1 Related Work

Research on anonymity has been carried out for many years now. In the applied-pi calculus, [16] verifies anonymity for the FOO protocol, [2] studies general unlinkability and shows that this implies anonymity, and [19] provides a model based on process algebra incorporating aspects of the underlying communication mechanism (anonymous channels in particular).

There are also many epistemic logic-based approaches. [14] provides a logical framework built on modal epistemic logic for anonymity in multiagent systems; [12,22] also define information-hiding properties in terms of agent knowledge; [15] provides a modular framework that allows one to analyze general unlinkability properties using function views, along with extensive case studies on anonymity and privacy.

Theorem provers have also been used to verify anonymity. [6] uses an automatic theorem prover MCMAS for verification; [3] also specifies general unlinkability as an extension to the Inductive Method for security protocol verification in the theorem prover Isabelle.

In this paper, we extract a logical core of reasoning about certificates, translate the typical constructs used for voting protocols into proof properties, and employ equivalence-based reasoning for verifying anonymity. We also apply this technique to model two voting protocols, namely FOO and Helios, and to analyze anonymity for FOO.

2   Modelling the FOO Protocol

2.1   Introduction to FOO

In [11], the authors introduce the FOO protocol for electronic voting, which has inspired many subsequent protocols. This protocol uses blinding functions and bit commitments in order to satisfy many desirable security properties, including anonymity. The voter V sends to the authority A his name, along with a blindsigned commitment to the vote v. The authority signs this term, and sends it back to V. V now unblinds this to obtain a signature on his commitment to the vote v, and sends that to the collector C. C adds the encrypted vote and V's commitment to the public bulletin board. V then sends to C the random bit r he used to create the vote commitment, so C can access the vote and update his tally. The protocol is presented in Fig. 1a (see [11,16] for a detailed explanation). Sends marked by $\looparrowright$ are over anonymous channels.

$$V \to A : V, [\text{blind}(\text{commit}(v,r),b)]_V$$

$$V \to A : \{v\}_{r_A}, V \text{ says } \{ \ \exists x, r : \{x\}_r = \{v\}_{r_A}$$
$$\wedge \ \text{valid}(x) \ \}$$

$$A : \text{deny} \ \exists x : \text{voted}(V, x)$$

$$A : \text{insert} \ \text{voted}(V, \{v\}_{r_A})$$

$$A \to V : [\text{blind}(\text{commit}(v,r),b)]_A$$

$$A \to V : A \text{ says}$$
$$[\ \text{elg}(V) \wedge \text{voted}(V, \{v\}_{r_A})$$
$$\wedge \ V \text{ says } \{ \ \exists x, r : \{x\}_r = \{v\}_{r_A}$$
$$\wedge \ \text{valid}(x) \ \} \ ]$$

$$V \looparrowright C : [\text{commit}(v,r)]_A$$
$$C \to \ : \text{list}, [\text{commit}(v,r)]_A$$
$$V \to C : r$$

$$V \looparrowright C : \{v\}_{r_C}, r_C,$$
$$\exists X \ \exists y, s : A \text{ says}$$
$$[\ \text{elg}(X) \wedge \text{voted}(X, \{y\}_s)$$
$$\wedge \ X \text{ says } \{ \ \exists x, r : \{x\}_r = \{y\}_s$$
$$\wedge \ \text{valid}(x) \ \} \ ]$$
$$\wedge \ y = v$$

(a) FOO Protocol with terms.
$[x]_A$ denotes x signed by A.

(b) FOO Protocol with assertions.

Fig. 1. FOO protocol: modelling with terms only and with assertions

2.2   Modelling FOO with Assertions

In Fig. 1b, we present the FOO protocol as modelled using assertions.

The voter V contacts the authority A with his vote v encrypted using a random key r_A. V also sends a certificate linking his name to his encrypted vote v. The V *says* prefix links V to the certificate about v, and thus informs the authority that V wishes to vote using the valid vote v, the encrypted form of which has been sent with the certificate. Note that this certificate automatically rules out replay attacks (of the kind where another agent V' copies V's published data off the bulletin board and replays it in her own name).

The authority A checks that the voter V has not voted earlier. If this check passes, A adds the fact that V has voted with the encrypted term $\{v\}_{r_A}$ to her database (so that V cannot vote again in the future) via an *insert* action. A then issues a certificate stating that V is a valid voter and wishes to vote with the encrypted term he sent A earlier, and that V claims that the term encrypted therein is a valid vote. The voter V now anonymously sends to the counter C the vote v encrypted in a new random key. This is accompanied by an existential assertion, which hides the voter's identity from C, while still convincing C that A has certified V and the sent vote to be valid.

We need three predicates here – valid, elg, and voted. The first two are predicates for stating the validity of the vote and the eligibility of the voter, respectively. The voted predicate is used for linking the voter and the vote. As we shall see in Sect. 4, we can add such protocol-specific predicates to the assertion language in order to communicate succinct certificates (for example, here we use valid(v), instead of providing a disjunction over the finite set of valid votes for the value of v, which would grow longer as the set of allowable values grows larger).

3   Modelling Helios 2.0

3.1   Introduction to Helios

[1] introduces the voting scheme called Helios which has the desirable property of public auditability, i.e., even if Helios is fully corrupt, one can verify the integrity of an election outsourced to it. Helios provides unconditional integrity as long as the bulletin board is trustworthy, while privacy is guaranteed if one trusts the Helios server, which doubles up as election administrator and trustee. The voter sends his vote to the Ballot Preparation System, which creates an encrypted ballot, which is then sealed and cast. The voter's identity and ballot are then posted on the public bulletin board. On closing the election, Helios removes voter names, shuffles all ballots, produces a proof of correct shuffling, and posts these on the board. After allowing some time for auditors to check the shuffling, Helios decrypts each ballot, produces a proof of correct decryption, and posts the tally on the bulletin board. Helios crucially uses auditing by various participants in order to guarantee correctness.

3.2   Helios 2.0

[9] demonstrates an attack on vote privacy in the basic Helios system in [1], where, by controlling more than half the voters, an adversary can get the compromised voters to copy a single (honest) voter's encrypted ballot off the bulletin board, and from the tally know whom that voter voted for. Note that this happens in spite of the Helios system itself being non-corrupt. In order to fix this, they introduce measures to weed out replayed ballots, and a linking mechanism between every ballot and the voter whose vote it is supposed to encrypt. They also replace the shuffling mechanism by a homomorphic encryption operation, and introduce trustees who are distinct from the election administrator. This introduces an extra assurance of vote privacy, since a corrupt administrator needs to corrupt some trustees in order to see a voter's unencrypted vote.

$$V \to S \quad : \quad v,\ V\ says\ \texttt{valid}(v)$$

$$S \to V \quad : \quad b,\ S\ says\ \{\exists v : b = ballot(v) \wedge V\ says\ \texttt{valid}(v)\}$$

$$V \to S \quad : \quad cast$$

$$S \to A \quad : \quad b,\ S\ says\ \{\exists v : b = ballot(v) \wedge V\ says\ \texttt{valid}(v)\}$$

$$A \quad : \quad deny\ \texttt{voted}(V)$$

$$A \quad : \quad insert\ \texttt{voted}(V)$$

$$A \to BB \quad : \quad b,\ A\ says\ S\ says\ \{\exists v : b = ballot(v) \wedge V\ says\ \texttt{valid}(v)\}$$

Suppose $b_1, \ldots, b_k$ were the ballots cast and published on the bulletin board.

$$A \to BB \quad : \quad t,\ A\ says\ [\exists s : t = ballot(s) \wedge$$

$$\{\exists v_1, \ldots, v_k : s = sum(v_1, \ldots, v_k) \wedge \bigwedge_{i=1}^{k} b_i = ballot(v_i)\}]$$

Fig. 2. Helios 2.0 protocol with assertions

3.3   Modelling Helios 2.0 with Assertions

The voter first inputs his vote to a script which creates his ballot and sends it back to him with an assertion stating correctness. The voter can then choose to cast this vote, at which point the script submits his ballot and the assertion to the administrator. The administrator publishes the ballot and the assertion on the bulletin board. After some known deadline, the administrator homomorphically combines all ballots, and publishes the encrypted tally along with an assertion stating correctness of the tally. The trustees can then decrypt this tally, and the administrator publishes the result.

In Fig. 2 we model Helios 2.0 with assertions. We do not include the final step, where the trustees decrypt the final encrypted tally and publish it onto the bulletin board. Note that this model, much like the terms-only model in [9], requires us to add a homomorphic encryption operation to our term algebra.

However, we can incorporate the weeding out of replayed ballots and establishing the link between ballots and voters by the use of assertions alone, instead of having to send extra terms. Note that in order for an agent V_2 to copy V_1's vote and replay it to A, V_2 would need to make an assertion of the form S *says* $\{\exists v : b = ballot(v) \wedge V_2$ *says* $\texttt{valid}(v)\}$, which would contradict the sending in V_1's name. Thus we can establish a link between vote and voter, while also disallowing replays. We merely need to add a homomorphic encryption operation to the term algebra, since our assertions, as of now, are not capable of capturing this operation.

4   Assertions: Theory

We fix the following countable sets – a set $\mathscr{V}$ of variables, a set Ag of agents, a set $\mathscr{N}$ of nonces, and a set of $\mathscr{K}$ of keys. We assume that every $k \in \mathscr{K}$ has an inverse key, denoted $inv(k)$. The set of basic terms $\mathscr{B}$ is defined to be $Ag \cup \mathscr{N} \cup \mathscr{K}$. The set of terms $\mathscr{T}$ is given by the following syntax:

$$t := m \mid (t_1, t_2) \mid \{t\}_k$$

where $m \in \mathscr{B} \cup \mathscr{V}$, and $k \in \mathscr{K} \cup \mathscr{V}$. A term with no variables occurring in it is called a *ground term*. The system of rules for deriving new ground terms from old is given in Table 1. The rules are presented in terms of sequents $X \vdash_{dy} t$ where X is a finite set of ground terms, and t is a ground term.

Table 1. The Dolev-Yao derivation system

$$\frac{}{X \cup \{t\} \vdash_{dy} t} \; ax$$

$$\frac{X \vdash_{dy} t_1 \quad X \vdash_{dy} t_2}{X \vdash_{dy} (t_1, t_2)} \; pair \qquad \frac{X \vdash_{dy} (t_1, t_2)}{X \vdash_{dy} t_i} \; split$$

$$\frac{X \vdash_{dy} t \quad X \vdash_{dy} k}{X \vdash_{dy} \{t\}_k} \; enc \qquad \frac{X \vdash_{dy} \{t\}_k \quad X \vdash_{dy} inv(k)}{X \vdash_{dy} t} \; dec$$

4.1   Assertions and Derivations

We now present the formal details of the model with assertions, a version of which was first proposed in [21]. The set of assertions, $\mathscr{A}$, is given by the following syntax (fixing a set of variables, and a set of predicates for each arity):

$$\alpha := t = t' \mid \alpha_1 \vee \alpha_2 \mid \alpha_1 \wedge \alpha_2 \mid \exists x : \alpha \mid m \; says \; \alpha$$
$$\mid \texttt{valid}(m) \mid \texttt{elg}(m) \mid \dots \mid m \; sent \; t \mid m \; sent \; \alpha$$

where $t \in \mathscr{T}$, $m \in Ag \cup \mathscr{V}$, and valid and elg are application-specific predicates. The ellipses signify that one may add more such predicates, depending on the application requirements (as in the FOO protocol, from Sect. 2.2). A *ground assertion* is one with no free variables.

The set of assertions is a positive fragment of existential first-order logic. The intention is that in addition to ground terms, agents also communicate ground assertions to each other. Agents are allowed to assert equality of terms, and basic predicates on terms, as well as disjunctions and conjunctions. They can also "sign" assertions by use of the *says* operator. They also have the capability of existentially abstracting some terms from an assertion, thereby modelling *witness hiding*. The sole use of the *sent* operator is to enable an observer to record who communicated a term or an assertion.

Table 2. Derivation rules for assertions. In the $\bullet$ rule, $x_i, y_i \in \mathscr{V}$. We assume that $X \vdash_{dy} x$ and $inv(x) = x$ for all $x \in \mathscr{V}$. In the $\exists e$ rule, $y \notin Vars(X, \Phi \cup \{\beta\})$.

$$\frac{X \vdash_{dy} m}{X, \Phi \vdash m = m} [m \in \mathscr{B} \cup \mathscr{V}] \qquad \frac{}{X, \Phi \cup \{\alpha\} \vdash \alpha} ax \qquad \frac{X, \Phi \vdash \alpha(t) \quad X, \Phi \vdash t = t'}{X, \Phi \vdash \alpha(t')}$$

$$\frac{X, \Phi \vdash s = t \quad X, \Phi \vdash t = u}{X, \Phi \vdash s = u} \qquad \frac{X, \Phi \vdash s = t}{X, \Phi \vdash t = s} \qquad \frac{X, \Phi \vdash (s_0, s_1) = (t_0, t_1)}{X, \Phi \vdash s_i = t_i}$$

$$\frac{X, \Phi \vdash s = s' \quad X, \Phi \vdash t = t'}{X, \Phi \vdash (s, t) = (s', t')} \qquad \frac{X, \Phi \vdash \{x_0\}_{x_1} = \{y_0\}_{y_1}}{X, \Phi \vdash x_i = y_i} \bullet \qquad \frac{X, \Phi \vdash s = s' \quad X, \Phi \vdash m = m'}{X, \Phi \vdash \{s\}_m = \{s'\}_{m'}}$$

$$\frac{X, \Phi \vdash m = n}{X, \Phi \vdash \alpha} \perp [m, n \in \mathscr{B}, m \neq n] \qquad \frac{X, \Phi \vdash \alpha \quad X \vdash_{dy} sk(A)}{X, \Phi \vdash A \ says \ \alpha} says_A$$

$$\frac{X, \Phi \vdash \alpha \quad X, \Phi \vdash \beta}{X, \Phi \vdash \alpha \wedge \beta} \wedge i \qquad \frac{X, \Phi \vdash \alpha_1 \wedge \alpha_2}{X, \Phi \vdash \alpha_i} \wedge e \qquad \frac{X, \Phi \vdash A \ says \ \alpha}{X, \Phi \vdash \alpha} strip$$

$$\frac{X, \Phi \vdash \alpha_i}{X, \Phi \vdash \alpha_1 \vee \alpha_2} \vee i \qquad \frac{X, \Phi \vdash \alpha \vee \beta \quad X, \Phi \cup \{\alpha\} \vdash \delta \quad X, \Phi \cup \{\beta\} \vdash \delta}{X, \Phi \vdash \delta} \vee e$$

$$\frac{X, \Phi \vdash \alpha(t)}{X, \Phi \vdash \exists x : \alpha(x)} \exists i \qquad \frac{X, \Phi \vdash \exists x : \alpha(x) \quad X, \Phi \cup \{\alpha(y)\} \vdash \beta}{X, \Phi \vdash \beta} \exists e$$

In the course of participating in a protocol, agents accumulate a database of ground terms and ground assertions communicated to them. The (natural deduction style) proof system for assertions is presented in Table 2. The rules are presented in terms of sequents $X, \Phi \vdash \alpha$, where X is a finite set of ground terms and Φ is a finite set of assertions (which are not necessarily ground).

Equality assertions form a central part of communications between agents. Note that an agent A can derive $t = t$ only when all basic subterms of t can be derived by A. The recipient of an equality assertion can use the rules provided in Table 2 to reason further about the terms involved therein. Our rules for equality are fairly intuitive and reflect basic properties of the pairing and encryption operations. Equality assertions are most likely to be used in existentially quantified assertions. Notable among the other rules are $says_A$, which allows the possessor of $sk(A)$ to "sign" an assertion in A's name, and $strip$, which allows one to strip the sign in A $says$ α and use α in local reasoning.

These rules allow agents to carry out non-trivial inferences, potentially learning more than was intended by the protocol. Suppose an agent A has a term $\{v\}_k$, which he knows be a nonce encrypted with some key, but whose inverse he does not have access to. One would presume that A therefore should have no idea about the value of v. However, it is possible for assertions about $\{v\}_k$ to reveal more information to A. Suppose A manages to obtain two certificates $\exists x, y : \{v\}_k = \{x\}_y \wedge (x = 0 \vee x = 1)$ and $\exists x, y : \{v\}_k = \{x\}_y \wedge (x = 0 \vee x = 2)$. Let us call these assertions $\exists x, y : \alpha(x, y)$ and $\exists x, y : \alpha'(x, y)$. These two assertions are in A's database of assertions Φ. Let a, b, a', b' be new variables that do not occur in Φ. Consider $\Phi \cup \{\alpha(a, b), \alpha'(a', b')\}$. From $\{v\}_k = \{a\}_b$ and $\{v\}_k = \{a'\}_{b'}$, we get $\{a\}_b = \{a'\}_{b'}$. Since $a, a', b, b' \in \mathcal{V}$, $a = a'$ and $b = b'$ using the $\bullet$ rule from Table 2. From the other parts of α and α', and using transitivity, we get $a = 0 \vee a = 1$ and $a = 0 \vee a = 2$. We use disjunction elimination to get $a = 0$. From this we conclude that $\{v\}_k = \{0\}_b$, and hence $\Phi \cup \{\alpha(a, b), \alpha'(a', b')\} \vdash \exists y : (\{v\}_k = \{0\}_y)$. Therefore, using the $\exists e$ rule, we get $\Phi \vdash \exists y : (\{v\}_k = \{0\}_y)$.

[4,5] use ZK terms, which we shall refer to as zkp terms, to encapsulate assertions about terms appearing in the protocol. Each zkp term proves a formula involving some private and some public variables. The recipient of a zkp term is deemed to have knowledge of the terms used in place of the public variables, but not the private ones. We adopt a similar convention here. For an assertion α, if an equality of the form $t = t'$ occurs in it, or if α involves the application of a predicate to a term t, then α reveals t. However, if a term of the form $\{v\}_k$, say, appears in α, then α does not reveal v. We also adopt the convention that every term revealed by an assertion is sent earlier in the protocol.

4.2   Actions, Roles and Protocols

There are six type of actions – send, anonymous send, receive, confirm, deny, and insert. Sends, anonymous sends, and receives are of the form $+A$: $(m)(t, \alpha)$, $+A^*$: $(m)(t, \alpha)$ and $-A$: (t, α) respectively, where $A \in Ag \cup \{id\}$ (where id is a dedicated variable that stands for the agent performing the action), $m \subseteq \mathcal{V} \cup \mathcal{N} \cup \mathcal{K}$ stands for nonces and keys that are $fresh$ which should be instantiated with hitherto unused values in each occurrence of this action, $t \in \mathcal{T}$ and $\alpha \in \mathcal{A}$. The A: $confirm$ α and A: $deny$ α actions allow A to branch on whether or not he can derive α, while A: $insert$ α allows A to add previously unknown true assertions into her database. For $A \in Ag \cup \{id\}$, an A-action is an action which involves A. A $ground$ $action$ is one without any variable occurrence. An A-role is a finite sequence of A-actions. A role is an A-role for some $A \in Ag \cup \{id\}$. A $protocol$ Pr is a finite set of roles.

Given a sequence of actions $\eta = a_1 \cdots a_n$, we say that the variable x *originates* at i if x occurs in a_i and does not occur in a_j for any $j < i$. A variable x occurring in a role η is said to be *bound* if it originates at i and either a_i is a receive action, or $a_i = +A$: $(\boldsymbol{y})(t, \alpha)$ is a send action with $x \in \boldsymbol{y}$.

As an example, we show the voter role for the FOO protocol from Sect. 2. In this role, v and id stand for the vote and voter respectively, while k, k' are fresh keys, and $auth$ is a bound variable (since it originates in a receive) which stands for the authority with whom the voter interacts. The authority and counter roles can also be extracted from the protocol description in a similar manner.

$$+id : (k)\ \{v\}_k, id\ says\ \{\exists x, r : \{x\}_r = \{v\}_k \wedge \mathtt{valid}(x)\}$$
$$-id : auth\ says\ [\mathtt{elg}(id)\ \wedge\ \mathtt{voted}(id, \{v\}_k)$$
$$\wedge\ id\ says\ \{\ \exists x, r : \{x\}_r = \{v\}_k \wedge\ \mathtt{valid}(x)\ \}\ ]$$
$$+id^* : (k')\ (\{v\}_{k'}, k'),$$
$$\exists X, y, s : auth\ says\ [\mathtt{elg}(X) \wedge \mathtt{voted}(X, \{y\}_s)$$
$$\wedge\ X\ says\ \{\exists x, r : \{x\}_r = \{y\}_s \wedge \mathtt{valid}(x)\}] \wedge\ y = v$$

4.3   Runs of a Protocol

Even though the roles of a protocol mention variables, its *runs* (or executions) consist only of ground terms and assertions exchanged in various *instances* of the roles. An instance of a role is formally specified by a *substitution* σ, which is a partial map from $\mathcal{V}$ to the set of all ground terms. We lift σ for terms, assertions and actions in the standard manner. σ is said to be *suitable* for an action a if $\sigma(a)$ is an action, i.e. a typing discipline is followed. A substitution is suitable for a role η if it is defined on all free variables of η and suitable for all actions in η.

A *session* of a protocol Pr is a sequence of actions of the form $\sigma(\eta)$, where $\eta \in Pr$ and σ is suitable for η.

A run of a protocol is an interleaving of sessions in which each agent can construct the messages that it communicates. This is formalized by a notion of *knowledge state*, which represents all the terms and assertions that each agent knows. A *control state* is a record of progress made by an agent in the various sessions he/she participates in.

A knowledge state ks is a tuple $((X_A, \Phi_A)_{A \in Ag})$, where X_A (resp. Φ_A) is the set of ground terms (resp. ground assertions) belonging to an agent A. A control state S is a finite set of sequences of actions. A protocol state is a pair (ks, S) where ks is a knowledge state and S is a control state.

Definition 1. *Let (ks, S) and (ks', S') be two states of a protocol Pr, and let b be a ground action. We say that $(ks, S) \xrightarrow{b} (ks', S')$ iff there is a session $\eta = a \cdot \eta' \in S$ and a substitution σ suitable for η' such that:*

- $b = \sigma(a)$
- $S' = (S \setminus \{\eta\}) \cup \{\sigma(\eta')\}$
- $ks \xrightarrow{b} ks'$ *as given in Table 3.*

In Definition 1, we add $\sigma(\eta')$ rather than η', in order to update the substitution associated with the session on executing the action. This update reflects the new values generated for each fresh nonce variable (in case the action is a send) or the new bindings for input variables (in case the action is a receive). For instance, if $\eta = a \cdot \eta'$ where $a = -A\!: ((x,y), \alpha(x,y))$ and $b = -A\!: ((t,t'), \alpha(t,t'))$, then $\sigma = [x := t, y := t']$. Any occurrence of x in η' is bound to t.

Table 3. Enabling conditions for $ks \xrightarrow{b} ks'$. For each agent A, (X_A, Φ_A) and (X'_A, Φ'_A) represent A's knowledge in ks and ks', respectively. I is the intruder.

Action b	Enabling conditions	Updates
$+A\!: (m)(t, \alpha)$	$X_A \cup m \vdash t$ $X_A \cup m, \Phi_A \vdash \alpha$	$X'_A = X_A \cup m \quad X'_I = X_I \cup \{t\}$ $\Phi'_I = \Phi_I \cup \{\alpha, A \text{ sent } t, A \text{ sent } \alpha\}$
$+A^*\!: (m)(t, \alpha)$	$X_A \cup m \vdash t$ $X_A \cup m, \Phi_A \vdash \alpha$	$X'_A = X_A \cup m \quad X'_I = X_I \cup \{t\}$ $\Phi'_I = \Phi_I \cup \{\alpha\}$
$-A\!: (t, \alpha)$	$X_I \vdash t$ $X_I, \Phi_I \vdash \alpha$	$X'_A = X_A \cup \{t\}$ $\Phi'_A = \Phi_A \cup \{\alpha\}$
$A\!: confirm\ \alpha$	$X_A, \Phi_A \vdash \alpha$	No change
$A\!: deny\ \alpha$	$X_A, \Phi_A \nvdash \alpha$	No change
$A\!: insert\ \alpha$	Always enabled	$\Phi'_A = \Phi_A \cup \{\alpha\}$

Note the crucial difference between the updates for sends and anonymous sends – in the former, the intruder updates its state with A *sent* t and A *sent* α, whereas in the latter, no sender information is available to any observer (including the intruder).

An *initial control state* of Pr is a finite set of sessions of Pr. In the *initial knowledge state*, each agent has her own secret keys and shared keys, all public keys in her database, and potentially some constants of Pr.

Definition 2. *A run of a protocol Pr is $(ks_0, a_1 \cdots a_n)$ such that ks_0 is an initial knowledge state, and there exist sequences $ks_1, \ldots, ks_n$ and $S_0, \ldots, S_n$ such that $(ks_{i-1}, S_{i-1}) \xrightarrow{a_i} (ks_i, S_i)$ for all $i \leq n$.*

4.4   Notes on Implementability

A central aspect of this model is that communicated assertions are "believed" by the recipients. This is reflected in the updates for receive actions. On the other hand, it is not possible for a malicious agent to inject "falsehoods" into the system, as evidenced by the enabling conditions which only allow derivable assertions to be communicated. How might all this be realized in practice?

An implementation is to demand that every communicated assertion be translated into an appropriate zero knowledge proof. But suppose an agent receives ZKPs for assertions α and β from A and B, and wishes to send $\alpha \wedge \beta$ to someone else. For this, she should have the capacity to produce a ZKP for $\alpha \wedge \beta$. This implements the $\wedge i$ rule in our system. Clearly this requires some mechanism for composing ZKPs. Such a system has been studied in [18], which proposes a logical language close to ours, and also discusses modular construction of ZKPs, based on the seminal work on composability of ZKPs [13].

However, [18] has some restrictions on the proof rules for which one can modularly construct ZKPs. For instance, they do not consider disjunction elimination or existential elimination. Nevertheless, we consider these rules since they are at the heart of potential attacks (as illustrated by the earlier example). This situation can be handled formally by making a distinction between rules that are "safe for composition" and rules that are not. A rule like $\wedge i$ is safe for composition, for example, whereas $\vee e$ might not be. We then adopt the restriction that we communicate assertions that are derived using only safe rules. If the derivation of an assertion necessarily involves unsafe rules, then it cannot be communicated to another agent, even though this derivation itself is allowed for local reasoning. In this paper, we therefore consider both local reasoning to derive more assertions (to gain more knowledge about some secrets, for instance) as well as deriving communicable assertions.

5   Formalizing Anonymity

Informally, we say that a voting protocol satisfies anonymity if in all executions of the protocol, no adversary can deduce the connection between a voter and her vote. One way to formalise it is to consider a run ρ where voter V_0 voted 0 and voter V_1 voted 1, and show that there is some run ρ' where the votes of V_0 and V_1 are swapped and every other voter acts the same as in ρ, such that even the most powerful intruder I (who has access to all keys of the authorities) cannot distinguish ρ from ρ'. (Note that we stick to this definition as in [16], but this captures anonymity only under a special class of tally functions.)

Definition 3. *Let* (ks, ρ) *and* (ks', ρ') *be two runs of* Pr, *where* $\rho = a_1 \cdots a_n$ *and* $\rho' = a'_1 \cdots a'_n$. *Let* t_i *and* t'_i *be the terms communicated in* a_i *and* a'_i, *respectively. Let* (X, Φ) *and* (X', Φ') *be the knowledge states of* I *at the end of each run.*

We say that (ks, ρ) *is* I-*indistinguishable from* (ks', ρ') – *denoted* $(ks, \rho) \sim_I$ (ks', ρ') – *if for all assertions* $\alpha(x_1, \ldots, x_k)$ *and all sequences* $i_1 < \cdots < i_k \leq n$:

$$X, \Phi \vdash \alpha(t_{i_1}, \ldots, t_{i_k}) \;\; iff \;\; X', \Phi' \vdash \alpha(t'_{i_1}, \ldots, t'_{i_k}).$$

One can view the parameters $x_1, \ldots, x_k$ occurring in the above definition as *handles*, and the mapping from $x_1, \ldots, x_k$ to $t_{i_1}, \ldots, t_{i_k}$ as an *active substitution*. Parametrized assertions $\alpha(x_1, \ldots, x_k)$ constitute *tests* on each run of the protocol. Thus the above notion is related to the notion of static equivalence that is central to protocol modelling in the applied-pi calculus [4,5,16]. Note that the notion of indistinguishability we use here is trace-based, as that fits naturally with our model. But it is also possible to have a bisimulation-based definition, and adapt our proof ideas.

Consider a voting protocol Pr with three roles – *voter*, *authority* and *counter*, and two phases: *authorization* and *voting*. For simplicity, we assume that there are two fixed agents A and C who play the authority and counter role, respectively. If there is only one voter in a run, then obviously his/her vote can be linked to him/her. If a voter's vote is counted during the authorization phase, then we might have a situation where a vote is cast by a voter before anyone else has been authorized. This again is an easy violation of anonymity. Therefore we assume that in any run of Pr, there are at least two agents playing the voter role, and all $V_i \rightarrow A$ actions precede all $V_j \rightarrow C$ actions.

Fix voter names V_0, V_1, and votes v_0 and v_1. A session η of Pr is said to be an (i,j)-session if η maps id to V_i and v to v_j.

Definition 4. *We say that Pr satisfies anonymity if for every initial knowledge state $ks = (X, \Phi)$ such that $X_A \cup X_C \subseteq X_I$, and for every run (ks, ρ) which includes a $(0,0)$-session and a $(1,1)$-session, there is a run (ks, ρ') which includes a $(1,0)$-session and a $(0,1)$-session such that $(ks, \rho) \sim_I (ks, \rho')$.*

Theorem 1. *The FOO protocol satisfies anonymity.*

Proof. Recall the voter role for FOO from Sect. 4.2. Consider a run (ks, ρ) of FOO whose initial control state is $S \cup \{\eta_0, \eta_1\}$, where η_0 is the $(0,0)$-session and η_1 is the $(1,1)$-session. Let η_2 and η_3 be the $(0,1)$-session and $(1,0)$-session, respectively. We construct a run ρ' which includes η_2 and η_3 such that $(ks, \rho) \sim_I$ (ks, ρ'). The session η_0 assigns values p and r to the keys k and k' from the role description, while η_1 assigns values q and s respectively. For ease of notation, we denote v_0 and v_1 by u and v respectively, and $d = \{u\}_p$ and $e = \{v\}_q$.

Suppose $\rho = a_1 \cdots a_n$. Assume without loss of generality that both sessions η_0 and η_1 are fully played out in ρ. Also without loss of generality, let $i < j < k < l$ be indices such that the send actions of η_0 are a_i and a_k, and the send actions of η_1 are a_j and a_l, where

$$a_i = +V_0\colon (p)(d, \beta(d)) \text{ and } a_k = +V_0^*\colon (r)((\{u\}_r, r), \gamma(u))$$
$$a_j = +V_1\colon (q)(e, \beta(e)) \text{ and } a_l = +V_1^*\colon (s)((\{v\}_s, s), \gamma(v))$$

We build $\rho' = b_1 \cdots b_n$ as shown in Fig. 3.

Observe that ρ' is also a run of FOO starting from the state $(ks, S \cup \{\eta_2, \eta_3\})$, where η_2 contains b_i and b_l, and η_3 contains b_j and b_k. We crucially use the fact that we do not fix the instances of the fresh nonces a priori, so we can swap the action containing p as a fresh nonce with the one containing q as a fresh nonce, for example.

For any term t (resp. assertion α), we define $\mathsf{swp}(t)$ (resp. $\mathsf{swp}(\alpha)$) to be the result of changing all occurrences of d to e and vice versa. swp is lifted to sets of terms and assertions as usual.

Let (X, Φ) and (X', Φ') be the knowledge states of I at the end of ρ and ρ' respectively. It is evident from the construction of ρ' that $X' = \mathsf{swp}(X)$.

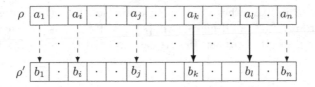

Fig. 3. The dashed arrows capture $b_m = a_m[d \mapsto e, e \mapsto d]$, for all $m \notin \{l, k\}$. For $m \in \{l, k\}$, the thick arrows stand for $b_m = a_m[V_0 \mapsto V_1, V_1 \mapsto V_0]$.

Furthermore, it is easy to see that neither X nor X' derive either p or q, and that $X \vdash_{dy} t$ iff $X' \vdash_{dy} \mathsf{swp}(t)$.

It can also be seen that $\Phi' = \mathsf{swp}(\Phi)$, as elaborated below. For every m, if a_m communicates α, then b_m communicates $\mathsf{swp}(\alpha)$. The other formulas added to Φ are *sent* assertions. For every action a_m other than a_k and a_l, the sender of b_m is unchanged from a_m. Therefore, a *sent* assertion with the same sender name would be added to Φ and Φ'. For a_k and a_l, no *sent* assertions are added since these are anonymous sends. Therefore, $\Phi' = \mathsf{swp}(\Phi)$.

We now prove that $X, \Phi \vdash \alpha(t_{i_1}, \ldots, t_{i_k})$ iff $X', \Phi' \vdash \alpha(t'_{i_1}, \ldots, t'_{i_k})$, for all assertions $\alpha(x_1, \ldots, x_k)$. It suffices to prove that $X, \Phi \vdash \alpha$ iff $X', \Phi' \vdash \mathsf{swp}(\alpha)$ for all α. For every $\exists : \delta$, let y_δ be a variable that does not occur in Φ. A set Θ is said to be *closed under witnesses* if $\delta(y_\delta) \in \Theta$ for all $\exists y : \delta \in \Theta$. Let Π be the smallest superset of Φ closed under witnesses. We use Π' to denote $\mathsf{swp}(\Pi)$. It can be shown by an analysis of derivations that $X, \Phi \vdash \alpha$ iff $X, \Pi \vdash_1 \alpha$ and $X', \Phi' \vdash \alpha$ iff $X', \Pi' \vdash_1 \alpha$, where $\vdash_1$ denotes derivability without using the $\exists e$ rule. Note that both X, Π and X', Π' are safe for d and e in the following sense. They do not derive equalities of the form $p = t$ or $q = t$ for any term t, and they do not derive equalities of the form $d = t'$ or $e = t'$ where t' is a term containing a non-variable. We now prove the final claim needed for indistinguishability of ρ and ρ'.

Claim. For any α, $X, \Pi \vdash_1 \alpha$ iff $X', \Pi' \vdash_1 \mathsf{swp}(\alpha)$.

Proof of Claim. We prove the implication from left to right, by induction on structure of derivations. The other direction holds by symmetry. Suppose π is a derivation of $X, \Pi \vdash \alpha$, with last rule r.

$r = ax$: Suppose $\alpha \in \Pi$. It follows that $\mathsf{swp}(\alpha) \in \Pi'$.
r **is equality of encrypted terms:** π looks as follows.

$$
\begin{array}{cc}
\pi_0 & \pi_1 \\
\vdots & \vdots \\
X, \Pi \vdash s = s' & X, \Pi \vdash m = m'
\end{array}
$$
$$
\overline{X, \Pi \vdash \{s\}_m = \{s'\}_{m'}}
$$

Suppose $\{s\}_m$ is either d or e. Then m is either p or q, and this would mean that $p = m'$ or $q = m'$ is derivable, contradicting safety of X, Π. Therefore

$\{s\}_m$ is not equal to either d or e. By induction hypothesis, $\mathsf{swp}(s = s')$ is derivable from X', Π', and hence $\mathsf{swp}(\{s\}_m = \{s'\}_{m'})$ is also derivable. r is equality of decrypted terms:] In this case, π is of the following form

$$
\begin{array}{ccc}
\pi_0 & \pi_1 & \pi_2 \\
\vdots & \vdots & \vdots
\end{array}
$$

$$
\frac{X, \Pi \vdash \{s\}_m = \{s'\}_{m'} \quad X \vdash_{dy} inv(m) \quad X \vdash_{dy} inv(m')}{X, \Pi \vdash s = s'}
$$

By induction hypothesis, it follows that $X', \Pi' \vdash \mathsf{swp}(\{s\}_m) = \mathsf{swp}(\{s'\}_{m'})$. Observe that neither $\{s\}_m$ nor $\{s'\}_{m'}$ is the same as d or e (for otherwise we would have that $X \vdash_{dy} p$ or $X \vdash_{dy} q$, which is an impossibility). Thus any occurrence of d or e in $\{s\}_m$ is inside s, and similarly for $\{s'\}_{m'}$. Thus $\mathsf{swp}(\{s\}_m) = \{\mathsf{swp}(s)\}_m$ and $\mathsf{swp}(\{s'\}_{m'}) = \{\mathsf{swp}(s')\}_{m'}$. Therefore $\mathsf{swp}(s) = \mathsf{swp}(s')$ is also derivable. ($inv(m)$ and $inv(m')$ are derivable from X' since they are derivable from X and do not mention d or e.)

The rest of the cases are along similar lines or appeal to induction hypothesis.⊣

6   Conclusion

In this paper, we extended the model of [21] by adding existential assertions to the language, as a tool to hide private data used to generate certificates. These assertions are especially useful in coding up constructs that are common to voting protocols. We showed how to specify protocols in this model, and formalised the notion of anonymity in terms of indistinguishability. In a non-trivial example of analysis in our model, we proved anonymity for the FOO protocol.

One way of extending this model is by adding a background theory of universally quantified sentences. Such a theory is a standard part of many authorization systems. For instance, if an agent A communicates to B the assertion $\exists x : \mathtt{voted}(V, x)$ and if the background theory contains the assertion $\forall X, x : \{\mathtt{voted}(X, x) \Rightarrow \mathtt{elg}(X)\}$ then B can conclude $\mathtt{elg}(V)$. More detailed examples are found in [4, 18]. It is an important ingredient in many systems, and we can easily incorporate it in our theoretical model.

Future work includes determining the complexity of this positive fragment of existential first-order logic, and automating the decision procedure for anonymity by extending some existing tool like Tamarin. Also, formalizing other security properties might allow us to prove some previously unknown properties about common protocols. We would also like to extract a canonical representation in this model for any protocol expressed in the terms-only formalism and vice versa.

References

1. Adida, B.: Helios: web-based open-audit voting. In: Proceedings of 17th Conference on Security Symposium (SS 2008), pp. 335–348 (2008)

2. Arapinis, M., Chothia, T., Ritter, E., Ryan, M.: Analysing unlinkability and anonymity using the applied Pi calculus. In: 23rd IEEE Computer Security Foundations Symposium, pp. 107–121 (2010)
3. Butin, D., Gray, D., Bella, G.: Towards verifying voter privacy through unlinkability. In: Jürjens, J., Livshits, B., Scandariato, R. (eds.) ESSoS 2013. LNCS, vol. 7781, pp. 91–106. Springer, Heidelberg (2013). https://doi.org/10.1007/978-3-642-36563-8_7
4. Backes, M., Hritcu, C., Maffei, M.: Type-checking zero-knowledge. In: Proceedings of 15th ACM CCS, pp. 357–370 (2008)
5. Backes, M., Maffei, M., Unruh, D.: Zero-knowledge in the applied Pi-calculus and automated verification of the direct anonymous attestation protocol. In: IEEE Symposium on Security and Privacy, pp. 202–215 (2008)
6. Boureanu, I., Jones, A.V., Lomuscio, A.: Automatic verification of epistemic specifications under convergent equational theories. In: Proceedings of 11th AAMAS, pp. 1141–1148 (2012)
7. Baskar, A., Ramanujam, R., Suresh, S.P.: A DEXPTIME-complete Dolev-Yao theory with distributive encryption. In: Hliněný, P., Kučera, A. (eds.) MFCS 2010. LNCS, vol. 6281, pp. 102–113. Springer, Heidelberg (2010). https://doi.org/10.1007/978-3-642-15155-2_11
8. Chaum, D.: Blind signatures for untraceable payments. In: Chaum, D., Rivest, R.L., Sherman, A.T. (eds.) Advances in Cryptology, pp. 199–203. Springer, Boston (1983). https://doi.org/10.1007/978-1-4757-0602-4_18
9. Cortier, V., Smyth, B.: Attacking and fixing Helios: an analysis of ballot secrecy. In: Proceedings of Computer Security Foundations Symposium, pp. 297–311 (2011)
10. Dolev, D., Yao, A.: On the security of public key protocols. IEEE Trans. Inf. Theory **29**, 198–208 (1983)
11. Fujioka, A., Okamoto, T., Ohta, K.: A practical secret voting scheme for large scale elections. In: International Workshop on the Theory and Application of Cryptographic Techniques, pp. 244–251 (1992)
12. Gray, J.W., Syverson, P.F.: A logical approach to multilevel security of probabilistic systems. Distrib. Comput. **11**, 73–90 (1998)
13. Groth, J., Sahai, A.: Efficient non-interactive proof systems for bilinear groups. In: Smart, N. (ed.) EUROCRYPT 2008. LNCS, vol. 4965, pp. 415–432. Springer, Heidelberg (2008). https://doi.org/10.1007/978-3-540-78967-3_24
14. Halpern, J.Y., O'Neill, K.R.: Anonymity and information hiding in multiagent systems. J. Comput. Secur. **13**(3), 483–514 (2005)
15. Hughes, D., Shmatikov, V.: Information hiding, anonymity and privacy: a modular approach. J. Comput. Secur. **12**(1), 3–36 (2004)
16. Kremer, S., Ryan, M.: Analysis of an electronic voting protocol in the applied Pi calculus. In: Sagiv, M. (ed.) ESOP 2005. LNCS, vol. 3444, pp. 186–200. Springer, Heidelberg (2005). https://doi.org/10.1007/978-3-540-31987-0_14
17. Lafourcade, P., Lugiez, D., Treinen, R.: Intruder deduction for the equational theory of Abelian Groups with distributive encryption. Inf. Comput. **205**(4), 581–623 (2007)
18. Maffei, M., Pecina, K., Reinert, M.: Security and privacy by declarative design. In: IEEE 26th CSF Symposium, pp. 81–96 (2013)
19. Mauw, S., Verschuren, J., de Vink, E.P.: Data anonymity in the FOO voting scheme. In: Electronic Notes in Theoretical Computer Science, pp. 5–28 (2007)
20. The Netflix Prize. http://www.netflixprize.com/index.html

21. Ramanujam, R., Sundararajan, V., Suresh, S.P.: Extending Dolev-Yao with assertions. In: Prakash, A., Shyamasundar, R. (eds.) ICISS 2014. LNCS, vol. 8880, pp. 50–68. Springer, Cham (2014). https://doi.org/10.1007/978-3-319-13841-1_4
22. Syverson, P.F., Stubblebine, S.G.: Group principals and the formalization of anonymity. In: Wing, J.M., Woodcock, J., Davies, J. (eds.) FM 1999. LNCS, vol. 1708, pp. 814–833. Springer, Heidelberg (1999). https://doi.org/10.1007/3-540-48119-2_45

Marked Mix-Nets

Olivier Pereira[1]([✉]) and Ronald L. Rivest[2]

[1] UCLouvain, Louvain-la-Neuve, Belgium
`olivier.pereira@uclouvain.be`
[2] MIT, Cambridge, MA, USA
`rivest@mit.edu`

Abstract. We propose a variant mix-net method, which we call a "marked mix-net". Marked mix-nets avoid the extra cost associated with verifiability (producing a proof of correct mixing operation), while offering additional assurances about the privacy of the messages, compared to a non-verifiable mix-net.

With a marked mix-net, each mix-server adds an extra secret mark in each ciphertext, and the input ciphertexts are made non-malleable but still re-randomizable (RCCA).

Marked mix-nets appear to be a good fit for the mix-net requirements of voting systems that need a mix-net for anonymity but where correctness is guaranteed through independent mechanisms. Our work investigates applications to STAR-Vote, but other applications could be explored, e.g., in Prêt-à-Voter, Selene or Wombat.

1 Introduction

1.1 Mix-Nets

Mix-nets were originally proposed by Chaum [12], then extended and elaborated by many others: additional details can be found in Adida [2], Sampigethaya and Poovendran [24], and Wikström [31], for instance. They are a central tool for anonymizing a set of messages, like votes for instance, by breaking any observable connection between the messages it receives, and those it outputs.

More precisely, a mix-net server, or *mixer*, takes a sequence of encrypted messages and outputs them in permuted order, according a secret permutation that only it knows (sometimes the message encryption and decryption process are also included in the mix-net definition). Since the objective is to hide the permutation, the inputs and outputs to the mix-net must be not only encrypted somehow, but the outputs should be re-encrypted or encrypted differently than the inputs, so that the outputs can not be trivially matched with the corresponding inputs. This places additional requirements on the encryption methods used.

A mix-net can be just a single server, or a sequence of k mixers for some $k > 1$, each permuting its inputs according to its own secret permutation before sending its outputs along to be the inputs to the next mixers.

In some cases one may worry about malicious mixers who do not actually permute their inputs, but perform some other operation instead. For example, in

© International Financial Cryptography Association 2017
M. Brenner et al. (Eds.): FC 2017 Workshops 2017, LNCS 10323, pp. 353–369, 2017.
https://doi.org/10.1007/978-3-319-70278-0_22

a voting context, a mixer could replicate some inputs and delete others, causing a change in the vote tally. Because of the encryption, such manipulations may be hard or impossible to detect; the only thing an observer can really tell is that the number of inputs is equal to the number of outputs.

For such applications one may use a *verifiable mix-net* [4,11,21,23,31]. Here each mixer produces an additional output, which is often a non-interactive zero-knowledge (NIZK) proof that it has operated correctly (i.e., that the set of messages one obtains by decrypting the inputs is the same as the set of messages one obtains by decrypting the outputs; the mixer only permuting things around). Anyone can verify the published NIZK proofs from each mixer.

The design of these NIZK proofs considerably improved over the years, and they certainly are among the most sophisticated cryptographic protocols deployed in real-world applications: they started to be increasingly used in private elections and trialed in public ones [9,14,27,28]. This sophistication also comes with computational complexity. For instance, Bayer and Groth [4] report in 2012 timings between 2 and 5 min for two types of state-of-the-art proofs computed for 100,000 ElGamal ciphertexts, computed in an order q subgroup of $\mathbb{Z}_p^*$ where $|q| = 160$ and $|p| = 1024$. More recently, the authors of Verificatum report timings around 12 min for the shuffle of 100,000 ElGamal ciphertexts, again in an order q subgroup of $\mathbb{Z}_p^*$, but with the more contemporary security parameters $|q| = 3247$ and $|p| = 3248$ [29].

While remarkably efficient, such numbers can become a potential obstacle when running a large-scale public election. Considering for instance an election in a mid-size city with 500,000 voters and 100 races that need to be mixed independently (in order to avoid pattern attacks), the computation of a proof would take between 16 and 100 h. In such a context, and given the typical time-frame of elections, organizers will require each mixer to use several powereful workstations in order to improve speed and parallelism. But such workstations increase the management load, the attack surface, and are likely to require IT staff, which need to be chosen independently for each mixer in order to avoid the creation of a single point of corruption. Overall, these requirements of hardware and experts can be expected to create important costs and organizational challenges.

Marked mix-nets aim at offering a considerably faster alternative that would be useful in some practical settings. Going back to our previous example, the 100 hours required when computing a proof of shuffle modulo a 3248 prime modulus become an online effort of around 13 min on a single laptop when using our marked mix-net, while maintaining all previous parallelism possibilities.

This speed improvement comes with a relaxation of the security guarantees offered by a fully verifiable mix-net.

1. The marked mix-net is only verifiable for privacy/anonymity, but not for correctness. If the marked mix-net verification procedure succeeds, then the link between the input and output ciphertexts is broken as soon as one mixer is honest, and assuming that correctness is verified independently (possibly in a statistical sense). There is indeed no guarantee that the output ciphertexts are a permutation of those at the input: a malicious mixer could remove some

ciphertexts and insert new ciphertexts of his own while remaining undetected by the statistical correctness test, due to luck.

2. A marked mix-net targets security in front of a covert adversary [3]. This means that the marked mix-net aims at making any privacy/anonymity violation likely to be visible to an auditor, and it is the expectation that the sanctions that would result from any evidence of malicious behavior would be high enough to deter any such behavior. (Note that organizational measures can be taken so that a single judge audits the data before they are released, so that any privacy violation would only be visible to that judge, and not to the malicious party.)

We believe that these security properties are satisfactory for some applications, and that the operational simplifications resulting from the lower computational requirements makes marked mix-net an interesting option for some voting systems.

1.2 Applications of Marked Mix-Nets

We were motivated to develop a marked mix-net by the need for a suitable mix-net in the STAR-Vote design [5]. However, other systems, including Selene [22], Wombat [6], or some variants of Prêt-à-Voter that use a human verifiable paper audit trail [16] could possibly adopt a marked mix-net as well.

In STAR-Vote, human-readable paper ballots are produced by ballot marking devices, together with an electronic and encrypted record of the votes. As ballots are collected, this electronic record is replicated and hash chained in various ways, in order to improve robustness and reliability. Furthermore, the content of some hash-chains is included in the voter take-home paper receipts, in order to support end-to-end verifiability. These features make it quite simple to identify which voter produced what ciphertext – and this is not meant to be a secret information.

STAR-Vote is designed to be end-to-end verifiable. Still, it is also designed to accommodate failures in the end-to-end verification process. For instance, the cast-as-indended audit process could fail to be performed on election day, or there might be a soundness issue in the zero-knowledge proofs that are used to prove the validity of the ballots. Therefore, STAR-Vote also supports an efficient ballot-level risk-limiting audit (RLA) [7], illustrated in Fig. 1, which proceeds by comparing paper ballots randomly picked from the urns against electronic ballot records. In order to perform a matching between electronic and paper ballots, the encrypted votes need to be decrypted, but they need to be made anonymous first. STAR-Vote requires the use of a mix-net for that purpose.

The original specification for STAR-Vote indicates that the mix-net should be verifiable. But is a verifiable mix-net *really* needed for STAR-Vote? Perhaps not, as the RLA that it serves compares electronic records against paper records in order to detect if there is any significant malfeasance that would cause divergence between these records, and as such would detect a divergence coming from an incorrect mixing process. So, for integrity purposes, a verifiable mix-net may not be needed.

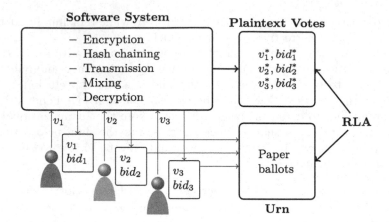

Fig. 1. Overview of the preparation of the inputs of the STAR-Vote risk limiting audit. Voters interact with the software system, which prints paper ballots. After voter verification, the paper ballots are placed into an urn. At the end of the election, the software outputs an anonymized list of plaintext votes. The risk limiting audit compares paper ballots and electronic ballots, referencing them by their ballot id.

Privacy is a different concern, though: STAR-Vote still relies on the electronic process, and on the mix-net in particular, to guarantee that the ballots that are decrypted are anonymous. And the use of a non-verifiable mix-net can raise important privacy issues. For instance, a corrupted last mixer could ignore the ciphertexts handed by the penultimate mixer, and mix those that were the input of the first mixer instead. As a result, this corrupted mixer would be able to deanonymize all cleartext votes after decryption, and this would be completely undetectable. Hence the initial recommendation of a verifiable mix in the STAR paper. But, as explained above, this is not an innocuous choice, both in terms of computational requirement and organizational complexity for the STAR-Vote implementers and auditors.

There are other systems that offer similar features, and for which the use of a marked mix-net could be envisioned.

For example, Wombat [6] is another system that uses both encrypted electronic records that are mixed, and human-readable paper records that can be used to verify the electronic tally. As such, using a marked mix-net in Wombat could increase the speed of the tally, as long as a (ballot polling) risk-limiting audit process is used to confirm the electronic tally based on the paper ballots. Note that the security model would be a bit different between Wombat and STAR-Vote: in STAR-Vote, the mix-net is only a component of the RLA that is applied on the result of a system that is end-to-end verifiable independently of it; while in Wombat, the verifiable mix-net is really a component of the end-to-end verifiability of the system, and moving to a non-fully verifiable mix makes the verification of the correctness of the election result rely on the RLA. Besides, the "delayed effect" attack detailed in Sect. 3.3 could apply.

Another example would be Selene [22], which uses two mix-nets: one for assigning tracker numbers to voters, and one for making the votes anonymous. While the use of a marked mix-net seems difficult for the tracker number assignment phase (e.g., duplication may be hard to detect), the use of a marked mix-net for the vote anonymization phase might be an interesting option. Similar observations can be made about a variant of Prêt-à-Voter proposed by Lundin and Ryan [16], that offers a human readable paper trail.

We do not make any claim about the exact consequences of using a marked mix-net in these systems, and leave these questions open for the moment, while focusing on STAR-Vote in this paper.

The following sections give details. Section 2 provides some background information on ElGamal encryption and an overview of the basic mix-nets techniques. Section 3 explains the design of our marked mix-net. Section 4 describes the risk-limiting process of STAR-Vote and how it could be adapted to use our marked mix-net, and Sect. 5 concludes.

2   Cryptographic Background

For concreteness, we present the new marked mix-net design using a variant of the ElGamal encryption scheme [15]. Our ideas should be portable to mix-nets based on other encryption schemes.

2.1   ElGamal Encryption

Assume that G is a group of prime order q, with generator g. The description of G, including q and g, are public parameters. An ElGamal secret key x is selected by drawing x uniformly at random from $F_q - 0$, and the corresponding public key is computed as $y = g^x$.

The encryption of a message m encoded as an element of G is computed as $E(y, m) = (mg^r, y^r)$ for a uniformly random element r from F_q. The decryption of a ciphertext (a, b) is easy using x: we can indeed define $D(x, a, b) = ab^{-1/x} = a(y^r)^{-1/x} = (mg^r)(g^{xr})^{-1/x} = m$ Note that x is invertible in F_q since x is nonzero. The security of the ElGamal encryption scheme relies on the hardness of the Decision Diffie-Hellman problem [8] in the group G.

There are various techniques for mapping bit strings into ElGamal messages in the group G, but these techniques depend on the choice of G. For the purposes of this paper, the specifics of this mapping do not matter and, when the context is clear, we will not make any distinction between m as a sequence of bits and m's encoding as an element of G.

ElGamal is (multiplicatively) *homomorphic*—the (componentwise) product of ciphertexts is a ciphertext for the product of the messages: $E(y, m_1) * E(y, m_2) = E(y, m_1 m_2)$. (Technically, the above means equality of sets of ciphertexts.) Because ElGamal is homomorphic, a ciphertext can be re-randomized knowing only the public key, by multiplying (componentwise) by an encryption of 1: $E(y, m) * E(y, 1) = E(y, m)$. Finally, ElGamal encryption is *malleable*. In particular, you can multiply the plaintext by a factor of b merely by multiplying one component of the ciphertext by b $(b,1) * E(y,m) = (b,1) * (mg^r, y^r) = ((bm)g^r, y^r) \in E(y, bm)$. We will make an intensive use of these two features in our marked mix-net. (These features are also present in many other encryption schemes, but ElGamal is probably the simplest and most common example.)

2.2   Mix-Nets

In *re-encryption mix-nets* (our focus here), each mixer receives a sequence of n ciphertexts as input, to which it applies a random permutation, after which it re-randomizes each ciphertext in order to make ciphertexts unlinkable, and then outputs the result for the next mixer.

The inputs of a re-encryption mic-net can simply be encrypted with a single public key y and, as explained above, the mix-servers do not need to know the corresponding secret key x in order to re-randomize. The outputs of the last mix-server can be decrypted by a party who knows x. (In some cases, x may be secret-shared [25] by several parties, and a threshold number of such parties cooperate to decrypt the mix-net outputs [18].)

Looking at the re-randomization process of ElGamal, we can observe an interesting feature: the re-randomization is essentially the multiplication of two ciphertexts that are independent of each other. This means that a mixer can, in an offline phase, before he sees any ciphertext, compute a collection of encryptions of "1" $\in G$. Then, the online phase can simply consist in ciphertext multiplications, which is orders of magnitude faster than computing a ciphertext (the exact factor being strongly dependent on the choice of G). This is the property we aim at preserving when designing our marked mix-net. In particular, this excludes so-called decryption mix-nets, in which each mixer would perform a partial decryption, as this would cause a latency of at least one modular exponentiation per ciphertext and per mixer.

Notation: We let k denote the number of mix servers. We let m_i denote the ith input message, for $1 \le i \le n$. We let $c_i^{(j)}$ denote the ith input to the jth mix server, for $1 \le i \le n$ and $1 \le j \le k$, and let $\hat{c}_i^{(j)}$ denote the ith output of the jth mix server. Since the outputs of server j are the inputs to server $j+1$, we have $\hat{c}_i^{(j)} = c_i^{(j+1)}$ for all i and $1 \le j < k$. Since there is no server $k+1$, the values $\{\hat{c}_i^{(k)}\}$ are the mix-net outputs.

3   Marked Mix-Nets

3.1   Privacy Issues with Non-verifiable Mix-Nets

Independently of the integrity properties, the use of the re-encryption mix-net outlined above raises several privacy concerns.

Mixer bypassing. First, when using k mixers in order to avoid the need to trust any particular one, there is no way to be sure that the mixers do not bypass each other during the mixing process. In particular, M_k could ignore the $\hat{c}_*^{(k-1)}$ ciphertexts and use the $c_*^{(1)}$ instead. As a result, M_k alone would be able to choose the permutation between the $c_*^{(1)}$ and the $\hat{c}_*^{(k)}$ ciphertexts, which is precisely what the use of k mixers is expected to avoid. And there would be no way to detect this manipulation.

One way to avoid this would be to require each mixer to apply, to each ciphertext, a *mark* that shows that it processed this ciphertext, and that can be removed after the end of the mixing process.

Ciphertext replication. At the other end of the chain of mixers, M_1 could also violate the privacy of some voters, by exploiting the homomorphic property of ElGamal. The ciphertexts in $c_*^{(1)}$ can be expected to have a known structure and, in some cases, they could contain elements that cannot be verified easily, or cannot be verified at all, like a random padding used in the message encoding. For instance, in STAR-Vote, each $c_i^{(1)}$ is actually made of two ElGamal ciphertexts, one of them encrypting a hash that can only be matched if the corresponding paper ballot is picked, which is extremely unlikely in a large-scale election. By relying on this, M_1 could target a ciphertext $c_i^{(1)}$ by replacing $c_j^{(1)}$ with a ciphertext $\bar{c}_j^{(1)} = Enc(y, d) \cdot c_i^{(1)}$ where d is a message carefully crafted by M_1 so that $\bar{c}_j^{(1)}$ looks like a perfectly plausible ciphertext, but can still be recognized after decryption of the outputs of M_k by looking for two messages with difference d.

This problem could be avoided by making the ciphertexts somehow non-malleable, so that any duplication or malicious manipulation of a ciphertext would become visible at time of audit. This requirement may seem to be contradictory with the requirement of being able to mark ciphertexts (outlined above), and the reconciliation of these two features is at the core of the design of our marked mix-net.

3.2   A Marked Mix-Net

Our marked mix-net aims to address these privacy issues (and others, which will be discussed later). Still, like the original mix-nets, it does not provide any correctness guarantees: mixers remain able to add or delete ciphertexts during the mixing process. However, contrary to the original mix-nets, these additions and deletions must be independent of the honest mix-net inputs, hence preventing the leakage of information about these inputs.

In order to obtain an extremely fast protocol, we address these issues in a covert adversary model [3], in which attacks can succeed with non negligible probablity, but will also be detected with a non negligible probability. Our assumption here (which is in line with the motivation of the covert adversary model) is that the mixing will be executed by well-defined public parties, and that any cheating detection would immediately trigger police investigation and important penalties, that would be sufficient to deter any such malicious behavior in the first place. Aumann and Lindell discuss a strong version of the covert adversary model in which, when an attack is detected, the adversary does not learn any undue infrormation (so, it is punished on top of having no benefits from his attack). Variants of our marked mix-net could offer this flavor of security, e.g., by using two layers of encryption, but the resulting protocol would be more expensive.

Non-malleability. The resistance to replication attacks suggests the use of an encryption scheme offering some form of non-malleability property that would guarantee that any unauthorized ciphertext manipulation would trigger an alert. However, we still need to be able to re-randomize ciphertexts, in order to be able to perform the mixing operations.

These properties are reminiscent of the notion of re-randomizable RCCA encryption, proposed by Canetti et al. [10], which requires the possibility to re-randomize ciphertexts while preventing any other homomorphic transformation. RCCA security of course does not prevent a mixer to make exact ballot copies (possibly re-randomized), and we will need a mechanism in order to detect these.

One efficient solution for building re-randomizable RCCA encryption has been proposed by Phan and Pointcheval [19], and consists in applying a transformation, called OAEP 3-Round (OAEP3 for short), to messages before encrypting them with a probabilistic encryption scheme like ElGamal.

This transformation assumes the availability of 3 independent random oracles, H_1, H_2 and H_3 (in practice, these can be implemented with a single hash function and 3 distinct prefixes). The OAEP3 transform processes a message m, represented as a bit-string, using a fresh random bit string r as follows:

$$s = m \oplus H_1(r) \quad t = r \oplus H_2(s) \quad u = s \oplus H_3(t)$$

and outputs the pair (t, u).

The OAEP3 transformed message can then be encrypted with ElGamal as usual, and the resulting scheme is shown to be RCCA secure [19], assuming the hardness of the gap Diffie-Hellman problem in G [17], a problem that consists in solving an instance of the computational Diffie-Hellman problem in the presence of a Decisional Diffie-Hellman oracle. The intuition underlying this result is common to the OAEP-style transformations: any change into t or u leads to message changes that are unpredictable without querying the H_i oracles first. So, a modification of a ciphertext can result in a recognizable modification of the corresponding plaintext only if this plaintext is known in the first place.

Still, it does not guarantee that mixers operate on the expected ciphertexts in the first place, without bypassing other mixers. This concern will be addressed below.

Marking. The mixer bypassing problem discussed above can be solved by requiring all mixers to add a secret mark on each of the ciphertexts that they process, on top of the OAEP3 transform.

Concretely, each of the k trustees proceeds as follows:

1. The encryption process is modified by requiring each party willing to submit an encryption of a message m to the first mixer to encrypt the message $\text{OAEP3}(m\|0^\mu)$ instead, where μ is a security parameter.
2. Each mixer $M_i \in \{M_1, \ldots, M_k\}$ chooses a secret mark $a_i \in \mathbb{Z}_q$, and broadcasts $E(y, \text{OAEP3}(a_i))$. (It may be appropriate to use a key y that is different of the one used to encrypt the messages.)
3. At mixing time, instead of simply re-randomizing each ciphertext by multiplying it with a ciphertext of the form (g^r, y^r), each mixer performs multiplications with ciphertexts of the form $(a_i g^r, y^r)$, hence multiplying the encrypted message by a_i.
4. When the whole mixing procedure is complete, the secret marks are decrypted, and the decrypted outputs of the last mixer are all divided by the product of all a_i's. It is then verified that the 0^μ sequence is present in all the plaintexts, and that the randomness used in OAEP3 is unique. An investigation is triggered otherwise.

The 0^μ string provides a baseline on top of which all marks are applied. If a decrypted ciphertexts fails to have been properly marked, there is a probability $2^{-\mu}$ that, after the removal of all expected marks, it would still end with the 0^μ sequence. So, in our covert adversary setting, a very short μ may be sufficient, e.g., $\mu = 1$ for having a probability around $1/2$ of detecting this kind of malfeasance.

In a similar way, if an adversary tries to perform a copy of a ciphertext, possibly rerandomized or modified in some way, the non-malleability property obtained from OAEP3 will either cause the repetition of the randomness used in the OAEP3 transform, which we require to be unique, or remove the 0^μ string with noticeable probability, leading to an invalid ciphertext.

Note also that we demand the encrypted marks of the initial broadcasts to be OAEP3 processed too, essentially to make sure that the encrypted mark that is broadcast cannot be used by a corrupted mixer to apply another mixer's mark (using the homomorphic property of ElGamal encryption for instance).

Thanks to this marking process, any mixer that would try to bypass other mixers and process ciphertexts that did no go through the expected path will fail to contain the marks that it should. This will also leave evidences through the list of ciphertexts, and the cheating mixer can then be identified. The marking mechanism used here is similar to that used by Chaum in the "dining cryptographer's problem" [13]. Here marks are also members of the underlying abelian group, and can be added or removed from the message in any order.

The resulting marked mix-net is described in Fig. 2.

3.3 Security Analysis

We discuss how our marked mix-net defeats the traditional attacks on mix-nets, including those discussed in the in-depth review of Adida [2], and leave

The marked mix-net proceeds as follows:

1. A public key y is made available to all message senders and mixers.
2. Each mixer M_i picks a random mark $a_i \in \mathbb{Z}_q$, and broadcasts $E(y, \text{OAEP3}(a_i))$.
3. In order to submit a message m to the first mixer, submit a ciphertext $E(y, \text{OAEP3}(m \| 0^\mu))$.
4. When all inputs have been submitted, each mixer M_i sequentially shuffles its input ciphertexts, multiplies each of them with a fresh ciphertexts $E(y, a_i)$, then passes the resulting ciphertexts to mixer M_{i+1}.
5. The ciphertexts produced by the last mixer are verifiably decrypted, producing a sequence $d_1, \ldots, d_n$.
6. The encrypted marks are verifiably decrypted, making the a_i's available.
7. The mixed messages $\hat{m}_1, \ldots, \hat{m}_n$ are retrieved by computing $(\hat{m}_i \| 0^\mu \| r_i) = \text{OAEP3}^{-1}(d_i/a)$ where $a = a_1 a_2 \cdots a_k$. If the 0^μ sequence is missing, or if any pair of ciphertexts shares the same r_i then an investigation is triggered in order to identify the cheating party.
8. The inputs and outputs of each mixer are tested to be made of elements of the group G, and the ZK proofs are verified.

Fig. 2. The marked mix-net

a rigorous specification and analysis of the security properties as an important and non trivial future work, that should be performed before any deployment.

1. **Related inputs.** In this attack, a corrupted party submits a ciphertext computed as a function of another one, in order to detect a know relation after decryption and de-anonymize targeted ciphertexts. As usual, we require the input ciphertexts to be submitted using a submission-secure scheme [30], which prevents related submissions. Still, if the first mixers are corrupted, they would be able to remove one ciphertext (or more) and replace it with a ciphertext related to the one that is targeted. The relation between the two ciphertexts can be of two types: either a direct (re-encrypted) copy, or an encryption of a modified ciphertext. Copies would cause the presence of messages with identical randomness (r_i) after decryption. Modifications would, thanks to the properties of the OAEP3 transform, result in the decryption of a random message, which would then contain the 0^μ message tag with probability $2^{-\mu}$ and be declared invalid with high probability. Both these attacks would be detected and investigated, in contradiction with our covert adversary security model.
2. **Attacks based on lack of semantic security.** Our ciphertexts remain standard ElGamal ciphertexts, which prevents any leakage of partial information that could be used to track ciphertexts.
3. **Attacks based on partial decryption during mixing.** Our marked mixnet only performs decryption after the completion of the mixing, preventing any coalition of mixers to take advantage of the partial decryption of others.

4. **Mixing cancellation.** We prevent mixers from canceling the permutation applied by other mixers (by mixing their inputs instead of their outputs) thanks to our marking mechanism: skipping any mixer will cause a missing mark, which will be spotted at decryption time.

5. **Proof wrapping.** Some mixes use double encryption layers, which may cause issues when proofs are provided about the outer layer only (e.g., an adversary could add a third encryption layer and make proofs about that last one). OAEP3 can be interpreted as an extra layer in the encryption mechanism. However, it is designed to prevent malleability, which is the core ingredient used in wrapping attacks.

6. **Subgroup tagging.** A corrupted mixer may lift some ciphertexts to another (possibly larger) group, and use this mechanism to circumvent the guarantees of semantic security and track a ballot throughout the mixing process. In order to prevent such attacks, we require the mix verification process to check that the outputs of each mixer indeed lie in the right group.

7. **Delayed effect.** Here, a corrupted first mixer uses the time between the closing of the polling places and the beginning of the mixing to replace some ciphertexts, possibly with the help of the parties who submitted them. This may make it possible to change or adapt votes after the closing of the votes, based on fresh information. Such a strategy would definitely pass our verification process and is the main reason that makes it non-verifiable in the traditional sense. Whether it matters is application dependent. In an application like STAR-Vote, in which the mixing-process is followed by a risk-limiting audit against the paper ballots that were submitted before the closing of the polling places, the RLA guarantees that this kind of attack will be limited to happen for a very small number of ciphertexts, small enough to make sure that it has no impact on the election outcome. Besides, any change would also create discrepancies with the results of the end-to-end verifiable tally.

8. **Input guessing.** This attack is similar to the previous one but, instead of colluding with a voter, the adversary (corrupting the first mixer, for instance) can try to guess someone's vote (or maybe just verify that a voter followed instructions) and replace the ciphertexts submitted by the targeted voter with fresh ciphertexts encrypting the expected vote intent. As before, this substitution cannot be detected as part of the mixing process. It is also benign in itself, as long as the adversary has no way to detect whether his guess was correct or not. This may not be the case however in an application like STAR-Vote, where the RLA may actually offer evidence of a ballot modification, which would happen as a the result of a wrong guess. But this communication channel, which may inform the adversary about the targeted voter intent, would at the same time offer evidence of malicious behaviour, and this attack strategy would therefore be excluded by our covert adversary model.

9. **Permutation guessing.** In another variation of the previous attacks, an attacker could make a guess on the mapping between an input ciphertext and an output ciphertext. If the guess is correct, then the division of these two ciphertexts would provide an encryption of the mark of that mixer, which

could be used to bypass him. However, this attack will be visible in the likely case of an incorrect guess, and is therefore excluded by the covert adversary model.

In terms of accountability, the use of a marked mix-net makes investigations more challenging than in the case of a fully verifiable mix-net: in the fully verifiable case, it is enough to check all proofs of shuffle and decryption in order to find out who cheated during the mixing process. A marked mix-net does not provide such features anymore. However, we require all mixers to keep track of their secret permutations and reencryption factors until the end of the audit process (e.g., by storing their random seed). These can be used in order to obtain the necessary accountability in case of discrepancy happening during decryption (e.g., the 0^μ sequence is missing) or if the RLA detects a problem. A simple strategy for making mixers accountable would be to ask them to provide their re-encryption factors related to problematic ciphertexts, proceeding by following the mixers in backwards order. This is extremely simple but may raise privacy concerns in some cases. Still, if the penalty of a cheating mixer is high enough, it is sufficient to deter from any temptation. A privacy-friendly solution would be, in case of problem, to ask the mixers to produce a traditional ZK proof of their correct behavior. Again, even if this is not desired due to the computational burden that it would bring, the perspective that this will happen and result in cheater detection can be expected to deter mixers from adopting any malicious behavior. A malicious vote submission device could also submit an invalid ballot as an input to the mix-net, in order to trigger the full proof process and slow down the mixing. Whether this is realistic or not is application dependent: ballots submitted to a mix-net are typically identifiable, and this may be enough to deter anyone from adopting this strategy, which offers fairly low benefits. Besides, when ballots are encoded by a DRE (as in STAR-Vote for instance), an invalid ballot also becomes a sign of a serious hacking in the system, which would trigger deep investigation anyway.

4   STAR-Vote

4.1   STAR-Vote's Risk Limiting Audit

As explained in Sect. 1.2, our motivation for marked mix-nets comes from the risk limiting audit process in STAR-Vote. We provide more details about the process proposed in the original paper, discuss how it can be adapted to use our marked mix-net, and the benefits that result from it. In order to simplify our discussion, we only focus on the aspects of STAR-Vote that are relevant to the RLA.

STAR-Vote ballots are prepared by ballot marking devices (BMD) all interconnected, inside each voting office, to a controller and an urn. When a voter prepares a ballot, two records are produced:

1. A paper record, which contains (among other things) the voter choices in human readable form, as well as a random, high-entropy, unique ballot id (or

bid). This *bid* is printed on the paper, but not otherwise known to the voters, election officials, or mix servers.

2. An electronic record, which contains (among other things):
   - An encryption of the voter choices, under the form of a counter set to "0" or "1" encrypted for each option that the voter can select. As a Texas election can contain 100 races, this can make a few hundreds ciphertexts.
   - An encryption of $H(bid\|r)$ for each race r to which the voter participates.

So, for each race r included in the ballot, ciphertexts of the form $E(y, H(bid\|r)), E(y, v)$ are produced, in which $E(y, v)$ encrypts the content of the vote v for race r.

The paper record is placed into an urn, making it human readable but anonymous, while the electronic record is fully encrypted but cannot be considered to be anonymous (including because various logs can make it quite easy to match the timing at which a ciphertext is produced and the one at which a voter is seen to produce his ballot).

When the polls are closed, the electronic record is used to compute the election tally very fast, by decrypting the homomorphic aggregation of the ciphertexts.

The mix-net permutes the $E(y, H(bid\|r)), E(y, v)$ tuples race by race (they are considered as a single big ciphertext from the mix-net point of view), and the outputs are then decrypted, revealing the plaintext items $H(bid\|r), v$.

This structure defeats "pattern attacks", also called "Italian attacks" [20], since it isn't obvious from the output which votes are from the same ballot (for different races) as long as the *bid* is not known.

The risk-limiting audit examines randomly selected paper ballots one at a time until enough evidence has been gathered to confirm the nominal (initial, reported) election outcome, or until all paper ballots have been examined. In the latter case, a full recount has been performed by the RLA.

When a paper ballot is selected, its *bid* is read. This allows $H(bid\|r)$ to be recomputed for each race, which allows the appropriate entries to be identified in the decrypted mix-net output, together with the corresponding vote v. The voter selections on the paper ballot for each race can then be examined for equality with the value v.

4.2   Using a Marked Mix-Net

STAR-Vote prescribes the use of a verifiable mix-net, for privacy reasons more than for verifiability reasons, since the output of the mix-net is already verified both against the homomorphic tally (at the global level) and through the RLA (at the ballot level). We suggested above that the use of a marked mix-net could provide a more efficient and simpler choice.

The specific structure of the messages mixed in STAR-Vote suggests further tweaks. First we may question the benefits of mixing tuples of ciphertexts instead of single ciphertext. STAR-Vote has distinct ciphertexts in order to be able to reuse the ciphertexts used in the homomorphic tally as part of the inputs of the mix-net, which provides some guarantees of consistency between the inputs of the mixnet and homomorphic tally. Having two ciphertexts per ballot and per race however potentially doubles the computational power that is required to decrypt the outputs of the mix-net, a task that we would like to keep short. The consistency guarantee may also not be critical since, in case of investigation, evidence of the discrepancies can still be collected.

The reuse of the ciphertexts produced for the homomorphic tally as inputs for the mix-net also raises difficulties for our marked mix-net described above, since plaintexts need to be OAEP3 processed before encryption. We therefore suggest to modify the STAR-Vote design to have one single ciphertext per ballot and per race, which can then be conveniently processed through the OAEP3 transform, as specified in Fig. 2.

The use of the OAEP3 transform does not raise any difficulty when the message space of the encryption scheme is large enough (for instance, when G is the subgroup of quadratic residues modulo a large p). However, the use of elliptic curve might raise some difficulties. Indeed, while the OAEP3 expansion is quite low (it does not require any strong redundancy, like OAEP for instance), there is still a length increase that comes from the randomness that is added, and which may look unnecessary in the context of an encryption scheme like ElGamal, which is already randomized. This randomness is however useful for at least two reasons: in general, it guarantees the non-malleability, by preventing an adversary to compute a table of all possible OAEP3 outputs in case of small message space and, in the context of a mixnet, it prevents the invisible inclusion in the mixing process of ciphertext copies.

We may however observe that the messages that we need to encrypt all contain a single unique component that is indistinguishable from a sequence of random bits: $H(bid\|r)$. We therefore suggest that the inputs of the mixnet could be computed as: $E(y, \mathrm{OAEP3}(v\|0^\mu; H(bid\|r)))$, where the message part of the inputs of OAEP3 is $v\|0^\mu$ and $H(bid\|r)$ is used as fresh randomness. It can be observed, as did Abe et al. for instance [1], that the OAEP3 transformation does not guarantee non-malleability with respect to the random part of the OAEP3 inputs (such non-malleability is provided by their OAEP-4X transformation). However, we really need the non-malleability with respect to the 0^μ part, which is sufficient to detect malicious behaviors. As a result, the message expansion resulting from the input pre-processing of the marked mix-net is only of μ bits, where μ can be just a small constant.

The modifications that we propose for the STAR-Vote RLA are summarized in Fig. 3.

4.3   Benefits of the Approach

The proposed approach considerably simplifies the risk-limiting process from an algorithmic point of view: it avoids the need to run a full verifiable mixnet for the sole purpose of the risk-limiting audit.

It also considerably decreases the computational power that is required from the mixers: their task can now be almost entirely precomputed and, in particular,

1. The ballot marking device produces a submission secure encryption $E(y, \mathrm{OAEP3}(v\|0^\mu; H(bid\|r)))$ instead of the encryption $E(y, H(bid\|r))$.
2. The marked mix-net of Figure 2 is used to process these ciphertexts (except for Step 3, which is performed as above), instead of a verifiable mix-net.

Fig. 3. Proposed changes in the STAR-Vote RLA.

no online modular exponentiation is required. This may enable to close the election audit process faster, reduce the computing infrastructure costs, and also reduce the organizational burden.

The latency before the beginning of the paper comparison phase of the RLA may not change, however: if a covert adversary setting is accepted, the mixers of the verifiable mix-net may simply shuffle the ciphertexts and pass them along, which would cost as much as our marked mix-net, and only start computing their proofs of shuffle after that, knowing that they will eventually need to produce them for audit. Note that, in a traditional adversary setting, proofs would need to be provided and verified before the beginning of the decryption phase, and the strong latency would be back.

5 Conclusions

We have described a new type of mix-net that offers weaker verifiability properties than a traditional verifiable mix-net, yet preserves privacy even when all public keys are known and when all but one mix server may act maliciously.

Our marked mix-net is considerably more efficient than a fully verifiable mix-net in terms of computational load: the online working load of each mixer is only 2 multiplications per ElGamal ciphertext, while recent proof of shuffle (e.g., [4,26]) require several online exponentiations per ciphertext. We can then expect to decrease the computational load by a factor at least 100. We believe that this is an appealing feature in large scale elections.

We suggest that STAR-Vote, and possibly other voting schemes, need not use a verifiable mix-net and may use the marked mix-net presented here instead. However, before any deployment, a rigorous analysis of the security properties of the marked mix-net would be needed.

Acknowledgement. We thank the anonymous reviewers for their helpful comments and suggestions.

The first author is grateful to the Belgian Fund for Scientific Research (F.R.S.-FNRS) for its financial support provided through the the SeVoTe project. The second author gratefully acknowledges support for his work on this project received from the Center for Science of Information (CSoI), an NSF Science and Technology Center, under grant agreement CCF-0939370, and from the Department of Statistics, University of California, Berkeley, which hosted his sabbatical visit during this work.

References

1. Abe, M., Kiltz, E., Okamoto, T.: Chosen ciphertext security with optimal ciphertext overhead. In: Pieprzyk, J. (ed.) ASIACRYPT 2008. LNCS, vol. 5350, pp. 355–371. Springer, Heidelberg (2008). https://doi.org/10.1007/978-3-540-89255-7_22
2. Adida, B.: Advances in cryptographic voting systems. Ph.D. thesis. MIT (2006)
3. Aumann, Y., Lindell, Y.: Security against covert adversaries: efficient protocols for realistic adversaries. In: Vadhan, S.P. (ed.) TCC 2007. LNCS, vol. 4392, pp. 137–156. Springer, Heidelberg (2007). https://doi.org/10.1007/978-3-540-70936-7_8
4. Bayer, S., Groth, J.: Efficient zero-knowledge argument for correctness of a shuffle. In: Pointcheval, D., Johansson, T. (eds.) EUROCRYPT 2012. LNCS, vol. 7237, pp. 263–280. Springer, Heidelberg (2012). https://doi.org/10.1007/978-3-642-29011-4_17
5. Bell, S., Benaloh, J., Byrne, M.D., DeBeauvoir, D., Eakin, B., Fisher, G., Kortum, P., McBurnett, N., Montoya, J., Parker, M., Pereira, O., Stark, P.B., Wallach, D.S., Winn, M.: STAR-vote: a secure, transparent, auditable, and reliable voting system. USENIX J. Election Technol. Syst. (JETS) **1**(1), 8 (2013)
6. Ben-Nun, J., Fahri, N., Llewellyn, M., Riva, B., Rosen, A., Ta-Shma, A., Wikström, D.: A new implementation of a dual (paper and cryptographic) voting system. In: E-VOTE (2012)
7. Benaloh, J., Jones, D., Lazarus, E.L., Lindeman, M., Stark, P.B.: Soba: secrecy-preserving observable ballot-level audit. In: EVT-WOTE 2011. USENIX (2011)
8. Boneh, D.: The decision Diffie-Hellman problem. In: Buhler, J.P. (ed.) ANTS 1998. LNCS, vol. 1423, pp. 48–63. Springer, Heidelberg (1998). https://doi.org/10.1007/BFb0054851
9. Bulens, P., Giry, D., Pereira, O.: Running mixnet-based elections with helios. In: Shacham, H., Teague, V. (eds.) Electronic Voting Technology Workshop/Workshop on Trustworthy Elections. USENIX (2011)
10. Canetti, R., Krawczyk, H., Nielsen, J.B.: Relaxing chosen-ciphertext security. In: Boneh, D. (ed.) CRYPTO 2003. LNCS, vol. 2729, pp. 565–582. Springer, Heidelberg (2003). https://doi.org/10.1007/978-3-540-45146-4_33
11. Chase, M., Kohlweiss, M., Lysyanskaya, A., Meiklejohn, S.: Verifiable elections that scale for free. In: Kurosawa, K., Hanaoka, G. (eds.) PKC 2013. LNCS, vol. 7778, pp. 479–496. Springer, Heidelberg (2013). https://doi.org/10.1007/978-3-642-36362-7_29
12. Chaum, D.: Untraceable electronic mail, return addresses, and digital pseudonyms. Commun. ACM **24**(2), 84–90 (1981)
13. Chaum, D.: The dining cryptographers problem: unconditional sender and recipient untraceability. J. Cryptol. **1**(1), 65–75 (1988)
14. Culnane, C., Ryan, P.Y.A., Schneider, S., Teague, V.: vVote: a verifiable voting system. ACM Trans. Inf. Syst. Secur. **18**(1), 3:1–3:30 (2015)
15. ElGamal, T.: A public key cryptosystem and a signature scheme based on discrete logarithms. IEEE Trans. Inform. Theory IT **31**(4), 469–472 (1985)
16. Lundin, D., Ryan, P.Y.A.: Human readable paper verification of prêt à voter. In: Jajodia, S., Lopez, J. (eds.) ESORICS 2008. LNCS, vol. 5283, pp. 379–395. Springer, Heidelberg (2008). https://doi.org/10.1007/978-3-540-88313-5_25
17. Okamoto, T., Pointcheval, D.: The gap-problems: a new class of problems for the security of cryptographic schemes. In: Kim, K. (ed.) PKC 2001. LNCS, vol. 1992, pp. 104–118. Springer, Heidelberg (2001). https://doi.org/10.1007/3-540-44586-2_8

18. Pedersen, T.P.: A threshold cryptosystem without a trusted party. In: Davies, D.W. (ed.) EUROCRYPT 1991. LNCS, vol. 547, pp. 522–526. Springer, Heidelberg (1991). https://doi.org/10.1007/3-540-46416-6_47

19. Phan, D.H., Pointcheval, D.: OAEP 3-round:a generic and secure asymmetric encryption padding. In: Lee, P.J. (ed.) ASIACRYPT 2004. LNCS, vol. 3329, pp. 63–77. Springer, Heidelberg (2004). https://doi.org/10.1007/978-3-540-30539-2_5

20. Popoveniuc, S., Stanton, J.: Undervote and pattern voting: vulnerability and a mitigation technique. In: Preproceedings of the 2007 IAVoSS Workshop on Trustworthy Elections (WOTE 2007) (2007)

21. Ren, J., Wu, J.: Survey on anonymous communications in computer networks. Comput. Commun. **33**(4), 420–431 (2010)

22. Ryan, P.Y.A., Rønne, P.B., Iovino, V.: Selene: voting with transparent verifiability and coercion-mitigation. In: Clark, J., Meiklejohn, S., Ryan, P.Y.A., Wallach, D., Brenner, M., Rohloff, K. (eds.) FC 2016. LNCS, vol. 9604, pp. 176–192. Springer, Heidelberg (2016). https://doi.org/10.1007/978-3-662-53357-4_12

23. Sako, K., Kilian, J.: Receipt-free mix-type voting scheme. In: Guillou, L.C., Quisquater, J.-J. (eds.) EUROCRYPT 1995. LNCS, vol. 921, pp. 393–403. Springer, Heidelberg (1995). https://doi.org/10.1007/3-540-49264-X_32

24. Sampigethaya, K., Poovendran, R.: A survey on mix networks and their secure applications. In: Proceedings of IEEE, vol. 94, no. 12, pp. 2142–2181 (2006)

25. Shamir, A.: How to share a secret. CACM **22**(11), 612–613 (1979)

26. Terelius, B., Wikström, D.: Proofs of restricted shuffles. In: Bernstein, D.J., Lange, T. (eds.) AFRICACRYPT 2010. LNCS, vol. 6055, pp. 100–113. Springer, Heidelberg (2010). https://doi.org/10.1007/978-3-642-12678-9_7

27. Tsoukalas, G., Papadimitriou, K., Louridas, P., Tsanakas, P.: From helios to zeus. USENIX J. Election Technol. Syst. **1**(1), 1–17 (2013)

28. Verificatum (2015). http://www.verificatum.org/

29. Verificatum: complexity analysis of the verificatum mix-net vmn version 3.0.2 (July 2016). http://www.verificatum.com/files/complexity-3.0.2.pdf

30. Wikström, D.: Simplified submission of inputs to protocols. In: Ostrovsky, R., De Prisco, R., Visconti, I. (eds.) SCN 2008. LNCS, vol. 5229, pp. 293–308. Springer, Heidelberg (2008). https://doi.org/10.1007/978-3-540-85855-3_20

31. Wikström, D.: Electronic election schemes and mix-nets (2015). http://www.csc.kth.se/~dog/esearch/

Pseudo-Code Algorithms for Verifiable Re-encryption Mix-Nets

Rolf Haenni$^{(\boxtimes)}$, Philipp Locher, Reto Koenig, and Eric Dubuis

Bern University of Applied Sciences, 2501 Biel, Switzerland
{rolf.haenni,philipp.locher,reto.koenig,eric.dubuis}@bfh.ch

Abstract. Implementing the shuffle proof of a verifiable mix-net is one of the most challenging tasks in the implementation of an electronic voting system. For non-specialists, even if they are experienced software developers, this task is nearly impossible to fulfill without spending an enormous amount of resources into studying the necessary cryptographic theory. In this paper, we present one of the existing shuffle proofs in a condensed form and explain all the necessary technical details in corresponding pseudo-code algorithms. The goal of presenting the shuffle proof in this form is to make it accessible to a broader audience and to facilitate its implementation by non-specialists.

1 Introduction

Various cryptographic techniques have been developed to guarantee vote privacy in verifiable electronic voting systems. In practice, processing the list of encrypted votes through a *verifiable re-encryption mix-net* has become the dominating approach in the last couple of years. Various systems developed by academics, practitioners, and vendors are based on this approach, which imitates the physical process of shaking a ballot box containing real votes on paper. While shuffling a list of encryptions is a simple process from a cryptographic point of view, proving that the shuffle has been preformed correctly is a much more difficult task.

For proving the correctness of a cryptographic shuffle, two provably secure proof techniques are dominant in the literature [2,8] (other methods exist, but many of them have been proven insecure). Due to the complexity of the underlying cryptography, implementing these techniques is almost impossible for non-specialists. Given the manifold subtleties and pitfalls that need to be considered in a cryptographic implementation of such a complexity, even an experienced software developer with a broad cryptographic background may struggle in getting everything right.

Alternatively, system developers may try to delegate the shuffle proof to an existing software library, but such libraries are not available in large numbers. To the best of our knowledge, the only professionally maintained implementation is the *Verificatum Mix-Net* (VMN), which exists since 2008 [10,11].[1] A few other

---

[1] See http://www.verificatum.com.

© International Financial Cryptography Association 2017
M. Brenner et al. (Eds.): FC 2017 Workshops 2017, LNCS 10323, pp. 370–384, 2017.
https://doi.org/10.1007/978-3-319-70278-0_23

shuffle proof implementations have been realized, for example as part of the *UniCrypt* library [6], but their intended area of application is mainly academic. In the context of political elections, a practical problem of using third-party libraries in an actual implementation is the complicated system certification process, which gets more difficult with every additional dependency. Having the smallest possible number of dependencies to non-standard libraries may therefore be a desirable strategy for both system developers and election administrations.

In this paper, we focus on the shuffle proof proposed by Wikström and Terelius [8,9,11]. In their original publications, the proof is split into an offline and online part and covers options such as restrictions on the set of possible permutations. Their approach also supports various types of objects to shuffle. Such features are interesting from a theoretical point of view, but they are less interesting for practical applications in the area of electronic elections. Tailored pseudo-code algorithms for writing a verifier for VMN are given in [11], but algorithms for generating the proofs are not included in that document.

In this paper, we describe both parts of the shuffle proof in one compact form, while restricting ourselves to the most common use case of single ElGamal encryptions. We summarize the cryptographic theory necessary to understand the core proof mechanisms and provide detailed and comprehensive pseudo-code algorithms for generating and verifying such proofs. The goal of presenting the proof in this form is to make it accessible to a broader audience and to facilitate its implementation by non-specialists. In this way, we hope to facilitate the dissemination of shuffle proofs in electronic voting applications. Even without presenting new results, we think this is an important contribution to the community.

The organization of the paper is as follows. In Sect. 2, we review the cryptographic background that is necessary to understand the summary of Wikström's proof mechanisms given in Sect. 3. The pseudo-code algorithms for building a verifiable ElGamal re-encryption mix-net are presented in Sect. 4. Enough details are given for a software developer with little cryptographic background to implement the proof without accomplishing a profound understanding of the underlying mechanisms. Sections 2 and 3 may therefore be skipped by readers focused in implementing the proof. Section 5 concludes the paper.

2   Cryptographic Background

Let $\mathcal{G}$ be a cyclic group of prime order q, for which the decisional Diffie-Hellman (DDH) assumption is believed to hold. Since q is prime, every $x \in \mathcal{G} \setminus \{1\}$ is a generator. Any such group would be suitable for Wikström's shuffle proof, but here we restrict ourselves to the subgroup $\mathbb{G}_q = \{x^2 \bmod p : 1 \leq x \leq p - 1\} \subset \mathbb{Z}_p^*$ of quadratic residues modulo a safe prime $p = 2q + 1$. This is the most common choice in practice. When working with $\mathbb{G}_q$, the corresponding prime field $\mathbb{Z}_q = \{0, \dots, q - 1\}$ of integers modulo q plays an important role to perform computations in the exponent.

2.1   ElGamal Encryption

An *ElGamal enryption scheme* is a triple (KeyGen, Enc, Dec) of algorithms, which operate on groups such as $\mathbb{G}_q \subset \mathbb{Z}_p^*$, for which DDH holds [3]. The public parameters of an ElGamal encryption scheme over $\mathbb{G}_q$ are the primes p and q and a generator $g \in \mathbb{G}_q \setminus \{1\}$. A suitable generator can be found by squaring an arbitrary value $x \in \mathbb{Z}_p^* \setminus \{1, p-1\}$, for example $g = 2^2 = 4$ is always a generator of $\mathbb{G}_q$ (except for $p = 5$).

An ElGamal key pair is a tuple $(sk, pk) \leftarrow$ KeyGen(), where $sk \in_R \mathbb{Z}_q$ is the randomly chosen private decryption key and $pk = g^{sk} \in \mathbb{G}_q$ the corresponding public encryption key. If $m \in \mathbb{G}_q$ denotes the plaintext to encrypt, then

$$\mathsf{Enc}_{pk}(m, r) = (m \cdot pk^r, g^r) \in \mathbb{G}_q \times \mathbb{G}_q$$

denotes the ElGamal encryption of m with randomization $r \in_R \mathbb{Z}_q$. Note that the bit length of an encryption $e \leftarrow \mathsf{Enc}_{pk}(m, r)$ is twice the bit length of p. For a given encryption $e = (a, b)$, the plaintext m can be recovered by using the private decryption key sk to compute

$$m \leftarrow \mathsf{Dec}_{sk}(e) = a \cdot b^{-sk}.$$

For any given key pair $(sk, pk) \leftarrow$ KeyGen(), it is easy to demonstrate that $\mathsf{Dec}_{sk}(\mathsf{Enc}_{pk}(m, r)) = m$ holds for all $m \in \mathbb{G}_q$ and $r \in \mathbb{Z}_q$.

The ElGamal encryption scheme is IND-CPA secure under the DDH assumption and homomorphic with respect to multiplication. Therefore, componentwise multiplication of two ciphertexts yields an encryption of the product of respective plaintexts:

$$\mathsf{Enc}_{pk}(m_1, r_1) \cdot \mathsf{Enc}_{pk}(m_2, r_2) = \mathsf{Enc}_{pk}(m_1 m_2, r_1 + r_2).$$

In a homomorphic encryption scheme like ElGamal, a given encryption $e \leftarrow \mathsf{Enc}_{pk}(m, r)$ can be *re-encrypted* by multiplying e with an encryption of the neutral element 1. The resulting re-encryption of e,

$$\mathsf{ReEnc}_{pk}(e, r') = e \cdot \mathsf{Enc}_{pk}(1, r') = \mathsf{Enc}_{pk}(m, r + r'),$$

is clearly an encryption of m with a fresh randomization $r + r'$.

2.2   Pedersen Commitments

The (extended) *Pedersen commitment scheme* is based on a cyclic group for which the discrete logarithm (DL) assumption holds. In this document, we use the same subgroup $\mathbb{G}_q \subset \mathbb{Z}_p^*$ of integers modulo $p = 2q + 1$ as in the ElGamal encryption scheme. Let $g, h_1, \ldots, h_N \in \mathbb{G}_q \setminus \{1\}$ be independent generators of $\mathbb{G}_q$, which means that their relative logarithms are provably not known to anyone.

The Pedersen commitment scheme consists of two deterministic algorithms, one for computing a commitment

$$\mathsf{Com}(\mathbf{m}, r) = g^r \prod_{i=1}^{N} h_i^{m_i} \in \mathbb{G}_q$$

to N messages $\mathbf{m} = (m_1, \ldots, m_N) \in \mathbb{Z}_q^n$ with randomization $r \in_R \mathbb{Z}_q$, and one for checking the validity of $c \leftarrow \mathsf{Com}(\mathbf{m}, r)$ when $\mathbf{m}$ and r are revealed (which we do not require in this paper). In the special case of a single message m, we write $\mathsf{Com}(m, r) = g^r h^m$ using a second generator h independent from g. The Pedersen commitment scheme is perfectly hiding and computationally binding under the DL assumption.

In Wikström's shuffle proof, we also require commitments to permutations $\psi : \{1, \ldots, N\} \to \{1, \ldots, N\}$. Let $\mathbf{B}_\psi = (b_{ij})_{N \times N}$ be the *permutation matrix* of ψ, which consists of bits

$$b_{ij} = \begin{cases} 1, & \text{if } \psi(i) = j, \\ 0, & \text{otherwise.} \end{cases}$$

Note that in each row and each column in $\mathbf{B}_\psi$, exactly one bit is set to 1. If $\mathbf{b}_j = (b_{1,j}, \ldots, b_{N,j})$ denotes the j-th column of $\mathbf{B}_\psi$, then

$$\mathsf{Com}(\mathbf{b}_j, r_j) = g^{r_j} \prod_{i=1}^N h_i^{b_{ij}} = g^{r_j} h_i, \text{ for } i = \psi^{-1}(j),$$

is a commitment to $\mathbf{b}_j$ with randomization r_j. By computing such commitments to all columns, we obtain a *permutation commitment*

$$\mathsf{Com}(\psi, \mathbf{r}) = (\mathsf{Com}(\mathbf{b}_1, r_1), \ldots, \mathsf{Com}(\mathbf{b}_N, r_N))$$

to ψ with randomizations $\mathbf{r} = (r_1, \ldots, r_N)$. Note that the size of such a $\mathbf{c} \leftarrow \mathsf{Com}(\psi, \mathbf{r})$ is $O(N)$.

2.3   Non-interactive Preimage Proofs

Non-interactive zero-knowledge proofs of knowledge are important building blocks in cryptographic protocol design. In a non-interactive *preimage proof*

$$NIZKP[(x) : y = \phi(x)]$$

for a one-way group homomorphism $\phi : X \to Y$, the prover proves knowledge of a secret preimage $x = \phi^{-1}(y) \in X$ for a public value $y \in Y$ without revealing anything about x [7].

The most common construction of a non-interactive preimage proof results from combining the so-called Σ-protocol with the Fiat-Shamir heuristic [4]. Generating a preimage proof $(t, s) \leftarrow \mathsf{GenProof}_\phi(x, y)$ for ϕ consists of picking a random value $w \in_R X$ and computing a commitment $t = \phi(w) \in Y$, a challenge $c = \mathsf{Hash}(y, t)$, and a response $s = w + c \cdot x \in X$. Verifying a proof includes computing $c = \mathsf{Hash}(y, t)$ and checking $t = y^{-c} \cdot \phi(s)$. For a given proof $\pi = (t, s)$, this process is denoted by $b \leftarrow \mathsf{CheckProof}_\phi(\pi, y)$, where $b \in \{0, 1\}$ indicates if the proof is valid or not. Clearly, we have

$$\mathsf{CheckProof}_\phi(\mathsf{GenProof}_\phi(x, y), y) = 1$$

for all $x \in X$ and $y = \phi(x) \in Y$. Proofs constructed in this way are perfect zero-knowledge in the random oracle model, which in practice is approximated with the use of a collision-resistant hash function.

3   Summary of Wikström's Shuffle Proof

A *cryptographic shuffle* of a list $\mathbf{e} = (e_1, \dots, e_N)$ of ElGamal encryptions $e_i \leftarrow \mathsf{Enc}_{pk}(m_i, r_i)$ is another list of ElGamal encryptions $\mathbf{e}' = (e_1', \dots, e_N')$, which contains the same plaintexts m_i in permuted order. Such a shuffle can be generated by selecting a random permutation $\psi : \{1, \dots, N\} \rightarrow \{1, \dots, N\}$ from the set Ψ_N of all such permutations (e.g., using Knuth's shuffle algorithm [5]) and by computing re-encryptions $e_i' \leftarrow \mathsf{ReEnc}_{pk}(e_j, r_j')$ for $j = \psi(i)$. We write

$$\mathbf{e}' \leftarrow \mathsf{Shuffle}_{pk}(\mathbf{e}, \mathbf{r}', \psi)$$

for an algorithm performing this task, where $\mathbf{r}' = (r_1', \dots, r_N')$ denotes the randomization used to re-encrypt the input ciphertexts.

Proving the correctness of a cryptographic shuffle can be realized by proving knowledge of ψ and $\mathbf{r}'$, which generate $\mathbf{e}'$ from $\mathbf{e}$ in a cryptographic shuffle:

$$NIZKP[(\psi, \mathbf{r}') : \mathbf{e}' = \mathsf{Shuffle}_{pk}(\mathbf{e}, \mathbf{r}', \psi)].$$

Unfortunately, since $\mathsf{Shuffle}_{pk}$ does not define a homomorphism, we can not apply the standard technique for preimage proofs. Therefore, the strategy of what follows is to find an equivalent formulation using a homomorphism.

The shuffle proof according to Wikström and Terelius consists of two parts, an offline and an online proof. In the offline proof, the prover computes a commitment $c \leftarrow \mathsf{Com}(\psi, \mathbf{r})$ and proves that c is a commitment to a permutation matrix. In the online proof, the prover demonstrates that the committed permutation matrix has been used in the shuffle to obtain $\mathbf{e}'$ from $\mathbf{e}$. The two proofs can be kept separate, but combining them into a single proof results in a slightly more efficient method. Here, we only present the combined version of the two proofs and we restrict ourselves to the case of shuffling ElGamal ciphertexts.

From a top-down perspective, Wikström's shuffle proof can be seen as a two-layer proof consisting of a top layer responsible for preparatory work such as computing the commitment $\mathbf{c} \leftarrow \mathsf{Com}(\psi, \mathbf{r})$ and a bottom layer computing a standard preimage proof.

3.1   Preparatory Work

There are two fundamental ideas behind Wikström's shuffle proof. The first idea is based on a simple theorem that states that if $\mathbf{B}_\psi = (b_{ij})_{N \times N}$ is an N-by-N-matrix over $\mathbb{Z}_q$ and $(x_1, \dots, x_N)$ a vector of N independent variables, then $\mathbf{B}_\psi$ is a permutation matrix if and only if $\sum_{j=1}^{N} b_{ij} = 1$, for all $i \in \{1, \dots, N\}$, and $\prod_{i=1}^{N} \sum_{j=1}^{N} b_{ij} x_i = \prod_{i=1}^{N} x_i$. The first condition means that the elements of each row of $\mathbf{B}_\psi$ must sum up to one, while the second condition requires that $\mathbf{B}_\psi$ has exactly one non-zero element in each row.

Based on this theorem, the general proof strategy is to compute a permutation commitment $\mathbf{c} \leftarrow \mathsf{Com}(\psi, \mathbf{r})$ and to construct a zero-knowledge argument that the two conditions of the theorem hold for $\mathbf{B}_\psi$. This implies then that $\mathbf{c}$ is a commitment to a permutation matrix without revealing ψ or $\mathbf{B}_\psi$.

For $\mathbf{c} = (c_1, \ldots, c_N)$, $\mathbf{r} = (r_1, \ldots, r_N)$, and $\bar{r} = \sum_{j=1}^{N} r_j$, the first condition leads to the following equality:

$$\prod_{j=1}^{N} c_j = \prod_{j=1}^{N} g^{r_j} \prod_{i=1}^{N} h_i^{b_{ij}} = g^{\sum_{j=1}^{N} r_j} \prod_{i=1}^{N} h_i^{\sum_{j=1}^{N} b_{ij}} = g^{\bar{r}} \prod_{i=1}^{N} h_i = \mathsf{Com}(1, \bar{r}). \quad (1)$$

Similarly, for arbitrary values $\mathbf{u} = (u_1, \ldots, u_N) \in \mathbb{Z}_q^N$, $\mathbf{u}' = (u_1', \ldots, u_N') \in \mathbb{Z}_q^N$, with $u_i' = \sum_{j=1}^{N} b_{ij} u_j = u_j$ for $j = \psi(i)$, and $\tilde{r} = \sum_{j=1}^{N} r_j u_j$, the second condition leads to two equalities:

$$\prod_{i=1}^{N} u_i' = \prod_{j=1}^{N} u_j, \quad (2)$$

$$\prod_{j=1}^{N} c_j^{u_j} = \prod_{j=1}^{N} (g^{r_j} \prod_{i=1}^{N} h_i^{b_{ij}})^{u_j} = g^{\sum_{j=1}^{N} r_j u_j} \prod_{i=1}^{N} h_i^{\sum_{j=1}^{N} b_{ij} u_j} = g^{\tilde{r}} \prod_{i=1}^{N} h_i^{u_i'}$$

$$= \mathsf{Com}(\mathbf{u}', \tilde{r}), \quad (3)$$

By proving that (1), (2), and (3) hold, and from the independence of the generators, it follows that both conditions of the theorem are true and finally that $\mathbf{c}$ is a commitment to a permutation matrix. In the interactive version of Wikström's proof, the prover obtains $\mathbf{u} = (u_1, \ldots, u_N) \in \mathbb{Z}_q^N$ in an initial message from the verifier, but in the non-interactive version we derive these values from the public inputs, for example by computing $u_i \leftarrow \mathsf{Hash}((\mathbf{e}, \mathbf{e}', \mathbf{c}), i)$.

The second fundamental idea of Wikström's proof is based on the homomorphic property of the ElGamal encryption scheme and the following observation for values $\mathbf{u}$ and $\mathbf{u}'$ defined in the same way as above:

$$\prod_{i=1}^{N} (e_i')^{u_i'} = \prod_{j=1}^{N} \mathsf{ReEnc}_{pk}(e_j, r_j')^{u_j} = \prod_{j=1}^{N} \mathsf{ReEnc}_{pk}(e_j^{u_j}, r_j' u_j)$$

$$= \mathsf{ReEnc}_{pk}(\prod_{j=1}^{N} e_j^{u_j}, \sum_{j=1}^{N} r_j' u_j) = \mathsf{Enc}_{pk}(1, r') \cdot \prod_{j=1}^{N} e_j^{u_j}, \quad (4)$$

for $r' = \sum_{j=1}^{N} r_j' u_j$. By proving (4), it follows that every e_i' is a re-encryption of e_j for $j = \psi(i)$. This is the desired property of the cryptographic shuffle. By putting (1) to (4) together, the shuffle proof can therefore be rewritten as follows:

$$NIZKP \left[(\bar{r}, \tilde{r}, r', \mathbf{u}') : \begin{array}{l} \prod_{j=1}^{N} c_j = \mathsf{Com}(1, \bar{r}) \\ \wedge \prod_{i=1}^{N} u_i' = \prod_{j=1}^{N} u_j \\ \wedge \prod_{j=1}^{N} c_j^{u_j} = \mathsf{Com}(\mathbf{u}', \tilde{r}) \\ \wedge \prod_{i=1}^{N} (e_i')^{u_i'} = \mathsf{Enc}_{pk}(1, r') \cdot \prod_{j=1}^{N} e_j^{u_j} \end{array} \right]. \quad (5)$$

The last step of the preparatory work results from replacing in the above expression the equality of products, $\prod_{i=1}^{N} u_i' = \prod_{j=1}^{N} u_j$, by an equivalent expression based on a chained list $\hat{\mathbf{c}} = \{\hat{c}_1, \ldots, \hat{c}_N\}$ of Pedersen commitments with different generators. For $\hat{c}_0 = h$ and random values $\hat{\mathbf{r}} = (\hat{r}_1, \ldots, \hat{r}_N) \in \mathbb{Z}_q^N$, we define $\hat{c}_i = g^{\hat{r}_i} \hat{c}_{i-1}^{u'_i}$, which leads to $\hat{c}_N = \mathsf{Com}(u, \hat{r})$ for $u = \prod_{i=1}^N u_i$ and

$$\hat{r} = \sum_{i=1}^N \hat{r}_i \prod_{j=i+1}^N u'_j.$$

Applying this replacement leads to the following final result, on which the proof construction is based:

$$NIZKP \left[(\bar{r}, \hat{r}, \tilde{r}, r', \hat{\mathbf{r}}, \mathbf{u}') : \begin{array}{l} \prod_{j=1}^N c_j = \mathsf{Com}(1, \bar{r}) \\ \wedge \hat{c}_N = \mathsf{Com}(u, \hat{r}) \wedge \left[\bigwedge_{i=1}^N (\hat{c}_i = g^{\hat{r}_i} \hat{c}_{i-1}^{u'_i}) \right] \\ \wedge \prod_{j=1}^N c_j^{u_j} = \mathsf{Com}(\mathbf{u}', \tilde{r}) \\ \wedge \prod_{i=1}^N (e'_i)^{u'_i} = \mathsf{Enc}_{pk}(1, r') \cdot \prod_{j=1}^N e_j^{u_j} \end{array} \right]. \quad (6)$$

To summarize the preparatory work for the proof generation, we give a list of all necessary computations:

- Pick $\mathbf{r} = (r_1, \ldots, r_N) \in_R \mathbb{Z}_q^N$ and compute $\mathbf{c} \leftarrow \mathsf{Com}(\psi, \mathbf{r})$.
- For $i = 1, \ldots, N$, compute $u_i \leftarrow \mathsf{Hash}((\mathbf{e}, \mathbf{e}', \mathbf{c}), i)$, let $u'_i = u_{\psi(i)}$, pick $\hat{r}_i \in_R \mathbb{Z}_q$, and compute $\hat{c}_i = g^{\hat{r}_i} \hat{c}_{i-1}^{u'_i}$.
- Let $\hat{\mathbf{r}} = (\hat{r}_1, \ldots, \hat{r}_N)$ and $\hat{\mathbf{c}} = (\hat{c}_1, \ldots, \hat{c}_N)$.
- Compute $\bar{r} = \sum_{j=1}^N r_j$, $\hat{r} = \sum_{i=1}^N \hat{r}_i \prod_{j=i+1}^N u'_j$, $\tilde{r} = \sum_{j=1}^N r_j u_j$, and $r' = \sum_{j=1}^N r'_j u_j$.

Note that $\hat{r}$ can be computed in linear time by generating the values $\prod_{j=i+1}^N u'_j$ in an incremental manner by looping backwards over $j = N, \ldots, 1$.

3.2 Preimage Proof

By rearranging all public values to the left-hand side and all secret values to the right-hand side of each equation, we can derive a homomorphic one-way function from the final expression of the previous subsection. In this way, we obtain the homomorphic function

$$\phi(x_1, x_2, x_3, x_4, \hat{\mathbf{x}}, \mathbf{x}')$$

$$= (g^{x_1}, g^{x_2}, \mathsf{Com}(\mathbf{x}', x_3), \mathsf{ReEnc}_{pk}(\prod_{i=1}^N (e'_i)^{x'_i}, -x_4), (g^{\hat{x}_1} \hat{c}_0^{x'_1}, \ldots, g^{\hat{x}_N} \hat{c}_{N-1}^{x'_N})), \quad (7)$$

which maps inputs $(x_1, x_2, x_3, x_4, \hat{\mathbf{x}}, \mathbf{x}') \in X$ of length $2N + 4$ into outputs

$$(y_1, y_2, y_3, y_4, \hat{\mathbf{y}}) = \phi(x_1, x_2, x_3, x_4, \hat{\mathbf{x}}, \mathbf{x}') \in Y$$

of length $N + 5$, i.e., $X = \mathbb{Z}_q^4 \times \mathbb{Z}_q^N \times \mathbb{Z}_q^N$ is the domain and $Y = \mathbb{G}_q^3 \times \mathbb{G}_q^2 \times \mathbb{G}_q^N$ the co-domain of ϕ. Note that we slightly modified the order of the five sub-functions of ϕ for better readability. By applying this function to the secret values $(\bar{r}, \hat{r}, \tilde{r}, r', \hat{\mathbf{r}}, \mathbf{u}')$, we get a tuple of public values,

$$(\bar{c}, \hat{c}, \tilde{c}, e', \hat{\mathbf{c}}) = \left(\frac{\prod_{j=1}^{N} c_j}{\prod_{j=1}^{N} h_j}, \frac{\hat{c}_N}{h^u}, \prod_{j=1}^{N} c_j^{u_j}, \prod_{j=1}^{N} e_j^{u_j}, (\hat{c}_1, \dots, \hat{c}_N) \right), \qquad (8)$$

which can be derived from the public values $\mathbf{e}$, $\mathbf{e}'$, $\mathbf{c}$, $\hat{\mathbf{c}}$, and pk (and from $\mathbf{u}$, which is derived from $\mathbf{e}$, $\mathbf{e}'$, and $\mathbf{c}$).

To summarize, we have a homomorphic one-way function $\phi : X \to Y$, secret values $x = (\bar{r}, \hat{r}, \tilde{r}, r', \hat{\mathbf{r}}, \mathbf{u}') \in X$, and public values $y = (\bar{c}, \hat{c}, \tilde{c}, e', \hat{\mathbf{c}}) = \phi(x) \in Y$. We can therefore generate a non-interactive preimage proof

$$NIZKP \left[(\bar{r}, \hat{r}, \tilde{r}, r', \hat{\mathbf{r}}, \mathbf{u}') : \begin{array}{c} \bar{c} = g^{\bar{r}} \wedge \hat{c} = g^{\hat{r}} \wedge \tilde{c} = \mathsf{Com}(\mathbf{u}', \tilde{r}) \\ \wedge \; e' = \mathsf{ReEnc}_{pk}(\prod_{i=1}^{N} (e_i')^{u_i'}, -r') \\ \wedge \left[\bigwedge_{i=1}^{N} (\hat{c}_i = g^{\hat{r}_i} \hat{c}_{i-1}^{u_i'}) \right] \end{array} \right], \qquad (9)$$

using the standard procedure from Sect. 2.3. The result of such a proof generation, $(t, s) \leftarrow \mathsf{GenProof}_\phi(x, y)$, consists of two values $t = \phi(w) \in Y$ of length $N + 5$ and $s = \omega + c \cdot x \in X$ of length $2N + 4$, which we obtain from picking $w \in_R X$ (of length $2N + 4$) and computing $c = \mathsf{Hash}(y, t)$. Alternatively, a different $c = \mathsf{Hash}(y', t)$ could be derived directly from the public values $y' = (\mathbf{e}, \mathbf{e}', \mathbf{c}, \hat{\mathbf{c}}, pk)$, which has the advantage that $y = (\bar{c}, \hat{c}, \tilde{c}, e', \hat{\mathbf{c}})$ needs not to be computed explicitly during the proof generation.

This preimage proof, together with the two lists of commitments $\mathbf{c}$ and $\hat{\mathbf{c}}$, leads to the desired non-interactive shuffle proof $NIZKP[(\psi, \mathbf{r}') : \mathbf{e}' = \mathsf{Shuffle}_{pk}(\mathbf{e}, \mathbf{r}', \psi)]$. We denote the generation and verification of a such proof $\pi = (t, s, \mathbf{c}, \hat{\mathbf{c}})$ by

$$\pi \leftarrow \mathsf{GenProof}_{pk}(\mathbf{e}, \mathbf{e}', \mathbf{r}', \psi)$$
$$b \leftarrow \mathsf{CheckProof}_{pk}(\pi, \mathbf{e}, \mathbf{e}').$$

respectively. Corresponding algorithms are depicted in Algorithms 3 and 6. Note that generating the proof requires $7N+4$ and verifying the proof $9N+11$ modular exponentiations in $\mathbb{G}_q$. The proof itself consists of $5N + 9$ elements ($2N + 4$ elements from $\mathbb{Z}_q$ and $3N + 5$ elements from $\mathbb{G}_q$).

4 Pseudo-Code Algorithms

Based on the background information given in the previous two sections, we will now transform the mathematical description of the proof into detailed pseudo-code algorithms. This will give us an even closer look at how the shuffle proof works. Algorithms 1, 3 and 6 are the three main algorithms for performing the shuffle, generating the proof, and checking the validity of a proof, respectively. We decided to give almost monolithic descriptions for each of these algorithms with little dependencies to sub-routines.

There are some public parameters, which we do not pass explicitly as arguments to each algorithm: the prime modulo p of the group $\mathbb{G}_q \subset \mathbb{Z}_p^*$, the group order $q = (p-1)/2$, the main independent group generators g and h, and N other independent generators $h_1, \ldots, h_N$. We do not give algorithms for finding suitable group parameters or give recommendations about their sizes, we simply assume that they are publicly known.[2] For a deterministic algorithm that generates an arbitrary number of independent generators, we refer to the NIST standard FIPS PUB 186-4 [1, Appendix A.2.3]. The deterministic nature of this algorithm enables the independence of the generators to be publicly verified.

Most numeric calculations in the given algorithms are either performed modulo p or modulo q. For maximal clarity, we indicate the modulus in each individual case. We suppose that efficient algorithms are available for computing modular exponentiations $x^y \bmod p$ and modular inverses $x^{-1} \bmod p$. Divisions $x/y \bmod p$ are handled as $xy^{-1} \bmod p$ and exponentiations $x^{-y} \bmod p$ with negative exponents as $(x^{-1})^y \bmod p$ or $(x^y)^{-1} \bmod p$. We also assume that readers are familiar with mathematical notations for sums and products, such that implementing expressions like $\sum_{i=1}^N x_i$ or $\prod_{i=1}^N x_i$ is straightforward.

An important precondition for every algorithm is the validity of the input parameters, for example that an ElGamal encryption $e = (a, b)$ is an element of $\mathbb{G}_q \times \mathbb{G}_q$ or that given input lists are of equal length. We specify all preconditions for every algorithm, but we do not give explicit code to perform corresponding checks. However, as many attacks on mix-nets are based on infiltrating invalid parameters, we stress the importance of conducting such checks in an actual implementation. For testing group membership $x \in \mathbb{G}_q$ of quadratic residues modulo p, we refer to algorithms for computing the Jacobi symbol $\left(\frac{x}{p}\right)$, for example in [1, pp. 76–77].

Finally, we assume that efficient and secure algorithms are available for computing cryptographic hash values $h \leftarrow \mathsf{Hash}(x)$ of arbitrary mathematical objects and for picking uniform elements $r \in_R \mathbb{Z}_q$ (or more generally $r \in_R [a, b]$). Writing such algorithms is a difficult problem on its own, which we cannot address here. However, such algorithms are usually available in standard cryptographic libraries of modern programming languages.

4.1   Generating the Shuffle

The input of a cryptographic shuffle $\mathbf{e}' \leftarrow \mathsf{Shuffle}_{pk}(\mathbf{e}, \mathbf{r}', \psi)$ is a list of $\mathbf{e} = (e_1, \ldots, e_N)$ encryptions e_i, in our case ElGamal encryptions $e_i = (a_i, b_i) \in \mathbb{G}_q^2$, which need to be re-encrypted and permuted. In Algorithm 1, we describe this procedure, which includes picking a random permutation $\psi = (j_1, \ldots, j_N) \in \Psi_N$ (line 2) and a list $\mathbf{r}' = (r_1', \ldots, r_N')$ of re-encryption randomizations (line 4). The re-encryptions are computed in a loop over all input encryptions (lines 3–7) and

---

[2] See https://www.keylength.com for current recommendations.

permuted by re-arranging them according to ψ (line 8). The random values ψ and $\mathbf{r}'$ are returned together with $\mathbf{e}'$, because they are required as secret inputs to the proof generation.

---

1 **Algorithm:** GenShuffle($\mathbf{e}, pk$)

   Input: ElGamal encryptions $\mathbf{e} = (e_1, \ldots, e_N)$, $e_i = (a_i, b_i) \in \mathbb{G}_q^2$
          Encryption key $pk \in \mathbb{G}_q$
2 $\psi \leftarrow$ GenPermutation(N)   // $\psi = (j_1, \ldots, j_N)$, see Algorithm 4.2
3 **for** $i = 1, \ldots, N$ **do**
4      $r_i' \in_R \mathbb{Z}_q$
5      $a_i' \leftarrow a_i \, pk^{r_i'} \bmod p$
6      $b_i' \leftarrow b_i \, g^{r_i'} \bmod p$
7      $e_i' \leftarrow (a_i', b_i')$
8 $\mathbf{e}' \leftarrow (e_{j_1}', \ldots, e_{j_N}')$
9 $\mathbf{r}' \leftarrow (r_1', \ldots, r_N')$
10 **return** $(\mathbf{e}', \mathbf{r}', \psi)$ // $\mathbf{e}' \in (\mathbb{G}_q^2)^N$, $\mathbf{r}' \in \mathbb{Z}_q^N$, $\psi \in \Psi_N$

Algorithm 1. Generates a random permutation $\psi \in \Psi_N$ and uses it to shuffle a given list $\mathbf{e}$ of ElGamal encryptions into a shuffled list $\mathbf{e}'$.

The above shuffling algorithm calls one sub-routine for generating a random permutation $\psi \in \Psi_N$. We present a procedure for this problem in Algorithm 2, which is essentially Knuth's shuffle algorithm [5, pp. 139–140]. The auxiliary variable I is an integer array of size N, which is addressed with indices $i, k \in \{1, \ldots, N\}$. After initializing the array with integers $1, \ldots, N$ (line 2), N swap operations are performed with indices chosen at random (lines 3–6). Knuth's algorithm is proven to implement a uniform distribution over all possible permutations.

4.2 Generating the Shuffle Proof

The mathematical description of the shuffle proof in Sect. 3 is the basis for procedure shown in Algorithm 3. The core of the algorithm is the preimage proof specified in (9), which requires some preparatory work. The first preparatory step is the generation of the permutation commitment $\mathbf{c}$ (line 2), which we delegate to a separate subroutine. The second preparatory step is the computation of values $\mathbf{u}$, which are derived from the public inputs $\mathbf{e}$ and $\mathbf{e}'$ and the permutation commitment $\mathbf{c}$, and which are permuted according to ψ into $\mathbf{u}'$ (lines 3–6). The next preparatory step is the computation of the commitment chain $\hat{\mathbf{c}}$ in a separate subroutine with $c_0 = h$ as initial value (line 7). Finally, the last step consists in computing the secret inputs $\bar{r}$, $\hat{r}$, $\tilde{r}$, and r' for the preimage proof (lines 8–14).

---

1 **Algorithm:** GenPermutation(N)

   Input: Permutation size $N \in \mathbb{N}$

2 $I \leftarrow \langle 1, \ldots, N \rangle$

3 **for** $i = 1, \ldots, N$ **do**

4      $k \in_R \{i, \ldots, N\}$

5      $j_i \leftarrow I[k]$

6      $I[k] \leftarrow I[i]$

7 $\psi \leftarrow (j_1, \ldots, j_N)$

8 **return** ψ // $\psi \in \Psi_N$

Algorithm 2. Generates a random permutation $\psi \in \Psi_N$ following Knuth's shuffle algorithm.

The implementation of the preimage proof starts on line 15, where $2N + 4$ values $w_i, \hat{w}_i, w_i' \in \mathbb{Z}_q$ are selected at random (lines 15–18). They are needed for the computation of the $N + 5$ commitments $t_i, \hat{t}_i \in \mathbb{G}_q$ (lines 19–25), which follows the definition of the homomorphic one-way function ϕ as specified in (7). The commitments and all public values are then used to compute the challenge c (lines 26–27), which determines to $2N + 4$ responses $s_i, \hat{s}_i, s_i' \in \mathbb{Z}_q$ (lines 28–33). The algorithm ends with returning the tuples t and s of all commitments and responses, respectively, together with the permutation commitment $\mathbf{c}$ and the commitment chain $\hat{\mathbf{c}}$.

Each of the two auxiliary algorithms called during the proof generation returns a list of Pedersen commitments. In the case of Algorithm 4, the return value is actually a commitment to the permutation ψ. The procedure for computing such a permutation commitment is described in Sect. 2.2. The return value of Algorithm 5 consists of Pedersen commitments that are linked over one of the two generators. The role of this commitment chain has been discussed in Sect. 3 and does not require further explanations.

4.3 Verifying the Shuffle Proof

A shuffle proof $\pi = (t, c, \mathbf{c}, \hat{\mathbf{c}})$ generated by Algorithm 3 consists of the result (t, s) of the preimage proof and the two lists of commitments $\mathbf{c}$ and $\hat{\mathbf{c}}$ obtained as a result of several preparatory steps. Algorithm 6 shows the necessary steps of checking the validity of such a proof. The additional input values of this algorithm are two lists of encryptions $\mathbf{e}$ and $\mathbf{e}'$ and the public key pk.

The first preparatory step in the algorithm is the derivation of the values $\mathbf{u}$ from the inputs $\mathbf{e}$, $\mathbf{e}'$, and $\mathbf{c}$ (lines 2–3). The second preparatory step is the computation of the public values $\bar{c}$, $\hat{c}$, $\tilde{c}$, and $e' = (a', b')$ (lines 5–9) according to their definition given in (8). Nothing else is needed to perform the verification of the preimage proof (t, s) according to the standard procedure described in Sect. 2.3. That is, the challenge c can be derived from the public values $\mathbf{e}$, $\mathbf{e}'$,

1 **Algorithm:** GenProof($\mathbf{e}, \mathbf{e}', \mathbf{r}', \psi, pk$)

Input: ElGamal encryptions $\mathbf{e} = (e_1, \ldots, e_N)$, $e_i = (a_i, b_i) \in \mathbb{G}_q^2$
Shuffled ElGamal encryptions $\mathbf{e}' = (e'_1, \ldots, e'_N)$, $e'_i = (a'_i, b'_i) \in \mathbb{G}_q^2$
Re-encryption randomizations $\mathbf{r}' = (r'_1, \ldots, r'_N)$, $r'_i \in \mathbb{Z}_q$
Permutation $\psi = (j_1, \ldots, j_N) \in \Psi_N$
Encryption key $pk \in \mathbb{G}_q$

2 $(\mathbf{c}, \mathbf{r}) \leftarrow$ GenCommitment(ψ)   // $\mathbf{c} = (c_1, \ldots, c_N)$, $\mathbf{r} = (r_1, \ldots, r_N)$

3 **for** $i = 1, \ldots, N$ **do**

4     $u_i \leftarrow$ Hash($(\mathbf{e}, \mathbf{e}', \mathbf{c}), i$)

5     $u'_i \leftarrow u_{j_i}$

6 $\mathbf{u} \leftarrow (u_1, \ldots, u_N)$, $\mathbf{u}' \leftarrow (u'_1, \ldots, u'_N)$

7 $(\hat{\mathbf{c}}, \hat{\mathbf{r}}) \leftarrow$ GenCommitmentChain($h, \mathbf{u}'$)   // $\hat{\mathbf{c}} = (\hat{c}_1, \ldots, \hat{c}_N)$, $\hat{\mathbf{r}} = (\hat{r}_1, \ldots, \hat{r}_N)$

8 $\bar{r} \leftarrow \sum_{i=1}^{N} r_i \bmod q$

9 $v_N \leftarrow 1$

10 **for** $i = N - 1, \ldots, 1$ **do**

11     $v_i \leftarrow u'_{i+1} v_{i+1} \bmod q$

12 $\hat{r} \leftarrow \sum_{i=1}^{N} \hat{r}_i v_i \bmod q$

13 $\tilde{r} \leftarrow \sum_{i=1}^{N} r_i u_i \bmod q$

14 $r' \leftarrow \sum_{i=1}^{N} r'_i u_i \bmod q$

15 **for** $i = 1, \ldots, 4$ **do**

16     $\omega_i \in_R \mathbb{Z}_q$

17 **for** $i = 1, \ldots, N$ **do**

18     $\hat{\omega}_i \in_R \mathbb{Z}_q$, $\omega'_i \in_R \mathbb{Z}_q$

19 $t_1 \leftarrow g^{\omega_1} \bmod p$

20 $t_2 \leftarrow g^{\omega_2} \bmod p$

21 $t_3 \leftarrow g^{\omega_3} \prod_{i=1}^{N} h_i^{\omega'_i} \bmod p$

22 $(t_{4,1}, t_{4,2}) \leftarrow (pk^{-\omega_4} \prod_{i=1}^{N} (a'_i)^{\omega'_i} \bmod p, g^{-\omega_4} \prod_{i=1}^{N} (b'_i)^{\omega'_i} \bmod p)$

23 $\hat{c}_0 \leftarrow h$

24 **for** $i = 1, \ldots, N$ **do**

25     $\hat{t}_i \leftarrow g^{\hat{\omega}_i} \hat{c}_{i-1}^{\omega'_i} \bmod p$

26 $y \leftarrow (\mathbf{e}, \mathbf{e}', \mathbf{c}, \hat{\mathbf{c}}, pk)$, $t \leftarrow (t_1, t_2, t_3, (t_{4,1}, t_{4,2}), (\hat{t}_1, \ldots, \hat{t}_N))$

27 $c \leftarrow$ Hash(y, t)

28 $s_1 \leftarrow \omega_1 + c \cdot \bar{r} \bmod q$

29 $s_2 \leftarrow \omega_2 + c \cdot \hat{r} \bmod q$

30 $s_3 \leftarrow \omega_3 + c \cdot \tilde{r} \bmod q$

31 $s_4 \leftarrow \omega_4 + c \cdot r' \bmod q$

32 **for** $i = 1, \ldots, N$ **do**

33     $\hat{s}_i \leftarrow \hat{\omega}_i + c \cdot \hat{r}_i \bmod q$, $s'_i \leftarrow \omega'_i + c \cdot u'_i \bmod q$

34 $s \leftarrow (s_1, s_2, s_3, s_4, (\hat{s}_1, \ldots, \hat{s}_N), (s'_1, \ldots, s'_N))$

35 $\pi \leftarrow (t, s, \mathbf{c}, \hat{\mathbf{c}})$

36 **return** π // $\pi \in (\mathbb{G}_q^3 \times \mathbb{G}_q^2 \times \mathbb{G}_q^N) \times (\mathbb{Z}_q^4 \times \mathbb{Z}_q^N \times \mathbb{Z}_q^N) \times \mathbb{G}_q^N \times \mathbb{G}_q^N$

Algorithm 3. Generates a proof of shuffle for given ElGamal encryptions $\mathbf{e}$ and $\mathbf{e}'$ according to Wikström's method.

---

1 **Algorithm:** GenCommitment(ψ)

   Input: Permutation $\psi = (j_1, \ldots, j_N) \in \Psi_N$

2 **for** $i = 1, \ldots, N$ **do**
3 | $r_{j_i} \in_R \mathbb{Z}_q$
4 | $c_{j_i} \leftarrow g^{r_{j_i}} h_i \bmod p$
5 $\mathbf{c} \leftarrow (c_1, \ldots, c_N)$
6 $\mathbf{r} \leftarrow (r_1, \ldots, r_N)$
7 **return** $(\mathbf{c}, \mathbf{r})$ $// \; \mathbf{c} \in \mathbb{G}_q^N, \mathbf{r} \in \mathbb{Z}_q^N$

Algorithm 4. Generates a commitment $\mathbf{c} = \mathsf{Com}(\psi, \mathbf{r})$ to a permutation ψ by committing to the columns of the corresponding permutation matrix.

---

1 **Algorithm:** GenCommitmentChain($c_0, \mathbf{u}$)

   Input: Initial commitment $c_0 \in \mathbb{G}_q$
               Public challenges $\mathbf{u} = (u_1, \ldots, u_N), u_i \in \mathbb{Z}_q$
2 **for** $i = 1, \ldots, N$ **do**
3 | $r_i \in_R \mathbb{Z}_q$
4 | $c_i \leftarrow g^{r_i} c_{i-1}^{u_i} \bmod p$
5 $\mathbf{c} \leftarrow (c_1, \ldots, c_N)$
6 $\mathbf{r} \leftarrow (r_1, \ldots, r_N)$
7 **return** $(\mathbf{c}, \mathbf{r})$ $// \; \mathbf{c} \in \mathbb{G}_q^N, \mathbf{r} \in \mathbb{Z}_q^N$

Algorithm 5. Generates a commitment chain $c_0 \rightarrow c_1 \rightarrow \cdots \rightarrow c_N$ relative to a list of public challenges $\mathbf{u}$ and starting with a given commitment c_0.

$\mathbf{c}, \hat{\mathbf{c}}$, and pk (line 11), which then leads to $N + 5$ values $t_i', \hat{t}_i' \in \mathbb{G}_q$ by applying the one-way function ϕ to s (lines 12–17). The resulting values are compared to respective values $t_i, \hat{t}_i \in \mathbb{G}_q$ included in the proof, and if all values match, the proof is valid (line 18).

5 Conclusion

In this paper, we have given a compact summary of Wikström's shuffle proof and a detailed description of the proof generation and verification processes in form of pseudo-code algorithms. The level of detail of these algorithms is such that even developers with little background in cryptography can implement to proof by coding carefully line after line. This solves an important problem of system developers in charge of such an implementation. In the past, many of them have struggled when facing the complexity of the underlying cryptography. With this paper at hand, they have now a detailed guideline which they can follow without

---

1 **Algorithm:** CheckProof$(\pi, \mathbf{e}, \mathbf{e}', pk)$

   Input: Shuffle proof $\pi = (t, s, \mathbf{c}, \hat{\mathbf{c}})$, $t = (t_1, t_2, t_3, (t_{4,1}, t_{4,2}), (\hat{t}_1, \ldots, \hat{t}_N))$,
         $s = (s_1, s_2, s_3, s_4, (\hat{s}_1, \ldots, \hat{s}_N), (s'_1, \ldots, s'_N))$, $\mathbf{c} = (c_1, \ldots, c_N)$,
         $\hat{\mathbf{c}} = (\hat{c}_1, \ldots, \hat{c}_N)$
         ElGamal encryptions $\mathbf{e} = (e_1, \ldots, e_N)$, $e_i = (a_i, b_i) \in \mathbb{G}_q^2$
         Shuffled ElGamal encryptions $\mathbf{e}' = (e'_1, \ldots, e'_N)$, $e'_i = (a'_i, b'_i) \in \mathbb{G}_q^2$
         Encryption key $pk \in \mathbb{G}_q$

2 **for** $i = 1, \ldots, N$ **do**

3    $u_i \leftarrow \mathsf{Hash}((\mathbf{e}, \mathbf{e}', \mathbf{c}), i)$

4 $\mathbf{u} \leftarrow (u_1, \ldots, u_N)$

5 $\bar{c} \leftarrow \prod_{i=1}^{N} c_i / \prod_{i=1}^{N} h_i \bmod p$

6 $u \leftarrow \prod_{i=1}^{N} u_i \bmod q$

7 $\hat{c} \leftarrow \hat{c}_N / h^u \bmod p$

8 $\tilde{c} \leftarrow \prod_{i=1}^{N} c_i^{u_i} \bmod p$

9 $(a', b') \leftarrow (\prod_{i=1}^{N} a_i^{u_i} \bmod p, \prod_{i=1}^{N} b_i^{u_i} \bmod p)$

10 $y \leftarrow (\mathbf{e}, \mathbf{e}', \mathbf{c}, \hat{\mathbf{c}}, pk)$

11 $c \leftarrow \mathsf{Hash}(y, t)$

12 $t'_1 \leftarrow \bar{c}^{-c} g^{s_1} \bmod p$

13 $t'_2 \leftarrow \hat{c}^{-c} g^{s_2} \bmod p$

14 $t'_3 \leftarrow \tilde{c}^{-c} g^{s_3} \prod_{i=1}^{N} h_i^{s'_i} \bmod p$

15 $(t'_{4,1}, t'_{4,2}) \leftarrow ((a')^{-c} pk^{-s_4} \prod_{i=1}^{N} (a'_i)^{s'_i} \bmod p, (b')^{-c} g^{-s_4} \prod_{i=1}^{N} (b'_i)^{s'_i} \bmod p)$

16 **for** $i = 1, \ldots, N$ **do**

17    $\hat{t}'_i \leftarrow \hat{c}_i^{-c} g^{\hat{s}_i} \hat{c}_{i-1}^{s'_i} \bmod p$

18 **return**
   $(t_1 = t'_1) \wedge (t_2 = t'_2) \wedge (t_3 = t'_3) \wedge (t_{4,1} = t'_{4,1}) \wedge (t_{4,2} = t'_{4,1}) \wedge \left[\bigwedge_{i=1}^{N} (\hat{t}_i = \hat{t}'_i) \right]$

Algorithm 6. Checks the correctness of a shuffle proof π generated by Algorithm 4.3. The public values are the ElGamal encryptions $\mathbf{e}$ and $\mathbf{e}'$ and the public encryption key pk.

fully understanding the theory. We expect that a robust implementation for someone that starts from scratch will now be possible within a matter of weeks (instead of months at least).

To verify the above claim, we have given a draft of this paper to an experienced software developer with no special education or experience in implementing cryptographic algorithms. Within approximately four weeks of part-time work, he managed to produce high-quality Java 8 code of everything that is needed for building a verifiable mix-net. Based on the precise description of our paper, he even managed—for a very small group $\mathbb{G}_q$—to calculate a shuffle proof entirely by hand, and his test suite reaches nearly 100% code coverage. Using the native GMP library for fast big integer calculations and parallel streams from Java 8 to exploit the power of all available cores, the performance of his code is already well-optimized. This work has been conducted in the context of the CHVote Internet voting project of the State of Geneva in Switzerland. The complete source code is available in a public repository on GitHub.[3] We have also assigned this implementation task to a group of students with little background knowledge in cryptography and security. This is an ongoing project, we expect the results in a couple of months in form of a Bachelor thesis. A goal of this work is to obtain a second independent implementation and to use it for mutual tests.

By compiling the theory of Wikström's shuffle proof into a single paper and by facilitating the implementation of verifiable mix-nets with pseudo-code algorithms, we hope that this paper will help to disperse this technology even further.

Acknowledgments. We thank the anonymous reviewers for their thorough reviews and appreciate their comments and suggestions.

References

1. Digital signature standard (DSS). FIPS PUB 186–4, National Institute of Standards and Technology (NIST) (2013)
2. Bayer, S., Groth, J.: Efficient zero-knowledge argument for correctness of a shuffle. In: Pointcheval, D., Johansson, T. (eds.) EUROCRYPT 2012. LNCS, vol. 7237, pp. 263–280. Springer, Heidelberg (2012). https://doi.org/10.1007/978-3-642-29011-4_17
3. ElGamal, T.: A public key cryptosystem and a signature scheme based on discrete logarithms. In: Blakley, G.R., Chaum, D. (eds.) CRYPTO 1984. LNCS, vol. 196, pp. 10–18. Springer, Heidelberg (1985). https://doi.org/10.1007/3-540-39568-7_2
4. Fiat, A., Shamir, A.: How to prove yourself: practical solutions to identification and signature problems. In: Odlyzko, A.M. (ed.) CRYPTO 1986. LNCS, vol. 263, pp. 186–194. Springer, Heidelberg (1987). https://doi.org/10.1007/3-540-47721-7_12
5. Knuth, D.E.: The Art of Computer Programming, Volume 2: Seminumerical Algorithms, 3rd edn. Addison Wesley, Boston (1997)
6. Locher, P., Haenni, R.: A lightweight implementation of a shuffle proof for electronic voting systems. In: Plödereder, E., Grunske, L., Schneider, E., Ull, D. (eds.) INFORMATIK 2014, 44. Jahrestagung der Gesellschaft für Informatik, pp. 1391–1400. No. P-232 in Lecture Notes in Informatics, Stuttgart, Germany (2014)
7. Maurer, U.: Unifying zero-knowledge proofs of knowledge. In: Preneel, B. (ed.) AFRICACRYPT 2009. LNCS, vol. 5580, pp. 272–286. Springer, Heidelberg (2009). https://doi.org/10.1007/978-3-642-02384-2_17
8. Terelius, B., Wikström, D.: Proofs of restricted shuffles. In: Bernstein, D.J., Lange, T. (eds.) AFRICACRYPT 2010. LNCS, vol. 6055, pp. 100–113. Springer, Heidelberg (2010). https://doi.org/10.1007/978-3-642-12678-9_7
9. Wikström, D.: A commitment-consistent proof of a shuffle. In: Boyd, C., González Nieto, J. (eds.) ACISP 2009. LNCS, vol. 5594, pp. 407–421. Springer, Heidelberg (2009). https://doi.org/10.1007/978-3-642-02620-1_28
10. Wikström, D.: User Manual for the Verificatum Mix-Net Version 1.4.0. Verificatum AB, Stockholm, Sweden (2014)
11. Wikström, D.: How to Implement a Stand-alone Verifier for the Verificatum Mix-Net: VMN Version 3.0.2. Verificatum AB, Stockholm, Sweden (2016)

---

[3] https://github.com/republique-et-canton-de-geneve/chvote-protocol-poc.

Using Selene to Verify Your Vote in JCJ

Vincenzo Iovino, Alfredo Rial, Peter B. Rønne$^{(\boxtimes)}$, and Peter Y.A. Ryan

University of Luxembourg, Esch-sur-Alzette, Luxembourg
vinciovino@gmail.com, {alfredo.rial,peter.roenne,peter.ryan}@uni.lu

Abstract. We show how to combine the individual verification mechanism of Selene with the coercion-resistant e-voting scheme from Juels, Catalano and Jakobsson (JCJ). This results in an e-voting scheme which allows the voter to check directly that her vote is counted as intended, but still allows her to mitigate coercion.

We also construct variants of the protocol which provide everlasting privacy or better verifiability. Further, both improvements of JCJ and Selene are discussed.

1   Introduction

Remote e-voting gives voters the opportunity to conveniently vote from home, work or even abroad. However, it also presents cryptographers with the difficult task of integrating both verifiability and privacy properties in a secure, efficient and usable e-voting protocol. One of the hardest problems of leaving the reassuring frame of a voting booth is to protect voters against coercion attempts. Juels, Catalano and Jakobsson (JCJ) [JCJ05] found a way to provide coercion-resistance across multiple elections, assuming only a single coercion-free registration. The registration provides the voters with credentials which they use for voting. Coerced voters can provide the coercer with a fake credential, and a vote cast using this will not be counted. The system was later implemented as Civitas [CCM08].

The JCJ-mechanism might be worrisome to the normal user. Was the credential entered correctly? Did someone else manage to override my vote? In the end, it would be reassuring for the voters to be able to directly check that their votes were counted correctly. However, providing voters with such a service endangers the receipt-freeness and coercion-resistance if not done carefully. Fortunately, Selene [RRI16] provides us with a mechanism for individual tallied-as-intended verifiability while being able to mitigate the coercion threat. This is done by giving each vote a unique tracking number, but first revealing this to the voter after the tally has been published. Unfortunately, Selene was developed for Helios style protocols, but in this paper we will show that the construction can also be applied to the coercion-resistant vote casting system from JCJ/Civitas. Indeed we will consider different variants of JCJ and show how Selene can be added to JCJ even in the case when we want to provide everlasting privacy via pseudonyms, or when we offer better verifiability properties. We will also see

M. Brenner et al. (Eds.): FC 2017 Workshops 2017, LNCS 10323, pp. 385–403, 2017.
https://doi.org/10.1007/978-3-319-70278-0_24

how to address the secure platform problem with the extra verifiability gained from Selene. Along the way we will discuss some problems and solutions of the JCJ construction with cross-election and dynamic coercion. Further, we will give a more efficient construction of the zero-knowledge proofs needed in Selene.

1.1   Related Work

Since the seminal paper defining coercion-resistance [JCJ05], there have been numerous paper analyzing the JCJ protocol and providing alternatives, see e.g. [NFVK13a] and references therein.

Selene [RRI16] is based on the idea of having trackers for the votes, an idea already suggested in Schneier's book [Sch94], which later independently also appeared in a scheme used for ANR (Agence National de la Recherche) funding committee meetings. Recently, sElect [KMST16] uses trackers to achieve good accountability. However, in all of these cases the tracker directly represents a receipt, whereas Selene mends this by delaying when the voter can obtain the tracker.

The idea of everlasting privacy goes back to Moran and Naor [MN06] and have been studied in several works, see e.g. [CPP13] for how to make perfectly private audit trails in general election schemes, or [ACKR13] for how to do automated verification of everlasting protocols. Here we focus on pseudonymity rather than anonymity. However, if we follow JCJ closely, this is the best we can do since the credentials themselves will be like pseudonyms to a future adversary.

The secure platform problem is one of the main problems in e-voting. One solution is to use out-of-band channels and code-voting, see [Cha01, RT09]. In e.g. Helios [Adi08] Benaloh challenges [Ben06] should help to detect malware, but are unfortunately not often used [KOKV11]. Relying on hardware tokens is yet another possibility, see [HK14, GRCC15], but is not always unproblematic, see [KR16].

2   Building Blocks

Our construction uses the following building blocks: a non-interactive zero-knowledge proof system (NIZK) [BFM88] in the random oracle model [BR93], the ElGamal public key encryption scheme [Gam85], threshold encryption with a plaintext equivalence test [JJ00], a verifiable re-encryption mixnet [SK95], the Pedersen commitment scheme [Ped91], a web bulletin board [HL09], untappable channels [HH07] and anonymous channels [Fre00].

3   System Model and Setup

We first describe the parties involved in an e-voting scheme.

Voters. The voters V_i $(i = 1, \ldots, n)$ register for voting, cast ballots, obtain trackers and verify the voting results.

Tally Tellers. The Tally Tellers T_j tally the cast ballots and publish the results.

Registration Tellers. The Registration Tellers RT_k register voters.

Tracker Tellers. The Tracker Tellers TT_l process trackers. They could be the same parties as the Tally Tellers or the Registration Tellers, but they are kept separate here due to the different trust assumptions.

Our e-voting scheme consists of the following phases.

Setup. In the setup phase, the parties generate secret and public keys. Each voter creates a designated verifier key. The Tally Tellers generate a public key pk_T for a threshold encryption scheme.

Registration. In the registration phase, a voter V_i and the registration tellers run a protocol. The designated verifier key dvk_i of V_i and pk_T are used as inputs. As a result of the protocol, the voter obtains a credential C_i. Additionally, the voter identifier V_i, the key dvk_i and an encryption of C_i under pk_T are published on the web bulletin board (BB).

Tracker Preparation. In this phase, the Tracker Tellers and the voters run a protocol. A set of trackers $\{n_i\}_{i=1,...,n}$, the designated verifier keys of the voters and pk_T are used as inputs. As a result of the protocol, each voter obtains a Pedersen commitment to its tracker. Additionally, an encryption under pk_T of the tracker associated with a voter V_i is appended to the row for voter V_i on the BB. In this protocol, the association between trackers and voters is not revealed to any party.

Vote Casting. In this phase, a voter V_i computes a ballot and publishes it on the BB. In our construction, the ballot contains an encryption under pk_T of the credential C_i and of the vote vote_i.

Tallying. In this phase, the Tally Tellers take as input the ballots published on the BB and run a protocol to output pairs (vote_a, n_a), which associate each valid vote with the tracker of the voter that cast that vote. Those pairs are published on the BB.

Tracker Retrieval. In this phase, a voter V_i and the tracker tellers run a protocol as a result of which V_i learns the tracker n with which it became associated in the tracker preparation phase.

Once a voter learns her tracker n_a, the voter can verify on the BB that the pair (vote_a, n_a) is correct.

Setup. Let G be a cyclic group of prime order q and g be a generator of G. In the setup phase, each voter creates designated verifier key $\mathsf{dvk}_i = g^{x_i}$. The designated verifier keys are used to provide deniability in the registration phase in JCJ and the implementation Civitas. We assume that the designated verifier key system is well setup, which includes that the voters have proven that they know their secret key. Additionally, we use the same designated verifier key in the Selene construction as the public key for the ElGamal encryption scheme. JCJ also suggest an alternative registration with an erasure function. In that case we need a PKI as in Selene where dvk_i is the voter's public key.

The Tally Tellers run the distributed key generation algorithm of the threshold encryption scheme to generate a public key pk_T and obtain each a private share of the secret key.

4   Description of the E-Voting Protocol

In this section, we describe the protocol combining JCJ and Selene in detail.

4.1   Registration

The registration is quite similar to JCJ/Civitas. Each voter has a designated verifier key dvk_i. The voter must prove (interactively in ZK) that she knows the secret key corresponding to dvk_i over an untappable channel during registration. This is to prevent a coercer from making a voter register a designated verifier key for which the secret key is unknown by the voter. For each eligible voter V_i, each Registration Teller RT_j randomly picks $C_{ij} \leftarrow_\$ G$ and publishes $\{C_{ij}\}_{\mathsf{pk}_T}$ on BB in a row marked for voter V_i. As discussed in Sect. 7.1, we could instead use pseudonyms PV_i if everlasting privacy is desired.

For each voter, the encryptions are multiplied together to homomorphically obtain a single credential C_i. On BB, we now have the following row for each voter

$$V_i, \mathsf{dvk}_i, \{C_{ij}\}_{\mathsf{pk}_T}, \prod_j \{C_{ij}\}_{\mathsf{pk}_T} = \{C_i\}_{\mathsf{pk}_T}$$

Here we deviate from JCJ/Civitas by also including the public key dvk_i in the row. This key will be the public key used by the voter in Selene.

The voter now receives the credential shares and designated verifier proofs from the Registration Tellers

$$RT_i \rightarrow V_i : C_{ij}, \pi_{ij}$$

where π_{ij} is a designated proof to the key dvk_i proving that $\{C_{ij}\}_{\mathsf{pk}_T}$, appearing on BB, is an encryption of C_{ij}. The voter can now calculate C_i and check the proofs.

If the voter is coerced, she chooses at random an alternative value C_i' in G and shows this to the coercer. The proofs can be faked with her designated verifier key. It is here of course essential that the voter knows the secret key, but a coerced voter can even reveal this secret key to the coercer, as long as the coercer does not cooperate with the registration tellers. It is important that the coercer is not present by the reception of all C_{ij}'s.

The credential can be reused for several elections, and could, in principle, be obtained in booth by the registration authorities.

4.2   Tracker Preparation

Whereas the previous part was very similar to JCJ/Civitas, we now add the main ingredient of Selene, namely, the personal voting trackers that each voter can use to check her tallied vote.

The trackers $\{n_i\}_{i=1,...,n}$ should be a negligible set of $\mathbb{Z}_q$ (i.e. the chance of a random element in $\mathbb{Z}_q$ being a tracker is negligible).

The Tracker Tellers first publish

$$n_i, \{g^{n_i}\}_{\mathsf{pk}_T}$$

on BB, where the encryption is with trivial randomness. The trackers are sent through a re-encryption mix and one anonymised tracker is added to each of the voters' rows to obtain

$$V_i, \mathsf{dvk}_i, \{C_i\}_{\mathsf{pk}_T}, \{g^{n_{\pi(i)}}\}_{\mathsf{pk}_T}$$

where π is the permutation used for mixing. In the following we will suppress π for easier notation. Note that, whereas credentials can be used for several elections, this tracker mixing needs to be renewed for each election.

Further each Tracker Teller TT_j randomly chooses $r_{ij} \leftarrow_\$ \mathbb{Z}_q$ for each voter and publishes

$$\{\mathsf{dvk}_i^{r_{ij}}\}_{\mathsf{pk}_T}, \{g^{r_{ij}}\}_{\mathsf{pk}_T}, \Pi_{ij}$$

where Π_{ij} is a non-interactive zero-knowledge proof that this is done correctly. The proof is presented in the Selene protocol, see [RRI15], Appendix A. As in Selene, the terms from each Teller are now homomorphically combined with the encryption of the tracker, and we obtain a trapdoor commitment to the tracker

$$\{g^{n_i}\}_{\mathsf{pk}_T} \prod_j \{\mathsf{dvk}_i^{r_{ij}}\}_{\mathsf{pk}_T} = \{g^{n_i} \mathsf{dvk}_i^{r_i}\}_{\mathsf{pk}_T}$$

with $r_i = \sum_j r_{ij}$. This is appended to each voter's row. Finally, the Tally Tellers decrypt the trapdoor commitment to the tracker, $g^{n_i} \mathsf{dvk}_i^{r_i}$, for each voter.

4.3   Vote Casting

Vote casting is done like in JCJ. Here we follow Civitas. If voter V_i wants to vote "vote$_i$", she anonymously sends to BB

$$(\{C_i\}_{\mathsf{pk}_T}, \{\mathsf{vote}_i\}_{\mathsf{pk}_T}, \pi)$$

where π is a zero-knowledge proof that the vote is well-formed together with a proof that C_i and vote$_i$ are simultaneously known, which prevents vote copying. To cast a vote in presence of a coercer, the fake credential given to the coercer is simply used in place of the real one.

4.4   Improving the Coercion Resistance of JCJ

The JCJ protocol has a tally procedure which leaves room for certain coercion attacks. Let us first remind ourselves how the tally procedure works. It relies heavily on the Tally Tellers performing Plaintext Equivalence Tests (PETs) on the encryption of the credentials, see e.g. [CCM08].

1. Zero-knowledge proofs of the cast ballots are checked, and invalid ballots are removed.
2. Duplicates, i.e., ballots that use the same credential, are removed according to the existing vote update policy. This is done using PETs among the ciphertexts of the credentials in the cast ballots. This means that the coercer cannot mark the vote with a chosen number of duplicates.
3. The list of ciphertexts of registered credentials is anonymized using a mix-net. Further, from the list of valid ballots after duplicate removal, we likewise use a parallel mix-net to anonymize the pairs of ciphertexts of credentials and votes.
4. Unauthorized votes, i.e., ballots that do not use a registered credential, are removed by performing PETs of the credentials from the cast votes with the list of registered credentials.
5. The remaining valid votes can now be decrypted to reveal the tally.

The duplicate removal can in certain quite special situations give the coercer unwanted information and correspondingly hinders coercion-resistance, as we will now see. This was discovered, but not analyzed, in [Roe16]. The problem appears when the coercion happens dynamically or across elections. Consider an uncoerced voter who has already voted. The coercer now detects this somehow, say by overhearing this or seeing this in the browsing history of the voter.[1] The coercer can now coerce the voter just before voting ends. The coerced voter now gives the coercer a fake credential, and they can sit down and cast an, in fact, invalid vote. However, in the duplicate removal phase, it will then be evident that the credential was fake, since no duplicates are detected for the fake vote. To circumvent this, all voters should start by casting fake votes if they want to be prepared for later coercion threats, which seems pretty complicated. Note that the protocol in [KHF11] actually does something similar to prevent board flooding attacks on JCJ, but the cost is a statistical coercion-resistance.

Another case is a voter which was coerced in an earlier election and gave the coercer a fake credential. At a later election, the coercer can now cast a vote using this credential and check whether this will have duplicates in the duplicate removal phase. If this does not happen, the coercer can conclude that either the credential was fake, or that the voter did not vote in the latter election, which might be improbable. This means that the coerced voter also needs to cast votes using the fake credential even at elections after being coerced to be on the safe side.

---

[1] We can assume that coerced voters are careful to use only devices out of the reach of the coercer or to delete browsing history, but this is more unlikely for uncoerced voters.

Note that it does not help to do a mix before performing the duplicate elimination since the groups of ballots could still be marked by a certain number of duplicates.

If vote updating is not intended, we can sidestep the issue by simply dropping the step of duplicate removal. After anonymizing both the registered credentials and the cast ballots, PETs are performed for each registered credential against the cast ballots until the first match comes up. We then pick this as the vote for the given credential. For the set of cast votes for a given valid credential this will pick one in the set at random. The method thus reveals a minimum amount of information, but makes vote updating harder to implement. Further it also decreases verifiability as discussed below, but Selene helps here.

4.5   Tallying with Selene

Tallying with Selene requires a minor modification. First, all proofs are checked and invalid votes are discarded. Then all cast pairs

$$(\{C_a\}_{\mathsf{pk}_T}, \{\mathrm{vote}_a\}_{\mathsf{pk}_T}) \mapsto (\{C_{\pi(a)}\}_{\mathsf{pk}_T}, \{\mathrm{vote}_{\pi(a)}\}_{\mathsf{pk}_T})$$

are re-encryption mixed.

Further the pairs of registered credentials and tracking numbers

$$(\{C_i\}_{\mathsf{pk}_T}, \{g^{n_i}\}_{\mathsf{pk}_T}) \mapsto (\{C_{\pi'(i)}\}_{\mathsf{pk}_T}, \{g^{n_{\pi'(i)}}\}_{\mathsf{pk}_T})$$

from each voter's column are re-encryption mixed in parallel. From each entry in this anonymised list of credential-tracker pairs, the Tally Tellers do PETs against the credentials from the anonymised list of cast votes. The first time we get a positive match, the corresponding vote is decrypted (verifiably) together with the corresponding tracker. If wanted, one can also do more elaborate PETs (like in JCJ-Civitas), first removing all duplicate votes, possibly with some vote update policy, as explained in Sect. 4.4.

The end result (after taking the discrete log of the trackers) is the Tally Board of valid vote-tracker pairs (since the set of trackers is small and known, it is easy to go from g^n to n)

$$(\mathrm{vote}_a, n_a).$$

4.6   Tracker Retrieval

Finally, the tracker retrieval happens like in Selene. Each Tracker Teller provides each voter with their share $g^{r_{ij}}$.

$$TT_j \to V_i : g^{r_{ij}}.$$

This happens according to some random time distribution a suitable time after the tally has been published, see [RRI16] and via, for the coercer, untappable channels.

The voter (or rather her device) combines these shares to get g^{r_i}. Together with the public trapdoor commitment $g^{n_i} \mathsf{dvk}_i^{r_i}$, the term g^{r_i} forms an ElGamal encryption of the tracker under the key dvk_i. The voter can now decrypt and directly check that her vote appears correctly on the Tally Board.

Trackers can be faked in the case of coercion, just like in Selene. That is, the voter finds the wanted fake tracker, n^*, on BB for the coercer's choice of vote and calculates

$$\left(g^{-n^*} g^{n_i} \mathsf{dvk}_i^{r_i} \right)^{x_i^{-1}} .$$

as the fake term to give to the coercer instead of g^{r_i}. Here x_i is the secret key of $\mathsf{dvk}_i = g^{x_i}$.

A potential attack would raise if an adversary, possibly colluding with all the Tracker Tellers, could make a voter get a fake g^{r_i} term that the voter decrypts to a valid tracker different from the true tracker of the voter with non-negligible probability. In [RRI15] it is proven that this is hard under a standard computational assumption.

5   More Efficient Zero-Knowledge Proofs in Selene

In the tracker preparation phase, the Tracker Tellers publish

$$\{\mathsf{dvk}_i^{r_{ij}}\}_{\mathsf{pk}_T}, \{g^{r_{ij}}\}_{\mathsf{pk}_T}, \Pi_{ij}$$

where the zero-knowledge proof was of the correctness of this construction, i.e. that the two generators are raised to the same known power. However, the term $\{g^{r_{ij}}\}_{\mathsf{pk}_T}$ is not really needed. In principle, it could be used for accountability if the Tracker Teller tries to send a wrong $g^{r_{ij}}$ to the voter. However, for deniability, the Tracker Teller sends this term without any proof to the voter. This means that there is no proof that the Teller sent a wrong message to the voter. Thus we suggest to only publish

$$\{\mathsf{dvk}_i^{r_{ij}}\}_{\mathsf{pk}_T}, \Pi'_{ij}$$

where Π'_{ij} is a shorter zero-knowledge proof, showing that the ciphertext indeed encrypts the key dvk_i to a known power. In a long version of this note we present this proof in details; it consists of 8 group elements in some group of prime order p and of 6 elements of $\mathbb{Z}_p^*$. We also prove in the long version that the adversary, also in this case, even when colluding with all Tellers, only has a negligible chance of constructing a fake term $g^{r_{ij}}$ that makes the voter decrypt to a valid tracker different from her real tracker.

6   Security Assumptions and Arguments for Security

In this section we will briefly mention the trust assumptions for the voting authorities and give brief explanations of why the different security properties hold.

6.1 Trust Assumptions for the Tellers

- The Registration Tellers are trusted individually for coercion-resistance and collectively for verifiability. For everlasting privacy via pseudonyms (see Sect. 7.1) they are individually trusted for everlasting privacy.
- The Tally Tellers are trusted collectively for privacy (and hence coercion-resistance) and verifiability. A threshold version follows directly. We will here assume that the verifiable reencryption mixes done in the protocol are performed by the Tally Tellers, and that these are private if at least one Teller is honest.
- The Tracker Tellers are trusted collectively for privacy. They are trusted individually for coercion-resistance since the voter needs to know which $g^{r_{ij}}$ to fake for the coercer (like for the Registration Tellers).

6.2 Verifiability

For verifiability, we assume that the voters keep their private designated verifier keys secret. An adversary colluding with all the Registration Tellers can however still obtain the credential of a voter, and cast votes on her behalf, violating at least eligibility verifiability. The same can happen if the adversary and all the Tally Tellers collude, see also Sect. 7.2 below how to mitigate this risk.

However, if such grand collusion do not happen, the only ballots on BB with a given voters correct credential are with overwhelming probability cast by the voter herself. That the correct vote is now chosen in the tally is secured by checking the zero-knowledge proofs of the verifiable PETs and verifying the correctness of the mixes. Finally, the actual decryption of the vote can also be verified.

The correctness of the individual verifiability of the Selene trackers, is very similar to the original Selene construction. The verification of the first mix of the trackers ensures that each voter gets a unique tracker, from the set of trackers. The pairwise mix of registered credentials and trackers, together with verification of the PETs ensure that this tracker is assigned to the voter's cast vote. Again, the correct decryption of the trackers can be verified. That the voters receive the correct trackers with overwhelming probability is discussed above.

6.3 Vote Privacy

If the Tally Tellers or Tracker Tellers collude they can easily break privacy. Otherwise privacy of the mixes and encryptions will ensure privacy. In general, ballot independence is ensured by the construction (at least if we do not do the duplicate weeding) if we check the proofs of the PETs. This also means that even if the Registration Tellers collude and can cast valid votes on behalf of voters, this does not violate privacy.

6.4   Coercion-Resistance and Coercion-Mitigation

Coercion-resistance and, related, receipt-freeness is a harder problem. The point is that even in the ideal version of the scheme, the voters will know exactly which vote is theirs in the final tally by checking their unique tracker. This is intended and gives the voter a reassurance of the correctness of the vote. However, each voter knowing their unique tracker does constitute a piece of information, not obtainable in standard voting schemes, and which is not foreseen in standard definitions of coercion-resistance and receipt-freeness.

Coerced voters however still have good options to *mitigate* coercion. They have algorithms to both fake their credential and the term to obtain their tracker number. The difference to standard coercion-resistance crystallizes when the voter shows a fake tracking number to the coercer, and it turns out to be the coercer's own tracker. This was analyzed in Selene [RRI15] where also several alternative versions without this drawback were discussed, but at the cost of a less clear Tally Board.

Another problem comes from a slight lack of coercion-resistance in the JCJ construction itself, which is then magnified by the addition of individual verifiability. JCJ, and any scheme which has voting authorised by a token which can be faked and provided to the coercer, is not strictly coercion-resistant at least if used across multiple elections. The point is that the coercer can cast votes using the token obtained from the voter for special candidates which are expected to get a low number of votes. In the extreme case where this candidate does not get any votes in the election, the coercer knows he was provided with a fake token. In less extreme cases, the coercer only gains statistical information of the validity of the token. Used across elections the statistical certainty can be improved. This is not so different from the coercer actually directly demanding the voter to vote for the corresponding candidate. However, the point is that the coercer can choose to follow this strategy completely without the voter's knowledge and thus without the voter having the choice to remain undetected by following the coercer's wish. The individual verifiability here worsens the situation[2] since the coercer can demand to know which candidate he chose, which the voter should know via the individual verifiability mechanism (here via the tracking number). Of course, the voter cannot reply with certainty due to the covert strategy of the coercer. However we will see in Subsect. 7.4 that we can change the tracker retrieval mechanism to allow the voter to answer the coercer's demand with a valid tracker thus successfully defending against this attack (unless the chosen candidate did not get any votes, in which case no defense would ever be possible for the chosen result function).

7   Extensions and Alternative Protocols

7.1   Everlasting Privacy via Pseudonyms

Privacy is easy to break for a future adversary who is able to break the employed encryption, e.g. because the DDH assumption happens to be broken or simply

---

[2] Thanks to Véronique Cortier for pointing this out.

by the expected increase in computational power over time. In general, we think about the future adversary as having unlimited computational power, but only being active after the election using the data from BB.

A quick and dirty way to obtain everlasting privacy is to use pseudonyms (see [LHK16] for a more advanced approach to everlasting privacy and coercion-resistance, however with an efficiency drawback). I.e., instead of labelling the rows on the bulletin board with the voter IDs, we use pseudonyms. We assume that only the Registration Tellers and the Tracker Tellers know the relation between the pseudonyms, designated verifier keys and the actual voter IDs. Especially, this information will not be public and not available to the future adversary.

Of course, pseudonyms are not the best way to preserve privacy, especially across elections. However, they are easy to implement with not too big usability costs. In particular, the JCJ construction works with credentials, which to the future adversary are just like pseudonyms labelling the voters, even though they only appear under encryption. As we show now, we can also use the Selene mechanism in this case with some modifications.

Registration with Pseudonyms. In the registration phase, we mark the voter's row on BB with the pseudonym PV_i instead of V_i

$$PV_i, (\mathsf{dvk}_i)^{s_{ij}}, \{C_{ij}\}_{\mathsf{pk}_T}, \prod_j \{C_{ij}\}_{\mathsf{pk}_T} = \{C_i\}_{\mathsf{pk}_T}$$

Note that each Registration Teller also takes the public key of the voter dvk_i and raises it to the random power s_{ij} before publishing it. For each voter, we can now collect the terms

$$PV_i, (\mathsf{dvk}_i)^{s_i} = \prod_j (\mathsf{dvk}_i)^{s_{ij}}, \prod_j \{C_{ij}\}_{\mathsf{pk}_T} = \{C_i\}_{\mathsf{pk}_T},$$

with $s_i = \sum_j s_{ij}$. The Registration Tellers now send both the credential shares C_{ij}, the random exponents r_{ij}, the pseudonym and the designated verifier proofs to the voter

$$RT_i \rightarrow V_i : C_{ij}, s_{ij}, \pi_{ij}, PV_i$$

where π_{ij} is a designated proof to the key dvk_i proving that $\{C_{ij}\}_{\mathsf{pk}_T}$, appearing on BB, is an encryption of C_{ij}. The voter checks the proofs and the validity of the values s_{ij}. Further, the voter can now calculate C_i and s_i. For internal purposes the voter can update her key to be $(\mathsf{dvk}_i)^{s_i}$.

The reason for raising dvk_i to s_i is two-fold. The first reason is to blind the public key from the future adversary. From $(\mathsf{dvk}_i)^{s_i}$, it is information-theoretically impossible to infer dvk_i. The second reason is to prevent the following verifiability attack. Suppose that all registration tellers collude. They could then point two or more voters to the same pseudonym and credential, which would only be detected if the attacked voters unlikely compare pseudonyms.

This would only give one vote to the two voters. Note that this verifiability is outside the scope of the JCJ assumptions, assuming at least one Registration Teller is honest. However, in [Roe16], it was shown that we can do better (see also below). However, by knowing the exponentials, the registration tellers would need to know a discrete logarithm relation between the attacked voters, which is infeasible by the hardness of the discrete logarithm problem, if we assume that the PKI has been set up properly.

The remainder of the protocol can now proceed as above with dvk_i replaced by $(\mathsf{dvk}_i)^{s_i}$. The future adversary will be able to relate a vote to the pseudonym and $(\mathsf{dvk}_i)^{s_i}$, but not directly to the voter. Note that the Tracker Tellers need to know the relation between pseudonyms and voters to return the random terms $g^{r_{ij}}$ to the voters. Like the Registration Tellers they are thus also assumed not to be colluding with the future adversary. This trust is one of the reasons to distinguish them from the Tally Tellers.

7.2   Stronger Verifiability

In [Roe16], a version of JCJ-Civitas was presented which has stronger security guarantees, and only changes the registration and voting procedure slightly. The main point is that the voters know the discrete logarithm of their credential, and this can be seen as a secret key. The cast ballots containing the encrypted credential are basically anonymously signed using this secret key. This prevents verifiability attacks where either all Tally Tellers or Registration Tellers are corrupted. In that case, they know the secret credentials, and could cast valid votes on behalf of any voter. If we use the duplicate removal step, which had slight coercion-resistance problems, as discussed above, this attack could be detectable by alert voters. However, even so, it could lead to unsolvable disputes about the validity of the election, see [Roe16].

Selene can also be added to this version of JCJ just as for standard JCJ. However, we can also create a new combination of JCJ and Selene where, post-registration, the voters only have to handle a single key (actually, coerced voters, of course, also need to handle the fake keys).

The registration works as follows. For a given voter V_i, all Registration Tellers RT_j choose random values $c_{ij} \in \mathbb{Z}_q$ and publish $\{g^{c_{ij}}\}_{\mathsf{pk}_T}$ on BB. The voter gets c_{ij} from RT_j together with a designated zero-knowledge proof to dvk_i, proving the correct encryption of $g^{c_{ij}}$.

The ciphertexts of the credential shares can now be multiplied together, but are further multiplied by $\{\mathsf{dvk}_i\}_{\mathsf{pk}_T}$, which for verifiability is encrypted with trivial randomness. Since ElGamal is homomorphic, the final ciphertext is an encryption of the voter credential $C_i = g^{c_i} := g^{\sum_j c_{ij} + x_i}$. However, in this case the voter, and only the voter, knows the discrete logarithm, since the Registration Tellers do not know the secret key of dvk_i.

In case of coercion, the voter will present the coercer with a random number c_i' and corresponding group element $C_i' = g^{c_i'}$ and claim this is the real credential – just like in JCJ, but now working with the discrete logarithms instead of the group elements.

After registration, BB contains

$$V_i, \{C_i\}_{\mathsf{pk}_T}$$

and the uncoerced voter only needs to store the discrete logarithm of C_i. We do not demand now V_i to store dvk_i separately. The Tracker Tellers can mix and add $\{g^{n_i}\}_{\mathsf{pk}_T}$ to each voter as above, but the Tracker Tellers can now only work with $\{C_i\}_{\mathsf{pk}_T}$. Due to the homomorphic property of ElGamal, this is however enough. To create the trapdoor commitment, the Tracker Teller TT_j randomly chooses $r_{ij} \leftarrow_\$ \mathbb{Z}_q$, and publishes for each voter

$$\{C_i\}_{\mathsf{pk}_T}^{r_{ij}} = \{C_i^{r_{ij}}\}_{\mathsf{pk}_T}, \Pi_{ij}$$

where again Π_{ij} is a NIZKPoK that this is done correctly. We have here chosen the version without publishing the encryption of $g^{r_{ij}}$, however this only changes for the proof.

Observe that we need a proof that an ElGamal ciphertext is raised to some known power and this accounts to a proof of knowledge of the randomness r in a DH-tuple. A NIZKPoK for it can be obtaining by applying the Fiat-Shamir's heuristic to the Chaum-Perdersen's proofs [CP93]. The coercion-resistance of the public information follows from the DH-assumption observing what follows. Let us assume for simplicity that there is only one teller. Then, the coercer can see $C_i^r g_i^n$ along with the ciphertext raised to r but not C_i and note also that the voter does not know r. Thus, under the DH-assumption we can conclude that this information consists of just random group elements.

By homomorphically multiplying $\{g^{n_i}\}_{\mathsf{pk}_T}$ with all the $\{C_i^{r_{ij}}\}_{\mathsf{pk}_T}$, we get the trapdoor commitment $\{g^{n_i} C_i^{r_i}\}_{\mathsf{pk}_T}$ where the trapdoor key now is c_i. The Tally Tellers decrypt these commitments verifiably.

Vote casting follows [Roe16] and works like before. The voter casts

$$(\{C_i\}_{\mathsf{pk}_T}, \{\mathsf{vote}_i\}_{\mathsf{pk}_T}, \pi)$$

anonymously to BB. The difference is that the zero-knowledge proof now also contains a proof of knowledge of the discrete logarithm in the encrypted credential, i.e. like an anonymous signature.

Tallying is just like before, and retrieving the trackers likewise. However, for coerced voters, faking the random term $g^{r_{ij}}$ is now different from standard Selene. The point is that, whereas in the standard case, the coerced voter will hand out the real secret key of dvk_i to the coercer, in this case the coercer will get a fake key $C_i' = g^{c_i'}$. The fake term g^{r_i} is thus calculated as

$$\left(g^{-n^*} g^{n_i} C_i^{r_i}\right)^{c_i'^{-1}}$$

since, when combining this with the commitment on BB, we get a ciphertext which decrypts to the wanted tracker n^* when we decrypt with the fake credential key given to the coercer. Actually, this construction is mildly better than standard Selene for coercion. The reason is that, if the coercer somehow manages to see the real term g^{r_i}, this will decrypt to the voter's correct tracker in standard Selene, but here it will decrypt to a random number, since the coercer is in the possession of a fake key. The voter can thus still claim that something must have gone wrong, or the system is corrupted, whereas in standard Selene the chance of this would be negligible. In real life, this is probably not a very usable defense for coerced voters.

Note that, if Tracker Tellers are corrupted, they can reveal relations on the credentials between voters from the decrypted commitments, since they know the random coins used in the commitments. This is however less of a problem in this version of JCJ since the discrete log of the credential is needed to break verifiability, and the Tracker Tellers are anyway trusted for coercion-resistance.

7.3   On the Secure Platform Problem

One of the main problems of e-voting is the secure platform problem. Very often this problem is ignored and the voter's computing platform is considered safe. An alternative useful approach is to use an out-of-band channel, e.g. using vote codes on paper, see e.g. Pretty Good Democracy [RT09].

Instead of resorting to out-of-band channels, one can also try to secure the device used by the voter, see e.g. [NV12] [NFVK13b] where simple smart cards are used. These are further used to improve usability for the voter. One drawback of dedicated hardware might be forced abstention attacks from local coercers, who simply seize the device from the coerced voter.

Instead, we can try to spread the risk of malware attacks to two independent devices, assuming that the adversary will not be able to control both. Further, we keep these devices general, i.e., it could be smartphones or laptops and not dedicated hardware. Keys could have backups on more devices if the voter is afraid of forced coercion. Due to the setup with two different credential/keys, the combination of JCJ and Selene (with two credential/keys) seems ideal for this task.

Let us assume that the voter has two computing devices D_1 and D_2. We store the secret key of the designated verifier key dvk_i on D_2. The voter now uses device D_1 for the registration where the voter gets the credential from the registration. The credential is then stored on D_1, and possibly with secure backups. Note that, during registration, only the public key dvk_i is needed, thus device D_2 can be excluded from this process.

A coerced voter can provide fake proofs without using device D_1, i.e., by only using the secret key on device D_2. Thus device D_2 does not learn the credential.

Vote-casting can be done on device D_1 since it holds the credential, but does not need device D_2. Finally, tracker retrieval and vote verification can be done on D_2 without using D_1.

In order to perform an undetected change of the vote, an adversary needs to infect both device D_1 to get the correct credential, and device D_2 in order to fake the verification of the final tallied vote with the Selene mechanism. Since the devices could be very independent, e.g. the check of the final vote could even be done on some public PC (with a threat of a privacy attack, of course), this seems to greatly reduce the danger from malware.

7.4   Using JCJ to Improve Selene

The combination of JCJ and Selene cannot only be used to add extra verifiability to JCJ, but can also provide a more secure tracker retrieval in Selene. The point is that the voter can authenticate herself with her credential. We can use this to make the tracker retrieval active. That is, instead of the Tracker Tellers sending out the $g^{r_{ij}}$ terms, with the risk of the coercer intercepting the message, the voter contacts the Tracker Tellers to obtain the terms. We will here briefly sketch the idea.

The voters can identify themselves to the Tracker Tellers with a ciphertext of the credential. Here and in the following such encrypted credentials should be followed by zero-knowledge proofs of plaintext knowledge of a special form that makes sure that it is not copied from e.g. already cast election ballots, or reused for ballots or authentication in later elections. For clarity we will suppress these proofs in the following. The Tally Tellers can now perform a PET with the registered credential (while also checking the zero-knowledge proof) to check the authenticity. After authentication, the terms $g^{r_{ij}}$ are handed out.

Coerced voters need to have a time window between the publication of the tally board and the start of the tracker retrieval, where they can upload a fake $g^{r_{ij}}$ term to each Tracker Teller. They do this via an anonymous channel

$$V_i \rightarrow TT_j : V_i, \{C_1\}_{\mathsf{pk}_T}, \{C_2\}_{\mathsf{pk}_T}, \{(g^{r_{ij}})_{\mathsf{fake}}\}_{\mathsf{pk}_T}.$$

The first plaintext is supposed to be the real credential, the second plaintext the faked credential (different from C_1) and the third plaintext is the faked term that will be shown, when someone with credential C_2 tries to retrieve their tracker share. The Tally Tellers need to be invoked to get this term. The fake term could also be sent in plain, if the channel is considered untappable for the coercer.

Now, if a coercer tries to retrieve the random term, the voter should have made a faking request beforehand, and the coercer gets the faked term.

However, we need to be careful since the coercer should not be able to use the update mechanism to discover that he is in the possession of a faked credential. We thus proceed as follows. After the time window, each Tracker Teller now has a database for each voter with rows of faking requests (which might come from the coercer as well). For understandability, we assume that each voter has maximally one coercer, and we can then weed this list so that the value of the first credential C_1 can only appear once, copies are removed via PETs. A retrieval request now takes the form of $V_i, \{C\}_{\mathsf{pk}_T}$. The Tracker Teller now processes this request via the following algorithm which has two memory slots. Before beginning, the ciphertext of the registered credential is loaded to memory slot 1 and the real value $g^{r_{ij}}$ is loaded to slot 2. For the given request TT_j requests a PET of the submitted ciphertext with the value in memory slot 1. If the PET is successful, it hands out the stored value in memory slot 2 and exits the algorithm. If not, it requests PETs against the database C_1s and the value in memory slot 1. If there is no success, it hands out a random number and exits the algorithm, but if there is a success it stores the corresponding C_2 ciphertext in memory slot 1, and the fake value in memory slot 2, suppresses the corresponding database row for the current session and reiterates the algorithm, now essentially acting as if the fake credential was a real credential, but with the fake value in memory slot 2. The algorithm stops since the database is finite.

The coercer only has a negligible chance of guessing the real credential. Thus with overwhelming probability, if the coercer asks for tracker retrieval, the algorithm will after its first step simulate that the credential, handed to the coercer by the voter, is the real one with a corresponding faked term. In this way the retrieval mechanism will act as if the coercer has a real credential. Note that timing might be a side channel attack here, so some default delay is required in the response time.

The advantage of the system is that also coerced voters can safely do verification of their votes, the disadvantage is a rather complicated system, and the voter still needs to be active to fake their trackers.

Another advantage is that the mechanism can also be used to defend against the attack mentioned in Subsect. 6.4. To do this, the retrieval mechanism also performs PETs of the registered fake credential (which was given to the coercer) and the credentials contained in the cast ballots. For a positive PET the corresponding vote can be disclosed to the voter, who can then calculate the fake term. This would require another step to update the fake term. Alternatively, the voter can even beforehand fake terms for all possible candidates and further PET checks between the vote cast by the coercer and these faked terms can then directly update the fake value.

A more careful description of this retrieval mechanism and corresponding security proofs are postponed for future work.

8 Conclusions and Future Work

We have shown that it is possible to use the Selene mechanism in JCJ, providing an e-voting protocol where voters can individually check that their vote was counted as intended, while still preserving a good level of coercion-resistance. Further, several alternatives were presented providing: better verifiability (while only handling a single key), everlasting privacy, a more secure tracker retrieval and better protection against malware on the voters' computing devices. Also improvements to Selene, in terms of efficiency, and JCJ, in terms of coercion-resistance, were presented.

This paper did not provide formal proofs of the security guarantees. These are currently under consideration for the classical Selene protocol in the UC framework, and should later be extended to also include this work.

Two main problems of JCJ were not touched upon, namely, efficiency and usability. Regarding usability, Selene, in some sense is a step backwards. The users (in the first version of the protocol at least) needs to handle two keys post-registration. And coerced voter have to careful when they retrieve the trackers. Further investigations are necessary to determine to which extent this can be handled by the voter assisting devices, and if the extra clarity and trust given by the check of the final vote will outweigh this. We however, also plan to increase the usability of JCJ in the future by allowing the voters to use short codes. Finally regarding efficiency, the versions of JCJ presented here still suffer from the tally time being quadratic in the number of voters, a problem we will also try to solve in future a work.

Acknowledgements. Vincenzo Iovino is supported by the Luxembourg National Research Fund (FNR grant no. 7884937). Further, this work is also supported by the INTER-Sequoia project from the Luxembourg National Research Fund, which is joint with the ANR project SEQUOIA ANR-14-CE28-0030-01.

References

[ACKR13] Arapinis, M., Cortier, V., Kremer, S., Ryan, M.: Practical everlasting privacy. In: Basin, D., Mitchell, J.C. (eds.) POST 2013. LNCS, vol. 7796, pp. 21–40. Springer, Heidelberg (2013). https://doi.org/10.1007/978-3-642-36830-1_2

[Adi08] Adida, B.: Helios: web-based open-audit voting. In: Proceeding of 17th USENIX Security Symposium, pp. 335–348 (2008)

[Ben06] Benaloh, J.: Simple verifiable elections. In: Wallach, D.S., Rivest, R.L. (eds.) 2006 USENIX/ACCURATE Electronic Voting Technology Workshop, EVT 2006, Vancouver, BC, Canada, 1 August 2006. USENIX Association (2006)

[BFM88] Blum, M., Feldman, P., Micali, S.: Non-interactive zero-knowledge and its applications (extended abstract). In: 20th Annual ACM Symposium on Theory of Computing, pp. 103–112. ACM Press, May 1988

[BR93] Bellare, M., Rogaway, P.: Random oracles are practical: a paradigm for designing efficient protocols. In: Ashby, V. (ed) ACM CCS 1993: 1st Conference on Computer and Communications Security, pp. 62–73. ACM Press, November 1993

[CCM08] Clarkson, M.R., Chong, S., Myers, A.C.: Civitas: a secure voting system. In: IEEE Symposium on Security and Privacy (2008)

[Cha01] Chaum, D.: Surevote: technical overview. In: Proceeding of Workshop on Trustworthy Elections (WOTE 2001) (2001)

[CMR+16] Clark, J., Meiklejohn, S., Ryan, P.Y.A., Wallach, D., Brenner, M., Rohloff, K. (eds.): FC 2016. LNCS, vol. 9604. Springer, Heidelberg (2016). https://doi.org/10.1007/978-3-662-53357-4

[CP93] Chaum, D., Pedersen, T.P.: Wallet databases with observers. In: Brickell, E.F. (ed.) CRYPTO 1992. LNCS, vol. 740, pp. 89–105. Springer, Heidelberg (1993). https://doi.org/10.1007/3-540-48071-4_7

[CPP13] Cuvelier, É., Pereira, O., Peters, T.: Election verifiability or ballot privacy: do we need to choose? In: Crampton, J., Jajodia, S., Mayes, K. (eds.) ESORICS 2013. LNCS, vol. 8134, pp. 481–498. Springer, Heidelberg (2013). https://doi.org/10.1007/978-3-642-40203-6_27

[Fre00] Freedman, M.J.: Design and analysis of an anonymous communication channel for the free haven project (2000). http://www.freehaven.net/doc/comm.ps

[Gam85] El Gamal, T.: A public key cryptosystem and a signature scheme based on discrete logarithms. IEEE Trans. Inf. Theory **31**(4), 469–472 (1985)

[GRCC15] Grewal, G.S., Ryan, M.D., Chen, L., Clarkson, M.R.: Du-vote: remote electronic voting with untrusted computers. In: Fournet, C., Hicks, M.W., Viganò, L. (eds.) IEEE 28th Computer Security Foundations Symposium, CSF 2015, Verona, Italy, 13–17 July 2015 (2015)

[HH07] Hans, D., Helmut, K.: Intorduction to cryptography-principles and applications (2007)

[HK14] Haenni, R., Koenig, R.: Voting over the Internet on an insecure platform. In: Design, Development, and Use of Secure Electronic Voting Systems, chapter IGI Global, March 2014

[HL09] Heather, J., Lundin, D.: The append-only web bulletin board. In: Degano, P., Guttman, J., Martinelli, F. (eds.) FAST 2008. LNCS, vol. 5491, pp. 242–256. Springer, Heidelberg (2009). https://doi.org/10.1007/978-3-642-01465-9_16

[JCJ05] Juels, A., Catalano, D., Jakobsson, M.: Coercion-resistant electronic elections. In: Proceedings of the 2005 ACM Workshop on Privacy in the Electronic Society, WPES 2005, Alexandria, VA, USA, 7 November 2005, pp. 61–70 (2005)

[JJ00] Jakobsson, M., Juels, A.: Mix and match: secure function evaluation via ciphertexts. In: Okamoto, T. (ed.) ASIACRYPT 2000. LNCS, vol. 1976, pp. 162–177. Springer, Heidelberg (2000). https://doi.org/10.1007/3-540-44448-3_13

[KHF11] Koenig, R., Haenni, R., Fischli, S.: Preventing board flooding attacks in coercion-resistant electronic voting schemes. In: Camenisch, J., Fischer-Hübner, S., Murayama, Y., Portmann, A., Rieder, C. (eds.) SEC 2011. IAICT, vol. 354, pp. 116–127. Springer, Heidelberg (2011). https://doi.org/10.1007/978-3-642-21424-0_10

[KMST16] Küsters, R., Mueller, J., Scapin, E., Truderung, T.: Select: a lightweight verifiable remote voting system. In: IEEE 29th Computer Security Foundations Symposium, CSF 2016, Lisbon, Portugal, 27 June-1 July 2016, pp. 341–354. IEEE Computer Society (2016)

[KOKV11] Karayumak, F., Olembo, M.M., Kauer, M., Volkamer, M.: Usability analysis of helios - an open source verifiable remote electronic voting system. In: Proceeding of Electronic Voting Technology Workshop/Workshop on Trustworthy Elections (EVT/WOTE 2011) (2011)

[KR16] Kremer, S., Rønne, P.B.: To du or not to du: a security analysis of du-vote. In: IEEE European Symposium on Security and Privacy, EuroS&P 2016, Saarbrücken, Germany, 21–24 March 2016, pp. 473–486. IEEE (2016)

[LHK16] Locher, P., Haenni, R., Koenig, R.E.: Coercion-resistant internet voting with everlasting privacy. In: Clark, J., Meiklejohn, S., Ryan, P.Y.A., Wallach, D., Brenner, M., Rohloff, K. (eds.) FC 2016. LNCS, vol. 9604, pp. 161–175. Springer, Heidelberg (2016). https://doi.org/10.1007/978-3-662-53357-4_11

[MN06] Moran, T., Naor, M.: Receipt-free universally-verifiable voting with everlasting privacy. In: Dwork, C. (ed.) CRYPTO 2006. LNCS, vol. 4117, pp. 373–392. Springer, Heidelberg (2006). https://doi.org/10.1007/11818175_22

[NFVK13a] Neumann, S., Feier, C., Volkamer, M., Koenig, R.E.: Towards a practical JCJ/civitas implementation. IACR Cryptology ePrint Archive **2013**, 464 (2013)

[NFVK13b] Neumann, S., Feier, C., Volkamer, M., Koenig, R.E.: Towards A practical JCJ/civitas implementation. In: Horbach, M. (ed) Informatik 2013, 43. Jahrestagung der Gesellschaft für Informatik e.V. (GI), Informatik angepasst an Mensch, Organisation und Umwelt, 16–20 September 2013, Koblenz, Deutschland, vol. 220 of LNI, pp. 804–818. GI (2013)

[NV12] Neumann, S., Volkamer, M.: Civitas and the real world: problems and solutions from a practical point of view. In: Seventh International Conference on Availability, Reliability and Security, Prague, ARES 2012, Czech Republic, 20–24 August 2012, pp. 180–185 (2012)

[Ped91] Pedersen, T.P.: Non-interactive and information-theoretic secure verifiable secret sharing. In: Feigenbaum, J. (ed.) CRYPTO 1991. LNCS, vol. 576, pp. 129–140. Springer, Heidelberg (1992). https://doi.org/10.1007/3-540-46766-1_9

[Roe16] Roenne, P.B.: JCJ with improved verifiability guarantees. In: The International Conference on Electronic Voting E-Vote-ID 2016, 18–21 October 2016, Lochau/Bregenz, Austria (2016)

[RRI15] Ryan, P.Y.A., Rønne, P.B., Iovino, V.: Selene: voting with transparent verifiability and coercion-mitigation. IACR Cryptology ePrint Archive, 2015:1105 (2015)

[RRI16] Ryan, P.Y.A., Rønne, P.B., Iovino, V.: Selene: voting with transparent verifiability and coercion-mitigation. In: Clark, J., Meiklejohn, S., Ryan, P.Y.A., Wallach, D., Brenner, M., Rohloff, K. (eds.) FC 2016. LNCS, vol. 9604, pp. 176–192. Springer, Heidelberg (2016). https://doi.org/10.1007/978-3-662-53357-4_12

[RT09] Ryan, P.Y.A., Teague, V.: Pretty good democracy. In: Christianson, B., Malcolm, J.A., Matyáš, V., Roe, M. (eds.) Security Protocols 2009. LNCS, vol. 7028, pp. 111–130. Springer, Heidelberg (2013). https://doi.org/10.1007/978-3-642-36213-2_15

[Sch94] Schneier, B.: Applied Cryptography (1994)

[SK95] Sako, K., Kilian, J.: Receipt-free mix-type voting scheme. In: Guillou, L.C., Quisquater, J.-J. (eds.) EUROCRYPT 1995. LNCS, vol. 921, pp. 393–403. Springer, Heidelberg (1995). https://doi.org/10.1007/3-540-49264-X_32

A Roadmap to Fully Homomorphic Elections: Stronger Security, Better Verifiability

Kristian Gjøsteen and Martin Strand[✉]

Norwegian University of Science and Technology, Trondheim, Norway
{kristian.gjosteen,martin.strand}@ntnu.no

Abstract. After the trials of remote internet voting for local elections in 2011 and parliamentary elections in 2013, a number of local referendums has renewed interest in internet voting in Norway.

The voting scheme used in Norway is not quantum-safe and it has limited voter verifiability. In this case study, we consider how we can use fully homomorphic encryption to construct a quantum-safe voting scheme with better voter verifiability.

While fully homomorphic cryptosystems are not efficient enough for the system we sketch to be implemented and run today, we expect future improvements in fully homomorphic encryption which may eventually make these techniques practical.

Keywords: Fully homomorphic encryption · Remote internet voting · Quantum-safe

1 Introduction

Norway conducted trials of remote internet voting for the 2011 local elections and the 2013 parliamentary elections. The government discontinued the trials in 2014, but a large number of local referendums in 2016 has caused renewed interest in remote internet voting, especially for less important elections.

There are two issues with the scheme used in 2013 that should be improved. The scheme is not quantum-safe, and voter verifiability is mostly lacking today, due to an auditing protocol that can only be run by accredited organisations. This is a study to see if we can improve on both of these shortcomings concurrently. There are still some primitives lacking before this roadmap can be implemented completely.

While it is unclear if a sufficiently large and reliable quantum computer will ever be built to threaten the security of discrete logarithm-based systems, the mere possibility that the encryption protecting ballot confidentiality may be compromised in 10–30 years from now is a serious problem that needs to be addressed.

Verifiability is difficult in Norway for two reasons. Revoting is used as an anti-coercion tactic, and Norwegian ballots are sufficiently complicated to allow Italian attacks, i.e., marking a ballot with a number of insignificant yet unique

© International Financial Cryptography Association 2017
M. Brenner et al. (Eds.): FC 2017 Workshops 2017, LNCS 10323, pp. 404–418, 2017.
https://doi.org/10.1007/978-3-319-70278-0_25

changes. Also, the entire ballot is required for the count, so the election can not be considered as a collection of independent races. Voter verifiability is in general not considered to be important by the Norwegian electorate (polls and other studies generally finds high levels of trust in Norwegian elections [20]), but even if there is no public demand for voter verifiability, better voter verifiability than in the 2013 scheme would still be an improvement.

There are many schemes in the literature that achieve better voter verifiability than the 2013 scheme, but in general, these are not quantum-safe and do not facilitate very complicated ballots. All of the mainstream fully homomorphic schemes are believed to be quantum-safe.

While the 2013 protocol [14] exploited the multiplicative structure of the ElGamal scheme, a fully homomorphic scheme can allow us to use both addition and multiplication. This enables much more flexible computations, which means that we can arrange the decryption and counting process such that it is more voter verifiable.

Alternative Approaches. There have been earlier attempts at completing election tallies while the ballots are still encrypted, but not at this level of complexity. Salamonsen [23] tried to apply Pailler encryption to Norwegian county elections, possibly the easiest variant, and timed the effort needed to compute ciphertexts and the necessary zero knowledge proofs, clocking in at between 2 and 5 h of work for the voter. Peeking ahead to Sect. 6.4, we see that our solution is far more efficient than this.

Benaloh et al. [4] have described how one can use single-operation homomorphic encryption to tally a single transferable vote election. However, we tackle a more intricate problem in this work that cannot be solved with the same techniques. Chilotti et al. [8] have constructed a LWE based voting system in detail, but assume that their bulletin board is honest. We remove that restriction, and also get a scheme that can handle more complex (yet compact) ballots.

Contributions. At a theoretical level, we are exploring a possible application of fully homomorphic encryption. The idea of FHE was first proposed in 1978 [22], but was first properly realised with Gentry's breakthrough [12]. There have been several proposed applications [1,19], but many of those are purely theoretical due to the tremendous amount of redundant data that would be needed per user.

Next, this is a case study on how FHE could be used to make future Norwegian elections both quantum-safe and more voter verifiable. Our proposed protocol is borderline practical, at least taking into account the number of zero knowledge proofs the existing protocol must check, and it can be further optimised by implementation experts. We provide some experimental data to give a rough estimate of the computation efforts needed. We expect further progress in fully homomorphic encryption, which means that this protocol can eventually become practical in the not-too-distant future.

Organisation. The next section provides an introduction to the technical nature of Norwegian elections, followed by an introduction to lattice cryptography and fully homomorphic encryption. In Sect. 4, we briefly recall the modelling done in previous work. Section 5 partially paves the way for our instantiation of local elections (Sect. 6) by discussing primitives we are going to need. Finally, we argue for the security of the protocol in Sect. 7. The formal security modelling and thus proofs have been omitted in this work due to space limitations.

2   Norwegian Elections

The main idea in this paper is to do most of the ballot processing as computations on encrypted data. This means that we need to give an arithmetic circuit for counting. In order for this circuit to make sense, we first need to explain the mechanics of Norwegian elections in some detail.

In all Norwegian elections, each district elects multiple members roughly as follows. Parties nominate lists of candidates for each district. The voter chooses one of these party lists as their ballot. Here we only discuss the details of the local elections. The full version of the paper will also contain a description of parliamentary elections and how to handle these with FHE.

Municipal Elections. To vote in a municipal election, the voter must first pick a party list. Choosing a given party list gives that party a certain number of *list votes*. The total number of list votes in a district will determine the number of members each party gets.

The voter can then give *person votes* to zero or more candidates on the list. The number of person votes each candidate gets determines which candidates are actually elected as members for that party.

The party may also *prefer* a subset of their candidates. These candidates will then automatically get an additional number of person votes equal to 25% of the number of ballots submitted for that party.

The voter can also optionally *write in* a certain number of candidates from other party lists. These candidates will then receive person votes. However, writing in a candidate from a different party list will also transfer a list vote from the voter's party of choice to the party that the write-in candidate belongs to.

Consider the example ballot from Fig. 1. If the number of members to be elected is 29, each submitted ballot will initially give 29 list votes to the indicated party, in this case the Crypto Party. But on this ballot, the voter has listed four candidates from other lists, which means that the Crypto Party only gets 25 list votes, while the Hacker Party (HP) gets two list votes, and the Analyst Party (AP) and the Eavesdropper Party (EP) gets one list vote each.

When tallying, one first counts the list votes each party gets, and decide how many representatives each party gets using a modified Sainte-Laguë's method. The original Sainte-Laguë's method is to create a table with one column for each party, and with each party's number of list votes written in the first row. In the ith row, the number from the first row of the same column divided by

Crypto Party
Candidate list for the local elections 2019

1. ☒ **Gaius Julius Caesar**
2. ☐ **Giovan Battista Bellaso**
3. ☒ Al-Khalil ibn Ahmad al-Farahidi
4. ☒ Leone Battista Alberti

⋮

34. ☐ Charles Wheatstone

Candidates from other lists

NAME	PARTY
Alan Turing	HP
Konrad Zuse	HP
Charles Babbage	AP
Eve Mallory	EP

Fig. 1. An example ballot for a local election

$2i - 1$ is written. The k representatives to be elected are then distributed to the parties with the k largest numbers. The modification used in Norway is that the numbers in the first row are divided by 1.4 before distributing candidates, a modification that slightly favours larger parties.

The next step when tallying is to decide which candidates are actually elected. To do this, one counts all person votes given by voters (either to a candidate on the party list, or by writing in a candidate from another party list) and the person votes resulting from party preference. The candidates are then ranked according to the number of person votes received. In the event of a tie, the order of the candidates on the party list is used.

3   Lattices and Fully Homomorphic Encryption

Lattices have long been important in cryptography, both as a tool to attack systems and as basis for new cryptographic systems. Two recent developments have made such lattice-based cryptography even more important, namely the development of *fully homomorphic encryption* (FHE) and the renewed interest in *quantum-safe cryptographic schemes.*

Fully homomorphic encryption is a form of encryption that allows one to do certain computations on encrypted data. While first defined [22], the first plausible solution was Gentry's breakthrough construction [12].

Fully homomorphic encryption allows us to evaluate a function described by a *circuit* on a set of encrypted inputs, resulting in an encryption (of size independent of the number of inputs and the circuit evaluated, called *compact*) of the result we would have gotten if we instead just computed the circuit on (unencrypted) inputs.

Lattice problems such as *(ring) learning with errors* ((R)LWE) are generally considered to be hard to solve, even for a large quantum computer.

Lattice cryptography has seen a tremendous development since Regev [21] found a quantum reduction from the natural lattice problems of finding the shortest vector (SVP) or finding a short basis of independent vectors (SIVP), to LWE.

Several authors have used LWE and RLWE to create fully homomorphic encryption. The main ideas remain the same as in Gentry's original construction. The plaintext is masked with *inner* and *outer* randomness, where the innermost one is denoted as noise. One can then typically perform additions and multiplications, though sometimes a NAND gate must be used. However, for each operation, the noise level grows. When it reaches the same size as the outer randomness, the ciphertext is no longer decryptable. Multiplications are usually expensive in terms of noise, causing the noise to grow quickly, while additions are cheap.

The noise problem can sometimes be solved using a technique called *bootstrapping*, during which a ciphertext is encrypted again (though this encryption could be done with no randomness), and the inner encryption is removed by running the decryption circuit in an encrypted state. One can fine-tune the parameters such that the resulting ciphertext has a lower noise level than the original one. However, the bootstrapping process is computationally expensive, so it is more common to select parameters based on the function one wants to compute, so as to achieve a designated *[multiplicative] depth* (so-called levelled fully homomorphic encryption). Many schemes have also provided solutions for limiting the noise growth, so that one can avoid bootstrapping further.

FHE has reached a level of maturity where it is practical for some applications and security levels [10]. We expect performance to increase still further. The BGV [5] cryptosystem has been implemented by Halevi and Shoup [16], and among others, Microsoft has also worked with implementations [18].

Formally, a FHE scheme consists of algorithms (Gen, Enc, Eval, Dec). The unusual member of the set is Eval, which accepts a special evaluation key evk, a circuit $\mathcal{C}$ and a number of ciphertexts $c_1, \ldots c_n$ such that

$$\mathsf{Dec}(sk, \mathsf{Eval}(evk, \mathcal{C}, c_1, \ldots, c_n)) = \mathcal{C}(\mathsf{Dec}(sk, c_1), \ldots, \mathsf{Dec}(sk, c_n)).$$

We will simplify this notation whenever it is convenient, and often just express the circuit (or function) directly on the ciphertexts, even when we really want them to be applied to the encrypted data.

The presentation of the circuits in this paper is fairly general, but we have made sure to only use features supported by the BGV scheme. We refer to the original publication [5] for the technical details, but quickly introduce some of the high-level features provided by the scheme.

Plaintext slots. Following an idea of Smart and Vercauteren [25], one can pack several plaintexts into a single ciphertext and do SIMD operations (single-instruction multiple-data) on the vector of plaintexts. The advantage is that one saves space, and that one can perform operations on tuples of data in the time it would to do it on a single value. All slots must have the same capacity. The plaintext space of the BGV scheme can thus be set to any space $\mathbb{F}_{q^\ell}^n$ for some integers q, ℓ and n, where n denotes the number of slots.

Noise management. The authors use a system of modulus reduction for each multiplication, such that the noise increases slower than it would otherwise do. Hence, one can have smaller ciphertexts. The number of times one can do the modulus reduction decides the maximal multiplicative depth.

Key switching. In addition to reducing the modulus, one can also efficiently transform ciphertexts from one key to another.

The term *fully homomorphic encryption* has two meanings, either that the scheme in question can process any circuits of any depth (typically by using boot-strapping) or that it can evaluate two operations, in contrast to group homomorphic schemes like ElGamal. In principle, we only need a levelled homomorphic scheme, but will use the word fully to denote the concept.

4 Modelling and Security Requirements

We model our system with the same players that already existed in the Norwegian e-voting project, namely the voter V with her computer and mobile phone, a ballot box B, a receipt generator R, a decryption service D and an auditor A. We quickly explain the existing motivation before proceeding. For more details, see Gjøsteen [14].

Gjøsteen acknowledged that the user may not be in control of her own equipment, for instance due to malware. One should therefore distinguish the voter's intention and what the computer actually does. When the ballot box receives an encrypted ballot from the voter's computer, it transforms and partially decrypts the ballot, and forwards it to the receipt generator. Then the transformed ballot is completely decrypted, and the correct receipt code is sent by SMS to the voter's mobile phone.

Both the ballot box and the receipt generator give the auditor information about everything they have seen, so that he can compare and make sure no one of them is ignoring information seen by the other. Any information dropped by the ballot box should ideally be detected by the voter, because of a missing receipt. (The soundness of this protocol is based on an assumption that the phone is independent of the device used to vote. While this may have been an acceptable assumption when the system was first introduced, it is less so today. Finding another solution may be necessary, but is outside the scope of this paper.)

Next consider what happens when the election closes. Then the ballot box should provide ciphertexts to the decryption service, which outputs the public result of the election. The auditor verifies that the decryption service got the right ciphertexts from the ballot box, and that the output was correct.

The security requirements can informally be summarised in the following list.

D-**privacy.** The decryption service should not be able to correlate its input to voter identities

B-**privacy.** The ballot box should not learn anything from the ciphertexts

R-**privacy.** The receipt generator should not be able to correlate return codes to what the voter chose

A-**privacy.** The auditor should not learn anything about how anyone voted

B-integrity. The ballot box must not be able to create a convincing encrypted
ballot such that its decryption is inconsistent with the related information
that is sent to the receipt generator

D-integrity. The decryption service must not be able to alter the election outcome

We conclude this section with a brief overview of some limitations that any
Norwegian voting system must deal with.

Privacy is important in Norwegian elections. The ballot should obviously be
confidential, but even the list of who voted is considered confidential in Norway. In particular, this means that any voter verifiable scheme that reveals the
identities of the voters is unacceptable in Norway.

A second constraint is coercion resistance. It seems like the main defence
against coercion must be revoting in Norway, and the revoting could possibly
be paper revoting. Paper voting cannot involve any secrets or other material
from previous electronic voting, and a paper ballot should also supercede any
subsequent electronic ballot submission.

Related to coercion resistance, Italian attacks are easy in Norway, since
adding a random set of marks to a ballot will most likely make it unique and
have negligible electoral effect. This means that any public verifiability must
avoid publishing complete ballots. Today, the election authorities publish lists
of vote sums per party and person.

Finally, it seems like electronic voting must coexist with paper voting for the
forseeable future. This means that the electronic count must somehow combine
with the paper count before the final result is declared.

5   Primitives

We assume the existence of several primitives in this work. Some of them have
not been described in the literature yet, and should be considered open, but
feasible problems.

The main primitive we need is an efficient zero knowledge proof or argument for correct decryption. These are well known for schemes such as ElGamal
[7], but for FHE, they only become efficient when applied to many ciphertexts
concurrently [2,3]. However, much of the work can be done ahead of time, and
the protocol also supports distributed decryption, which will essentially guarantee the security of the complete scheme. Note that one possible instantiation
of the following protocol would only require the verifiable decryption of a single
ciphertext. Providing an efficient zero knowledge proof for that case can still be
considered an open problem.

Next, we also need a number of subroutines. Equality checking will be used
throughout the whole routine, and has been provided by Kim et al. [17]. We will
denote it as a function

$$\mathsf{Eq}(a,b) = \begin{cases} 1 & \text{if } a = b \\ 0 & \text{otherwise.} \end{cases}$$

The multiplicative depth for equality checking in the BGV scheme is given as $\lceil \log(p-1) \rceil + \lceil \log \ell \rceil$ where p is the characteristic of the field and ℓ is the order of the extension. Although this will be a fairly high number, most equality checks will run in parallell, which will help keep the noise under control.

If we want to implement the whole tallying as operations on encrypted data (which we do not propose to do) we would also need sorting and division by rational numbers. Both of these primitives exist. Emmadi et al. [11] analysed a number of algorithms and concluded that Odd-Even Merge sort would work best for the Smart-Vercauteren scheme [24]. It is reasonable that some of their results will apply to the BGV scheme as well. Chung and Kim proposed that one can use a continued fraction representation of rational numbers to reduce the storage requirement for rational numbers with a given precision, and also described how to perform divisions [9]. Cetin et al. [6] have demonstrated that it is possible to compute fractions and even square roots by applying numerical methods to the encrypted data.

6 Instantiation

Recall the BGV scheme introduced in Sect. 3. Let m be the number of parties taking part in the election and n be the total number of candidates from all the parties. We use the BGV cryptosystem with multiple plaintext slots, and the goal is to get an encryption of the following tuple for each ballot posted by a voter.

$$(p_1, \ldots, p_m, p_1', \ldots, p_m', p_1'', \ldots, p_m'', c_1, \ldots, c_n) \tag{1}$$

The tuple requires $3m + n$ slots. Although they will hold data of different length, the BGV system requires them to be the same size.

Let v be the maximal number of voters from the voting district, and let k be the number of candidates. The voter may list up to $k/4$ candidates from other lists, which also places an upper bound on how many list votes that may be transferred from the chosen party to another. The first m slots will hold the number of times a list is selected, the next section holds the number of list votes given away, and the final section of m slots holds the number of list votes received. Finally, the last n items will hold person votes. The upper bound for the plaintext space is then the maximal number of list votes that can be transferred, $vk/4$, and the characteristic of the slots should in principle not be chosen smaller, although it is very unlikely that one will ever reach this bound.

Remark 1. One can possibly save some storage overhead by using several independent ciphertexts instead of larger ciphertexts with slots, or some combination of slots and separate ciphertexts, so that no slots have higher capacity than needed.

To vote, the voter must encrypt her ballot with a symmetric scheme, and attach the key encrypted under the FHE scheme [13]. Assume that the voter ciphertext encodes the vector

$$b = (p, s_1, \ldots, s_{n_p}, e_1, \ldots, e_{n'}), \tag{2}$$

where p is the index of the chosen party list, s_i is a bit indicating whether candidate i on the list receives a person vote and $e_1, \ldots, e_{n'}$ are the indices of the representatives from different lists that have been written in on this ballot.

Remark 2. It is natural to ask why the voter simply cannot encrypt a vector of the form (1). The reason is that we want to be able to validate the ballot efficiently, something which would add considerable extra work if we had to check ranges for vectors like the one above. Note that we need to check that $s_1, \ldots, s_{n_p}$ are actual bits. One way to do this is to compute the product $s(\mathsf{Enc}(1) - s)$ for each slot, and verify that it decrypts to 0. (There is an obvious weakness to this, which is that if it does not decrypt to 0, then information will leak. We can avoid this problem by normalising using the algorithm of Kim et al. [17], which depends on the Frobenius automorphism $x \mapsto x^q$. This particular exponentiation can be done for free in the BGV system. Of course, we may not care about the privacy of malformed ballots.)

The ballot box should perform a bootstrapping after transforming the ciphertext to the FHE scheme. This guarantees that the voter cannot introduce too much noise, which in turn can make the end result impossible to decrypt.

We now explain how to transform a ballot of the form in (2) to the form of (1). Recall the function Eq that returns 1 whenever the two input values are equal. Define $\mathsf{In}(a, S) = \sum_{s \in S} \mathsf{Eq}(a, s)$, which will return 1 if and only if a is a member of set the S.

Let $\{P_i\}$ denote all parties taking part in the election, and let p_i'' be the number of list votes transferred to party P_i. By abuse of notation, let P_i also denote the set of indexes for the candidates on the party list of party i. The number p_i'' of list votes transferred is then easily computed as

$$p_i'' \leftarrow \mathsf{In}(e_1, P_i) + \mathsf{In}(e_2, P_i) + \cdots + \mathsf{In}(e_{n'}, P_i)$$

Note that each equality and membership check requires some multiplications, but since they can all be done in parallell, the overall noise remains manageable.

To compute the number p_i' of list votes given away, we need to identify the right party, and then add the sum of all p_i'' for that ballot,

$$p_i' \leftarrow \mathsf{Eq}(i, p) \cdot \sum_{j=1}^{m} p_j''.$$

The values p_i are easily decided with $\mathsf{Eq}(i, p)$.

Finally, compute person votes to candidates from other lists. Let P_j be the party that the candidate c_j belongs to, and recall that p was the party selected by the voter.

$$c_j \leftarrow (1 - \mathsf{Eq}(p, P_j)) \left(\mathsf{Eq}(j, e_1) + \mathsf{Eq}(j, e_2) + \cdots + \mathsf{Eq}(j, e_{n'}) \right)$$

The first factor ensures that the candidates really are from a different list, in order to avoid a situation where a candidate could get a person vote in two different ways.

Remark 3. Note that we do not check for this when we are counting person votes in and out. The reason is that it does not change the balance, and it should thus not create any problems for the validity of the ballot or the count in general. We aim at a forgiving system such that only destructive changes could cause a ballot to be discarded.

Use a similar technique as above to add the person votes to the candidates from the list chosen by the voter. One can also convert the whole vector into a ciphertext, and use SIMD techniques [25] to add them as one. Note, however, that one should still do basic range checking on the values as described in the remark above.

Finally, we want to verify that a ballot is valid, by computing the polynomial

$$\prod_{i \leq j} (e_i - e_j),$$

which will be zero if and only if one candidate is listed more than once. This polynomial requires many multiplications, so we propose that the end result is decrypted publicly, so that the selection bit can be public. One can normalise any non-zero value to 1.

6.1   Selecting Votes to Be Counted

Since we allow voters to vote multiple times and even override all electronic votes by voting on paper, we need a way to identify the ballots that should be included in the final tally, while providing both voter verifiability and coercion resistance. While in theory it is possible to do everything with FHE, it would probably be more expensive than anything else in this paper, so we have opted for a more classical solution, where the ballot box selects the ballots to be counted and uses a combination of auditing and FHE to prove that its selection is correct.

1. The ballot box stores a secret record (v_i, c_i, s_i) for each ballot, where v_i is the voter's identity, c_i is the encrypted vote and s_i is a sequence number, or equivalently, a timestamp.
2. When voting closes, for each voter v_i that also submitted a paper ballot, the ballot box adds a triple (v_i, c_i, s_i) where c_i encodes a blank vote and s_i is a sequence number greater than the highest inserted in the ballot box.
3. The ballot box shuffles all identities and sends the list to the auditor.
4. The ballot box publishes a list $\{(c_i, \tilde{s}_i, \tilde{v'}_i)\}$, where the tilde indicates that the value has been encrypted using a FHE scheme and the identities $\{v_i\}$ have been replaced with pseudonyms $\{v'_i\}$. The list is ordered by identity and sequence number. The end points may still leak secret information, so the list should be treated as something circular. Concretely, we select a random item on the list, and move the records following that item to the front of the list instead.
5. The ballot box sends the randomness used to generate the new ciphertexts to the auditor for verification.

6. Define a function f by

$$f(v_i, v_j, s_i, s_j) = \begin{cases} 1 & \text{if } v_i \neq v_j \text{ or } s_i < s_j; \text{ and} \\ 0 & \text{otherwise.} \end{cases}$$

The ballot box computes $\tilde{u}_i = \mathsf{Eval}(evk, f, \tilde{v}_i, \tilde{v}_{i+1}, \tilde{s}_i, \tilde{s}_{i+1})$ for all i, and counting modulo the number of ballots, such that the last item on the list is compared to the first. The function f can be implemented by combining the equality checker described above with an inequality function [11].
7. The ballot box multiplies all $\tilde{u}_i$. This value should later be decrypted. Any auditing parties should accept that the list is correctly ordered if the product decrypts to 1.
8. Next define a function g such that $g(v_i, v_j)$ is 1 if and only if $v_i \neq v_j$ and 0 otherwise. The ballot box computes selection values $\tilde{z}_i = \mathsf{Eval}(evk, g, \tilde{v}_i, \tilde{v}_{i+1})$, cycling to the top of the list as above. The list of ciphertexts that should be counted is $\{c'_i = \tilde{z}_i c_i\}$.

6.2   Tally

The final tally now becomes trivial. The ballot box simply adds all the encrypted vectors $\{c'_i\}$. We suggest to pass these sums on to the decryption service for decryption and deciding which candidates are elected based on cleartext vote counts (number of list votes and number of person votes).

Of course, it is possible to do Sainte-Laguë's method with encrypted data. While we do not recommend this, since the paper ballots must also be counted, we note that it is possible, and simply an engineering problem to analyse the complexity and then adjust the parameters to allow for the circuit depth. We note, however, that it may result in even bigger ciphertexts. Possibly the most interesting challenge would be to handle the precision of the rational numbers that necessarily would occur, and then handling the sorting.

6.3   Receipts

Sending a receipt to the voter becomes easy when using an FHE scheme. The ballot box homomorphically applies a voter-specific one-way transformation on the ballot, followed by a key-switch, a feature offered by the BGV cryptosystem. We do not propose such a function here, other than to state that a light-weight keyed hash function would do the job nicely. While the main purpose is to facilitate a greater multiplicative depth, the transformation key can only be built using both of the secret keys, but it leaks neither. Hence, we can give the transformation key exclusively to the ballot box (and the auditor), while the receipt generator is the only party to know the decryption key for the transformed ciphertexts.

After the receipt generator decrypts, it sends an SMS with a value derived from the transformed ballot, with which the voter can verify that the ballot has been received correctly. The auditor should be sent a copy of all ciphertexts received by the receipt code generator.

Due to the problem of phones being closely linked to the user's other equipment, the receipt system should as a whole be put under closer scrutiny.

6.4   Parameter Selection

Using the above algorithms, we can estimate the parameters needed for the protocol. For a conservative estimate, we can look at the numbers for the largest municipality, Oslo. There are about 500,000 eligible voters, and the last local election saw 17 different party lists with a total of 659 candidates. The city council consists of 59 members. This means that the voter can list at most 15 names from other parties on her ballot, so the greatest number we need to handle is about $7,500,000 \approx 2^{23}$. Then equality checks will need a depth 23 circuit. We can now compute how much depth we will need after converting from the symmetric ciphertext.

- p_i'' can be computed with many equality checks in parallell, but no other multiplications, hence depth 23. The same holds for p_i.
- p_i' is one equality check multiplied with a sum of p_i'', so we need 24 multiplications. The candidate slots are also the result of a multiplication of two equality checks.
- Computing the validity check requires $\binom{15}{2}$ multiplications. However, they can be arranged in a tree of depth 7.
- Each value $\tilde{u}_i$ requires an equality check and an inequality check. After that, all such ciphertexts must be multiplied, which can be done with depth of approximately 20.
- The selection bit $\tilde{z}_i$ takes a single comparison, and is multiplied to the rest of the ballot, adding one level to some of the previous results.

In addition comes the depth required to send the receipt, but that is dependent of the function employed to generate the return codes. Note that those computations will be in parallell to those above.

Finally, we can conclude that no part of the computation requires a depth greater than 50.

The number of slots needed in the Oslo case is $3 \cdot 17 + 659 = 710$.

We ran the bundled general test program of HElib [15,16] with the above parameters on a server running Ubuntu 14.04 on Intel Xeon 2.67 GHz processors with a total of 24 cores and 256 GB of memory. The program ran the key generation on a single core, and used a maximum of 8 cores for some sample ciphertext operations. The maximum memory usage was in the order of 20 GB. The complete process took 4:52 min, with key generation taking about half of that time. While this order of magnitude is unreasonable for a single voter, it may be feasible for an election system, as long as the feedback to the voter is sufficiently quick. Implementing the above algorithms efficiently is an open problem.

7 Security

A formal security proof along the lines of Gjøsteen [14] is too long for this paper, and we defer such a proof for a full version of this paper. However, we briefly discuss the general security properties, and then discuss coercion resistance in some detail.

The system is not designed to be secure if two or more of the ballot box, receipt generator, decryptor or auditor are corrupt. However, when at most one of them is corrupt, encryption and careful use of key-switching ensures that the receipt generator and the decryptor cannot decrypt public ciphertexts containing sensitive information (such as ballots and voter identities), ensuring that we have both R-privacy and D-privacy. (For instance, the published ciphertexts only contain ballots and pseudonyms, so while a corrupt decryption service could decrypt them, it would learn nothing about which voters these ballots came from.) The encryption itself and the general features of the protocol ensure B-privacy and A-privacy.

Since the computation on encrypted data can be redone by any interested party using published information, the scheme is trivially almost end-to-end verifiable, and also has B-integrity. This follows from the correctness of the selection and counting circuit we have designed, and the correctness of the FHE scheme in use. An interested voter can verify that the ciphertext she submitted is listed in the public record and then redo the computation of the counting circuit, recreating the ciphertexts containing the results. The zero knowledge proofs will then ensure that the published election results are consistent with the verified encrypted results. This gives us D-integrity.

The gap in verifiability lies in the selection of votes to be counted, where a corrupt ballot box may insert fake votes that a corrupt auditor may choose to ignore. (An honest auditor should either notice that electronic votes lack a valid digital signature, or that fake paper votes have been inserted.) Even with this gap, however, our proposal is a significant improvement on previous schemes used in Norway.

- If the ballot box alters a ballot before forwarding it to the receipt generator, then the voter should get an incorrect receipt. If the ballot box alters a ballot after the receipt generator has seen it, the auditor will notice.
- The receipt generator cannot alone compromise the integrity of the election. Privacy follows from careful use of key-switching and using an appropriate function to generate receipts with a per-voter key.
- The decryption service must prove correctness of decryption, and the integrity of the result follows from this proof.
- The cryptosystem ensures that an auditor cannot read any individual votes.

We defend against coercion by letting a voter revote electronically any number of times, and decreeing that a paper ballot will override any earlier or later electronic votes. This is within the requirement of the Norwegian Election Act, which states that "[t]he purpose of this Act is to establish such conditions that citizens shall be able to elect their representatives to the Storting, county councils and municipal councils by means of a secret ballot in free and direct elections." [26] Let us now consider how a coercer could be able to succeed.

It is clear that any coercer cooperating with a corrupt ballot box or auditor will be able to defeat revoting as an anti-coercion strategy. We therefore assume a coercer that sits next to the voter as she casts her ballot, and assume that the coercer is also able to record the precise ciphertext, and himself transform it into the FHE ciphertext c_i that will appear in the public records.

If the voter now revotes electronically, and the coercer afterwards returns and forces her to vote under surveillance again, then the public list of ciphertexts will reveal that the voter revoted. However, any paper vote will be sorted after the last electronic vote, so it cannot be discovered by the adversary. Also note that since the identities are permuted and encrypted, he cannot guarantee that a paper vote will be sandwiched between an electronic vote and the first vote of someone of whom he knows the identity, making the paper ballot truly anonymous.

Acknowledgements. The authors wish to thank the anonymous reviewers for constructive and useful suggestions.

References

1. Armknecht, F., Boyd, C., Carr, C., Gjøsteen, K., Jäschke, A., Reuter, C.A., Strand, M.: A guide to fully homomorphic encryption. Cryptology ePrint Archive, Report 2015/1192 (2015). http://eprint.iacr.org/
2. Baum, C., Damgård, I., Toft, T., Zakarias, R.: Better preprocessing for secure multiparty computation. In: Manulis, M., Sadeghi, A.-R., Schneider, S. (eds.) ACNS 2016. LNCS, vol. 9696, pp. 327–345. Springer, Cham (2016). https://doi.org/10.1007/978-3-319-39555-5_18
3. Baum, C., Damgård, I., Oechsner, S., Peikert, C.: Efficient commitments and zero-knowledge protocols from ring-sis with applications to lattice-based threshold cryptosystems. Cryptology ePrint Archive, Report 2016/997 (2016). http://eprint.iacr.org/2016/997
4. Benaloh, J., Moran, T., Naish, L., Ramchen, K., Teague, V.: Shuffle-sum: coercion-resistant verifiable tallying for STV voting. IEEE Trans. Inf. Forensics Secur. 4(4), 685–698 (2009)
5. Brakerski, Z., Gentry, C., Vaikuntanathan, V.: Fully homomorphic encryption without bootstrapping. In: Electronic Colloquium on Computational Complexity (ECCC), vol. 18, p. 111 (2011)
6. Cetin, G.S., Doroz, Y., Sunar, B., Martin, W.J.: Arithmetic using word-wise homomorphic encryption. Cryptology ePrint Archive, Report 2015/1195 (2015). http://eprint.iacr.org/2015/1195
7. Chaum, D., Pedersen, T.P.: Wallet databases with observers. In: Brickell, E.F. (ed.) CRYPTO 1992. LNCS, vol. 740, pp. 89–105. Springer, Heidelberg (1993). https://doi.org/10.1007/3-540-48071-4_7
8. Chillotti, I., Gama, N., Georgieva, M., Izabachène, M.: A homomorphic LWE based E-voting scheme. In: Takagi, T. (ed.) PQCrypto 2016. LNCS, vol. 9606, pp. 245–265. Springer, Cham (2016). https://doi.org/10.1007/978-3-319-29360-8_16

9. Chung, H.W., Kim, M.: Encoding rational numbers for FHE-based applications. Cryptology ePrint Archive, Report 2016/344 (2016). http://eprint.iacr.org/
10. Dowlin, N., Gilad-Bachrach, R., Laine, K., Lauter, K., Naehrig, M., Wernsing, J.: Cryptonets: applying neural networks to encrypted data with high throughput and accuracy. Technical report, Microsoft Research (2016)
11. Emmadi, N., Gauravaram, P., Narumanchi, H., Syed, H.: Updates on sorting of fully homomorphic encrypted data. Cryptology ePrint Archive, Report 2015/995 (2015). http://eprint.iacr.org/
12. Gentry, C.: A fully homomorphic encryption scheme. Ph.D. thesis, Stanford University (2009). http://crypto.stanford.edu/craig
13. Gentry, C., Halevi, S., Smart, N.P.: Homomorphic evaluation of the AES circuit. In: Safavi-Naini, R., Canetti, R. (eds.) CRYPTO 2012. LNCS, vol. 7417, pp. 850–867. Springer, Heidelberg (2012). https://doi.org/10.1007/978-3-642-32009-5_49
14. Gjøsteen, K.: The Norwegian internet voting protocol. Cryptology ePrint Archive, Report 2013/473 (2013). http://eprint.iacr.org/
15. Halevi, S., Shoup, V.: Algorithms in HElib. In: Garay, J.A., Gennaro, R. (eds.) CRYPTO 2014. LNCS, vol. 8616, pp. 554–571. Springer, Heidelberg (2014). https://doi.org/10.1007/978-3-662-44371-2_31
16. Halevi, S., Shoup, V.: Bootstrapping for HElib. In: Oswald, E., Fischlin, M. (eds.) EUROCRYPT 2015. LNCS, vol. 9056, pp. 641–670. Springer, Heidelberg (2015). https://doi.org/10.1007/978-3-662-46800-5_25
17. Kim, M., Lee, H.T., Ling, S., Wang, H.: On the efficiency of FHE-based private queries. IEEE Trans. Dependable Secur. Comput. $\mathbf{PP}(99)$ (2016)
18. Lauter, K.: Practical applications of homomorphic encryption (2015)
19. Naehrig, M., Lauter, K.E., Vaikuntanathan, V.: Can homomorphic encryption be practical? In: Cachin, C., Ristenpart, T. (eds.) Proceedings of the 3rd ACM Cloud Computing Security Workshop, CCSW, pp. 113–124. ACM (2011)
20. OSCE Office for Democratic Institutions and Human Rights. Norway, Parliamentary Elections 9 September 2013, Final Report. Technical report, December 2013
21. Regev, O.: On lattices, learning with errors, random linear codes, and cryptography. In: Gabow, H.N., Fagin, R. (eds.) Proceedings of the 37th Annual ACM Symposium on Theory of Computing, pp. 84–93. ACM (2005)
22. Rivest, R., Adleman, L., Dertouzos, M.: On data banks and privacy homomorphisms. In: Foundations of Secure Computation, pp. 169–179. Academia Press, Cambridge (1978)
23. Salamonsen, K.: A security analysis of the helios voting protocol and application to the Norwegian county election (2014)
24. Smart, N.P., Vercauteren, F.: Fully homomorphic encryption with relatively small key and ciphertext sizes. In: Nguyen, P.Q., Pointcheval, D. (eds.) PKC 2010. LNCS, vol. 6056, pp. 420–443. Springer, Heidelberg (2010). https://doi.org/10.1007/978-3-642-13013-7_25
25. Smart, N.P., Vercauteren, F.: Fully homomorphic SIMD operations. Des. Codes Cryptography $\mathbf{71}(1)$, 57–81 (2014)
26. Lov om valg til stortinget, fylkesting og kommunestyrer (valgloven). http://lovdata.no, sep 2002. Translation at https://www.regjeringen.no/globalassets/upload/KRD/Kampanjer/valgportal/Regelverk/Representation_of_the_People_Act170609.pdf

Enabling Vote Delegation for Boardroom Voting

Oksana Kulyk[1(✉)], Stephan Neumann[1],
Karola Marky[1], and Melanie Volkamer[1,2]

[1] Technische Universität Darmstadt, Darmstadt, Germany
{oksana.kulyk,stephan.neumann,karola.marky,melanie.volkamer}@secuso.org
[2] Karlstad University, Karlstad, Sweden

Abstract. A lot of decisions are made during boardroom meetings. After a discussion, the head of the board often asks for a quick poll. But what if you cannot join the meeting? So called boardroom voting schemes have been proposed to conduct the poll over the Internet and thereby enabling also those who are not present but available online to participant in the poll. But what if you are not available at this point in time? For important decisions you may want to delegate your vote to a present and trusted board member. In this paper, we show how to extend an existing boardroom voting scheme towards delegation functionality. The new scheme is evaluated against security requirements determined for boardroom voting and security requirements tailored to the delegation process.

1   Introduction

Boardroom voting schemes are one of the new research directions in electronic voting and a number of approaches have been proposed [2, 12–14, 16, 20, 27]. Some of these approaches provide the possibility to participate in the polls remotely. However, time and geographical restrictions often prevent absent board members from participating in the poll. Consequently, decisions are often not supported by a required quorum. For such situation, it is worth considering the possibility to delegate ones' vote to a trusted board member that is present, the so-called *proxy*.

We extend the boardroom voting approach described in [20] to enable delegation. To do so we introduce so so-called *delegation token*, that is sent by the voter who wants to delegate. The rest of the board members get a random value that is indistinguishable from the authorised delegation token. The authorised delegation token is also distributed via secret sharing among all the of board members. In this way, during the voting the board members can validate the votes cast with an authorised delegation token, without revealing the identity of the board member who received the authorised delegation token, and thus was trusted by the voter to cast a delegated ballot on her behalf.

Note that an alternative solution would be to let the voters jointly establish a a public-key encryption system used in the election before the election, so that the delegating voters could use it to encrypt their delegation tokens, and the

© International Financial Cryptography Association 2017
M. Brenner et al. (Eds.): FC 2017 Workshops 2017, LNCS 10323, pp. 419–433, 2017.
https://doi.org/10.1007/978-3-319-70278-0_26

majority of present voters could use the corresponding private key in order to decrypt the data sent within an election. However, our delegated voting scenario assumes, that all the setup that is required for a specific election occurs within the meeting, since it is not always practical to demand that the present board members gather together in advance to conduct election setup before each election. Hence, the way for the absent voters to delegate to a trusted board member of her choice prior to the election is needed, which is achieved by our proposal. Therefore,

The paper is structured as follows. We describe the requirements on delegated voting found in the literature in Sect. 2 and the background for our scheme in Sect. 3. We describe our solution for delegating in boardroom voting setting in Sect. 4, followed by the security evaluation in Sect. 5. We describe the related work in Sect. 6 and conclude in Sect. 7.

2   Security Requirements

For the security requirements that are related to *direct voting* as opposed to delegating, we rely on the list of security requirements for boardroom voting given in [20][1].

Voter eligibility. Only the votes from eligible voters, and only one vote from each voter, should be included in the result.

Vote integrity. Each cast vote (direct or delegated) of an eligible voter should be correctly included in the tally.

Robustness. After the vote casting has finished, the election result can be computed even in case where some of the scheme components are faulty.

Vote privacy. The voting scheme should not provide any more information that enables establishing a link between the honest voter[2] and her vote (delegated or direct) aside from the information that would be output by the ideal proxy boardroom voting scheme.

Fairness. The voting scheme should not reveal partial election results before all the votes have been cast.

The security requirements on the *delegation process* are based on the available literature concerning delegated voting [18,19,30]. Note we provide informal definitions for these requirements, since no formalization of the requirements on delegation process either in form of legal or technical definitions exist.

---

[1] As opposed to [20], similar to the proposal in [5] we consider verifiability to be a part of integrity, and not a separate requirement. We furthermore consider uniqueness a part of eligibility.

[2] We refer to a voter or a proxy as *honest* if she behaves according to the scheme specification.

Delegation eligibility. Only the delegated ballots on behalf of eligible voters, and only one delegated ballot per voter, should be included in the tally.

Delegation integrity. No proxy can vote on the voter's behalf unless authorised by the voter.

Delegation privacy. The voting scheme should not provide any information to the public or to the proxies themselves, that identifies whether a particular voter has delegated to a particular proxy.[3]. We further require that the voter should not be able to use her private data from the election to construct the proof for delegating to a specific proxy herself by divulging this data to an adversary.

Delegation power privacy. The voting scheme should not reveal, how many voters have delegated to a specific proxy.

3   Background

In this section we describe the background required for our scheme.

3.1   Cryptographic Primitives

The public-key *ElGamal* cryptosystem [11] is used in our scheme for encrypting the cast votes and other data that is exchanged during the election.

In order to prove the validity of statements in our scheme without revealing any information beyond that, *zero-knowledge proofs* are used. Namely, we will use the methods described in [6] in order to construct the zero-knowledge proofs of statements about discrete logarithms. In this, we use the following notation in our paper: for example, given the public values g, h, y_1, y_2, the notation $PoK\{x_1, x_2 : y_1 = g^{x_1} \wedge y_2 = g^{x_2} h^{x_1}\}$ denotes the proof of knowledge of secret values x_1, x_2 so that $y_1 = g^{x_1}$ and $y_2 = g^{x_2} h^{x_1}$ holds.

The non-interactive version for zero-knowledge proofs is computed using the strong Fiat-Shamir heuristic as described in [4] with $\mathcal{H}$ as a cryptographic hash function.

For the delegation process, our scheme relies on distribution of secret delegation tokens among multiple voters, which is done using *threshold secret sharing*. This secret can then be reconstructed only if at least the threshold of all the voters collaborates. A number of proposals have been made for this purpose, with our scheme relying on a proposal in [26][4].

---

[3] Note, that the relevancy of this requirement might be debated, since in some cases it is reasonable to assume, that other boardroom members know whom the delegating voter trusts anyway. Still, we choose to include this requirement for the case, when the voter does not wish to publicly disclose his support for a particular proxy to others, or even to the proxy herself.

[4] While there are extensions of [26] that ensure verifiability to protect against dishonest dealers (e.g. [24]), this protection is not required in our scheme, since the dealer has no incentive to cheat during secret sharing. Hence, for the sake of simplicity we chose to use a less complex variant.

Another application of threshold secret sharing techniques in our scheme is the *distributed generation of a public ElGamal key* used for encryption within the election, and a set of private key shares distributed among the voters. The distributed key generation occurs as described in [23]. The threshold t is being chosen so that the collaboration of at least t voters is required to reconstruct the secret key or decrypt a ciphertext. The secret key shares are then used to distributively decrypt the encrypted data by applying the scheme as described in [23]. A zero-knowledge proof is used to prove the decryption validity.

In order to commit to a value without revealing it, in our scheme we use *Pedersen commitments* [24], that are unconditionally hiding and computationally binding under the assumption that the discrete logarithm is hard in the chosen group.

In order to anonymize a list of ElGamal ciphertexts by removing the link between each ciphertext and its sender, a *re-encryption mix net* scheme is being applied. The mix net consists of several mix nodes, in which each mix node shuffles the ciphertexts in turn, and provides the output as an input to the next mix node. It holds that the ciphertexts are anonymized, as long as at least one mix node does not reveal its secret values used for shuffling. For the sake of preventing manipulation (i.e. that no ciphertexts have been replaced during the shuffling), various methods for proving the validity of the shuffle have been proposed, such as [3, 29].

In order to check, whether two ElGamal ciphertexts e_1, e_2 encrypt the same value, without revealing any other information about corresponding plaintexts, we use the technique described in [15], the *plaintext equivalence test (PET)*, denoted as $\mathsf{PET}(e_1, e_2)$. This test is distributively performed by the participants who hold the shares of a secret decryption key and outputs 1 in case e_1 and e_2 encrypt the same plaintext, or a random value otherwise.

3.2 Boardroom Voting Scheme from [20]

We briefly describe the boardroom voting scheme proposed in [20] and used as a basis for our proxy boardroom voting extension. The scheme in [20] is based upon the proposal in [8] and adjusted towards decentralized setting, where the voters take over the role of the trustees. The election runs as follows.

Setup. Prior to the election, the voters exchange their public signing keys in order to enable authenticated message exchange. For this purpose they conduct the decentralized key exchange as described in [22], so that the correctness of the exchanged keys is established by manual verification of the so-called short authentication strings via an out-of-band channel (e.g. phone conference or physical proximity). After exchanging the signing keys, each pair of voters runs the Diffie-Hellman key [10] exchange in order to establish the symmetric secret keys for private communication. After the public signing keys and the symmetric secret keys have been established, the voters run the distributed threshold secret sharing as described in [23] in order to generate a public election key pk and share the corresponding private election key sk.

Voting. Once the election key has been generated, one voter takes over the role of the election organizer and initializes the voting. In order to vote, each voter encrypts her chosen voting option with the public election key pk and broadcasts it as her ballot to other voters.

Tallying. Once all the ballots have been cast, the voter jointly perform the tallying. For this, they shuffle the ballots with a verifiable re-encryption mix net [29], where each voter acts as a mix node. After the shuffling, the voters jointly run the distributed threshold decryption as described in [23] in order to reveal the election result.

4   Our Scheme

We are now ready to provide a description of our scheme for proxy voting in boardroom voting setting. We assume the existence of a trustworthy public-key infrastructure among all eligible voters, established either via decentralized key exchange as in [20] or in any other appropriate way[5]. Furthermore, the PKI is used to establish private communication channels between the voters, and a reliable broadcast channel for present voters is established (e.g. via Byzantine agreement [21]). For the sake of simplicity, we describe the tallying with the anonymization performed via mix net shuffle. However, the scheme can be easily modified for supporting homomorphic tallying.

In further descriptions we imply that every message is signed by its sender id_i with a private signing key sk_{id_i}. In order to prevent the reuse of old signatures, the signature should furthermore incorporate timestamps and/or other specific information about the election.

4.1   Pre-election

A list of all the eligible voters $id_1, ..., id_N$ is made available [6], with a list of their public signing keys pk_{id_i} (the corresponding private signing keys sk_{id_i} are possessed only by the voters). Furthermore, each voter broadcasts a pair of keys (g_i, h_i) with $x_i = \log_{g_i} h_i$ known only to the voter id_i. The list of voters that are about to be present at the meeting is known in advance, so that the majority of them are actually present.

4.2   Delegation

The delegation can occur before as well as during the election, prior to the voting. We define $V_d \subset \{id_1, ..., id_N\}$ as a set of voters who delegate, and

---

[5] Note that as this PKI can used independently of any specific election, it can be prepared well in advance and reused subsequently.

[6] This list, for example, could be a list of board members who have a right to participate in the meeting.

$V_p = \{id_1, ..., id_N\} \setminus V_d$ as the voters who decide to vote directly (referred to as present voters, or as proxies).

The threshold t is defined as $\lfloor N_p/2 \rfloor + 1$, with $N_p = |V_p|$ as the number of present voters. If a voter $id_i \in V_d$ decides to delegate, following steps are required:

The voter id_i selects a random value $m_i \in \mathbb{Z}_q$, which serves as her delegation token. She then shares $g_i^{m_i}$ among present voters as follows:

- Compute the shares of m using Shamirs secret share scheme: select a random polynomial $f_i(x) \in \mathbb{Z}_q[x]$ with degree $t-1$ and $f_i(0) = m_i$. For each voter $id_j \in V_p$, compute secret share $m_{i,j} = f_i(j)$.
- For each voter $id_j \in V_p$, furthermore compute commitments $c_{i,j} = (c_{i,j}^{(1)}, c_{i,j}^{(2)})$ with $c_{i,j}^{(1)} = g_i^{r_{i,j}} h_i^{u_{i,j}}$, $c_{i,j}^{(2)} = g_i^{m_{i,j}} h_i^{r_{i,j}}$ for random $r_{i,j}, u_{i,j} \in \mathbb{Z}_q$, and a digital signature on $c_{i,j}$, $s_{i,j} = \mathsf{Sign}(\mathsf{sk}_{id_i}, c_{i,j})$.
- For each voter $id_j \in V_p$, set $m'_{i,j}$ to m_i if the voter id_j is chosen as a proxy, and a random value in $\mathbb{Z}_q$ otherwise. If the voter does not want to choose a proxy and wants to abstain instead, she sets $m'_{i,j}$ to a random value in $\mathbb{Z}_q$ for each voter.

The tuple $(g_i^{m_{i,j}}, m'_{i,j}, s_{i,j}, r_{i,j}, u_{i,j})$ is being sent to each voter $id_j \in V_p$ over a private channel. Note that id_j can compute $c_{i,j}^{(1)}, c_{i,j}^{(2)}$ herself.

4.3   Setup

At this point, any voter id_i who delegated her voting right can change her mind and attend the meeting; in that case, id_i is excluded from V_d and added to V_p prior to voting.

During the election, the distributed threshold secret sharing is being executed by the present voters $id_j \in V_p$ to establish the public election key $\mathsf{pk}_v = (g_v, h_v)$ and the corresponding private election key sk_v with $h_v = g^{\mathsf{sk}_v}$. At this point the list of valid voting options is being made available, as $\mathbb{V} = \{v_1, ..., v_L\} \subset \mathbb{Z}_q^L$.

Furthermore, for all the delegating voters $id_i \in V_d$ an encryption of the delegation token m_i with pk_v is jointly calculated, whereby each voter $id_j \in V_p$ performs the following steps, given the tuple $(g_i^{m_{i,j}}, m'_{i,j}, c_{i,j}, r_{i,j}, u_{i,j})$ as received during the delegation:

- Encrypt her share of $g_i^{m_i}$ resulting in $e_{i,j}^{(d)} = \mathsf{Enc}(\mathsf{pk}_v, g_i^{m_{i,j}})$,
- Compute the proof of knowledge $\chi_{i,j}$, which is constructed using the technique in [7] and proves that $e_{i,j}^{(d)}$ encrypts the same value that is committed in $c_{i,j} = (c_{i,j}^{(1)}, c_{i,j}^{(2)})$ (i.e. $\chi_{i,j} = PoK\{r_{i,j}, u_{i,j}, r'_{i,j} : a_{i,j} = g_v^{r'_{i,j}} \wedge b_{i,j}/c_{i,j}^{(2)} = h_v^{r'_{i,j}} h_i^{-r_{i,j}} \wedge c_{i,j}^{(1)} = g_i^{r_{i,j}} h_i^{u_{i,j}}\}$ for $e_{i,j}^{(d)} = (a_{i,j}, b_{i,j})$).
- Broadcast the tuple $(id_i, e_{i,j}^{(d)}, c_{i,j}, \chi_{i,j})$.

Given that for each i, at least t of the values of $e_{i,j}^{(d)}$ with valid proofs, $j \in Q_i \subset \{1, ..., N\}$, $|Q_i| \geq t$ are broadcast, these values are combined as

$$e_i^{(d)} = \prod_{j \in Q_i} (e_{i,j}^{(d)})^{\lambda_{i,j}}$$

with $\lambda_{i,j} := \sum_{k \in Q_i, k \neq j} \frac{j}{j-k}$. The resulting value of $e_i^{(d)}$ thus corresponds to the encryption of $g_i^{m_i} = g_i^{\sum_{j \in Q_i} m_{i,j} \lambda_{i,j}}$ with the public signing key pk_v.

4.4   Voting

The voters who are present in the meeting (i.e. $id_j \in V_p$) cast their ballots directly by submitting $E_j^{(p)} = \mathsf{Enc}(\mathsf{pk}_v, v_j)$ with v_j signifying their choice, and the accompanying well-formedness proof σ_j that proves the knowledge of v_j and, in case of anonymization via homomorphic tallying, that $v_j \in \mathbb{V}$. Furthermore, for each delegating voter $id_i \in V_d$, each present voter $id_j \in V_p$ calculates a value $\hat{e}_{i,j}^{(d)} = \mathsf{Enc}(\mathsf{pk}_v, g_i^{m'_{i,j}})$. Note that $\hat{e}_{i,j}^{(d)}$ encrypts m_i only in case that the voter id_j is in possession of a token m_i (i.e. $m'_{i,j} = m_i$). For the sake of ensuring soundness, the voter further calculates $\pi_{i,j}$ as a proof of knowledge of plaintext discrete logarithm for $m'_{i,j}$ constructed using the technique described in [7] (i.e. $\pi_{i,j} = PoK\{w_{i,j}, m_{i,j} : a_{i,j}^{(d)} = g_v^{w_{i,j}}, b_{i,j}^{(d)} = g_i^{m_{i,j}} h_v^{w_{i,j}}\}$ with $\hat{e}_{i,j}^{(d)} = (a_{i,j}^{(d)}, b_{i,j}^{(d)})$), calculates $E_{i,j}^{(d)}$ as $\mathsf{Enc}(\mathsf{pk}_v, v_{i,j}^{(d)})$ with $v_{i,j}^{(d)}$ as her chosen option to cast on behalf of the delegating voter id_i, $\sigma_{i,j}$ as the proof of plaintext knowledge for $E_{i,j}^{(d)}$, and broadcasts the tuple $(\hat{e}_{i,j}^{(d)}, E_{i,j}^{(d)}, \pi_{i,j}, \sigma_{i,j})$.

4.5   Tallying - Weeding Duplicates and Invalid Delegations

In the next stage, the delegated ballots are jointly processed by the present voters. First, the delegated ballots with invalid proofs of knowledge $\pi_{i,j}, \sigma_{i,j}$ are removed. Then, the vote updating policy is applied. Namely, the given two ballots cast as direct ballots by the same voter, or two delegated ballots cast on behalf of the same voter by the same proxy, either all but the last (if vote updating is allowed) or all by the first (if vote updating is not allowed) cast ballot are excluded from further processing.

The next step removes the delegated ballots if they have canceled by the voter, i.e. if the voter cast a direct ballot instead. Namely, out of all the delegated ballots tuples $(\hat{e}_{i,j}^{(d)}, E_{i,j}^{(d)}, \pi_{i,j})$, the ballots with $id_i \in V_p$ are removed.

The remaining delegated ballots are being anonymized via verifiable re-encryption mix net with each present voter acting as a mix node, resulting in an anonymized list $V = \{(\hat{e'}_{i,j}^{(d)}, E'_{i,j}^{(d)})\}_{id_i \in V_d, id_j \in V_p}$. The values $e_i^{(d)}$ that encrypt the voters delegation tokens m_i are also processed through the mix net resulting in an anonymized list $V' = \{e'_i^{(d)}\}_{id_i \in V_d}$. The next step removes the delegated ballots cast with an invalid delegation token. For this, the following procedure is performed for each anonymized tuple $(\hat{e'}_{i,j}^{(d)}, E'_{i,j}^{(d)}) \in V$:

- Calculate $\mathsf{PET}(\hat{e'}_{i,j}^{(d)}, e'_i^{(d)})$ for each $e'_i^{(d)} \in V'$.
- If the PET is positive for some $e'_i^{(d)}$, add $E'_{i,j}^{(d)}$ to the list V'' for further tallying and remove $e'_i^{(d)}$ from V'.

4.6 Tallying - Mixing and Decrypting

After that, the list of ciphertexts $\{E_j^{(p)}\}_{id_j \in V_p} \cup \{E'_i^{(d)}\} \in V''$ is being anonymized with another mix net shuffle. The anonymized result is being decrypted via distributed decryption.

5 Security

We now conduct an informal security evaluation of the proposed scheme. Namely, we argue that the security requirements outlined in Sect. 2 are fulfilled under the following assumptions[7]:

(A1) Out of N_p present voters, at least $N_p - t + 1$ are honest and do not divulge their private information to the adversary.

(A2) The devices of honest voters are trustworthy.

(A3) At least t of present voters are available, capable to communicate with each other, and produce valid output during the election.

(A4) The PKI is trustworthy.

(A5) The adversary is computationally restricted, the decisional Diffie-Hellman problem is hard in the selected group, and the signature scheme used in the PKI is reliable. The random oracle is instantiated by the hash function $\mathcal{H}$.

(A6) No coercion takes place.

We start off with evaluating the security requirement related to direct voting.

Voter eligibility. This requirement is ensured as long as the PKI used to authenticate the voters is trustworthy (A4). Furthermore, the duplicate votes submitted by voters are removed throughout the tallying phase. Unless the PKI is not trustworthy (A4), dishonest voters cannot cast multiple votes. If a voter delegates her right to vote and additionally casts a vote personally, then the voter's delegation is invalidated throughout the tallying phase if the PKI is trustworthy (A4).

Vote integrity. For direct votes, this requirement can be violated by replacing a cast vote with another ciphertext at the time of vote casting. Alternatively, the adversary could drop the messages with cast votes from particular voters at vote casting, thus excluding these votes from the tally. However, given a trustworthy voting device, such a manipulation will be detected by the voter, since her result would not fit with the result of other voters (A2). Another way to manipulate the tally would be to replace the ballots during the shuffling or to produce an

---

[7] Note, that these assumptions are common within e-voting systems, e.g. Helios [1].

incorrect decryption result. Both possibilities are prevented by the soundness of the zero knowledge proofs of shuffle validity and decryption validity (A5).

We now consider the integrity of delegated votes. Note, in case the voter has delegated her vote to multiple proxies, only a vote from one of them is included into the tallying. Hence, in this way excluding the votes of other proxies from being included in the tallying is not considered a violation of delegation integrity for proxies. Similarly, excluding the votes cast on behalf of dishonest voters does not violate the requirement.

A dishonest majority of present voters might prevent the delegated ballot on behalf of the particular voter from being included in the tally by refusing to publish their values $e_{i,j}^{(d)}$ and preventing the reconstruction of $e_i^{(d)}$. While this is prevented by the assumption that more than half of all the present voters are honest (A5), we still do not consider it to be a violation of vote integrity, since the misbehaviour of dishonest voters would be detected.

On the other hand, publishing the invalid values $e_{i,j}^{(d)}$, so that the reconstructed $e_i^{(d)}$ does not encrypt the value of $g_i^{m_i}$ for a valid delegation token m_i, would indeed be a violation of vote integrity, if undetected. However, the soundness of zero-knowledge proof $\chi_{i,j}$ that accompanies $\hat{e}_{i,j}^{(d)}$ and the computational binding property of the commitment $c_{i,j}$ (A5) that holds unless the secret x_i is leaked (A2) ensure, that each $e_{i,j}^{(d)}$ encrypts the value $g_i^{m_{i,j}}$ contained in $c_{i,j}$. Since $c_{i,j}$ is signed by the voter (and a lack of a valid signature would be noticeable to the honest present voters, as well as to the delegating voters who verify the election data), the unforgeability of the signature (A5) ensures that $c_{i,j}$ was sent by the voter herself, hence, it contains the valid value of $g_i^{m_{i,j}}$. Hence, the reconstructed value $e_i^{(d)}$ encrypts the same $g_i^{m_i}$ that is shared by the voter id_i.

Another way to prevent the delegated votes from an honest proxy to be included in the tally is to ensure that the result of $\mathsf{PET}(\hat{e}'^{(d)}_{i,j}, e'^{(d)}_i)$ outputs some value other than 1. This is prevented due to the soundness of the zero-knowledge proofs accompanying the PETs. Furthermore, analogously to the case of direct ballots, the soundness of zero knowledge proofs regarding shuffle validity and decryption validity prevent the manipulation of cast ballots (A5).

Robustness. Violating robustness would mean, that either the mixing, the weeding of invalid delegations or the decryption has failed to output a valid output. This is prevented if at least t present voters are available and provide the required output during the tallying (A3).

Vote privacy. This requirement is violated if the adversary corrupts voting devices, which then leak the choices made by the voters. This is prevented as long as the honest voters' devices are not compromised (A2). Furthermore, the voters themselves do not leak the randomness used by encrypting the vote (A2).

Another way to violate vote privacy of honest voters is to decrypt the encrypted votes prior to their anonymization (i.e. before mixing). This, however, requires breaking the encryption of the votes (A5), or obtaining at least t shares of a private election key from the present voters (A1,A2).

Furthermore, vote privacy can be violated by revealing the secret permutation used by each voter during the mixing. However, as long as at least one voter keeps this permutation secret (A1), the permutation between the resulting output and the input ciphertexts remains secret as well.

Fairness. As the cast ballots are attached to the voter's identities until the tallying, violating fairness would also imply violating vote privacy. Hence, fairness is ensured under the same assumptions as vote privacy: namely, that the voting devices of honest voters are trustworthy (A2), at least $N_p - t + 1$ of N_p present voters are honest (A1), and the underlying encryption cannot be broken (A5).

We further evaluate the security requirements related to delegated voting.

Delegation eligibility. Casting a delegated ballot on behalf of a non-eligible voter would require forging the signatures on the commitments $c_{i,j}$ sent to the present voters (prevented by the assumptions (A4) and (A5)). Furthermore, multiple delegated ballots on behalf of the same voter are dismissed during tallying.

Delegation integrity. One way to violate this requirement would be to cast delegated votes on behalf of non-eligible voters. Given the fact that delegations are accompanied by signed values $c_{i,j}$, this attack strategy is prevented unless the underlying PKI is not trustworthy (A4). Furthermore, reusing old signatures on $c_{i,j}$ would be prevented, since the election information and the timestamp are incorporated in the signature.

Another way to violate this requirement for a proxy id_j who wants to vote on behalf of the voter id_i without being authorised, is to find out the value of m_i, shared by id_i to the present voters during the delegation. This would require either corrupting the voting device of id_i (A2) or eavesdropping on the communication between id_i and a proxy chosen by her (prevented due to private communication channels, i.e. the trustworthiness of the PKI (A4)). Note that even if the adversary succeeds in obtaining at least t shares of $g_i^{m_{i,j}}$ from the present voters, she would still require to compute the discrete logarithm $m_{i,j}$ (A5).

Alternatively, an adversary can attempt manipulating the computation of $e_i^{(d)}$, so that it encrypts a plaintext $g^{m_i'}$ chosen by her. As shown in the evaluation of vote integrity, however, the assumptions (A4, A5) ensure than $e_i^{(d)}$ encrypts the same value $g_i^{m_{i,j}}$ sent by the voter.

Finally, delegation integrity can be violated, if the proxy id_j submits a value $\hat{e}_{i,j}^{(d)}$ which is accepted during the weeding of invalid delegations. The soundness of the proof of knowledge of plaintext discrete logarithm $\pi_{i,j}$ ensures (A5), that the proxy knows the discrete log m_i of the plaintext $g_i^{m_i}$ encrypted in $\hat{e}_{i,j}^{(d)}$. As shown above, the assumptions (A4) and (A5) ensure that the reconstructed values $e_i^{(d)}$ encrypt the delegation tokens submitted by the voters to their chosen proxies. The soundness of the proof of shuffle ensures (A5), that the anonymized encrypted delegation tokens $e_i'^{(d)}$ encrypt the same values as $e_i^{(d)}$.

Delegation privacy. The delegation privacy requirement would be violated if it is revealed which proxy possesses the value m_i that was shared by the voter id_i among other present voters. This can be achieved either by corrupting the voting device of id_i that stores m_i (A2), coercing the present voters into disclosing all the shares $m_{i,j}$ with the adversary (A6), getting access to at least t shares of $g_i^{m_i}$ (i.e. corrupting at least t present voters (A1), their voting devices (A2) or the communication channels between the present and the delegated voters (A4)), or decrypting $e_i^{(d)}$ and the values of $\hat{e}_{i,j}^{(d)}$ (i.e. either breaking encryption (A5) or obtaining at least t shares of a secret key sk_v by corrupting at least t present voters (A1) or their voting devices (A2)).

Furthermore, the delegating voter herself cannot construct a proof that she delegated to a specific proxy, even if she provides all the shares $g_i^{m_{i,j}}$ and the value of m_i to the adversary. Namely, given that the voter knows the discrete logarithm $x_i = \log_{g_i} h_i$, she can provide fake values of $g_i^{m_{i,j}}$, m_i instead. As such, for every values $m_{i,j}, r_{i,j}$ and $u_{i,j}$ (thus, for every pair of commitments $c_{i,j}^{(1)}, c_{i,j}^{(2)}$) and every value $m'_{i,j} \neq m_{i,j}$ the voter can find $r'_{i,j}, u'_{i,j}$ so that $x_i r_{i,j} + m_{i,j} = x_i r'_{i,j} + m'_{i,j}$ and $x_i u_{i,j} + r_{i,j} = x_i u'_{i,j} + r'_{i,j}$ (thus, $c_{i,j}^{(1)} = g_i^{r_{i,j}} h_i^{u_{i,j}}$ and $c_{i,j}^{(2)} = g_i^{m_{i,j}} h_i^{r_{i,j}}$). She can then fake the receipt by sending a random value m'_i and a set of shares $m'_{i,j}$ that reconstruct to m'_i together with the corresponding values of $r'_{i,j}, u'_{i,j}$ to the present voter who requests such a receipt. Given t as threshold and N_p as the total amount of present voters among which g^{m_i} is shared, the voter would have to fake at least $N_p - t + 1$ shares $m_{i,j}$. Hence, as long as at least $N_p - t + 1$ present voters are honest, and that the delegating voter knows the identities of the honest present voters, the adversary would not be able to distinguish between the fake values $g_i^{m_{i,j}}$, m_i that from the real ones.

Note, however, that in case one of the voters $id_j \in V_p$ (i.e. who received delegations) is not available in the meeting, our scheme reveals the number of delegating voters who either abstained (but still participated in the delegation by issuing invalid delegation tokens $m'_{i,j} \neq m_i$ to all the voters in V_p) or delegated to id_j. We do not consider such a case to be a violation of delegation privacy, since, as shown above, the scheme does not reveals the identities of the voters who either issued invalid delegation tokens or delegated to id_j and does not make it possible to tell whether a given voter issued a valid token to id_j or not (under the assumptions (A1, (A2), (A4), (A5), and (A6)). At the same time, in order to reduce the information leakage in our scheme, we would suggest actively encouraging that the voters in V_d who decide to abstain still participate in the delegation phase of the election by issuing invalid delegation tokens $m'_{i,j} \neq m_i$ to all the voters in V_p. Furthermore, the voters in V_p can be encouraged to re-delegate by forwarding their delegation token to another trusted present voter, if they think they would not be able to participate in the meeting.

Delegation power privacy. Given $N_d = N - N_p$ delegating voters, each present voter should posses N_d delegation tokens. Violating delegation power privacy would mean estimating, possibly with the help of the proxy herself who tries to prove her delegation power, how many of those tokens are valid. However, given that the delegation privacy requirement is fulfilled, a proxy herself does not know which ones of the delegation tokens she received are valid. Hence, under the assumptions that at least $N_p - t + 1$ of the present voters are honest (A1), the PKI is trustworthy (A4), the voting devices of the delegating voters and honest proxies are trustworthy (A2), the voters do not collaborate with the proxy to prove that they delegated their voting right to her (A6) and the encryption is not broken (A5), delegation power privacy is ensured.

Note that as already mentioned in the evaluation of delegation privacy, if a proxy $id_j \in V_p$ does not participate in the election, our scheme could reveal the number of voters N_j who either delegated to id_j or issued invalid delegation tokens $m_{i,j}$ to all the proxies. However, since the scheme does not reveal, how many voters out of N_j abstained, delegation power privacy is not violated, especially if the voters who want to abstain are encouraged to issue invalid delegation tokens instead of not participating at all.

6 Related Work

A number of proposals considered decentralised elections, i.e. the boardroom voting setting. The first proposal was made in [9] using decryption mix net. Several proposals focused on self-tallying approach, based upon self-dissolving commitments [12–14,16,17,27]. Other approaches to boardroom voting have extended the decentralised tallying scheme proposed in [8] and partially implemented in the Helios voting system [1]. The variant of this approach using homomorphic tallying has been proposed in [25], and the variant using mix net and decentralised PKI establishment has been proposed and implemented in [20]. A boardroom voting system described and evaluated in [2] implements a boardroom voting scheme that does not rely on cryptography.

Several schemes with delegated voting functionality have been proposed in the literature. The proposal by Kulyk et al. [19] addresses coercion resistance in delegated voting by extending the well-known coercion-resistant JCJ/Civitas theme for electronic voting towards delegated voting. A further proposal in [18] extends the Helios voting system with delegated voting functionality. Their approach, however, only allows to delegate after the election setup has been conducted (i.e. after the election key has been generated) which is not suitable to the boardroom voting setting that we consider in this work. Tchorbadjiiski [28] introduces hash chains to compute "connected" credentials on the client side to enable a transitive and revocable delegation process, and the proposal by Zwattendorfer et al. [30] uses blind signatures to enable delegation privacy.

7 Conclusion

We proposed an electronic voting scheme that facilitates delegated voting in the boardroom voting setting. The scheme enforces both general security requirements on electronic voting, such as vote privacy and integrity of the election, and security requirements that are specifically tailored to the delegation process.

As such, the scheme ensures delegation privacy by hiding the link between the voter and the identity of her chosen proxy, delegation integrity by ensuring that a proxy can only cast a ballot on some voter's behalf if authorised by the voter, delegation eligibility to ensure that only the delegated ballots on behalf of the eligible voters are included in the tally and delegation power privacy to ensure, that the scheme does not reveal how many voters have delegated to a particular proxy.

In the future, we plan to extend our security evaluation and provide formal security proofs for the proposed delegated boardroom voting scheme. For this, the formal definitions for security requirements specific to delegated voting should be established.

Another direction of future work would be to address the attack vectors on vote secrecy, delegation privacy and delegation power privacy that exploit the information revealed by the election result. Due to the relatively small number of voters in boardroom voting, these attacks might have more impact than they have in large scale elections. Hence, we plan to consider ways to minimize information revealed by the result during the course of the delegation.

Finally, a direction of future work would be focusing on the efficiency of the scheme. While the scheme is designed for small-scale elections , it nonetheless requires a relatively high level of interaction among the present voters (the bottleneck being the weeding of invalid delegated ballots during the tallying). Therefore, methods for improving the efficiency by reducing the required communications and computations are required.

Acknowledgements. This paper has been partially developed within the project (HA project no. 435/14-25) funded in the framework of Hessen ModellProjekte, financed with funds of LOEWE –Landes-Offensive zur Entwicklung Wissenschaftlich-ökonomischer Exzellenz, Förderlinie 3: KMU-Verbundvorhaben (State Offensive for the Development of Scientific and Economic Excellence). It has also been partially developed within the project 'VALID' - Verifiable Liquid Democracy - which is funded by the Polyas GmbH. This work has also been supported by the German Federal Ministry of Education and Research (BMBF) as well as by the Hessen State Ministry for Higher Education, Research and the Arts within CRISP.

References

1. Adida, B.: Helios: web-based open-audit voting. In: Proceedings of 17th Conference on Security Symposium, SS 2008, pp. 335–348. USENIX, July 2008
2. Arnaud, M., Cortier, V., Wiedling, C.: Analysis of an electronic boardroom voting system. In: Heather, J., Schneider, S., Teague, V. (eds.) Vote-ID 2013. LNCS, vol. 7985, pp. 109–126. Springer, Heidelberg (2013). https://doi.org/10.1007/978-3-642-39185-9_7
3. Bayer, S., Groth, J.: Efficient zero-knowledge argument for correctness of a shuffle. In: Pointcheval, D., Johansson, T. (eds.) EUROCRYPT 2012. LNCS, vol. 7237, pp. 263–280. Springer, Heidelberg (2012). https://doi.org/10.1007/978-3-642-29011-4_17

4. Bernhard, D., Pereira, O., Warinschi, B.: How not to prove yourself: pitfalls of the Fiat-Shamir heuristic and applications to Helios. In: Wang, X., Sako, K. (eds.) ASIACRYPT 2012. LNCS, vol. 7658, pp. 626–643. Springer, Heidelberg (2012). https://doi.org/10.1007/978-3-642-34961-4_38

5. Budurushi, J., Neumann, S., Olembo, M.M., Volkamer, M.: Pretty understandable democracy-a secure and understandable internet voting scheme. In: Proceedings of 8th International Conference on Availability, Reliability and Security, ARES 2013, pp. 198–207. IEEE (2013)

6. Camenisch, J., Stadler, M.: Efficient group signature schemes for large groups. In: Kaliski, B.S. (ed.) CRYPTO 1997. LNCS, vol. 1294, pp. 410–424. Springer, Heidelberg (1997). https://doi.org/10.1007/BFb0052252

7. Camenisch, J., Stadler, M.: Proof systems for general statements about discrete logarithms. Technical report, Citeseer (1997)

8. Cramer, R., Gennaro, R., Schoenmakers, B.: A secure and optimally efficient multi-authority election scheme. Eur. Trans. Telecommun. **8**(5), 481–490 (1997)

9. DeMillo, R.A., Lynch, N.A., Merritt, M.J.: Cryptographic protocols. In: Proceedings of 14th Annual ACM Symposium on Theory of Computing, STOC 1982, pp. 383–400. ACM (1982)

10. Diffie, W., Hellman, M.: New directions in cryptography. IEEE Trans. Inf. Theor. **22**(6), 644–654 (1976)

11. ElGamal, T.: A public key cryptosystem and a signature scheme based on discrete logarithms. In: Blakley, G.R., Chaum, D. (eds.) CRYPTO 1984. LNCS, vol. 196, pp. 10–18. Springer, Heidelberg (1985). https://doi.org/10.1007/3-540-39568-7_2

12. Giustolisi, R., Iovino, V., Rønne, P.B.: On the possibility of non-interactive e-voting in the public-key setting. In: Clark, J., Meiklejohn, S., Ryan, P.Y.A., Wallach, D., Brenner, M., Rohloff, K. (eds.) FC 2016. LNCS, vol. 9604, pp. 193–208. Springer, Heidelberg (2016). https://doi.org/10.1007/978-3-662-53357-4_13

13. Groth, J.: Efficient maximal privacy in boardroom voting and anonymous broadcast. In: Juels, A. (ed.) FC 2004. LNCS, vol. 3110, pp. 90–104. Springer, Heidelberg (2004). https://doi.org/10.1007/978-3-540-27809-2_10

14. Hao, F., Ryan, P.Y., Zielinski, P.: Anonymous voting by two-round public discussion. IET Inf. Secur. **4**(2), 62–67 (2010)

15. Jakobsson, M., Juels, A.: Mix and match: secure function evaluation via ciphertexts. In: Okamoto, T. (ed.) ASIACRYPT 2000. LNCS, vol. 1976, pp. 162–177. Springer, Heidelberg (2000). https://doi.org/10.1007/3-540-44448-3_13

16. Khader, D., Smyth, B., Ryan, P.Y., Hao, F.: A fair and robust voting system by broadcast. In: Proceedings of 5th International Conference on Electronic Voting, EVOTE 2012, vol. 205, pp. 285–299. Gesellschaft für Informatik (2012)

17. Kiayias, A., Yung, M.: Self-tallying elections and perfect ballot secrecy. In: Naccache, D., Paillier, P. (eds.) PKC 2002. LNCS, vol. 2274, pp. 141–158. Springer, Heidelberg (2002). https://doi.org/10.1007/3-540-45664-3_10

18. Kulyk, O., Marky, K., Neumann, S., Volkamer, M.: Introducing proxy voting to Helios. In: Proceedings of 11th International Conference on Availability, Reliability and Security, ARES 2016, pp. 98–106. IEEE, September 2016

19. Kulyk, O., Neumann, S., Marky, K., Budurushi, J., Volkamer, M.: Coercion-resistant proxy voting. In: Hoepman, J.-H., Katzenbeisser, S. (eds.) SEC 2016. IAICT, vol. 471, pp. 3–16. Springer, Cham (2016). https://doi.org/10.1007/978-3-319-33630-5_1

20. Kulyk, O., Neumann, S., Volkamer, M., Feier, C., Koster, T.: Electronic voting with fully distributed trust and maximized flexibility regarding ballot design. In: Proceedings of 6th International Conference on Electronic Voting, Verifying the Vote, EVOTE 2014, pp. 1–10. IEEE (2014)
21. Lamport, L., Shostak, R., Pease, M.: The Byzantine generals problem. ACM Trans. Program. Lang. Syst. **4**(3), 382–401 (1982). TOPLAS 1982
22. Nguyen, L.H., Roscoe, A.W.: Efficient group authentication protocol based on human interaction. In: Proceedings of Workshop on Foundation of Computer Security and Automated Reasoning Protocol Security Analysis, FCS-ARSPA 2006, pp. 9–33, August 2006
23. Pedersen, T.P.: Distributed provers and verifiable secret sharing based on the discrete logarithm problem. DAIMI Rep. Ser. **21**(388) (1992)
24. Pedersen, T.P.: Non-interactive and information-theoretic secure verifiable secret sharing. In: Feigenbaum, J. (ed.) CRYPTO 1991. LNCS, vol. 576, pp. 129–140. Springer, Heidelberg (1992). https://doi.org/10.1007/3-540-46766-1_9
25. Ritter, J.: Decentralized e-voting on android devices using homomorphic tallying. Master's thesis, Bern University of Applied Sciences, Biel, Switzerland (2014)
26. Shamir, A.: How to share a secret. Commun. ACM **22**(11), 612–613 (1979)
27. Szepieniec, A., Preneel, B.: New techniques for electronic voting. JETS 2015: USENIX J. Elect. Technol. Syst. pp. 46–69 (2015)
28. Tchorbadjiiski, A.: Liquid democracy diploma thesis. RWTH AACHEN University, Germany (2012)
29. Terelius, B., Wikström, D.: Proofs of restricted shuffles. In: Bernstein, D.J., Lange, T. (eds.) AFRICACRYPT 2010. LNCS, vol. 6055, pp. 100–113. Springer, Heidelberg (2010). https://doi.org/10.1007/978-3-642-12678-9_7
30. Zwattendorfer, B., Hillebold, C., Teufl, P.: Secure and privacy-preserving proxy voting system. In: Proceedings of IEEE 10th International Conference on e-Business Engineering, ICEBE 2013, pp. 472–477. IEEE, September 2013

Practical Governmental Voting with Unconditional Integrity and Privacy

Nan Yang and Jeremy Clark[✉]

Concordia University, Montreal, Canada
na_yan@encs.concordia.ca, j.clark@concordia.ca

Abstract. Throughout the years, many cryptographically verifiable voting systems have been proposed with a whole spectrum of features and security assumptions. Where the voter casts an in-person (and possibly paper) ballot and leaves, as is common in a governmental election, the majority of the proposals fall in the category of providing unconditional integrity and computational privacy. A minority of papers have looked at the inverse scenario: everlasting privacy with computational integrity. However as far as we know, no paper has succeeded in providing both unconditional integrity and privacy in this setting—it has only been explored in boardroom voting schemes where voters participate in the tallying process. Our paper aims for a two-level contribution: first, we present a concrete system with these security properties (one that works as a backend for common ballot styles like Scantegrity II or Prêt à Voter); and second, we provide some insight into how different combinations of security assumptions are interdependent.

1 Introduction

An end-to-end verifiable (E2E) voting system uses cryptography to provide a verifiable tally while maintaining the secrecy of each voter's ballot. Over decades of research in this area, one trend to emerge is a move toward real-world voting systems suitable for common election scenarios, including governmental elections. For our purposes, we consider a system to be suitable for a governmental election if it has two properties:

1. **Vote-and-go**: once a voter has completed and submitted their ballot, they do not need to be involved in the tallying process.
2. **Human-votable**: a voter can cast a vote without having to perform any computations (bare-handed) through a process similar to a traditional (non-verifiable) voting system, such as DRE or optical scan voting

Many E2E systems are designed within these constraints and some have been used in governmental elections [6,7]. The governmental setting is contrasted with other practical settings, such as a boardroom vote, where all voters might be physically present in the same room with their own trusted computational devices. This setting is less constrained and allows different cryptographic techniques to be used—e.g., an unconditionally secure multiparty computation.

© International Financial Cryptography Association 2017
M. Brenner et al. (Eds.): FC 2017 Workshops 2017, LNCS 10323, pp. 434–449, 2017.
https://doi.org/10.1007/978-3-319-70278-0_27

In the governmental setting, vote-and-go requires a third party election authority to collect a representation of the voter's ballot. This representation is often an encryption or commitment to the voter selections for DRE-based systems, or for optical scan systems, a paper-based obfuscation (e.g., code substitution, permutation, split) that is accompanied by some encryption or commitment value on the ballot or in the backend data. Standard encryption and commitment schemes are not secure against a computationally unbounded adversary. Such an adversary can either recover the message (Elgamal or Paillier), change the message (Pedersen commitment) or both (hash-based commitments). When the message is a vote, this translates into, respectively, breaking election integrity or ballot secrecy or both.

Computational assumptions underly nearly all real-world cryptographic applications, whether it is HTTPS, password hashing, or secure messaging. However the exact assumptions evolve over time as new attacks are found, as do the security parameters that realize them. An unconditionally secure protocol alleviates us from monitoring the validity of these assumptions over time and future-proofs the protocol against new innovations like quantum computing.

2   Prior Work

There are hundreds of papers proposing voting schemes and it is not possible to review even all the relevant ones. Instead, we have broken the literature into four broad categories that classify a majority of the proposals. Table 1 provides a summary of the election integrity and ballot secrecy assumptions for each cluster.

Distributed EA. Beginning with Cramer et al. [16], many systems homomorphically encrypt ballots under a public key that is distributed amongst a set of trustees forming an election authority (EA). If an unbounded adversary attacks a transcript of the election, they can learn how every voter voted by breaking the encryption key but cannot change the value that is encrypted. Further, assuming true zero knowledge proofs are used, unbounded adversaries cannot undetectably change the tally. Note that in practice, many of these systems use non-interactive zero knowledge proofs based on the Fiat-Shamir heuristic — this enables an unbounded adversary (whether a voter or a trustee) to lie [21] in a way that can undetectably change a tally, however this assumption is practical to avoid [19, 26]. If a suitable threshold of trustees are corrupted, they may recover how each voter voted but they cannot change the tally. A few notable systems of this type include: MarkPledge [33], Prêt à Voter [12], Voter-initiated auditing [3], Helios [1], STAR-Vote [2], and vVote [6].

Chaumian. Beginning with Chaum [9], a series of systems also use a distributed election authority much like above. However these systems add an additional assumption: trustees can use a special computational device, called a blackbox, to perform computations such that the inputs and intermediate values are not leaked to any participant. This enables an election system based solely

Table 1. A comparison of computational and collusion security assumptions in four common categories of proposed cryptographic voting systems, plus our own system. Note: this table does not attempt to capture all desirable features of a voting system. We acheive the same security assumptions as boardroom voting systems, plus we allow human-voteable ballots and vote-and-go tallying. The 'special assumption' used in Chaumian systems (and this work) is a blackbox assumption.

Category	Examples	Secrecy — Resilient to Unbounded Adversary	Secrecy — Resilient to Full Collusion	Secrecy — No Special Assumptions	Integrity — Resilient to Unbounded Adversary	Integrity — Resilient to Full Collusion	Integrity — No Special Assumptions
Distributed EA	Pret a Voter, Helios			•	•	•	•
Chaumian	Punchscan, Scantegrity				•	•	•
Everlasting Privacy	Moran-Naor	•		•		•	•
Boardroom	Broadbent-Tapp	•		•	•		•
This work		•			•		•

on cryptographic commitments and commitment-based cut-and-choose proofs. Assuming the commitment scheme is perfectly binding, an adversary can break ballot secrecy by breaking the commitment scheme (if unbounded), corrupting a sufficient number of trustees to recover the input to the blackbox, or by breaking the blackbox hardware assumption. However an unbounded adversary cannot undetectably change the values committed to, all modifications to the tally are detectable even if made by a fully colluding election authority, and the soundness of the blackbox computations are verifiable and not assumed to be done correctly. Notable systems of this type include Punchscan [34], Scantegrity I/II [10,11], Eperio [18], and Remotegrity [41].

Everlasting Privacy. Beginning with Cramer et al. [15] (and related to earlier work by Chaum [8]), a reasonable observation was made that integrity need only last the lifetime of the election but ballot secrecy could be relevant for decades or centuries. It is possible to invert the resistance of a voting scheme to computationally unbounded adversaries from integrity to privacy. Most modern work uses perfectly hiding homomorphic commitments in lieu of homomorphic encryption, however this creates a dilemma: if the random factors of the commitments are unknown, a tally cannot be computed (and if they are known, then the commitment's hiding property no longer resists an unbounded adversary). Most systems compromise by using untappable channels to communicate random factors amongst trustees— thus it does not retain unconditional ballot secrecy under collusion. Notable systems of this type include Moran-Naor [31], split-ballot voting [32], and extensions to distributed EA systems [17]. Recent work from Locher et al. has examined the removal of the collusion assumption, presenting schemes [27,28] that have everlasting privacy under *both* an unbounded and fully colluding EA (with computational integrity).

Boardroom Voting. The term boardroom voting was suggested by Benoloh and Fisher [4] to categorize systems where voters participate in the tallying process (i.e., are not vote-and-go). Like the general literature on unconditionally secure protocols, these schemes tend to use multiparty computation based on verifiable secret sharing. Note that not all boardroom voting schemes are unconditional—many boardroom systems use computational assumptions to be more practical [22,25,38,39]. However the ones that are resist unbounded adversaries for both integrity and privacy (but collusion between them can break either property). One way to frame our contribution is porting the security properties of these systems to a governmental election. This has been explored [5] and the *vote-and-go* property is achieved, voters need to perform computations in the booth (and it is thus not *human voteable*). One might argue that ThreeBallot [37] is a human-voteable instantiation of secret sharing. Indeed, its properties are very close to what we want to achieve. Unfortunately ThreeBallot is not fully private [23].

3   Framing Our Contribution

It has long been asserted within our community that perfect ballot secrecy and perfect election integrity cannot be simultaneously achieved. This trade-off is quite true under certain assumptions but it is often repeated as a simple fact without internalizing the fine print. As it turns out, if you read the fine print, it is possible to achieve both—indeed many boardroom voting systems already do. The challenge is achieving these security properties while also allowing the voter to deposit their ballot with the EA and leave. If the deposited ballot is an encryption or computational commitment, it must be either computationally binding or hiding but not both. If the ballot is secret shared to the trustees, however, it can be perfectly hiding and binding under an assumption about the number of honest trustees. The immediate difficulty here is that secret sharing a vote will require a computational device.

This paper is intended as exploratory research to understand better how far unconditional privacy and integrity can be extended to a practical governmental voting system. We are not insisting that our system is immediately better than existing approaches because we require certain trade-offs that might be less desirable (discussed below). However we think this area deserves exploration.

In our approach, we begin in the Chaumian model. We noted in our literature review that systems in this model primarily rely on a commitment scheme. As we discuss in Sect. 4.1, verifiable secret sharing can be used as a perfectly hiding commitment that is also perfectly binding but only to the participants in the secret sharing scheme. We take a simple system from this model, Eperio [18], which is already just a backend tallying system that can interface with a variety of paper ballots (permutation-based ballots like Prêt à Voter and code-based ballots like Scantegrity), and we replace the commitment scheme with a protocol based on verifiable secret sharing. We then show that the cut-and-choose protocols continue to provide election integrity, assuming an honest threshold of trustees (which is already assumed in computational Eperio for ballot privacy). The result is an interesting protocol that achieves unconditional privacy and integrity, plus voters can vote with paper ballots.

Universal verification. We pay a price for unconditional secrecy and privacy, namely we have to sacrifice universal verification. Chevallier-Mames et al. prove that achieving unconditional privacy is sufficient to thwart universal verification (if it is possible for voters to choose to abstain from voting) [13]. Under slightly different definitions, Vora and Hosp show an impossibility 'triangle:' it is only possible to achieve two of the three properties: perfect integrity, perfect privacy, and universal verification [24]. They define integrity and privacy in an information-theoretical sense. We also note that attempts of adding it to the basic primitive we use (VSS) generally has only been achieved with computationally secure primitives [38,40]. In our protocol, voters can still perform the traditional *cast-as-intended* and *recorded-as-cast* checks but voters have to trust that a threshold of trustees are honest in reporting that ballots were *tallied-as-recorded*. It is not clear this trade-off is worth the gain in security against unbounded adversaries, but we will say that it is not that different from cryptographic election where voters defer to others (say each political party) to perform the cryptographic election audit of the tally. Finally, our approach of using paper ballots does not preclude traditional risk-limiting manual recounts done in conjunction with the cryptographic election if the ballots have a cryptographic overlay (as in Scantegrity II).

Blackbox assumption. Finally, like Punchscan, Scantegrity and Eperio, we do make a blackbox assumption that a perfectly private computation can be performed on a tamper-resistant device. Blackboxes are stateless devices without any non-volatile memory. The simply compute an output from a set of inputs without revealing any intermediary values in the function. They could be implemented as a hardware circuit, FPGA, or in software in a trusted execution environment such as Intel TXT (c.f., [30]).

Future work might explore the removal of this assumption, through a distributed computation, however we rely on it for this initial work in the area. We do note however that it is not immediately clear that a distributed computation is necessarily better. If an adversary wanted to attack the election by corrupting computational devices, it seems logical that compromising n devices is harder than compromising 1—in fact, this reasoning is seductive enough that the shareholders might use standard computers without extra precautions to perform their computations. In such case, compromising n devices might be as easy as compromising one (e.g., through an exploit for a common operating system) and might indeed be easier if the single blackbox device (it does not even need to be a full fledged computer) is given a lot of attention in terms of hardening it against attack.

Human-voteable and vote-and-go. Some voting schemes require the voter to participate in some multi-party computation. For example, [5] requires that voters take their vote and secret-share it with different election authorities. Even [29], a voting scheme "without cryptography," requires the voter to perform an amount of arithmetic which is arguably unreasonable in practice. In contrast, a human-voteable (also called barehanded [36]) voting scheme is one which does not require any kind of computational device to vote (such as a trusted computer).[1] Vote-and-go refers to the fact that individual voters are not expected to assist in any kind of post-ballot computations, such as computing the tally. All major governmental elections today are have both properties. It is difficult to see how a scheme that does not have both can escape being an impractical academic exercise. While smartphones are ubiquitous, their use opens up new attack vectors and is little better than trusting a polling machine or a physical ballot counted by humans.

4 Protocol Components

4.1 Verifiable Secret-Sharing and Commitment

A (k, n) verifiable secret-sharing (VSS) scheme is a multi-party protocol between a *dealer* and n *shareholders* that consists of two functions $\langle$Share, Recover$\rangle$. When invoking share, the dealer distributes some secret string x among the shareholders such that no subset of shareholders less than k can jointly output x and the dealer proves that each share can be consistently used to reconstruct some secret without an error. When invoking Recover, k or more shareholders combine their shares to recover x (if less than k shareholders honestly contribute their shares, $\perp$ is recovered instead).

The guarantees of a VSS scheme can be made information-theoretic while tolerating up to $k < n/2$ malicious shareholders, assuming the existence of a broadcast channel. A broadcast channel is already a standard assumption in an E2E voting scheme. Many VSS schemes exist, each targeting different efficiency metrics. For our purposes, we assume the use of a standard scheme due to Rabin and Ben Or [35].

The relationship between a VSS scheme and a commitment function was explored recently by Garay et al. [20]. They observe that VSS is typically used a distributed 'analogue' to a commitment scheme and prove that VSS realizes a commitment-like properties. Informally speaking, the two main properties of bit-commitment are binding and hiding, which respectively mean that the sender can only open the commitment in one way, and that the receiver is unable to distinguish between (chosen) committed messages m_0 or m_1.

The respective properties of VSS which will act as the binding and hiding conditions are:

---

[1] Note we do not refer to assistive technology (AT) that helps voters with disabilities cast a vote—for this reason, we dislike the term barehanded. Rather we mean devices that are trusted to perform a computation for the voter, not navigate an interface.

- If no strict majority of shareholder's shares uniquely defines a secret, then there will be an abort. In other words, the dealer is unable to either create a commitment that they cannot open, or a commitment that can be opened in more than one way.
- No strict minority subset of shareholders can reconstruct the secret, or prevent an honest strict majority from reconstructing the secret. If a secret fails to be reconstructed, then the faulty shares can be identified. In other words, no strict minority subset of colluding sShareholders can change an existing commitment, or prevent the honest shareholders from opening the commitment.
- The secret will only be reconstructed when the majority of honest shareholders come to an agreement. In contrast to a two-party bit-commitment, the dealer is not involved in the opening process. Some pre-agreed condition will trigger the honest shareholders to divulge their shares. In our case, they are triggered by an auditor.

Concretely, given a (n,k)-VSS scheme, our commitment scheme will consist of two function ⟨Commit, Open⟩ realized as follows.

- Commit(x): The dealer takes a secret x and invokes Share(x) with the shareholders and proves that the shares are consistent. A failure of the secret-sharing is considered a failure of commitment. If successful, the dealer announces a commitment identifier id to the shareholders used to identify the commitment that should be opened. This identity is output as commitment value c (in a standard commitment, c would be functionally dependent on x).
- Open(c): The auditor sets $id = c$ broadcasts to the shareholders Recover(id). The honest shareholders follow the protocol to determine if the commitment should be opened or not. If so, they execute the reconstruct protocol and send to the auditor their shares, who reconstructs the secret. The honest majority will identify any dishonest shareholders, whose shares the auditors will ignore.

4.2   Eperio

Our voting protocol is based on the Eperio voting system [18]. Technically Eperio is a backend component that can realizes a variety of voting systems. We summarize some details of that protocol which we will augment with VSS in Sect. 5.

Ballots. Eperio can utilize different ballot types. We use a ballot in the style of Prêt à Voter (see Fig. 1): a permuted list of candidates with a serial number. The ballot is assumed to be physically unforgeable and is marked by the voter and split along the dotted line. The candidate ordering is shredded, while the mark position and serial number is optically scanned and then kept by the voter as a privacy-preserving receipt. In Fig. 1, we also show a tabular form of the ballot that is exactly equivalent. This form of the ballot could be printed out and given

Bob	☐
Alice	☐
Charlie	☐
	1234

U	M	S
1234.01	☐	Bob
1234.02	☐	Alice
1234.03	☐	Charlie

Fig. 1. A Prêt à Voter ballot with 3 candidates. Each ballot has a randomly shuffled order of candidates. Left side: the ballot as received by the voter. Right side: an equivalent formulation of the same ballot information in tabular form.

to voters, however it would be a poor design relative to the ballot form on the lefthand side of the figure.

The tabular form of the ballot consists of 3 columns and $\mathcal{C}$ rows, where $\mathcal{C}$ is the number of candidates in the election. The first column, which we denote by $\mathbf{U}$, are Unique IDs which contains a unique ballot identifier and a choice identifier. In the example ballot of Fig. 1, the ballot number is 1234 and the suffixes identify each of the $\mathcal{C}$ markable positions on ballot 1234. So in this case, markable position 1234.01 would count for Bob. On a different ballot, say 1235, position 1235.01 might correspond to a different candidate.

The second column is the *Marks List* column, which we denote by $\mathbf{M}$. In this column, the voter places a checkmark at exactly one spot, indicating the row corresponding to the candidate the voter wishes to vote for. The last column is the *Candidate Selection* column, which we will denote by $\mathbf{S}$. This is a list of the candidates in a randomly permuted (per-ballot) order.

Eperio Tables. An Eperio table is a data structure that encodes the ballot information. If you were to take every ballot in tabular form, concatenate them end-to-end, you would end up with the 'canonical' Eperio table. This canonical table is never used directly, but many (e.g., 20) instances of it are created which are row-wise shuffles the table. In the original Eperio protocol, the $\mathbf{U}$ and $\mathbf{S}$ columns are individually encrypted for each instance of an Eperio table prior to the election to be used in the post-election audit.

Eperio Protocol. Prior to the election, a set of trustees use a blackbox device (trusted for ballot secrecy but not integrity) to generate a canonical Eperio table for an election with $\mathcal{C}$ candidates and $\mathcal{V}$ voters. All randomness used by the blackbox is deterministically derived from seeds provided by the trustees. The canonical table will be $3 \times \mathcal{C}\mathcal{V}$. The canonical table is provided to the printers for printing the ballots. As in almost all paper-based E2E voting systems, printing is assumed to be a trustworthy process (at least with respect to ballot secrecy— a print audit will establish the correctness of the printed ballots but cannot distinguish between a malicious printer or honest printers being provide the wrong information to print).

A set of ℓ Eperio tables are generated by applying a random permutation to the rows of the canonical table by the blackbox. ℓ is a security parameter where an attack that moves a vote from Alice to Bob will be detected (given adequate receipt checks and print audits) with probability $1 - 2^{-\ell}$. The **U** and **S** columns of each Eperio table is publicly committed prior to voting.

During voting, voters may request a ballot to be print audited (we defer to the paper the discussion of the print audit—we can handle more simply in our protocol). They then fill out their ballots for their selected candidates and have the mark position portion of their ballot recorded (they can keep this lefthand side of the ballot as a receipt). After the election, the trustees input into the blackbox their random seeds and the scanned ballots (**U** and **M**). The blackbox reconstructs all the tables and asserts an **M** column for each Eperio table. These **M** columns and an assertion of the final tally is published.

After the results have been asserted, a random beacon is used to select an ℓ-bit string; one bit for each Eperio table. If the bit for a given table is 0, the blackbox (again reseeded by the trustees) reveals the **U** column and if it is 1, it reveals the **S** column (the **M** column for each is already public). For each **UM**-revealed table, voters can check their receipt and everyone can check for consistency across each table. For each **MS**-revealed table, anyone can check that it matches the asserted tally. The specific reasoning for each of the three possible audits can be found in [18]. For any particular committed Eperio table, if only one of these combinations is opened, privacy is preserved.

5   Our Protocol

Our observation is that the encryption in Eperio is used as a commitment scheme and can be changed to any type of commitments. The authors themselves make this observation suggesting that the perfectly-binding commitment scheme (based on encryption) could be replaced with Pedersen commitments for everlasting privacy. We observe here that the commitments could be replaced with a VSS-style commitment to provide unconditional integrity and everlasting privacy (but sacrificing universal verifiability). Our protocol is given in Fig. 2.

Verification. In our protocol, voters may engage in three checks. The first is a receipt check, which applies to any tables opened **UM**. External auditors may also check with these tables that no ballot is over-voted. The second check is a print audit, which applies to all rows in each table corresponding to a print audited ballot opened **UMS**. The final check is the correctness of the tally, checked with **MS**. Note all **UM** tables are shuffled but otherwise identical versions of the same data, and likewise with all **MS** tables. The basic integrity attack a malicious blackbox can conduct is changing the tally, which constitutes moving marks in the **M**. However it must guess which tables will be opened **UM** and leave these unmodified (or the moved marks will be detectable via a receipt check), and guess exactly which tables will be opened **MS** to move the marks (or the tally will be unmodified, or inconsistent across tables). The probability of guessing correctly is $2^{-\ell}$ where ℓ is the number of tables. For $\ell = 20$ (a parameter used in Scantegrity for effectively the same purposes), the probability of guessing

Pre-Casting

1. Voters register with a local election authority. Issues of voter registration fraud are handled by the EA and are beyond the scope of this work.
2. The EA publishes the number of candidates C and number of ballots to print (e.g., $2 \cdot V$ where V is the voting age population and the scalar 2 allows for, on expectation, one print audit per voter). The EA sets security parameter ℓ.
3. The blackbox uses local randomness to create the canonical Eperio table (which is provided to the printers) and ℓ permutations of it. It then uses VSS to commit the permuted tables to the shareholders, cell by cell. Each table's format and index is published. Upon completion, the shareholders purge the memory of the blackbox.

Vote Casting and Tallying

1. Voters show up and register at the designated voting locations. For each voter, the EA will give the voter a paper ballot, such as the one in Figure 1, assuming they have not voted already.
2. The voter may optionally choose to print audit the ballot. The scanner notes the serial number and its status as audited. The ballot is voided for voting purposes, and the voter is given the next ballot with the same option to audit or vote.
3. Once the voter decides to vote, she marks her ballot and destroys the portion of the ballot containing the candidate ordering. The other portion, containing the serial number and marked position, is copied by the scanner and the original is kept by the voter as a privacy-preserving receipt.
4. After the election, the scanners publish what they received: the **M** column of the canonical table.
5. A quorum of at least k honest shareholders submit their shares of all tables to the blackbox, which reconstructs the canonical table (by sorting each Eperio table and checking for consistency). It also takes as input the scanner data. It outputs an asserted **M** column for each of the ℓ tables and an asserted final tally. The shareholders publish the output and purge the blackbox's memory.

Audit

1. An unpredictable ℓ-bit value is publicly generated by a beacon (e.g., using stock prices [14]).
2. For bit i of the beacon value, a quorum of at least k honest shareholders publish their shares of each cell in the **U** column in the i-th Eperio table if the bit is 0, and each cell in the **S** column if the bit is 1. For print audited ballots (only), they publish both the **U** and **S** cells.
3. The shareholders securely delete all unused shares.

Fig. 2. Our variant of Eperio using VSS.

correct is less than a thousandth of a percentage. Importantly, this probability is independent of the adversary's computational power.

Discussion: Minimizing blackbox usage. The shareholders in our scheme are involved in three phases of the protocol: (1) preelection to use the blackbox to instantiate the election data, (2) after the election to use the blackbox to assert the mark column for each table, and (3) after the challenge to open up the data. In original Eperio, the blackbox must be used in all three steps. In our protocol, (3) can be accomplished by the shareholders directly without requiring the blackbox. In a variation of our protocol, we could also eliminate the blackbox from step (2). In step 2, the blackbox is required to permute a list of marks. The shareholders could do this directly if in step (1), the blackbox gave them each (in a specified order) a permutation to apply such that the composition of all these permutations is the permutation that was used. The issue is that this requres n-out-of-n shareholders in step (2) instead of k (however only k are required in step 3).[2]

6   Proof of Security Sketch

In our security proof sketch, we will reduce a breaking of either privacy or integrity to the breaking of one or more properties of the VSS scheme. We assume that the blackbox's computations are unobservable, and that the broadcast and private channels between shareholders are secure. In practice, these channels need not introduce extra cryptographic (and hence computational) assumptions, since they can be implemented as physical channels such as trusted couriers. In short, breaking either privacy or integrity will imply that strictly more than half of shareholders are malicious. Put differently, if a majority of shareholders collude (violating our assumptions), then they can determine how each voter voted (link ballot IDs to candidates voted for) and can modify the tally to anything they want and have it accepted by the verification step. If the blackbox assumption fails, the adversary can determine how each voter voted but cannot undetectably modify the tally.

6.1   Privacy

It was shown in Eperio [18] that violating privacy reduces to a number of assumptions including breaking the *hiding* property of the commitment. Since we effectively only change the commitment scheme, we can ask ourselves: "If a cabal of malicious shareholders, auditors and voters collude, can they break the hiding property of the VSS-commitment?" Assuming, as always, that the number of malicious shareholders is a strict minority, the answer to the above question is no.

We do not pursue a full simulation-based proof but we comment that VSS-commitments have an additional property that should streamline such a proof,

---

[2] Future work might explore the possibility of giving each shareholder a matrix that interpolates to the correct permutation matrix under the sequential composition of any k-out-of-n interpolations.

relative to the computational commitments used in Eperio. As a cut-and-choose protocol, Eperio faces a standard problem of simulateability: as the challenge space grows, the ability for the simulator to anticipate the correct challenge decreases exponentially (if it rewinds the verifier, it must do it an exponentially-increasing number of times which is not permissible). This can be side-stepped by, say, letting the simulator program the beacon value (by running it through a random oracle) or by repeating the protocol with one-bit challenges. In our case, a VSS-commitment is effectively a trapdoor commitment scheme for any majority of the shareholders. During the audit phase, the simulator can open a commitment in such a way that is perfectly consistent with any tally constraints imposed onto it.

Finally, we must also take care that each random choice (permutation in the tables) is truly random and not the result of a deterministic random generator (as in the original Eperio) or else the the permutations will not have a perfectly uniform distributed (which could be distinguished by an unbounded adversary). We modify Eperio along these lines—the shareholders do not contribute randomness, rather they remember shares of the randomness used (in the form of shuffled tables which can be resorted to recover the permutation).

6.2   Integrity

As in Eperio, the integrity of the election is reduced to a number of assumptions including the *binding* property of the commitment. We have replaced the commitment used by VSS, and in Sect. 4.1 we have argued that VSS has properties which corresponds to the binding property of a commitment scheme.

The auditing process remains the same. For each of the permuted Eperio tables, an auditor will ask the shareholders to open the commitments in such a way that corresponds to the three audits, as discussed in Sect. 4.2. Assuming that the number of malicious shareholders are strictly less than half, the VSS binding property guarantees that they cannot change the commitment that has been successfully executed.

In fact, let us suppose that the malicious shareholders can arbitrarily control where the marks go in the permuted Eperio tables. However, since there is at least one honest shareholder, the malicious shareholders do not know how to consistently mark the votes. Therefore, with high probability increasing exponentially to one in the number of Eperio tables, either a voter will detect that his vote is inconsistent with his receipt when the U columns are opened during the auditing process, or an auditor will discover inconsistencies across different Eperio tables opened the same way. In either way, the malicious shareholders' cheating is detected.

7   Conclusion

We present a system, based on Eperio, that offers integrity and ballot secrecy against computationally unbounded adversaries, regardless of whether such an adversary is a voter, verifier, or election trustee. Further, our system enables voters to cast paper-based ballots, such as an optical scan ballot overlay as used in Scantegrity II or a permutation-style optical scan ballot as used in Prêt à Voter. Once the ballot is cast, the voter may leave and does not have to participate in tallying the election (in contrast to the other category of systems providing unconditional security: boardroom voting schemes).

To be even-handed, we point out that our system introduces several drawbacks. We rely on private and broadcast channels which, in practice, require computational cryptography, thereby negating information-theoretic security. We have argued that these channels may be implemented physically as untappable channels and in fact, for elections such as the Scantegrity II municipal election at Takoma Park, MD, election officials did meet in person in the same room to set-up the election and to compute the final tally. Like other paper ballot systems, the physical ballots are assumed to be unforgeable (therefore malicious voters cannot repudiate a correct audit) and we trust the EAs to not peek at the printed physical ballots before issuing them to voters (which would break privacy). Both of these issues could be mitigated to a large extent by using Scantegrity II ballots, however in Scantegrity II the scanner learns how the vote was cast (as it is a cryptographic overlay and not a replacement system).

Most importantly in terms of drawbacks, our system removes the ability for voters to independently verify the election results. They must trust that a majority of shareholders are honest. While we have no data on how many voters do a full cryptographic check of the election results in a typical E2E-verifiable election, we expect that many will already defer to someone else to check (whether by running their software without validating it or simply believing their assertions). That said, universal verification provides the agility to decide who you trust after the election and even do it yourself if you do not adequately trust anyone else who can perform the check. We are not advocating that unconditional security trumps universal verification, but we believe it is important to provide viable solutions for both sides of this trade-off. This way, readers can decide which is most appropriate for their election requirements.

Acknowledgements. We thank Claude Crépeau for helpful insights. We thank the anonymous reviewers who pointed out relevant work, suggested interesting ideas, and showed us where our paper needed more clarity. The second author acknowledges funding for this work from NSERC and FQRNT.

References

1. Adida, B.: Helios: web-based open-audit voting. In: USENIX Security (2008)
2. Bell, S., Benaloh, J., Byrne, M.D., Debeauvoir, D., Eakin, B., Kortum, P., McBurnett, N., Pereira, O., Stark, P.B., Wallach, D.S., Fisher, G., Montoya, J., Parker, M., Winn, M.: Star-vote: a secure, transparent, auditable, and reliable voting system. JETS **1**, 8 (2013)
3. Benaloh, J.: Simple verifiable elections. In: EVT (2006)
4. Cohen, J.D., Fisher, M.J.: A robust and verifiable cryptographically secure election scheme. In: SFCS (1985)

5. Broadbent, A., Tapp, A.: Information-theoretically secure voting without an honest majority. In: WOTE (2008)
6. Burton, C., Culnane, C., Schneider, S.: Verifiable electronic voting in practice: the use of vvote in the victorian state election. In: IEEE Security and Privacy (2016)
7. Carback, R.T., Chaum, D., Clark, J., Conway, J., Essex, A., Hernson, P.S., Mayberry, T., Popoveniuc, S., Rivest, R.L., Shen, E., Sherman, A.T., Vora, P.L.: Scantegrity II election at Takoma Park. In: USENIX Security Symposium (2010)
8. Chaum, D.: Elections with unconditionally-secret ballots and disruption equivalent to breaking RSA. In: Barstow, D., et al. (eds.) EUROCRYPT 1988. LNCS, vol. 330, pp. 177–182. Springer, Heidelberg (1988). https://doi.org/10.1007/3-540-45961-8_15
9. Chaum, D.: Secret-ballot receipts: true voter-verifiable elections. IEEE Secur. Priv. **2**(1), 38–47 (2004)
10. Chaum, D., Carback, R., Clark, J., Essex, A., Popoveniuc, S., Rivest, R.L., Ryan, P.Y.A., Shen, E., Sherman, A.T.: Scantegrity II: end-to-end verifiability for optical scan election systems using invisible ink confirmation codes. In: EVT (2008)
11. Chaum, D., Essex, A., Carback, R., Clark, J., Popoveniuc, S., Sherman, A.T., Vora, P.: scantegrity: end-to-end voter verifiable optical-scan voting. IEEE Secur. Priv. **6**(3), 40–46 (2008)
12. Chaum, D., Ryan, P.Y.A., Schneider, S.: A practical voter-verifiable election scheme. In: di Vimercati, S.C., Syverson, P., Gollmann, D. (eds.) ESORICS 2005. LNCS, vol. 3679, pp. 118–139. Springer, Heidelberg (2005). https://doi.org/10.1007/11555827_8
13. Chevallier-Mames, B., Fouque, P.-A., Pointcheval, D., Stern, J., Traoré, J.: On some incompatible properties of voting schemes. In: Chaum, D., Jakobsson, M., Rivest, R.L., Ryan, P.Y.A., Benaloh, J., Kutylowski, M., Adida, B. (eds.) Towards Trustworthy Elections. LNCS, vol. 6000, pp. 191–199. Springer, Heidelberg (2010). https://doi.org/10.1007/978-3-642-12980-3_11
14. Clark, J., Hengartner, U.: On the use of financial data as a random beacon. In: EVT/WOTE (2010)
15. Cramer, R., Franklin, M., Schoenmakers, B., Yung, M.: Multi-authority secret-ballot elections with linear work. In: Maurer, U. (ed.) EUROCRYPT 1996. LNCS, vol. 1070, pp. 72–83. Springer, Heidelberg (1996). https://doi.org/10.1007/3-540-68339-9_7
16. Cramer, R., Gennaro, R., Schoenmakers, B.: A secure and optimally efficient multi-authority election scheme. In: Fumy, W. (ed.) EUROCRYPT 1997. LNCS, vol. 1233, pp. 103–118. Springer, Heidelberg (1997). https://doi.org/10.1007/3-540-69053-0_9
17. Demirel, D., van de Graaf, J., dos Santos Araujo, R.S.: Improving Helios with everlasting privacy towards the public. In: EVT/WOTE (2012)
18. Essex, A., Clark, J., Hengartner, U., Adams, C.: Eperio: mitigating technical complexity in cryptographic election verification. In: EVT/WOTE (2010)
19. Gallegos-Garcia, G., Iovino, V., Rial, A., Ronne, P.B., Ryan, P.Y.A.: (Universal) unconditional verifiability in e-voting without trusted parties. Technical report, IACR Eprint Report 2016/975 (2016)
20. Garay, J., Givens, C., Ostrovsky, R., Raykov, P.: Broadcast (and round) efficient verifiable secret sharing. In: ICITS (2014)

21. Goldwasser, S., Kalaj, Y.: On the (in)security of the Fiat-Shamir paradigm. In: FOCS (2003)
22. Hao, F., Zieliński, P.: A 2-round anonymous veto protocol. In: Christianson, B., Crispo, B., Malcolm, J.A., Roe, M. (eds.) Security Protocols 2006. LNCS, vol. 5087, pp. 202–211. Springer, Heidelberg (2009). https://doi.org/10.1007/978-3-642-04904-0_28
23. Henry, K., Stinson, D.R., Sui, J.: The effectiveness of receipt-based attacks on threeballot. IEEE TIFS **4**(4), 699–707 (2009)
24. Hosp, B., Vora, P.L.: An information-theoretic model of voting systems. Math. Comput. Model. **48**, 1628–1645 (2008)
25. Kiayias, A., Yung, M.: Self-tallying elections and perfect ballot secrecy. In: Naccache, D., Paillier, P. (eds.) PKC 2002. LNCS, vol. 2274, pp. 141–158. Springer, Heidelberg (2002). https://doi.org/10.1007/3-540-45664-3_10
26. Kiayias, A., Zacharias, T., Zhang, B.: End-to-end verifiable elections in the standard model. Technical report 2015/346, IACR Eprint Report (2015)
27. Locher, P., Haenni, R.: Verifiable internet elections with everlasting privacy and minimal trust. In: Haenni, R., Koenig, R.E., Wikström, D. (eds.) VOTELID 2015. LNCS, vol. 9269, pp. 74–91. Springer, Cham (2015). https://doi.org/10.1007/978-3-319-22270-7_5
28. Locher, P., Haenni, R., Koenig, R.E.: Coercion-resistant internet voting with everlasting privacy. In: Clark, J., Meiklejohn, S., Ryan, P.Y.A., Wallach, D., Brenner, M., Rohloff, K. (eds.) FC 2016. LNCS, vol. 9604, pp. 161–175. Springer, Heidelberg (2016). https://doi.org/10.1007/978-3-662-53357-4_11
29. Malkhi, D., Margo, O., Pavlov, E.: E-voting without 'Cryptography'. In: Blaze, M. (ed.) FC 2002. LNCS, vol. 2357, pp. 1–15. Springer, Heidelberg (2003). https://doi.org/10.1007/3-540-36504-4_1
30. Mannan, M., Kim, B.H., Ganjali, A., Lie, D.: Unicorn: two-factor attestation for data security. In: CCS (2011)
31. Moran, T., Naor, M.: Receipt-free universally-verifiable voting with everlasting privacy. In: CRYPTO (2006)
32. Moran, T., Naor, M.: Split-ballot voting: everlasting privacy with distributed trust. In: CCS (2007)
33. Neff, C.A.: A verifiable secret shuffle and its application to e-voting. In: CCS (2001)
34. Popoveniuc, S., Hosp, B.: An introduction to punchscan. In: WOTE (2006)
35. Rabin, T., Ben-Or, M.: Verifiable secret sharing and multiparty protocols with honest majority. In: Proceedings of the Twenty-first Annual ACM Symposium on Theory of Computing, STOC 1989, New York, NY, USA, pp. 73–85. ACM (1989)
36. Riva, B., Ta-Shma, A.: Bare-handed electronic voting with pre-processing. In: Proceedings of the USENIX Workshop on Accurate Electronic Voting Technology, EVT 2007, Berkeley, CA, USA, pp. 15–15. USENIX Association (2007)
37. Rivest, R.L., Smith, W.D.: Three voting protocols: threeballot, VAV, and twin. In: EVT (2007)
38. Schoenmakers, B.: A simple publicly verifiable secret sharing scheme and its application to electronic voting. In: Wiener, M. (ed.) CRYPTO 1999. LNCS, vol. 1666, pp. 148–164. Springer, Heidelberg (1999). https://doi.org/10.1007/3-540-48405-1_10
39. Schoenmakers, B.: Fully auditable electronic secret-ballot elections. Xootic Mag. **8**, 5 (2000)

40. Stadler, M.: Publicly verifiable secret sharing. In: Maurer, U. (ed.) EUROCRYPT 1996. LNCS, vol. 1070, pp. 190–199. Springer, Heidelberg (1996). https://doi.org/10.1007/3-540-68339-9_17

41. Zagórski, F., Carback, R.T., Chaum, D., Clark, J., Essex, A., Vora, P.L.: Remotegrity: design and use of an end-to-end verifiable remote voting system. In: Jacobson, M., Locasto, M., Mohassel, P., Safavi-Naini, R. (eds.) ACNS 2013. LNCS, vol. 7954, pp. 441–457. Springer, Heidelberg (2013). https://doi.org/10.1007/978-3-642-38980-1_28

Trusted Smart Contracts

Findel: Secure Derivative Contracts
for Ethereum

Alex Biryukov, Dmitry Khovratovich, and Sergei Tikhomirov[✉]

SnT, University of Luxembourg, Esch-sur-Alzette, Luxembourg
alex.biryukov@uni.lu, khovratovich@gmail.com,
sergey.s.tikhomirov@gmail.com

Abstract. Blockchain-based smart contracts are considered a promising technology for handling financial agreements securely. In order to realize this vision, we need a formal language to unambiguously describe contract clauses. We introduce Findel – a purely declarative financial domain-specific language (DSL) well suited for implementation in blockchain networks. We implement an Ethereum smart contract that acts as a marketplace for Findel contracts and measure the cost of its operation. We analyze challenges in modeling financial agreements in decentralized networks and outline directions for future work (See the author's post-print at https://orbilu.uni.lu/handle/10993/30975 and the related source code at https://github.com/cryptolu/findel).

Keywords: Blockchain · Smart contracts · Financial engineering · Domain-specific language

1 Introduction

Financial derivatives – contracts defined in terms of other contracts – play a major role in modern economy[1]. Financial industry lacks a universal domain-specific language. Natural language is unsuitable for expressing contracts due to its inherent ambiguity. An influential paper [JES00] is one of many attempts to create a rigorous DSL that would mitigate disputes and stimulate automated processing of complex derivatives. It leverages ideas from functional programming and uses a succinct set of basic building blocks to express financial agreements. A key feature of this notation is composability: new indefinitely complex derivatives can be defined based on existing ones. Due to their nested structure, contracts in this DSL are well-suited for automated processing, including valuation. The authors do not specify an enforcement mechanism though: execution is performed by an implicit environment. This work forms the basis for research [Gai11, Sch14] and commercial [FSNB09, Mor16] projects.

The idea of smart contracts – computer programs for (semi-)automatic enforcement of agreements – dates back to mid-1990s [Sza97]. Blockchain networks, notably Ethereum, became the first practical implementation of this idea and fueled interest in the concept [dC16]. Ethereum is a network of mutually

---

[1] The derivatives market is comparable in size to the world's GDP. The gross market value of all outstanding over-the-counter derivatives is $20.7 trillion [Bis16] (2016). The world GDP in 2015 is $73,9 trillion [Wor16].

© International Financial Cryptography Association 2017
M. Brenner et al. (Eds.): FC 2017 Workshops 2017, LNCS 10323, pp. 453–467, 2017.
https://doi.org/10.1007/978-3-319-70278-0_28

distrusting nodes, which nevertheless establish consensus on the results of computations without the need of a trusted third party.

An obvious use case for blockchain-based smart contracts is to securely manage financial agreements. A naive approach to doing so is to encode the entire logic of an agreement inside a smart contract. Expressing complex clauses in a general-purpose programming language, like Ethereum's Solidity, is error-prone [ABC16, Sir16]. We propose a safer approach that separates the description of a contract from its execution. A user only defines what a contract *is* ("I owe you \$10 tomorrow"), not *how* it is executed ("if the timestamp is greater than t_0, ..."). The entire execution logic is implemented inside a smart contract, which is executed by nodes of a blockchain network. Thus we take the best of both worlds: unambiguity and composability of a concise declarative DSL, and trustless execution of blockchain-based smart contracts.

We introduce **Findel** (Financial Derivatives Language) – a declarative financial DSL (Sect. 2) capable of expressing most common derivatives (Appendix A). We implement an Ethereum contract that manages Findel contracts (Sect. 3) and prove our approach viable in terms of cost (Sect. 4).

2   Findel Contracts Syntax

2.1   Definitions

Definition 1. *A **Findel contract**[2] C is a tuple (D, I, O), where D is the **description**, I is the **issuer**, and O is the **owner** (collectively called parties).*

Definition 2. *A **description** of a Findel contract is a tree with **basic primitives** as leaves and **composite primitives** as internal nodes. The following BNF grammar defines primitives:*

$\langle basic \rangle ::= $ Zero $|$ One ($\langle currency \rangle$)

$\langle scale \rangle ::= $ Scale ($\langle number \rangle$, $\langle primitive \rangle$)

$\langle scaleObs \rangle ::= $ ScaleObs ($\langle address \rangle$, $\langle primitive \rangle$)

$\langle give \rangle ::= $ Give ($\langle primitive \rangle$)

$\langle and \rangle ::= $ And ($\langle primitive \rangle$, $\langle primitive \rangle$)

$\langle or \rangle ::= $ Or ($\langle primitive \rangle$, $\langle primitive \rangle$)

$\langle if \rangle ::= $ If ($\langle address \rangle$, $\langle primitive \rangle$, $\langle primitive \rangle$)

$\langle timebound \rangle ::= $ Timebound ($\langle timestamp \rangle$, $\langle timestamp \rangle$, $\langle primitive \rangle$)

$\langle composite \rangle ::= \langle scale \rangle | \langle scaleObs \rangle | \langle give \rangle | \langle and \rangle | \langle or \rangle | \langle if \rangle | \langle timebound \rangle$

$\langle primitive \rangle ::= \langle basic \rangle | \langle composite \rangle$

---

[2] We may refer to Findel contracts simply as contracts, when the distinction between them and Ethereum smart contracts is clear from the context.

We distinguish between composite and basic primitives, because the former contain other primitives as sub-nodes while the latter do not. *Currency*, *number*, *address*, and *timestamp* are implementation dependent data types. D and I can not be modified after a contract is created.

A financial company typically has templates for common contracts. Parties who wish to sign an agreement write their names on a copy of a template and sign it, making it unique and legally binding. In our model, Findel contracts represent signed copies while their descriptions represent blank templates.

Traditional contracts usually contain clauses that regulate sub-ideal situations, i.e., a breach of contract. Findel does not distinguish between "ideal" and "sub-ideal" situations. All right and obligations are expressed uniformly. Section 3.3 discusses issues related to contract enforcement.

Table 1 informally defines the primitives' execution semantics.

Table 1. Findel contract primitives

Primitive	Informal semantics
Basic	
Zero	Do nothing
One($currency$)	Transfer 1 unit of $currency$ from the issuer to the owner
Composite	
Scale(k, c)	Multiply all payments of c by a constant factor k
ScaleObs($addr, c$)	Multiply all payments of c by a factor obtained from $addr$
Give(c)	Swap parties of c
And(c_1, c_2)	Execute c_1 and then execute c_2
Or(c_1, c_2)	Give the owner the right to execute either c_1 or c_2 (not both)
If($addr, c_1, c_2$)	If b is true, execute c_1, else execute c_2, where b is a boolean value obtained from $addr$
Timebound(t_0, t_1, c)	Execute c, if the current timestamp is within $[t_0, t_1]$

Table 2 illustrates the composability of Findel[3].

2.2 Execution Model

Findel contracts have the following lifecycle:

1. The first party **issues** the contract by specifying D, becoming its issuer. This is a mere declaration of the issuer's desire to conclude an agreement and entails no obligations.

---

[3] INF is a symbol representing infinite time, i.e., $t_0 < INF$ for every t_0. δ is an implementation dependent constant intended for handling imperfect precision of time signal in distributed networks.

Table 2. Examples of custom Findel contracts

Contract	Definition
$\text{At}(t_0, c)$	$\text{Timebound}(t_0 - \delta, t_0 + \delta, c)$
$\text{Before}(t_0, c)$	$\text{Timebound}(now, t_0, c)$
$\text{After}(t_0, c)$	$\text{Timebound}(t_0, INF, c)$
$\text{Sell}(n, CURR, c)$	$\text{And}(\text{Give}(\text{Scale}(n, \text{One}(CURR))), c)$

2. The second party **joins** the contract, becoming its owner. As a result, both parties accept certain rights and obligations.
3. The contract is **executed** immediately as follows:
   (a) Let the root node of the contract's description be the current node.
   (b) If the current node is either `Or` or `Timebound` with $t_0 > now$, postpone the execution: issue a new Findel contract with the same parties and the current node as root. The owner can later demand its execution.
   (c) Otherwise, execute all sub-nodes recursively[4].
   (d) Delete the contract.

The execution outcome is fully determined by description D, execution time t, and external data S retrieved at time t.

2.3 Example

Suppose Alice sells to Bob a zero-coupon (i.e., paying no interest) bond that pays \$11 in one year for \$10: s

$$c_{zcb} = \text{And}(\text{Give}(\text{Scale}(10, \text{One}(USD))), \text{At}(now+1 \text{ years}, \text{Scale}(11, \text{One}(USD))))$$

We now show how c_{zcb} is executed step by step.

1. And executes; Bob temporarily owns two new contracts:

Alice's contracts	
Alice's balance	100
Bob's contracts	$\text{Give}(\text{Scale}(10, \text{One}(USD)))$
	$\text{At}(now + 1 \text{ years}, \text{Scale}(11, \text{One}(USD)))$
Bob's balance	10

2. Give executes; Alice owns a new contract:

Alice's contracts	$\text{Scale}(10, \text{One}(USD))$
Alice's balance	100
Bob's contracts	$\text{At}(now + 1 \text{ years}, \text{Scale}(11, \text{One}(USD)))$
Bob's balance	10

---

[4] In case of `Or`, execute exactly one of the sub-nodes, according to the owner-submitted value indicating the choice; delete the other one. It is the only primitive that requires an additional user-supplied argument for execution.

3. Scaled One transfers $10 go from Bob to Alice:

Alice's contracts	
Alice's balance	110
Bob's contracts	At(now + 1 years, Scale(11, One(USD)))
Bob's balance	0

4. In one year Bob claims $11 from Alice:

Alice's contracts	
Alice's balance	99
Bob's contracts	
Bob's balance	11

3   Implementation

We develop an Ethereum smart contract, referred to as marketplace, that keeps track of users' balances and lets them create, trade, and execute Findel contracts. The Findel DSL is network-agnostic and can be implemented on top of any blockchain with sufficient programming capabilities.

3.1   Ethereum Overview

Ethereum is a decentralized smart contracts platform [But14, Woo14]. Ethereum full nodes store data, perform computations, and maintain consensus about the state of all accounts using a proof-of-work mechanism similar to that in Bitcoin. Programs (Ethereum smart contracts) are stored on the blockchain as Ethereum virtual machine (EVM) bytecode, a Turing-complete language. Programmers write contracts in high-level languages targeting EVM, most popular being Solidity and Serpent (we use the former).

A contract can call other contracts' functions and send them units of Ether – the Ethereum native cryptocurrency. To launch a particular function of a contract, a user must send a well-formed transaction to the Ethereum network.

Each EVM operation has a fixed cost in *gas*. A user pays upfront for the maximum amount of gas the computation is expected to consume and gets a partial refund after a successful execution. If an exception (including "out of gas") occurs, all changes are reverted, but the gas is not refunded.

3.2   Implementation Details

Users and Balances. We implement the objects defined in Sect. 2.1 with struct data types `Description` and `Fincontract`. We also introduce the `User` type that contains the user's Ethereum address and balances in all supported currencies. Users, descriptions and contracts are stored in their respective mappings (a generic key-value storage type in Solidity) in the marketplace's storage.

The ultimate effect of every financial agreement is changing the parties' balances (with clauses specifying when and under what conditions it should occur).

We stick to a naive approach: each user is assigned an array of balances for each supported currency. Although easily implementable, it introduces a single point of failure: the marketplace holds users' deposits.

The only primitive that actually transfers value is One. The `enforcePayment` function implements its execution. It subtracts a given amount in a given currency from the issuer's balance and adds it to the owner's balance. Our current implementation does not enforce any constraints on users' balances that would prevent them from building up too much debt.

Ownership Transfer. In addition to `issuer` and `owner` (see Definition 1), a `Fincontract` contains an auxiliary `proposedOwner` field. On contract creation, `issuer`, `owner`, and `proposedOwner` are initialized to `msg.sender`. To transfer ownership, the owner sets `proposedOwner` either to the address of the proposed new owner or to `0x0`. Only the proposed owner can (but does not have to) `join` the contract; `0x0` means anyone can do so[5].

Data Sources and Gateways. Ethereum contracts are intentionally isolated from the broader Internet and can not pull data from the Web, as it can not be consistently replicated [Gre16]. Asynchronous requests usually solve the problem: a smart contract records an Ethereum event with request parameters properly encoded. A daemon process at an Ethereum node listens for such events, parses requests, and sends them to the Web. The responses are then sent to the requesting smart contract on behalf of an Ethereum account affiliated with the daemon. The submitted data may be accompanied by a proof of authenticity (say, digital signature on a pre-approved public key)[6].

Financial derivatives often use external data. To prevent a malicious or careless user from creating a Findel contract using untrusted sources, we need to guarantee data authenticity.

Definition 3. *A **gateway** is a smart contract that conforms to the API:*

- *int **getValue()** Get the latest observed value[7].*
- *uint **getTimestamp()** Get the timestamp at which the latest value was observed.*
- *bytes **getProof()** Get the authenticity proof for the latest value.*
- ***update()** Update the value.*

---

[5] Beware of front-runners: Bob can monitor the network and try to join a contract as soon as he sees Alice's attempt to do so. Depending on the network latency and miner's behavior, either transaction can be confirmed.

[6] BTCRelay is a prominent example: users submit Bitcoin block headers to a smart contract, which implies their authenticity from the validity of easily verifiable proof-of-work. After a header is stored on the Ethereum blockchain, users check with a Merkle proof that the Bitcoin block contains a given transaction.

[7] For simplicity, we only consider 256-bit integers as observable values. Boolean values can be trivially simulated via integers.

A gateway connects to an external data source and stores the latest value observed along with the time of observation, and, optionally, a cryptographic proof of authenticity. We do not specify the type of proof a gateway provides. Possible options include Oraclize [Ora16]/TLSNotary [Tls16] and Reality Keys [Rea16].

The marketplace queries a gateway at execution time, if necessary. If the value is fresh and the proof is valid, the execution proceeds, otherwise it is aborted and all changes are reverted. Since a Findel contract may use multiple gateways, the owner is advised to update them all shortly before execution.

A possible improvement would be for a gateway to store not only the latest observed value, but a sequence of historical data. This would allow for more straightforward modeling of derivatives that depend on multiple data points, such as barrier options (execute either c_1 or c_2 depending on whether an observable value touches a pre-defined threshold between acquisition and maturity).

We assume that the original data sources (e.g., feeds of reputable financial media) are trustworthy. An extra safety catch would be to query multiple sources, exclude outliers and return an aggregated value. Authenticity of data sources is guaranteed by a secure connection (e.g., TLS) and the existing PKI for authentication ([CF14,LC16] propose blockchain-based PKI architectures).

Gateways without publicly available source code should not be trusted.

Execution Implementation. The executeRecursively function implements the execution logic defined in Sect. 2.2 and returns true if executed completely (without creating new contracts) and false otherwise. The execution of an expired contract ($t_0 < now$) returns true unconditionally[8] and deletes the contract[9]. Every step in the life cycle of a Findel contract issues a system-wide notification (Event), allowing users to keep track of contracts they are interested in.

Our implementation deviates from the model (Sect. 2.1) in that the execution of contracts is not guaranteed. Ethereum contracts can not act on their own: the owner must issue a transaction to trigger execution. The owner may be unable to do so due to either opportunistic behavior, or technical problems, such as loss of connectivity or lack of ether. Thus we presume that Findel contracts are not guaranteed to execute[10]. We discuss this issue in Sect. 3.3.

We model unbounded Findel contracts (i.e., with INF as the upper time bound) using a global *expiration* constant inside the marketplace contract.

---

[8] By definition, an expired contract is equivalent to Zero.

[9] An expired contract should also be deleted even if its owner is offline forever. Our current implementation does not handle the latter case, though it may be considered an attack vector due to increasing storage usage. A possible approach is for a marketplace to offer rewards for keeping track of expired contracts and triggering their deletion.

[10] Compare to [JES00]: "If you acquire *(c1 or c2)* you must immediately acquire either *c1* or *c2* (but not both)". We can not force a user to make this decision.

Every Findel contract in the Ethereum implementation can only be executed within *expiration* time units after creation (e.g., 10 years).

3.3   Possible Improvements

We now discuss the shortcomings of our model and ways to improve it.

Enforcement. As mentioned in Sect. 3.2, Findel contracts are not guaranteed to execute. At first sight, it is a major problem, as contract must impose obligations on parties. In traditional finance, a trusted third party and, ultimately, the state law enforcement are responsible for punishing violators. The closest we can arguably get to enforcement is a conditional penalty implemented inside a Findel contract itself.

Assume Alice issues and Bob joins the following contract:

$$C = Before(t_0, Or(Give(One(USD)), Give(One(EUR))))$$

C obliges Bob to give Alice either \$1 or €1 before time t_0. If Bob fails to make a choice on time, Alice does not get the money she was planning to receive[11]. To prevent it, Alice attaches a "penalty" clause:

$$P = After(t_0, If(c_{executed}, Zero, Scale(2, One(USD))))$$

$c_{executed}$ is the address of a gateway that indicates whether a particular Findel contract was executed. When Bob joins $C_{penalty} = And(C, Give(P))$, Alice obtains the right to claim \$2 from Bob if he fails to fulfil his obligations.

Note that $C_{penalty}$ references $C_{executed}$, which in turn must be aware of $C_{penalty}$. Thus the gateway should be either adjustable (with Alice tuning the gateway with a special transaction) or generic (reports the state of a Findel contract taking its id as an argument).

Defaulting on Debt. A concise financial DSL does not prevent borrowers from defaulting on their debt. It is up to a marketplace to solve this problem.

Requiring a 100% guarantee deposit seems safe, but is questionable from an economical standpoint. People and organizations borrow money to invest it. The no-arbitrage principle states that there is no guaranteed way to make a profit. The investor reward, e.g. interest, is the premium for taking the inevitable risk of business failure. Thus, this approach hardly makes economical sense.

A marketplace can also mimic the fractional reserve banking model by requiring users to always be able to pay at least $n\%$ of their debt and punishing violators (e.g., by withholding their guarantee deposit). It does not solve the problem of defaults completely though. In legacy finance, users have a fixed government-issued identity, allowing banks to maintain a common database of their credit

---

[11] In this particular case, an equivalent contract $Give(Or(One(USD), One(EUR)))$ solves the issue. In more complex cases this is not necessarily the case.

history. In a decentralized setting, users can create a practically indefinite number of identities. A production-ready marketplace should therefore take measures to combat Sybil attacks.

Modeling Balances with Tokens. A more refined approach to modeling users' balances is to use **tokens** – a de-facto standard API [Tok16] for implementing transferable units of value in Ethereum. Tokens are primarily used to represent company shares during so-called initial coin offerings [Ico17]. We assume that tokens can be freely exchanged to any currency the marketplace operates with. Given the address T of the Ethereum token contract, any Ethereum contract can query the balance of any user U, and transfer its tokens (if it has any) to an arbitrary address. Suppose Alice and Bob are token holders. Alice calls a standard API function `approve` to allow Bob to withdraw a certain amount of tokens from her account. Bob later calls `transferFrom` to transfer the tokens. The transfer succeeds if Alice has enough funds.

We suggest the following procedure. A Findel contract's issuer approves the marketplace with the number of tokens he is potentially liable with. The marketplace implements `enforcePayment` by calling `transferFrom` thus trying to withdraw tokens from the issuer and send them to the owner. Certainly, for the execution to complete, the owner must either have enough tokens in the account, or execute another Findel contract to fill it up. Thus we delegate the banking functionality to the token smart contract and free the marketplace from holding and transferring money [Kho16].

Multi-party Contracts. We might want to extend the Findel contracts model to support more than two parties. An example of a three-party contract is buying a car with insurance. A user can only buy a car while simultaneously signing an insurance contract. We can express the two contracts (buyer – car dealer, buyer – insurance company) in Findel DSL, but executing them atomically is non-trivial. A possible way would be to use a gateway that keeps track of the state of Findel contracts. If *insuranceSigned* indicates whether a user joined the insurance contract, then buying with insurance looks like this (assuming CAR is a token representing the ownership over a car):

$$\text{If}(insuranceSigned, \text{And}(\text{Give}(\text{Scale}(P, \text{One}(USD))), \text{One}(CAR))), \text{Zero})$$

Local Client. In order to communicate with a Findel marketplace, users need client-side software. Besides communicating with the Ethereum network, it might also implement other functions:

- Create and store Findel contracts locally.
- Calculate the current value and other properties of Findel contracts based on assumptions about external data (e.g., the €/$ exchange rate is between 1.0 and 1.2) or valuation techniques such as the lattice binomial model [CRR79].

- Keep track of relevant Findel contracts and perform actions depending on their state (e.g., if c_1 gets executed, join c_2).
- Store a predefined list of addresses of trusted gateways, similar to a list of trusted certificate authorities in web browsers.

3.4 Platform Limitations

A Turing-complete programming language does not mean that all a programmer can think of can be implemented inside an Ethereum contract. Gas costs aside, the Ethereum network architecture implies certain limitations.

Lack of Precise Clock. Timing is important for almost all financial contracts. Clock synchronization is a hard problem in decentralized systems, even more so if participants can profit from manipulating timestamps. Blocks in Ethereum are produced every 15 s; block timestamps provide causal ordering. Solidity contains keywords for time units, but timestamps are ultimately controlled by miners.

Imperative Paradigm. Functional programming paradigm is well suited for developing embedded DSLs [Gib13]. The original papers by Peyton Jones et al. as well as all existing implementations of their DSL use functional languages (Haskell [JES00, JE03, vS07], OCaml [Lex00], Scala [Wal12, Cha15]). In contrast, Solidity and Serpent are imperative. Functional languages for Ethereum are in a very early stage of development [FpE17].

Underdeveloped Type System. Ethereum supports neither decimal nor floating-point types[12], which often model amounts of money and currency exchange rates respectively. The only numeric data types in Solidity are integers of various bit lengths. Moreover, Solidity lacks type parameters, which could be useful for Gateways (i.e., `Gateway<int>`).

4 Gas Costs

Every computational step in Ethereum is charged in terms of gas. Despite the use of expensive permanent storage operations, the cost of running our implementation is not prohibitively high for a proof-of-concept.

We measure gas costs of managing common Findel contracts as assessed by the Browser-solidity compiler [Bro16][13] for a marketplace supporting two currencies (referred to as USD and EUR and not tied to any asset). The difference between transaction and execution cost is that the former includes the overhead of creating a transaction (i.e., a call from a client) and the latter does not (i.e., a call from another contract) [Rev16].

---

[12] A likely rationale: rounding issues break consensus.
[13] Solidity version: 0.4.4+commit.4633f3de.Emscripten.clang.

4.1   Setup and Helper Functions

Registering a user implies initializing the user's balances to zero for all supported currencies. For testing purposes, we implement a gateway that uses the current timestamp as data source and calculates a single `keccak256` hash as a dummy authenticity proof (Table 3).

Table 3. Cost of setup and helper functions (in gas units)

Operation	Transaction cost	Execution cost
Create a marketplace smart contract	2221599	1681095
Register a user	79462	58190
Check user's balance	47667	26395
Get contract info	24407	959
Get description info	24706	1258
Update a gateway	36922	15650

4.2   Managing Common Derivatives

In our measurements, we omit cases where parties split the execution cost. We assume that the issuer only pays for contract creation and issuance whereas the owner pays for the execution. For simple Findel contracts, two Ethereum transactions (one from each party) represent the whole lifecycle of a Findel contract. In more complex cases, when a contract executes in multiple steps, we sum up all costs that the owner bears to execute it completely. We also do not account for gateway update costs (Table 4).

Table 4. Cost of handling Findel contracts for common derivatives (in gas units)

Operation	Create and issue		Join and execute	
	Tx cost	Exec cost	Tx cost	Exec cost
One	184239	177967	58493	93602
Currency exchange (fixed rate)	663149	656877	101878	138430
Currency exchange (market rate)	300842	294570	59822	96196
Zero-coupon bond	373783	367511	143891	201750
Bond with two coupons	939566	933294	346871	477100
European option	519628	513356	278191	411103
Binary option	402359	396087	59826	96204

As of January 2017, the gas cost 10^{-9} ether per unit [Eth17]; the price of ether fluctuated around \$10 [Wor17]. That brings the cost of a typical Findel contract operation (10^5–10^6 gas units) to 1.8–18 US cent.

5   Related Work

[Sch13, Hvi10] review financial DSLs and related projects. [STM16, CBB16] explore approaches to smart contract programming languages.

5.1   Composable Contracts by Peyton Jones et al.

Our work is inspired by the composable contracts as defined in [JE03], from which we borrow some of our primitives (Zero, One, Scale, And, Or). It turns out though that this notation is not directly transferable to blockchain environments (at least to Ethereum) due to the way it formalizes temporal conditions (*when*, *until*). Blockchains differ substantially from traditional centralized marketplaces in how they model conditions. For this reason we introduced *If* and Timebound primitives to express causal and temporal conditions respectively.

5.2   Logic Portfolio Theory by Steffen Schuldenzucker

Steffen Schuldenzucker in [Sch16] proposes an axiomatic approach to proving no-arbitrage relationships between contracts based on the notation from [JE03]. Using a rigorously defined algebra of contracts, he proves well-known financial theorems, such as the put-call parity. Formal semantics of Findel can be introduced using a similar approach. This would enable formal verification techniques that could substantially increase confidence in the safety of our language.

5.3   Preliminary Draft by Nick Szabo

Smart contracts pioneer Nick Szabo in [Sza02] presents "a mini-language" that can be characterized as a middle ground between programming and legal speak. The basic building block is a *right* (e.g., to receive $100 now). Rights are combined using well-defined operators (*when, then, also, with* – analogous to our primitives) and *performed* depending on external events. Parties are assumed to have a trusted source of real-world information. The language is not purely declarative: contracts may perform calculations and save values in state variables, which allows for more flexibility[14].

6   Conclusion

Smart contracts in public blockchain networks seem to be a perfect match for modeling financial agreements. Their unique value proposition is trustless execution, which reduces counterparty risks. We introduced Findel – a declarative financial DSL built upon ideas from previous research in financial engineering. Formalizing contract clauses using Findel makes them unambiguous and

---

[14] Szabo makes a case against state variables in general, stating that "they should be avoided unless utterly necessary".

machine-readable. We proved Ethereum to be a suitable platform for trading and executing Findel contracts.

Nevertheless, the whole smart contract field is still in its infancy. Programmers who wish to implement a usable smart contract for handling financial agreements need to be aware of the forthcoming challenges: from fundamental limitations of the blockchain network architecture to imperfect development environment.

A   Examples

- A **fixed-rate currency exchange**: the owner sells €10 for $11.

$$\text{And}(\text{Give}(\text{Scale}(10, \text{One}(EUR))), \text{Scale}(11, \text{One}(USD))$$

- A **market-rate currency exchange**: the owner sells €10 at market rate as reported by the gateway at *addr*.

$$\text{Scale}(10, \text{And}(\text{Give}(\text{One}(EUR)), ScaleObs(addr, \text{One}(USD)))))$$

- A **zero-coupon bond**: the owner receives $100 at t_0.

$$\text{Timebound}(t_0 - \delta, t_0 + \delta, \text{Scale}(100, \text{One}(USD)))$$

- A **bond with coupons**: the owner receives $1000 (face value) in three years (maturity date) and two coupon payments of $50 at regular intervals before the maturity date.

$$\text{And}(\text{At}(\text{now} + 3 \text{ years}, c_{face}), \text{And}(\text{At}(\text{now} + 1 \text{ years}, c_{cpn}), \text{At}(\text{now} + 1 \text{ years}, c_{cpn})))$$

where

$$c_{face} = \text{Scale}(1000, \text{One}(USD)), \quad c_{cpn} = \text{Scale}(50, \text{One}(USD))$$

- A **future** (a **forward**[15]): parties agree to execute the underlying contract c at t_0.

$$\text{Timebound}(t_0 - \delta, t_0 + \delta, c)$$

- An **option**: the owner can choose at (European option) or before (American option) time t_0 whether to execute the underlying contract c.

$$\text{Timebound}(t_0 - \delta, t_0 + \delta, \text{Or}(c, \text{Zero}))$$

$$\text{Timebound}(now, t_0 + \delta, \text{Or}(c, \text{Zero}))$$

- A **binary option**: the owner receives $10 if a predefined event took place at t_0 and nothing otherwise.

$$\text{If}(addr, \text{Scale}(10, \text{One}(USD)), \text{Zero})$$

---

[15] In traditional finance, a future is a standardized contract while a forward is not. This distinction is not relevant for our model.

References

[ABC16]   Atzei, N., Bartoletti, M., Cimoli, T.: A survey of attacks on ethereum smart contracts. IACR Cryptol. ePrint Arch. **2016**, 1007 (2016)

[Bis16]   Statistical release. OTC derivatives statistics at end-june 2016 (2016). https://www.bis.org/publ/otc_hy1611.pdf

[Bro16]   Browser-solidity online compiler (2016). https://ethereum.github.io/browser-solidity/

[But14]   A next-generation smart contract and decentralized application platform (2014). https://github.com/ethereum/wiki/wiki/White-Paper

[CBB16]   Clack, C.D., Bakshi, V.A., Braine, L.: Smart contract templates: foundations, design landscape and research directions. CoRR, abs/1608.00771 (2016)

[CF14]   Yakoubov, S., Fromknecht, C., Velicanu, D.: A decentralized public key infrastructure with identity retention. Cryptology ePrint Archive, Report 2014/803 (2014). http://eprint.iacr.org/2014/803

[Cha15]   Chaudhary, S.: Adventures in financial and software engineering (2015). https://falconair.github.io/2015/01/30/composingcontracts.html

[CRR79]   Cox, J.C., Ross, S.A., Rubinstein, M.: Option pricing: a simplified approach. J. Finan. Econ. **7**(3), 229–263 (1979)

[dC16]   del Castillo, M.: JP Morgan, credit suisse among 8 in latest bank blockchain test (2016). http://www.coindesk.com/jp-morgan-credit-suisse-among-8-in-latest-bank-blockchain-test/

[Eth17]   Ethstats (2017). https://ethstats.net/

[FpE17]   Functional programming for ethereum (2017). https://github.com/fp-ethereum/fp-ethereum

[FSNB09]   Frankau, S., Spinellis, D., Nassuphis, N., Burgard, C.: Commercial uses: going functional on exotic trades. J. Func. Program. **19**(01), 27–45 (2009)

[Gai11]   Gaillourdet, J.-M.: A software language approach to derivative contracts in finance (2011). http://ceur-ws.org/vol-750/yrs06.pdf

[Gib13]   Gibbons, J.: Functional programming for domain-specific languages. In: Zsók, V., Horváth, Z., Csató, L. (eds.) CEFP 2013. LNCS, vol. 8606, pp. 1–28. Springer, Cham (2015). https://doi.org/10.1007/978-3-319-15940-9_1

[Gre16]   Greenspan, G.: Why many smart contract use cases are simply impossible (2016). http://www.coindesk.com/three-smart-contract-misconceptions/

[Hvi10]   Hvitved, T.: A survey of formal languages for contracts. In: Fourth Workshop on Formal Languages and Analysis of Contract-Oriented Software (FLACOS 2010), pp. 29–32. Citeseer (2010)

[Ico17]   Icos, token sales, crowdsales (2017). https://www.smithandcrown.com/icos/

[JE03]   Peyton Jones, S.L., Eber, J.-M.: How to write a financial contract, The Fun of Programming (2003)

[JES00]   Peyton Jones, S.L., Eber, J.-M., Seward, J.: Composing contracts: an adventure in financial engineering, functional pearl. In: ICFP, pp. 280–292. ACM (2000)

[Kho16]   Khovratovich, D.: debt.sol (2016). https://gist.github.com/khovratovich/45f68082b556b45eb64e8e1c3eb82892

[LC16]   Lewison, K., Corella, F.: Backing rich credentials with a blockchain PKI (2016). https://pomcor.com/techreports/BlockchainPKI.pdf

[Lex00]   Ocaml at lexifi (2000). https://www.lexifi.com/blogs/ocaml

[Mor16] Mortensen, S.: Universal contracts (2016). https://github.com/corda/corda/tree/master/experimental/src

[Ora16] Oraclize (2016). http://www.oraclize.it/

[Rea16] Reality keys (2016). https://www.realitykeys.com/

[Rev16] Revere, R.R.: What is the difference between transaction cost and execution cost in browser solidity? (2016). https://ethereum.stackexchange.com/q/5812/5113

[Sch13] Schiller, T.: Financial domain-specific language listing (2013). http://www.dslfin.org/resources.html

[Sch14] Schuldenzucker, S.: Decomposing contracts (2014). http://www.ifi.uzh.ch/ce/people/schuldenzucker/decomposingcontracts.pdf

[Sch16] Schuldenzucker, S.: An axiomatic framework for no-arbitrage relationships in financial derivatives markets (2016). http://www.ifi.uzh.ch/ce/publications/LPT.pdf

[Sir16] Gün Sirer, E.: Thoughts on the dao hack (2016). http://hackingdistributed.com/2016/06/17/thoughts-on-the-dao-hack/

[STM16] Seijas, P.L., Thompson, S., McAdams, D.: Scripting smart contracts for distributed ledger technology. Cryptology ePrint Archive, Report 2016/1156 (2016). http://eprint.iacr.org/2016/1156

[Sza97] Szabo, N.: Formalizing and securing relationships on public networks (1997). http://journals.uic.edu/ojs/index.php/fm/article/view/548

[Sza02] Szabo, N.: A formal language for analyzing contracts (2002). http://nakamotoinstitute.org/contract-language/

[Tls16] Tlsnotary (2016). https://tlsnotary.org/

[Tok16] Ethereum improvement proposal: Token standard (2016). https://github.com/ethereum/EIPs/issues/20

[vS07] van Straaten, A.: Composing contracts (2007). https://web.archive.org/web/20130814194431/http://contracts.scheming.org

[Wal12] Walton, C.: Scala contracts project (2012). https://github.com/channingwalton/scala-contracts/wiki

[Woo14] Wood, G.: Ethereum: a secure decentralised generalised transaction ledger (2014). http://gavwood.com/paper.pdf

[Wor16] Gross domestic product 2015 (2016). http://databank.worldbank.org/data/download/GDP.pdf

[Wor17] Worldcoinindex (2017). https://www.worldcoinindex.com/coin/ethereum

Decentralized Execution of Smart Contracts: Agent Model Perspective and Its Implications

Lin Chen[✉], Lei Xu, Nolan Shah, Zhimin Gao, Yang Lu, and Weidong Shi

Department of Computer Science, University of Houston, Houston, TX 77004, USA
chenlin198662@gmail.com

Abstract. Smart contracts are one of the most important applications of the blockchain. Most existing smart contract systems assume that for executing contract over a network of decentralized nodes, the outcome in accordance with the majority can be trusted. However, we observe that users involved with a smart contract may strategically take actions to manipulate execution of the contract for purpose to increase their own benefits. We propose an agent model, as the underpinning mechanism for contract execution over a network of decentralized nodes and public ledger, to address this problem and discuss the possibility of preventing users from manipulating smart contract execution by applying principles of game theory and agent based analysis.

Keywords: Smart contract · Blockchain · Public ledger · Game theory

1 Introduction

In recent years, there have been papers and articles focusing on improving our understanding of blockchain based crypto-currency using game theory [7,8,16]. The assumption behind these crypto-currency systems, e.g., Bitcoin, is that participating users are financially driven. If a user has no interest in gaining rewards from the system (e.g., mining, executing contract), he/she has no incentive of staying in the system. Therefore, users should not be considered as merely machines that have resources to execute the protocols of such system. By nature, they are more like players/economic agents who attempt to maximize their profits through participation. This motivates the use of game theory to study blockchain-based smart contract and transaction systems. For instance, in this line of research, a recent paper of Kiayias et al. studies mining as a game in Bitcoin and analyzes the best strategy for users [7]. However, little research has been done for understanding the behaviors of smart contract execution over decentralized blockchain and public ledger under agent based model, which is the main focus of this paper.

As such, we consider the strategic behavior of users in smart contracts. Briefly speaking, a smart contract is a computerized transaction protocol that executes the terms of a contract [19]. It could be viewed as a counterpart to a physical-world contract in a decentralized system. Like a contract in the physical world,

© International Financial Cryptography Association 2017
M. Brenner et al. (Eds.): FC 2017 Workshops 2017, LNCS 10323, pp. 468–477, 2017.
https://doi.org/10.1007/978-3-319-70278-0_29

a smart contract may specify different conditions and define the payoffs for users under each condition. The following is a simple example: if a random dice returns 0, then A pays one coin to B; if it returns 1, then B pays A one coin. Though electronic commerce applications or contracts can be supported using centralized systems, smart contract mostly relies on decentralized network of participants where no single participant is necessarily trusted. A hallmark of smart contracts is that enforcement is achieved through consensus.

A smart contract can involve multiple users/participants and large amounts of crypto-currency. Thus, it has the potential to be more critical than mining in pure crypto-currency systems (e.g., Bitcoin), in which only a fixed reward is paid to successful miners. The amount of crypto-currency involved in a contract may be many times and significantly higher than the cost of running the contract itself. Therefore, users involved in a smart contract may strategically take actions to maximize their own profits, which can cause significant problems and cast doubt to the fundamental assumption of smart contract execution model based on consensus or majority accepted outcome.

Considering the example mentioned above, suppose that A represents a set of users. If the random dice returns 0, A has the incentive of lying and claiming that it returns 1, and plays strategically according to the protocols of the system. If the system applies Byzantine agreement protocols or alike to reach consensus, then A plays as the set of malicious nodes in the Byzantine problem who attempt to prevent a consensus on 0 (i.e., A tries to impose a consensus on the wrong value 1 or prevent the entire system from reaching a consensus at all). If the system allows temporary branches and uses the longest chain rule to eventually resolve branches, then A adds a block containing the wrong value of the dice and tries to make it into the longest chain. The strategies that A may take are dependent on the protocols of the system. In this paper, we do not necessarily restrict our attention to one specific protocol or one specific embodiment of smart contract system. Therefore we do not specify the actions of A but rather say whether A lies or not. When we say A lies, we mean A plays strategically to produce contract execution outcome that favors him/her financially regardless the true result of the contract. Otherwise, we say A does not lie or A tells the truth - always producing or accepting the outcome based on truthful execution of the contract. The goal of this paper is to discuss the possibility and feasible strategies to prevent users involved in smart contracts from lying or manipulating contract execution outcome for personal financial gains.

It is worth pointing out that the risk of accepting the rogue outcome of contract execution increases when a large percentage of nodes of a smart contract system have direct or indirect financial involvement in a smart contract. Even for contracts only directly involving few or just two participants, there is a possibility that a subset of these directly involved participants can manipulate the outcome by creating dependent contracts that distributes financial rewards to other nodes of the system if they accept certain contract execution result, a form of bribing in contract execution and outcome confirmation. There is no trivial solution or prevention mechanism to this problem. In the worst case, every node may have either direct or indirect conflict of interests in terms of contract execution. In addition, the anonymous nature of smart contract users/accounts and crypto-currency wallets make it almost impossible to detect conflict of interests when comes to contract execution.

Our Contributions. We suggest that participants of a smart contract based system using blockchain and public ledger be considered as economic agents. As a consequence, execution of smart contract over a network of untrusted nodes using blockchain is better to be understood and studied under the framework of agents with the assumption that their participation is motivated by self-interests and financial benefits. When participants of a smart contract system (e.g., miners, nodes for executing contracts) are involved in a smart contract, they may have incentives and engage in negative behaviors (e.g., lying or manipulation) to maximize their own interests. These include producing or accepting contract execution outcome that favors themselves by ignoring or discarding results of truthful execution of the contract. Furthermore, we discuss the feasibility of preventing such behaviors through proper design of smart contract based systems.

We show that, in general, there is no guaranteed way to prevent users from lying or engaging in bad behaviors in a smart contract system, and there exist scenarios where lying on outcome of contract execution could be the dominant strategy for a user (i.e., the user will lie regardless of the actions of other users). To solve this problem, we introduce payment in the game, that is, we discuss the scheme that can penalize a node by fining him/her some amount of coins if the result of a smart contract execution is different from that of the majority. This is a straightforward approach that works for many problems in game theory. However, we show that, if all users are not only rational but also fall into a class called *superrationality*, then there exist scenarios in which they will always lie or behave badly regardless of how high the penalty or fine would be.

Our negative results rely heavily on the rationality assumption of the users and participants of a smart contract system. However, rationality is a debatable concept in game theory. There exists a line of research focusing on irrational behaviors of people. It suggests that a person, even with perfect rationality of himself/herself, might not fully trust the rationality of others. We show that the problem changes significantly if we assume that users are not fully confident in the rationality of others. We also characterize the amount of the penalty that can prevent users from lying on contract execution outcome given that the users' belief in the rationality of others is reflected by some known probability distribution.

The remainder of the paper is organized as follows: In Sect. 2 we give a short review of smart contract and describe the problem we address in this paper. Section 3 describes the agent model for smart contract execution over a network of decentralized participants and the role of penalty. In Sect. 4 we discuss the way to implement penalty in decentralized smart contract execution environment. Section 5 discusses related work, and we conclude the paper in Sect. 6.

2   Smart Contract and Problem Statement

We begin by defining smart contracts. The definition provided by Szabo [18] is:

Definition 1. *A smart contract is a set of promises, specified in a digital form, including protocols within which the parties perform on these promises.*

However, this definition potentially covers a broad range of already existing centralized and client-server based e-commerce systems (e.g., Ebay), which fundamentally distinguishes from blockchain based smart contracts that rely on a decentralized network of untrusted nodes/participants and crypto-currency (e.g., Ethereum [1]). Blockchain can enforce smart contracts in a decentralized way without assuming any single trusted party. This is especially attractive in scenarios where users involved in a contract do not necessarily trust each other. As long as the entire blockchain system is "trusted" as a whole, it is guaranteed that execution results of a smart contract could be trustworthy. Most of existing works assume that when the majority of participating nodes in a blockchain system are honest, the system is trusted.

However, the situation is more complex in reality. Each node of the blockchain may adopt different action strategies for different smart contracts to maximize their own interests. This makes smart contract execution process more like an economic game. We use the definition of a normal form game by Osborne [13]:

Definition 2. *A normal form game Γ consists of:*

- *A finite set N of players (agents).*
- *A nonempty set Q_i of strategies available for each player $i \in N$.*
- *A preference relation $\preceq_i$ on $Q = \times_{j \in N} Q_j$ for each player i.*

We restrict our attention to normal form games in this paper. For simplicity, when we say a game, we mean a normal form game.

A strategy $q_i \in Q_i$ is called a (weakly) dominant strategy for player i if no matter what strategies are chosen by other players, choosing q_i always gives i an outcome that is not worse than any other strategy.

The Agent Model for Smart Contract. We consider the following model, which we call an agent model for smart contracts. There is a smart contract which involves N users (players). Each user j has a weight w_j. The smart contract specifies a set of possible future states of the system, depending on which each user either gains or loses coins (crypto-currency). For simplicity we assume that there are only two possible states S_0 and S_1. If a state S_i occurs ($i = 0$ or 1), user j will get z_j^i coins (specifically, if $z_j^i < 0$, then it means that user j loses $-z_j^i$ coins). Once the smart contract starts to be executed, the state of the system is unique and clear to all users/participants, and we call this state as the true state. In a decentralized system for contract execution and confirmation, however, all the users shall agree to a certain state based on which the smart contract is executed; and this state may not necessarily be the true state because of the agent assumption. We assume that every user will vote for/accept one state, and if users who vote for/accept a certain state S_i have a total weight at least αW where $W = \sum_{j=1}^{N} w_j$, then the smart contract will be executed based on the state S_i. We discuss, under the described agent model, the possibility of preventing users from lying on contract execution outcome by voting for/accepting incorrect state.

Remark on the Model. A user may have different identities (pseudonyms) in a public blockchain based smart contract system. For simplicity, in this paper, we assume that each user owns exactly one identity, whereas identities and users are used interchangeably. Depending on the protocols used in a blockchain based contract system, parameters may have different meanings. For example, if the system uses proof of work and longest chain rule (e.g., Bitcoin), then w_j corresponds to the computation power of user j, and voting for a state S_i means generating a block that executes the smart contract based on S_i (this may yield a branch, though), and keeping adding blocks to make it into the longest chain. For ease of presentation, we assume that there are only two possible states S_0 and S_1. However, our result can be easily extended to the case where there are more possible states.

3   An Agent Model for Smart Contract Execution with Penalty

We start with the following simple observation.

Observation 1. *In the agent model, voting for the state that the user most prefers is the dominant strategy.*

Consider an arbitrary scenario in which every user votes for S_0 or S_1. If user j prefers S_1 most and does not vote for S_1, then he/she can simply switch and vote for S_1 instead. Switching only decreases the utility of j if originally S_1 is the state based on which the smart contract is executed, and after switching it becomes S_0. However, this is impossible. Hence the observation is true. Note that if S_1 is not the true state, then user j always lies.

A common approach that prevents agents from lying in a game is to introduce payments. We consider the most straightforward way of adding the payment to the agent model, that is, if a user votes for a state that is different from the state based on which the smart contract is executed, he/she will be penalized, i.e., he/she will be fined a certain amount of coins.

Adding payment might prevent some users from lying on execution outcome. Specifically, if the number of extra coins that a user gets by outputting wrong outcome or lying is less than the penalty, he/she may choose to vote for the true state. However, it is still possible that users are lying no matter how large the penalty is. Consider the following scenario: The true state is S_0. There are users who strictly prefer S_1 than S_0. Let U be the set of them and suppose $\sum_{j \in U} w_j \geq \alpha W$. Focusing on users in U, there are two Nash equilibria, every user in U voting for S_0 or every user in U voting for S_1. Consider an arbitrary user $j \in U$. When making his/her own decision, user j guess the decisions of other players. If j is optimistic and assumes every other player in U are voting for S_1, he/she will vote for S_1, otherwise if he/she is pessimistic and assumes every other player in U are voting for S_0, he/she will vote for S_0. In such a scenario, users may still lie. Furthermore, we have the following claim.

Theorem 2. *In the agent model with penalty, if j is superrational and knows that $\sum_{j \in U} w_j \geq \alpha W$, then no matter how high the penalty is, j will always lie.*

We provide the definition of superrationality as follows.

Definition 3 [6]. *A player (agent) is called superrational if he/she has perfect rationality (and thus maximize his/her own utility), assumes that all other players are superrational, and that a superrational player will always come up with the same strategy as any other superrational player when facing the same problem.*

We remark that, superrationality is also called renormalized rationality in literature. According to the definition, if j is superrational, then he/she assumes that any other user in U would behave in the same way as he/she does, in this case, he/she will always vote for S_1, hence Theorem 2 is true.

Our above arguments show that, in general, introducing payment does not prevent users from lying. There exist scenarios in which users lie regardless of how high the penalty is. However, superrationality or rationality may not apply to real world application scenarios. As we have discussed, the incentive of lying relies crucially on a user's belief in certain behaviors of others. Specifically, he/she believes that other users are all rational. However, rationality itself is one of the most debatable issues in game theory in the sense that it seems to contradict a lot of laboratory experiments, which suggests that people often fail to conform to some of the basic assumptions of rationality. The "Centipede Game", which was constructed by Rosenthal [15] in 1982, is one of the most well-known examples that illustrate such a phenomenon.

The centipede game is carried out between two players, say, A and B in a fixed number of rounds which is known to both players. Initially both A and B own 1 coin. At the beginning of round i, let a_i and b_i be the number of coins owned by A and B respectively. If i is odd, A makes the decision of yes or no, otherwise, B makes the decision. If A or B decides on yes, then the game moves to round $i+1$, $a_{i+1} = a_i + 1$, $b_{i+1} = b_i + 1$. If A or B decides on no, then the game stops. If it is A that decides on no (i.e., i is odd), then $a_{i+1} = a_i + 2$, $b_{i+1} = b_i - 1$. Otherwise it is B that decides on no, then $a_{i+1} = a_i - 1$, $b_{i+1} = b_i + 2$.

Assuming that A is rational and he/she believes the rationality of B, then A will decide on no at round 1 and the centipede game ends at the beginning. The reasoning is that at the last round regardless of whose turn it is, the decision will be no. Therefore, at the second to last round the opponent will decide no to make sure that the number of his/her coins does not decrease. Iteratively carrying out this argument we get the conclusion. However, this does not coincide with the experiment results. For example, McKelvey and Palfrey [10] reported that only 15% of the players chose to end the game at the beginning in the experiments they carried out. That means, in most of these experiments, people do exhibit behaviors that contradict the traditional rationality assumptions in game theory. More experimental results and discussions on the centipede game and irrationality could be found in [11, 20].

The experimental results suggest that people often do not have fully trust in the rationality of the others. Notice that even if player A has perfect rationality, however, if he/she does not believe in the rationality of B, then A may still choose to continue the centipede game. Users involved in a smart contract may encounter a similar situation. Consider user $j \in U$, whether j votes for S_1 or not depends on his/her belief in the other users. Following the studies on irrationality in centipede game [2], we define the parameter $\tau_j(k)$, which indicates user j's belief in a certain behavior of user k, that is, user j believes that with probability $\tau_j(k)$, user k will vote for S_1, and with probability $1 - \tau_j(k)$, user k will vote for S_0. Based on such assumptions, user j's decision is based on the following.

For $k \neq j$, we define X_k as a 0-1 random variable such that:

$$Pr(X_k = 1) = \tau_j(k), \quad Pr(X_k = 0) = 1 - \tau_j(k).$$

Suppose user j votes for S_1, then based on j's belief, the probability that the smart contract is executed based on S_1 is $Pr(\sum_{k \neq j} X_k + w_j \geq \alpha W)$. Let p_j be the penalty if the smart contract is executed based on S_0, then the expected reward of j by lying (voting for S_1) is

$$z_j^1 Pr(\sum_{k \neq j} w_j X_j \geq \alpha W - w_j) - p_j(1 - Pr(\sum_{k \neq j} X_j \geq \alpha W - w_j))$$

$$= (z_j^1 + p_j) Pr(\sum_{k \neq j} w_j X_j \geq \alpha W - w_j) - p_j$$

The expected reward of j by telling the truth is

$$z_j^0 Pr(\sum_{k \neq j} w_j(1 - X_j) \geq \alpha W - w_j) = z_j^0 Pr(\sum_{k \neq j} w_j X_j \leq (1 - \alpha)W)$$

Therefore, as long as

$$z_j^0 Pr(\sum_{k \neq j} w_j X_j \leq (1 - \alpha)W) \geq (z_j^1 + p_j) Pr(\sum_{k \neq j} w_j X_j \geq \alpha W - w_j) - p_j,$$

is true, the rational user j will not lie. This means, if j does not fully believe in the rationality of other users, then sufficient penalty can prevent j from lying. Overall, the following is true:

Theorem 3. *In the agent model with penalty, if a user does not fully believe in the rationality of others, then a sufficient penalty can prevent him/her from outputting incorrect contract execution outcome or lying.*

4   Implementation of Contract Execution with Penalty

Penalty plays a central role in the agent model of smart contract execution as shown in the previous section's analysis. We discuss the enforcement of penalty in this section.

There are several strategies to eliminate disagreement in blockchain branches. These strategies are also used to determine smart contract execution results when there is disagreement. Common rules include longest-chain which is used by Bitcoin [12], and GHOST which is used by Ethereum [17]. No matter what strategy is used, we add following functions to support penalty in a decentralized smart contract system:

- Recording users' choices. Existing blockchain systems usually records only one identity for each block and ignores supporters of the block. Recording supporters is necessary for implementing penalty schemes. When a user accepts a block, he/she should generate a signature of the block and broadcast it to the network. Therefore, everyone can track users' choices of the smart contract execution outcome;
- Distribution of penalty. When a group of users supporting the wrong result need to be penalized, users supporting the correct result can submit a penalty request to the blockchain. The collected fine is distributed to them.

5   Related Work

We provide a brief overview on blockchain based smart contract and game theory studies on these systems.

Ethereum is the most popular smart contract system [1]. It is based on proof-of-work, but is planning to move to proof-of-stake. Luu et al. proposed a formal method to analyze Ethereum smart contracts to detect potential vulnerabilities [9].

The consequence of decentralization is subtle. Garay [5] and Pass et al. [14] showed that, several important security properties defined in the work of Nakamoto [12] are true, given the assumption that the majority of mining power in the Bitcoin system is controlled by the honest miners. Without such an assumption, however, security is not guaranteed. However, the assumption itself is questionable. For example, in 2014, the mining pool GHash.io exceeded 50% of the computational power in Bitcoin [3]. Thus, it becomes important to understand the behavior of users that participate in the system and study mechanisms that would motivate them to behave in an honest way.

There are a series of studies focusing on game theory aspects of users involved in mining. From a game theory perspective, Eyal and Sirer [4] showed that even a majority of honest miners is not enough to guarantee the security of the Bitcoin protocol. Sapirshtein et al. [16] and Kiayias et al. [7] studies mining as a game in Bitcoin and analyzes the best strategy of users.

6 Conclusion and Future Work

In this paper, we establish an agent based framework to model smart contract execution over a decentralized network of nodes/participants using blockchain and public ledger. In contrast to the commonly accepted assumption that smart contract execution outcome accepted by the majority can be trusted, agent based model of smart contract execution assumes that nodes may have incentive to manipulate or lie on outcome of contract execution in return for personal benefits or financial gains even they are not directly involved in a contract. We observe that users who are directly or indirectly involved in a smart contract may strategically take actions to manipulate smart contract execution outcome (e.g., produce or accept outcome that favors their own interests). In accordance with agent based model, we discuss the possibility of preventing users from engaging in bad behaviors in terms of contract execution or lying on contract outcome. We provide negative results for general smart contract execution models. We also show that if penalty is introduced in contract execution and assume that users are not fully confident in the rationality of other participants, then it is plausible to prevent users from lying on outcome or manipulating result of contract execution. Furthermore, we believe that, irrationality is an important subject that would contribute to better understanding of user behaviors in a decentralized cryptocurrency or smart contract system. A systematic investigation of irrationality in the context of smart contract execution and consensus is an important open problem. Another interesting open problem is whether it is possible to use other mechanisms, rather than financial penalty, to prevent users from lying on contract outcome when it favors them the most.

References

1. Buterin, V.: A next-generation smart contract and decentralized application platform. White Paper (2014)
2. Dunbar, G., Wang, R., Wang, X.: Rationalizing irrational beliefs. Theor. Econ. Lett. **6**(06), 1219 (2016)
3. Duong, T., Fan, L., Zhou, H.S.: 2-hop blockchain: Combining proof-of-work and proof-of-stake securely (2016)
4. Eyal, I., Sirer, E.G.: Majority is not enough: bitcoin mining is vulnerable. In: Christin, N., Safavi-Naini, R. (eds.) FC 2014. LNCS, vol. 8437, pp. 436–454. Springer, Heidelberg (2014). https://doi.org/10.1007/978-3-662-45472-5_28
5. Garay, J., Kiayias, A., Leonardos, N.: The bitcoin backbone protocol: analysis and applications. In: Oswald, E., Fischlin, M. (eds.) EUROCRYPT 2015. LNCS, vol. 9057, pp. 281–310. Springer, Heidelberg (2015). https://doi.org/10.1007/978-3-662-46803-6_10
6. Hofstadter, D.R.: Dilemmas for superrational thinkers, leading up to a luring lottery. Sci. Am. **6**, 267–275 (1983)
7. Kiayias, A., Koutsoupias, E., Kyropoulou, M., Tselekounis, Y.: Blockchain mining games. In: Proceedings of the 2016 ACM Conference on Economics and Computation, pp. 365–382. ACM (2016)

8. Lewenberg, Y., Bachrach, Y., Sompolinsky, Y., Zohar, A., Rosenschein, J.S.: Bitcoin mining pools: a cooperative game theoretic analysis. In: Proceedings of the 2015 International Conference on Autonomous Agents and Multiagent Systems, pp. 919–927. International Foundation for Autonomous Agents and Multiagent Systems (2015)

9. Luu, L., Chu, D.H., Olickel, H., Saxena, P., Hobor, A.: Making smart contracts smarter. In: Proceedings of the 2016 ACM SIGSAC Conference on Computer and Communications Security, pp. 254–269. ACM (2016)

10. McKelvey, R.D., Palfrey, T.R.: An experimental study of the centipede game. Econometrica: J. Econ. Soc. 803–836 (1992)

11. McKelvey, R.D., Palfrey, T.R.: Quantal response equilibria for extensive form games. Exp. Econ. **1**(1), 9–41 (1998)

12. Nakamoto, S.: Bitcoin: a peer-to-peer electronic cash system (2008)

13. Osborne, M.J., Rubinstein, A.: A Course in Game Theory. MIT Press, Cambridge (1994)

14. Pass, R., Seeman, L., Shelat, A.: Analysis of the blockchain protocol in asynchronous networks. IACR Cryptol. ePrint Arch. **2016**, 454 (2016)

15. Rosenthal, R.W.: Games of perfect information, predatory pricing and the chainstore paradox. J. Econ. Theory **25**(1), 92–100 (1981)

16. Sapirshtein, A., Sompolinsky, Y., Zohar, A.: Optimal selfish mining strategies in bitcoin. arXiv preprint arXiv:1507.06183 (2015)

17. Sompolinsky, Y., Zohar, A.: Secure high-rate transaction processing in bitcoin. In: Böhme, R., Okamoto, T. (eds.) FC 2015. LNCS, vol. 8975, pp. 507–527. Springer, Heidelberg (2015). https://doi.org/10.1007/978-3-662-47854-7_32

18. Szabo, N.: Formalizing and securing relationships on public networks. First Mon. **2**(9) (1997)

19. Tapscott, D., Tapscott, A.: Blockchain Revolution: How the Technology Behind Bitcoin is Changing Money, Business, and the World. Penguin, Westminster (2016)

20. Zauner, K.G.: A payoff uncertainty explanation of results in experimental centipede games. Games Econ. Behav. **26**(1), 157–185 (1999)

A Concurrent Perspective on Smart Contracts

Ilya Sergey[1]([✉]) and Aquinas Hobor[2]

[1] University College London, London, UK
i.sergey@ucl.ac.uk
[2] Yale-NUS College and School of Computing, National University of Singapore,
Singapore, Singapore
hobor@comp.nus.edu.sg

Abstract. In this paper, we explore remarkable similarities between multi-transactional behaviors of smart contracts in cryptocurrencies such as Ethereum and classical problems of shared-memory concurrency. We examine two real-world examples from the Ethereum blockchain and analyzing how they are vulnerable to bugs that are closely reminiscent to those that often occur in traditional concurrent programs. We then elaborate on the relation between observable contract behaviors and well-studied concurrency topics, such as atomicity, interference, synchronization, and resource ownership. The described *contracts-as-concurrent-objects* analogy provides deeper understanding of potential threats for smart contracts, indicate better engineering practices, and enable applications of existing state-of-the-art formal verification techniques.

1 Introduction

Smart contracts are programs that are stored on a blockchain, a distributed Byzantine-fault-tolerant database. Smart contracts can be triggered by blockchain transactions and read and write data on their blockchain [38]. Although smart contracts are run and verified in a distributed fashion, their semantics suggest that one can think of them as of *sequential* programs, despite the existence of a number of complex interaction patterns including *e.g.*, reentrancy and recursive calls. This mental model simplifies both formal and informal reasoning about contracts, enabling immediate reuse of existing general-purpose frameworks for program verification [5,16,31,32] that can be employed to verify smart contracts written in *e.g.* Solidity [15] with only minor adjustments.

Although all computations on a blockchain are deterministic,[1] a certain amount *non-determinism* still occurs due to races between transactions themselves (*i.e.* which transactions are chosen for a given block by the miners). We will show in that non-determinism can be exploited by adversarial parties and makes reasoning about contract behavior particularly subtle, reminiscent to known challenges involved in conventional concurrent programming.

---

[1] This requirement stems from the way the underlying Byzantine distributed ledger consensus protocol enables all involved parties to agree on transaction outcomes.

© International Financial Cryptography Association 2017
M. Brenner et al. (Eds.): FC 2017 Workshops 2017, LNCS 10323, pp. 478–493, 2017.
https://doi.org/10.1007/978-3-319-70278-0_30

In this paper we outline a model of smart contracts that emphasizes the properties of their *concurrent* executions. Such executions can span *multiple* blockchain transactions (within the same block or in multiple blocks) and thereby violate desired safety properties that cannot be stated using only the contract's implementation and local state—precisely what the existing verification methodologies focus on [5,32]. To facilitate the reuse of the common programming intuition, we propose the following analogy:

Accounts using smart contracts in a blockchain
are like
threads using concurrent objects in shared memory.

Threads using concurrent objects in shared memory. By *concurrent objects* we mean the broad class of data structures that are employed to exchange data between and manage the interaction of multiple *threads* (processes) running concurrently [20]. Typical examples of concurrent objects are locks, queues, and atomic counters—typically used via popular libraries such as `java.util.concurrent`. At runtime, these concurrent objects are allocated in a block of *shared memory* that is accessible to the running threads. The behavior resulting from the threads accessing the objects simultaneously—*i.e. interference*—can be extremely unpredictable and thus extremely difficult to reason about.

Concurrent objects whose implementation does not utilize proper synchronization (*e.g.*, with *locks* or *barriers*) can manifest *data races*[2] under interference leading to a loss of memory integrity. Even for race-free objects the observed behavior under interference may be erroneous from the perspective of one or more clients. For example, a particular thread may not "foresee" the actions taken by the other threads with a shared object and thus may not expect for that object to change in all of the ways that it does change under interference.

Accounts using smart contracts in a blockchain. Smart contracts are analogous to concurrent objects. Instead of residing in a shared memory they live in the blockchain; instead of being used by threads they are invoked by *accounts* (users or other contracts). Like concurrent objects, they have internal mutable state, manage resources (*e.g.* funds), and can be accessed by multiple parties both within a block and in multiple blocks. Unlike traditional concurrent objects, a smart contract's methods are atomic due to the transactional model of computation. That is, a single call to a contract (or a chain of calls to a series of contracts calling each other), is executed *sequentially*—without interrupts—and either terminates after successfully updating the blockchain or aborts and rolls back to its previous configuration before the call.

The notion of "atomicity for free" is deceptive, however, as concurrent behavior can still be observed *at the level of the blockchain*:

---

[2] That is, unsynchronized concurrent accesses by different threads to a single memory location when at least one of those accesses is a write.

- The order of the transactions included to a block is not determined at the moment of a transaction execution, and, thus, the outcome can largely depend on the ordering with respect to other transactions [27].
- Several programming tasks require the contract logic to be spread across several blockchain transactions (*e.g.*, when contracts "communicate" with the world outside of the blockchain), enabling true concurrent behavior.
- Calling other contracts can be considered to be a kind of *cooperative multitasking*. By cooperative multitasking we mean that multiple threads can run but do not get interrupted unless they explicitly "yield". That is, a call from contract A to contract B can be considered to be a yield from contract A's perspective, with contract B yielding when it returns. The key point for smart contracts is that **contract B can run code that was unanticipated by contract A's designer**, which makes the situation much closer to a concurrent setting than a typical sequential one.[3] In particular, contract B can modify state that contract A may assume is unchanged during the call. This is the essence of The DAO bug [9], in which contract B made a call back into contract A to modify A's local state before returning [27]. However, reentrancy is not the only way this kind of error can manifest, since:
- It is not difficult to imagine a scenario in which a certain contract is used as a *service* for other parties (users and contracts), managing the access to a shared resource and, in some sense, serving as a concurrent library. As multi-contract transactions are becoming more ubiquitous, various interference patterns can be observed and, thus, should be accounted for.

Our goals and motivation. Luckily, the research in concurrent and distributed programming conducted in the past three decades provides a large body of theoretical and applied frameworks to code, specify, reason about, and formally verify concurrent objects and their implementations. The goal of this paper is thus twofold. First, we are going to provide a brief overview of some known concurrency issues that can occur in smart contracts, characterizing the problems in terms of more traditional concurrency abstractions. Second, we are aiming to build an intuition for "good" and "bad" contract behaviors that can be identified and verified/detected correspondingly, using existing formal methods developed for reasoning about concurrency.

2   Deployed Examples of *Concurrentesque* Behavior

Here we discuss two contracts that have been deployed on the Ethereum blockchain that each illustrate different aspects of concurrent-type behavior. The BlockKing contract, like many others on the Ethereum blockchain today, implements a simple gambling game [2]. Although BlockKing is not heavily used, we study it because it showcases a potential use of the Oraclize service [4], which is a service that allows contracts to communicate with the world outside of the blockchain and thus invites true concurrency. Since the early adopters of the

---

[3] A better term would be "uncooperative multitasking" under the circumstances.

Oraclize service wrote it as a demonstration of the service and has made its source code freely available, it is likely that many other contracts that wish to use Oraclize will mirror it in their implementations.

The second example we discuss is the widely-studied bug in the DAO contract [1]. The DAO established an owner-managed venture capital fund with more than 18,000 investors; at its height it attracted more than 14% of all Ether coins in existence at that time. The subsequent attack on it cost investors approximately 3.6 million Ether, which at that time was worth approximately USD 50 million. The DAO employed what we call "uncooperative multitasking", in that when the DAO sent money to a recipient then that recipient was able to run code that interfered (via reentrancy) with the DAO's contract state that the DAO assumed would not change during the call.

2.1   The BlockKing Contract

The gamble in BlockKing works as follows. At any given time there is a designated "Block King" (initially the writer of the contract). When money is sent to the contract by a sender s, a random number j is generated between 1 and 9. If the current block number modulo 10 is equal to j then s becomes the new Block King. Afterwards, the Block King gets sent a percentage of the money in the contract (from 50% to 90% depending on various parameters), and the writer of the contract gets sent the balance.

Generation of good quality random numbers is often difficult in deterministic systems, especially in a context in which all data is publicly stored—and in which there are financial incentives for attackers. Accordingly, BlockKing utilizes the services of a trusted party, Wolfram Alpha, to generate its random numbers using the Oraclize service. Assuming Oraclize is well-behaved, this strategy for random number selection should be very difficult for attackers to predict.

The code for BlockKing is 365 lines long, but the lines of particular interest are given in Fig. 1; line numbers here refer to the actual source code of the contract as given by Etherscan [2]. The enter function is called when money is sent to the contract. It sets some contract variables (lines 299–301) and then sends a query to the Oraclize service (line 303).

The `oraclize_query` function raises an event visible in the "real world" before returning to its caller, which then exits (line 304). In the real world the Oraclize servers monitor the event logs, service the request (in this case by contacting the Wolfram Alpha web service), and then make a fresh call into the originating contract at a designated callback point (line 306 in BlockKing). Between the event and its callback, many things can occur, in the sense that the the blockchain can advance several blocks between the call to `oraclize_query` and the resumption of control at `__callback`. During this time the state of the blockchain, and even of the BlockKing contract itself, can have changed drastically. In other words, *this is true concurrent behavior on the blockchain.*

What can go wrong? Suppose that multiple gamblers wish to try their luck in a short period of time (even within the same block). The contract makes no attempt to track this behavior. Accordingly, each new contestant will overwrite

```
293    function enter() {
294      // 100 finney = .05 ether minimum payment otherwise refund payment and stop contract
295      if (msg.value < 50 finney) {
296        msg.sender.send(msg.value);
297        return;
298      }
299      warrior = msg.sender;
300      warriorGold = msg.value;
301      warriorBlock = block.number;
302      bytes32 myid =
303        oraclize_query(0,"WolframAlpha","random number between 1 and 9");
304    }
305
306    function __callback(bytes32 myid, string result) {
307      if (msg.sender != oraclize_cbAddress()) throw;
308      randomNumber = uint(bytes(result)[0]) - 48;
309      process_payment();
310    }
311
312    function process_payment() {

         . . .

339      if (singleDigitBlock == randomNumber) {
340        rewardPercent = 50;
341        // If the payment was more than .999 ether then increase reward percentage
342        if (warriorGold > 999 finney) {
343          rewardPercent = 75;
344        }
345        king = warrior;
346        kingBlock = warriorBlock;
347      }
```

Fig. 1. BlockKing code fragments [2].

the previous one's data (the critical warriorBlock and warrior variables) in lines 299–301. When the callbacks do eventually occur, the last contestant in the batch will enjoy multiple chances to win the throne curtesy of the earlier contestants in that batch who payed for the other callbacks! The culprit is lines 339–347 from the process_payment function, called as the last line of the __callback function in line 309.

Each time the process_payment function is called the least significant digit of warriorBlock is computed and stored into the variable singleDigitBlock.[4] Each time the process_payment function is called by __callback he has a new chance to match the random number in line 339. If the numbers do match, then that final contestant is crowned on line 345.

2.2 The DAO Contract

The source code for the DAO is 1,239 lines and markedly more complex than BlockKing [23]. Since much has already been written about this bug (e.g. [9,27]), we present in Fig. 2 only the key lines. The problem is the order of line 1012, which (via a series of further function calls) sends Ether to msg.sender, and line 1014, which zeros out the balance of msg.sender's account.

In a sequential program, reordering two independent operations has no effect on the ultimate behavior of the program. However, in a concurrent program

---

[4] For reasons that seem rather strange to us, this modulus is computed very inefficiently in lines 315–338 of the contract, which we elide to save space.

```
1010    // Burn DAO Tokens
1011    Transfer(msg.sender, 0, balances[msg.sender]);
1012    withdrawRewardFor(msg.sender); // be nice, and get his rewards
1013    totalSupply -= balances[msg.sender];
1014    balances[msg.sender] = 0;
1015    paidOut[msg.sender] = 0;
1016    return true;
1017  }
```

Fig. 2. DAO code fragment [23].

the effect of a sequentially-harmless reorder can have significant effect since the order in which operations occur can affect how the threads interfere. In the DAO, sending the Ether in line 1012 "yields" control, in some multitasking sense, to any arbitrary (and thus potentially malicious) contract located at msg.sender.

Unfortunately, the DAO internal state still indicates that the account is funded since its account balance has not yet been zeroed out in line 1014. Accordingly, a malicious msg.sender can initiate a second withdrawal by calling back into the DAO contract, which will in turn send a second payment when control reaches line 1012 again. In fact, the malicious msg.sender can then initiate a third, fourth, *etc.* withdrawal, all of which will result in payment. Only at the end is his account zeroed out, after being paid many multiples of its original balance.

Previous analyses of this bug have indicated that the problem is due to recursion or unintended reentrancy. In a narrow sense this is true, but in a wider sense what is going on is that sequential code is running in what is in many senses a concurrent environment.

3   Interference and Synchronization

Having showed that concurrent-type behavior exists and causes problems in real contracts on the Blockchain, we will now examine other ways that our *concurrent-objects-as-contracts* viewpoint can help us understand how contracts can behave on the blockchain.

3.1   Atomic Updates in Shared-Memory Concurrency

Figure 3 depicts a canonical example (presented in a Java 8-like pseudocode) of a wrongly used concurrent object, which is supposed to implement an "atomic" counter with methods get and set. The implementation of the concurrent counter on the left is obviously *thread-safe* (*i.e.*, *data race*-free), thanks to the use of synchronized primitives [17]. What is problematic, though, is how an instance of the Counter class is used in the multithreaded client code on the right.

Specifically, with two threads running in parallel and their operations interleaving, the call to incr() within thread2's body could happen, for instance, between the assignment to a and the call c.set(a + 1) within the incr() call of

```
class Counter {
  private int x = 0;

  /** Return current value */
  synchronized int get() {
    return x;
  }

  /** Set x to be v */
  synchronized int set(int v) {
    int t = x;
    x = v;
    return t;
  }
}
```

```
final Counter c = new Counter();

void incr() {
  int a = c.get();
  int b = c.set(a + 1);
  assert (a == b);
}

// In the main method
Runnable thread1 = () ->
  { incr(); }

Runnable thread2 = () ->
  { incr(); }

thread1.run(); thread2.run();
```

Fig. 3. A concurrent counter (left) and its two-thread client application (right).

thread1. This would invalidate the condition in the following assert statement, making the overall program fail *non-deterministically* for a certain execution!

The issue arises because the implementation of incr() on top of Counter does not provide the *atomicity guarantees*, expected by the client code. Specifically, the code on the right is implemented in the assumption that there will be *no interference* between the statements of incr(), hence the counter c is going to be incremented by 1, and a and b will be the same by the end of its execution. Indeed, this is not always the case in the presence of concurrently running thread2, and not only a and b will be different, the later call to c.set() will also "overwrite" the result of the earlier one.

A better designed implementation of Counter could have instead provided an *atomic* implementation of incr(), implemented via a version of *fetch-and-increment* operation [20, §5.6], via explicit locking, or by means of Java's synchronized keyword. However, given the only two methods, get and set, the implementation of Counter has synchronization properties of an atomic register whose *consensus number* [20, §5.1] (*i.e.*, the number of concurrent threads that can unambiguously agree on the outcomes of get and set) is exactly 1. Therefore, it is fundamentally impossible to implement an atomic incrementation of c by using only get and set, and without relying on some additional synchronization, by giving priorities to certain preordained threads.

Perhaps a bit surprisingly, even though the implementation of Counter from Fig. 3 is not flawed by itself, its weak atomicity properties render it quite useless in the presence of an unbounded number of threads, making it virtually impossible to make any *stable* (*i.e.*, resilient with respect to concurrent changes) assumptions about its internal state.

3.2   Atomic Updates in Concurrent Blockchain Transactions

The left part of Fig. 4 shows a smart contract, implemented in Solidity [15], with functionality and methods reminiscent to those of an atomic concurrent counter. The function `get` allows one to query the contract for the current balance, associated with some fixed address `id`, whereas the `set` function allows one to update balance with the new balance, taken from the message via `msg.value`, sending back the old amount and returning it as a result.

```
contract Counter {                      // ...
  address public id;                    // Same code as in Counter
  uint private balance;
                                        function testAndSet(uint expected)
  function get() returns (uint) {         returns (uint) {
    return balance;                       uint t = balance;
  }                                       if (t == expected) {
                                            balance = msg.value;
  function set() returns (uint) {         msg.sender.send(t);
    uint t = balance;                       return t;
    balance = msg.value;                } else {
    msg.sender.send(t);                   throw;
    return t;                           }
}}                                      }
```

Fig. 4. A counter contract (left) and a synchronizing `testAndSet` method (right).

Since the bodies of both `get` and `set` are going to be executed sequentially in the course of some transactions, neither there is any need to synchronized them, nor there is any explicit way to do so in Solidity. However, it is not difficult to observe that as an implementation of the simplest possible storage (*e.g.*, for some `id`-related funds), used by multiple different parties to update it's balance, the `Counter` contract is as useless as its Java counterpart from Fig. 3.

For instance, imagine that two parties, unaware of each other try to increment the amount, stored by an instance of `Counter` by a certain value. Since the contract does not provide a way for them to do it in one operation, they will have to first query the amount via `get` and then try to change it via `set` function, following the same pattern as the implementation of `incr` from Fig. 3. Indeed, both these calls can be accomplished in a single transaction, which would make the execution sequential. However, because of the limited gas requirement,[5] it is ill-advised to call more than one external contract in the course of execution. Furthermore, the call to `get` can be performed by a client, external to the blockchain, which would mean that the consecutive calls to `get` and `set` will end up in *two different* transactions. If this is the case, those calls might interfere with other transactions, launched by multiple parties trying to modify `Counter`

---

[5] This is a standard way in Ethereum to ensure that execution of a contract terminates: by supplying it with a limited amount of "gas", used as a fuel for execution steps.

at the same time, making us face the familiar problem: the result of calling the function set cannot be predicted out of the local observations.

The cause of the described problem, both in the shared-memory and blockchain cases, is the lack of *strong synchronization primitives*, allowing one to simultaneously observe and manipulate with the counter in the presence of concurrent executions. One solution to the problem, which would make it possible to increment the counter atomically, is to enhance the counter with the testAndSet function (right part of Fig. 4). This function implements the check/update logic similar to the *compare-and-swap* primitive [20, §5.8], (known as CMPXCHG, on the Intel x86 and Itanium architectures), as a way to implement synchronization between multiple threads. The consensus number of testAndSet (and some other similar *Read-Modify-Write* primitives) is known to be ∞, hence it is strong enough to allow an arbitrary number of concurrent parties agree on the outcome of the operation.

Notes on formal reasoning and verification. The modern formal approaches for runtime concurrency verification, based on exploring dynamic execution traces and summarizing their properties, provide efficient tools for detecting the violations of atomicity assumptions, and the lack of synchronization [26]. For instance, by translating our contract to the corresponding shared-memory concurrent object, one would be able to use the existing tools to summarize its traces [13], thus, making it possible to observe undesired interaction patterns.

4   State Ownership and Permission Accounting

A different way to prohibit the unwelcome interference on a contract's state is to engineer a tailored permission accounting discipline, controlling the set of operations allowed for different parties.

Let us first notice that the problems exhibited by the two-thread example in Fig. 3 and preventing one from asserting anything about its state x could be avoided if we enforced a restricted access discipline: for instance, by stating that at any moment at most one thread can query/modify its state. This would grant the corresponding thread an exclusive *ownership* [30] over the object, thus, justifying any assertions made locally from this thread about the object's state.

The unique ownership is traditionally ensured in Ethereum's contracts by disallowing any other party, but a dedicated *owner*, make critical changes in the contract state. For instance, Fig. 5 (left) shows an altered version of the Counter contract, so no other party can interact with it but its "owner". The ownership discipline is enforced by Solidity's mechanism of modifiers, allowing one to provide custom dynamically checked pre-/postconditions for functions. In our example, the byOwner modifier will enforce that the functions get and set will be only invoked on behalf of a fixed party—the owner of the contract.

This is a rather crude solution to the interference problem, as it would mean to exclude any concurrent interaction at a contract whatsoever. It is quite illuminating, though, from a perspective on thinking of contracts as concurrent

```
contract Counter {
  address public owner;
  uint private balance;

  modifier byOwner() {
    if (msg.sender != owner) throw;
    _
  }

  function get() external byOwner
    returns (uint) {
    return balance;
  }

  function set() external byOwner
    returns (uint) {
    uint t = balance;
    balance = msg.value;
    msg.sender.send(t);
    return t;
}}
```

```
// Same declarations as in Counter

mapping (address => bool) readers;

// Initialized with 0x0
address writer;

modifier canRead() {
  if (msg.sender != writer ||
      !readers[msg.sender]) throw;
  _
}

modifier canWrite() {
  if (msg.sender != writer) throw;
  _
}

function acquireReadLock() returns (bool) {
  if (writer == 0x0) {
    readers[msg.sender] = true;
  } else return false;
}

// ... Other synchronization primitives
```

Fig. 5. An exclusively-owned (left) and Read/Write-locked (right) contract.

objects, allowing us to immediately apply our analogy: *accounts are threads.* Indeed, by imposing a specific ownership discipline on a contract as shown in Fig. 5 is similar to enhancing its Java counterpart with an explicit check of `Thread.currentThread().getId()`.

Let us now try to push the analogy between accounts and threads a bit further by designing a version of a counter with more elaborated access rights. In particular, we are going to ensure that as long as there are accounts (aka "threads") "interested" in having its value immutable (as their internal logic might rely on its immutability), no other party may be allowed to modify it. Similarly, if at the moment there is exactly one party that holds a unique permission to modify the counter, no other parties may be allowed to read it. The solution to this synchronization problem is well-known in a concurrency community by the name *Read/Write lock* [6]. Its implementation requires keeping track of threads currently reading and writing to the shared object, so a thread should explicitly *acquire* the corresponding permission before performing a read/write operation, and then should *release* it upon finishing.

The right part of Fig. 5 shows the essential fragments of the Read/Write-locked contract implementation. The two new fields, `readers` and `writer` keep track of the currently active readers and writers. The new modifiers `canRead` and `canWrite` are to be used for the omitted `get` and `set` operations correspondingly. Finally, `acquireReadLock` allows its caller to acquire the lock as long as there is no active writer in the system, by registering it in the `readers` mapping.

As we can see, the accounts-as-threads is a rather powerful analogy, suggesting a number of solutions to possible synchronization problems that can be taken verbatime from the concurrency literature. The only drawback of the presented solution is the fact that it is rather monolithic: the contract now combines the functionality of the data structure (*i.e.*, the counter) and that of a synchronization primitive (*i.e.*, a lock). We will discuss possible ways to improve the modularity of the implementation in Sect. 5.

Notes on formal reasoning and verification. Formal reasoning about permission accounting and separation of state access is a long studied topic in the shared-memory concurrency literature (see, *e.g.*, [8] for an overview). Formalisms, such as Concurrent Separation Logic and [30] Fractional/Counting permissions [6] provide a flexible way to define the abstract ownership discipline and verify that a particular implementation follows it faithfully. For instance, our Read/Write lock contract can be formally proven *safe* (*i.e.*, prohibiting concurrent write-modifications) using a formal model of permissions by Bornat *et al.* [6].

5 Discussion

5.1 Composing the Contracts

The locking contract "pattern", considered in Sect. 4, has a significant drawback: its design is *non-modular*. That is, the locking machinery is implemented by the contract itself rather than by a third-party library. This is at odds with good practices of software engineering, in which it is advised to implement synchronization primitives, such as ordinary and reentrant locks, as standalone libraries, which can be used for managing access client-specific resources.

But once the lock logic is factored out of the contract, the reasoning about the contract's behavior becomes significantly more difficult, as, in order to prove the preservation of its internal invariants, one needs to be aware of the properties of the extracted locking protocol, such as, *e.g.*, uniqueness of a writer, which are external to the contract. In other words, verification of a contract can no longer be conduced in an *isolated* manner and will require building a model that allows reasoning about a contract interacting with other, rigorously specified contracts. The idea of disentangling the logic of contracts is not inherent to our concurrent view and is paramount in the existing good practices of contract development. For instance, the same idea is advocated as a way to implement *upgradable* contracts in Ethereum through introducing and additional level of indirection [11]. Having a "contract factory", implemented as another contract, which can be invoked by any party, poses verification challenges similar to those of proving the safety properties of *higher-order* concurrent object (*i.e.*, an object, that is manipulating with other objects) [19].

The idea of compositional reasoning and verification of mutually-dependent and higher-order concurrent objects using concurrency logics has been a subject of a large research body in the past decade [12,33,34,37]. Most of those approaches focus on a notion of *protocol*, serving as an abstract interface of an object's behavior in the presence of concurrent updates, while hiding low-level implementation details (*i.e.*, the actual code). We believe, that by leveraging our analogy, we will be able to develop a method for modular verification of such multi-contract interactions.

5.2 Liveness Properties

With the introduction of locks and exclusive access, another concurrency-related issue arises: reasoning about *progress* and *liveness* properties of contract implementations. For instance, it is not difficult to imagine a situation, in which a particular account, registered as a "reader" in our example from Fig. 5, might never release the reader-lock, thus, blocking everyone else from being able to change the contract's state in the future. The liveness in this setting would mean that *eventually something good happens*, meaning that any party is properly incentivised to release the lock. In a concurrency vocabulary, such an assumption can be rephrased as *fairness* of the system scheduler, making it possible to reuse existing proof methods for modular reasoning about progress [25] and termination [18] in of single- and multi-contract executions.

6 Related Work

Formal reasoning about smart contracts is an emerging and exciting topic, and suitable abstractions for describing a contract's behavior are a subject of active research. In this section, we relate our observations to the existing results in formalizing and verifying contract properties, outlining promising areas that would benefit from our concurrency analogy.

6.1 Verifying Contract Implementations

Since the DAO bug [9], the Ethereum community has been focusing on preventing similar errors, with the aid of general-purpose tools for program verification.

At the moment, contracts written in Solidity can be annotated with Hoare-style pre/postconditions and translated down to OCaml code [32], so they become amenable to verification using the Why3 tool, which uses automation to discharge the generated verification conditions [16]. This approach is efficient for verifying basic safety properties of Solidity programs, such as particular variables always being within certain array index boundaries, and preservation of general contract invariants (typically stated in a form if linear equations over values of `uint`-valued variables) at the method boundaries and before performing external contract calls—precisely what was violated by the DAO contract.

Bhargavan *et al.* have recently implemented a translation from a subset of Solidity (without loops and recursion) [5] into F*—a programming language and verification framework, based on dependent types [35]. They also provided a translator from EVM bytecode to F* programs. Both these approaches made it possible to use F* as a uniform tool for verification of contract properties, such as invariant preservation and absence of unhandled exceptions, which were encoded as an effect via F*'s support for indexed Hoare monad [36]. A similar approach to specify the behavior of contracts and based on dependent types has been adopted by Pettersson and Edström [31], who implemented a small effect-based contract DSL as a shallow embedding into Idris [7], with the executable code extracted to Serpent [14], a Python-style contract language.

Hirai has recently formalized the entire specification of Ethereum Virtual Machine [22] in Lem [28] with extraction to the Isabelle/HOL proof assistant, allowing mechanized verification of contracts, compiled to EVM bytecode, for a number of safety properties, including assertions on mutable state and the absence of potential reentrancy. Unlike the previous approaches, Hirai's formalization does not provide a syntactic way to construct and compose proofs (*e.g.*, via a Hoare-style program logics), and all reasoning about contract behavior is conducted out of the low-level execution semantics [38].

In contrast with these lines of work, which focus predominantly on *low-level* safety properties and invariant preservation, our observations hint a more high-level formalism for capturing the properties of a contract behavior and its communication patterns with the outside world. In particular, we consider communicating state-transition systems (STSs) [29] with abstract state as a suitable formalism for proving, *e.g.*, trace and liveness properties of contract executions using a toolset of established tools, such as TLA+ [24]. In order to connect such an abstract representation with low-level contract code, one will have to prove a *refinement* [3] between the high-level and the low-level representations, *i.e.*, between an STS and the code. In some sense, finding a suitable contract invariant and proving it via Why3 or F* may be considered as proving a refinement between a *one-state* transition system, such that the only state is what is described by the invariant, and an implementation that preserves it. However, we expect more complicate STSs will be required in order to reason about contracts with preemptive concurrency.

6.2   Reasoning About Global Contract Properties

The observation about some contracts being prone to unintentional or adversarial misuse due to the interference phenomenon has been made by Luu *et al.* [27]. They characterised the problem similar to what's exhibited by our counter example in Sect. 3 as *transaction-ordering dependency* (TOD), which under our concurrency analogy can be generalized as a problem of unrestricted interference. The solution to the TOD-problem, suggested by Luu *et al.*, required changing the semantics of Ethereum transactions, providing a primitive, similar to our testAndSet from Fig. 4. While the advantage of such an approach is the absence of the need to modify the already deployed contracts (only the client code interacting with them needs to be changed), it requires all involved users to upgrade their client-side applications, in order to account for the changes. In essence, Luu *et al.*'s solution targets a very specific concurrency pattern: strengthening synchronization, provided by atomic registers, by adding a blockchain-supported *read-modify-write* primitive. Realizing the nature of the problem, hinted by our analogy, might instead suggest alternative *contract-based* solutions, such as, *e.g.*, engineering a locking proxy contract. The disadvantage of this approach is, however, the need to foresee this behavior at the moment of designing and deploying a contract. That said, such an ability to model this behavior is precisely what, we believe, our analogy enables.

7   Conclusion

We believe that our analogy between *smart contracts* and *concurrent objects* can provide new perspectives, stimulate research, and allow effective reuse of existing results, tools, and insights for understanding, debugging, and verifying complex contract behaviors in a distributed ledger. As any analogy, ours should not be taken verbatim: on the one hand, there are indeed issues in concurrency, which seem to be hardly observable in contract programming; on the other hand, smart contract implementers should also be careful about notions that do not have direct counterparts in the concurrency realm, such as gas-bounded executions and management of funds.

To conclude, we leave the reader with several speculations, inspired by our observations, but neither addressed nor disproved:

- A common concurrency challenge in non garbage-collected languages is to track the uniqueness of heap locations, which can be later reclaimed and repurposed—an issue dubbed *the ABA problem* [10]. With the lack of due caution, the ABA problem may lead to the violation of the object's state integrity. Can we imagine a similar scenario in a multi-contract setting?
- Continuing the analogy, if one sees a blockchain as a shared state, then the mining protocol defines the priorities for scheduling. Can we leverage the insights from efficient concurrent thread management in order to analyze and improve the existing distributed ledger implementations?
- *Linearizability* [21] (aka *atomicity*) is a standard notion of correctness for specifying high-level behavior of lock-free concurrent objects. What would be an equivalent de-facto notion of consistency for composite contracts with multi-transactional operations, such as BlockKing?

Acknowledgements. Sergey's research is supported by EPSRC grant EP/P009271/1. Hobor's research is funded by Yale-NUS College R-607-265-045-121.

References

1. The DAO. https://en.wikipedia.org/wiki/The_DAO_(organization)
2. BlockKing contract (2016). https://etherscan.io/address/0x3ad14db4e5a658d8d20 f8836deabe9d5286f79e1
3. Abadi, M., Lamport, L.: The existence of refinement mappings. In: LICS, pp. 165–175. IEEE Computer Society (1988)
4. Bertani, T.: Oraclize (2016). http://www.oraclize.it
5. Bhargavan, K., Delignat-Lavaud, A., Fournet, C., Gollamudi, A., Gonthier, G., Kobeissi, N., Kulatova, N., Rastogi, A., Sibut-Pinote, T., Swamy, N., Zanella-Béguelin, S.: Formal verification of smart contracts: short paper. In: PLAS, pp. 91–96. ACM (2016)
6. Bornat, R., Calcagno, C., O'Hearn, P.W., Parkinson, M.J.: Permission accounting in separation logic. In: POPL, pp. 259–270. ACM (2005)
7. Brady, E.: Programming and reasoning with algebraic effects and dependent types. In: ICFP, pp. 133–144. ACM (2013)

8. Brookes, S., O'Hearn, P.W.: Concurrent separation logic. ACM SIGLOG News **3**(3), 47–65 (2016)
9. Buterin, V.: Critical update re: DAO vulnerability. https://blog.ethereum.org/2016/06/17/critical-update-re-dao-vulnerability
10. Dechev, D., Pirkelbauer, P., Stroustrup, B.: Understanding and effectively preventing the ABA problem in descriptor-based lock-free designs. In: ISORC, pp. 185–192. IEEE Computer Society (2010)
11. Dimitrova, E.: Writing upgradable contracts in Solidity. https://blog.colony.io/writing-upgradeable-contracts-in-solidity-6743f0eecc88. Accessed 3 Feb 2017
12. Dinsdale-Young, T., Dodds, M., Gardner, P., Parkinson, M.J., Vafeiadis, V.: Concurrent abstract predicates. In: D'Hondt, T. (ed.) ECOOP 2010. LNCS, vol. 6183, pp. 504–528. Springer, Heidelberg (2010). https://doi.org/10.1007/978-3-642-14107-2_24
13. Emmi, M., Enea, C.: Symbolic abstract data type inference. In: POPL, pp. 513–525. ACM (2016)
14. Ethereum Foundation: The Serpent Contract-Oriented Programming Language. https://github.com/ethereum/serpent
15. Ethereum Foundation: The Solidity Contract-Oriented Programming Language. https://github.com/ethereum/solidity
16. Filliâtre, J.-C., Paskevich, A.: Why3—where programs meet provers. In: Felleisen, M., Gardner, P. (eds.) ESOP 2013. LNCS, vol. 7792, pp. 125–128. Springer, Heidelberg (2013). https://doi.org/10.1007/978-3-642-37036-6_8
17. Goetz, B., Peierls, T., Bloch, J., Bowbeer, J., Holmes, D., Lea, D.: Java Concurrency in Practice. Addison-Wesley, Boston (2006)
18. Gotsman, A., Cook, B., Parkinson, M.J., Vafeiadis, V.: Proving that non-blocking algorithms don't block. In: POPL, pp. 16–28. ACM (2009)
19. Hendler, D., Incze, I., Shavit, N., Tzafrir, M.: Flat combining and the synchronization-parallelism tradeoff. In: SPAA, pp. 355–364 (2010)
20. Herlihy, M., Shavit, N.: The Art of Multiprocessor Programming. M. Kaufmann, Burlington (2008)
21. Herlihy, M., Wing, J.M.: Linearizability: a correctness condition for concurrent objects. ACM Trans. Prog. Lang. Syst. **12**(3), 463–492 (1990)
22. Hirai, Y.: Formalization of Ethereum Virtual Machine in Lem. https://github.com/pirapira/eth-isabelle. Accessed 3 Feb 2017
23. Jentzsch, C.: The DAO (2016). https://etherscan.io/address/0xffbd72d37d4e7f64939e70b2988aa8924fde48e3
24. Lamport, L.: Specifying Systems: The TLA+ Language and Tools for Hardware and Software Engineers. Addison-Wesley, Boston (2002)
25. Liang, H., Feng, X.: A program logic for concurrent objects under fair scheduling. In: POPL, pp. 385–399. ACM (2016)
26. Lin, Y., Dig, D.: CHECK-THEN-ACT misuse of java concurrent collections. In: ICST, pp. 164–173. IEEE Computer Society (2013)
27. Luu, L., Chu, D., Olickel, H., Saxena, P., Hobor, A.: Making smart contracts smarter. In: CCS, pp. 254–269. ACM (2016)
28. Mulligan, D.P., Owens, S., Gray, K.E., Ridge, T., Sewell, P.: Lem: reusable engineering of real-world semantics. In: ICFP, pp. 175–188. ACM (2014)
29. Nanevski, A., Ley-Wild, R., Sergey, I., Delbianco, G.A.: Communicating state transition systems for fine-grained concurrent resources. In: Shao, Z. (ed.) ESOP 2014. LNCS, vol. 8410, pp. 290–310. Springer, Heidelberg (2014). https://doi.org/10.1007/978-3-642-54833-8_16

30. O'Hearn, P.W.: Resources, concurrency, and local reasoning. Theor. Comp. Sci. **375**(1–3), 271–307 (2007)
31. Pettersson, J., Edström, R.: Safer smart contracts through type-driven development. Master's thesis, Chalmers University of Technology, Department of Computer Science and Engineering, Sweden (2016)
32. Reitwiessner, C.: Formal Verification for Solidity Contracts. https://forum. ethereum.org/discussion/3779/formal-verification-for-solidity-contracts. Accessed 3 Feb 2017
33. Sergey, I., Nanevski, A., Banerjee, A.: Mechanized verification of fine-grained concurrent programs. In: PLDI, pp. 77–87. ACM (2015)
34. Svendsen, K., Birkedal, L., Parkinson, M.: Modular reasoning about separation of concurrent data structures. In: Felleisen, M., Gardner, P. (eds.) ESOP 2013. LNCS, vol. 7792, pp. 169–188. Springer, Heidelberg (2013). https://doi.org/10. 1007/978-3-642-37036-6_11
35. Swamy, N.,Chen, J., Fournet, C., Strub, P., Bhargavan, K., Yang, J.: Secure distributed programming with value-dependent types. In: ICFP, pp. 266–278. ACM (2011)
36. Swamy, N., Hritcu, C., Keller, C., Rastogi, A., Delignat-Lavaud, A., Forest, S., Bhargavan, K., Fournet, C., Strub, P., Kohlweiss, M., Zinzindohoue, J.K., Béguelin, S.Z.: Dependent types and multi-monadic effects in F*. In: POPL, pp. 256–270. ACM (2016)
37. Turon, A., Dreyer, D., Birkedal, L.: Unifying refinement and hoare-style reasoning in a logic for higher-order concurrency. In: ICFP, pp. 377–390. ACM (2013)
38. Wood, G.: Ethereum: a secure decentralised generalised transaction ledger (2014). http://gavwood.com/paper.pdf

An Empirical Analysis of Smart Contracts: Platforms, Applications, and Design Patterns

Massimo Bartoletti$^{(\boxtimes)}$ and Livio Pompianu

Università degli Studi di Cagliari, Cagliari, Italy
{bart,livio.pompianu}@unica.it

Abstract. Smart contracts are computer programs that can be consistently executed by a network of mutually distrusting nodes, without the arbitration of a trusted authority. Because of their resilience to tampering, smart contracts are appealing in many scenarios, especially in those which require transfers of money to respect certain agreed rules (like in financial services and in games). Over the last few years many platforms for smart contracts have been proposed, and some of them have been actually implemented and used. We study how the notion of smart contract is interpreted in some of these platforms. Focussing on the two most widespread ones, Bitcoin and Ethereum, we quantify the usage of smart contracts in relation to their application domain. We also analyse the most common programming patterns in Ethereum, where the source code of smart contracts is available.

1 Introduction

Since the release of Bitcoin in 2009 [40], the idea of exploiting its enabling technology to develop applications beyond currency has been receiving increasing attention [26]. In particular, the public and append-only ledger of transaction (the *blockchain*) and the decentralized consensus protocol that Bitcoin nodes use to extend it, have revived Nick Szabo's idea of *smart contracts*—i.e. programs whose correct execution is automatically enforced without relying on a trusted authority [47]. The archetypal implementation of smart contracts is Ethereum [28], a platform where they are rendered in a Turing-complete language. The consensus protocol of Ethereum ensures that all and only the valid updates to the contract states are recorded on the blockchain, so ensuring their correct execution.

Besides Bitcoin and Ethereum, a remarkable number of alternative platforms have flourished over the last few years, either implementing crypto-currencies or some forms of smart contracts [1, 7, 9, 30, 37]. For instance, the number of crypto-currencies hosted on coinmarketcap.com has increased from 0 to more than 600 since 2012; the number of github projects related to blockchains and smart contracts has reached, respectively, $2,715$ and 445 units (see Fig. 1). In the meanwhile, ICT companies and some national governments have started dealing with these topics [41, 48], also with significant investments.

© International Financial Cryptography Association 2017
M. Brenner et al. (Eds.): FC 2017 Workshops 2017, LNCS 10323, pp. 494–509, 2017.
https://doi.org/10.1007/978-3-319-70278-0_31

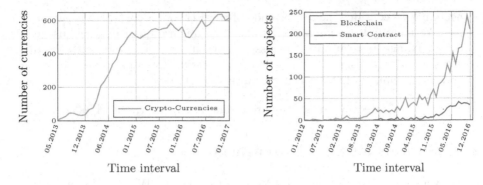

Fig. 1. On the left, monthly trend of the number of crypto-Currencies hosted on coinmarketcap.com. On the right, number of new projects related to blockchains and smart contracts which are created every month on github.com.

Despite the growing hype on blockchains and smart contracts, the understanding of the actual benefits of these technologies, and of their trustworthiness and security, has still to be assessed. In particular, the consequences of unsafe design choices for the programming languages for smart contracts can be fatal, as witnessed by the unfortunate epilogue of the DAO contract [13], a crowdfunding service plundered of ∼ 50M USD because of a programming error. Since then, many other vulnerabilities in smart contract have been reported [12,14,18,37].

Understanding how smart contracts are used and how they are implemented could help designers of smart contract platforms to create new domain-specific languages (not necessarily Turing complete [27,29,33,42]), which *by-design* avoid vulnerabilities as the ones discussed above. Further, this knowledge could help to improve analysis techniques for smart contracts (like e.g.the ones in [25,37]), by targeting contracts with specific programming patterns.

Contributions. This paper is a methodic survey on smart contracts, with a focus on Bitcoin and Ethereum—the two most widespread platforms currently supporting them. Our main contributions can be summarised as follows:

– in Sect. 2 we examine the Web for news about smart contracts in the period from June 2013 to September 2016, collecting data about 12 platforms. We choose from them a sample of 6 platforms which are amenable to analytical investigation. We analyse and compare several aspects of the platforms in this sample, mainly concerning their usage, and their support for programming smart contracts.
– in Sect. 3 we propose a taxonomy of smart contracts, sorting them into categories which reflect their application domain. We collect from the blockchains of Bitcoin and Ethereum a sample of 834 smart contracts, which we classify according to our taxonomy. We then study the usage of smart contracts, measuring the distribution of their transactions by category. This allows us to compare the different usage of Bitcoin and Ethereum as platforms for smart contracts.

– Section 4 we consider the source code of the Ethereum contracts in our sample. We identify 9 common design patterns, and we quantify their usage in contracts, also in relation to the associated category. Together with the previous point, ours constitutes the first quantitative investigation on the usage and programming of smart contract in Ethereum.

All the data collected by our survey are available online at: goo.gl/pOswL8.

2   Platforms for Smart Contracts

In this we analyse various platforms for smart contracts. We start by presenting the methodology we have followed to choose the candidate platforms Sect. 2.1. Then we describe the key features of each platform, pinpointing differences and similarities, and drawing some general statistics Sect. 2.2.

2.1   Methodology

To choose the platforms subject of our study, we have drawn up a candidate list by examining all the articles of coindesk.com in the "smart contracts" category[1]. Starting from June 2013, when the first article appeared, up to the 15th of September 2016, 175 articles were published, describing projects, events, companies and technologies related to smart contracts and blockchains. By manually inspecting all these articles, we have found references to 12 platforms: Bitcoin, Codius, Counterparty, DAML, Dogeparty, Ethereum, Lisk, Monax, Rootstock, Symbiont, Stellar, and Tezos.

We have then excluded from our sample the platforms which, at the time of writing, do not satisfy one of the following criteria: (i) have already been launched, (ii) are running and supported from a community of developers, and (iii) are publicly accessible. For the last point we mean that, e.g., it must be possible to write a contract and test it, or to explore the blockchain through some tools, or to run a node. We have inspected each of the candidate platforms, examining the related resources available online (e.g., official websites, white-papers, forum discussions, *etc.*) After this phase, we have removed 6 platforms from our list: Tezos and Rootstock, as they do not satisfy condition (i); Codius and Dogeparty, which violate condition (ii), DAML and Symbiont, which violate (iii). Summing up, we have a sample of 6 platforms: Bitcoin, Ethereum, Counterparty, Stellar, Monax and Lisk, which we discuss in the following.

2.2   Analysis of Platforms

We now describe the general features of the collected platforms, focussing on:(i) whether the platform has its own blockchain, or if it just piggy-backs on an already existing one; (ii) for platforms with a public blockchain, their consensus

---

[1] http://www.coindesk.com/category/technology/smart-contracts-news

protocol, and whether the blockchain is public or private to a specific set of nodes; (iii) the languages used to write smart contracts.

Bitcoin [40] is a platform for transferring digital currency, the bitcoins (BTC). It has been the first decentralized cryptocurrency to be created, and now is the one with the largest market capitalization. The platform relies on a public blockchain to record the complete history of currency transactions. The nodes of the Bitcoin network use a consensus algorithm based moderately hard *"proof-of-work"* puzzles to establish how to append a new block of transactions to the blockchain. Nodes work in competition to generate the next block of the chain. The first node that solves the puzzle earns a reward in BTC.

Although the main goal of Bitcoin is to transfer currency, the immutability and openness of its blockchain have inspired the development of protocols that implement (limited forms of) smart contracts. Bitcoin features a non-Turing complete scripting language, which allows to specify under which conditions a transaction can be redeemed. The scripting language is quite limited, as it only features some basic arithmetic, logical, and crypto operations (e.g., hashing and verification of digital signatures). A further limitation to its expressiveness is the fact that only a small fraction of the nodes of the Bitcoin network processes transactions whose script is more complex than verifying a signature[2].

Ethereum [28] is the second platform for market capitalization, after Bitcoin. Similarly to Bitcoin, it relies on a public blockchain, with a consensus algorithm similar to that of Bitcoin[3]. Ethereum has its own currency, caller *ether* (ETH). Smart contracts are written in a stack-based bytecode language [49], which is Turing-complete, unlike Bitcoin's. There also exist a few high level languages (the most prominent being *Solidity*[4]), which compile into the bytecode language. Users create contracts and invoke their functions by sending transactions to the blockchain, whose effects are validated by the network. Both users and contracts can store money and send/receive ETH to other contracts or users.

Counterparty [32] is a platform without its own blockchain; rather, it embeds its data into Bitcoin transactions. While the nodes of the Bitcoin network ignore the data embedded in these transactions, the nodes of Counterparty recognise and interpret them. Smart contracts can be written in the same language used by Ethereum. However, unlike Ethereum, no consensus protocol is used to validate the results of computations[5]. Counterparty has its own currency, which can be transferred between users, and be spent for executing contracts. Unlike Ethereum, nodes do not obtain fees for executing contracts; rather, the fees paid

---

[2] As far as we know, currently only the *Eligius* mining pool accepts more general transactions (called *non-standard* in the Bitcoin community). However, this pool only mines ∼ 1% of the total mined blocks [20].

[3] The consensus mechanism of Ethereum is a variant of the GHOST protocol in [46].

[4] Solidity: http://solidity.readthedocs.io/en/develop/index.html.

[5] See FAQ: How do Smart Contracts "form a consensus" on Counterparty? http://counterparty.io/docs/faq-smartcontracts/#how-do-smart-contracts-form-a-consensus-on-counterparty.

by clients are destroyed, and nodes are indirectly rewarded from the inflation of the currency. This mechanism is called *proof-of-burn*.

Stellar [10] features a public blockchain with its own cryptocurrency, governed by a consensus algorithm inspired to federated Byzantine agreement [11]. Basically, a node agrees on a transaction if the nodes in its neighbourhood (that are considered more trusted than the others) agree as well. When the transaction has been accepted by enough nodes of the network, it becomes infeasible for an attacker to roll it back, and it is considered as confirmed. Compared to *proof-of-work*, this protocol consumes far less computing power, since it does not involve solve cryptographic puzzles. Unlike Ethereum, there is no specific language for smart contracts; still, it is possible to gather together some transactions (possibly ordered in a chain) and write them atomically in the blockchain. Since transactions in a chain can involve different addresses, this feature can be used to implement basic smart contracts. For instance, assume that a participant A wants to pay B only if B promises to pay C after receiving the payment from A. This behaviour can be enforced by putting these transactions in the same chain. While this specific example can be implemented on Bitcoin as well, Stellar also allows to batch operations different from payments[6], e.g.creating new accounts. Stellar features special accounts, called *multisignature*, which can be handled by several owners. To perform operations on these accounts, a threshold of consensus must be reached among the owners. Transaction chaining and multisignature accounts can be combined to create more complex contracts.

Monax [8] supports the execution of Ethereum contracts, without having its own currency. Monax allows users to create private blockchains, and to define authorisation policies for accessing them. Its consensus protocol[7] is organised in rounds, where a participant proposes a new block of transactions, and the others vote for it. When a block fails to be approved, the protocol moves to the next round, where another participant will be in charge of proposing blocks. A block is confirmed when it is approved by at least 2/3 of the total voting power.

Lisk [6] has its own currency, and a public blockchain with a *delegated proof-of-stake* consensus mechanism[8]. More specifically, 101 active delegates, each one elected by the stakeholders, have the authority to generate blocks. Stakeholders can take part to the electoral process, by placing votes for delegates in their favour, or by becoming candidates themselves. Lisk supports the execution of Turing-complete smart contracts, written either in JavaScript or in Node.js. Unlike Ethereum, determinism of executions is not ensured by the language: rather, programmers must take care of it, e.g.by not using functions like *Math.random*. Although Lisk has a main blockchain, each smart contract is executed on a separated one. Users can deposit or withdraw currency from a contract to the main chain, while avoiding double spending. Contract owners can

---

[6] https://www.stellar.org/developers/guides/concepts/operations.html.
[7] https://tendermint.com/.
[8] https://lisk.io/documentation?i=lisk-handbooks/DelegateHandbook.

customise their blockchain before deploying their contracts, e.g.choosing which nodes can participate to the consensus mechanism.

Table 1. General statistics of platforms for smart contracts.

Platform	Blockchain			Contract Language	Total Tx	Volume	Marketcap
	Type	Size	Block int.			(K USD)	(M USD)
Bitcoin	Public	96 GB	10 min	Bitcoin scripts + signatures	184,045,240	83,178	15,482
Counterparty				EVM bytecode	12,170,386	33	4
Ethereum	Public	17–60 GB	12 s	EVM bytecode	14,754,984	10,354	723
Stellar	Public	?	3 s	Transaction chains + signatures	?	35	17
Monax	Private	?	Custom	EVM bytecode + permissions	?	n/a	n/a
Lisk	Private	?	Custom	JavaScript	?	45	15

Table 1 summarizes the main features of the analysed platforms. The question mark in some of the cells indicates that we were unable to retrieve the information (e.g., we have not been able to determine the size of Monax blockchains, since they are private). The first three columns next to the platform name describe features of the blockchain: whether it is public; its size; the average time between two consecutive blocks. Note that Bitcoin and Counterparty share the same cell, since the second platform uses the Bitcoin blockchain. Measuring the size of the Ethereum blockchain depends on which client and which pruning mode is used. For instance, using the Geth client, we obtain a measure of 17GB in "fast sync" mode, and of 60GB in "archive" mode[9]. In platforms with private blockchains, their block interval is custom. The fifth column describes the support for writing contracts. The sixth column shows the total number of transactions[10]. The last two columns show the daily volume of currency transfers, and the market capitalisation of the currency (both in USD, rounded, respectively, to thousands and millions)[11]. All values reported on Table 1 are updated to January 1st, 2017.

3 Analysing the Usage of Smart Contracts

In this we analyse the usage of smart contracts, proposing a classification which reflects their application domain. Then, focussing on Bitcoin and Ethereum, we quantify the usage of smart contracts in relation to their application domain. We start by presenting the methodology we have followed to sample and classify Bitcoin and Ethereum smart contracts (Sect. 3.1). Then, we introduce our classification and our statistical analysis (Sects. 3.2 and 3.3).

---

[9] https://redd.it/5om2lw.

[10] Sources: https://blockchain.info/charts/n-transactions-total (for Bitcoin), https://blockscan.com (Counterparty), and https://etherscan.io (Ethereum).

[11] Market capitalization estimated by http://coinmarketcap.com.

3.1   Methodology

We sample contracts from Bitcoin and Ethereum as follows:

- for Ethereum, we collect on January 1st, 2017 all the contracts marked as "verified" on the blockchain explorer etherscan.io. This means that the contract bytecode stored on the blockchain matches the source code (generally written in a high level language, such as Solidity) submitted to the explorer. In this way, we obtain a sample of 811 contracts.
- for Bitcoin, we start by observing that many smart contracts save their metadata on the blockchain through the OP_RETURN instruction of the Bitcoin scripting language [1,2,7,23]. We then scan the Bitcoin blockchain on January 1st 2017, searching for transactions that embed in an OP_RETURN some metadata attributable to a Bitcoin smart contract. To this purpose we use an explorer[12] which recognises 23 smart contracts, and extracts all the transactions related to them.

3.2   A Taxonomy of Smart Contracts

We propose a taxonomy of smart contracts into five categories, which describe their intended application domain. We then classify the contracts in our sample according to the taxonomy. To this purpose, for Ethereum contracts we manually inspect the Solidity source code, while for Bitcoin contracts we search their web pages and related discussion forums. After this manual investigation, we distribute all the contracts into the five categories, that we present below.

Financial. Contracts in this category manage, gather, or distribute money as preeminent feature. Some contracts certify the ownership of a real-world asset, endorse its value, and keep track of trades (e.g., Colu currently tracks over 50,000 assets on Bitcoin). Other contracts implement crowdfunding services, gathering money from investors in order to fund projects (the Ethereum DAO project was the most representative one, until its collapse due to an attack in June 2016). High-yield investment programs are a type of Ponzi schemes [22] that collect money from users under the promise that they will receive back their funds with interest if new investors join the scheme (e.g., Government, KingOfTheEtherThrone). Some contracts provide an insurance on setbacks which are digitally provable (e.g., Etherisc sells insurance policies for flights; if a flight is delayed or cancelled, one obtains a refund). Other contracts publish advertisement messages (e.g., PixelMap is inspired to the Million Dollar Homepage).

Notary. Contracts in this category exploit the immutability of the blockchain to store some data persistently, and in some cases to certify their ownership and provenance. Some contracts allow users to write the hash of a document on the blockchain, so that they can prove document existence and integrity (e.g., Proof of Existence). Others allow to declare copyrights on digital arts files,

---

[12] https://github.com/BitcoinOpReturn/OpReturnTool

like photos or music (e.g., Monegraph). Some contracts (e.g., Eternity Wall) just allow users to write down on the blockchain messages that everyone can read. Other contracts associate users to addresses (often represented as public keys), in order to certify their identity (e.g., Physical Address).

Game. This category gathers contracts which implement *games of chance* (e.g., LooneyLottery, Dice, Roulette, RockPaperScissors) and *games of skill* (e.g., Etherization), as well as some games which mix chance and skill (e.g., PRNG challenge pays for the solution of a puzzle).

Wallet. The contracts in this category handle keys, send transactions, manage money, deploy and watch contracts, in order to simplify the interaction with the blockchain. Wallets can be managed by one or many owners, in the latter case requiring multiple authorizations (like, e.g.in Multi-owned).

Library. These contracts implement general-purpose operations (like e.g., math and string transformations), to be used by other contracts.

3.3   Quantifying the Usage of Smart Contracts by Category

We analyse all the transactions related to the 0 smart contracts in our sample. Table 2 displays how the transactions are distributed in the categories of Sect. 3.2. For both Bitcoin and Ethereum, we show the number of detected contracts (third column), and the total number of transactions (fourth column).

Overall, we have 1,673,271 transactions. Notably, although Bitcoin contracts are fewer than those running on Ethereum, they have a larger amount of transactions each. A clear example of this is witnessed by the financial category, where

Table 2. Transactions by category.

Category	Platform	Contracts	Transactions
Financial	Bitcoin	6	470, 391
	Ethereum	373	624, 046
Notary	Bitcoin	17	443, 269
	Ethereum	79	35, 253
Game	Bitcoin	0	0
	Ethereum	158	58, 257
Wallet	Bitcoin	0	0
	Ethereum	17	1, 342
Library	Bitcoin	0	0
	Ethereum	29	37, 034
Unclassified	Bitcoin	0	0
	Ethereum	155	3, 679
Total	Bitcoin	23	913, 660
	Ethereum	811	759, 611
	Overall	834	1, 673, 271

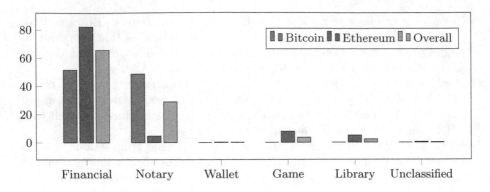

Fig. 2. Distribution of transactions by category.

6 Bitcoin contracts[13] totalize two thirds of the transactions published by the 373 Ethereum contracts in the same category (Fig. 2).

While both Bitcoin and Ethereum are mainly focussed on financial contracts, we observe major differences about the other categories. For instance, the Bitcoin contracts in the Notary category[14] have an amount of transactions similar to that of the Financial category, unlike in Ethereum. The second most used category in Ethereum is Game. Although some games (e.g., lotteries [16,17,19,24] and poker [36]) which run on Bitcoin have been proposed in the last few years, the interest on them is still mainly academic, and we have no experimental evidence that these contracts are used in practice. Instead, the greater flexibility of the Ethereum programming language simplifies the development of this kind of contracts (although with some quirks [31] and limitations[15]).

Note that in some cases there are not enough elements to categorise a contract. This happens e.g., when the contract does not link to the project webpage, and there are neither comments in online forums nor in the contract sources.

4   Design Patterns for Ethereum Smart Contracts

In this we study design patterns for Ethereum smart contracts. To this purpose, we consider the sample of 811 contracts collected through the methodology described in Sect. 3. By manually inspecting the Solidity source code of each of these contracts, we identify some common design patterns. We start in Sect. 4.1

---

[13] Bitcoin financial contracts: Colu, CoinSpark, OpenAssets, Omni, SmartBit, BitPos.

[14] Bitcoin notary contracts: Factom, Stampery, Proof of Existence, Blocksign, Crypto-Copyright, Stampd, BitProof, ProveBit, Remembr, OriginalMy, LaPreuve, Nicosia, Chainpoint, Diploma, Monegraph, Blockai, Ascribe, Eternity Wall, Blockstore.

[15] Although the Ethereum virtual machine is designed to be Turing-complete, in practice the limitations on the amount of gas which can be used to invoke contracts also limit the set of computable functions (e.g., verifying checkmate exceeds the current gas limits of a transaction [35]).

by describing these patterns. Then, in Sect. 4.2 we measure the usage of the patterns in the various categories of contracts identified in Sect. 3.

4.1 Design Patterns

Token. This pattern is used to distribute some fungible goods (represented by tokens) to users. Tokens can represent a wide variety of goods, like e.g.coins, shares, outcomes or tickets, or everything else which is transferable and countable. The implications of owning a token depend on the protocol and the use case for which the token has been issued. Tokens can be used to track the ownership of physical properties (e.g., gold [3]), or digital ones (e.g., cryptocurrency). Some crowdfunding systems issue tokens in exchange for donations (e.g., the Congress contract). Tokens are also used to regulate user authorizations and identities. For instance, the DVIP contract specifies rights and term of services for owners of its tokens. To vote on the poll ETCSurvey, users must possess a suitable token. Given the popularity of this pattern, its standardisation has been proposed [5]. Notably, the majority of analysed Ethereum contracts which issue tokens already adhere to it.

Authorization. This pattern is used to restrict the execution of code according to the caller address. Majority of the analysed contracts check if the caller address is that of the contract owner, before performing critical operations (e.g., sending ether, invoking suicide or selfdestruct). For instance, the owner of Doubler is authorized to move all funds to a new address *at any time* (this may raise some concerns about the trustworthiness of the contract, as a dishonest owner can easily steal money).
Corporation checks addresses to ensure that every user can vote only once per poll. CharlyLifeLog uses a white-list of addresses to decide who can withdraw funds.

Oracle. Some contracts may need to acquire data from outside the blockchain, e.g.from a website, to determine the winner of a bet. The Ethereum language does not allow contracts to query external sites: otherwise, the determinism of computations would be broken, as different nodes could receive different results for the same query. Oracles are the interface between contracts and the outside. Technically, they are just contracts, and as such their state can be updated by sending them transactions. In practice, instead of querying an external service, a contract queries an oracle; and when the external service needs to update its data, it sends a suitable transaction to the oracle. Since the oracle is a contract, it can be queried from other contracts without consistency issues. One of the most common oracles is Oraclize[16]: in our sample, it is used by almost all the contracts which resort to oracles.

Randomness. Dealing with randomness is not a trivial task in Ethereum. Since contract execution must be deterministic, all the nodes must obtain the same value when asking for a random number: this struggles with the randomness requirements wished. To address this issue, several contracts (e.g., Slot) query

---

[16] http://www.oraclize.it/.

oracles that generate these values off-chain. Others (e.g., Lottery) try to generate the numbers locally, by using values not predictable *a priori*, as the hash of a block not yet created. However, these techniques are not generally considered secure [18].

Poll. Polls allows users to vote on some question. Often this is a side feature in a more complex scenario. For instance, in the Dice game, when a certain state is reached, the owner issues a poll to decide whether an emergency withdrawal is needed. To determine who can vote and to keep track of the votes, polls can use tokens, or they can check the voters' addresses.

Time constraint. Many contracts implement time constraints, e.g.to specify when an action is permitted. For instance, BirthdayGift allows users to collect funds, which will be redeemable only after their birthday. In notary contracts, time constraints are used to prove that a document is owned from a certain date. In game contracts, e.g.Lottery, time constraints mark the stages of the game.

Termination. Since the blockchain is immutable, a contract cannot be deleted when its use has come to an end. Hence, developers must forethink a way to disable it, so that it is still present but unresponsive. This can be done manually, by inserting ad-hoc code in the contract, or automatically, calling `selfdestruct` or `suicide`. Usually, only the contract owner is authorized to terminate a contract (e.g., as in SimpleCoinFlipGame).

Math. Contracts using this pattern encode the logic which guards the execution of some critical operations. For instance, Badge implements a method named `subtractSafely` to avoid subtracting a value from a balance when there are not enough funds in an account.

Fork check. The Ethereum blockchain has been forked four times, starting from July 20th, 2016, when a fork was performed to contrast the effect of the DAO attack [4]. To know whether or not the fork took place, some contracts inspect the final balance of the DAO. Other contracts use this check to detect whether they are running on the main chain or on the fork, performing different actions in the two cases. AmIOnTheFork is a library contract that can be used to distinguish the main chain from the forked one.

4.2   Quantifying the Usage of Design Patterns by Category

We now study how the design patterns identified in Sect. 4.1 are used in smart contracts. Out of the 811 analysed contracts, 648 use at least one of the 9 patterns presented, for a grand total of 1427 occurrences of usage.

Table 3 shows the correlation between the usage of design patterns and contract categories, as defined in Sect. 3. A cell at row i and column j shows a pair of values: the first value is the percentage of contracts of category i that use the pattern of column j; the second one is the percentage of contracts with pattern j which belongs to category i. So, for instance, 24% of the contracts in the financial category use the token pattern, and 51% of all the contracts with the token pattern are financial ones.

Table 3. Relations between design patterns and contract categories. A pair (p, q) at row i and column j means that $p\%$ of the contracts in category i use the pattern of column j, and $q\%$ of contracts with pattern j belong to category i.

	Token	Auth.	Oracle	Random.	Poll	Time	Termin.	Fork	Math	None
Financial	24-51	51-39	2-15	1-2	5-29	23-31	14-30	8-69	4-47	29-66
Notary	13-6	52-9	1-2	0-0	8-9	20-6	29-13	0-0	1-3	30-15
Game	3-3	84-27	25-74	72-93	25-57	73-43	21-19	1-3	2-9	1-1
Wallet	18-2	100-3	0-0	0-0	0-0	94-6	100-10	0-0	12-6	0-0
Library	0-0	31-2	0-0	14-3	0-0	24-3	24-4	34-24	21-19	17-3
Unclassified	43-39	66-21	3-9	1-1	3-6	18-10	28-25	28-25	1-5	15-15
Total	*21-100*	*61-100*	*7-100*	*15-100*	*9-100*	*33-100*	*22-100*	*5-100*	*4-100*	*20-100*

We observe that *token, authorization, time constraint*, and *termination* are generally the most used patterns. Some patterns are spread across several categories (e.g., *termination* and *time constraint*), while others are mainly adopted only in one. For instance, *oracle* and *randomness* patterns are peculiar of game contracts, while the *token* pattern is mostly used in financial contracts. Although *math* is the less used, it appears in each category. Some contracts do not use any pattern (29% of financial and 30% of notary); almost all the contracts in game and wallet categories uses at least one. Further, only 15% of all the unclassified contracts do no use any pattern at all.

The most frequent patterns in financial contracts are *token* (24%), *authorization* (51%), and *time constraint* (23%). Due to the presence of contracts which implement assets and crowdfunding services, we have that half of contracts using *token* and *math* patterns belong to the financial category. For instance, these services use *token* for representing goods or developing polls. Moreover, a great 69% of contracts that use the *fork check* pattern is financial. This is caused by the necessity of knowing the branch of the fork before deciding to move funds. Finally, several financial applications (29%) perform simple operations (e.g.sending a payment) without using any of our described patterns.

The *authorization* pattern is used in many notary contracts to ensure that only the owner of a document can add or modify its data, in order to avoid tampering. Most gambling games involve players who pay fees to join the game, and rewards that can be collected by the winner. *Authorization* pattern is used to let the owner to be the only one able to redeem participants' fees or to perform administrative operations, and to let the winner withdraw his reward. The *time constraint* pattern is used to distinguish the different phases of the game. For instance, within a specific time interval players can join the game and/or bet; then, bets are over, and the game determines a winner. To choose the winner, some gambling games resort to random numbers, which are often generated through an oracle. Indeed, 25% of games use the *oracle* pattern, and the pattern itself is used 74% of cases by a game contract. Since *all* game contracts invoking an *oracle* (25%) ask for random values, and since 72% of contracts use the *random* pattern, we can deduce that 47% of them generate random numbers without resorting to oracles.

Notably, 100% of wallet contracts adopt both *authorization* and *termination* design patterns. A high 94% also uses *time constraint*. On the contrary, *oracle*, *poll*, and *randomness* patterns are of little use when developing a wallet, while *math* is sometimes used for securing operations on the balance.

5 Conclusions

We have analysed the usage of smart contracts from various perspectives. In Sect. 2 we have examined a sample of 6 platforms for smart contracts, pinpointing some crucial technical differences between them. For the two most prominent platforms—Bitcoin and Ethereum—we have studied a sample of 0 contracts, categorizing each of them by its application domain, and measuring the relevance of each of these categories (Sect. 3). The availability of source code for Ethereum contracts has allowed us to analyse the most common design patterns adopted when writing smart contracts (Sect. 4).

We believe that this survey may provide valuable information to developers of new, domain-specific languages for smart contracts. In particular, measuring what are the most common use cases allows to understand which domains deserve more investments. Furthermore, our study of the correlation between design patterns and application domains can be exploited to drive the correct choice of programming primitives of domain-specific languages for smart contracts.

Due to the mixed flavour of our analysis, which compares different platforms and studies how smart contracts are interpreted on each them, our work relates to various topics. The work [38] proposes design patterns for altering and undoing of smart contracts; so far, our analysis in Sect. 4.2 has not still found instances of these patterns in Ethereum. Among the works which study blockchain technologies, [15] compares four blockchains, with a special focus on the Ethereum one; [45] examines a larger set of blockchains, including also some which does not fit the criteria we have used in our methodology (e.g., RootStock and Tezos). Many works on Bitcoin perform empirical analyses of its blockchain. For instance, [43,44] study users deanonymization, [39] measures transactions fees, and [21] analyses Denial-of-Service attacks on Bitcoin. The work [34] investigates whether Bitcoin users are interested more on digital currencies as asset or as currency, with the aim of detecting the most popular use cases of Bitcoin contracts, similarly to what we have done in Sect. 3.3. Our classification of Bitcoin protocols based on OP_RETURN transactions is inspired from [23], which also measures the space consumption and temporal trend of OP_RETURN transactions.

Recently, some authors have started to analyse the security of Ethereum smart contracts: among these, [18] surveys vulnerabilities and attacks, while [37] and [25] propose analysis techniques to detect them. Our study on design patterns for Ethereum smart contracts could help to improve these techniques, by targeting contracts with specific programming patterns.

Acknowledgments. This work is partially supported by Aut. Reg. of Sardinia project P.I.A. 2013 "NOMAD".

References

1. Bitcoin contract. https://en.bitcoin.it/wiki/Contract. Accessed 14 Jan 2017
2. Bitcoin OP_RETURN wiki page. https://en.bitcoin.it/wiki/OP_RETURN. Accessed 14 Jan 2017
3. Dgx website. https://www.dgx.io/. Accessed 14 Jan 2017
4. Ethereum hard fork 20 July 2016. https://blog.ethereum.org/2016/07/20/hard-fork-completed/. Accessed 14 Jan 2017
5. Ethereum request for comment 20. https://github.com/ethereum/wiki/wiki/Standardized_Contract_APIs. Accessed 14 Jan 2017
6. Lisk. https://lisk.io/. Accessed 14 Jan 2017
7. Making sense of blockchain smart contracts. http://www.coindesk.com/making-sense-smart-contracts/. Accessed 14 Jan 2017
8. Monax. https://monax.io/. Accessed 14 Jan 2017
9. Smart contracts: The good, the bad and the lazy. http://www.multichain.com/blog/2015/11/smart-contracts-good-bad-lazy/. Accessed 14 Jan 2017
10. Stellar. https://www.stellar.org/. Accessed 14 Jan 2017
11. The Stellar consensus protocol. https://www.stellar.org/papers/stellar-consensus-protocol.pdf. Accessed 14 Jan 2017
12. Thinking about smart contract security. https://blog.ethereum.org/2016/06/19/thinking-smart-contract-security/. Accessed 14 Jan 2017
13. Understanding the DAO attack. http://www.coindesk.com/understanding-dao-hack-journalists/. Accessed 14 Jan 2017
14. Another bug in the ens, you can win with an unlimited high bid without paying for it (2017). https://www.reddit.com/r/ethereum/comments/5zctus/another_bug_in_the_ens_you_can_win_with_an/. Accessed 17 Mar 2017
15. Anderson, L., Holz, R., Ponomarev, A., Rimba, P., Weber, I.: New kids on the block: an analysis of modern blockchains. CoRR abs/1606.06530 (2016)
16. Andrychowicz, M., Dziembowski, S., Malinowski, D., Mazurek, L.: Secure multiparty computations on Bitcoin. In: IEEE S & P, pp. 443–458 (2014)
17. Andrychowicz, M., Dziembowski, S., Malinowski, D., Mazurek, L.: Secure ultiparty computations on Bitcoin. Commun. ACM **59**(4), 76–84 (2016). http://doi.acm.org/10.1145/2896386
18. Atzei, N., Bartoletti, M., Cimoli, T.: A survey of attacks on ethereum smart contracts (SoK). In: Maffei, M., Ryan, M. (eds.) POST 2017. LNCS, vol. 10204, pp. 164–186. Springer, Heidelberg (2017). https://doi.org/10.1007/978-3-662-54455-6_8
19. Back, A., Bentov, I.: Note on fair coin toss via Bitcoin (2013). http://www.cs.technion.ac.il/~idddo/cointossBitcoin.pdf
20. Banasik, W., Dziembowski, S., Malinowski, D.: Efficient zero-knowledge contingent payments in cryptocurrencies without scripts. In: Askoxylakis, I., Ioannidis, S., Katsikas, S., Meadows, C. (eds.) ESORICS 2016. LNCS, vol. 9879, pp. 261–280. Springer, Cham (2016). https://doi.org/10.1007/978-3-319-45741-3_14
21. Baqer, K., Huang, D.Y., McCoy, D., Weaver, N.: Stressing out: Bitcoin "stress testing". In: Clark, J., Meiklejohn, S., Ryan, P.Y.A., Wallach, D., Brenner, M., Rohloff, K. (eds.) FC 2016. LNCS, vol. 9604, pp. 3–18. Springer, Heidelberg (2016). https://doi.org/10.1007/978-3-662-53357-4_1

22. Bartoletti, M., Carta, S., Cimoli, T., Saia, R.: Dissecting Ponzi schemes on Ethereum: identification, analysis, and impact. CoRR abs/1703.03779 (2017). https://arxiv.org/abs/1703.03779

23. Bartoletti, M., Pompianu, L.: An analysis of Bitcoin OP_RETURN metadata. CoRR abs/1702.01024 (2016). To appear in Bitcoin Workshop 2017. https://arxiv.org/abs/1702.01024

24. Bentov, I., Kumaresan, R.: How to use Bitcoin to design fair protocols. In: Garay, J.A., Gennaro, R. (eds.) CRYPTO 2014. LNCS, vol. 8617, pp. 421–439. Springer, Heidelberg (2014). https://doi.org/10.1007/978-3-662-44381-1_24

25. Bhargavan, K., Delignat-Lavaud, A., Fournet, C., Gollamudi, A., Gonthier, G., Kobeissi, N., Rastogi, A., Sibut-Pinote, T., Swamy, N., Zanella-Beguelin, S.: Formal verification of smart contracts. In: PLAS (2016)

26. Bonneau, J., Miller, A., Clark, J., Narayanan, A., Kroll, J.A., Felten, E.W.: SoK: research perspectives and challenges for Bitcoin and cryptocurrencies. In: IEEE S & P, pp. 104–121 (2015)

27. Brown, R.G., Carlyle, J., Grigg, I., Hearn, M.: Corda: an introduction (2016). http://r3cev.com/s/corda-introductory-whitepaper-final.pdf

28. Buterin, V.: Ethereum: a next generation smart contract and decentralized application platform (2013). https://github.com/ethereum/wiki/wiki/White-Paper

29. Churyumov, A.: Byteball: a decentralized system for transfer of value (2016). https://byteball.org/Byteball.pdf

30. Clack, C.D., Bakshi, V.A., Braine, L.: Smart contract templates: foundations, design landscape and research directions. CoRR abs/1608.00771 (2016)

31. Delmolino, K., Arnett, M., Kosba, A., Miller, A., Shi, E.: Step by step towards creating a safe smart contract: lessons and insights from a cryptocurrency lab. In: Clark, J., Meiklejohn, S., Ryan, P.Y.A., Wallach, D., Brenner, M., Rohloff, K. (eds.) FC 2016. LNCS, vol. 9604, pp. 79–94. Springer, Heidelberg (2016). https://doi.org/10.1007/978-3-662-53357-4_6

32. Dermody, R., Krellenstein, A., Slama, O., Wagner, E.: Counterparty: Protocol specification (2014). http://counterparty.io/docs/protocol_specification/. Accessed 14 Jan 2017

33. Frantz, C.K., Nowostawski, M.: From institutions to code: towards automated generation of smart contracts. In: Workshop on Engineering Collective Adaptive Systems (eCAS) (2016)

34. Glaser, F., Zimmermann, K., Haferkorn, M., Weber, M.C.: Bitcoin - asset or currency? revealing users' hidden intentions. In: European Conference on Information Systems (ECIS) (2014)

35. Grau, P.: Lessons learned from making a chess game for Ethereum (2016). https://medium.com/@graycoding/lessons-learned-from-making-a-chess-game-for-ethereum-6917c01178b6#.fwtdwly6e. Accessed 14 Jan 2017

36. Kumaresan, R., Moran, T., Bentov, I.: How to use Bitcoin to play decentralized poker. In: ACM CCS, pp. 195–206 (2015)

37. Luu, L., Chu, D.H., Olickel, H., Saxena, P., Hobor, A.: Making smart contracts smarter. In: ACM CCS (2016). http://eprint.iacr.org/2016/633

38. Marino, B., Juels, A.: Setting standards for altering and undoing smart contracts. In: Alferes, J.J.J., Bertossi, L., Governatori, G., Fodor, P., Roman, D. (eds.) RuleML 2016. LNCS, vol. 9718, pp. 151–166. Springer, Cham (2016). https://doi.org/10.1007/978-3-319-42019-6_10

39. Möser, M., Böhme, R.: Trends, tips, tolls: a longitudinal study of Bitcoin transaction fees. In: Brenner, M., Christin, N., Johnson, B., Rohloff, K. (eds.) FC 2015. LNCS, vol. 8976, pp. 19–33. Springer, Heidelberg (2015). https://doi.org/10.1007/978-3-662-48051-9_2

40. Nakamoto, S.: Bitcoin: a peer-to-peer electronic cash system (2008). https://bitcoin.org/bitcoin.pdf

41. Nomura Research Institute: Survey on blockchain technologies and related services. http://www.meti.go.jp/english/press/2016/pdf/0531_01f.pdf

42. Popejoy, S.: The Pact smart contract language (2016). http://kadena.io/pact

43. Reid, F., Harrigan, M.: An analysis of anonymity in the Bitcoin system. In: Altshuler, Y., Elovici, Y., Cremers, A., Aharony, N., Pentland, A. (eds.) Security and Privacy in Social Networks, pp. 197–223. Springer, Heidelberg (2013). https://doi.org/10.1007/978-1-4614-4139-7_10

44. Ron, D., Shamir, A.: Quantitative analysis of the full Bitcoin transaction graph. In: Sadeghi, A.-R. (ed.) FC 2013. LNCS, vol. 7859, pp. 6–24. Springer, Heidelberg (2013). https://doi.org/10.1007/978-3-642-39884-1_2

45. Seijas, P.L., Thompson, S., McAdams, D.: Scripting smart contracts for distributed ledger technology. Cryptology ePrint Archive, Report 2016/1156 (2016). http://eprint.iacr.org/2016/1156

46. Sompolinsky, Y., Zohar, A.: Secure high-rate transaction processing in Bitcoin. In: Böhme, R., Okamoto, T. (eds.) FC 2015. LNCS, vol. 8975, pp. 507–527. Springer, Heidelberg (2015). https://doi.org/10.1007/978-3-662-47854-7_32

47. Szabo, N.: Formalizing and securing relationships on public networks. First Monday 2(9) (1997). http://firstmonday.org/htbin/cgiwrap/bin/ojs/index.php/fm/article/view/548

48. UK Government Chief Scientific Adviser: Distributed ledger technology: beyond block chain. https://www.gov.uk/government/uploads/system/uploads/attachment_data/file/492972/gs-16-1-distributed-ledger-technology.pdf

49. Wood, G.: Ethereum: a secure decentralised generalised transaction ledger (2014). http://gavwood.com/paper.pdf

Trust in Smart Contracts is a Process, As Well

Firas Al Khalil(✉), Tom Butler, Leona O'Brien, and Marcello Ceci

Governance, Risk, and Compliance Technology Center, University College Cork,
Cork, Ireland
{firas.alkhalil,tbutler,leona.obrien,marcello.ceci}@ucc.ie

Abstract. Distributed ledger technologies are rising in popularity, mainly for the host of financial applications they potentially enable, through smart contracts. Several implementations of distributed ledgers have been proposed, and different languages for the development of smart contracts have been suggested. A great deal of attention is given to the practice of development, i.e. programming, of smart contracts. In this position paper, we argue that more attention should be given to the *"traditional developers"* of contracts, namely the lawyers, and we propose a list of requirements for a human and machine-readable contract authoring language, friendly to lawyers, serving as a common (and a specification) language, for programmers, and the parties to a contract.

1 Introduction

The emergence of distributed ledger technology, due to the development of Bitcoin [22], sparked a lot of interest in different communities: from academia to industry, and from technological and financial circles to philosophical ones [24, 27].

The amount of enthusiasm generated around distributed ledgers is indicative of the potentialities that are waiting to be tapped into. What is undeniable, today, is that the financial industry is paying very close attention to cryptocurrencies, especially Bitcoin, but also to other financial applications enabled by distributed ledgers.

Which brings us to *smart contracts*, a concept first envisioned by Szabo [29], as far as 1995 so is claimed, and now believed to be enabled by the advent of distributed ledgers. Several definitions for smart contracts exist, varying in their faithfulness to the original concept, and some of them only adding to the existing confusion surrounding them. We will stand by the original definition of Szabo: *"[s]mart contracts [. . .] facilitate all steps of the contracting process"*; search, negotiation, commitment, performance, and adjudication are all parts of the contracting process he mentioned [28].

Bitcoin, as a platform, is able to model and execute smart contracts, but with a lot of restrictions due to its limited scripting language. This limitation, along with the observation that cryptocurrencies can be viewed as "just another kind of smart contracts", led eventually to the development of Ethereum [31]: a decentralised platform where smart contracts are first-class citizens; the distributed

© International Financial Cryptography Association 2017
M. Brenner et al. (Eds.): FC 2017 Workshops 2017, LNCS 10323, pp. 510–519, 2017.
https://doi.org/10.1007/978-3-319-70278-0_32

ledger is equipped with a Turing complete programming language that enables developers to write *"arbitrary"* contracts/code. More recently, platforms built on top of Bitcoin and supporting a Turing complete smart contracts language were developed (e.g. Rootstock [11]), and maybe more interestingly, platforms for smart contracts with non Turing complete languages were also developed, i.e. τ-Chain [6].

It is not a surprise that traditional programmers, if one may call them so, are unable to carry out *"economical thinking"* [10]; indeed, they are also, in our experience, ill-equipped to capture legal or regulatory thinking. The inverse can be said of *subject-matter experts*, i.e. business analysts and lawyers; they are most certainly unable to carry out *"computational thinking"*.

How to carry out the development of smart contracts in large financial institutions, where, traditionally, contracts are drafted by subject-matter experts? More importantly, how can we reason on the legality of developed contracts? Either manually by a lawyer, or automatically using a tool for compliance checking? A failure to answer these questions inevitably contributes to the scepticism of the financial industry – which has been put under the microscope by regulators since 2008 – about the future of smart contracts, and the industry's reluctance in adopting it.

In this position paper, we argue that trust in smart contracts, is *also* a process; a bridge is needed to connect both sides of the abyss.

The rest of this paper is organised as follows: Sect. 2 shows how diverse is the scene of distributed ledger technologies; Sect. 3 shows how irreconcilable are the languages of programmers and subject-matter experts; Sect. 4 develops our views on how can we build a bridge that enables trust, from an institutional perspective, in smart contracts; we finally conclude in Sect. 5.

2   On Distributed Ledger Technologies

The introduction of Bitcoin by Satoshi Nakamoto [22] polarised the actors in the financial industry since the beginning: some were extremely enthusiastic about it, to the point where they claimed that Bitcoin is the *"next big thing"*, and others were extremely sceptical about it.

The innovation of Bitcoin is not limited to the currency; the idea of a shared ledger itself proved to be very powerful and sprung many platforms rivalling or even complementing Bitcoin. The interested reader can refer to Tschorsch and Scheuermann [30] for an excellent technical survey on distributed ledger technologies. Moreover, a quick look at the currently available platforms inspired by Bitcoin, gives a good idea on the rising popularity of the technology: for instance, `coinmarketcap.com`, a site that tracks market capitalisation of different cryptocurrencies, lists 719 platforms.

Since its inception, Bitcoin provided a stack-based scripting language that allowed developers to define the conditions to spend Bitcoins (e.g. requiring multiple signatures), which revived the vision of smart contracts. However, this scripting language is purposefully not Turing complete, which ultimately means that it is limited in expressivity. In the following, we will take a look at four different platforms that are meant to overcome Bitcoin's scripting limitations, illustrating the different technical choices one can make, regarding the development of smart contracts.

The first platform we are going to look at, which is currently almost synonymous to "smart contracts", is Ethereum [31]. Ethereum was proposed as a distributed platform independent of – yet very similar to – Bitcoin. To create distributed trust-less consensus and solve the double-spending problem, Ethereum uses proof-of-work, just like Bitcoin, however, it provides the Ethereum Virtual Machine (EVM) that runs a Turing complete stack based language, which opens the doors to a hypothetically unlimited number of applications. Developers are not forced to use the EVM's opcode to write smart contracts. Indeed, they can use Solidity or Serpent, which are high-level programming languages, similar to javascript or python, respectively, that can compile to EVM byte code.

The second platform we are going to look at is Nxt[1], one of the earliest smart contract platforms. Unlike Bitcoin and Ethereum, Nxt uses proof-of-stake to achieve consensus and solve the double-spending problem. Moreover, Nxt does not provide a scripting language to smart contract developers; instead, it provides a RESTful API exposing a set of primitive operations (like spending, storing strings, sending messages, etc.) that developers can invoke.

The third platform we will consider is Rootstock [11]. Unlike Ethereum, and Nxt, Rootstock was developed to complement Bitcoin (as a *sidechain* [12]) and provides its own Turing complete virtual machine (the RVM) to enable smart contracts.

The fourth and final platform we will examine is τ-Chain [6]. The authors of this platform argue that Turing completeness is not necessary for distributed ledgers, because with Turing completeness comes undecidability, i.e. smart contracts can go in an infinite loop and the network will never be able to predict this behaviour. Indeed, Ethereum overcomes the problem of undecidability by forcing the caller of the smart contract to provide *gas* with the transaction (bought with *ether*, Ethereum's own cryptocurrency); every instruction on the EVM consumes a predefined amount of gas, and they are non-refundable, i.e. if the gas is totally consumed and the smart contract didn't finish execution, the gas is never returned to the caller.

However, Asor [6] proposes the use of an ontology [2] of rules, along with a reasoner, to enable computations on the network. Authors of smart contracts would write them in a totally functional programming language, like Idris [7], that will be ultimately translated into the ontology. This approach will not only make computations decidable, but it also allows the assertion of properties of smart contracts that were impossible with Turing complete languages, e.g. if the contract connects to the Internet or not, or if the contract fulfils some interfaces/requirements/etc.

The interested reader can refer to the survey written by Seijas et al. [25] for more information on scripting languages for distributed ledgers. The

---

[1] https://nxt.org/.

aforementioned platforms illustrate some of the variations that exist in distributed ledger technology's ecosystem. These platforms can differ not only in the tooling and the language they expose for smart contract development, but also in the paradigms that govern them. The development of smart contracts thus requires a deep and serious understanding of the target platform. In the following section, we will examine what hinders a fast adoption of such an enabling technology by the financial industry.

3   Staring into the Abyss

A close inspection of the literature shows that effort is being put in helping developers author smart contracts, by either developing tools, or creating abstractions.

Recently, Delmolino et al. [10] reported on their experience in teaching smart contract programming, using Ethereum, to undergraduate students at the University of Maryland. The authors concluded that smart contract programming *requires an "economic thinking" perspective that traditional programmers may not have acquired.* Indeed, students repeatedly made logical errors that ultimately lead to money leaks, failed to use cryptographic primitives to secure the contracts from attackers, failed to account for the incentives of contract callers, and even made mistakes directly related to Ethereum.

This observation lead to the development of a Masters thesis by Pettersson and Edström [23], and their objective was to help said programmers to develop safer smart contracts. Their aim is to prevent 3 kinds of mistakes contract developers fall in: unexpected states, failure to use cryptography, and overflowing the EVM's stack. They propose to use of a functional programming language, namely Idris. They developed a code generator that transforms code produced by an Idris compiler to Serpent code, which can be subsequently compiled into EVM bytecode.

In a different, yet related work, Luu et al. [21] noted that a class of security-related bugs in smart contracts are due to the gaps in the understanding of the distributed semantics of the underlying platform.

Another interesting work is that of Florian et al. [20], who propose the use of logic-based smart contracts. They showed that this approach can complement smart contracts written in procedural code, in terms of contract negotiation, formation, storage/notarizing, enforcement, monitoring and activities related to dispute resolution.

In a different take, García-Bañuelos et al. [16] showed how the business process language BPMN can be mapped into executable smart contracts on the Ethereum. This development lead Hull et al. [19] to propose a *Business Collaboration Language* (BCL) for shared ledgers. Indeed, this BCL can be thought of as the equivalent of SQL for relational databases, targeting shared ledgers, regardless of implementation-specific details.

As far as we know, the only works that consider the issue of authoring smart contracts from the subject-matter expert's perspective are those proposed by Frantz and Nowostawski [14] and Clack et al. [9].

Frantz and Nowostawski [14] propose a semi-automated method for the translation of human readable contracts to smart contracts on Ethereum. The authors develop a domain specific language for contract modelling, where statements are rules expressed in English, and that translates into `Solidity`. However, this solution is very tied to Ethereum, and it is not clear how extensible or adaptable it is. Additionally, it doesn't cover the legal language that a lawyer would be accustomed to.

Clack et al. [9] rightly identify two semantics of contracts:

Operational semantics: concerned with the execution of the contract on a specific platform.

Denotational semantics: that capture the *"legal meaning"* of the contract, as understood by a lawyer.

The authors envision the use of smart contract templates, based on the idea of Ricardian Contracts [17,18]. A Ricardian Contract is a digitlly signed triple $\langle P, C, M \rangle$, where P is the legal prose, capturing denotational semantics, C is the platform specific code expressing operational semantics, and M is a map (key-value pairs) of parameters used in P and C.

While the use of smart contract templates, based on Ricardian Contracts, looks like a move towards the right direction, we argue that prose should not be tied to code:

- While the semantics of legal language can be expressed as a set of deontic defeasible rules, the code is rather procedural. The order of the instructions in the procedure does not reflect the natural order of the contract clauses expressed in natural language [20].
- The life-cycle of legal prose is independent from the life-cycle of the code. For example, a lawyer might describe the terms of a contract in prose and never come back to it, while a developer will – most likely – iterate through different implementations (e.g. bug fixes).
- There is not a single smart contract platform, which ultimately means that different parameters (key-value pairs of M) will be needed for different platforms. For example, several works (e.g. [1,3,32]) describe data feed systems that enable smart contracts to consume data feeds from outside the distributed ledger (e.g. a stock market index); while the notion of an external feed might be familiar to a lawyer, its technical details, thus the choices related to the adoption of one method over another, and eventually the parametrisation is definitely out of her/his reach and/or interest.

In the following section, we will identify the key issues, as we see them, regarding the adoption of smart contracts, and how we envision to solve them.

4   Trusting Smart Contracts

In Sect. 2 we tried to show, through a non-exhaustive list of examples, how distributed ledgers can differ on a deep technical level, which requires a very intimate technological knowledge by the *implementer* of the smart contract. Afterwards, we showed, in Sect. 3, how current effort is mostly focused on developing technical tools and infrastructure aimed at facilitating the technical implementation of smart contracts. However, there is a major lacuna in all this: that is the translation, or mapping, of the contract's denotational semantics to its operational semantics.

We share the view of Clack et al. [9] on the separation between operational and denotational semantics of contracts. In fact, we argue that trust in smart contracts can only stem from the ability of lawyers in financial institutions to understand, express, and ultimately validate the denotational semantics of a contract. However, we disagree on the assumption they make on the languages expressing these semantics, i.e. any assumption on the correspondence between a *"legal language"* and the *"technical language"* cannot be taken for granted, as the lawyer cannot predict the behaviour of the code; this is an open question that deserves further research and validation.

What is missing from all of the described work, is the realisation that the involvement of a lawyer, especially in the heavily regulated financial industry, in the authoring of contracts, not only smart contracts, is paramount, for her/his knowledge on the regulation governing said contracts dictates the denotational semantics. A lawyers' knowledge of the explicit and implicit rights and obligations, counterparties, stakeholders, schedules and penalties, and regulations governing a financial contract needs to be represented.

Indeed, the financial crisis of 2008 was in part caused by the sub-prime lending practice that encouraged high credit risk borrowers to take on mortgages at high interest rates that they had little ability to repay. These debts were pooled together and engineered to be offered as low risk asset-backed securities. These were heavily traded because of the *perceived* low risk while providing high returns. The housing market in the US slumped setting off a chain reaction that ultimately meant the mortgage-backed securities became worthless having direct effect on the capital of the major global banks. Funding dried up and more importantly, the trust that keeps the financial system performing dissolved. As a result, regulation in the financial industry has grown exponentially.

There are two scenarios where the lawyer's involvement is unavoidable:

- When the contract is partly fulfilled through code, because the lawyer can only validate its textual version [20], i.e. the prose.
- When assessing the compliance of the contract with regulations, from the point of view of both the legal requirements introduced by the regulation (e.g. on financial activities, anti-money laundering, or consumer protection), and of the effects that these regulations automatically bind to the contract (*naturalia negotii* [15]).

Therefore, we think that proper authoring of smart contracts should involve two main agents: the lawyer and the developer. The interaction between both agents should be governed by a common language. The lawyer authors and consumes contracts written in that language, while the developer uses it as a specification guiding her/his implementation. This common language should have the following properties:

– It should not alienate the lawyer, i.e. it should be as close as possible to the language of contracts s/he is used to.
– It should be expressive enough to allow the authoring of smart and *"not-so-smart"* contracts.
– It should be a Controlled Natural Language (CNL) with an unambiguous grammar. The CNL should be mappable to a logical formalism which will facilitate compliance checking with existing regulations.
– The concepts and actions described in the contract (i.e. the vocabulary) along the clauses of the contract (i.e. the rules) should be shareable across the network, which is important for both *discoverability* and *negotiation* – two defining aspects of smart contracts – by human and autonomous agents.
– It should be able to represent the actions coded in the smart contract [9], the duties and powers arising from the contract [14], and the meta-rules governing it (e.g. regulation on financial activities, Anti-Money Laundering or consumer protection).

In our previous work [8] we describe Mercury, a language to capture regulations for the purpose of compliance checking, alongside a methodology [4] to capture legal knowledge and translate it to OWL [5]. Mercury is based on the Semantics for Business Vocabulary and Business Rules [26] (SBVR), but the language of smart contracts should not forcibly be based on SBVR, as long as it can be mapped to a logical formalism, e.g. OWL, where reasoning on compliance is feasible.

In a recently published technical report, English et al. [13] investigated how distributed ledger technologies and the Semantic Web can affect one another. Indeed, the blockchain can provide secure resource identifiers (by ensuring authenticity, human-readability, and decentralisation), and ontologies can provide a unified way to understand blockchain concepts between humans, and exposing blockchain data according to an ontology enables the interlinking with other linked data and to perform reasoning.

Our proposal improves transparency, which is one of the major luring qualities of distributed ledgers, and a determining factor of the trust-less trust in the network. But doubt rises when it comes to the trust in the fact that the contract, as written by the lawyer, was correctly translated into code, i.e. the trust in the fact operational semantics faithfully represent denotational semantics. One may argue that this trust can be guaranteed if there is a mechanism $\mathcal{G}$ that automatically generates code from prose and/or a mechanism $\mathcal{C}$, potentially the inverse of $\mathcal{G}$, that proves the correspondence of the code to the prose, but a closer inspections shows that:

1. There is evidence from the literature that $\mathcal{G}$ and $\mathcal{C}$ can exist, especially from [20] and τ-Chain [6]. Indeed, if the vision of τ-Chain is possible, then there is an opportunity to go directly from denotational to operational semantics using our approach, but this *may* imply the restriction of said trust to one specific distributed ledger technology.

2. It is not really clear, at least for us, if $\mathcal{G}$ and $\mathcal{C}$ exist for shared ledgers that use stack-based languages. This is an open question that deserves closer attention, and can have one of two clear answers:
   (a) It is possible, or practically feasible, which is great news for everyone, or
   (b) It is impossible, or practically infeasible. Then it is only reasonable to ask: *is the existence of $\mathcal{G}$ and $\mathcal{C}$ a prerequisite for the establishment of said trust?* We conjecture that it is not, for two reasons:
       i. The implementation processes of existing financial contracts in the form of software is already opaque, especially to the consumer, and our proposed approach would only facilitate transparency.
       ii. Trust can be gained through the establishment of reputation: the better you are in effectively transforming your specification to code, the more reputable you are; the more reputable you are, the more trustworthy you are perceived to be.

5 Conclusion

In this position paper, we expressed our point of view on how trust in smart contrast, from a financial institution's point of view, can be enabled. It is true that cryptographic guarantees are enablers of, and integral to, trust in distributed ledger technology, but we argue that another kind of trust is needed; one that is established by a process involving lawyers.

We showed how distributed ledger technologies can vary on a deep technical level, which led to the development of tools and abstractions to help developers in programming smart contracts. These developments are essential for the technological ecosystem, but we show how most of the existing work do not take into account compliance with existing (and ever growing) regulations.

To that end, we set a list of criteria for a language necessary for the development of contracts, executed on the ledger, or not, that is close to the legal prose, transparent, and rooted in formal logic. We also identify a key research challenge, which is the ability to translate the aforementioned language to executable code.

References

1. Oraclize: The provably honest oracle service. http://www.oraclize.it/. Accessed 30 Jan 2017
2. OWL 2 Web Ontology Language Document Overview (Second Edition). https://www.w3.org/TR/2012/REC-owl2-overview-20121211/. Accessed 30 Jan 2017
3. PriceFeed smart contract. http://feed.ether.camp/. Accessed 30 Jan 2017
4. Abi-Lahoud, E., O'Brien, L., Butler, T.: On the road to regulatory ontologies. In: Casanovas, P., Pagallo, U., Palmirani, M., Sartor, G. (eds.) AICOL -2013. LNCS, vol. 8929, pp. 188–201. Springer, Heidelberg (2014). https://doi.org/10.1007/978-3-662-45960-7_14
5. Al Khalil, F., Ceci, M., Yapa, K., O'Brien, L.: SBVR to OWL 2 mapping in the domain of legal rules. In: Alferes, J.J.J., Bertossi, L., Governatori, G., Fodor, P., Roman, D. (eds.) RuleML 2016. LNCS, vol. 9718, pp. 258–266. Springer, Cham (2016). https://doi.org/10.1007/978-3-319-42019-6_17

6. Asor, O.: About Tau-Chain. ArXiv e-prints (February 2015)
7. Brady, E.: Idris, a general-purpose dependently typed programming language: design and implementation. J. Funct. Program. **23**(5), 552–593 (2013)
8. Ceci, M., Al Khalil, F., O'Brien, L.: Making sense of regulations with SBVR. In: RuleML 2016 Challenge, Doctoral Consortium and Industry Track hosted by the 10th International Web Rule Symposium (RuleML 2016) (2016)
9. Clack, C.D., Bakshi, V.A., Braine, L.: Smart contract templates: essential requirements and design options. ArXiv e-prints (August 2016). https://arxiv.org/abs/1608.00771v2
10. Delmolino, K., Arnett, M., Kosba, A., Miller, A., Shi, E.: Step by step towards creating a safe smart contract: lessons and insights from a cryptocurrency lab. In: Clark, J., Meiklejohn, S., Ryan, P.Y.A., Wallach, D., Brenner, M., Rohloff, K. (eds.) FC 2016. LNCS, vol. 9604, pp. 79–94. Springer, Heidelberg (2016). https://doi.org/10.1007/978-3-662-53357-4_6
11. Lerner, S.D.: Rootstock. bitcoin powered smart contracts. white paper (November 2015). https://uploads.strikinglycdn.com/files/90847694-70f0-4668-ba7f-dd0c6b0b00a1/RootstockWhitePaperv9-Overview.pdf
12. Lerner, S.D.: Drivechains, sidechains, and 2-way hybrid peg designs (January 2016). https://uploads.strikinglycdn.com/files/27311e59-0832-49b5-ab0e-2b0a73899561/Drivechains_Sidechains_and_Hybrid_2-way_peg_Designs_R9.pdf
13. English, M., Auer, S., Domingue, J.: Block chain technologies and the semantic web: a framework for symbiotic development. Technical report, University of Bonn, Germany (2016)
14. Frantz, C.K., Nowostawski, M.: From institutions to code: towards automated generation of smart contracts. In: 2016 IEEE 1st International Workshops on Foundations and Applications of Self* Systems (FAS*W), pp. 210–215 (September 2016)
15. Frignani, A.: Some Basic Differences between the Common Law and the Civil Law Approach. http://www.jus.unitn.it/CARDOZO/Review/Comparative/Frignani-1997/Washingt.htm (1996). Accessed 02 Feb 2017
16. García-Bañuelos, L., Ponomarev, A., Dumas, M., Weber, I.: Optimized execution of business processes on blockchain. In: Carmona, J., Engels, G., Kumar, A. (eds.) BPM 2017. LNCS, vol. 10445, pp. 130–146. Springer, Cham (2017). https://doi.org/10.1007/978-3-319-65000-5_8
17. Grigg, I.: The Ricardian contract. In: Proceedings of 2004 First IEEE International Workshop on Electronic Contracting, pp. 25–31 (July 2004)
18. Grigg, I.: On the intersection of Ricardian and Smart Contracts. http://iang.org/papers/intersection_ricardian_smart.html (February 2017). Accessed 30 Jan 2017
19. Hull, R., Batra, V.S., Chen, Y.-M., Deutsch, A., Heath III, F.F.T., Vianu, V.: Towards a shared ledger business collaboration language based on data-aware processes. In: Sheng, Q.Z., Stroulia, E., Tata, S., Bhiri, S. (eds.) ICSOC 2016. LNCS, vol. 9936, pp. 18–36. Springer, Cham (2016). https://doi.org/10.1007/978-3-319-46295-0_2
20. Idelberger, F., Governatori, G., Riveret, R., Sartor, G.: Evaluation of logic-based smart contracts for blockchain systems. In: Alferes, J.J.J., Bertossi, L., Governatori, G., Fodor, P., Roman, D. (eds.) RuleML 2016. LNCS, vol. 9718, pp. 167–183. Springer, Cham (2016). https://doi.org/10.1007/978-3-319-42019-6_11
21. Luu, L., Chu, D.H., Olickel, H., Saxena, P., Hobor, A.: Making smart contracts smarter. In: CCS 2016 Proceedings of the 2016 ACM SIGSAC Conference on Computer and Communications Security, pp. 254–269. ACM, New York, NY, USA (2016). http://doi.acm.org/10.1145/2976749.2978309

22. Nakamoto, S.: Bitcoin: a peer-to-peer electronic cash system (2008)
23. Pettersson, J., Edström, R.: Safer smart contracts through type-driven development. Ph.D. thesis, Master's thesis, Department of CS and E, Chalmers University of Technology and University of Gothenburg, Sweden (2015)
24. Reijers, W., O'Brolcháin, F., Haynes, P.: Governance in blockchain technologies and social contract theories. Ledger **1**, 134–151 (2016). http://www.ledgerjournal. org/ojs/index.php/ledger/article/view/62
25. Seijas, P.L., Thompson, S., McAdams, D.: Scripting smart contracts for distributed ledger technology. Cryptology ePrint Archive, Report 2016/1156 (2016). http:// eprint.iacr.org/2016/1156
26. Semantics of Business Vocabulary and Business Rules (SBVR) Version 1.3, May 2015. http://www.omg.org/spec/SBVR/1.3/PDF
27. Swan, M.: Blockchain temporality: smart contract time specifiability with blocktime. In: Alferes, J.J.J., Bertossi, L., Governatori, G., Fodor, P., Roman, D. (eds.) RuleML 2016. LNCS, vol. 9718, pp. 184–196. Springer, Cham (2016). https://doi. org/10.1007/978-3-319-42019-6_12
28. Szabo, N.: Formalizing and Securing Relationships on Public Networks. https:// web.archive.org/web/20050217172626/.   http://www.firstmonday.dk/ISSUES/ issue2_9/szabo/index.html (1997). Accessed 25 Jan 2017
29. Szabo, N.: The Idea of Smart Contracts. https://web.archive.org/web/ 20160831070942/. http://szabo.best.vwh.net/smart_contracts_idea.html (1997). Accessed 25 Jan 2017
30. Tschorsch, F., Scheuermann, B.: Bitcoin and beyond: a technical survey on decentralized digital currencies. IEEE Commun. Surv. Tutor. **18**(3), 2084–2123 (2016). http://dx.doi.org/10.1109/COMST.2016.2535718
31. Wood, G.: Ethereum: a secure decentralised generalised transaction ledger. Ethereum Project Yellow Paper 151 (2014)
32. Zhang, F., Cecchetti, E., Croman, K., Juels, A., Shi, E.: Town crier: an authenticated data feed for smart contracts. In: CCS 2016 Proceedings of the 2016 ACM SIGSAC Conference on Computer and Communications Security, pp. 270–282. ACM, New York, NY, USA (2016). http://doi.acm.org/10.1145/2976749.2978326

Defining the Ethereum Virtual Machine for Interactive Theorem Provers

Yoichi Hirai[✉]

Ethereum Foundation, Berlin, Germany
yoichi@ethereum.org

Abstract. Smart contracts in Ethereum are executed by the Ethereum Virtual Machine (EVM). We defined EVM in Lem, a language that can be compiled for a few interactive theorem provers. We tested our definition against a standard test suite for Ethereum implementations. Using our definition, we proved some safety properties of Ethereum smart contracts in an interactive theorem prover Isabelle/HOL. To our knowledge, ours is the first formal EVM definition for smart contract verification that implements all instructions. Our definition can serve as a basis for further analysis and generation of Ethereum smart contracts.

1 Introduction

Ethereum is a protocol for executing a virtual computer in an open and distributed manner. This virtual computer is called the *Ethereum Virtual Machine* (EVM). The programs on EVM are called Ethereum *smart contracts*. A deployed Ethereum smart contract is public under adversarial scrutiny, and the code is not updatable. Most applications (auctions, prediction markets, identity/reputation management etc.) involve smart contracts managing funds or authenticating external entities. In this environment, the code should be trustworthy.

The developers and the users of smart contracts should be able to check the properties of the smart contracts with widely available proof checkers. Our EVM definition is written in Lem, which can be translated into popular interactive theorem provers Coq [1], Isabelle/HOL [19] and HOL4 [23]. We used our EVM definition and proved safety properties of some smart contracts in Isabelle/HOL.

Our contributions are as follows:

- we gave a formal specification of the interface between a smart contract execution and the rest of the world (Sect. 4);
- we defined EVM in a way portable to different interactive theorem provers (Isabelle/HOL and HOL4) and a programming language OCaml, during which we found some subtle differences between the specification (the Yellow Paper [26]) and the implementations (Sects. 5 and 6);
- we tested the executable part of our EVM definition against the VM test suite, which validates existing Ethereum node implementations (Subsect. 5.3); we found unsearched corner cases in the test suite;
- we used our EVM definition to prove invariants and safety properties of Ethereum smart contracts (Sect. 7).

© International Financial Cryptography Association 2017
M. Brenner et al. (Eds.): FC 2017 Workshops 2017, LNCS 10323, pp. 520–535, 2017.
https://doi.org/10.1007/978-3-319-70278-0_33

2   Choice of the Goal and the Tool

2.1   Goal: Which Programming Language to Formalize

Considerations Around Solidity. Although ultimately all Ethereum smart contracts are deployed as EVM bytecode, the bytecode is rarely directly written. The most popular programming language Solidity [3] has a rich syntax but no specification. The only definition of Solidity is the Solidity compiler implementation, which compiles Solidity programs into EVM bytecode.

The Solidity compiler is written in C++. Importing the C++ code in a theorem prover is nearly impossible because the definition of the whole C++11 language has not been formalized although some of the hardest aspects of the language have been addressed: concurrency [6], inheritance [21] etc.

It is feasible to verify a compiler with optimization (e.g. CompCert [14] and CakeML [13]). Something similar for Solidity would require formalization of both Solidity and EVM before correctness of the compiler can be stated.

Considerations on EVM. There are drawbacks of verifying EVM bytecode:

- most developers and users do not read EVM bytecode;
- the EVM architecture might become obsolete after the protocol adopts one of the proposed new architectures (EVM 1.5 that introduces function calls or EVM 2.0 which is based on WebAssembly [4]).

The first point can be, in the future, mitigated by translating static assertions in Solidity into EVM bytecode. The second point is, in fact, milder compared with the fast changes of the Solidity compiler. When the virtual machine architecture changes, all Ethereum implementations need to implement the change. This makes EVM change slower than the Solidity compiler.

EVM is an attractive formalization target. It is a stack-machine with a simple instruction-encoding and fully sequential execution. The simplicity of the EVM architecture resulted in just over 2,000 lines of formal definition. EVM has an English specification called the Yellow Paper (Fig. 1) clear enough to allow multiple implementations to be developed independently[1]. Also, since any disagreements among implementations hurt the availability of the network, the community has implemented test suites to compare EVM implementations. We use one of these test suites to test our EVM definition.

2.2   Tool: Formalization in Which Language

We intend our EVM definition as a basis for smart contract verification. The verification should be done in a precise manner. Model checkers are not capable of doing this because they cannot treat the huge state space: a smart contract can store up to 2^{256} 256-bit machine words permanently (the resource usage is limited

---

[1] Several entities develop Ethereum clients in Python, C++, Rust, Java, Scala and Go, and each contains its own EVM implementation.

0s: Stop and Arithmetic Operations

All arithmetic is modulo 2^{256} unless otherwise noted.

Value Mnemonic δ α Description

0x01 ADD   2 1 Addition operation.

$$\boldsymbol{\mu}_s'[0] \equiv \boldsymbol{\mu}_s[0] + \boldsymbol{\mu}_s[1]$$

⋮

0x08 ADDMOD   3 1 Modulo addition operation.

$$\boldsymbol{\mu}_s'[0] \equiv \begin{cases} 0 & \text{if } \boldsymbol{\mu}_s[2] = 0 \\ (\boldsymbol{\mu}_s[0] + \boldsymbol{\mu}_s[1]) \mod \boldsymbol{\mu}_s[2] & \text{otherwise} \end{cases}$$

All intermediate calculations of this operation are not subject to the 2^{256} modulo.

Fig. 1. A short excerpt from the Yellow Paper [26]. The symbol δ (resp. α) stands for the number of deleted (resp. added) stack elements. $\boldsymbol{\mu}_s[i]$ is the i-th stack element before the instruction execution. $\boldsymbol{\mu}_s'[i]$ is the i-th stack element afterwards.

only economically). Such big state spaces can better be dealt with interactive theorem provers. Instead of specifying EVM in one particular theorem prover, we chose a framework called Lem [16] because definitions in Lem can be translated into some popular theorem provers: Coq [1], Isabelle/HOL [19] and HOL4 [23].

One potential alternative is the K-Framework [22]. The K-Framework is a tool specifically engineered for defining programming languages. We chose Lem and its translation targets for their larger user base[2] and their longer history.

3   A Brief Description of the Ethereum Virtual Machine

Some of our design choices and challenges can be described only after an overview of EVM. We just describe EVM as a state machine that executes programs. We omit the underlying techniques that support distributed execution.

3.1   States

In EVM, apart from several global parameters, most states are stored in accounts. EVM has a partial map from *addresses* (160-bit words) to account states. An *account state* contains code, storage, nonce and the balance. The *code* is a sequence of bytes. The *storage* is a mapping from a machine word (an EVM *machine word* has 256 bits) to a machine word. The *nonce* is an ever-increasing machine word. The *balance* is also a machine word, representing some transferable value that can be paid as fees to run EVM. When the code is not empty, the code controls the account; such an account is called a *contract*. Otherwise,

---

[2] The Coq users' mailing list has 1,404 subscribers while the K-Framework's has 127 at the time of writing.

the account is controlled by the holder of a private key corresponding to the address; such an account is called an *external account*. The code, when exists, encodes a sequence of instructions. Instructions are all encoded in a single byte except for the PUSH instructions, which contain immediate values.

3.2 State Transitions

An external account can initiate a *transaction* either by creating a contract or by calling an account. Once a transaction is initiated, the whole state transition of EVM is deterministic. We do not describe the contract creation by an external account because a contract's state after creation is publically checkable.

Both external accounts and contracts can *call* an account. When an account calls an account, the call is accompanied with transferred balance, gas, and data. The transferred balance is deposited to the called account. The gas regulates the resource consumption during the call. When the called account is an external account, a simple balance transfer happens. Otherwise, when the called account is a contract, after the balance transfer, the called contract's code is executed. The code execution can alter the storage of the executing account. The execution can read all accounts' balances and codes.

The resource consumption of the code execution is capped by the amount of gas that the initiating external account pays for. Executing an instruction consumes some amount of gas. When the gas is exhausted, the execution fails (*out-of-gas failure*). Such failures revert all state changes performed during the current call, except gas consumption.

A contract can call an account by executing the CALL instruction. The ensuing balance transfer and code execution belong to the same transaction as the calling code execution. The calling contract can limit the resource consumption in the called contract by choosing the amount of gas passed on. When the inner call fails, the side-effects of the inner call is reverted (except gas consumption) but the side-effects of the outer call remains intact. The outer call is informed of such a failure through a return value of the CALL instruction.

A transaction belongs to a block. A *block* is a unit of agreement among Ethereum nodes. EVM has special instructions that reads the *block number* and the cryptographic hash values of some previous blocks. Since a block specifies a previous block but not a unique successor, blocks in the network form a tree in general, but, as far as the states of EVM are concerned, only one branch in the tree matters. Because of this, we can think of EVM as a sequentially executed machine.

4 Interface of a Contract Invocation

4.1 Boundary Between the System and the Environment

We are interested in propositions of the form: whatever the environment does, the system responds in a desired manner. Before we try to specify the desired behavior, we need to identify the system and the environment. The choice is not straightforward because multiple parties are involved in EVM.

One way is to say that the system is the contract. In that case, the environment contains anything out of EVM and all accounts on EVM except the contract under verification. In our development, the system is a single contract invocation, which is even narrower than a single account (Fig. 2(b)). The difference can be seen in the following scenario. The environment can call into the contract. The contract can reply by calling an account. The environment can, depending on the states of accounts that we do not control, call our contract again. This is called *reentrancy*. During reentrancy, the storage and the balance of our contract might change. We chose to model the reentrancy as part of the environment. We explain this choice in Subsect. 6.3.

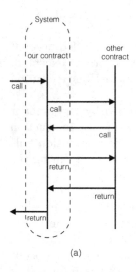 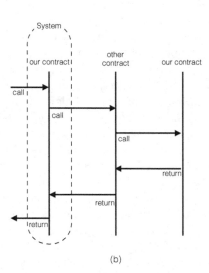

(a)   (b)

Fig. 2. Different choices of system-environment boundaries during reentrancy. Both pictures describe the same situation, but have different boundaries between the system and the environment. (a) When the system is our contract, the reentrant call is a part of the system. (b) When the system is a single invocation of our contract, the reentrant call is a part of the environment. Both are sound, but we chose (b) because it matches the program syntax where `CALL` instructions are followed by the next operations in the same message call, not the next operations in the reentrant call.

4.2   Input and Output of a Deployed Ethereum Smart Contract

In Subsect. 4.1, we have set the boundary between the smart contract and the environment. Next, we identify their interaction. The specification of the interface is particularly important because it can be used to specify higher level languages for Ethereum smart contracts. Our most concrete contribution is our EVM definition in Lem, so we show some snippets in this section and explain the syntax.

The interaction between the contract and the environment always starts with the environment's call into the contract. The environment can call into the contract with the following information:

```
type CALL_ENV = ⟨
  callenv_gaslimit : W₂₅₆;              (* the current invocation's gas limit *)
  callenv_value   : W₂₅₆;                 (* the amount of Eth sent along*)
  callenv_data   : LIST BYTE;               (* the data sent along *)
  callenv_caller  : ADDRESS;              (* the caller's address *)
  callenv_timestamp : W₂₅₆;        (* the timestamp of the current block *)
  callenv_blocknum : W₂₅₆;     (* the block number of the current block *)
  callenv_balance : ADDRESS → W₂₅₆; (* the balances of all accounts. *) ⟩
```

The whole syntax defines a *record* type with seven *fields*. A value of CALL_ENV consists of seven values each accessible under a field name. The field names are italicized. Each field name is annotated with a type of the associated value. W_{256} denotes the type of 256-bit machine words and ADDRESS 160-bit machine words. LIST BYTE is the type of lists of bytes. The arrow type ADDRESS → W_{256} is the type of total functions that take an ADDRESS and return a W_{256}. This definition is useful not only for reasoning about EVM bytecodes but also for designing high level languages that would be compiled into EVM. Ethereum contracts written in any language needs to take the combination of data above.

The environment can also make a called account return or fail after our contract makes a call. Together, the environment's possible actions are described by the following *variant type* ENVIRONMENT_ACTION, whose value can be the label ENVIRONMENTCALL together with a value of CALL_ENV, the label ENVIRONMENTRET together with a value of RETURN_RESULT, or the label ENVIRONMENTFAIL. It is automatically understood that values with different labels are different. This definition describes everything that can happen to an Ethereum contract. If we have checked these cases, we have enumerated all possibilities.

```
type ENVIRONMENT_ACTION =
| ENVIRONMENTCALL of CALL_ENV (* the environment calls the contract *)
| ENVIRONMENTRET of RETURN_RESULT     (* the environment returns *)
| ENVIRONMENTFAIL                   (* the environment fails *)
```

We omit the definition of RETURN_RESULT and many other symbols. The whole formalization is publicly available[3].

The contract can also make its move: calling another account, making a delegate call, creating a contract, failing, destroying itself, or returning. A *delegate call* runs a potentially different account's code on the caller's account.

---

[3] https://github.com/pirapira/eth-isabelle/tree/wtsc01.

```
type CONTRACT_ACTION =
| CONTRACTCALL of CALL_ARGUMENTS              (* calling an account *)
| CONTRACTDELEGATECALL of CALL_ARGUMENTS         (* library call *)
| CONTRACTCREATE of CREATE_ARGUMENTS     (* deploying a contract *)
| CONTRACTFAIL                        (* failing back to the caller *)
| CONTRACTSUICIDE  (* destroying itself and returning to the caller *)
| CONTRACTRETURN of LIST BYTE            (* returning to the caller *)
```

This definition describes everything that an Ethereum contract can do. When a high level language is designed for Ethereum, it's desirable that the language can cause all of these actions. Moreover, since the input-output interface is defined in an interactive theorem prover, the actions can be universally ($\forall$) or existentially ($\exists$) quantified in logical formulas that specify Ethereum smart contracts.

5   Formalizing the Deterministic Contract Execution

The Yellow Paper [26] specifies EVM's behavior uniquely for all possible inputs (either a contract creation or a message call) coming from external accounts. After no state transitions, the resulting state is left ambiguous. The original purpose of such determinism is to prevent the nodes from disagreeing, but the determinism also simplifies the formalization. We were able to formalize consecutive execution of instructions in our contract as a total function that produces a state. The deterministic definitions of the program semantics occupy 2,000 lines of Lem code. The determinism also made it straightforward to test this part of the EVM definition against a standard test suite (Subsect. 5.3)[4].

We initially tried to implement EVM available in the latest Ethereum network. During the VM tests we found that EVM should price instructions differently depending on block numbers, so we modeled this as to pass the tests.

5.1   Defining Execution Contexts

During the formalization, we have identified the runtime state of EVM. While EVM is executing an account's code, EVM has access to the stack, the memory, the memory usage counter, the storage, the program counter, the balances of all accounts, the caller, the value sent along the current call, the data sent along the current call, the initial state kept for reverting into, the external account that originated the transaction, the codes on all addresses, the current block, the remaining gas, existence of accounts, and the list of touched storage indices. Everything except the last one is necessary for EVM execution. The last piece spares enumerating all storage indices while testing. These data are packed into a record type VARIABLE_CTX. Moreover, EVM can read the program and the address of the currently running contract. These data are packed into a record type CONSTANT_CTX.

---

[4] If nondeterminism existed in the EVM execution, at least, we would need to choose a representation of nondeterminism that works both in interactive theorem provers and in OCaml.

An instruction can result in the following cases:

```
type INSTRUCTION_RESULT =
| INSTRUCTIONCONTINUE of VARIABLE_CTX (* the execution continues. *)
| INSTRUCTIONANNOTATIONFAILURE          (* annotation was false. *)
| INSTRUCTIONTOENVIRONMENT of
    CONTRACT_ACTION                     (* the contract's move *)
  * STORAGE                            (* the new storage content *)
  * (ADDRESS  →  W₂₅₆)              (* the new balance of all accounts *)
  * LIST W₂₅₆         (* the list of possibly changed storage indices *)
  * MAYBE (VARIABLE_CTX * INTEGER * INTEGER)     (* continuation *)
```

The asterisk $*$ composes the type of *tuples*.

5.2   Defining Deterministic Contract Execution

Using the above definitions, we can define a function that operates an instruction on the execution environments:

```
val instruction_sem  :  VARIABLE_CTX  →  CONSTANT_CTX  →  INST  →
INSTRUCTION_RESULT
```

```
let instruction_sem v c inst₁ =
subtract_gas (meterGas inst₁ v c)
(match inst₁ with
| Arith ADD  →  stack_2_1_op v c (fun a b  →  a + b)
| Arith ADDMOD  →  stack_3_1_op v c
  (fun a b divisor  →
   (if divisor = 0 then 0
    else word256FromInteger ((uint a + uint b) mod (uint divisor))))
  ⋮
end)
```

where meterGas calculates the exact gas consumption of the executed instruction. We can repeat the semantics of single instructions to define the semantics of a whole program (JUMP instruction is not special because all instructions, including JUMP, change the program counter).

The type PROGRAM_RESULT is similar to INSTRUCTION_RESULT. The program semantics takes artificial step counters that disallow infinite execution because, in Isabelle/HOL, every function must be provably terminating[5]. This does not cause imprecision because any actual execution can be simulated with a sufficiently large step counter value.

```
val program_sem  :  VARIABLE_CTX  →  CONSTANT_CTX  →  INT  →  NAT  →
PROGRAM_RESULT
```

---

[5] We can guarantee termination by the gas, but the proof is non-trivial (currently 980 lines of Isabelle code).

During the modeling, we found that the Yellow Paper computes gas differently from the implementations. The subtlest case was the computation of gas for memory accesses: when a contract accesses the memory on addresses spanning from $2^{256} - 255$ to 1, the gas calculation differed in the Yellow Paper and in implementations. The Yellow Paper used 1 as the maximal touched address while all checked implementations used $2^{256} + 1$ instead. Since all implementations agreed, we filed a fix in the Yellow Paper.

5.3 Testing the Deterministic Contract Interpreter

We tested our definition against a test suite called VM tests [2]. The test suite (together with other test suits) keep different Ethereum implementations conformant. We used VM tests to ensure conformance of our EVM definition. Lem automatically translated the definition into OCaml. The OCaml translation was then combined with a test case runner we wrote in OCaml (Fig. 3).

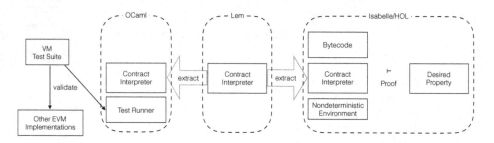

Fig. 3. Our Lem definition can be extracted into OCaml and Isabelle/HOL. We tested the OCaml extraction against the standard VM test suite. Using the Isabelle/HOL extraction, we proved safety properties about some bytecodes. In this figure, the VM test suite and other EVM implementations are not our contributions.

During the testing, we uncovered problems like:

– wrong word-to-integer conversion during ADDMOD in our EVM definition;
– different endianness between OCaml extraction and Isabelle/HOL extraction, due to our wrong direction; and
– small mistakes in the Yellow Paper, in most cases about modulo-2^{256}.

The number of successful test cases is 40,619 while no tests fail. We skipped 24 test cases because they involve running multiple contracts, and we chose to model only a single contract's execution deterministically. Running these 24 cases would involve major enhancements in our test runner: emulating multiple instances of our EVM model and communication among them.

In addition, we measured the code coverage of the VM test suite on the generated OCaml code. We found that DELEGATECALL instruction is never called, that CALL instruction is never called with insufficient balance to be transferred, that some instructions were never called with insufficient stack elements, and that the gas calculation after the latest changes is not tested. Although recent protocol changes are often tested in other test suites, the VM test suite can be complemented with these cases.

6   Formalizing the Nondeterministic Environment

We define the nondeterministic environment as a binary relation between a prestate of type (ACCOUNT_STATE * PROGRAM_RESULT) and a poststate of type (ACCOUNT_STATE * VARIABLE_CTX). This binary relation encodes the environment's freedom. The binary relation is parametrized with an invariant (to be speculated by the verification practitioner) of the contract under verification, which limits the state changes on the contract during reentrancy. If this limitation makes the same speculated invariant provable, the invariant can be deemed established following an informal argument given in Subsect. 6.3.

6.1   Implicit Balance Changes

We assume that the balances of accounts change freely while our contract is not executed. This assumption subsumes the payment for the gas. The storage of other accounts might change too. However, the balance of our contract is assumed not to decrease when there are no calls being executed on it[6]
    On the other hand, the balance of our contract might increase when another account executes SUICIDE instruction, specifying our account as the recipient of the remaining balance. So the environment can freely increase the balance of our contract. We are assuming that the balance increase does not overflow (which seems to hold currently because the total balance of all accounts is below 2^{80} while the balances can be counted up to $2^{256} - 1$).

6.2   Gas Consumption During Calls

When our contract calls an account, the available amount of gas might decrease. We modeled this as a completely nondeterministic change. This treatment admits the actual gas decrease as one possibility, and it shortens the proof goals during brute-force proving. Without this treatment, during the symbolic execution described in Sect. 7, we saw the symbolic states grow rapidly because the remaining gas was represented as a long sequence of subtractions. With the nondeterministic choice, the remaining gas in the symbolic state is reduced into one variable after each call.

---

[6] This property can be established only by checking all lines in the Yellow Paper that changes the balance.

6.3   Modeling of Reentrancy as an Adversarial Environment's Step

We have freedom: the nested execution under reentrancy can either be a part of the system or the environment. The choice influences the proof structure. If the reentrancy is part of the system, proofs of safety properties need to explore all possibilities in the nested reentrant calls. If the reentrancy is part of the environment, the reentrancy is an adversarial step that changes the account state in some arbitrary ways. We chose the latter way because this matches better with the syntax of EVM bytecode, and it serves as the first approximation before building a bigger EVM definition involving call stacks.

We assume that the reentrancy can change the contract's account state (the balance and the storage) following a speculated invariant. Using this assumption, we prove the same invariant on the outer call. If we finish proving this, we can perform mathematical induction over the number of nesting reentrancy to check that all message calls keep the invariant. This mathematical induction has not been formalized in any interactive theorem provers only because substantial development is required before stating the goal.

6.4   Cleanup of an Account After Self-destruction

When a contract executes SUICIDE instruction, the storage and the code of the account are cleared not immediately but at the end of a transaction. The timing of this cleanup is determined by the adversarial environment. However, we know that the cleanup does not occur while a contract is still running.

7   Example Verification of Smart Contracts

To show the utility of our definitions, we have developed three example proofs in Isabelle/HOL.

Invariant of a Program that Always Fails. As the shortest example, we prepared a smart contract that always fails. We proved that the code remains intact forever; in other words the contract does not execute SUICIDE operations.

Invariant of a Program that Fails on Reentrance. The next example features reentrancy, which enabled an external account "to put ∼$60M under her control" [5] during "the DAO" incident, where a coding mistake in a contract allowed leakage of the fund. We implemented a contract (Fig. 4) that calls an account but fails on reentrance. We proved that its storage values always stay within the specified values (Fig. 5) even when reentrant calls are attempted.

Safety Property of a Compiled Program. We proved a safety property of a realistic Ethereum contract with 501 instructions produced by the Solidity compiler. The safety property states that, if the storage has a flag set, only the owner recorded in the storage can decrease the balance or change the storage.

```
abbreviation fail_on_reentrance_program :: "inst list"
where
"fail_on_reentrance_program ==
  Stack (PUSH_N [0]) # Storage SLOAD # Dup 1 # Stack (PUSH_N [2]) #
  Pc JUMPI # Stack (PUSH_N [1]) # Arith ADD # Stack (PUSH_N [0]) #
  Storage SSTORE # Stack (PUSH_N [0]) # Stack (PUSH_N [0]) #
  Stack (PUSH_N [0]) # Stack (PUSH_N [0]) # Stack (PUSH_N [0]) #
  Stack (PUSH_N [0xabcdef]) # Stack (PUSH_N [30000]) # Misc CALL #
  Arith ISZERO # Stack (PUSH_N [2]) # Pc JUMPI # Stack (PUSH_N [0]) #
  Stack (PUSH_N [0]) # Storage SSTORE # Misc STOP # []"
```

Fig. 4. An Ethereum smart contract that calls an account but fails on reentrancy. The expression in this figure defines a list of instructions in Isabelle/HOL. See the Yellow Paper [26] for intuitive descriptions of instructions.

```
inductive fail_on_reentrance_invariant :: "account_state ⇒ bool"
where
  depth_zero:
    "account_address st = fail_on_reentrance_address ⟹
    account_storage st 0 = 0 ⟹
    account_code st = program_of_lst
      fail_on_reentrance_program program_content_of_lst ⟹
    account_ongoing_calls st = [] ⟹ account_killed st = False ⟹
    fail_on_reentrance_invariant st"
| depth_one:
    "account_code st = program_of_lst
      fail_on_reentrance_program program_content_of_lst ⟹
    account_storage st 0 = 1 ⟹
    account_address st = fail_on_reentrance_address ⟹
    account_ongoing_calls st = [(ve, 0, 0)] ⟹
    account_killed st = False ⟹
    vctx_pc ve = 28 ⟹ vctx_storage ve 0 = 1 ⟹
    vctx_storage_at_call ve 0 = 0 ⟹
    fail_on_reentrance_invariant st"
```

Fig. 5. An invariant of the contract that fails on reentrancy, expressed in Isabelle/HOL. The whole invariant is a disjunction of two clauses: **depth_zero** holds when the contract is not running while **depth_one** holds when the contract has called an account.

The proof is a brute-force symbolic execution in Isabelle/HOL. The proof contains repetitive 5,000 lines. It takes three hours for Isabelle to check the proof. There is huge room of improvements. Since the contract contains no loops, it should be possible to automate the whole proof. The proof checking time would be much shorter with more advanced techniques that appear in the next section.

8   Related Work

The idea and the techniques in this paper are not new, except that we apply these to EVM. Boyer and Yu [9] used a theorem prover Nqthm to model MC68020 processor, and checked correctness of a binary search implementation. Fox [10] modeled the ARM6 micro-architecture, which is far more complex than EVM, in HOL and validated it against the instruction set architecture. The deterministic part of our EVM definition happens to be in the form of functional big-step semantics [20] although our proof development is not advanced enough to enjoy its merits. The idea of combining theorem proving and testing is not new either even in the industry [7].

The literature suggests our future paths as well. Myreen et al. [18] defined Hoare logic for ARM machine code. Myreen et al. [17] further developed techniques for decompiling machine code with loops into recursive HOL functions. The approach of Kennedy et al. [11] is to formalize the machine code and then to build gradually structured programming method in Coq. Alternatively, we might try to build a higher level language that compiles into EVM. Jinja (Jinja is not Java) [12] demonstrates language specification and implementation in Isabelle/HOL. CakeML [13] is a programming language defined in Lem with a verified compiler into x86-64.

Some automatic analysis tools have been developed for Ethereum smart contracts. Oyente [15] implements abstract interpretation of EVM in Python with constraint solving using Z3. The tool can automatically detect several classes of vulnerabilities with false positives. Removing these classes of vulnerabilities does not guarantee lack of bugs. The tool does not implement all instructions. Bhargavan et al. [8] define translations from a fragment of Solidity and from EVM into F*, a functional programming language with a rich type system. They can detect diversion from certain programming disciplines in Solidity. They can also estimate an upper bound of gas consumption of an EVM program. They do not mention testing their translations against implementations[7].

9   Challenges and Future Work

Currently, verifying a realistic contract take around three hours on a Lenovo Ideapad 500S. Most of the time is spent in out-of-gas failures at various points in the program. One way to improve the situation is to set up a semantics that squashes all out-of-gas failures as a single case.

Another direction is to make the reasoning compositional. In other words, we should enable carrying over verification of small program snippets into verification of larger programs. This involves developing a syntax for properties (program logics) that is robustly concise during the compositional reasoning. Some program logics for machine code exist: e.g. Tan and Appel [24] and Myreen et al. [18].

---

[7] One of the authors explained that the work had been done in a hackathon and the codebase had not been touched since.

We have not tested the nondeterministic parts of our development. Also we have not validated our development against the blockchain history of the Ethereum network. The executable part of our model is considerably smaller than the whole EVM. If we model the whole EVM, we can try more standard test suites on our EVM definition. The modelling of the whole EVM would be the first step towards implementing a reference EVM out of our definitions.

The interactive theorem provers are designed for honest users. When a proof assistant admits a theorem that looks like falsehood, the proof assistant is called *Pollack-super-inconsistent*. Coq and Isabelle are known to be Pollack-super-inconsistent with auxiliary definitions and notations [25]. When falsehood seems provable, subtler errors can also creep in. For protecting users from malicious verification results, we need faithful presentation of the proven properties.

For verifying smart contracts in more human-friendly languages, we can either formalize existing languages or build a compiler gradually in a theorem prover. The first approach poses the burden of developing and maintaining an up-to-date machine-readable definition of the language. The second approach poses the burden of integration with the ecosystem, where the contracts need to interface with JavaScript libraries and where developers need to be familiarized.

10   Conclusion

We defined EVM so that interactive theorem provers can reason about Ethereum smart contracts. Our EVM definition contains all instructions. We used our EVM definition in Isabelle/HOL and proved safety properties and invariants of Ethereum contracts in the presence of reentrancy. As a side effect, we discovered several problems in the specification; we requested eleven fixes to the Yellow Paper. We found thirteen code paths in our model that the VM test suite did not touch. We demonstrated formal executable specification is effective for verifying smart contracts, for testing the specification, and for measuring code coverage of virtual machine tests. We expect our development to be a basis for more sophisticated smart contract verification frameworks and for verified compilers from/to EVM bytecode.

Acknowledgments. We thank Sami Mäkelä for enabling Isabelle and Coq extractions and finding mistakes in our formalization. We thank Sidney Amani, Christian Reitwießner and the anonymous referees for their time and valuable comments on this paper.

References

1. The Coq proof assistant. https://coq.inria.fr/. Accessed 19 Dec 2016
2. Ethereum VM tests. https://github.com/ethereum/tests/tree/develop/VMTests. Accessed 02 Jan 2017
3. Solidity 0.4.8-develop documentation. https://solidity.readthedocs.io/. Accessed 19 Dec 2016

4. WebAssembly. http://webassembly.org/. Accessed 16 Dec 2016
5. Atzei, N., Bartoletti, M., Cimoli, T.: A survey of attacks on Ethereum smart contracts. Cryptology ePrint Archive (2016). http://eprint.iacr.org/2016/1007
6. Batty, M., Owens, S., Sarkar, S., Sewell, P., Weber, T.: Mathematizing C++ concurrency. SIGPLAN Not. **46**(1), 55–66 (2011)
7. Becker, H., et al.: Combining mechanized proofs and model-based testing in the formal analysis of a hypervisor. In: Fitzgerald, J., Heitmeyer, C., Gnesi, S., Philippou, A. (eds.) FM 2016. LNCS, vol. 9995, pp. 69–84. Springer, Cham (2016). https://doi.org/10.1007/978-3-319-48989-6_5
8. Bhargavan, K., Delignat-Lavaud, A., Fournet, C., Gollamudi, A., Gonthier, G., Kobeissi, N., Kulatova, N., Rastogi, A., Sibut-Pinote, T., Swamy, N., Zanella-Béguelin, S.: Formal verification of smart contracts: short paper. In: PLAS 2016, pp. 91–96. ACM (2016)
9. Boyer, R.S., Yu, Y.: Automated proofs of object code for a widely used microprocessor. J. ACM **43**(1), 166–192 (1996)
10. Fox, A.: Formal specification and verification of ARM6. In: Basin, D., Wolff, B. (eds.) TPHOLs 2003. LNCS, vol. 2758, pp. 25–40. Springer, Heidelberg (2003). https://doi.org/10.1007/10930755_2
11. Kennedy, A., Benton, N., Jensen, J.B., Dagand, P.E.: Coq: the world's best macro assembler? In: PPDP 2013, pp. 13–24. ACM (2013)
12. Klein, G., Nipkow, T.: A machine-checked model for a Java-like language, virtual machine and compiler. ACM Trans. Program. Lang. Syst. **28**(4), 619–695 (2006)
13. Kumar, R., Myreen, M.O., Norrish, M., Owens, S.: CakeML: a verified implementation of ML. In: POPL 2014, pp. 179–191. ACM, New York (2014)
14. Leroy, X.: Formal verification of a realistic compiler. Commun. ACM **52**(7), 107–115 (2009)
15. Luu, L., Chu, D.H., Olickel, H., Saxena, P., Hobor, A.: Making smart contracts smarter. In: CCS 2016, pp. 254–269. ACM (2016)
16. Mulligan, D.P., Owens, S., Gray, K.E., Ridge, T., Sewell, P.: Lem: reusable engineering of real-world semantics. SIGPLAN Not. **49**(9), 175–188 (2014)
17. Myreen, M.O., Gordon, M.J.C., Slind, K.: Decompilation into logic-improved. FMCAD **2012**, 78–81 (2012)
18. Myreen, M.O., Fox, A.C.J., Gordon, M.J.C.: Hoare logic for ARM machine code. In: Arbab, F., Sirjani, M. (eds.) FSEN 2007. LNCS, vol. 4767, pp. 272–286. Springer, Heidelberg (2007). https://doi.org/10.1007/978-3-540-75698-9_18
19. Nipkow, T., Wenzel, M., Paulson, L.C. (eds.): Isabelle/HOL: A Proof Assistant for Higher-Order Logic. LNCS, vol. 2283. Springer, Heidelberg (2002). https://doi.org/10.1007/3-540-45949-9
20. Owens, S., Myreen, M.O., Kumar, R., Tan, Y.K.: Functional big-step semantics. In: Thiemann, P. (ed.) ESOP 2016. LNCS, vol. 9632, pp. 589–615. Springer, Heidelberg (2016). https://doi.org/10.1007/978-3-662-49498-1_23
21. Ramananandro, T., Dos Reis, G., Leroy, X.: Formal verification of object layout for C++ multiple inheritance. SIGPLAN Not. **46**(1), 67–80 (2011)
22. Roşu, G., Şerbănuţă, T.F.: An overview of the K semantic framework. J. Log. Algebr. Program. **79**(6), 397–434 (2010)
23. Slind, K., Norrish, M.: A brief overview of HOL4. In: Mohamed, O.A., Muñoz, C., Tahar, S. (eds.) TPHOLs 2008. LNCS, vol. 5170, pp. 28–32. Springer, Heidelberg (2008). https://doi.org/10.1007/978-3-540-71067-7_6
24. Tan, G., Appel, A.W.: A compositional logic for control flow. In: Emerson, E.A., Namjoshi, K.S. (eds.) VMCAI 2006. LNCS, vol. 3855, pp. 80–94. Springer, Heidelberg (2005). https://doi.org/10.1007/11609773_6

25. Wiedijk, F.: Pollack-inconsistency. Electron. Notes Theor. Comput. Sci. **285**, 85–100 (2012)
26. Wood, G.: Ethereum: a secure decentralised generalised transaction ledger-EIP-150 revision. http://paper.gavwood.com/. Accessed 19 Dec 2016

SmartCast: An Incentive Compatible Consensus Protocol Using Smart Contracts

Abhiram Kothapalli[✉], Andrew Miller, and Nikita Borisov

University of Illinois at Urbana-Champaign, Urbana, IL, USA
{kothapa2,soc1024,nikita}@illinois.edu

Abstract. Motivated by the desire for high-throughput public databases (i.e., "blockchains"), we design incentive compatible protocols that run "off-chain", but rely on an existing cryptocurrency to implement a reward and/or punishment mechanism. Our protocols are incentive compatible in the sense that behaving honestly is a weak Nash equilibrium, even in spite of potentially malicious behavior from a small fraction of the participants (i.e., the BAR model from Clement et al. [7]). To show the feasibility of our approach, we build a prototype implementation, called SmartCast, comprising an Ethereum smart contract, and an off-chain consensus protocol based on Dolev-Strong [10]. SmartCast also includes a "marketplace" smart contract that randomly assigns workers to protocol instances. We evaluate the communication costs of our system, as well as the "gas" transaction costs that are involved in running the Ethereum smart contract.

Keywords: Atomic broadcast · TRB · Game theory · Ethereum · Smart contracts

1 Introduction

Bitcoin and related cryptocurrencies have sparked renewed interest in decentralized consensus protocols, as exemplified by the so-called blockchain technologies. It turns out that many applications (including complementary currencies, certificate revocation [6,14], directory authorities for p2p networks like Tor [9]), benefit from a globally agreed-upon sequence of transactions. Currencies such as Bitcoin and Ethereum use the proof-of-work mining to distribute the responsibility for maintaining the blockchain integrity to a large collection of parties; the integration of mining with a financial reward makes this collection difficult to subvert. However, the global nature of this ledger creates some inherent costs, both in terms of transaction costs and the agreement latency. An alternative approach is what has been termed a *permissioned ledger*, where the role of miners is taken by a trusted coalition of parties, whose motivation to properly follow the protocol is assumed to come externally.

Several applications of blockchains, however, would benefit from a middle ground between these two extremes. Loosely defined coalitions, such as food

© International Financial Cryptography Association 2017
M. Brenner et al. (Eds.): FC 2017 Workshops 2017, LNCS 10323, pp. 536–552, 2017.
https://doi.org/10.1007/978-3-319-70278-0_34

banks, cooperatives, or student organizations, are some times in need of a blockchain-like ledger for tracking membership benefits or exchanges between sister organizations; however, they would not have the resources to directly operate a reliable collection of "miners," nor, necessarily agree on a set of trusted parties. At the same time, directly using cryptocurrency for account deposits might limit their accounting flexibility and incur non-trivial transaction costs.

Our approach creates a system where workers who act to enforce integrity are financially rewarded for their correct participation in the process, as monitored by other workers and enforced through an Ethereum smart contract. Our protocol draws inspiration from a consensus protocol designed by Clement et al. [7], where honest participation is shown to be a *rational* strategy for participants trying to maximize their utility. Their protocol, however, assumes that workers derive *intrinsic* utility from the correct functioning of the protocol and requires an infinite time horizon; in our scenario, which we believe to be more realistic, we expect consensus to be enforced by inherently disinterested parties whose only motivation is financial. This *extrinsic* reward dramatically simplifies the protocol design and improves its efficiency. Our protocol requires only occasional communication with the Ethereum blockchain through the smart contract, thus minimizing transaction costs.

To design our protocol, we create a *generic* transform that renders any existing protocol where communication is the dominant cost *incentive-compatible*. We show that, under this transform, honest participation is a weak Nash equilibrium in a worst-case utility model, which was previously used by Clement et al. [7].

To show the feasiblity of our approach, we build a prototype implementation, called SmartCast, comprising an Ethereum smart contract and an "off-chain" consensus protocol (based on the Dolev-Strong [10] broadcast protocol). We evaluate the communication costs of our system, as well as the "gas" transaction costs that are involved in running the Ethereum smart contract. We additionally describe how these protocols can be deployed in practice with random consensus nodes.

1.1   Related Works

Several previous works have proposed using cryptocurrencies to enforce properties in off-chain protocols. Bentov and Kumaresan's protocol [1] guarantees either a fair output or else financial compensation to each honest party, but requires significant collateral deposits. In contrast, our weak Nash equilbirium notion guarantees that parties cannot benefit by deviating. In a separate line of work, Garay et al. design a general framework to build protocols that are resilient against rational adversaries [11]. We instead design a protocol transformer that can achieve resilience for a certain class of protocols. To the best of our knowledge, we are the first to harness smart contracts for the purpose of Byzantine fault tolerance.

2   Background and Preliminaries

2.1   Network Model

Our basic computation model is the standard point-to-point network setting with synchronous authenticated channels. We consider a fixed set of parties $\mathcal{N}$, where an individual party is denoted $p \in \mathcal{N}$. The protocol proceeds in rounds of communication, with the exact order of messages in each round may be arbitrary (i.e., chosen by the adversary). Messages not delivered within the round are invalid. Each party is associated with a common-knowledge public signing key to send authenticated messages. Our model accounts for Byzantine failures. The adversary can choose to corrupt a subset of nodes $\mathcal{B} \subset \mathcal{N}$, giving them complete control over these nodes. $|\mathcal{B}|$ is bounded by a parameter b.

2.2   Smart Contract Protocols

Public cryptocurrencies [4] (or "blockchain") systems, such as Bitcoin [17] and Ethereum [20], provide a decentralized platform for programmable money. These can be used as general-purpose trusted third parties, but with caveats. For instance, they can be trusted for correctness, but do not provide any inherent privacy. For some applications, privacy can be provided by a layer of multi-party computations and zero-knowledge proofs [1,12]. A second caveat is that blockchain transactions are expensive (because they are fully replicated throughout the entire cryptocurrency network), so it typically is not cost-effective to carry out protocols directly on top of the blockchain.

A protocol in the smart contract model is therefore most effective with two components: (1) A smart contract program, which receives reports from nodes about each other, and dispenses rewards at the end; and (2) Local code for each of the parties to execute, including interactions with the smart contract and participation in "off-chain" subprotocols. We also assume a rushing adversary, who can observe the smart contract transactions sent by non-Byzantine parties before submitting transactions on behalf of the Byzantine parties.

2.3   Utilities in the BAR Model

We adapt the The Byzantine-Altruistic-Rational (BAR) fault tolerance model from Clement et al. [7] to the smart contract setting. The BAR model is a game-theoretic layer on top of the standard distributed protocol execution model. That is, we view the choice of what code to run (i.e., either following the protocol or deviating in some arbitrary way) as a strategic decision.

We associate each "off-chain" protocol message with a *cost* to the sender of that message, determined by the total size of the messages sent. However, we ignore any other costs of computation, storage, and other resources. We thus assume that the total utility of each party therefore depends on the monetary payments disbursed by the smart contract, minus the cost of the messages they send. Since the protocol execution is probabilistic, unless indicated otherwise we are concerned with the expected utility.

As Clement identifies, in an ordinary protocol (i.e., without the smart contract incentive mechanism in place), parties may be able to profit by deviating from the protocol—in particular by withholding messages to reduce their costs (i.e., by acting "lazy"). Thus the high level approach is to punish lazy nodes.

A strategy profile $\boldsymbol{\sigma}$ defines a program for each party p in $\mathcal{N}$ to run. Given a protocol ρ, we use the symbol $\boldsymbol{\rho}$ to denote the *prescribed strategy*, in which every party follows the protocol correctly.

While standard distributed systems models feature a worst-case adversary, and standard game models feature a set of strategic (i.e., "rational") players, the intersection of these has yet to be studied widely. Clement proposes the following notion of "worst-case utility," which we also adopt.

Definition 1. *Worst-case Utility. The worst case utility $\bar{u}_p(\sigma)$ for a rational player $p \in \mathcal{N}$ is where p follows strategy σ, every non-Byzantine player in $N - \mathcal{B} - \{p\}$ follows the prescribed strategy, $\boldsymbol{\rho}_{N-\mathcal{B}}$, and the choice of Byzantine players $\mathcal{B}$ and their strategies $\bar{\tau}_\mathcal{B} \in \mathcal{S}_\mathcal{B}$ are chosen to minimize the resulting utility u_p. This is defined more precisely as:*

$$\bar{u}_p(\sigma) \triangleq \min_{\mathcal{B} \subset \mathcal{N}:|\mathcal{B}| \leq b} \circ \min_{\tau \in S_\mathcal{B}} \circ \, u_p(\boldsymbol{\rho}_{\mathcal{N}-\mathcal{B}-\{p\}} + \sigma + \boldsymbol{\tau}_\mathcal{B}) \tag{1}$$

Our goal is then to show that the prescribed strategy is a worst-case *weak Nash equilibrium*, i.e., $\bar{u}_p(\rho_p) \geq \bar{u}_p(\sigma)$ for any σ. That is, a rational party cannot *improve* their expected utility by following any other deviant protocol σ. This solution concept could be thought of as modeling paranoid players who think that other parties (up to b of them colluding) are "out to get them."

2.4   Synchronous Byzantine Agreement

Alternative definitions of consensus primitives abound in the distributed systems literature. Perhaps the strongest of these—and the one most naturally suited to our application scenario—is "atomic broadcast." This primitive allows any of the N protocols parties to submit input values, and the parties all reach agreement on an ordered sequence of values that at least includes the inputs from each honest party. Atomic broadcast could thus be described as the "blockchain" primitive in today's post-Bitcoin parlance.

Below we provide a more formal definition of this primitive, adapted for the synchronous setting. We assume that each input value is bounded by a maximum message size C, and that the protocol finally terminates after a maximum number of rounds $r^\dagger$.

Definition 2. *Bounded Atomic Broadcast: Given a set of players $\mathcal{N}$, each process p in $\mathcal{N}$ receives inputs $m_{p,r} \in \{0,1\}^C$ in round r.*

– *(Termination): after a bounded number of rounds $r^\dagger$, each correct process terminates.*

- *(Agreement):* The sequence of outputs $V_{p,r}$ in round r by each correct process p are all identical, i.e. $\forall r, \forall p, q \in \mathcal{N} - \mathcal{B}.V_{p,r} = V_{q,r}$.
- *(Validity):* every input from a correct node (received before $r \leq r^\dagger$) is included in $V_{r^\dagger}$.

Looking ahead, in Sect. 3.4 we implement an atomic broadcast protocol by composing a simpler primitive, called Terminating Reliable Broadcast (TRB). In TRB, one of the parties is designated as the leader, and only the leader may input messages. Thus in TRB there is no need to apply an ordering to messages from different sources, and if the leader is faulty then the parties may need to output a default value $\bot$.

Definition 3. *Terminating Reliable Broadcast Given a set of players $\mathcal{N}$, among which one, D, is designated the leader and receives an input $m \in \{0,1\}^C$ (i.e., within some bounded message size of C bits), a Terminating Reliable Broadcast protocol must satisfy the following properties:*

- *(Termination):* Every correct process p delivers some value $m \in \{0,1\}^C \cup \{\bot\}$ after a bounded time r^*.
- *(Agreement):* If any correct process delivers m, then all correct processes deliver m.
- *(Validity):* If the leader D is correct, then every correct process delivers D's input m.

Alternative network models. Although our SmartCast protocol relies on a synchronous network model. This is generally considered a strong assumption. Other protocols such as PBFT [5] provide security in the more challenging weakly synchronous setting—they meet the lower bound in this model, which is $b \leq N/3$.

However, synchrony is an assumption we must take anyway if we rely on a smart contract system in the style of Bitcoin and Ethereum. It is not clear how to adapt our protocol to the asynchronous setting, since we would not be able to detect whether a message was omitted by a party or just delayed in the network.

3   Smart Contracts for Incentive Compatible Protocols

In this section we present our main contribution, a protocol transformer, SmartBAR(·), which transforms an arbitrary synchronous protocol with costly communication, π into an incentive compatible protocol SmartBAR(π). As an application, in Sect. 3.4 we apply this transformation to yield an incentive-compatible consensus protocol, called SmartCast.

At a high level, SmartBAR(·) adds a smart contract layer to π that implements a reward/punishment mechanism. In an ordinary protocol (i.e., without this incentive mechanism in place), parties may be able to profit by deviating from the protocol—in particular by withholding messages to reduce their costs (i.e., by acting "lazy"). To ensure that laziness is not profitable, our protocol enlists the honest parties to detect lazy nodes and the smart contract to punish them.

The transformation works for an arbitrary synchronous protocol π that satisfy the following assumptions. First, each correct party in π terminates after a bounded number of rounds r^*, for some parameter r^*. Second, the total number of bits between any pair of parties is bounded by a value M. We call a protocol that satisfies these an $(r^*, M)-bounded$ synchronous protocol.

Since the transformation runs π in place, any fault tolerance properties of π still carry over to SmartBAR(π). In particular, if π tolerates b faults, and we prove that running is a b-worst-case equilibrium, then the security of the overall protocol security reduces to the assumption of strategic behavior among the rational remaining parties.

3.1   The Protocol Transformer SmartBAR($\cdot$)

The transformed protocol SmartBAR(π) runs π with the following minimal modifications:

- Modification 1: We impose a predictable communication pattern so that nodes can detect if another is cutting costs by not forwarding messages. Our predictable communication pattern requires that in each protocol instance, node p must send every node q the maximum possible total message size M. If fewer than M message bits are sent by the end of the protocol, then dummy messages are sent to make up the difference.
- Modification 2: We impose a penalty on nodes that fail to forward messages, by implementing the following rules:
  - Each node keeps track of the total message bits received from each other node.
  - At the end of the protocol, if fewer than M bits have been received by p from q, then p sends a report $R_{p,q} = $ enemy to the smart contract. Otherwise, if at least M bits have been received, then p sends a report $R_{p,q} = $ friend.
  - The smart contract waits until the final round of the protocol r^* to collect status reports from all nodes $p \in \mathcal{N}$. Finally, the smart contract determines the payout to each party by deducting a penalty of θ (a parameter discussed shortly) for each enemy report about that party.

Alternative definitions of enemy. Note that we propose a relatively lenient definition for enemy as a node that does not send at least M bits. This protects honest nodes with harmless or negligible deviations from being marked as dishonest by other honest nodes. On the other hand, we can follow a much stricter definition of enemy by marking nodes that do not send at least M bits, send incorrect bits, send more than M bits, and so on. This leads to additional protocol security by barring more forms of misbehavior, but may unnecessarily penalize honest nodes that perform harmless or negligible deviations.

The entire SmartBAR$(\cdot)$ protocol is defined in Fig. 1. For simplicity, we assume the smart contract is initialized with an endowment $E \geq N(N-1) \cdot \theta$. In practice, this endowment might be provided by collecting collateral deposits from

Protocol $\mathsf{Smart}(\pi)$ for a bounded synchronous protocol π, a set of parties $\mathcal{N}$, and a maximum number of Byzantine nodes $b < |\mathcal{N}| - 2$.

Let r^* be a bound on the final round before π terminates.
Let M bound the total size of messages sent between any pair of parties in π.

Local program (for node p).

- Run the given protocol π_p.
- For each received message m, parse m as either an ordinary message $\mathsf{PASS}(m')$ (in which case pass m' through to π_p) or else a padding message $\mathsf{DUMMY}(0^*)$, in which case discard this message.
- For each outgoing message m generated by π_p, intended for player q, send $\mathsf{PASS}(m)$ to q.
- At the final round r^*, let $M_{p,q}$ be the total size of messages sent so far to q (including any messages sent during this round). If $M_{p,q} < M$, then send a padding message $\mathsf{DUMMY}(0^{M-M_{p,q}})$.
- After r^*, for each player $q \neq p$, let $M_{q,p}$ be the total size of messages received from q. If $M_{q,p} < M$, then set $R_{p,q} := 0$ (an enemy report). Otherwise, set $R_{p,q} := \theta$ (a friend report). Finally, send a transaction containing $\mathsf{report}(R_p)$ to the smart contract, where $R_p = \{R_{p,q}\}_{q \neq p}$ is the vector of all of the reports from p about each other player q.

Smart contract program.

- The contract is parameterized by a set of players $\mathcal{N}$, identified by their addresses (i.e., public keys).
- The contract must be initialized with an endowment (a quantity of digital currency) of at least $E \geq (|\mathcal{N}|)(|\mathcal{N}| - 1) \cdot \theta$, where $\theta = \frac{|\mathcal{N}|-1}{|\mathcal{N}|-1-b} M$.
- The contract contains an entry point $\mathsf{report}(R_p)$, which when invoked by party p, stores the argument vector R_p.
- By a fixed deadline time T, the contract receives a report $R_{p,q} \in [0, \theta]$ from each party $p \in \mathcal{N}$ about each other party $q \in \mathcal{N}$. Any reports that are not received in time are treated as a default value of 0.
- After time T, for each $p \in N$,
    - determine the reward as the sum of reports about p, so $\mathsf{reward}_p := \sum_{q \in \mathcal{N} | q \neq p} R_{q,p}$, and send reward_p to player p

Fig. 1. Our protocol transformer, $\mathsf{Smart}(\cdot)$, which provides incentive-compatibility for an arbitrary synchronous protocol. Each party pads outgoing messages to the maximum size, and reports to the smart contract about any "lazy" peers.

the participants or collecting usage fees from users of the system, as described shortly in Sect. 3.5. We next describe how the parameter θ is determined in order to satisfy the worst-case equilibrium notion.

3.2   Rationality Analysis

We now prove that following the SmartBAR protocol is a worst-case weak Nash equilibrium.

The utility for party $p \in N$ as a function of a strategy vector $\boldsymbol{\sigma}$ is $u_p(\boldsymbol{\sigma}) = benefits_p(\boldsymbol{\sigma}) - costs_p(\boldsymbol{\sigma})$. The overall benefits will be decided by $reward_p$ and the overall cost is $cost_{msg} + cost_{report}$. In the following, we use the notation $\boldsymbol{\sigma}_{N-\{p\}} + \boldsymbol{\sigma}_p$ to denote the union of the strategy vectors $\boldsymbol{\sigma}_{N-\{p\}} + \boldsymbol{\sigma}_p$.

In order to prove that rational parties gain the highest utility by following the recommended protocol, we take the following steps:

First we show a lower bound that following the protocol earns p a minimum utility u^*, regardless of the adversary's choice of strategies.

Next, we partition the space of alternative strategies into classes based on how they behave towards honest nodes. We define a simple family of strategies, called the "indiscriminate" strategies, which act as representatives of these classes. We can prove that the indiscriminate strategies perform just as well (in the worst-case) as any other strategy.

Finally, we show how to choose the protocol parameter θ so that u^* is an upper bound for the utility of any indiscriminate strategy. The setting of θ directly determines the overall collateral cost (i.e., the required endowment) for the protocol.

Lemma 1. *Regardless of the strategy τ_B followed by Byzantine parties, if p follows ρ_p, then p obtains at least*
$$\bar{u}_p(\rho) \geq u^*$$
where
$$u^* \triangleq (N-1)\theta - (N-1)M - b\theta.$$

Proof. The ideal reward of the protocol is initially set to be $(N-1)\theta$. The prescribed strategy sends all possible messages, incurring the maximum message cost $(N-1)M$. Since all the non-Byzantine nodes report p as a `friend`, the maximum report cost can be at most $b\theta$, which occurs when all b Byzantine nodes report `enemy`.

This bound holds regardless of how the protocol parameter θ is chosen. This worst-case utility is incurred when the Byzantine parties follow the spiteful strategy.

The indiscriminate strategies, α_γ. We next turn towards proving an upper bound on the utility of deviating from the prescribed strategy ρ.

We first define a family of simple strategies, α, which we call the indiscriminate strategies. Looking ahead, these strategies will serve as representatives for a partitioning of the overal strategy space. The indiscriminate strategies α by a fraction $0 \leq \gamma \leq 1$, such that α_γ misbehaves towards each other node with probability γ. More precisely, α_γ is defined as follows: At the beginning of the game, for each other party q a coin is flipped with probability γ (for some arbitrary percentage γ). If the coin flip succeeds, then p refuses to send any messages to q; otherwise p sends messages to q according to the ordinary protocol.

The strategy α_γ clearly causes p to incur a message cost of $(1 - \gamma)(N - 1)M$. Since this strategy witholds messages from exactly $\gamma(N - 1 - b)$ honest uncorrupted parties in expectation, the worst-case expected report cost is $(b + \gamma(N - 1 - b))\theta$. We therefore have the following claim:

Claim. The worst-case expected utility for the strategy α_γ is

$$\bar{u}_p(\alpha_\gamma) = (N - 1)\theta - (N - 1)(1 - \gamma)M - (b + \gamma(N - 1 - b))\theta \qquad (2)$$

The Spiteful Strategy, δ. Following Clement et al. [7], we define a particular adversarial strategy, called the spiteful strategy, which serves as a worst-case adversary (as we will see shortly). The spiteful strategy initially behaves according to the prescribed strategy, but in the final round it always reports **enemy** for player p, causing p to be punished.

If rational party p could determine which nodes were corrupted, then p would be able to cut his losses by withholding messages from just the nodes in $\mathcal{B}$. The spiteful strategy, however, blends in with the honest parties. As shown by the following lemma, this means p can do no better than to withhold messages from other nodes chosen uniformly at random, as with the indiscriminate strategy α_γ. In the following, we say that player p follows an *acceptable message sequence* towards player q if p sends q a total of at least M bits.

Lemma 2. *Consider a strategy σ_γ, such that in an execution with all honest parties (i.e., with the strategy vector $\{\sigma_\gamma\} + \rho_{\mathcal{N}-\{p\}}$), party p sends an unacceptable message sequence to exactly $\gamma(N - 1)$ nodes in expectation. Then the worst-case utility $\bar{u}(\sigma_\gamma)$ is at most $\bar{u}(\alpha_\gamma)$.*

Proof. Let γ_q be the probability that σ_γ sends an unacceptable message sequence to party $q \in \mathcal{N} - \{p\}$ when all parties besides p follow the protocol. By assumption, we know that

$$\sum_{q \in \mathcal{N}-\{p\}} \gamma_q = \gamma.$$

First, note that against the spiteful adversary, p incurs an expected message cost of at least $(1 - \gamma)(N - 1)M$. Next, to bound the report cost, we will choose $\mathcal{B} \subseteq \mathcal{N}-\{p\}$, with $|\mathcal{B}| = b$, such that we minimize $\sum_{q \in \mathcal{B}} \gamma_q$. This minimization guarantees that p sends an unacceptable message sequence to at least $(N - 1 - b)\gamma$ honest nodes in expectation, resulting in an expected report cost of at least $(b + (N - 1 - b)(\gamma))\theta$. $\qquad \square$

Note the above proof above holds regardless of whether probabilities γ_q are independent.

Choosing the parameter θ. We want to choose θ so that deviating from ρ cannot improve the worst-case expected utility. Starting from Lemma 2, it will suffice if we can guarantee that $\bar{u}_p(\rho) \geq \bar{u}_p(\alpha_\gamma)$ for all γ. We therefore solve the following:

$$\bar{u}_p(\rho) \geq \bar{u}_p(\alpha_\gamma) \tag{3}$$
$$(N-1)M + b\theta \leq (N-1)(1-\gamma)M + (b + (N-1-b)(\gamma))\theta \tag{4}$$
$$\theta \geq \frac{N-1}{N-1-b}M \tag{5}$$

Theorem 1. *If* π *is a synchronous protocol that terminates after* r^* *rounds and each party sends a maximum of* M *message bits to each other party, then the transformed protocol* Smart(π) *is a worst-case weak Nash equilibrium.*

Proof. When the SmartTRB protocol is instantiated with θ defined as in Eq. 5, from Lemma 1 we have that the worst-case expected utility when p follows the protocol $\bar{u}_p(\rho)$ is at least as good as any indiscriminate strategy $\bar{u}_p(\alpha_\gamma)$. And from Lemma 2, we know that the indiscriminate strategies perform as well in the worst-case as any other strategies.

3.3   Comparison with the BAR Primer [7]

Our protocol and analytical framework is adapted from the bar model of Clement et al. [7], but with several significant differences.

While Clement's model requires an infinitely repeated game, our model considers the bounded case. In the infinite settings, rational parties simply play tit-for-tat, immediately and irrevocably "retaliating" against nodes that misbehave, preventing them from all future rewards. In a finite setting, a node could misbehave in the final round without fear of retaliation.

Additionally Clement's model assumes that nodes gain a positive utility from the correction execution of the protocol itself. Alternatively, in our model, nodes gain a positive utility monetary payments disbursed by the smart contract. We believe our utility model is more realistic, especially in a marketplace setting (like that discussed in Sect. 3.5) where the participants in a protocol instance are randomly assigned from some population of available workers.

Together, these two modelling differences require a significant change to the protocol and proof. First, while "retaliation" in Clement's model involves requiring nodes to send expensive "penance" messages (since that is the only way to inflict a punishment in their model), the smart contract provides a direct alternative. Second, in the finite setting we must rule out deviant strategies that withhold messages in a possibly randomized way, even in the last round, as though "guessing" at which parties might be corrupted. We overcome this by introducing a new family of "indiscriminate strategies" that serve as simple representatives of the full strategy space. Finally, like Clement, our proof involves a "spiteful strategy," that acts as a worst case adversary. However, the "spiteful strategy" is different in our model: it misbehaves only in the final round, after it is too late for the victim p to retaliate.

3.4   SmartCast: An Incentive Compatible Consensus Protocol

As an application of our general protocol transformation, we now describe how to apply our SmartBAR$(\cdot)$ transformation to a classic synchronous protocol, DolevStrong [10], in order to obtain an incentive-compatible off-chain consensus protocol.

The Dolev-Strong protocol for Terminating Reliable Broadcast. The Dolev-Strong protocol is a classic algorithm for synchronous byzantine agreement using signatures, that achieves optimal resilience by tolerating $N-1$. However, it provides no explicit incentives for participants to follow. As seen in Clements et al., individual participants in the protocol can reduce their computational cost by omitting messages.

The protocol runs for $b+1$ rounds, where the leader D sends a signed message containing its input to each of the other nodes in the first round. Each node that receives the leader's message in the first round "accepts" the message, and then appends their own signature and relays the message to every other node. If the leader fails to send a message to some node p, some other node q will relay the message to p in any round r, as long as the relay contains at least r signatures. p will then continue to relay the message. If the leader equivocates, it is possible that a node accepts two or more distinct values. In this case, a node outputs $\perp$, and only relays the first two such values received. In total, each node must therefore send a maximum of $2N$ total messages, each containing an input value and up to $b+1$ signatures.

We provide a listing of the Dolev-Strong algorithm in Fig. 2, adapted from Kumaresan's thesis [13]. For a proof of security we refer the reader to [10,13].

We let $D \in \mathcal{N}$ denote a designated leader. We let $m \in \{0,1\}^C$ denote the sender D's input, and sk_D its secret key.

- (Stage 1): The leader D sends $(m, \mathsf{sign}_{\mathsf{sk}_D}(m))$ to every party. It then outputs m and terminates the protocol. Each other party p initializes $\mathsf{ACC}_p := \emptyset$, and $\mathsf{SET}_p := (v \mapsto \emptyset)$, a mapping from values to (initially empty) sets of signatures.
- (Stage 2): In rounds $r = 1, ..., b+1$, perform the following:
  - If a pair (v, SET) is received from some q, with $v \in \{0,1\}^C$, and if SET contains valid signatures on v from at least r distinct parties including the leader D, and if ACC_p contains only 0 or 1 values, then p updates $\mathsf{ACC}_p := \mathsf{ACC}_p \cup \{v\}$, and $\mathsf{SET}_p[v] := \mathsf{SET}_p[v] \cup \mathsf{SET}$.
  - Each party p checks whether any value $v \in \{0,1\}^C$ was newly added to the set of accepted values ACC_p during round $r-1$. In this case, p computes $\mathsf{sign}_{\mathsf{sk}_p}(v)$, and sends $(v, \mathsf{SET}_p[v] \cup \{\mathsf{sign}_{\mathsf{sk}_p}(v)\}$ to every other party.
- (Stage 3): If $\mathsf{ACC}_p = \{v\}$ for some v, then p outputs v. Otherwise p outputs $\perp$.

Fig. 2. Definition of the DolevStrong protocol [10] for Terminating Reliable Broadcast (adapted from Kumaresan [13])

From Reliable Broadcast to Atomic Broadcast. Atomic broadcast further guarantees that messages can be committed by any node, not just a leader. In a synchronous network, atomic broadcast can be easily built from terminating reliable broadcast, simply by having nodes take turns becoming leaders. In brief, each node maintains a buffer of input values that have not been committed yet. When it is node p's turn as leader, p broadcasts the set of elements in its buffer. When each turn ends, the nodes remove any newly committed elements from their buffers.

3.5   Deploying Consensus Protocols with Smart Contracts

So far, we have discussed protocols assuming a fixed set of parties, with collateral provided abstractly by a benefactor. We now describe an alternative deployment scenario where many independent SmartCast instances are run concurrently, and where the participants in each are randomly drawn from a large population of potential workers. Our idea is to build a smart contract-based marketplace, SmartCast-Market, that matches up workers to protocol instances.

A naïve approach might be to allow participants to join a SmartCast instance a first-come-first-serve basis. This naïve solution would be vulnerable to Sybil attacks, where malicious nodes join as fast as they can with numerous pseudonyms, hoping to fill up all of the slots in a protocol and therefore crowd out honest nodes. Instead, our solution is to allow nodes to join a pool of workers, and to allow task creators to deposit collateral and add to a pool of pending tasks. Every epoch, workers are assigned to tasks in a randomized batch. This prevents nodes from gaining too much influence within any particular protocol instance.

If all participants in an instance follow the protocol, then the total payment for a task must be $P = N(N - 1)\theta$. In principle, this could be collected from a combination of up-front payment from the task creator, along with collateral deposits from the participants themselves.

Since participation is voluntary, we should ensure as a guideline that workers never lose money by participating in the protocol. Thus if they deposit collateral, they must get at least that collateral back (in expectation) despite a worst-case adversary. However, since the parameter $\theta = \frac{N-1}{N-1-b}M$ is chosen minimally, in the worst-case each honest party just breaks even, receiving only $(N - 1 - b)\theta$ in payment but incurring an equal message cost of $(N - 1)M$. Therefore there is no opportunity for collateral deposits to contribute to the necessary endowment.

Thus the task creator must pay up-front the maximum payment $N(N - 1)\theta$, although the maximum total message cost is only $N(N - 1)M$. Hence, the task creator potentially pays an overhead of $\frac{N-1}{N-1-b}$ above the raw cost of the resources used.

4   Implementation and Evaluation

To evaluate the practical limitations of the SmartCast protocol, we develop a prototype implementation of both the Dolev-Strong consensus algorithm and

```
contract SmartCast {
    mapping(address => uint) playermap;
    bool[] reported;
    address[] players;
    uint[] rewards;
    uint theta;
    uint deadline; // Deadline to receive reports

    function assert(bool b) internal { if (!b) throw; }
    modifier after_ (uint T) { if (block.number < T) throw; }
    modifier before(uint T) { if (block.number >= T) throw; }
    modifier onlyplayer() { if (playermap[msg.sender] == 0) throw; }

    function SmartCast(address[] _players, uint _theta, uint _dline) {
        var N = players.length;
        // Each player earns up to N * theta
        assert(msg.value == N * N * _theta);
        theta = _theta;
        deadline = _dline;
        for (var p = 0; p < _players.length; p++) {
            players.push(_players[p]);
            rewards.push(0);
            playermap[_players[p]] = (p+1);
        }
    }
    function report(uint[] reports) onlyplayer before(deadline) {
        var p = playermap[msg.sender] - 1;
        assert(!reported[p]); reported[p] = true; // only report once
        assert(penalties.length == players.length);
        for (var q = 0; q < reports.length; q++) {
            var report = reports[q];
            assert(report >= 0);
            assert(report <= theta);
            rewards[q] += report;
        }
    }
    function withdraw() onlyplayer after_(deadline) {
        var i = playermap[msg.sender];
        if (!msg.sender.send(balance[i])) throw;
        balance[i] = 0;
    }
}
```

Fig. 3. Implementation of the Smart contract in Solidity.

an Ethereum smart contract capable of assigning various nodes to arbitrary consensus tasks.

Our Dolev-Strong implementation is written in Python, using ordinary threads and TCP sockets, with messages signed using the `ed25519` signature scheme. We evaluated our protocol by running on a network of up to 16 Amazon EC2 instances. To simulate realistic network delays, we used the Linux traffic control tool to limit bandwidth to 5mbps and impose a 100ms latency per message.

In the synchronous network model, messages between honest parties are simply guaranteed to be delivered within a given time bound. However, in reality, it is necessary to choose this timeout parameter concretely, based on estimates of network performance and on a tolerance for failure. Too short a timeout, and messages between otherwise-honest parties may fail to be delivered in time.

In our experiments the payload for each broadcast is a constant size of 1 megabyte (i.e., the size of a Bitcoin block today). We benchmarked the network and computation load by performing several trial computations and measuring the resulting message delivery time, and then fitting a normal distribution to the results.

We first analyze the effects of message failure on the individual participants bottom line. If a node p fails to deliver a message to q in time, then q will inflict a punishment on p. Since each node is required to send 2 messages, if each message fails with probability ζ, we expect the expected cost of punishments to be $(N-1)(1-(1-\zeta)^2)$. In Fig. 4 we compare the actual punishment incurred in our experiment with this expected line.

Message delivery failures can also lead to inconsistent outputs. In the worst case, if the maximum number of b nodes are actively attacking the network, then even a single failed message among the remaining nodes can lead to inconsistency. This occurs in the following scenario: suppose b nodes (including the leader) are corrupted, and send no messages at all until round b (the next-to-last round). At the beginning of round b, one of the corrupted nodes sends a message to a single honest node p containing a value v and b signatures. The node p will accept (and output) the value v, and relay it to the remaining $N-1-b$ honest nodes. If even one of these nodes fails to receive this final-round message, then it will output an inconsistent value $\bot$. Thus given b malicious nodes, and assuming messages fail independently with probability ζ, the uncorrupted nodes could output inconsistent values with probability $1-(1-N^2)$ probability (these are plotted in Fig. 5).

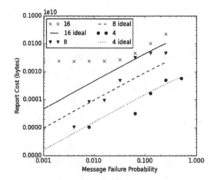

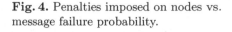

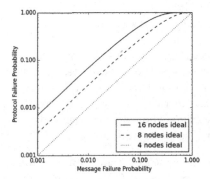

Fig. 4. Penalties imposed on nodes vs. message failure probability.

Fig. 5. Consistency failure vs. message failure probability (analytic only).

4.1 Ethereum Smart Contract

We implemented the smart contract component of SmartCast in Ethereum's Solidity programming language. Our implementation includes:

- A smart contract for collecting reports, and handling payments. The entire program listing is shown in Fig. 3.

- A smart contract implementing the "Marketplace" described in Sect. 3.5.
- A test framework using `pyethereum`, allowing us to measure the "gas costs" (i.e., transaction fees) for varying numbers of parties.

The Solidity language syntax resembles Javascript, and the intended effect of each line should be clear in context (though we imagine readers may be skeptical of the details, given several recent high-profile failures caused by subtle Solidity quirks [8,15,16]). Fortunately, the Smart Contract program listing in 3 fairly closely matches the pseudocode in Fig. 1. We explain a few Solidity idioms that readers are likely to be unfamiliar with. Solidity supports "modifier" macros, which are convenient for specifying preconditions which must hold before a function is called (or else they `throw` an error). Furthermore, although the pseudocode disburses all rewards immediately upon the deadline, Ethereum does not directly support time-triggered events, thus the indirect `withdraw` function is necessary.

The Marketplace Contract. We also implemented a Solidity version of the "marketplace" smart contract described in Sect. 3.5. Below we describe its high level functions. For space, we omit the full Solidity code listing; the full code will be made available online.

- `registerTask`: creates a new task, configured with any application-specific parameters (e.g., description of a validation condition or a list of approved clients). The task creator must include payment sufficient to pay the workers for the task.
- `registerWorker`: allows a worker to sign up, depositing any necessary collateral.
- `finalize`: shuffles the list of workers and list of tasks, and then assigns workers to tasks until either (a) no tasks are remaining, or (b) not enough workers are available to fill the remaining task. For each fully-assigned task, spawn a new instance of the SmartCast contract. Return any deposited collateral to workers who were not assigned to a task, and refund payment to task creators whose tasks were not fulfilled.

Our protocol relies on a random beacon; our prototype simply uses `block.blockhash(0)` as a source of randomness, although this is known to be manipulable by miners [3,18].

Ethereum Benchmarks. We tested our smart contract implementation using the `pyethereum.tester` framework. Table 1 shows the required gas costs for varying configurations of our application. We show results for only a few possible configurations: we increase the number of parties P, but always fill two tasks with two workers left over. The `finalize` method is the most expensive, since it grows with $O(N)$ when shuffling the list of workers. However, the `registerWorker` and `registerTask` methods are each invoked N times, and thus contribute about equally to the total.

Ethereum imposes a per-block (and hence, per-transaction) gas limit, which miners can vote to change gradually over time. Although the simulator easily supports these large transactions, today's Ethereum blockchain enforces a limit of approximately 2 million gas units, which the `finalize` operation busts when $P \geq 20$ (as underlined in Table 1). To avoid this limit, an alternative approach would be to spread the `finalize` operation over several contract invocations. This would require more complicated code, since each invocation would need to explicitly load and save its internal state. Our application provides a motivation for higher-level programming abstractions for transactions spanning multiple blocks.

Table 1. Smart contract gas costs (normalized to dollars, based on current Ethereum parameters and price (as of Nov 14 2016)). Underlined costs are infeasible, exceeding Ethereum's current per-block gas limit.

(N,P,T)	registerWorker		registerTask		finalize		Tot	
	Gas	(USD)	Gas	(USD)	Gas	(USD)	Gas	(USD)
(4, 10, 2)	110743	2.7¢	153347	3.8¢	1215702	30.4¢	2614826	65.4¢
(8, 18, 2)	110743	2.7¢	153347	3.8¢	1863111	46.6¢	4234665	$1.05
(16, 34, 2)	110743	2.7¢	153347	3.8¢	2966784	74.0¢	6678740	$1.70
(32, 66, 2)	110743	2.7¢	153347	3.8¢	5271727	$1.32	12047459	$3.01

Alternative implementation in Bitcoin. Our SmartBar protocol could still function using only Bitcoin's multi-signature transactions. The parties and the benefactor would generate N^2 transactions, where each transaction $T_{p,q}$ rewards θ to party q conditionally on a signature from p.

5   Conclusion and Future Work

We have adapted the work of Clement et al. [7] to the "smart contract" world, using cryptocurrencies to provide incentive compatibility for off-chain consensus protocols. Though we give a specific instantiation based on the Dolev-Strong protocol for reliable broadcast, our protocol is expressed as a generic transformation for arbitrary synchronous protocols.

Although the incentive compatibility notion we have adapted from Clement et al. [7] is described as "worst-case," modeling arbitrary Byzantine failures, many plausible attacks yet lie outside this model. In particular, our definition counterintuitively rules out "bribery" attacks, which are well-known though have not been observed in practice [2,19]. Notice that the "worst-case" notion is from the point of view of an individual participant; since accepting a bribe makes an individual party richer, this is excluded by definition. Additionally, our utility model assumes unilateral deviation, which rules out collusion attacks. Incorporating both bribery and collusion into our model remains an important open problem.

References

1. Bentov, I., Kumaresan, R.: How to use bitcoin to design fair protocols. In: Garay, J.A., Gennaro, R. (eds.) CRYPTO 2014. LNCS, vol. 8617, pp. 421–439. Springer, Heidelberg (2014). https://doi.org/10.1007/978-3-662-44381-1_24
2. Bonneau, J.: Why buy when you can rent? Bribery attacks on Bitcoin consensus. In: Bitcoin Research Workshop (2016)
3. Bonneau, J., Clark, J., Goldfeder, S.: On bitcoin as a public randomness source. Cryptology ePrint Archive, Report 2015/1015 (2015). http://eprint.iacr.org/2015/1015
4. Bonneau, J., Miller, A., Clark, J., Narayanan, A., Kroll, J.A., Felten, E.W.: Research perspectives and challenges for bitcoin and cryptocurrencies. In: IEEE Symposium on Security and Privacy (2015)
5. Castro, M., Liskov, B., et al.: Practical byzantine fault tolerance. In: OSDI, vol. 99, pp. 173–186 (1999)
6. Chase, M., Meiklejohn, S.: Transparency overlays and applications. In: Proceedings of the 2016 ACM SIGSAC Conference on Computer and Communications Security, pp. 168–179. ACM (2016)
7. Clement, A., Li, H., Napper, J., Martin, J.P., Alvisi, L., Dahlin, M.: BAR primer. In: 2008 IEEE International Conference on Dependable Systems and Networks With FTCS and DCC (DSN), pp. 287–296. IEEE (2008)
8. Delmolino, K., Arnett, M., Kosba, A.E., Miller, A., Shi, E.: Lessons and insights from a cryptocurrency lab. In: Bitcoin Research Workshop, Step by Step Towards Creating a Safe Smart Contract (2016)
9. Dingledine, R., Mathewson, N., Syverson, P.: Tor: the second-generation onion router. Technical report, DTIC Document (2004)
10. Dolev, D., Strong, H.R.: Authenticated algorithms for byzantine agreement. SIAM J. Comput. 12(4), 656–666 (1983)
11. Garay, J., Katz, J., Maurer, U., Tackmann, B., Zikas, V.: Rational protocol design: cryptography against incentive-driven adversaries. Cryptology ePrint Archive, Report 2013/496 (2013). http://eprint.iacr.org/2013/496
12. Kosba, A., Miller, A., Shi, E., Wen, Z., Papamanthou, C.: Hawk: the blockchain model of cryptography and privacy-preserving smart contracts. In: 2016 IEEE Symposium on Security and Privacy (SP), pp. 839–858 (May 2016)
13. Kumaresan, R.: Broadcast and Verifiable Secret Sharing: New Security Models and Round Optimal Constructions (2012)
14. Laurie, B., Langley, A., Kasper, E.: Certificate transparency. In: Network Working Group Internet-Draft, v12, work in progress (2013). http://tools.ietf.org/html/draft-laurie-pki-sunlight-12
15. Luu, L., Chu, D.H., Olickel, H., Saxena, P., Hobor, A.: Making smart contracts smarter. In: Proceedings of the 2016 ACM SIGSAC Conference on Computer and Communications Security, pp. 254–269. ACM (2016)
16. Morris, D.Z.: Blockchain-based venture capital fund hacked for $60 million (June 2016). http://fortune.com/2016/06/18/blockchain-vc-fund-hacked/
17. Nakamoto, S.: Bitcoin: a peer-to-peer electronic cash system (2008). http://bitcoin.org/bitcoin.pdf
18. Pierrot, C., Wesolowski, B.: Malleability of the blockchain's entropy. Cryptology ePrint Archive, Report 2016/370 (2016). http://eprint.iacr.org/2016/370
19. Teutsch, J., Jain, S., Saxena, P.: When cryptocurrencies mine their own business. In: Bitcoin Research Workshop (2016)
20. Wood, G.: Ethereum: a secure decentralized transaction ledger (2014). http://gavwood.com/paper.pdf

On the Feasibility of Decentralized Derivatives Markets

Shayan Eskandari[1], Jeremy Clark[2(✉)], Vignesh Sundaresan[1], and Moe Adham[1]

[1] Bitaccess, Ottawa, Canada
[2] Concordia University, Montreal, Canada
j.clark@concordia.ca

Abstract. In this paper, we present Velocity, a decentralized market deployed on Ethereum for trading a custom type of derivative option. To enable the smart contract to work, we also implement a price fetching tool called PriceGeth. We present this as a case study, noting challenges in development of the system that might be of independent interest to whose working on smart contract implementations. We also apply recent academic results on the security of the Solidity smart contract language in validating our code's security. Finally, we discuss more generally the use of smart contracts in modelling financial derivatives.

1 Introductory Remarks

The introduction of Bitcoin [9] in 2009 led to a new frontier in decentralizing technologies, both in finance and elsewhere. Of the many implementations, we note a few: file systems like The InterPlanetary File System (IPFS) [2], dynamic name servers like DNSChain [13] and MaidSafe, a fully distributed platform [6]. For our purposes, the most interesting technology is Ethereum [4,11]—a decentralized general transaction ledger. Ethereum in simple words is a decentralized computer that can run code, called smart contracts, which enforce the performance of an agreed upon set of negotiated standards in an automated and immutable way. Smart contracts can be designed to disintermediate traditional trusted parties, replacing them with pre-defined logical parameters. The smart contract concept is not new and was introduced by Szabo in 1997 [10], however there has not been any real implementation of it until Bitcoin, and then in a much more flexible and verbose fashion: Ethereum.

Under the umbrella of "fintech", "blockchain", and "distributed ledger technology", many legacy entities in the financial world (investment banks, security exchanges, clearinghouses, etc.) have expressed interest (through whitepapers and commercial partnerships and consortiums) in decentralizing financial markets. Derivative markets are often cited as a potential target. From the other end, papers on Ethereum and tutorials on Solidity (a high level programming language for Ethereum) often use derivatives as an example application. So there is a degree of consensus that derivatives running on Ethereum is an interesting application to study, but we are not aware of any public projects to attempt to build a derivative market in a serious way. This paper is a first step in that direction.

© International Financial Cryptography Association 2017
M. Brenner et al. (Eds.): FC 2017 Workshops 2017, LNCS 10323, pp. 553–567, 2017.
https://doi.org/10.1007/978-3-319-70278-0_35

1.1 Scope and Contributions

A simplification of a derivative is as follows: two parties enter an agreement where the first stands to profit if a specified security (*e.g.,* stock) appreciates in value over a specified time-period and the second stands to profit if it falls. Since the profitability of the agreement is derived directly from the price of the security, it is called a derivative instrument. The exact operational details that realize this property differs between types of derivatives. The most common derivative is a put/call option which gives the second party (called the *buyer*) the opportunity (but not obligation) to buy/sell a security at a specified price (*strike price*) at (*American*) or within (*European*) a specified time (*expiration*). The buyer pays the first party (the *seller*) a flat fee (*option price*) when purchasing the option. Derivatives are generally held to hedge risks in price movements or for speculation.

In a decentralized derivative system, a buyer and seller can have fast and automatic clearing and settlement (straight through processing) of the derivative without trusting a third party. However the design of a market must consider the following challenges:

1. **Terms of the Contract.** The terms of derivative must be expressible in the smart contract language. In this paper, we write contracts in Solidity for the Ethereum blockchain which is sufficient for describing the core aspects of the contract. We present a full implementation stack (from the smart contracts to a UI) for buying/selling a special type of derivative instrument. We pay special attention to common security risks in developing Solidity-based contracts.
2. **Counterparty Risk.** In most derivatives, the seller is obliged to buy/sell securities upon request of the buyer subject to the terms of the derivative. A seller might choose to not follow through with her obligations. In a centralized setting, identity, reputation and legal recourse are used to combat this. In a decentralized environment, this problem must be addressed. In this paper (and the reason we position it as a first step), we start with derivatives that are fully collateralized—meaning the full settlement amount under all outcomes is capped and this amount is locked to the contract at initiation time and distributed under the conditions of the contract. This means we do not implement a traditional put/call option but rather a tweaked version we describe below. In future work, we will consider counterparty risk broadly and how mitigating it can be combined with our framework to offer more traditional derivatives.
3. **Price Feed.** In a derivative where settlement is fully automated, either the underlying security (or a token representing it) needs to be on the blockchain already or the blockchain needs to be able to assign a value to the security— or more precisely, be fed the price it should use in evaluating the code of the contract. In practice, an entity feeding prices (or any external information) into a smart contract is called an oracle. Some related work has examined oracles, and we present our decentralized design in Subsect. 4.2 called PriceGeth, which we have made freely available.[1]

---

[1] https://github.com/VelocityMarket/pricegeth.

4. **Underlying Financial Model.** The buyer and seller of a derivative, whether implicitly or explicitly, must have some sense of what the probabilistic behaviour of the underlying security must be to determine the terms of the contract. This is the purpose of the infamous Nobel-awarded Black-Scholes model for stock prices—now obsolete but influential for decades. In our system, such a model is not baked into the functioning of the smart contract but would be used externally to decide favourable terms before buying/selling derivatives. For stocks, modern models (like jump-diffusion) might be used. For derivatives on cryptocurrencies or more esoteric securities, models simply do not exist yet and are an open area of research. Finally, we note that the derivative ultimately settles in Ether and so inflations/deflation of the currency might erode an otherwise profitable derivative.

In summary, we limit our contributions to (1) and (3) in this work, but also propose this fuller landscape as a useful research agenda for future researchers.

2 Related Work

Work on trusted oracles and price feeds, in the Ethereum eco-system, include TownCrier [12] which acts as an attested bridge (running within an SGX enclave) between trusted sources of information and the Ethereum blockchain. Oraclizeit[2] is another price feed which uses the similar workflow to fetch the requested information. Our approach differs from these as PriceGeth publishes the data to the Ethereum blockchain from the trusted source of information and the historical data is available to all smart contracts, however in comparison with the other approaches, is limited to only the published data (Price pairs).

Equibit [7] proposes a method to issue, create, disseminate and maintain equity across a broad base of investors without the need of intermediaries for record keeping. It is conceivable that derivative smart-contracts could utilize Equibit equity as payment or settlement method, as opposed to simply using Bitcoin or Ethereum's native digital currencies.

Bentov et al. [3] note than an extension to their work on decentralized prediction markets can be a derivative instruments they call a *capped contracts for difference*. It is similar to the one implemented in Velocity (their paper is not an implementation but a study of game theoretic properties).

Recent attacks on smart-contracts, such as TheDAO attack [14] attracted security researchers to analyze further on this era. Solidity security and survey of the attacks by Atzei et al. [1] lists some of the known security vulnerabilities and Luu et al. Developed a tool for static analysis on smart contract codes [8] which we used.

3 Materials and Methods

Smart Contracts. A *contract* is a written or spoken agreement between two or more parties that is intended to be enforceable by law. In a *smart contract*,

---

[2] http://www.oraclize.it/.

terms are written in code and executed by machines, removing the human performance component (unless if such a component is specified). We can consider our main smart contract as a black box: the inputs are investors' deposited *ether* (Ethereum's cash) and their position on the future price of an asset, either short or long. The smart contract will retain the deposit in escrow and execute a payout calculation and the payout itself when the expiry date comes. The payout is in Ether only, no actual shares are exchanged (a *contract for difference*) and the maximum payout is capped (*limit up/down*). Due to the deposit, there is no counter-party risk however the contract requires a trustworthy price feed and the investors earn zero interest for the duration of the contract. For this reason, we consider this a first step toward more flexible arrangements. The contract disintermediates the trusted role of the exchange (or broker for over-the-counter) and settling/clearing entities.

Types of Options. We implement a non-standard option that is similar to a collar or hedge wrapper. It is non-standard due to our requirement of escrowing money, which we make to side-step counter-party risk and enable a fully autonomous and disintermediated contract. The contract collects funds from the hedgers/speculators who take opposing positions on the future prospects of an asset: one takes the short position when they believe the underlying asset's value will lose value from its current price, and other takes the opposite long position speculating a rise in the price. In its simplest form, the collar options pay out $1 for every $1 change in the underlying asset (the payout can be made dependent on a drift term or even made non-linear). The payout is limited by the amount of money held in escrow—if the price rises beyond the limit, it is said to be limit up (or limit down in the opposite case) and the payout will be fixed (see Fig. 1). This kind of payout capping helps the contract holders stay immune to systemic risks and extreme jumps.

Development and Deployment. There are a few blockchains that would let us code an autonomous smart contracts: Ethereum, RSK [15] and more. The decision to work on Ethereum blockchain rather than others solely came from the

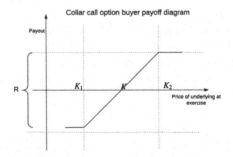

Fig. 1. Our collar-esque option with maximum long payout scenario. K1 is the initial price, K2 is the price at expiry time and R is the pre-defined collar for payouts

fact that there are more active developers in the community and maturity of the platform. Even though Ethereum is in early stages, it is more mature than other smart contract compatible platforms. The programming language used for smart contract development is Solidity in most of these platforms. All smart contracts developed and used in this paper has been deployed and tested by our beta testers on Ethereum testnet. In Ethereum blockchain, transactions and processing power costs some small amount of ether called *gas*[3]. For each transaction, the sender defines the gasLimit and also gasPrice for processing that transaction and miners decide to include those transactions in the blocks they mine or not. The concept of gas has many angles to discuss which falls outside of the scope of this paper. We will discuss some more in Sect. 5.

4   Implementation

We call our platform Velocity. We tried to model the real-life scenario of buying an options derivatives. Consider the case where Alice goes to a broker and buys an options contract from Bob. The broker is the one that handles the money transfer and also execute the options contract at the contract expiry time. Now our goal is to replace the broker with a smart contract. For the purpose of a proof of concept, **the smart contract will also act as Bob**, meaning if Alice buys a short call option, the Velocity smart contract will put a long call against her short call. This can be generalized so that other entities can fund the contract but for the rest of this paper, Velocity acts as a market maker. This might lead to users gaming the system, however it's trivial to change the smart contract to wait for the other opponent to enter the contract. We discuss this more in Sect. 5.

4.1   Velocity Main Smart Contract

A Velocity smart contract can be used for speculation on the price of any two assets[4], although the Ethereum price is always exposed as the deposits and the withdrawals are done in ETH[5]. As for this experiment, we use the price pair of Bitcoin (XBT/BTC) and Ethereum (ETH). If we used price pairs not involving ETH, for example the CAD/USD exchange rate, it would suffice to use two contracts for CAD/ETH and ETH/USD. Or the payout function could be changed to specify how it relates to numbers it is given. Note that in either case, the payout will always be in ETH. In its full generality, any number that changes over time and has a suitable feed (we describe feeds below) can be used: price (stocks, bonds, commodities, etc.), rate (interest, inflation, population, etc.), or something else (average global temperature, number of days without rain, etc.).

---

[3] What   is   gas?   http://ethdocs.org/en/latest/contracts-and-transactions/ account-types-gas-and-transactions.html#what-is-gas.

[4] or any other events that an options contract can be based on.

[5] Ethereum symbol.

Smart Contract. The way Velocity smart contract is implemented, one party purchases a contract by sending a nominal amount of ethereum (0.1 ETH) to the contract's ethereum address. Once confirmed by the network, the contract will fetch a starting price from the price feed, PriceGeth, and run for a period of time to reach the expiry time. The smart contract would put the same amount of ETH from its pool of funds into escrow for the payout. In the PoC demo, we use 5 ethereum blocks (approximately 1 min) to settle a contract. When the expiry time reaches, the same party must send another transaction to the contract and call the settlement function to settle the contract which leads to sending the payouts by the smart contract. While this experiment was going under beta testings, we found out that if the user loses the contract, there is no incentive to call the settle function as it would use up some ETH in gas and would not pay the user. This would lead stale money held in the escrow of the smart contract. This made us redesign our settlement functions and write one centralized cron job script to go through the unsettled contracts once a day and call the settle function on the ones that have been expired.

```
modifier checkMargin(uint amount) {
    if (amount == (applyLOT(Margin)))
    { _ ;} else {
        Error("Invalid Margin!");
        immediateRefund();}
    }
function goLong() public hasEnoughFunds(msg.value) checkMargin(msg.value)
payable returns(uint) {
    lastOptionId = newOption(msg.sender, msg.value, true);
    LongOption(lastOptionId, msg.sender, msg.value, block.number);
    return lastOptionId;
    }
```
Code 1 : Velocity Main Smart Contract - Long Option Call, The sender of a transaction to goLong() function has to send exactly the Margin value and with that he enters the option contract for Margin value with the smart Contract

Settle Function. exercise() is responsible in settling the options contract and pay out both parties (see Code 2), in which here is the user and the Velocity smart contract. Most of the functions are responsible to find the appropriate option contract and calculate the pay outs. However there are some functions that were added later on for security measurements, such as isOpen modifier. Modifiers in Solidity are functions that can check some statements before executing the main function. The first deployed version of Velocity main contract was vulnerable to a similar (but not the same) attack as the DAO attack, see Sect. 5. It was possible for an attacker to call an option contract and upon settling and winning, keep calling the exercise() function using his OptionId and get more of the same amount of payout over and over again. The code was patched and a new smart contract was deployed later in the experiment[6]. send() is a built-in function in

---

[6] Fix for the multiple payout bug: https://github.com/VelocityMarket/Options-Contract/commit/f3c8d0ef66b886c9ee8b432e92c83f3a4fb525ba.

Solidity which handles the sending of funds to other ethereum addresses or contracts. There are known vulnerabilities on how send() function works in solidity which should be appropriately handled. One can use a smart contract address as his option payout address which would execute some code upon receiving any funds and use that code flow to drain the sender's contract. payAndHandle() function tried to use the best security practices to prevent such attacks (see Code 5 for the source code).

```
modifier isOpen(uint optionId) {if (AllOptions[optionId].closed) throw; _ ;}
function exercise() public {
  exercise(findOptionId(msg.sender));
}
function exercise(uint optionId) public isOpen(optionId) returns(bool) {
  // REMOVED SOME CODE TO SAVE SPACE, FULL SOURCE CODE ON  GITHUB
  AllOptions[optionId].closed = true; //before payouts to prevent replay attacks
  LockedBalance -= AllOptions[optionId].amount; //release escrow
  // Payout calculation
  if (pricesToCheck.pricediff >= (int(Margin))) { // Pay Long
      //pay long
      return payAndHandle(optionId, AllOptions[optionId].Long,
2 * AllOptions[optionId].amount);
  }
  if ((0 < pricesToCheck.pricediff) && (pricesToCheck.pricediff < (int(Margin)))) {
      return (payAndHandle(optionId, AllOptions[optionId].Long,
        (AllOptions[optionId].amount + pricesToCheck.priceDiffLOT)) &&
            payAndHandle(optionId, AllOptions[optionId].Short,
            (AllOptions[optionId].amount - pricesToCheck.priceDiffLOT)));
  }
}
```
Code 2: Settle function of main options contract

Source Code. API documentation for other smart contracts to use the functionality and also Python and NodeJS clients to communicate with the main smart contract are available on Github[7].

4.2   Price Feed

A decentralized Price feed is an essential requirement for having a decentralized derivative market. There are a few proposals on how to fetch the price in a smart contract. One is using *Smart Contract* oracles[8], they offer daily updates for the price using a predefined data source. This was not an option to be used for our purpose as a daily update is not sufficient for short term derivative markets. Another option that could be used was Oraclizeit. They way Oraclizeit works is that the client smart contract, Velocity main contract in our case, sends a transaction to Oraclizeit smart contract with the required API url and the fields it needs, sometime after the confirmation by the network, Oraclizeit smart contract sends a callback transaction to Velocity smart contract with the requested data (Fig. 2).

---

[7] Simple collared option smart contract: https://github.com/VelocityMarket/Options-Contract.

[8] Data and Payments for your Smart Contracts https://smartcontract.com/.

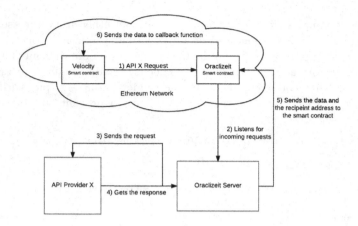

Fig. 2. Oraclizeit work flow

For the first implementation of Velocity smart contract we used Oraclizeit method to fetch the price.

As mentioned before, most of the decentralized application infrastructure on Ethereum blockchain are in Beta state and might not work as intended. This applies for Oraclizeit, specially as by design they have a central server which can stop working without any notice or visible signs. The red boxes in Fig. 2 indicates the centralized parts of the system. As you can see in (code 3), Oraclizeit will send the price to the callback function at the time of the call and also execute the exercise() function which is responsible for saving the price and calculating the payout amounts. This makes the callback function one of the important functions which should be called at the specific time.

```
oraclize_setProof(proofType_TLSNotary | proofStorage_IPFS);
//oraclize_setNetwork(2); //
priceUrl = "json(https://www.bitstamp.net/api/v2/ticker/btcusd).last";
function updateBTCUSDFromFeed(uint delay){
  oraclize_query(delay, "URL",
    priceUrl, 400000);
  }
function __callback(bytes32 myid, string result, bytes proof) {
  if (msg.sender != oraclize_cbAddress()) throw;
    uint BTCUSDFeed;
    BTCUSDFeed = parseInt(result, 2);
  exercise() // this function exercises the contract to calculate the payouts
  }
Code 3 : Implementation of Oraclizeit price feed in Velocity smart contract
```

In our testing period, we encountered multiple problems with this design:

1. The callback would not happen at all, which would result in an unsettled options contract. Oraclizeit support team were helpful and fixed this issue later on.

2. The callback would happen with some delays, which would result in inconsistency in the fetched price with the the the options contract expiry date. Decentralized networks have some latency by design, realtime does not really mean anything in such networks, hence counting on a transaction to happen at a exact time is not the best solution.
3. The callback would happen with insufficient gas, which would result in the failure to properly run exercise() function and thus failure to settle the options contract. Oraclizeit library offers a way to send more gas than needed in case the callback function needs more gas, however on the time of this experiment that functionality was not working properly.

PriceGeth. We designed PriceGeth[9] to publish (almost) realtime price pairs to Ethereum blockchain. This is how PriceGeth works (also see Fig. 3):

1. PriceFetcher server is saving an exchange Prices (USDBTC, BTCETH, BTCETC, BTCDOGE) every 1 s in a database
2. BlockListener is listening on using Geth[10] for new blocks
3. When BlockListener sees a new block it fetches the price at the Blocktime from PriceFetcher Module
4. PriceGeth server sends the data to PriceGeth smart contract (Code 4) and updates the latest price.

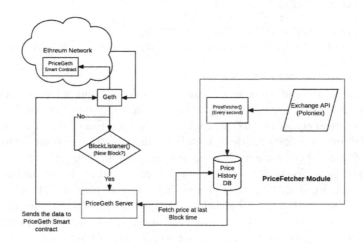

Fig. 3. PriceGeth Work Flow (Color figure online)

PriceGeth smart contract would keep all the historical prices and all would be available to all smart contracts on Ethereum blockchain for free (no gas needed

---

[9] Price API for Smart-Contracts on Ethereum Blockchain https://github.com/VelocityMarket/pricegeth.

[10] Official Go implementation of the Ethereum protocol https://geth.ethereum.org.

to fetch the price). The reason this is almost realtime, goes back to the nature of blockchains. Time units as in seconds and minutes are not meaningful for most of the blockchain applications, but the block height can be used as the time unit, meaning the time of each block is known to all users of the blockchain, but before a block is published no other time units can be used. This is why we designed PriceFetcher module to connect to an exchange API and saves the price pairs every second, to have the price for the previous block time anytime a new Ethereum block is generated.

```
struct Feed {
      uint    USDBTC;
      uint40    BTCETH;
      uint40    BTCETC;
      uint40    BTCDOGE;
      uint40  timestamp;
      uint    blockNumber;
    }
mapping (uint => Feed) priceHistory;
function setPrice(uint40 timestamp, uint40 blocknumber, uint USDBTC,
uint40 BTCETH, uint40 BTCETC, uint40 BTCDOGE) ifOwner() {
    if (firstBlock == 0) firstBlock = blocknumber;
    priceHistory[lastBlock].timestamp = timestamp;
    priceHistory[lastBlock].blockNumber = blocknumber;
    priceHistory[lastBlock].USDBTC = USDBTC;
    priceHistory[lastBlock].BTCETH = BTCETH;
    priceHistory[lastBlock].BTCETC = BTCETC;
    priceHistory[lastBlock].BTCDOGE = BTCDOGE;
    PriceUpdated(timestamp, blocknumber, USDBTC, BTCETH, BTCETC, BTCDOGE);
}
```

Code 4 : Pricegeth Main Smart contract

PriceGeth is a proof of concept implementation of having a trusted entity publishing price pairs to the blockchain and we are aware of the implications of trusting the PriceFetcher not to manipulate the prices. PriceFetcher is the central point of failure in PriceGeth design and should be addressed in future work. However after further research, it is almost impossible to have a truly trustless decentralized price feed unless we have a decentralized exchange infrastructure on the blockchain. This exchange can be used as the price oracle as the order books would be stored on the blockchain and hence there is no one single point of trust. The red boxes in Fig. 3 are indicating the centralized parts of this implementation. PriceGeth is released as a stand alone smart contract and also a library to be used in other smart contracts to use the price feed free of charge[11]. Another challenge of PriceGeth design is that PricePublisher is paying the gas for publishing and storing all the price pairs, and as there is no incentive of doing so, it is not an inefficient way of offering price oracles. PriceGeth can be implemented in a way that clients should use a token issued to them beforehand to fetch the price, or require payments to release the price data.

---

[11] PriceGeth Library https://github.com/VelocityMarket/pricegeth.

By design PriceGeth operator should not be able to use Velocity options as he can manipulate the price to game the system.

There is a similar work on price feeds titled Town Crier [12], which uses TLS security to prove the fact that the data sent to the smart contract is exactly as the one provided by the API, conceptually similar to Oraclizeit TLSNotary-proof[12]. TownCrier uses Intel SGX in their central server which insures the integrity of hardware used and thus insures no manipulation is done on the server. Even though one can argue that the data provider is a trusted entity, one of the goals to have a decentralized application is to have no trusted entity in the infrastructure and to have a trustless system.

5   Discussion

Security. Smart contracts have introduced some new security concerns to developers. Notions like gas usage and consensus and most importantly a function that pays out irreversible money are new to most of the developers hence the ability to develop a secure smart contract is hard to grasp. One of the visible examples of security issues is the attack on The DAO, Decentralized Autonomous Organization[13]. The goal of the DAO was to remove all the need for any venture capital intervention or any other third party for fundraising on a new idea or a company through crowdfunding and giving the investors tokens (shares) of the company. However due to an issue splitDAO function which was responsible to manage and fund new child DAOs or projects, an attacker was able to take one third of the money in the original DAO, worth approximately 86 million USD [16] at the time of the attack, this vulnerability is dubbed *Reentrancy Vulnerability*.

Luu et al. [8] developed a symbolic execution tool called "Oyente" to find potential security bugs, which they proved effective by running on Ethereum blockchain and successfully identifying The DAO vulnerability. We used this tool to analyze our code (see Fig. 4).

Another family of vulnerabilities that have caused some of the known attacks are *Mishandled Exceptions*, which mostly has caused Denial of Service attacks on individual smart contracts. In Velocity main contract we used *modifier* functions to sanitize the inputs to narrow down the probability of such exceptions. Another set of attacks *Timestamp Dependence* and *Transaction-Ordering Dependence* are interesting to ponder, however due to the design of Velocity and PriceGeth, they are not applicable to these smart contracts. As an example, usage of timestamp was replaced by Ethereum blocknumber and smart contracts time is based on the block number rather than seconds and minutes. There has been more security bugs in solidity compiler, a few related bugs were explained in Sect. 4.1.

---

[12] https://docs.oraclize.it/#security-tlsnotary-proof.
[13] https://github.com/slockit/DAO.

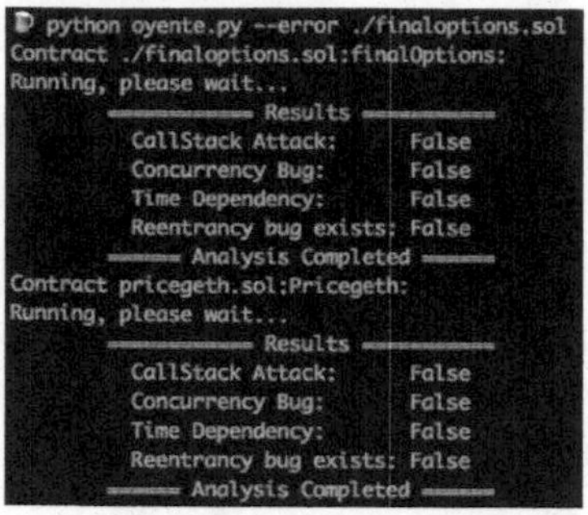

Fig. 4. Results of Smart Contract analysis tool called Oyente [12] to find security bugs

```
    function payAndHandle(uint optionId, address addr, uint amount)
  private returns (bool success) {
      if (addr.send(amount)) {
            optionPaid(optionId, addr, amount); //event for successful payment
      } else { throw;}
      return true;
  }
Code 5 : Secure payouts in smart contracts
```

Gas Sustainability. The concept of gas usage for processing power is not easy to grasp even for long term developers. People might be familiar with limited computational or storage resources, but the concept of passing gasLimit to a function to use to process inputs is a new concept. Each step has its own estimated gas usage, as an example to store a value in a variable, you have to pay *100 Wei*[14] for each *sstore* call[15]. This should be considered that there's a cap for gas usage for each transaction and block, thus complex computation should be split into multiple transactions which makes smart contract design more complicated than they are. Also we should mention that function calls can fail due to the fact that they run out of gas and they don't have enough gas to finish their required computation or storage. This can cause unpredicted behaviour from the smart contract as there would be broken flows in the code which should have been handled by the developer. The gas usage could change as there are updates and security patches to Ethereum protocol, e.g. transaction spam attack[16]. It might take multiple implementation of the same function to find an equilibrium between readability and gas efficiency.

Misuse of the Contract. In the current implementation of Velocity smart contract, one can call the Long option when he is sure of the price increase

---

[14] Wei: Smallest unit of Ethereum, equevalent to 0.000000000000000001 ETH.

[15] put into permanent storage.

[16] Long-term gas cost changes for IO-heavy operations to mitigate transaction spam attacks https://github.com/ethereum/EIPs/issues/150.

between the start time and expiry time and keep on doing this until there is no money left in the smart contract's pool of funds. This is because the smart contract calls the opposite of the incoming option call blindly. However in future work, there should be market scoring rule which depends on how many short option calls are placed comparing to the long calls and make it more expensive to call short when there are more short option calls than long calls.

Collar Option Library. Velocity smart contract can be used as a module in any other smart contract to handle option calls and execute some functions on the expiry time. This smart contract was written as a proof of concept and was released under *GPL* license[17].

6   Future Work

As discussed in Subsect. 4.2, fully decentralized Price feeds and oracles are needed in order to have a trustless decentralized financial market. This can be done by having a decentralized exchange to extract prices from using smart contracts. Even though there has been many price feed methods discussed, none of them seem to have trustless infrastructure. Smart contracts security is not well practiced and there are many unknown attack vectors in the eco system, from solidity compiler security bugs [17] to best practice security implementations [18], there is work to be done and tests to have a more mature secure eco-system to work with, Specially if the end goal is to have a decentralized financial application in place where money is at stake.

As for the options contracts, there should be more research and work on the payouts to make them smarter. One proposed solution is to have market scoring rules in place, which means if there are more open short option calls than long calls, it should get more expensive to call short options and vice-versa. Smart contracts are unchangeable piece of code that run autonomously, meaning if there's a market crash or systematic error, there cannot be anything to do to suspend the payouts and shut down the application, unless with pre-defined functions in the smart contract which only the owner can trigger, which would be a double standard in the trustless eco-system.

7   Conclusion

Even though the idea of having a fully autonomous and decentralized derivative market is intriguing, the infrastructure to reach this goal is still missing from the underlying network. As for example, price feed is one of the essentials of such a market and it should be done in a fully decentralized trustless way to prevent fraud and market manipulation by the feed provider. All the existing solutions today, have a central point that can manipulate data, it is either the exchange

---

[17] https://github.com/VelocityMarket/Options-Contract.

API or the component responsible to publish the price. As discussed before, one of the only solutions to this problem is to have a fully decentralized exchange on the network to provide realtime price feed for other smart contracts. There are some work done on decentralized exchanges [5], although there is no real world deployment of such a system at the time of writing. Smart contracts are fascinating idea that can revolutionize the technology by removing the middlemen, however the underlying technology is more on the proof of concept level than mature enough to be used on the real world scenarios. We should also mention that the barrier for people to have the relevant crypto-currency to work with such systems still exists.

A   Demo Website (UI) for the Velocity Smart Contract

See Fig. 5.

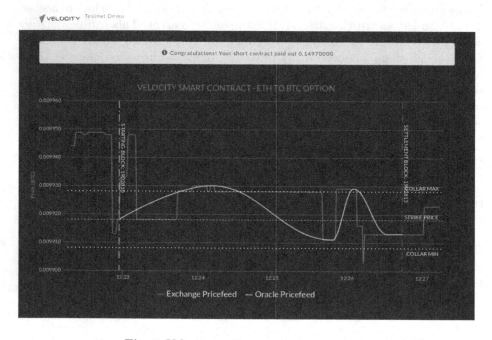

Fig. 5. Velocity options smart contract demo

References

1. Atzei, N., Bartoletti, M., Cimoli, T.: A survey of attacks on ethereum smart contracts (SoK). In: Maffei, M., Ryan, M. (eds.) POST 2017. LNCS, vol. 10204, pp. 164–186. Springer, Heidelberg (2017). https://doi.org/10.1007/978-3-662-54455-6_8

2. Benet, J.: Ipfs-content addressed, versioned, p2p file system (2014). arXiv:1407.3561
3. Bentov, I., Mizrahi, A., Rosenfeld, M.: Decentralized prediction market without arbiters (2017). arXiv:1701.08421
4. Buterin, V., et al.: A next-generation smart contract and decentralized application platform (2014)
5. Clark, J., Bonneau, J., Felten, E.W., Kroll, J.A., Miller, A., Narayanan, A.: On decentralizing prediction markets and order books. In: WEIS (2014)
6. Irvine, D.: Maidsafe distributed file system. Technical report, maidsafe.net limited (2010)
7. Kievit-Kylar, B., Horlacher, C., Godard, M., Saucier, C.: Equibit: a peer-to-peer electronic equity system (2016). arXiv:1612.06953
8. Luu, L., Chu, D.-H., Olickel, H., Saxena, P., Hobor, A.: Making smart contracts smarter. In: Proceedings of 2016 ACM SIGSAC Conference on Computer and Communications Security, pp. 254–269. ACM (2016)
9. Nakamoto, S.: Bitcoin: a peer-to-peer electronic cash system (2008)
10. Szabo, N.: The idea of smart contracts (1997)
11. Wood, G.: Ethereum: a secure decentralised generalised transaction ledger. Ethereum Project Yellow Paper (2014)
12. Zhang, F., Cecchetti, E., Croman, K., Juels, A., Shi, E.: Town crier: an authenticated data feed for smart contracts. In: Proceedings of 2016 ACM SIGSAC Conference on Computer and Communications Security, pp. 270–282. ACM (2016)
13. okturtles: A blockchain-based DNS, http server that fixes https security (2014)
14. Finley, K.: A 50 million dollar hack just showed that the DAO was all too human. Wired (2016)
15. Demian Lerner, S.: Rootstock: bitcoin powered smart contracts. Whitepaper (2015)
16. Daian, P.: Analysis of the DAO exploit. Hacking, Distributed (2016)
17. Reitwiessner, C.: Security alert: solidity variables can be overwritten in storage. Ethereum Blog (2016)
18. ConsenSys: Ethereum contract security techniques and tips. ConsenSys (2016)

A Proof-of-Stake Protocol for Consensus on Bitcoin Subchains

Massimo Bartoletti[(✉)], Stefano Lande, and Alessandro Sebastian Podda

Università degli Studi di Cagliari, Cagliari, Italy
bart@unica.it

Abstract. Although the transactions on the Bitcoin blockchain have the main purpose of recording currency transfers, they can also carry a few bytes of metadata. A sequence of transaction metadata forms a *subchain* of the Bitcoin blockchain, and it can be used to store a tamper-proof execution trace of a smart contract. Except for the trivial case of contracts which admit any trace, in general there may exist *inconsistent* subchains which represent incorrect contract executions. A crucial issue is how to make it difficult, for an adversary, to subvert the execution of a contract by making its subchain inconsistent. Existing approaches either postulate that subchains are always consistent, or give weak guarantees about their security (for instance, they are susceptible to Sybil attacks). We propose a consensus protocol, based on Proof-of-Stake, that incentivizes nodes to consistently extend the subchain. We empirically evaluate the security of our protocol, and we show how to exploit it as the basis for smart contracts on Bitcoin.

1 Introduction

Recently, cryptocurrencies like Bitcoin [26] have pushed forward the concept of decentralization, by ensuring reliable interactions among mutually distrusting nodes in the presence of a large number of colluding adversaries. These cryptocurrencies leverage on a public data structure, called *blockchain*, where they permanently store all the transactions exchanged by nodes. Adding new blocks to the blockchain (called *mining*) requires to solve a moderately difficult cryptographic puzzle. The first miner who solves the puzzle earns some virtual currency (some fresh coins for the mined block, and a small fee for each transaction included therein). In Bitcoin, miners must invert a hash function whose complexity is adjusted dynamically in order to make the average time to solve the puzzle ∼10 min. Instead, removing or modifying existing blocks is computationally unfeasible: roughly, this would require an adversary with more *hashing power* than the rest of all the other nodes. If modifying or removing blocks were computationally easy, an attacker could perform a *double-spending* attack where he pays some amount of coins to a merchant (by publishing a suitable transaction in the blockchain) and then, after he has received the item he has paid for, removes the block containing the transaction. According to the folklore, Bitcoin would resist to attacks unless the adversaries control the majority

© International Financial Cryptography Association 2017
M. Brenner et al. (Eds.): FC 2017 Workshops 2017, LNCS 10323, pp. 568–584, 2017.
https://doi.org/10.1007/978-3-319-70278-0_36

of total computing power of the Bitcoin network. Even though some vulnerabilities have been reported in the literature (see Sect. 4), in practice Bitcoin has worked surprisingly well so far: indeed, the known successful attacks to Bitcoin are standard hacks or frauds [19], unrelated to the Bitcoin protocol.

The idea of using the Bitcoin blockchain and its consensus protocol as foundations for *smart contracts*—namely, decentralized applications beyond digital currency [29]—has been explored by several recent works. For instance, [3,5,7,9,22–24] propose protocols for secure multiparty computations and fair lotteries; [13] implements decentralised authorization systems on Bitcoin, [28,30] allow users to log statements on the blockchain; [10] is a key-value database with get/set operations; [14] extends Bitcoin with advanced financial operations (like e.g., creation of virtual assets, payment of dividends, *etc.*), by embedding its own messages in Bitcoin transactions.

Although the Bitcoin blockchain is primarily intended to trade currency, its protocol allows clients to embed a few extra bytes as metadata in transactions. Many platforms for smart contracts exploit these metadata to store a persistent, timestamped and tamper-proof historical record of all their messages [1,6]. Usually, metadata are stored in OP_RETURN transactions [2], making them meaningless to the Bitcoin network and unspendable. With this approach, the sequence of platform-dependent messages forms a *subchain*, whose content can only be interpreted by the nodes that execute the platform (we refer to them as *meta-nodes*, to distinguish them from Bitcoin nodes). However, since the platform logic is separated from the Bitcoin logic, a meta-node can append to the subchain transactions with metadata which are meaningless for the platform—or even *inconsistent* with the intended execution of the smart contract. As far as we know, none of the existing platforms use a secure protocol to establish if their subchain is consistent. This is a serious issue, because it either limits the expressiveness of the smart contracts supported by these platforms (which must consider all messages as consistent, so basically losing the notion of state), or degrades the security of contracts (because adversaries can manage to publish inconsistent messages, so tampering with the execution of smart contracts).

Contributions. We propose a protocol that allows meta-nodes to maintain a consistent subchain over the Bitcoin blockchain. Our protocol is based on *Proof-of-Stake* [8,21], since extending the subchain must be endorsed with a money deposit. Intuitively, a meta-node which publishes a consistent message gets back its deposit once the message is confirmed by the rest of the network. In particular, our protocol provides an economic incentive to honest meta-nodes, while disincentivizing the dishonest ones. We empirically validate the security of our protocol by simulating it in various attack scenarios. Notably, our protocol can be implemented in Bitcoin by only using the so-called *standard* transactions[1].

---

[1] This is important, because non-standard transactions are discarded by nodes running the official Bitcoin client.

2   Bitcoin and the Blockchain

Bitcoin is a cryptocurrency and a digital open-source payment infrastructure that has recently reached a market capitalization of almost \$30 billions[2]. The Bitcoin network is peer-to-peer, not controlled by any central authority [26]. Each Bitcoin user owns one or more personal wallets, which consist of pairs of asymmetric cryptographic keys: the public key uniquely identifies the user *address*, while the private key is used to authorize payments. *Transactions* describe transfers of bitcoins ($\mathbb{B}$), and the history of all transactions, which recorded on a public, immutable and decentralised data structure called *blockchain*, determines how many bitcoins are contained in each address.

To explain how Bitcoin works, we consider two transactions t_0 and t_1, which we graphically represent as follows:[3]

t_0
in: $\cdots$
in-script: $\cdots$
out-script(t, σ): $ver_k(t, \sigma)$
value: v_0

t_1
in: t_0
in-script: $sig_k(\bullet)$
out-script$(\cdots)$: $\cdots$
value: v_1

The transaction t_0 contains $v_0\mathbb{B}$, which can be *redeemed* by putting on the blockchain a transaction (e.g., t_1), whose in field is the cryptographic hash of the whole t_0 (for simplicity, just displayed as t_0 in the figure). To redeem t_0, the in-script of t_1 must contain values making the out-script of t_0 (a boolean programmable function) evaluate to true. When this happens, the value of t_0 is transferred to the new transaction t_1, and t_0 is no longer redeemable. Similarly, a new transaction can then redeem t_1 by satisfying its out-script.

In the example displayed above, the out-script of t_0 evaluates to true when receiving a digital signature σ on the redeeming transaction t, with a given key pair k. We denote with $ver_k(t, \sigma)$ the signature verification, and with $sig_k(\bullet)$ the signature of the enclosing transaction (t_1 in our example), including *all* the parts of the transaction *except* its in-script.

Now, assume that the blockchain contains t_0, not yet redeemed, when someone tries to append t_1. To validate this operation, the nodes of the Bitcoin network check that $v_1 \leq v_0$, and then they evaluate the out-script of t_0, by instantiating its formal parameters t and σ, to t_1 and to the signature $sig_k(\bullet)$, respectively. The function ver_k verifies that the signature is correct: therefore, the out-script succeeds, and t_1 redeems t_0.

Bitcoin transactions may be more general than the ones illustrated by the previous example: their general form is displayed in Fig. 1. First, there can be multiple inputs and outputs (denoted with array notation in the figure). Each output has an associated out-script and value, and can be redeemed independently from others. Consequently, in fields must specify which output they are

---

[2] Source: crypto-currency market capitalizations http://coinmarketcap.com.

[3] in-script and out-script are respectively referred as scriptPubKey and scriptSig in the Bitcoin documentation.

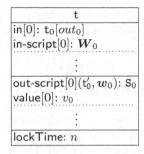

Fig. 1. General form of transactions.

redeeming ($t_0[out_0]$ in the figure). Similarly, a transaction with multiple inputs associates an in-script to each of them. To be valid, the sum of the values of all the inputs must be greater or equal to the sum of the values of all outputs. In its general form, the out-script is a program in a (not Turing-complete) scripting language, featuring a limited set of logic, arithmetic, and cryptographic operators. Finally, the lockTime field specifies the earliest moment in time (block number or UNIX timestamp) when the transaction can appear on the blockchain.

The Bitcoin network is populated by a large set nodes, called *miners*, which collect transactions from clients, and are in charge of appending the valid ones to the blockchain. To this purpose, each miner keeps a local copy of the blockchain, and a set of unconfirmed transactions received by clients, which it groups into *blocks*. The goal of miners is to add these blocks to the blockchain, in order to get a revenue. Appending a new block B_i to the blockchain requires miners to solve a cryptographic puzzle, which involves the hash $h(B_{i-1})$ of block B_{i-1}, a sequence of unconfirmed transactions $\langle T_i \rangle_i$, and some salt R. More precisely, miners have to find a value of R such $h(h(B_{i-1})\|\langle T_i \rangle_i\|R) < \mu$, where the value μ is adjusted dynamically, depending on the current hashing power of the network, to ensure that the average mining rate is of 1 block every 10 min. The goal of miners is to win the "lottery" for publishing the next block, i.e. to solve the cryptopuzzle before the others; when this happens, the miner receives a reward in newly generated bitcoins, and a small fee for each transaction included in the mined block. If a miner claims the solution of the current cryptopuzzle, the others discard their attempts, update their local copies of the blockchain with the new block B_i, and start mining a new block on top of B_i. In addition, miners are asked to verify the validity of the transactions in B_i by executing the associated scripts. Although verifying transactions is not mandatory, miners are incentivized to do that, because if in any moment a transaction is found invalid, they lose the fee earned when the transaction was published in the blockchain.

If two or more miners solve a cryptopuzzle simultaneously, they create a *fork* in the blockchain (i.e., two or more parallel valid branches). In the presence of a fork, miners must choose a branch wherein carrying out the mining process; roughly, this divergence is resolved once one of the branches becomes longer than the others. When this happens, the other branches are discarded, and all the orphan transactions contained therein are nullified.

Overall, this protocol essentially implements a *"Proof-of-Work"* system [15].

3   A Protocol for Consensus on Bitcoin Subchains

We define the notions of subchain and consistency in Sect. 3.1. In Sect. 3.2 we describe our protocol to embed consistent subchains on the Bitcoin blockchain; we examine some of its properties in Sect. 3.3. Finally, in Sect. 3.4 we show how to implement our protocol in Bitcoin.

3.1   Subchains and Consistency

We assume a set $A, B, \ldots$ of participants, who want to append messages $a, b, \ldots$ to the subchain. A *label* is a pair containing a participant A and a message a, written $A : a$. *Subchains* are finite sequences of labels, written $A_1 : a_1 \cdots A_n : a_n$, which are embedded in the Bitcoin blockchain. The intuition is that A_1 has embedded the message a_1 in some transaction t_1 of the Bitcoin blockchain, then A_2 has appended some transaction t_2 embedding a_2, and so on. For a subchain η, we write $\eta\, A : a$ for the subchain obtained by appending $A : a$ to η.

In general, labels can also have side effects on the Bitcoin blockchain: we represent with $A : a(v \to B)$ a label which also transfers $v\text{\textBitcoin}$ from A to B. When this message is on the subchain, it also acts as a standard currency transfer on the Bitcoin blockchain, which makes $v\text{\textBitcoin}$ in a transaction of A redeemable by B. When the value v is zero or immaterial, we simply write a instead of $a(v \to B)$.

A crucial insight is that not all possible sequences of labels are valid subchains: to define the *consistent* ones, we interpret subchains as traces of *Labelled Transition Systems* (LTS). Formally, an LTS is a tuple $(Q, L, q_0, \to)$, where:

- Q is a set of states (ranged over by $q, q', \ldots$);
- L is a set of labels (in our case, of the form $A : a$);
- $q_0 \in Q$ is the initial state;
- $\to\, \subseteq Q \times L \times Q$ is a transition relation.

As usual, we write $q \xrightarrow{A:a} q'$ when $(q, A : a, q') \in\, \to$, and, given a subchain $\eta = A_1 : a_1 \cdots A_n : a_n$, we write $q \xrightarrow{\eta} q'$ whenever there exist $q_1, \ldots, q_n$ such that:

$$q \xrightarrow{A_1:a_1} q_1 \xrightarrow{A_2:a_2} \cdots \xrightarrow{A_n:a_n} q_n = q'$$

We require that the relation $\to$ is *deterministic*, i.e. if $q \xrightarrow{A:a} q'$ and $q \xrightarrow{A:a} q''$, then it must be $q' = q''$.

The intuition is that the subchain has a state (initially, q_0), and each message updates the state according to the transition relation. More precisely, if the subchain is in state q, then a message a sent by A makes the state evolve to q' whenever $q \xrightarrow{A:a} q'$ is a transition in the LTS.

Note that, for some state q and label $A : a$, it may happen that no state q' exists such that $q \xrightarrow{A:a} q'$. In this case, if q is the current state of the subchain, we want to make hard for a participant (possibly, an adversary trying to tamper with the subchain) to append such message. Informally, a subchain $A_1 : a_1 \cdots A_n : a_n$ is *consistent* if, starting from the initial state q_0, it is possible to find states $q_1, \ldots, q_n$ such that from each q_i there is a transition labelled $A_{i+1} : a_{i+1}$ to q_{i+1}.

Definition 1 (Subchain consistency). *We say that a subchain η is consistent whenever there exists q such that $q_0 \xrightarrow{\eta} q$.*

Note that, if a subchain is consistent, then by determinism we have that the state q_n exists and is unique. In other words, a consistent sequence of messages uniquely identifies the state of the subchain.

Example 1. To illustrate consistency, consider a smart contract $\mathtt{FACTORS}_n$ which rewards with 1₿ each participant who extends the subchain with a new prime factor of n. The contract accepts two kinds of messages:

- $\mathbf{send}_p$, where p is a natural number;
- $\mathbf{pay}_p(1 \to A)$, meaning that A receives a reward for the factor p;

The states of the contract can be represented as sets of triples (A, p, b), where b is a boolean value indicating whether A has been rewarded for the factor p. The initial state is $\emptyset$. We define the transition relation of $\mathtt{FACTORS}_n$ as follows:

- $S \xrightarrow{A:\mathbf{send}_p} S'$, iff p is a prime factor of n, $(B, p, b) \notin S$ for any B and b, and $S' = S \cup \{(A, p, 0)\}$;
- $S \xrightarrow{F:\mathbf{pay}_p(1 \to A)} S'$, iff $(A, p, 0) \in S$ and $S' = (S \setminus \{(A, p, 0)\}) \cup \{(A, p, 1)\}$.

Consider now the following subchains for $\mathtt{FACTORS}_{330}$, where F is the participant who issues the contract, and M is an adversary:

1. $\eta_1 \;=\; A : \mathbf{send}_{11} \quad B : \mathbf{send}_2 \quad F : \mathbf{pay}_{11}(1 \to A) \quad F : \mathbf{pay}_2(1 \to B)$
2. $\eta_2 \;=\; A : \mathbf{send}_{11} \quad F : \mathbf{pay}_{11}(1 \to A) \quad M : \mathbf{send}_{11}$
3. $\eta_3 \;=\; M : \mathbf{send}_{229} \quad F : \mathbf{pay}_{229}(1 \to M)$
4. $\eta_4 \;=\; A : \mathbf{send}_{11} \quad F : \mathbf{pay}_{11}(1 \to M)$

The subchain η_1 is consistent, because both A and B send new factors and get their rewards. The subchains η_2 and η_3 are inconsistent, because 11 sent by M is not fresh, and 229 is not a factor of 330. Finally, the subchain η_4 is inconsistent, because M gets the reward that should have gone to A. □

Similarly to Bitcoin, we do not aim at guaranteeing that a subchain is *always* consistent. Indeed, also in Bitcoin a miner could manage to append a block with invalid transactions: in this case, as discussed in Sect. 2, the Bitcoin blockchain forks, and the other miners must choose which branch to follow. However, honest miners will neglect the branch with invalid transactions, so eventually (since honest miners detain the majority of computational power), that branch will be abandoned by all miners.

For subchain consistency we adopt a similar notion: we assume that an adversary can append a label $A : a$ such that $q_n \not\xrightarrow{A\,:\,a}$, so making the subchain inconsistent. However, upon receiving such label, honest nodes will discard it. To formalise their behaviour, we define below a function Γ that, given a subchain η (possibly inconsistent), filters all the invalid messages. Hence, $\Gamma(\eta)$ is a consistent subchain.

Definition 2 (Branch pruning). *We inductively define the endofunction Γ on subchains as follows, where ϵ denotes the empty subchain:*

$$\Gamma(\epsilon) = \epsilon \qquad \Gamma(\eta\, A : a) = \begin{cases} \Gamma(\eta)\, A : a & if \exists q, q' : q_0 \xrightarrow{\Gamma(\eta)} q \xrightarrow{A\,:\,a} q' \\ \Gamma(\eta) & otherwise \end{cases}$$

In order to model which labels can be appended to the subchain without breaking its consistency, we introduce below the auxiliary relation $\models$. Informally, given a consistent subchain η, the relation $\eta \models A : a$ holds whenever the subchain $\eta\, A : a$ is still consistent.

Definition 3 (Consistent update). *We say that $A : a$ is a* consistent update *of a subchain η, denoted with $\eta \models A : a$, iff the subchain $\Gamma(\eta)\, A : a$ is consistent.*

Example 2. Recall the subchain $\eta_2 = A : send_{11}\ F : pay_{11}(1 \to A)\ M : send_{11}$ from Example 1. We have that $B : send_2$ is a consistent update of η_2, because $\Gamma(\eta_2)\, B : send_2 = A : send_{11}\ F : pay_{11}(1 \to A)\ B : send_2$ is consistent.   □

3.2   Description of the Protocol

Assume a network of mutually distrusted nodes $N, N', \ldots$, that we call *meta-nodes* to distinguish them from the nodes of the Bitcoin network. Meta-nodes receive messages from participants (also mutually distrusting) which want to extend the subchain. Our goal is to allow honest participants (i.e., those who follow the protocol) to perform consistent updates of the subchain, while disincentivizing adversaries who attempt to make the subchain inconsistent.

To this purpose, we propose a protocol based on *Proof-of-Stake* (PoS). Namely, we rely on the assumption that the overall stake retained by honest participants is greater than the stake of dishonest ones[4]. The stake is needed by meta-nodes, which have to vote for approving messages sent by participants. These messages are embedded into Bitcoin transactions, which we call *update requests*. We denote by $UR[A : a]$ the update request issued by A to append the message a to the subchain. In order to vote an update request, a meta-node must invest $\kappa \math̄{B}$ on it, where κ is a constant specified by the protocol. An update

---

[4] Note that a similar hypothesis, but related to computational power rather than stake, holds in Bitcoin, where honest miners are supposed to control more computational power than dishonest ones.

1. Upon receiving an update request UR[A : a], a meta-node checks its consistency, $\eta \models A : a$. If so, it votes the request, and adds it to the request pool;
2. when Δ expires, the arbiter signs all the well-formed UR in the request pool;
3. all requests signed by the arbiter are sent to the Bitcoin miners, to be published on the blockchain. The first to be mined, indicated with UR_i, is the i-th label of the subchain.

Fig. 2. Summary of a protocol stage i.

request needs the vote of a single meta-node. The protocol requires meta-nodes to vote a request UR[A : a] only if A : a is a consistent update of the current subchain η, i.e. if $\eta \models A : a^5$. To incentivize meta-nodes to vote their update requests, participants pay them a *fee* (smaller than κ), which can be redeemed by meta-nodes when the update request is appended to the subchain.

We define our protocol in Fig. 2. It is organised in *stages*. The protocol ensures that *exactly one* label A : a is appended to the subchain for each stage i. This is implemented by appending a corresponding transaction $UR_i[A : a]$ to the Bitcoin blockchain. To guarantee its uniqueness, the protocol exploits an *arbiter* T, namely a distinguished node of the network which is assumed honest (we discuss this hypothesis in Sect. 3.3). We now describe the main steps of the protocol.

At step 1 of the stage i of the protocol, a meta-node (say, N) votes an update request (as detailed in Sect. 3.4). In order to do this, N must confirm a previous update UR_j in the subchain, by paying κ ฿ (plus the participant's fee) to the meta-node N′ who appended UR_j to the subchain. To avoid the *self-compensation attack* discussed later on in Sect. 3.3, the protocol only allows to confirm one of the past C updates, where $C \geq 2$ is a constant fixed by the protocol (called *checkpoint offset*). Summing up, the value j is such that: (i) $j < i$; (ii) $|i - j| < C$; (iii) $UR_j[A : a]$ is consistent. In this way the protocol incentivizes meta-nodes to vote consistent updates only, since inconsistent ones are not likely to be confirmed. If all the last C updates in the subchain are inconsistent, then N chooses the last one. Then, N adds UR[A : a] to the *request pool*, i.e. the set of all voted requests of the current stage (emptied at the beginning of each stage). This voting step has a fixed duration Δ, specified by the protocol (the choice of Δ is discussed in Sect. 5).

At step 2, which starts when Δ expires, the arbiter T signs all *well-formed* request transactions, i.e., those respecting the format defined in Sect. 3.4.

At step 3, meta-nodes send the requests signed by T to the Bitcoin network. The mechanism described in Sect. 3.4 ensures that, at each stage i, exactly one transaction, denoted $UR_i[A : a]$, is put on the Bitcoin blockchain. When this happens, the label A : a is appended to the subchain.

---

[5] We assume that all meta-nodes agree on the Bitcoin blockchain; since η is a projection of the blockchain, they also agree on η.

3.3 Basic Properties of the Protocol

We now establish some basic properties of our protocol. Hereafter, we assume that honest nodes control the majority of the total stake of the network[6], hereafter denoted by S. Further, we assume that the overall stake required to vote pending update requests is greater than the overall stake of honest meta-nodes.

Adversary power. An honest meta-node votes as many requests as is allowed by its stake. Hence, if its stake is h, it votes h/κ requests per stage. Consequently, the rest of the network—which may include dishonest meta-nodes not following the protocol—can vote at most $(S - h)/\kappa$ requests. Then:

Proposition 1. *The probability that an honest meta-node with stake h updates the subchain is at least h/S at each stage.*

Since we assume that honest meta-nodes control the majority of the stake, Proposition 1 also limits the capabilities of the adversary:

Proposition 2. *If the global stake of honest meta-nodes is S_H, then dishonest ones update the subchain with probability at most $(S - S_H)/S$ at each stage.*

Although inconsistent updates are ignored by honest meta-nodes, their side effects as standard Bitcoin transactions (i.e. transfers of $v\Bitcoin$ from A to B in labels $A : a(v \to B)$) cannot be revoked once they are included in the Bitcoin blockchain. We now show how the incentive system in our protocol reduces the feasibility of such inconsistent updates.

Assume that an adversary M manages to append 2 updates to the subchain: an inconsistent update at index j, and a consistent one at index $i > j$. Since M does not follow the protocol, she can exploit UR_i to redeem the $\kappa\Bitcoin$ she put on UR_j. Later on, the adversary will be able to redeem the $\kappa\Bitcoin$ she put on UR_i: indeed, honest meta-nodes will vote UR_i, as it is consistent. We call the above behaviour of M *self-compensation attack.*

Now, according to Proposition 2, if M has stake m, and the other meta-nodes are honest, then M has probability at most m/S of extending the subchain in a given stage of the protocol. Since stages can be seen as independent events, and since M has to publish at least 2 updates over the most recent checkpoint to perform the attack, we obtain the following:

Proposition 3. *The probability that an adversary with stake m succeeds in a self-compensation attack is at most:*

$$\binom{C}{2} \cdot \mu^2 (1 - \mu)^{C-2}$$

where C is the checkpoint offset, and $\mu = m/S$.

---

[6] Under this assumption, meta-nodes can ensure that the arbiter is honest.

Since the probability to publish inconsistent updates without losing $\kappa\ddot{\text{B}}$ grows with C, it is crucial to keep this value small. For instance, if $\mu = 0.1$ an adversary could perform the attack with probability bounded by (i) 0.01 if $C = 2$; (ii) 0.027 if $C = 3$; (iii) 0.0486 if $C = 4$.

Observe that if the attack succeeds once, then the attack probability slightly increases, since the stake m is charged by the client fees of the published updates. This is not an issue if the fee is small compared to S.

Trustworthiness of the arbiter. Our protocol uses in arbiter T to ensures that exactly one transaction per stage is appended to the blockchain, as well its choice is random. In order to simplify the description of the protocol, we have assumed the arbiter T to behave honestly. However, our arbiter does not play the role of a trusted authority: indeed, the update requests to be voted are chosen by the meta-nodes, and once they are added to the request pool, the arbiter is expected to sign all of them, without taking part on the validation nor in the voting. Since everyone can inspect the request pool, any misbehaviour of the arbiter can be detected by the meta-nodes, which can proceed to replace it.

3.4   Implementation in Bitcoin

In this section we show how our protocol can be implemented in Bitcoin. A label $\text{A} : \text{a}(v \rightarrow \text{B})$ at position i of the subchain is implemented as the Bitcoin transaction $\text{UR}_i[\text{A} : \text{a}(v \rightarrow \text{B})]$ in Fig. 3a, with the following outputs:

- the output of index 0 embeds the label $\text{A} : \text{a}$. This is implemented through an unspendable OP_RETURN script [6][7].
- the output of index 1 links the transaction to the previous element of the subchain, pointed by in[2]. This link requires the arbiter signature. Note that, since all the update requests in the same stage redeem the same output, exactly one of them can be mined.
- the output of index 2 implements the incentive mechanism. The script rewards the meta-node N' which has voted a preceding UR_j in the subchain. Meta-node N' can redeem from this output $\kappa\ddot{\text{B}}$ plus the participant's fee, by providing his signature.
- the output of index 3 is only relevant for messages $\text{a}(v \rightarrow \text{B})$ where $v > 0$. Participant B can redeem $v\ddot{\text{B}}$ from this output by providing his signature.

All transactions specify a lockTime $n + k$, where n is the current Bitcoin block number, and k is a positive constant. This ensures that a transaction can be mined only after k blocks. In this way, even if a transaction is signed by the arbiter and sent to miners before the others, it has the same probability as the others of being appended to the blockchain.

To initialise the subchain, the arbiter puts the Genesis transaction on the Bitcoin blockchain. This transaction secures a small fraction of bitcoin, which

---

[7] The OP_RETURN instruction allows to save 80 bytes metadata in a transaction; an out-script containing OP_RETURN always evaluates to false, hence it is unspendable.

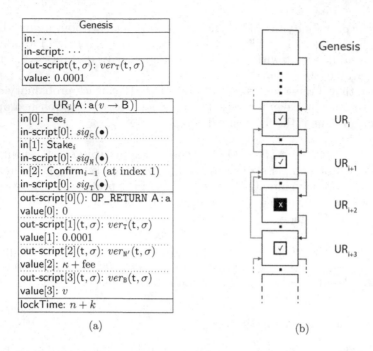

Genesis

Genesis
in: $\cdots$
in-script: $\cdots$
out-script(t, σ): ver_T(t, σ)
value: 0.0001

$UR_i[A : a(v \rightarrow B)]$
in[0]: Fee_i
in-script[0]: $sig_C(\bullet)$
in[1]: $Stake_i$
in-script[0]: $sig_N(\bullet)$
in[2]: $Confirm_{i-1}$ (at index 1)
in-script[0]: $sig_T(\bullet)$
out-script[0](): OP_RETURN A : a
value[0]: 0
out-script[1](t, σ): ver_T(t, σ)
value[1]: 0.0001
out-script[2](t, σ): $ver_{N'}$(t, σ)
value[2]: κ + fee
out-script[3](t, σ): ver_B(t, σ)
value[3]: v
lockTime: $n + k$

(a)   (b)

Fig. 3. In (a), format of Bitcoin transactions used to implement our protocol. In (b), a subchain maintained through our protocol. Since UR_{i+2} contains an inconsistent update, the meta-node which voted it is not rewarded.

can be redeemed by UR_1 through the arbiter signature. This value is then transferred to each subsequent update of the subchain (see Fig. 3b). At each protocol stage, participants send incomplete UR transactions to the network. These transactions contain only in[0] and out[0], specifying the fee and the message for the subchain (including the value to be transferred). To vote, meta-nodes add in[1], in[2] and out[2] to these transactions, to, respectively, put the required κ (from some transaction $Stake_i$), declare they want extend the last published update $Confirm_{i-1}$, and specify the previous update to be rewarded. All the in[1] fields in a stage of the protocol must be different, to prevent attackers to vote more URs with the same funds.

4   Evaluation of the Protocol

In this section we evaluate the security of our protocol, providing some experimental results. We also investigate how possible attacks to Bitcoin may affect subchains built on top of its blockchain.

Attack scenario. We assume an adversary who can craft any update (consistent or not), and controls one meta-node M with stake μS, where $\mu \in [0; 1]$ and S

is the total stake of the network[8]. We suppose that each meta-node can vote as many update requests as possible, spending all its stake, and that the network is always saturated with pending updates, which globally amount to the entire stake of honest meta-nodes[9]. We also assume that M gets an additional extra revenue r for each inconsistent update, modelling the case where she manages to induce a victim to publish an inconsistent payment $\mathsf{a}(r \to \mathsf{M})$. The goal of M is to append at least 2 updates to the blockchain (one of which inconsistent) every C published updates. She can use any possible strategy to achieve this goal.

We simulate the protocol under the attack scenario described above. Each simulation runs the protocol to generate a subchain with 10,000 messages, setting the client fee to 0.1κ and the checkpoint offset to 3. To this purpose we use DESMO-J [18], a discrete event simulator for Java.

Experimental results. Figure 4b measures the attacker revenue as μ increases. In particular, it shows that if the stake threshold κ is ten times greater than r, M gains only if she owns at least $\sim$40% of the global stake (i.e., $\mu \geq 0.4$). Therefore, under such assumption about the attacker stake, the security of our protocol is comparable with that of the Bitcoin *Proof-of-Work* protocol [17]. Instead, if $\kappa = r$, the attacker needs only $\sim$15% of the global stake to profit from the attack. Figure 4a shows that, in the absence of attackers ($\mu = 0$), the revenue of

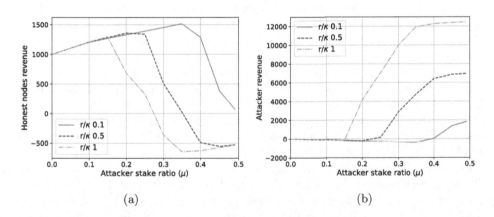

(a)   (b)

Fig. 4. Revenue of honest nodes (a) and of the attacker M (b) for increasing values of the attacker stake ratio μ. The curves represent different values of r/κ (the ratio between the attack revenue r, given by inconsistent $\mathsf{a}(r \to \mathsf{M})$ updates, and the cost of the vote).

---

[8] Assuming a single adversary is not less general than having many non-colluding meta-nodes which carry on individual attacks. Indeed, in this setting meta-nodes do not join their funds to increase the stake ratio μ.

[9] Note that saying the update queue is not always saturated is equivalent to model an adversary with a stronger μ: this because honest meta-nodes cannot spend all their stake in a single protocol stage, i.e. reducing their actual *power*. Thus, studying this particular case will not give any additional contribution to the analysis.

honest nodes is essentially the client fee times the number of updates published, as expected. Further, μ is below the threshold required to perform a profitable attack, the revenue of honest nodes increases: this happens because inconsistent updates voted by M reward honest ones, whereas the opposite cannot occur. Summing up, our protocol is secure only if, for updates on the form $\mathsf{a}(r \rightarrow \mathsf{A})$, we have that $r \leq \kappa$. Hence, if r is close to 0, the behaving dishonestly is not economically advantageous.

Security of the underlying Bitcoin blockchain. So far we have only considered direct attacks to our protocol, assuming the underlying Bitcoin blockchain to be secure. However, although Bitcoin has been secure in practice till now, some works have spotted some potential vulnerabilities of its protocol. These vulnerabilities could be exploited to execute *Sybil attacks* [4] and *selfish-mining attacks* [16], which might also affect subchains built on top of the Bitcoin blockchain.

In Sybil attacks on Bitcoin, honest nodes are induced to believe that the network is populated by many distinct participants, which instead are controlled by a single malicious entity. This attack is usually exploited to quickly propagate malicious information on the network, and to disguise honest participants in a consensus/reputation protocol, e.g. by overwhelming the network with votes of the adversary. In the selfish-mining attack [16], small groups of colluding miners manage to obtain a revenue larger than the one of honest miners. More specifically, when a selfish-mining pool finds a new block, it keeps it hidden to the rest of the network. In this way, selfish miners gain an advantage over honest ones in mining the next block. This is equivalent to keep a private fork of the blockchain, which is only known to the selfish-mining pool. Note that honest miners still mine on the public branch of the blockchain, and their hash rate is greater than selfish miners' one. Since, in the presence of a fork, the Bitcoin protocol requires to keep mining on the longest chain, selfish miners reveal their private fork to the network just before being overcome by the honest miners. Eyal and Sirer in [16] show that, under certain assumptions, this strategy gives better revenues than honest mining: in the worst scenario (for the adversary), the attack succeeds if the selfish-mining pool controls at least 1/3 of the total hashing power. Rational miners are thus incentivized to join the selfish-mining pool. Once the pool manages to control the majority of the hashing power, the system loses its decentralized nature. Garay, Kiayias and Leonardos in [17] essentially confirm these results: considering a core Bitcoin protocol, they prove that if the hashing power γ of honest miners exceeds the hashing power β of the adversary pool by a factor λ, then the ratio of adversary blocks in the blockchain is bounded by $1/\lambda$ (which is strictly greater than β). Thus, as β (the adversary pool size) approaches 1/2, they control the blockchain.

Although these attacks are mainly related to Bitcoin revenues, they can affect the consistency of any subchain built on top of its blockchain. In particular, suitably adapted versions of these attacks allow adversaries to cheat meta-nodes about the current subchain state, forcing them to synchronize their local copy of the Bitcoin blockchain with invalid forks that will be discarded by the network in the future. To protect against such attacks, meta-nodes should consider only *l-confirmed* transactions. Namely, if the last published blockchain block is B_n, they consider only those transactions appearing in blocks B_j with $j \leq n - l$. This means that an attacker would have to mine at least l blocks to force the revocation of a *l-confirmed* transaction. Rosenfeld [27] shows that, if an attacker controls at most the 10% of the network hashing power, $l = 6$ is sufficient for reducing the risk of revoking a transaction to less than 0.1%.

5 Discussion

We have proposed a protocol to reach consensus on subchains, i.e. chains of platform-dependent messages embedded in the Bitcoin blockchain. Our protocol incentivizes nodes to validate messages before appending them to the subchain, making economically disadvantageous for an adversary to append inconsistent messages. To confirm this intuition we have measured the security of our protocol over different attack scenarios. Our simulations show that, under conservative assumptions, its security is comparable to that of Bitcoin.

Performance of the protocol. As seen in Sect. 3.2, the protocol runs in periods of duration Δ. Due to the mechanism for choosing the message to append to the subchain from the request pool, the protocol can publish at most one transaction per Bitcoin block. This means that a lower bound for Δ is the Bitcoin block interval ($\sim$10 min). To monitor the arbiter behaviour throughout protocol stages, all meta-nodes must share a coherent view of the request pool. Then, Δ needs to be large enough to let each node synchronize the request pool with the rest of the network. A possible approach to cope with this issue is to make meta-nodes broadcast their voted updates, and to keep a list of other ones (considering only those which satisfy the format of transactions, as in Sect. 3.4). More efficient approaches could exploit distributed shared memories [12, 20].

Overcoming the metadata size limit. As noted in Sect. 3.4, we use OP_RETURN unspendable scripts to embed metadata in Bitcoin transactions. Since Bitcoin limits the size of such metadata to 80 bytes, this might not be enough to store the data needed by platforms. To overcome this issue, one can use distributed hash tables [25] maintained by meta-nodes. In this way, instead of storing full message data in the blockchain, OP_RETURN scripts would contain only the corresponding message digests. The unique identifier of the Bitcoin transaction can be used as the key to retrieve the full message data from the hash table.

Smart contracts over subchains. The model of subchains defined in Sect. 3.1, based on LTSs, can be easily extended to model the computations of smart contracts over the Bitcoin blockchains. A platform for smart contracts could exploit our model to represent the state of a contract as the state of the subchain, and model its possible state updates through the transition relation.

Implementing a platform for smart contracts would require a language for expressing them. To bridge this language with our abstract model, one can provide the language with an operational semantics, giving rise to an LTS describing the computations. Note that our assumption to model computations as a single LTS does not reduce the generality of the system, since a set of LTSs, each one modelling a contract, can be encoded in one LTS as their parallel composition. If the language is Turing-complete, an additional problem we would have to face is the potential non-termination. This issue has been dealt with in different ways by different platforms. E.g., the approach followed by Ethereum [11] is to impose a fee for each instruction executed by its virtual machine. If the fee does not cover the cost of the whole computation, the execution terminates.

A usable platform must also allow to create new contracts at run-time. Since in our model the LTS representing possible computations is fixed, we would need a mechanism to "extend" it. To handle the publication of new contracts, we could modify the protocol so that UR may contain its code, and the unique identifier of the transaction also identifies the contract. In this extended model, update requests would also contain the identifier of the contract to be updated, so that meta-nodes can execute the corresponding code.

Acknowledgments. This work is partially supported by Aut. Reg. of Sardinia grant P.I.A. 2013 "NOMAD". Alessandro Sebastian Podda gratefully acknowledges Sardinia Regional Government for the financial support of her PhD scholarship (P.O.R. Sardegna F.S.E. Operational Programme of the Autonomous Region of Sardinia, European Social Fund 2007-2013 - Axis IV Human Resources, Objective l.3, Line of Activity l.3.1).

References

1. Making sense of blockchain smart contracts. http://www.coindesk.com/making-sense-smart-contracts/. Accessed 14 Jan 2017
2. opreturn.org. http://opreturn.org/. Accessed 15 Dec 2016
3. Andrychowicz, M., Dziembowski, S., Malinowski, D., Mazurek, Ł.: Fair two-party computations via Bitcoin deposits. In: Böhme, R., Brenner, M., Moore, T., Smith, M. (eds.) FC 2014. LNCS, vol. 8438, pp. 105–121. Springer, Heidelberg (2014). https://doi.org/10.1007/978-3-662-44774-1_8
4. Babaioff, M., Dobzinski, S., Oren, S., Zohar, A.: On Bitcoin and red balloons. In: ACM Conference on Electronic Commerce (EC), pp. 56–73 (2012)
5. Banasik, W., Dziembowski, S., Malinowski, D.: Efficient zero-knowledge contingent payments in cryptocurrencies without scripts. In: Askoxylakis, I., Ioannidis, S., Katsikas, S., Meadows, C. (eds.) ESORICS 2016. LNCS, vol. 9879, pp. 261–280. Springer, Cham (2016). https://doi.org/10.1007/978-3-319-45741-3_14
6. Bartoletti, M., Pompianu, L.: An analysis of Bitcoin OP_RETURN metadata. In: Financial Cryptography Workshops (2017). Also available as CoRR abs/1702.01024
7. Bartoletti, M., Zunino, R.: Constant-deposit multiparty lotteries on Bitcoin. In: Financial Cryptography Workshops (2017). Also available as IACR Cryptology ePrint Archive 955/2016

8. Bentov, I., Gabizon, A., Mizrahi, A.: Cryptocurrencies without proof of work. In: Clark, J., Meiklejohn, S., Ryan, P.Y.A., Wallach, D., Brenner, M., Rohloff, K. (eds.) FC 2016. LNCS, vol. 9604, pp. 142–157. Springer, Heidelberg (2016). https://doi.org/10.1007/978-3-662-53357-4_10

9. Bentov, I., Kumaresan, R.: How to use Bitcoin to design fair protocols. In: Garay, J.A., Gennaro, R. (eds.) CRYPTO 2014. LNCS, vol. 8617, pp. 421–439. Springer, Heidelberg (2014). https://doi.org/10.1007/978-3-662-44381-1_24

10. Blockstore: key-value store for name registration and data storage on the Bitcoin blockchain (2014). https://github.com/blockstack/blockstore

11. Buterin, V.: Ethereum: a next generation smart contract and decentralized application platform (2013). https://github.com/ethereum/wiki/wiki/White-Paper

12. Cai, M., Chervenak, A., Frank, M.: A peer-to-peer replica location service based on a distributed hash table. In: ACM/IEEE Conference on High Performance Networking and Computing, p. 56. IEEE Computer Society (2004)

13. Crary, K., Sullivan, M.J.: Peer-to-peer affine commitment using Bitcoin. In: ACM PLDI, pp. 479–488 (2015)

14. Dermody, R., Krellenstein, A., Slama, O., Wagner, E.: CounterParty: protocol specification (2014). http://counterparty.io/docs/protocol_specification/

15. Dwork, C., Naor, M.: Pricing via processing or combatting junk mail. In: Brickell, E.F. (ed.) CRYPTO 1992. LNCS, vol. 740, pp. 139–147. Springer, Heidelberg (1993). https://doi.org/10.1007/3-540-48071-4_10

16. Eyal, I., Sirer, E.G.: Majority is not enough: Bitcoin mining is vulnerable. In: Christin, N., Safavi-Naini, R. (eds.) FC 2014. LNCS, vol. 8437, pp. 436–454. Springer, Heidelberg (2014). https://doi.org/10.1007/978-3-662-45472-5_28

17. Garay, J., Kiayias, A., Leonardos, N.: The Bitcoin backbone protocol: analysis and applications. In: Oswald, E., Fischlin, M. (eds.) EUROCRYPT 2015. LNCS, vol. 9057, pp. 281–310. Springer, Heidelberg (2015). https://doi.org/10.1007/978-3-662-46803-6_10

18. Göbel, J., Joschko, P., Koors, A., Page, B.: The discrete event simulation framework DESMO-J: review, comparison to other frameworks and latest development. In: European Conference on Modelling and Simulation (ECMS), pp. 100–109. European Council for Modeling and Simulation (2013)

19. Hern, A.: A history of Bitcoin hacks. March 2014. http://www.theguardian.com/technology/2014/mar/18/history-of-bitcoin-hacks-alternative-currency

20. Iyer, S., Rowstron, A., Druschel, P.: Squirrel: a decentralized peer-to-peer web cache. In: PODC, pp. 213–222. ACM (2002)

21. Kiayias, A., Konstantinou, I., Russell, A., David, B., Oliynykov, R.: Ouroboros: a provably secure proof-of-stake blockchain protocol (2016). IACR Cryptology ePrint Archive, 2016:889

22. Kiayias, A., Zhou, H.-S., Zikas, V.: Fair and robust multi-party computation using a global transaction ledger. In: Fischlin, M., Coron, J.-S. (eds.) EUROCRYPT 2016. LNCS, vol. 9666, pp. 705–734. Springer, Heidelberg (2016). https://doi.org/10.1007/978-3-662-49896-5_25

23. Kumaresan, R., Bentov, I.: How to use Bitcoin to incentivize correct computations. In: ACM CCS, pp. 30–41 (2014)

24. Kumaresan, R., Moran, T., Bentov, I.: How to use Bitcoin to play decentralized poker. In: ACM CCS, pp. 195–206 (2015)

25. Maymounkov, P., Mazières, D.: Kademlia: a peer-to-peer information system based on the XOR metric. In: Druschel, P., Kaashoek, F., Rowstron, A. (eds.) IPTPS 2002. LNCS, vol. 2429, pp. 53–65. Springer, Heidelberg (2002). https://doi.org/10.1007/3-540-45748-8_5

26. Nakamoto, S.: Bitcoin: a peer-to-peer electronic cash system (2018). https:// bitcoin.org/bitcoin.pdf
27. Rosenfeld, M.: Analysis of hashrate-based double spending (2014). CoRR, abs/1402.2009
28. Ruffing, T., Kate, A., Schröder, D.: Liar, liar, coins on fire!: penalizing equivocation by loss of Bitcoins. In: ACM CCS, pp. 219–230 (2015)
29. Szabo, N.: Formalizing and securing relationships on public networks. First Monday, 2(9) (1997)
30. Tomescu, A., Devadas, S.: Catena: efficient non-equivocation via Bitcoin. In: IEEE Symposium on Security and Privacy (2017)

Targeted Attacks

X-Platform Phishing: Abusing Trust for Targeted Attacks Short Paper

Hossein Siadati$^{(\boxtimes)}$, Toan Nguyen, and Nasir Memon

New York University, New York City, USA
{hossein,toan.v.nguyen,memon}@nyu.edu

Abstract. The goal of anti-phishing techniques is to reduce the delivery rate of phishemails, and anti-phishing training aims to decrease the phishing click-through rates. This paper presents the *X-Platform Phishing Attack*, a deceptive phishing attack with an alarmingly high delivery and click-through rates, and highlights a subclass of phishing attacks that existing anti-phishing methods do not seem to be able to address. The main characteristic of this attack is that an attacker is able to embed a malicious link within a legitimate message generated by service providers (e.g., Github, Google, Amazon) and sends it using their infrastructure to his targets. This technique results in the bypassing of existing anti-phishing filters because it utilizes reputable service providers to generate seemingly legitimate emails. This also makes it highly likely for the targets of the attack to click on the phishing link as the email id of a legitimate provider is being used. An X-Platform Phishing attack can use email-based messaging and notification mechanisms such as friend requests, membership invitations, status updates, and customizable gift cards to embed and deliver phishing links to their targets. We have tested the delivery and click-through rates of this attack experimentally, based on a customized phishing email tunneled through GitHub's *pull-request* mechanism. We observed that 100% of X-Platform Phishing emails passed the anti-phishing systems and were delivered to the inbox of the target subjects. All of the participants clicked on phishing messages, and in some cases, forwarded the message to other project collaborators who also clicked on the phishing links.

Keywords: Targeted attack · Phishing · Cross-platform attack

1 Introduction

Social engineering has become a core component of cyberattacks with financial and political incentives. Recent high profile attacks, such as the Target [20] and Sony [3] attacks used phishing emails to steal credentials of employees to infect their machines and establish a foothold inside a target network. *Business Email Compromise* (BEC) scams use phishing emails to deceive employees of a target company into transferring money to scammers' accounts [4]. *Political and celebrity hacks* such as recent attacks on the Democratic National Committee

M. Brenner et al. (Eds.): FC 2017 Workshops 2017, LNCS 10323, pp. 587–596, 2017.
https://doi.org/10.1007/978-3-319-70278-0_37

(DNC) [12] have used multistage phishing techniques to access confidential information. These phishing attacks focus on social engineering of a certain person or population and therefore are referred to as *targeted attacks*.

Advances in techniques for phishing detection impede the *delivery* of phishing emails. Security awareness improves the users' vigilance and therefore decreases the *click-through* rate on phishing emails. For example, Sender Policy Framework (SPF) [10] and DomainKey Identified Mail (DKIM) [1] have made it harder for the attackers to spoof a sender's email, and *Blacklist* of IP addresses has made it harder to use botnets for sending phishing emails. In addition, content-based anti-phishing engines combined with other signals have been successful in stopping large volume of phishing emails. Moreover, companies have invested in phishing training campaigns, that improve the overall awareness and resilience of their users. As a result, it is harder to deceive enterprise users. Therefore, it is natural for attackers to invest in devising new ways for delivering and luring victims to respond to phishing emails. For security researchers, it is important to be ahead of the curve, predict potential attacks, and provide required fixes.

This paper describes an advanced form of targeted attack which we call *X-Platform Phishing* (XPP)[1] that can bypass existing phishing filtering techniques and is able to elicit a high amount of responses from victims. This attack exploits the email-based messaging and notification mechanism of reputable platforms and leverages the trust of the end-users to the services they use, to deliver customized phishing messages to a target victim and deceive her/him into clicking on the phishing links. Examples of customizable messages sent by platforms include Github notifications, Google Scholar alerts, LinkedIn friend requests, Dropbox notifications, and Amazon gift card notifications. These messages are sent from a fixed email address of a reputable platform or service (e.g., notification@[domain name of the service provider]) and therefore are trusted by email services. Moreover, users have subscribed for the service, trust the emails from the service provider, and frequently receive and therefore expect to receive such emails. Consequently, it is very likely for them to read the phishing email and visit the malicious link.

To demonstrate the possibility of XPP, we ran a pilot study on the Github platform. We used the pull request functionality of Github to send customized phishing messages to subjects of our experiment. The results show that 100% of the subjects clicked on the phishing links. More surprisingly, not only did these subjects click on the links, they also forwarded the email to their colleagues, who in turn, fell for the attack.

Existing anti-phishing mechanisms are not able to detect and block this type of phishing attack. The main reason is that the email filtering mechanisms do not differentiate between emails from an enterprise and a customized email containing user messages delivered by an enterprise email address. This is very similar to X-Site Scripting (XSS) attack where a user-generated input containing a malicious script is allowed to run in the context and origin of the service provider on a browser. A potential remedy to stop X-Platform Phishing includes sanitizing

---

[1] It is pronounced Cross-Platform Phishing.

the contents of user messages before embedding them in the emails. Another possible approach is creating and exchanging a user trust score between service providers to facilitate the assessment of emails delivered by service providers.

The main contributions of this paper are the introduction of X-Platform Phishing and preliminary measurement of its delivery and click-through rates. We also discuss the shortcomings of anti-phishing mechanisms and propose remediation.

2 Background

X-Platform Phishing as described in this paper has the capability of bypassing existing email filtering mechanisms as well as driving high click-through rates when customized for specific targets. In this section, we discuss the methods of phishing email filtering, and characteristics of targeted phishing attacks in connection with XPP.

2.1 Anti-Phishing Techniques

Unwanted emails initially were used for advertising and later for spreading malware, phishing, and scamming people [14]. The traditional approach of filtering unwanted emails rely on blacklisting spamming IP addresses [9]. These lists are updated quickly with a median of 1.5 h to include new spamming IPs in the blacklist. Spammers have responded to blacklisting using a "Snowshoe spam" strategy that spreads the workload of spamming IPs by sending very short bursts of spam from several IPs [15]. Blacklisting IPs is not effective against XPP since the emails are originated and sent from IP address of legitimate service providers such as Github, Amazon, and LinkedIn.

Another approach is content-based spam filtering, that is mostly effective when the content of spamming messages are distinguishable from normal conversational emails due to the usage of words and links [11]. In the XPP, content of the phishing email is a mix of content from legitimate service provider and a portion customized by the attacker. This combination of good and bad content makes the task of classification for text-based classification more challenging. Moreover, previous work has shown that content-based filtering can be easily circumvented [13].

Email source authentication is another anti-spam mechanism, which has reduced the possibility of spoofing dramatically. These mechanisms include Sender Policy Framework (SPF) [10], DomainKey Identified Mail (DKIM) [1], and Domain-based Message Authentication, Reporting, and Conformance (DMARC) [2]. In a XPP attack, phishing email is sent from a reputable service provider by all valid signatures and from a legitimate IP address. This makes it very easy for XPP emails to get delivered into the Inbox of the victims. Therefore, more advanced tools and techniques are required to detect and block delivery of XPP.

2.2   Targeted Phishing Attacks

A targeted attack is a form of phishing attacks that includes deceptive messages and links customized for a high value target (e.g., staff of a financial company, a politician) in order to increase the yield of the attack response. This method has been used extensively as a starting point of many high profile attacks. In fact, Verizon's Data Breach Investigations Report has listed phishing as the favorite method used by attackers [17]. Existing targeted attacks usually spoof the email address of a well-known service providers to appear legitimate. For example, a phishing email sent to John Podesta [5] spoofed "googlemail.com" domain that belongs to Google. Spoofing is becoming harder due to the deployment of more strict email rejection policies by domains. One logical move of the attackers then, as envisioned in this paper, would be to piggy-back over the trust of messaging between legitimate service providers to deliver their phishing emails.

In a 2011 report [6], Cisco reported that 70% of users who receive targeted phishing emails open and read them. In comparison, only 3% for traditional mass phishing emails are read by users. This shows the comparably higher persuasiveness of targeted phishing emails. In that report, however, Cisco has considered the block rate of both types of phishing attack as 99%, meaning that the majority of the mass as well as targeted phishing emails are blocked by anti-phishing engines. The attack discussed in this paper proves this otherwise by experimenting a phishing attack that can not be blocked by existing anti-phishing engines and yields open rate and click-through rate of 100%. This calls for new anti-phishing approaches.

3   X-Platform Phishing

X-Platform Phishing, analogous to the X-Site Scripting (XSS) attack, exploits the email-based messaging and notification mechanism of a legitimate service to deliver phishing messages to target victims. For example, an attacker can send an electronic gift-card to victim with a customized message that includes a phishing link. Since the gift-card is sent by the email address of a reputable service provider (e.g., Amazon, Starbucks), the receiving email domain delivers it to the Inbox of the target.

Many service providers use email-based messaging and notification mechanisms for different purposes including *friend requests* (e.g., Linkedin), *membership invitations* (e.g. Telegram), *status updates* (e.g., Github pull request, Google Scholar notification), and Gift Card (e.g., Amazon, Starbucks). These communications are feasible even between users that do not trust each other. Further, the messages themselves are customizable by the attackers and the final message is embedded in a template prepared by the sending service provider.

Users usually respond to benign messages from service providers in a certain way. For example, users click on "Apply to your Amazon Account" button when they open an Amazon Gift Card. In the XPP, an attacker customizes the message in a way that deceives the targeted victim to click on elements they control. The content of the message sent to victims are highly customizable. The attacker can link an HTML tag or an image that loads in the email client of the target. For example, an attacker may create an "Apply to your Amazon Account" button inside the message section of the email and link it to a phishing website.

The phishing link bundled in a message sent by a reputable service provider will be delivered by an email address owned by service provider. This kind of email addresses is highly trusted and therefore the email will be delivered to the target's Inbox. Moreover, users find these messages as routine due to the trust built over years. The high delivery rate mixed with the trust of users, result in a very powerful attack. In the rest of this section, we detail use cases of this attack on users of two well-known platform with big user-bases and potentially high impact.

Use Case I. *Github* is a platform for collaborative software development. It has about 14 million users and more than 35 million repositories [18]. Security of this platform and its users are very important, specifically because software bundled and distributed based on Github projects are installed on millions of devices around the world. For example, half a million servers were identified to be vulnerable due to Heartbleed [19], a critical security bug discovered in OpenSSL, which has been developed and maintained on Github. Attackers are very interested in injecting vulnerabilities in software by compromising platforms such as Github [16]. Indeed, Free Software Foundation's repository was under the control of hackers for more than two months and potentially served backdoored versions of GNU software to millions of users [7]. Therefore, stealing credentials of Github developers can be disastrous.

An attacker who targets a developer is able to use XPP to launch a phishing attack by abusing the pull request on Github. This is because the messages of such requests are customizable by the person who creates them. An attacker who uses XPP technique customizes the message in the pull request and adds malicious content. Upon issuing the pull request, an email containing the malicious message will be delivered via *notifications@github.com* email address to the Inbox of target. It should be noted that any Github user can create a pull request for any public project and *mention* a specific user as the receiver of the request. For example, an attacker pulls a request on a project of his target on Github and provides following message. "I've found a critical security vulnerability in your project. Detail and a proof-of-concept are provided *[link]*," in which *link* can lead the target to a phishing website that requires Github login credential to access the proof-of-concept code or to a drive-by-download malware. The attacker then mentions the target using @ + target's Github username. After this pull request is submitted by the attacker, Github will send an email which contains the message and the link to the target. As shown in our experiment later, this attack yields very high delivery and click-through rates.

Use Case II. *Google Scholar* is one of the services provided by Google, specialized in indexing research publications and scholarly books. The number of publications indexed by this service is estimated to be 160 million documents as of May 2014. Millions of researchers from academia and industry use this service to access scholarly materials. Google indexes material from reputable publishers as well as open publication websites. Users of Google Scholar can subscribe to alerts to receive a notification when a new publication of their interest gets published. Notification emails of this type typically contain links to published documents or sources of documents. An attacker who targets researchers of special interest can create a Google Scholar account and create a fake publication in the topic of his target's interest and uploads to a website in his control. Once he adds this publication to his profile, Google Scholar will index and notify the interested users via emails. When the targets click on the link in the emails, they are directed to the attacker's website where the attacker may present them with a fake Google Scholar login page which asks the targets to login to view the document or plant a malicious document (a rouge PDF or DOC file) for the targets to download. This attack scenario, without doubt, leads to innocent clicks and resultant compromise.

4   Experiment

To demonstrate the feasibility of launching an XPP attack and measure its delivery and click-through rate, we ran a pilot study on a small population of users of the Github platform.

4.1   Attack Setup

The instance of X-Platform Phishing used in our experiment has several steps as depicted in Fig. 1. We describe each step in this subsection.

Fig. 1. Steps of X-Platform Phishing in our experiment

Attack Account Creation. We created a Github account and set up the profile of this account to appear as a developer from our institution.

Target Reconnaissance. XPP is a targeted attack meaning that the attacker uses contextual information about the target to improve yield. For each subject in this experiment, we found a Github project that she/he had been working on recently. We adjusted the phishing messages in the context of this project to make it more likely that the target would respond.

Project Creation. We cloned the active project of each subject, selected in the step above, and sent phishing messages to the subject by pulling a request from this project.

Content Customization. The content of a message sent to a Github developer is customizable. We used Markdown [8] to customize the text, add an image for tracking user, and put a click-able hyperlink to the message. One aspect of customization of the phishing message was to push Github's default message down to an invisible area so the subjects do not get distracted. For this, we added a number of newline tags <br/> to the end of the phishing message.

Message Delivery. There are several ways to send an email message using Github. In this experiment, we used Github's Pull Request (PR) to send phishing messages. A pull request allows a member of a project to receive notification about changes that other contributors make and want to merge them into the project source. We created a pull request on projects that we cloned from the subjects in our experiment, customized the message in the pull request using Markdown, and mentioned subject's Github handler[2] in the pull request. Github automatically sent the customized phishing message to their email addresses. Other possible methods of sending messages include adding target users as collaborator of a project, creating an issue report, or adding comment and mentioning their Github handler.

4.2   Phishing Message Design

We experimented the effect of two different story lines in the context of X-Platform Phishing. The first story line was *an approaching NSF grant proposal*. In this variation, we mentioned victims, who were graduate students, in a Github project with a message asking them to follow a todo-list regarding a grant proposal. A snapshot of this attack message is shown in Fig. 2(a). The second story line was *a bug report* in which we notified subjects to fix a bug in their project. A snapshot of this attack is shown in Fig. 2(b).

(a) Storyline 1   (b) Storyline 2

Fig. 2. The content of the messages in the story lines used in the experiment

4.3   Subject Recruitment

We selected 20 subjects from a convenient pool of students from our institution. Candidate subjects were selected because they had active Github accounts working on some projects over the past few months. All these students were graduate

---

[2] A user identifier of users inside Github starting with @.

students, five of which were doctoral and the rest of them were master students. NSF grant message was used for doctoral students, and bug report message was used for master students. Subjects were not notified prior to the experiment but were debriefed and interviewed afterward.

4.4   Collected Data

We collected data about two different aspects of the users response to XPP namely *message delivery* and *phishing click*. To know if a message was delivered, we added an invisible 1x1 image in the phishing message to notify our server whenever the message was loaded in a browser or application. A separate project was created for each subject so a customized link could easily identify the click-responses of subjects.

4.5   Result

The first scenario (i.e., NSF Grant) yielded 100% message delivery as well as 100% phishing click-through rates. For this case, we added a link to a website in our control on the description of the Github project page. When a subject clicks on this link, a request is sent to our website where we log the event (timestamp, subject ID, etc.). In a real attack, this link might lead to a fake Github login page or to a drive-by-download malware which may cause harms to the subjects or victims. We observed that all of the subjects clicked on this link. In one case, the email was circulated among other members of the projects and we observed multiple clicks on the link embedded in that project's description. This was confirmed later by interviewing the subject.

In the second scenario (i.e., bug fix), we also observed that all subjects opened the phishing emails and clicked on the phishing links embedded in the emails. In both scenarios, the victims clicked on the phishing links and visited our Github profile within an hour since the pull requests were submitted.

5   Discussions, Limitations, and Conclusion

Github is only one example of the platforms that can be misused for launching XPP attacks. Many other collaborative software development platforms such as Bitbucket, SourceForge, and Gitlab with millions of users, as well as any other platforms including LinkedIn, Amazon, Telegram, Google Scholar, Research-Gate, Academia.edu that have methods for email-based message exchange using a fixed identity of service provider are susceptible to be used for X-Platform Phishing attack.

It is challenging for an email platform to verify the legitimacy of user generated messages sent across platforms using service provider's email address. First of all, the messages are sent from a trustworthy domain. In addition, email services do not have fine grained information about the sender and the context of which users communicate on other platforms. Lack of information makes the usage of user-based trust score for filtering such massages challenging.

Possible countermeasures to XPP attacks include spam filtering mechanisms that consider trust relations of entities mentioned in delivered messages (e.g., handlers in form of @ in the Github pull requests) as a feature in email filtering. Another approach is extension of email delivery protocols to exchange user trust scores between sender and receiver domains. Such scores can be incorporated in the phishing classifiers. Lastly, having a cyberspace resilient to social engineering is the duty of all parties. All platforms have to employ anti-phishing mechanisms for both outgoing and incoming messages.

The pilot experiment described in this paper and the reported results are based on a limited pool of subjects and scenarios. Therefore, more extensive experiments are required to provide deeper insight about the effect of X-Platform Phishing, as we plan to explore in future. Designing countermeasures also is a high priority.

In conclusion, we have identified the possibility of a targeted phishing attack with potentially high impact in real-world. Success of this attack can be attributed to the trust between platforms to deliver messages and the trust of users on messages coming from reputable service providers. Leveraging this trust, an attacker can achieve high delivery and click-through rates. This calls for improved methods for detection of targeted phishing emails.

References

1. RFC 6376: DomainKeys Identified Mail (DKIM) Signatures. https://tools.ietf.org/html/rfc6376. Accessed 20 Dec 2016
2. Domain-based message authentication, reporting, and conformance (DMARC) (2015). https://tools.ietf.org/html/rfc7489. Accessed 17 Apr 2016
3. Bisson, D.: Sony Hackers Used Phishing Emails to Breach Company Networks. https://www.tripwire.com/state-of-security/latest-security-news/sony-hackers-used-phishing-emails-to-breach-company-networks/. Accessed 20 Dec 2016
4. Krebs, B.: FBI: $1.2B Lost to Business Email Scams. https://krebsonsecurity.com/2015/08/fbi-1-2b-lost-to-business-email-scams/. Accessed 20 Dec 2016
5. CBS: The phishing email that hacked the account of John Podesta. http://www.cbsnews.com/news/the-phishing-email-that-hacked-the-account-of-john-podesta/. Accessed 20 Dec 2016
6. CISCO: Email Attacks: This Time Its Personal. http://www.cisco.com/c/dam/en/us/products/collateral/security/email-security-appliance/targeted_attacks.pdf. Accessed 20 Dec 2016
7. Geek.com: Major Open Source code repository hacked for months, says FSF. https://www.geek.com/news/major-open-source-code-repository-hacked-for-months-says-fsf-551344/. Accessed 20 Dec 2016
8. Github: Mastering Markdown. https://guides.github.com/features/mastering-markdown/. Accessed 20 Dec 2016

9. Jung, J., Sit, E.: An empirical study of spam traffic and the use of DNS black lists. In: Proceedings of the 4th ACM SIGCOMM Conference on Internet Measurement, pp. 370–375. ACM (2004)
10. Kitterman, S.: Sender Policy Framework (SPF) for Authorizing Use of Domains in Email, Version 1. https://tools.ietf.org/html/rfc7208. Accessed 20 Dec 2016
11. Metsis, V., Androutsopoulos, I., Paliouras, G.: Spam filtering with naive bayes- which naive bayes? In: CEAS, pp. 27–28 (2006)
12. Motherboard: The hack we can't see: All Signs Point to Russia Being Behind the DNC Hack. https://motherboard.vice.com/read/all-signs-point-to-russia-being-behind-the-dnc-hack. Accessed 20 Dec 2016
13. Palka, S., McCoy, D.: Fuzzing e-mail filters with generative grammars and n-gram analysis. In: 9th USENIX Workshop on Offensive Technologies (WOOT 2015) (2015)
14. Jakobsson, M.: Traditional countermeasures to unwanted email. In: Jakobsson, M. (ed.) Understanding Social Engineering Based Scams, pp. 51–62. Springer, New York (2016). https://doi.org/10.1007/978-1-4939-6457-4_5
15. Symantec: Internet security threat report (ISTR) (2016). https://www.symantec.com/content/dam/symantec/docs/reports/istr-21-2016-en.pdf. Accessed 20 Dec 2016
16. Torres-Arias, S., Ammula, A.K., Curtmola, R., Cappos, J.: On omitting commits and committing omissions: preventing git metadata tampering that (re) introduces software vulnerabilities. In: 25th USENIX Security Symposium, USENIX Security, vol. 16, pp. 10–12 (2016)
17. Verizon: 2016 Data Breach Investigations Report. http://www.verizonenterprise.com/resources/reports/rp_dbir-2016-executive-summary_xg_en.pd. Accessed 20 Dec 2016
18. Wikipedia: Github. https://en.wikipedia.org/wiki/Github. Accessed 20 Dec 2016
19. Wikipedia: Half a million widely trusted websites vulnerable to Heartbleed bug. https://news.netcraft.com/archives/2014/04/08/half-a-million-widely-trusted-websites-vulnerable-to-heartbleed-bug.html. Accessed 20 Dec 2016
20. ZDNet: Anatomy of the Target data breach. http://www.zdnet.com/article/anatomy-of-the-target-data-breach-missed-opportunities-and-lessons-learned/. Accessed 20 Dec 2016

What to Phish in a Subject?

Ana Ferreira[1]([✉]) and Rui Chilro[2]

[1] CINTESIS - Center for Health Technologies and Services Research,
Faculty of Medicine, University of Porto, Porto, Portugal
`amlaf@med.up.pt`
[2] Universidade Digital, University of Porto, Porto, Portugal

Abstract. Phishing emails have come to stay. They have evolved and adapted to become more sophisticated and targeted so to appear more realistic and, therefore, more effective. But why does a user decide to open such emails? This paper focuses on the content of subject lines from phishing emails, a main piece which can trigger the user into deciding whether to (potentially) become a victim. The authors analyzed 788 subject lines from phishing emails collected over a one year period and found that the most common subject lines pretend to come from government or well known organizations and mostly integrate the authority and distraction principles of persuasion. The majority of subject lines include targeted keywords/expressions that provide the recipient with a feeling of social presence that heightens the realization that a message comes from a trustworthy person. This study shows that a small sentence can go a long way. An email subject line can include a high persuasive power to more successfully grab users' attention and increase the likelihood of that email being opened and responded to.

1   Introduction

Emails with fraudulent content have been around for a long time but there are still no effective ways to prevent or even minimize them. Every year, security reports alert that phishing is very common and a swift and easy way to bypass security measures within businesses and organizations [1–3]. Phishing emails can quickly provide attackers with open doors to more dangerous and disruptive attacks. Phishing has evolved and adapted to better target victims and maximize its attack success rate [1,2]. This more sophisticated type of phishing (e.g., spear phishing) has been associated with the largest cyberattacks in recent history. As such, 84% of the analyzed companies had a spear phishing attack penetrate their organization security and the average cost of a spear phishing attack is 1.6 million dollars [2]. Moreover, 90% of the detected attacks are performed using email.

Although there are now more awareness and tools to identify, alert and even eliminate scam and phishing emails, *why* and *how* do users still fall for such attacks? This report [3] calculated that the median time for the first user of a phishing campaign to open a malicious email was 1 min and 22 s.

© International Financial Cryptography Association 2017
M. Brenner et al. (Eds.): FC 2017 Workshops 2017, LNCS 10323, pp. 597–609, 2017.
https://doi.org/10.1007/978-3-319-70278-0_38

The first message conveyed by any email, stating its objective, is within the content of a subject line. This is the first interaction between an email phisher and his/her victim and the main piece that triggers the user into deciding whether an email is relevant, should be opened and paid attention to [4]. Once the action of opening the email is taken, the user is a step closer to becoming a phishing victim. So phishers can focus on devising directed, objective but incisive subject lines to increase their degree of persuasiveness and the probability of being taken seriously [5].

There are some works available that study email header content to better identify phishing attacks [6,7]. However, those do not typically specify results for the subject line element and, the analyzed information comprised in an email header is usually hidden from the user who, without much time in hand, will only focus on the commonly available information (e.g., the email fields: *From*, *Subject* and *Date*) to make his/her decision about opening an email.

The authors only found one research work in the literature that concluded that the level of attention to a phishing email subject line is positively related to an individual's likelihood to respond to that email [8]. Such conclusion interferes with measures to ensure that email users should only allow the text of emails to be visible and block graphics from automatically being loaded [9]. Even if the identified elements of emails that have a very high degree of persuasiveness (e.g., spelling, design and links [10], or rich content such as logos, graphics and personal data [9]) are blocked, these can be considered as just a complement of the email attractiveness. Users first need to peruse email subject lines alone, which do not include such elements, to decide to open that email and only then see the other elements it contains. Despite only containing text, the authors believe that email subject lines can still be cleverly crafted to increase the probability of a user to open the corresponding email.

This paper focuses on the content of subject lines from phishing emails to investigate what type and amount of information can be obtained only by looking at their text. The authors analyzed 788 subject lines from phishing emails, collected over a one year period, to verify what categories of phishing were used according to their objective and context, and if it was possible to distinguish targeted and more personal messages. In addition, subject lines were perused for their persuasion content as well as their usage trends over the referred time period.

The next section introduces some background regarding phishing categories and how principles of persuasion are used within phishing emails. Section 3 describes the analyzed sample and how that analysis was performed while Sect. 4 presents the obtained results. Section 5 presents a discussion of results and the last section concludes the paper.

2   Background

The authors found various websites that describe the importance of email subject lines and how they can affect phishing attacks success rate. Some sites even identify the most used subject lines, which they conclude to be the most dangerous [5]. However, the authors could not find scientific evidence of these results in the literature or similar works that studied how the content in a subject line of a phishing email can affect users' decision to open that email. The only work found (and already introduce) concluded that the more email subject lines can grab users' attention, the more persuasive power those can have in order to make email recipients respond to that email [8].

There are, nevertheless, research works that focus on email subject lines to verify: if they can influence response rates to email invitations to participate in surveys or interviews [11]; if they can help in the management of complex collaborative work [12]; or if past subject lines can help predict email opening rates [4].

Even with not much work available that focus specifically on phishing email subject lines, the authors believe in the importance of this topic and of further investigating its contents and to what degree these can be persuasive.

In order to recognize the type of content of email subject lines and what data phishers are after, there is the need to use a categorization that will allow to perform that distinction with the least possible ambiguity. The authors decided to base this categorization in this work [13], which has already made a systematization of the various available scam/fraud taxonomies, eliminating this way some of its repetitions and inconsistencies. Also, the authors of that work consider phishing as one category of the scam taxonomy. In the current paper, the authors assume that both terms, phishing and scam, are synonyms. When they mention phishing emails they consider all emails that fraudulently try to collect users' personal and/or private information or make them perform some dangerous action like clicking on a link or visiting a specific web page. So phishing, in the present study, is considered a more wide scam term and not a single/separate scam category.

Figure 1 presents the scam email categorization used for the phishing email subject lines analysis in this paper [13]. Both categories *Authority* and *Money Transfer* include sub-categories to better describe the type of·data asked by the phishing emails.

The persuasive content that email subject lines may include can be one explanation to the previously posed question (e.g., *Why* and *how* do users still fall for phishing attacks?). When humans interact they influence each other everyday. This influence can be legitimate but it can also be used as a tool to trick and manipulate people to perform unwanted actions that can lead to some kind of loss. Phishing can take advantage of a widely used platform of communication that reaches almost everybody in the world today: *Email Messaging*. Since this tool can simulate human interactions and dialogs, most of the persuasion principles that are present in a physical dialog can also be used in the virtual world. Phishers know this and, purposely or not, use techniques to manipulate and persuade email users to act as they want.

The current paper focuses on the definition and systematization of the principles of persuasion in social engineering described in [14] because it integrates most relevant works in this field [15–17]. Figure 2 presents the description and examples of those principles of persuasion.

Categories
Non-Targeted • Authority [Bank – Government – Organization] • Loan • Lottery • Money Transfer [Charity, Dead, Next of kin, Widow, Business commodity]
Targeted • Business Email Compromise • Rental • Romance
Both • Employment • Sales
Others

Fig. 1. Scam categories used in the content analysis of phishing email subject lines.

Principle of persuasion	Description and examples
AUTHORITY	Society trains people not to challenge authority but to respond without questioning. People usually follow an expert or a figure of authority and will do a great deal for who they think is in charge. *Ex: an email purporting to be from the victim's bank and including the bank's name in the subject line stating their account has been limited and requiring urgent action to change this status.*
SOCIAL PROOF	People tend to mimic what the majority of people around do or seem to be doing, so they let their guard and suspicion down and prefer to share the same responsibility and risks. *Ex: an email from an alleged system administrator with an email address of the company where the recipient works asking them to test a link that supposedly takes the user to his/her mailbox.*
LIKING, SIMILARITY & DECEPTION	People prefer to follow or relate to other people whom they know, like, are attracted to, or who seem familiar or similar to themselves. *Ex: an email from a supposed friend of the recipient asking him/her to visit an interesting website.*
COMMITMENT, RECIPROCATION & CONSISTENCY	Reciprocating a favor or responding to some action can be an automatic response that is linked to some previous commitment or consistent with a previous situation. *Ex: an email where the sender knows beforehand that the recipient is looking to buy a house and which promises a very good price for a house with the same characteristics and on the same location the recipient wants (consistency). To secure it (commitment), recipient needs to urgently pay for a deposit (reciprocation).*
DISTRACTION	When people focus on what they can gain, lose, or need, or on whether an item will be soon unavailable, is restricted, or will be more expensive later, this can heighten people's emotional state and make them forget other important considerations when making decisions. *Ex: an email acknowledging that the recipient has won a substantial lottery prize. The victim's focus is directed to how s/he can have access to the money and diverts attention from other details such as for instance, that a lottery ticket was never bought.*

Fig. 2. Principles of persuasion used in the content analysis of phishing email subject lines.

3   Materials and Methods

The analyzed sample comprises a text file with complete phishing emails aggregated from half-dozen account domains that belonged to one real person, with the purpose to collect spam email. The emails were manually identified as phish. Since there are hundreds of emails, the file needed to be processed to verify and eliminate cascading emails as well as make sure that all subject lines correspond to different email messages. After this trimming, all subject lines were compiled as one text. The performed analysis included the frequency analysis of most common words using a free online tool (OUTA) [18]. This utility allows to find the most frequent phrases and frequencies of words in a text, and non-English languages are also supported. OUTA counts the number of words, characters, sentences and syllables and calculates the lexical density (e.g., the number of lexical words/content divided by the total number of words). An extract of a small example of an OUTA output can be seen in Fig. 3.

Number of characters (including spaces) :	164605
Number of characters (without spaces) :	129888
Number of words :	21420
Lexical Density :	18.7628
Number of sentences :	3169
Number of syllables :	40520

Some top phrases containing 8 words (without punctuation marks)	Occurrences
someone is using your account without your knowledge	26
subject we're concerned that someone is using your	23
paypal to resolve a limitation on your account	22
in to paypal to resolve a limitation on	22
subject log in to paypal to resolve a	22
log in to paypal to resolve a limitation	22
to resolve a limitation on your account line	22
to paypal to resolve a limitation on your	22
that someone is using your account without your	18
concerned that someone is using your account without	18
we're concerned that someone is using your account	18
your account has been limited until we hear	16
account has been limited until we hear from	16

Fig. 3. Example of an output from the online text analyzer tool [18].

The advantage of this type of text analysis is that it is drawn from the text itself and not from words or terms that we may think could or should appear in phishing subject lines. This way, we are not prone to miss searching relevant expressions or words that otherwise could have been missed.

Still, OUTA only provides the most common occurrences of phrases and not all the possible occurrences, a further manual analysis of the rest of the subject lines, which occur less frequently and are not contemplated by OUTA, was processed to make sure that not other relevant data was missed. Moreover, since OUTA processes phrases with a different number of words, many repeated phrases can occur with the sub-parts of the same phrase. For example, a 6 word phrase will be repeated in the 5, 4, 3 and 2 words tables of occurrences. All repeated phrases were identified and discarded.

After obtaining the final tables of occurrences of the subject lines the authors associated the corresponding phrases/occurrences with categories and principles of persuasion as described in Figs. 1 and 2. To do this, the most common phrases and words (with the highest number of occurrences) were selected and their text verified, this time manually, to check whether they corresponded to the definition of any of the phishing categories and principles of persuasion. As an example, the phrase "your account has been limited until we hear" can be easily related to the *Authority Scam Category*, most probably in the Bank or Organization sub-category (second column, first row of Fig. 1). More information to confirm which of the two, could be easily obtained from other email fields (e.g., *From* field). Further, the same phrase is related to the *Authority Principle of Persuasion* (first row of Fig. 2) since it includes words to urge for an action from the receiver in order to unlock the service provided by the responsible or authority in that context.

Complementing this primary analysis, the content of subject lines can include secondary principles of persuasion. For the same given example, there is also a sense of impossibility that may cause the recipient to believe that something s/he owned was taken without previous warning (e.g., *Distraction*). The same subject line includes the principle of *Reciprocation* by instilling the potential victim to reply to the email message so that the problem can be resolved.

A different analysis will verify if subject lines include words/phrases that express targeted actions which are directed to the recipient, making him/her feel that they are very personal (e.g., using the pronoun "you" and posses-sive determiner "your"). These words can instill a sense of social presence [19], heightening the realization that the message is from a reliable human being. To clarify, the authors consider that email subject lines, independently of the phishing category, can include targeting content. More about this in Sect. 5.

Finally, the analysis will verify if there are any trends for specific subject lines per month and/or trimester.

4   Results

The analyzed sample included a total of 788 subject lines. The yearly distribution of the sample is shown in Fig. 4.

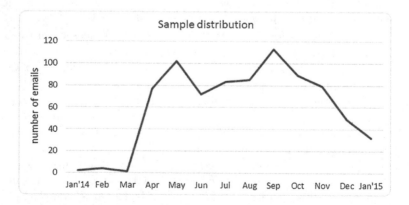

Fig. 4. Sample yearly distribution, with the number of emails, per month.

The average number of words per email subject line is 5,4 while the average number of characters is 37.

After processing the text using OUTA and deleting repeated lines, the most common phrases within the analyzed subject lines are presented in Table 1. These correspond to 33% (n = 257) of the total sample.

Table 1. Most common phrases in email subject lines of the analyzed sample. *This row was translated from German to "Account Activation Notice".

Email subject lines	Occurrences
1. Tax refund notification	48
2. Log in to PayPal to resolve a limitation on your account	22
3. Account status update	19
4. Your account has been limited until we hear from you	19
5. We're concerned that someone is using your account without your knowledge	18
6. Recent activity on your account	14
7. Response required	10
8. Your Netflix account requires validation	10
9. Submit your tax refund	9
10. Your AppleID has been suspended [#981317]	9
11. Fraud alert: irregular card activity	9
12. Konto Aktivierungs-Hinweis*	9
13. Please log in to confirm your identity and update your account information	8
14. Someone is using your account without your knowledge	8
15. Recently, there's been activity in your account that seems unusual compared to your normal account activities	7
16. Royal bank of scotland secure notification	7
17. Your Amazon.co.uk account	7
18. Please log in to PayPal to confirm your identity and update your password and security questions	6
19. Halifax internet banking customer service message	6
20. Important notice/Avis important	6
21. Log in to your account as soon as possible	6

The most common single words in the total sample of the email subject lines are: *your* with 383 occurrences; *account* with 303 occurrences; *notification* with 88 occurrences; *tax* with 81 occurrences; *update* with 70 occurrences; and *refund* with 68 occurrences. Moreover, *security* and *alert* had 41 occurrences.

Each of the 21 most common email subject lines was associated with the corresponding phishing category, main principle of persuasion, secondary principles of persuasion (if available), the identification if the subject line includes targeted, directed or personal words/expressions and the singling out of keywords and phrases that better express the data upon which the phishers focus their attacks (Table 2). From these 21 subject lines, 13 (62%) include targeted words/expressions.

Table 2. Categorisation and analysis of persuasive content in the most common email subject lines. (PC-Phishing Category; PPP-Primary Principle of Persuasion; SPP-Secondary Principle of Persuasion; Auth-Authority; Org-Organization; Gov-Government).

	PC	PPP	SPP	Targeted	Keywords/Phrases
1	Auth-Gov	Auth	Distraction	-	Tax - refund
2	Auth-Org	Auth	Reciprocation + Distraction	y	Log in - limitation your account
3	Auth-Org	Auth	-	-	Account - update
4	Auth-Org	Auth	Reciprocation + Distraction	y	Your - account - limited until hear from you
5	Auth-Org	Auth	Distraction	y	Concerned - your - account without your knowledge
6	Auth-Org	Auth	Distraction	y	Activity - your - account
7	Auth-Org	Auth	Reciprocation		Response - required
8	Auth-Org	Auth	Reciprocation	y	Your - account - requires
9	Auth-Gov	Auth	Commitment + Reciprocation	y	Submit - your - refund
10	Auth-Org	Auth	Distraction	y	Your - apple - suspended
11	Auth-Bank	Auth	Distraction	-	Fraud alert - card irregular activity
12	Auth-Bank	Auth	-	-	Account - activation
13	Auth-Org	Auth	Commitment + Reciprocation	y	Log in - confirm - your identity - update - account
14	Auth-Org	Auth	Distraction	y	Using - your - account without your knowledge
15	Auth-Org	Auth	Distraction	y	Activity - your account - unusual
16	Auth-Bank	Auth	Distraction		Secure - notification - bank
17	Auth-Org	Auth	Distraction	y	Your - account
18	Auth-Org	Auth	Commitment + Reciprocation	y	Log in - confirm - your identity - update - password security
19	Auth-Bank	Auth	-	-	Customer - service - banking
20	Auth-Bank	Auth	Distraction	-	Important - notice
21	Auth-Org	Auth	Distraction + Reciprocation	y	Log in - your - account as soon as possible

The analysis per month was performed from April 2014 until December 2014 since the first three months of the sample (e.g., January 2014, February 2014 and March 2014) had very few emails and the last month (e.g., January 2015) did not include a minimum number of common subject lines (at least 3 repeated ones) (Fig. 4). There was no linear trend for the most common email subject lines. Throughout the analyzed year, subject lines had an erratic behavior and the analysis per month included very small occurrences of all subject lines. These appear with some frequency one month and then completely disappear for the next few. With such small number of occurrences it is not possible to show the trends of subject lines per month or even per trimester. Only the trends for the most common subject line (e.g., Tax Refund Notification) is presented, though it also includes two months without any occurrence (Fig. 5).

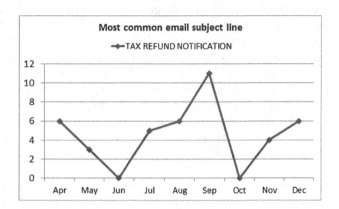

Fig. 5. Yearly variation of the most common subject line in the sample: *Tax refund notification.*

5   Discussion

According to the obtained results, the analyzed sample included, on average, 5 word long email subject lines that contained a wide range of information. The sample shows that five subject lines are very common but there is a big variety of lines since the most common one appears only 48 times (6%) in the universe of 788. However, this was just a preliminary analysis as it is possible to verify that there are similar (e.g., belong to the same phishing category and integrate the same principles of persuasion) lines but they are written with different words or expressions (synonyms) (ex: lines 1 and 9 or lines 5, 6, 14 and 15 of Table 1). A more detailed analysis of the other fields within the email is required to perform an aggregation of similar subject lines and this will increase the number of occurrences. Also, it will help verify the many variations of the same line that are used by phishers and understand if there is any pre-defined strategy in how they choose them.

In terms of phishing categorization, analyzed subject lines fall in only one of the presented categories: *Authority*, with the sub-categories: *Organization, Government* and *Bank* (Table 2). From these, the most frequently used is the

Organization, which can be explained by the fact that most devastating and largest attacks are made within major well known organizations that provide services to millions of users [2].

Such organizations are very attractive to phishers and that is why these mostly focus on how quickly can they obtain users' account information. Phishers only need to break into one of the accounts with more privileges to reach and exploit millions of others. The use of email subject lines that implicitly exercise a sense of authority (with the use of human's principles of persuasion) by exerting the fact that access to a user account is limited/blocked can certainly press their recipients to act as fast as possible to solve this issue.

To increase their odds in Auth-Org category, phishers complement persuasion with two more principles, e.g., the fact that a limitation or impossibility to use a service is present can heighten the emotional response by the recipients to focus only on what they are (supposedly) missing (e.g., the principle of distraction) as well as urgently take action (as requested by the phisher) to make things right again (e.g., the principle of reciprocation). The authors believe that the more principles are present in a subject line the more persuasive it can get as it includes various types of influence and target a more diversified number of victims, so exploiting more types of vulnerabilities. For this reason, specific combinations of principles of persuasion within email subject lines content can potentially be more dangerous.

A similar discussion can be done for the Auth-Bank's category, since subject lines are similar, but only adapted to a specific type of organization (e.g., Banks).

Even though the most common category of phishing emails present in the sample is Auth-Organization, the most used email subject line (e.g., Tax Refund Notification) is from another figure of authority, the Government. This can be explained by the fact that every working citizen has to abide and comply to the law and pay their taxes. Emails that focus on providing extra refunds on these matters can generate a high interest in their recipients and have, this way, a higher persuasive power. For this reason (and besides using the authority principle), this three word subject line expresses another principle of persuasion, the principle of distraction. These two principles combined in just three words is a clever and simple way for phishers to easily target billions of users all over the world.

The most common words/expressions found in the sample make phishing emails more targeted and personal. Words such as *your* and *account* with a presence of 50% and 40%, respectively, in the sample, help to set a social presence context [9,19]. Social presence is the sense of being with another person that apparently knows you or what you do; or being co-present with others and thereby overlooking the mediation by the technology (in this case the email platform). Those most common two words (e.g., *your* and *account*) can, almost by themselves, suggest the phishing category (Auth-Org or Auth-Bank) and main principle of persuasion (Authority) comprised within a subject line. Those two words, together with other common words in the sample such as *update* or *confirm* can express the principle of Reciprocation; or together with the words *limited* or *suspended*, express the principle of Distraction. This shows that just a few words (a small sentence) can contain a high persuasive power in themselves. This confirms the relevance of the presented work and the need to apply further resources in pursuing this topic.

In addition, in terms of persuasion, all phishing emails have a content of deception (3rd row, Fig. 2) in them, or they would not be classified as scams. They pretend to be from reliable sources and try to reach recipients with something that may be known or familiar to them. However, since all emails have this principle in the same implicit way, it is not useful in this study in order to characterize and distinguish email subject lines.

Also to notice that other relevant content can be derived from email subject lines, so opening the possibility for other types of analysis. Other clues can be found in the text of subject lines such as 'Re:' or 'Fwd:'. These can give more information regarding the origin of the email and, together with other characteristics, provide a more accurate perception of how the email was crafted and with what purpose. Another important factor is the use of visual clues. The character '!' is used 56 (7%) times in the sample while subject lines written in only capital letters appear 72 (9%) times. These features can heighten the sense of importance and urgency (Distraction) as well as the need for Reciprocation if that is expressed in the rest of the text, which usually is. Both features are used in the sample most common subject line (TAX REFUND NOTIFICATION !). This shows that, in spite of including text only, email subject lines can also cause a visual impact and, with it, complement the use of principles of persuasion, potentially increasing the influence these have in the recipients' decision to open an email.

Finally, though it was not possible to provide trends for types of email subject lines over the analyzed period, just by looking at one of the most common subject lines (Fig. 5) is possible to have an idea of the email traffic variation. There are periods with a lot of emails while other times they almost do not exist. Other analysis could be done to verify if the peaks correspond, for instance, to the real times when tax refund forms need to be submitted or refunds received by tax payers. If so, it could be possible to automatically predict and identify specific times for higher floods of certain types of phishing emails. Further, the integration of data from breaking news or trending headlines can also complement and help in the identification of trends of phishing themes. Data from current headlines that focus on business, big organizations, major events, economic crashes or any situation that may involve the interest of thousands to millions of users, may be used by phishers to craft phishing emails specifically targeted to exploit these issues, while they are trending.

Limitations - the sample size is a limitation of this work since a larger number of emails could include a more variety of subject lines, from different sources and complement the obtained results. However, the authors believe that this work shows a method and a proof of concept that can be reproduced with bigger and more varied samples. Also, related to this limitation, is the fact that it was not possible to perform a yearly trend analysis. Still, this can be overcome in future work with the possibility to aggregate lines that are different (use different words and expressions) but similar in what they transmit and ask from the recipient.

6   Conclusions and Future Work

So, *What to phish in a subject?* This study shows that a small sentence can go a long way. With a simple analysis and simple tools, it is possible to extract diversified and relevant content from only one of the phishing email fields: the subject line. Small but targeted text sentences, as well as other characteristics such as punctuation or capitalization, can include a high persuasive power and can better succeed in grabbing users' attention to influence them into opening a phishing email.

The authors believe that it is worth focusing more resources into analyzing subject lines content using a socio-technical approach. This can help integrating technical means, with knowledge from human persuasion and human characteristics that are commonly used within human interactions. This knowledge can help getting more diverse data more quickly and provide alternative means to distinguish directed and possibly more dangerous types of phishing.

As future work, the authors plan to collect bigger samples with more heterogeneous sources of phishing emails and perform a similar analysis of subject lines to compare results for different data sources. With a wider data sample, they plan to test if phishers use data from the daily headlines that affect a large number of populations in order to craft more targeted phishing or if that is not used at all. Further complementary studies are needed to verify what principles and/or combination of principles of persuasion, together with other features present in subject lines, are more successful in grabbing users' attention, make them open more emails and be, potentially, more dangerous. These studies are very difficult to accomplish due mainly to ethical and legal reasons. Succeeding in getting authorization to perform ethical attacks without users' consent is a problem. Nevertheless, it is possible, with adequate means of monitoring and auditing, which are (or should be) compulsory security requirements for any organization, to verify when users open or reply to an email and how long they take to do this. These log actions can then be associated to the type of email (if it is a phishing or scam email), what principles of persuasion their subject lines commonly use and, therefore, which can be more effective and why.

Acknowledgments. The authors would like to thank Professor Richard Clayton for kindly supplying the sample used in this study.

This work was supported by the project "NORTE-01-0145-FEDER-000016" (NanoSTIMA) that is financed by the North Portugal Regional Operational Programme (NORTE 2020), under the PORTUGAL 2020 Partnership Agreement, and through the European Regional Development Fund (ERDF).

References

1. Symantec: Internet security threat report. Technical report 21, April 2016. https://www.symantec.com/content/dam/symantec/docs/reports/istr-21-2016-en.pdf

2. Cloudmark Security Blog: Survey reveals spear phishing as a top security concern to enterprises (2016)
3. Verizon: 2015 data breach iinvestigation report. Technical report (2015). https://msisac.cisecurity.org/whitepaper/documents/1.pdf
4. Balakrishnan, R., Parekh, R.: Learning to predict subject-line opens for large-scale email marketing. In: 2014 IEEE International Conference on Big Data (Big Data), pp. 579–584, October 2014
5. Olsen, E.: New phishing research: 5 most dangerous email subjects, top 10 hosting countries. Technical report, Websense Security Labs (2013). https://blogs.forcepoint.com/security-labs/new-phishing-research-5-most-dangerous-email-subjects-top-10-hosting-countries-0
6. Hamid, A., Kim, T.-H.: Using feature selection and classification scheme for automating phishing email detection. Stud. Inf. Control **22**(1), 61–70 (2013). ISSN 1220-1766
7. Islam, R., Abawajy, J.: A multi-tier phishing detection and filtering approach. J. Netw. Comput. Appl. **36**(1), 324–335 (2013)
8. Vishwanath, A., Herath, T., Chen, R., Wang, J., Rao, H.R.: Why do people get phished? Testing individual differences in phishing vulnerability within an integrated, information processing model. Decis. Support Syst. **51**(3), 576–586 (2011)
9. Harrison, B., Vishwanath, A., Jie, N., Ragov, R.: Examining the impact of presence on individual phishing victimization. In: Hawaii International Conference on System Sciences (2015)
10. Jakobsson, M., Tsow, A., Shah, A., Blevis, E., Lim, Y.-K.: What instills trust? A qualitative study of phishing. In: Dietrich, S., Dhamija, R. (eds.) FC 2007. LNCS, vol. 4886, pp. 356–361. Springer, Heidelberg (2007). https://doi.org/10.1007/978-3-540-77366-5_32
11. Sappleton, N., Lourenco, F.: Email subject lines and response rates to invitations to participate in a web survey and a face-to-face interview: the sound of silence. Int. J. Soc. Res. Methodol. **19**(5), 611–622 (2016)
12. Jones, S., Payne, S., Hicks, B., Gopsill, J., Snider, C.: Subject lines as sensors: co-word analysis of email to support the management of collaborative engineering work. In: International Conference on Engineering Design 2015 (ICED 2015), July 2015
13. Jakobsson, M.: Understanding Social Engineering Based Scams. Springer, New York (2016). https://doi.org/10.1007/978-1-4939-6457-4
14. Ferreira, A., Coventry, L., Lenzini, G.: Principles of persuasion in social engineering and their use in phishing. In: Tryfonas, T., Askoxylakis, I. (eds.) HAS 2015. LNCS, vol. 9190, pp. 36–47. Springer, Cham (2015). https://doi.org/10.1007/978-3-319-20376-8_4
15. Cialdini, R.B.: Influence: The Psychology of Persuasion (Revision Edition). Harper Business (2007)
16. Gragg, D.: A multi-level defense against social engineering. Technical report, SANS Institute - InfoSec Reading Room (2003)
17. Stajano, F., Wilson, P.: Understanding scam victims: seven principles for systems security. Commun. ACM **54**(3), 70–75 (2011)
18. Online-Utility.org: Text analyzer. https://www.online-utility.org/text/analyzer.jsp
19. Minsky, M.: Telepresence. OMNI Mag. **3**, 45–51 (1980)

Unpacking Spear Phishing Susceptibility

Zinaida Benenson[1(✉)], Freya Gassmann[2], and Robert Landwirth[1]

[1] Friedrich-Alexander-Universität Erlangen-Nürnberg, Erlangen, Germany
{zinaida.benenson,robert.landwirth}@fau.de
[2] Universität des Saarlandes, Saarbrücken, Germany
f.gassmann@mx.uni-saarland.de

Abstract. We report the results of a field experiment where we sent to over 1200 university students an email or a Facebook message with a link to (non-existing) party pictures from a non-existing person, and later asked them about the reasons for their link clicking behavior. We registered a significant difference in clicking rates: 20% of email versus 42.5% of Facebook recipients clicked. The most frequently reported reason for clicking was curiosity (34%), followed by the explanations that the message fit recipient's expectations (27%). Moreover, 16% thought that they might know the sender. These results show that people's decisional heuristics are relatively easy to misuse in a targeted attack, making defense especially challenging.

Keywords: Spear phishing · Facebook · Decisional heuristics

1 Introduction

Phishing attacks that persuade users to click on malicious attachments or links have become a standard means of gaining an entry point into the systems during the APT (Advanced Persistent Threat) attacks and data breaches, and also have recently caused substantial damage in form of ransomware infections. The popularity of this attack vector has inspired numerous research efforts on susceptibility of the users to different targeting techniques and on user education [16]. Most of this research concentrated on link clicking in emails and submission of information on phishing webpages.

However, although harvesting users' login details via phishing websites and spreading malware through attachments remain important attack vectors, also just clicking on a link can result in a security incident. For example, according to two surveys published in 2016, email links leading to infected websites accounted for around 30% of malware infections in organizations [32,43].

Along with the phishing messages that address general Internet population, several variants of the so-called *spear phishing* evolved [10,17,30]. This term refers to phishing attacks targeted at specific individuals or groups, for example

Targeted Attacks Workshop at Financial Cryptography and Data Security 2017. ©IFCA.

customers of a specific organization (bank, online retailer, telecommunications company) or employees in a specific department (human resources, accounting, customer support). Spear phishing messages can address victims by names, refer to their immediate interests or job tasks and appear to come from trusted senders [15, 42].

Considering previous research, two areas remain relatively unexplored. Firstly, different media by which the phishing message could be received, such as email, Facebook or Twitter, could make a difference in success rates. Although phishing attacks via Facebook happen in practice [23], the first step towards direct comparisons of success rates between email and Facebook was made in our previous study in 2014 [4]. Secondly, researchers rarely directly asked users to explain the reasons behind their reactions to "suspicious" messages. Although some small-scale studies with 20 or less participants [6, 13] interviewed users to find out how they would decide in a hypothetical scenario whether an email is legitimate or not, we are not aware of large-scale behavioral studies on this topic. In this work, we make the following contributions:

- We show in a between subjects field experiment with 1255 users that receiving the same message with a "suspicious" link via Facebook or via email leads to significantly different click rates. Our study partially replicates our previous study [4] and validates its results.
- We analyze the reasons for clicking and not clicking reported by the participants in a post-experiment survey and discuss how lessons learned from this experiment can be applied to a broader range of scenarios involving spear phishing attacks.

This paper is organized as follows. We present related work in the next section, and research questions and hypotheses in Sect. 3. We then elaborate on study method in Sect. 4. We present results of the behavioral field experiment in Sect. 5 and results of the post-experimental survey in Sect. 6. We discuss our findings and their implications in Sect. 7 and conclude in Sect. 8.

2   Related Work

Early works in the mid 2000's investigated the criteria according to which users categorize incoming emails as genuine messages or scam. Downs et al. [13] used interviews and role plays to analyze how users classify emails. Jakobsson and Ratkiewicz conducted so-called "context-aware" experiments in which they used publicly available data as well as the communication patterns of Ebay users to increase the plausibility of emails [20]. In another field experiment by Jagatic et al. [19], sending a phishing email that spoofed a social network friend increased the success rate from 16% (for emails from unknown senders) to 72%.

The results of these works indicate that users have difficulties in recognizing malicious emails, and that their corresponding decision criteria do not fit the problem. Five years later, a phishing study conducted by Blythe et al. [6] came to the conclusion that users still have the same difficulties, as they consider sender address, design and language of an email as criteria for genuineness. They also cannot interpret technical details such as the composition of links.

Recognition of phishing websites also has been difficult for non-expert users. Their strategies, first uncovered in 2006 [12], still remained unsuccessful in 2015 [1]. Help provided by technical tools is also limited. Whereas passive indicators are rarely noticed by the users, active warnings are more often heeded [14,25,47]. Unfortunately, technical recognition of phishing websites, which is a precondition for effective warnings, still remains a challenging task. Most tools appear to have too high false positive and/or false negative detection rates [24,48].

Considering inability of non-expert users and of technical tools to reliably detect phishing attacks, education and training constitute alternative anti-phishing measures. Prominent academic tools for supporting anti-phishing user education and training are "Anti-Phishing Phil" [37] and "PhishGuru" [26]. In a comparative study of both systems [28], their developers found that both measures reduced the numbers of victims. The ability of non-experts to recognize (mostly non-targeted) phishing emails could be significantly increased from guessing (approx. 50% detection rates) to detection rates of 75–85%. Detection rates for users with initially higher expertise could be improved, using different education techniques, to nearly 100% [9,28,39].

Interestingly, similar educational efforts in a corporate environment proved to be unexpectedly challenging: majority of the users who clicked on a "suspicious" link that in reality led to training materials did not read these materials [10,27]. Moreover, although training effects were evident after one week in one study [27], these effects seemed to be lost after three months in another study [10].

Numerous studies measured factors that influence users' ability to recognize phishing emails, such as age, gender and technical background of the recipients, sender's gender and familiarity to the recipient, or design, spelling and content of the message. These measurements were conducted via surveys (e.g., [6,36,45]) or in behavioral studies that simulated phishing attacks (e.g., [10,19,20,28,31]). For example, emails with logos of the corresponding companies were significantly more difficult for the users to recognize as phish [6]. Some studies did not find any correlations between demographic factors and vulnerability for malicious messages [12,37], whereas others found that younger people (between 18 and 25) are more vulnerable than the middle-aged, and that women are more susceptible than men [5,19,36]. However, older adults (especially women) seem to be more vulnerable than younger adults [31].

Susceptibility of users to phishing attacks on various social media has been investigated to a lesser degree than susceptibility via email. Some studies considered acceptance rates of friend requests from strangers or from spoofed acquaintances on Facebook and other social networks, and the amount of information that can be gained from the users via this attack [5,38]. Another interesting research direction created fake social network profiles and observed which kind of friend requests they receive [18,40]. An automated infiltration attack built a network of fake accounts that successfully befriended more than 3000 users [7].

Also leveraging social network information for crafting spear phishing emails has been investigated [8, 19]. A highly sophisticated method of leveraging Twitter for spear phishing was presented at BlackHat USA 2016 [35]. To the best of our knowledge, our research group conducted the first study that directly compared phishing susceptibility between email and Facebook [4].

As mentioned previously, although some small-scale studies interviewed users to find out how they *would* decide whether an email is legitimate or not [6, 13], we are not aware of large-scale *behavioral* phishing studies that directly asked participants for the reasons of their clicking behavior.

Two studies combined a social engineering field experiment with a subsequent questionnaire similarly to our study. Vidas et al. [44] distributed flyers with "suspicious" QR-codes in different locations. Users that scanned a QR-code were taken to a website with a survey that asked them to indicate the main reason for their scanning action. Tischer et al. [41] distributed "suspicious" USB sticks on a university campus in a similar fashion. Users that found a stick and inserted it into a computer were also asked for reasons of their action. We further discuss their findings in Sect. 7. In contrast to our study, these two studies could only ask for the reasons of unsafe behavior, as users who behaved securely could not be reached by their surveys.

3   Research Questions and Hypotheses

The present study is a follow-up to a similar study we conducted in 2014 [4]. We partially replicate this previous study by considering its research question and the hypotheses H1–H5 presented below.

Research Question 1: Do people react to a "suspicious" link differently depending on whether the link was received via Facebook or via email?

Hypotheses: The following factors will be correlated to the higher success rate of the attack:

- H1: Message reception via Facebook,
- H2: Friend request from the sender,
- H3: Message sent from an open Facebook profile,
- H4: Female gender of the sender,
- H5: Female gender of the recipient.

These hypotheses were grounded in the previous work on demographic characteristics of phishing victims [36] and on social network phishing [5]. In study [4], none of the hypotheses could be supported. Whereas hypotheses H2-H5 did not yield any statistically significant results, the effect of Facebook was highly significant, but reversed: 56% of email recipients, but only 38% of Facebook recipients clicked on the "suspicious" link. Therefore, we decided to conduct a follow-up study to validate the findings of the previous study.

Moreover, effect sizes in the statistical analysis in study [4] were small, indicating that some other factors, unrelated to our hypotheses, led to clicking. This assumption resulted in the second research question for the present study:

Research Question 2: How do people explain their reasons for clicking or not clicking on a link?

To answer the above research questions, we designed a field experiment and a follow-up survey presented below.

4   Method

Win the following we present design of our study. In a nutshell, we conducted a field experiment where we sent to the participants an email or a personal Facebook message with a link from a non-existing person, claiming that the link leads to the pictures from a party. When clicked, the corresponding webpage showed the "access denied" message. We registered the click rates, and later sent to the participants a questionnaire that asked about the reasons for their clicking behavior.

4.1   Ethical Considerations

Jakobsson et al. [20,21] discuss the ethical issues of phishing studies in depth and arrive at the conclusion that, under certain circumstances, it is ethically permissible to conduct phishing studies without participants' consent and without debriefing. The above position is controversial, however, as experimenting with humans without their consent can negatively influence participants. For example, one of the first phishing experiments at the Indiana University [19] resulted in a serious controversy and media outcry as the students found out that they unwittingly participated in the study [29].

Therefore, we recruited the participants for a "cover story" survey of their Internet habits in order not to prime them about phishing. To offer an incentive for participation, we drew ten online shopping vouchers with the value of 10 EUR each. We fully debriefed participants after their participation by sending to them cumulative anonymized statistics about the study results and explaining why clicking on a link might result in a security incident. We also provided a possibility for anonymous study feedback, as well as a contact person for further questions. Our study plan was approved by the data protection office of the University of Erlangen-Nuremberg that verified its compliance with the German data protection laws and ethics.

4.2   Experimental Design

For sending the messages with links we created three email accounts (a male, a female and an anonymous account with unidentifiable gender) at a popular German provider, and four Facebook accounts, two male and two female. We used first names that were most popular in Germany around 1990 (the estimated years of birth of our participants, university students in their twenties), and the most popular German surnames, ending up with attacker names such as Sabrina Müller and Frank Bauer.

One male and one female Facebook account were "closed", that is, they contained only names and a symbolic male or female profile picture that Facebook shows by default. Two other profiles were "open", containing a profile photo, some other pictures, postings and friends, see Fig. 1.

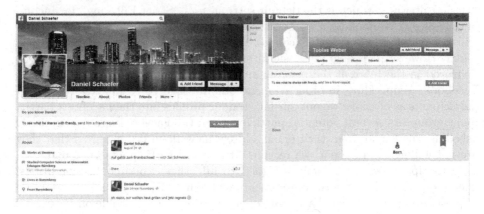

Fig. 1. Fake Facebook senders in the study: an open profile of Daniel Schäfer and a closed profile of Tobias Weber.

The field experiment started in the first week of January 2014. The participants were sent the following message with an individualized link via email or as a personal message on Facebook. The link contained an IP address from our university:

Hey!

The New Year's Eve party was awesome! Here are the pictures:

http://<*IP address*>/photocloud/page.php?h=<*participant ID*>

But please don't share them with people who have not been there!

See you next time!

<*sender's first name*>

When the users clicked on the link, their participant ID (a randomly assigned 7-digit number) was recorded in the database, and the website showed an "access denied" message.

4.3   Recruitment

The participants for the email-based study were recruited using the internal student mailing list of our university, whereas the participants for the Facebook-based study were recruited via the Facebook student groups of several German universities[1].

---

[1] We could not recruit enough Facebook participants at a single university and therefore used several universities.

We had a technical reason for recruiting Facebook participants via a Facebook group. At the time of the study, there were three folders in Facebook accounts into which new personal messages could be delivered: "Inbox", "Others" and "Spam". Users are only notified about new messages that are delivered into the Inbox. Furthermore, the users could choose between two settings called "Basic Filtering", which is the default setting, and "Strict Filtering" for incoming messages. We found out by experiment that users that chose strict filtering will always receive personal Facebook messages from strangers in the Others folder. However, if people use basic filtering, a message from a stranger will be delivered in the Inbox if the receiver and the sender are members of the same Facebook group. Thus, in order to make our message go to Inbox for as many participants as possible, we put our fake sender profiles into the Facebook participant group. As several potential participants in the Facebook groups explicitly asked us whether we want their email address as well, and commented that they are not willing to provide it, we recruited the email participants via email.

Participants were randomly assigned to all other experimental conditions: gender of the sender on both communication channels, friend request or no friend request from the sender on Facebook, open or closed sender profile on Facebook.

4.4   Sample Characteristics

We recruited 280 Facebook users (80 male, 200 female) and 975 email users (265 male, 710 female). Groups have a comparable gender structure with 27% and 29% of male participants, respectively.

Table 1. Key demographic facts about the participants. σ denotes standard deviation.

	All users	Email group	Facebook group
Recruited participants	1255 (28% male)	975 (27% male)	280 (29% male)
Survey response rate	57% (22% male)	56% (21% male)	62% (28% male)
Average age (survey)	23.1 ($\sigma = 4.4$)	23.2 ($\sigma = 4.1$)	22.9 ($\sigma = 5.1$)
% of students (survey)	93%	96%	86%

Other demographic characteristics of participants were not collected at the time of recruitment, but later during the survey. Therefore, these characteristics are only known for the survey participants. As presented in Table 1, response rate for the survey was 57%. The differences in response rates between the groups (56% for email and 62% for Facebook) are not statistically significant (Pearson's $\chi^2 = 2.98$, $p < 0.10$). Both groups have a comparable age structure (the differences are not statistically significant) and a strong majority of students. The number of students is significantly higher in the email group, although the effect is relatively small ($\chi^2(1) = 8.93$, $p < 0.001$, Cramer's V $\varphi_c = 0.162$).

5   Behavioral Clicking Results: Facebook vs. Email

We extracted the behavioral clicking data from the web server logs. During this process, page requests by bots, such as Facebook or Google, were removed. We used the same statistical analysis method as in the previous study [4].

The descriptive results and the Pearson chi-squared (χ^2) test results with the effect size reported using Cramer's V (φ_c) are presented in Table 2. Just as in the previous study, hypotheses H2–H5 were not supported. However, H1 was supported. Thus, in both studies, the only significant clicking factor is the communication channel. In our study, 20% of email versus 42.5% of Facebook users clicked on the link. However, the channel effect in [4] was reversed: 56% of email users versus 38% of Facebook users clicked. We discuss this difference further in Sect. 7.

Table 2. Statistics for clicking rates. The only significant factor ($p < 0.001$) in the present study is the communication channel (Facebook versus email).

Factor	Clicked	χ^2	df	p	φ_c
Communication channel	Email: 194/975 (20%) FB: 119/280 (42.5%)	59.365	1	**0.000**	0.218
Sender's gender (email)	Female: 72/325 (22.1%) Male: 59/326 (18.1%) Undefined: 63/324 (19.4%)	1.742	2	0.419	0.042
Sender's gender (Facebook)	Female: 64/140 (45.7%) Male: 55/140 (39.3%)	1.184	1	0.277	0.065
Receiver's gender (email)	Female: 152/710 (21.4%) Male: 42/265 (15.8%)	3.742	1	0.053	0.062
Receiver's gender (Facebook)	Female: 86/200 (43.0%) Male: 33/80 (41.2%)	0.144	1	0.704	0.023
Friend request (FR) from sender (Facebook)	With FR: 58/120 (48.3%) no FR: 61/160 (38.1%)	2.924	1	0.087	0.102
Profile information of the sender (Facebook)	Closed: 64/140 (45.7%) Open: 55/140 (39.3%)	1.184	1	0.277	0.065

6   Reported Reasons for Clicking Behavior

In the survey, 117 out of 720 participants reported that they clicked, and 502 participants reported that they did not click. These participants were asked in a subsequent open-ended question to explain in their own words why they clicked or did not click. The rest of the participants reported that they either could not remember whether they clicked, or that they did not receive the message.

We analyzed participants' explanations of their clicking behavior according to principles of qualitative content analysis [34]. First, two researchers independently worked through the responses, identifying relevant topics and labeling them. These topics and labels were discussed and an initial coding frame was designed. This initial coding frame was used in a first trial coding, spanning over the first one hundred responses, coded independently by both researchers.[2] During this process, each researcher took note of occurring coding problems. Post coding, these problems were discussed and the coding frame and its categories were revised accordingly. The refined coding frame was used to recode the initially coded replies and to also code the next hundred replies. This process was repeated until no more coding frame related problems arose during trial coding. After that, all data was coded by two independent raters using the final coding frame. To assess inter-rater reliability, Cohen's Kappa κ was calculated [11], and afterwards the cases with conflicting codes were discussed to produce agreement. During this discussion, full inter-rater agreement could be reached.

Replies of clickers were coded with seven categories. Cohen's κ for four categories indicated excellent agreement (over 0.75), while the remaining three showed good agreement (over 0.6).[3] Answers of non-clickers were coded with 20 categories. 19 categories had excellent Cohen's κ (over 0.75), and the remaining category had a good one (0.62). For interpretation purposes, we clustered some of these categories into more general categories.

6.1   Reasons for Clicking

The reported reasons for clicking were similar for the email and the Facebook groups (Table 3). By far the most frequent reason was *Curiosity*. These participants explained that they knew that the pictures cannot be for them, but were interested in the supposedly funny or private content.

Table 3. Categories for the clicking reasons (117 answers). Cohen's Kappa $\kappa > 0.75$ indicates excellent inter-rater agreement, $\kappa > 0.6$ means good agreement. Some participants reported more than one category.

Category	N	%	κ	Explanation
Curiosity	40	34.2	0.91	Curios about the pictures, interested to see their content
Context	32	27.4	0.82	Reception of the message fits the situation of the New Year's Eve celebration
Investigation	21	17.9	0.84	Wish to find out more about the situation that caused this message
Known sender	19	16.2	0.62	Certainty or assumption that one knows the sender
Technical context	13	11.1	0.9	Technical features (operating system, browser, antivirus, university's network) will thwart threats
Fear	8	6.8	0.92	Fear that a stranger may have pictures of the receiver
Automatic	4	3.4	0.71	Clicked without thinking, impulsively

---

[2] As the first question elicited only 117 responses, all these responses were processed during each coding step.

[3] We follow the interpretation of Cohen's Kappa by Banerjee et al. [3].

The second place was taken by the explanations that the message fits the *Context* of the New Year's Eve celebration, for example P151: *"I thought these were the pictures from the company's celebration, and all of us have been waiting for them."* P483 explained: *"I did not know many people from the New Year [...] and I thought it was one of them"*.

Some participants clicked in the course of an *Investigation*, as they wanted to find out more about the situation, and maybe to correct the "mistake": *"I wanted to see to whom the message was actually addressed and forward it if possible"* (P16). Users also thought that the message is from a *Known sender*, so P8 explained: *"I thought the message was from a friend whose name is also Sabrina by chance"*. This indicates that choosing most popular German names was a good strategy for targeting. Interestingly, two users explained that they thought it was some friend who used a pseudonymous account.

Participants also expressed trust into some technical measures, or in the ability of the university to protect them, so P711: *"I have never received spam at the university email address before"*, or P461: *"I knew that my Kaspersky will protect me"*. P490 considered the combination of Mac OS and Firefox "safe enough" for clicking. Four participants stated that as the IP address belonged to the university, they considered the link to be safe.

Eight participants said that they were anxious that a stranger might actually have pictures of them (*Fear* category), so P32: *"Although I felt unsafe, my fear that a stranger might have my pictures was very strong. There are so many possibilities nowadays to make photos that one never knows who might have made them, and under which circumstances"*.

Automatic reaction was also reported: *"I first clicked on the link and then it came to me that no person with this name was actually present"* (P33).

6.2   Reasons for Not Clicking

The most prominent reason for not clicking was the *Unknown sender* name (Table 4). Although unknown sender name is an important indicator of scam messages, only three users explicitly commented that one cannot fully rely on it, as dangerous messages can also arrive from known senders.

Many participants indicated that they suspected the link to contain malware or be fraudulent without explaining how they arrived at this conclusion (*Suspicion of Fraud* category). It seems that they relied on their intuition: *"I thought is was a virus"* (P137), *"Might have been a 'spy' link"* (P196), *"I knew immediately that this was spam"* (P385).

Some people reasoned that the context of the message reception did not fit. For example, *Situation context* was an important indicator, where users explained that no pictures were made at their party, or that they spent the New Year's Eve alone. Unfitting *Life context* means that there are no people or circumstances in the person's life that would cause such a message to be sent: *"My friends would not contact me in this way"* (P36), *"I do not receive this kind of mails"* (P238). Some people also remarked that they never share pictures via email (or via Facebook), or that they do not use this particular email address

Table 4. Categories for the reasons not to click (502 answers).

Category	N	%	κ	Explanation
Unknown sender	254	50.6	0.90	Sender of the message is unknown
Suspicion of Fraud[a]	250	49.8	0.93	Assumption that the message is fraudulent, phishing, might contain a virus
Situation context[a]	195	38.8	0.96	Reception of the message does not fit the situation of the New Year's Eve celebration
Life context[a]	58	11.6	0.75	There are no circumstances in the life of the recipient that would cause such a message
Rule of conduct	47	9.4	0.91	A behavioral rule prohibits clicking on links in such messages
Privacy	28	5.6	0.93	Private message sent to a wrong person
Message context[a]	27	5.4	0.87	Wrong communication channel or email address for a message like this
Message form[a]	25	5.0	0.91	Anonymous message, not addressed by name
Link form	20	4	0.93	Link looks suspicious
Bad experience	11	2.2	0.8	Unpleasant experience in a similar situation

[a]Indicates a merged category. Some participants reported more than one category.

for communication with their friends (category *Message context*), or that the message did not address them by name, or was "anonymous" (*Message form*).

Almost 10% of users said that they acted according to a specific *Rule of conduct*, for example they never open emails from unknown senders, or never click on "such" links. Some users mentioned the "strange" link (it contained a bare IP address, *Link form* category), or that they already had an unpleasant experience with clicking on a link (e.g., the link led to a porn site), or caught a virus after clicking on a link in a similar situation (*Bad experience*).

Respecting *Privacy* of other people was stated as a reason by 5.6% of users, for example P708 said: *"I do not look up a private message that was obviously not addressed to me"*. This reason can be considered as an antipode to the most frequently stated reason for clicking (curiosity).

7   Discussion

Although this study has some limitations, we think that useful preliminary conclusions can be drawn from our study and from its comparison to study [4]. Especially the highly significant difference between the communication channels and the reasons for clicking provide important insight into targeting strategies, as we discuss in the following.

7.1   Limitations

Findings of this study have several limitations. Thus, we did not assign the communication channel (Facebook or email) randomly to participants, and moreover, email and Facebook groups were recruited at different universities. We also had different sample sizes for email (975) and for Facebook (280). Both user groups are skewed towards female participants. However, this bias might not be important as recipients' sex did not play any role in our and in the previous study [4].

Furthermore, reported reasons for actions do not always correspond to the real reasons, as people make many decisions based on intuition or subconsciously [22,46]. Thus, although we now know more about how people reason about targeted attacks, we might still not be able to predict their behavior. This should be verified in future studies.

7.2   Facebook versus Email

In the present study, 42.5% of Facebook users, but 20% of email users clicked on the link. We hoped to find the reasons for this statistically highly significant difference in the reasons for clicking and not clicking provided by the users. Surprisingly, reasons did not differ statistically across the platforms, although a small amount of non-clickers commented that they did not expect this kind of message to arrive via email, and a small amount of clickers commented that receiving pictures via Facebook seemed plausible to them.

Several factors might be responsible for susceptibility of Facebook users. Firstly, social networks such as Facebook or LinkedIn might be considered trustworthy by users, as Kirlappos and Sasse indicate [25]. Secondly, the special characteristics of the Facebook platform, such as informal communication and easy ways to find the profile of a recent acquaintance, might have made our message especially plausible there. Thirdly, handling the messages on Facebook might be different from handling the emails, such that the users scan through their many notifications very quickly, without paying attention to what they are actually doing.

7.3   How Powerful is Personalization?

Our previous study [4] provided inspiration for the present study, although we did not strictly replicate it. As mentioned above, 56% of email participants clicked in study [4], whereas only 20% of email participants clicked in our study. Clicking rates on Facebook were comparable: 38% in [4] and 42.5% in the present study. Due to differences in experimental setup, direct statistical comparison of the two studies is problematic, and therefore we consider mainly qualitative arguments in the following.

According to Table 5, Facebook groups in both studies have comparable sizes, but the email group in our study has significantly more participants. The participants in both studies have comparable age and occupation demographics, but study [4] has significantly more male participants. However, in both studies, participants' sex did not correlate to their clicking probability, and therefore, gender differences of the samples are unlikely to have influenced the differences in results. Messages sent on both studies were similar, but not identical. Especially, participants in study [4] were addressed by first name.

Table 5. Comparison of key features between study [4] and our study.

	Study [4]	Our study
Time frame	Summer 2013	Winter 2013/14
Participants	398 (61% male) 240 Facebook/158 email	1255 (28 % male) 280 Facebook/975 email
Average age	22 ($\sigma = 4.5$)	23 ($\sigma = 4.4$)
% of students	96%	93%
Message	Pictures from party last week	Pictures from New Year's Eve party (sent on January 7th)
Addressing	Hey <*receiver's first name*>	Hey!
Clicking rates	38% Facebook/56% email	42.5% Facebook/20% email

We hypothesize that addressing by first name plays the most important role in the differences between two studies in the email clicking rates. Indeed, for many years, the traditional security advice to consumers had been that legitimate emails would address them by names, but the scams would not. Recently, this advice has changed. For example, at the time of writing, the Anti-Phishing Working Group (APWG) states: *"Typically, phisher emails are not personalized, but they can be"* [2]. The 56% clicking rate in study [4] as opposed to 20% clicking rate in the present study, although the messages were fairly similar, indicates that personalization is especially important for targeted email-based attacks. On Facebook, however, addressing by first name does not seem to play an important role. This could be connected to the difference in user interface, as names of recipients are clearly visible for the senders, and therefore are not perceived by the recipients as something that a stranger cannot find out. Moreover, receiving an informally addressed message via Facebook might be more common than receiving such a message via email. We note, however, that these assumptions are not supported by evidence so far and need further investigation.

7.4   Lessons About Targeting and Spear Phishing Susceptibility

Curiosity seems to be a very powerful driver of risky Internet behavior. This was also noticed in the previous studies: 64% of survey respondents in study by Vidas et al. [44] scanned "suspicious" QR codes out of curiosity, and 18% of survey respondents in the study by Tischer et al. [41] plugged in a "suspicious" USB stick for this reason.[4] At the same time, a small amount of participants in our study was protected from the would-be danger by their lack of curiosity, or the wish to respect the privacy of the others.

Also the fitting the content and the context of the message to the current life situation of a person plays an important role. Many people did not click because

---

[4] Both of these studies could not reach participants that behaved in a safe manner, as they did not have any opportunity to provide them with a survey.

they learned to avoid messages from unknown senders, or with an unexpected content, as it might give them an unpleasant experience, such as a virus. For some participants, however, the same heuristic ("does this message fit my current situation?") led to the clicks, as they thought that the message might be from a person from their New Year's Eve party, or that they might know the sender.

7.5 Defense Against Spear Phishing

Defense against spear phishing and other targeted attacks seems to be especially challenging because of the ambiguity of the situations that they create, making the context and content of the message look plausible and legitimate. Because of this ambiguity, asking people to be permanently vigilant when they process their messages might have unintended negative consequences.

For example, if a person's job requires processing a lot of invoices sent via email, they might click on a ransomware-infected file called "invoice", as this fits their job expectations. And if they are taught to be "careful" with invoices, they might start missing or delaying the real ones, which stands in a direct conflict with the requirements of their job. Under these circumstances, the employees are likely to disregard this kind of user education attempts, because the only way for them to get their job done *in time* is to process their emails as quickly as possible, without "wasting" time with extra security checks.

In general, being suspicious of every message that was maybe sent in a hurry with typos from a mobile device, or is otherwise a bit strange, will deprive people from (usually reliable) decision heuristics such as "this message fits my current expectations" or "I know the sender", making them less efficient in their jobs, especially if these jobs require processing of a high number of messages.

In security practice, sending fake phishing emails to employees has become a popular method of assessing their security awareness, with numerous commercial tools designed for this purpose. However, trying to involve users into perimeter defense by means of catching them on dangerous actions, such as link clicking in fake phishing emails, might have unintended negative consequences. For example, employees of an organization may become disgruntled and unmotivated if they find out that they are being attacked by their own security staff [33], or start blaming themselves for inability to make a correct decision in an ambiguous and difficult situation [10]. Moreover, sending employees messages from spoofed colleagues, friends and bosses, although might raise their security awareness, may also seriously hamper their work effectiveness, and also social relationships within the organization, promoting the atmosphere of distrust.

We note, however, that although our study led us to hypothesize about negative consequences of the above human-centered defenses against spear phishing attacks, we do not have enough evidence to support these hypotheses. Thus, one of the most important directions for future research is development of study designs and measurement procedures for assessing not only effectiveness of anti-phishing measures, but also their impact on the work and life environment of people, and on their psychological well-being.

8   Conclusion

We conducted a study consisting of a link clicking field experiment on Facebook and via email, and a follow-up survey that investigated the reasons for clicking behavior. An important future work question is whether awareness of danger ("links can lead to infected sites") helps, and to what extent can people be expected to act rationally when they feel curiosity, or any other strong emotion. We think that expecting the full impulse control from the users is unrealistic.

This particular study revealed susceptibilities to scam in some people, and the reasons behind their susceptibility, but we think that the lesson learned is broader. By a careful design and timing of a message, it should be possible to make virtually any person click on a link, as any person will be curious about something, or interested in some topic, or find themselves in a life situation that fits the message's content and context. For example, the message might come from a known sender, or refer to a previous experience in a plausible way. In the long run, relying on technical in-depth defense may be a better solution, and more research and evidence is needed to determine which level of defense non-expert users are able to achieve through security education and training.

Acknowledgments. We thank Nadina Hintz, Andreas Luder and Gaston Pugliese for their invaluable help in data gathering and analysis. Zinaida Benenson and Robert Landwirth were supported by the Bavarian State Ministry of Education, Science and the Arts within the scope of research association FORSEC (www.bayforsec.de).

References

1. Alsharnouby, M., Alaca, F., Chiasson, S.: Why phishing still works: user strategies for combating phishing attacks. Int. J. Hum. Comput. Stud. **82**, 69–82 (2015)
2. Anti-Phishing Working Group (APWG): How to avoid phishing scams. http://www.apwg.org/resources/overview/avoid-phishing-scams
3. Banerjee, M., Capozzoli, M., McSweeney, L., Sinha, D.: Beyond kappa: a review of interrater agreement measures. Can. J. Stat. **27**(1), 3–23 (1999)
4. Benenson, Z., Girard, A., Hintz, N., Luder, A.: Susceptibility to URL-based Internet attacks: Facebook vs. email. In: 6th IEEE International Workshop on SEcurity and SOCial Networking (SESOC), pp. 604–609. IEEE (2014)
5. Bilge, L., Strufe, T., Balzarotti, D., Kirda, E.: All your contacts are belong to us: automated identity theft attacks an online social networks. In: 18th International Conference on World Wide Web (2009)
6. Blythe, M., Petrie, H., Clark, J.A.: F for fake: four studies on how we fall for Phish. In: Proceedings of the SIGCHI Conference on Human Factors in Computing Systems, CHI 2011, pp. 3469–3478 (2011)
7. Boshmaf, Y., Muslukhov, I., Beznosov, K., Ripeanu, M.: The socialbot network: when bots socialize for fame and money. In: Proceedings of the 27th Annual Computer Security Applications Conference, pp. 93–102. ACM (2011)
8. Brown, G., Howe, T., Ihbe, M., Prakash, A., Borders, K.: Social networks and context-aware spam. In: Proceedings of the 2008 ACM Conference on Computer Supported Cooperative Work, pp. 403–412. ACM (2008)

9. Canova, G., Volkamer, M., Bergmann, C., Borza, R., Reinheimer, B., Stockhardt, S., Tenberg, R.: Learn to spot phishing URLs with the Android NoPhish App. In: Bishop, M., Miloslavskaya, N., Theocharidou, M. (eds.) WISE 2015. IAICT, vol. 453, pp. 87–100. Springer, Cham (2015). https://doi.org/10.1007/978-3-319-18500-2_8

10. Caputo, D.D., Pfleeger, S.L., Freeman, J.D., Johnson, M.E.: Going spear phishing: exploring embedded training and awareness. IEEE Secur. Priv. **12**(1), 28–38 (2014)

11. Cohen, J.: A coefficient of agreement for nominal scales. Educ. Psychol. Measur. **20**(1), 36–47 (1960)

12. Dhamija, R., Tygar, J.D., Hearst, M.: Why phishing works. In: Proceedings of the SIGCHI Conference on Human Factors in Computing Systems, CHI 2006, pp. 581–590 (2006)

13. Downs, J.S., Holbrook, M.B., Cranor, L.F.: Decision strategies and susceptibility to phishing. In: Proceedings of the Second Symposium on Usable Privacy and Security, SOUPS 2006, pp. 79–90 (2006)

14. Egelman, S., Cranor, L.F., Hong, J.: You've been warned: an empirical study of the effectiveness of web browser phishing warnings. In: Proceedings of the SIGCHI Conference on Human Factors in Computing Systems, CHI 2008, pp. 1065–1074 (2008)

15. Goodin, D.: Crypto ransomware targets called by name in spear-phishing blast. Ars Technica, 4 April 2016

16. Hong, J.: The state of phishing attacks. Commun. ACM **55**(1), 74–81 (2012)

17. Infosec Institute: Spear Phishing: Real Life Examples. http://resources.infosecinstitute.com/spear-phishing-real-life-examples. Accessed Mar 2017

18. Irani, D., Balduzzi, M., Balzarotti, D., Kirda, E., Pu, C.: Reverse social engineering attacks in online social networks. In: Holz, T., Bos, H. (eds.) DIMVA 2011. LNCS, vol. 6739, pp. 55–74. Springer, Heidelberg (2011). https://doi.org/10.1007/978-3-642-22424-9_4

19. Jagatic, T.N., Johnson, N.A., Jakobsson, M., Menczer, F.: Social phishing. Commun. ACM **50**(10), 94–100 (2007)

20. Jakobsson, M., Ratkiewicz, J.: Designing ethical phishing experiments: a study of (ROT13) rOnl query features. In: 15th International Conference on World Wide Web (2006)

21. Jakobsson, M., Johnson, N., Finn, P.: Why and how to perform fraud experiments. IEEE Secur. Priv. **6**(2), 66–68 (2008)

22. Kahneman, D.: Thinking, Fast and Slow. Macmillan, Basingstoke (2011)

23. Kaspersky Lab Exposes Facebook Phishing Attacks: 10,000 Victims in Two Days June 2016. http://www.kaspersky.com/about/news/virus/2016/10000-Victims-in-Two-Days

24. Khonji, M., Iraqi, Y., Jones, A.: Phishing detection: a literature survey. IEEE Commun. Surv. Tutor. **15**(4), 2091–2121 (2013)

25. Kirlappos, I., Sasse, M.A.: Security education against phishing: a modest proposal for a major rethink. IEEE Secur. Priv. Mag. **10**(2), 24–32 (2012)

26. Kumaraguru, P., Cranshaw, J., Acquisti, A., Cranor, L.F., Hong, J., Blair, M.A., Pham, T.: School of Phish: a real-world evaluation of anti-phishing training. In: Symposium On Usable Privacy and Security (SOUPS) (2009)

27. Kumaraguru, P., Sheng, S., Acquisti, A., Cranor, L., Hong, J.: Lessons from a real world evaluation of anti-phishing training. Anti-Phishing Working Group (2008)

28. Kumaraguru, P., Sheng, S., Acquisti, A., Cranor, L.F., Hong, J.: Teaching Johnny not to fall for phish. ACM Trans. Internet Technol. (TOIT) **10**(2), 7 (2010)

29. Lenz, R.: In Indiana phishing study, students take the bait. USA Today, 23 July 2007. http://usatoday30.usatoday.com/tech/news/computersecurity/2007-07-23-phishing-study_N.htm
30. Northcutt, S.: Spear Phishing (Methods of Attack Series). https://www.sans.edu/cyber-research/security-laboratory/article/spear-phish. Accessed Mar 2017
31. Oliveira, D., Rocha, H., Yang, H., Ellis, D., Dommaraju, S., Muradoglu, M., Weir, D., Soliman, A., Lin, T., Ebner, N.: Dissecting spear phishing emails for older vs young adults: on the interplay of weapons of influence and life domains in predicting susceptibility to phishing. In: Proceedings of the SIGCHI Conference on Human Factors in Computing Systems, CHI 2017 (2017)
32. Osterman Research Survey: Understanding the Depth of the Global Ransomware Problem (2016)
33. Sasse, A.: Scaring and bullying people into security won't work. IEEE Secur. Priv. **13**(3), 80–83 (2015)
34. Schreier, M.: Qualitative Content Analysis in Practice. Sage Publications, Thousand Oaks (2012)
35. Seymour, J., Tully, P.: Weaponizing Data Science for Social Engineering: Automated E2E Spear Phishing on Twitter. Black Hat USA (2016)
36. Sheng, S., Holbrook, M., Kumaraguru, P., Cranor, L.F., Downs, J.: Who falls for phish?: a demographic analysis of phishing susceptibility and effectiveness of interventions. In: Proceedings of the SIGCHI Conference on Human Factors in Computing Systems, pp. 373–382. ACM (2010)
37. Sheng, S., Magnien, B., Kumaraguru, P., Acquisti, A., Cranor, L.F., Hong, J., Nunge, E.: Anti-phishing phil: the design and evaluation of a game that teaches people not to fall for phish. In: Proceedings of the 3rd Symposium on Usable Privacy and Security, SOUPS 2007, pp. 88–99 (2007)
38. Sophos: Facebook users at risk of "rubber duck" identity attack. https://www.sophos.com/en-us/press-office/press-releases/2009/12/facebook.aspx
39. Stockhardt, S., Reinheimer, B., Volkamer, M., Mayer, P., Kunz, A., Rack, P., Lehmann, D.: Teaching phishing-security: which way is best? In: Hoepman, J.-H., Katzenbeisser, S. (eds.) SEC 2016. IAICT, vol. 471, pp. 135–149. Springer, Cham (2016). https://doi.org/10.1007/978-3-319-33630-5_10
40. Stringhini, G., Kruegel, C., Vigna, G.: Detecting spammers on social networks. In: 26th Annual Computer Security Applications Conference (2010)
41. Tischer, M., Durumeric, Z., Foster, S., Duan, S., Mori, A., Bursztein, E., Bailey, M.: Users really do plug in USB drives they find. In: 2016 IEEE Symposium on Security and Privacy (SP), pp. 306–319. IEEE (2016)
42. Vaas, L.: Beware the latest tax-season spear-phishing scam. https://nakedsecurity.sophos.com/2017/02/08/beware-the-latest-tax-season-spear-phishing-scam. Accessed Mar 2017
43. Verizon 2016 Data Breach Investigations Report (2016)
44. Vidas, T., Owusu, E., Wang, S., Zeng, C., Cranor, L.F., Christin, N.: QRishing: the susceptibility of smartphone users to QR code phishing attacks. In: Adams, A.A., Brenner, M., Smith, M. (eds.) FC 2013. LNCS, vol. 7862, pp. 52–69. Springer, Heidelberg (2013). https://doi.org/10.1007/978-3-642-41320-9_4
45. Vishwanath, A., Herath, T., Chen, R., Wang, J., Rao, H.R.: Why do people get phished? Testing individual differences in phishing vulnerability within an integrated, information processing model. Decis. Support Syst. **51**(3), 576–586 (2011)
46. Wilson, T.D.: Strangers to Ourselves. Harvard University Press, Cambridge (2004)

47. Wu, M., Miller, R.C., Garfinkel, S.L.: Do security toolbars actually prevent phishing attacks? In: Proceedings of the SIGCHI Conference on Human Factors in Computing Systems, pp. 601–610. ACM (2006)
48. Zhang, Y., Egelman, S., Cranor, L., Hong, J.: Phinding phish: evaluating antiphishing tools. In: Proceedings of the 14th Annual Network and Distributed System Security Symposium (NDSS) (2007)

Poster Papers

Scripting Smart Contracts for Distributed Ledger Technology

Pablo Lamela Seijas[1(✉)], Simon Thompson[1], and Darryl McAdams[2]

[1] University of Kent, Canterbury, UK
{pl240,S.J.Thompson}@kent.ac.uk
[2] San Francisco, CA, USA
darryl.mcadams@iohk.io

Distributed Ledger Technology (DLT) offers a way of maintaining a synchronised log in a non-centralised, distributed way; notably, this allows the implementation of cryptocurrencies and, more recently self-enforcing smart contracts. Bitcoin is the first widely-used implementation of a cryptocurrency but it has very limited scripting capabilities in practice. Ethereum allows smart contracts to contain arbitrary time-bounded turing-computable code that is executed and validated in a virtual machine. Nxt moves scriptability to clients and provides a delimited functionality through an API.

Because smart contracts can control money and potentially other assets, it is crucial that they behave as expected, not only in normal conditions, but also when attacked by malicious agents. In particular, contracts must be *reentrant* if they call unknown code, they must gracefully handle all kinds of *execeptions*, they must not expect agents to collaborate (in some cases by including *rewards and penalties* to deter attacks).

Designers of smart-contract languages and cryptocurrencies may mitigate the likelihood of errors being made by their users by carefully designing them to be intuitive, explicit, and by providing well-tested artefacts. Some examples of effort in this direction include: the use of *zero-knowledge proofs* for providing anonymity (see Zerocash); the use of *SNARKS* to hide private inputs (Hawk allows to design contracts by separating private and public parts); and allowing the use and enforcement of *higher-level specifications*, like the use of polymorphic types, combinators, finite-state machines (FSMs), or domain specific languages (DSLs). Additionally, there are many open challenges that are specific to DLT systems, like the design of ways for *amending the rules* (see Tezos), the *unpredictability* of the initial execution state derived from the decentralisation, the need for a safe *source of randomness*, the *cost of validating* the contracts (which could be mitigated through the use of verifiable computation), the amount of work required by *proof-of-work* (see *proof-of-stake*), and the need to preserve the delicate *equilibrium of incentives* that keeps block-chains secure.

In the full paper[1], we provide references for all the work mentioned here, we survey these and other representative examples of the advanced use of

---

[1] Pablo Lamela Seijas, Simon Thompson, and Darryl McAdams. *Scripting smart contracts for distributed ledger technology*. 2016. URL: https://eprint.iacr.org/2016/1156.pdf.

© International Financial Cryptography Association 2017
M. Brenner et al. (Eds.): FC 2017 Workshops 2017, LNCS 10323, pp. 631–??, 2017.
https://doi.org/10.1007/978-3-319-70278-0

cryptocurrencies and blockchains beyond their basic usage as a payment method, and we analyse existing scripting solutions, their strengths and weaknesses, and some existing solutions for known problems with them. Through our work, we have seen that, while there have been many diverse efforts in different directions, there are still many open questions, no universal solutions, and lots of room for future research and experimentation.

ZeroTrade: Privacy Respecting Assets Trading System Based on Public Ledger

Lei Xu[✉], Lin Chen, Nolan Shah, Zhimin Gao, Yang Lu, and Weidong Shi

University of Houston, Houston, TX 77004, USA

Motivation. Public ledger is a decentralized book keeping technology and is believed to have the potential to revolutionize many areas. Besides handling crypto-currency, public ledger can be used to tokenize arbitrary assets, and then support trading of these asset tokens in a decentralized manner. With public ledger based token trading system, users do not necessarily convert their assets to currencies, but can exchange assets directly. It also avoids unnecessary transportation as the asset only needs to be physically transferred to its last owner. Furthermore, utilization of the public ledger does not require that users have to trust each other in order to trade tokens safely. However, using decentralized public ledger for trading asset tokens raises serious privacy concerns. Because token ownership information is stored on the public ledger and disclosed to the public, anyone can uncover users trading activities and history. For a token based asset trading platform, all tokens are unique and transactions are usually two-ways or multi-ways. In response to these challenges, we propose ZeroTrade, a privacy respecting heterogeneous assets trading system that leverages various cryptography tools to conceal the exchange trace of asset tokens and takes advantage of public ledger for guaranteeing fairness of asset token exchange.

Solution. ZeroTrade involves trusted hubs that are responsible for converting assets to tokens and back, where trusted means that hubs will generate/accept valid tokens, and uses the public ledger to record all token exchange information. When two or more users want to exchange tokens with each other, each user picks an agent for the exchange. Asset tokens are first poured into a pool and users leverage agents to obliviously retrieve tokens from the pool in order to finish the exchange. The oblivious retrieving process cut off the connection between the original user and the agent. Therefore, one cannot determine the relationship between the original users who want to exchange tokens by observing information recorded on the public ledger.

To implement the design, ZeroTrade leverages different cryptography tools including zero-knowledge proof and various encryption techniques. Considering various demands in token trade, ZeroTrade also supports operations like partial token trade and revocation. A preliminary evaluation of the performance shows that ZeroTrade only adds limited burden on top of the public ledger. More detailed information can be found in the full version of the paper.

Conclusion. ZeroTrade provides a privacy friendly platform for asset trading based on public ledger. For the next step, we plan to implement a fully functional prototype and considering more complex token trading scenarios.

© International Financial Cryptography Association 2017
M. Brenner et al. (Eds.): FC 2017 Workshops 2017, LNCS 10323, p. 633, 2017.
https://doi.org/10.1007/978-3-319-70278-0

Author Index

in the United States
masters